PATRICK O'BRIAN

The Making of the Novelist

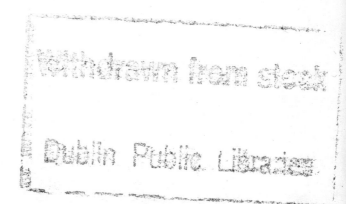

PATRICK O'BRIAN

The Making of the Novelist

Nikolai Tolstoy

Century · London

Published by Century in 2004

1 3 5 7 9 10 8 6 4 2

Century Books
The Random House Group Limited
20 Vauxhall Bridge Road, London, SW1V 2SA

Random House Australia (Pty) Limited
20 Alfred Street, Milsons Point, Sydney
New South Wales 2061, Australia

Random House New Zealand Limited
18 Poland Road, Glenfield
Auckland 10, New Zealand

Random House (Pty) Limited
Endulini, 5a Jubilee Road, Parktown 2193, South Africa

The Random House Group Limited Reg. No. 954009

www.randomhouse.co.uk

A CIP catalogue record for this book is available from the British Library

Papers used by Random House are natural, recyclable products
made from wood grown in sustainable forests. The manufacturing processes
conform to the environmental regulations of the country of origin

ISBN 0 7126 7025 4

Typeset by SX Composing DTP, Rayleigh, Essex
Printed and bound in Great Britain by
Mackays of Chatham plc, Chatham, Kent

CONTENTS

Prologue ix

1. Embarkation 1
2. Nooks and Corners 28
3. Strange Schooldays 61
4. A Literary Prodigy 80
5. In the Doldrums 106
6. Bohemian Days 128
7. First Love 152
8. Troubled Times 173
9. Broken Marriages 211
10. Arms and the Man 244
11. The Secret War 269
12. Trouble and Strife 295
13. A New Beginning 315
14. 'The smallest habitation I had ever seen' 341
15. The Untamed Land 363
16. Father and Son: A Tormented Relationship 398
17. The Long Day Running 424
18. Moelwyn Bank 440
19. The End of the Road 469
20. A Place in the Sun 483

Bibliographical Note 501
Acknowledgements 504
Index 506

In fondest memory of my mother and Patrick

I particularly stress his [Picasso's] *early days, partly because they are of course essential to an understanding of the man & partly because they are very little known – not a single one of the authorities has much to say, & what little they do produce is invariably inaccurate. At least this book will establish who, what & when he was as a boy & a young man, & I believe that it will give a truer, more living picture than any that has yet been written.*

Patrict O'Brian to William Targ of G. P. Putnam's, 13 May 1974

PROLOGUE

Patrick O'Brian's novels, above all his twenty-volume Aubrey–Maturin *œuvre*, have received critical acclaim in which superlatives compete with each other to an extent making it hard to choose among appreciations. In a highly influential review in the *New York Times Book Review* (6 January 1991) entitled 'An Author I'd Walk the Plank For', Richard Snow described them as 'the best historical novels ever written'. John Bayley, whose wife Iris Murdoch was an equally devoted admirer, wrote of 'the incomparable Patrick O'Brian':

> His ships are as intimate to us as are Sterne's Shandy Hall or Jane Austen's village of Highbury in *Emma*. Like Jane Austen, O'Brian is really happiest working on two or three inches of ivory and turning into art the daily lives of two or three or four families in a locality – except that his village happens to be a wooden ship of war at the apogee of a great Navy's world sea power in the days of sail, and famous for the skill and discipline of its officers and men. Jane Austen, two of whose brothers ended up as admirals, would have understood all this very well, and would no doubt warmly have approved O'Brian's spacious but modest undertaking . . . Patrick O'Brian has contrived to invent a new world that is almost entirely in this sense a world of enchanting fictional surfaces, and all the better for it. As narrator he never obtrudes his own personality, is himself never present in the role of author at all; but we know well what most pleases, intrigues, and fascinates him; and there is a kind of sweetness in his books, an enthusiasm and love for the setting of the fiction, which will remind older readers of Walter Scott.[1]

For A.S. Byatt, 'The writing is as strong and delightfully various as the people and plots. And everything – skies and seas and ports and creatures – is vividly and sensuously present', while T.J. Binyon extolled his wonderful evocation of another world: 'To have succeeded in conveying in so utterly convincing a manner the feel of the period is one of the author's greatest triumphs. It is achieved partly through the marvellously flexible language in which the novels are written, never obtrusively stylised yet

[1] *The New York Review*, 7 November 1991.

never jarringly modern, but chiefly through the recreation of a contemporary consciousness.'[1]

Yet it was not until the last decade of his long life, with a dozen or so of the series already published, that Patrick's readers became transformed from what one of his publishers once described to me as 'a small but faithful clique of admirers' into worldwide adulation recently reflected in Peter Weir's beautiful film adaptation of *The Far Side of the World*. The same publisher regretfully assured me that his readership would never extend beyond its then restricted 'cult' status. As one of his most stalwart admirers, the actor Charlton Heston, expressed it as late as 1994: 'The wonder is that it has taken so long for O'Brian's talents to be adequately recognised. Happily, I think that is now happening. He is more than a merely popular writer. He is a *very*, *very* fine one.'[2]

Ironically, the acclaim for which Patrick had worked so hard over six decades brought him personal distress more acute than any he had known in a singularly fraught life. Readers belatedly became eager to learn something of Patrick the man: not only his approach to writing, reading, and the sources of his encyclopædic knowledge of so wide a range of subjects, but also the personal aspects of a life of which the world knew little or nothing. Many authors are happy to lay bare their intimate thoughts and experiences, their principal regret being that a writer's life frequently tends towards dullness. Writing is hard and solitary work, and a repetitive round of sitting at a desk does not make for entertaining description.

Patrick's reaction to this curiosity was one of indignation and horror. He must surely have been one of the most secretive authors who ever lived, and he dreaded from the bottom of his soul any invasion of his privacy. In a rare television programme, in which he afterwards bitterly regretted participating, the baffled interviewer at one point asked him how long he had been living in his house. 'I'm not going to answer that,' snapped Patrick. 'The next thing you'll be wanting to know is how much I paid for it!'

He disapproved attempts to pry behind the scenes of an author's creative processes, on the grounds that it gravely detracted from the finished piece, which so often reflects a *mélange* of false starts, egregious misjudgements, and major shifts in perspective and treatment.[3] However, this was as nothing

[1] Byatt, 'Salts of the earth', *Evening Standard*, 14 February 1991; Binyon, 'The man with his eye on the mast', *Independent*, 23 February 1991.

[2] 'Virgil's challenge more than ably met', *Telegraph*, 14 May 1994.

[3] It is this that makes current plans by those who gained control of his literary estate to publish the scrappy opening draft of the novel on which he had begun working shortly before his death such an unforgivable betrayal in my opinion. My mother assured an American friend in 1995 'that he had never shared his work with anyone before completion' (*Latitude 38*, Mill Valley, CA, August 2000).

compared to his dread of exposure of his private life. Apologists for investigation have suggested that as the author of an admired life of Picasso (described by Kenneth Clark as 'much the best biography of Picasso that I have read') Patrick was not in a position to criticise those who sought to investigate an artist's private life. This is scarcely fair. There can be no general rule about such matters: Picasso's private life was largely played out with a publicity he plainly relished, while at the same time he pursued an active and controversial political career.

Fundamentally, however, Patrick's desperate concern to preserve his privacy did not stem from general principles, however much he sought to justify it on such grounds. In 1945, at the age of thirty, he consciously decided to obliterate his previous existence from memory. Although immediate members of his family were naturally aware (though for the most part little concerned about the matter) that he changed his name in that year by deed poll from Russ to O'Brian, when first made public in 1998 it provoked headline news around the globe. Much worse, it was declared that he had abandoned his first wife because he was unwilling to accept responsibility for a baby daughter suffering from an incurable illness, that he assumed the surname O'Brian initially to conceal responsibility for this inhuman action and then falsely passed himself off as an Irishman, and equally untruthfully claimed to have worked on board a sailing ship in his youth. In short, he was a bad husband, a callous father, and a calculating fraud.

Not long before the press attacks Patrick had learned to his alarm that an American, Dean King, was questioning friends and acquaintances with a view to writing his biography. Fortunately the British edition did not appear until shortly after Patrick's death. Although King's book presented a much fuller and more measured account of his life, the principal accusations were repeated in more detailed and permanent form. Patrick himself was too proud and introverted to attempt to counter the accusations (despite the fact that all, save for his having left his first wife, as I will show, were wholly or largely untrue), and in consequence he died two years later at the height of his literary fame a lonely, tortured, and at the last possibly paranoid figure.

As Patrick's stepson I observed these developments at close quarters with increasing distress and indignation. However, there appeared to be nothing that could be done to counter the wave of vilification, since he could not bring himself to speak even privately about the issues. At one point he contemplated taking legal action, but as he was well aware of my own unfortunate experiences at the hands of the English judiciary I was able to dissuade him.

Patrick married my mother Mary in 1945, a fortnight before he changed his name. Theirs was a love affair which lasted for six decades until her death in 1998. As my mother had deserted my father, under court rulings she was forbidden any access to me. Even her letters were intercepted and destroyed, so that she never knew whether or not I had received them. No photograph was ever sent to her, and consequently she did not even known what I looked like throughout my schooldays.

As I was aged four when she disappeared from my life, I retained only fleeting memories of her from my infancy. However, once I left school I saw no reason why I should continue not to know my own mother, and on an emotional day in the summer of 1955 I arrived at the home where she and Patrick lived in the south of France. Thereafter, year after year I spent long holidays living with them, and also saw them frequently during their regular visits to England and Ireland. My father had remarried in 1943, when he sadly fell under the influence of a new wife who I felt bitterly resented me. Consequently, though I remained fond of my father, I came rather to regard my mother and Patrick as my parents, and it is as such that I refer to them in this book.

It would be absurd to deny that Patrick could be quirky, hypersensitive, and not infrequently extremely difficult. On the other hand he was acutely sensitive to human relations, proving a deeply sympathetic and wise adviser to whom I would regularly turn when faced by problems ranging from troubled youthful love affairs to my own literary endeavours. We shared many tastes, above all an absorbing love of literature and history. He was generous to a fault, frequently presenting me with treasured books, and eventually gave me his entire library.

This is a book I had never dreamed of writing. I was well aware of Patrick's detestation of the idea of a biography, and at the time of his death was preoccupied with a succession of projected works on subjects with which I remain deeply concerned. On 27 May 1998 he had written to me, asking that when he died 'may I beg you to come over as quickly as ever you can (I enclose a cheque in case you should be short of money) and have me buried . . . and please, when you come down, destroy my diaries (if I have not already done it) and any private, intimate correspondence'. When that melancholy day arrived I found almost nothing that fell within this description. It may be that he had already destroyed much himself, and later I discovered that a few months before his death his literary agent had persuaded him to let her remove his diaries.

A few weeks after Patrick's sudden death in Dublin in the New Year of 2000 I unexpectedly found myself faced with a grave dilemma. I was asked to review Dean King's biography, which I read with growing astonishment and dismay. The Patrick who emerged from the book bore scarcely any resemblance to the man I had known so intimately for forty-five years, and accounts of major events in his private life were more often than not factually wrong. Although King is a sincere admirer of Patrick's works, and I am sure sought to be fair, such serious distortions were inevitable in view of the fact that he never met Patrick or my mother, most of Patrick's few intimate friends honoured his request not to speak with King, and at Patrick's request I had declined to discuss him or any aspect of my mother's life with him. Nor, naturally, did King possess access to any of Patrick's private papers. Finally, he relied heavily for his account of Patrick's early life on interviews with Richard Russ, Patrick's son by his first marriage, who in 1964 had become estranged from his father, and even before that saw him only on brief occasions after his final visit to Collioure in 1955. As contemporary records and his own letters show, Richard's memory occasionally played him false (understandably, when recollecting events which occurred in his infancy), and his testimony with regard to the break-up of his parents' marriage is of very restricted worth. Though of course his experience and memory are of independent value, ironically I knew Patrick much longer and better than did his own son.

When I found King's book described by well-intentioned reviewers (some of whom claimed close acquaintance with Patrick) on both sides of the Atlantic as a fair and well-researched account of his life, I felt it had become impossible to leave his imaginative version uncorrected. No longer was it a case of there being no biography, as Patrick had vainly wished, but an entirely false impression would be retained for posterity. I decided it was my duty to counter this by describing the Patrick I had known so well.

What he himself would have wished me to do I cannot say, but circumstances had changed so much since he asked me to destroy his papers that I cannot believe he would not now wish me to put the record straight. On reflection it seemed too that his request had been somewhat ambivalent. Why did he not destroy them himself, when chance might have led someone other than me to be first to enter the house after his death? Then again, Patrick cannot have overlooked the fact that I owned far more of his personal papers than he did. Not only was there the voluminous body of letters he had sent me over the years, but at different times he had given me personal documents, memoranda, odd pieces of his writing and the like when planning our respective labours, which frequently overlapped.

My original intention was to write a purely personal memoir of the man I knew. For his life before I came to know him, I was content to refer the reader to King's account, which I assumed he must have researched as thoroughly as possible. However, before long I began to find that he had perpetrated egregious errors, even in respect of such mundane and readily established matters as where and when Patrick was living at given times. Paradoxically this proved fortunate, since it impelled me to conduct my own researches, with gratifying results. On re-examination I found the papers in my possession to be far more informative and revealing than I had recalled, and I also received invaluable help from many members of the Russ family. One pleasant consequence of this was establishing contact and in several cases lasting friendships with my hitherto unknown 'cousins'.

Patrick O'Brian's unusually idiosyncratic character derived in large part from the exceptional circumstances of his childhood and youth. This consideration affords particular problems for his biographer, since he was at great pains to suppress or distort almost everything to do with his life before 1945, when he married my mother and changed his name. Patrick like the rest of us was not perfect, and not everything I have learned redounds to his credit. My purpose is not to provide an apologia, but as full and truthful an account of his life as is humanly possible. I suspect that he might now approve his admired Dr Johnson's response, when 'asked, if it was not wrong in Orrery to expose the defects of a man with whom he lived in intimacy. – *Johnson.* "Why no, sir, after the man is dead; for then it is done historically."'[1] I have suppressed nothing, save what I consider entirely personal and of no concern to the outside world. I believe it will be seen that much of what he was so determined to conceal was in fact innocuous or even praiseworthy. As a prime example, the extreme paucity and lack of success of his formal education, of which he was profoundly ashamed, when understood makes his life's achievement the more astonishing.

While writing I had before me constantly in mind the living Patrick whom I first met on the doorstep of our little home in the rue Arago in Collioure on 1 September 1955. Johnson further pronounced that 'nobody can write the life of a man but those who have eat and drunk and lived in social intercourse with him'.[2] Clearly he did not mean this to be taken literally, since he wrote numerous biographies of people he had never met. Nevertheless it is true that direct intimacy with the subject transmutes second-hand testimony, oral or literary, into a lively picture which imaginative empathy cannot provide to

[1] James Boswell, *The Journal of a Tour to the Hebrides with Samuel Johnson, LL.D.* (London, 1785), p. 291. 'If we owe regard to the memory of the dead, there is yet more respect to be paid to knowledge, to virtue, and to truth' (Arthur Murphy, ed., *The Works of Samuel Johnson, LL.D. with an Essay on his Life and Genius* (London, 1824), iv, p. 386). 'If a man is to write *A Panegyrick*, he may keep vices out of sight; but if he professes to write *A Life*, he must represent it really as it was' (*The Life of Samuel Johnson, LL.D.* (London, 1793), ii, pp. 538–39).

[2] Ibid., p. 22.

anything approaching the same extent.[1] Although I trust I have not allowed my affection to influence my judgement, I believe that evocative memory has proved an invaluable aid to understanding. If I can convey something of this to readers of this book, I shall be content.

Finally, for those who dislike epigraphs, my excuse is that my selection derives almost exclusively from books which Patrick himself owned and loved. In summary, it is hard to think of a more apt application of Madame de Staël's oft-quoted aphorism:

Tout comprendre rend très indulgent.

[1] '. . . most accounts of particular persons are barren and useless. If a life be delayed till interest and envy are at an end, we may hope for impartiality, but must expect little intelligence; for the incidents which give excellence to biography are of a volatile and evanescent kind, such as soon escape the memory, and are rarely transmitted by tradition' (Murphy, ed., *The Works of Samuel Johnson*, iv, pp. 382–86).

CHAPTER ONE

Embarkation

My mother groan'd, my father wept,
Into the dangerous world I leapt;
Helpless, naked, piping loud,
Like a fiend hid in a cloud.
(William Blake, 'Infant Sorrow')

For much of his life Patrick O'Brian was widely reputed to be of Irish ancestry and brought up and educated in that country. In fact he was born and educated in England, possessed not a drop of Irish blood, did not visit Ireland before his early twenties, and assumed the surname O'Brian by deed poll in 1945. It was not until October 1998 that anyone, beyond a diminishing circle of close relatives and friends old enough to have known him before his transformation, became aware of the fact that this aspect of his persona represented a fiction as imaginative as anything found in his novels. In that year, however, his innocuous pretence was exposed to worldwide publicity and strangely ill-informed comment.

Patrick's paternal ancestry was in reality German. His grandfather, Karl Russ, was born in 1842 at Braudis, near Leipzig in Saxony. According to family tradition the family had migrated some generations earlier from Eastern Europe, which may account for their surname, *Russe* being German for 'Russian'. For several generations the family had conducted business as furriers. Young Karl possessed an adventurous spirit, and after completing his apprenticeship travelled to Belgium and France, before eventually settling in Britain in 1862. After working for a number of City firms, he followed the family tradition by setting himself up as a furrier. His industry and enterprise made business so profitable that in 1874 he was able to buy a shop in the West End, at 70 New Bond Street, where the fine quality of his garments swiftly attracted the custom of the fashionable world. Four years later he was awarded a Gold

Medal at the Paris Exhibition, and before long amassed a considerable fortune.

In 1870 Karl had become a naturalised British subject, anglicising his name to Charles, and two years later married a charming twenty-two-year-old girl, Emily Callaway. He bought and furnished lavishly a large house in St John's Wood, and became a characteristic figure of solid Victorian prosperity and respectability. His wife fulfilled another familiar aspect of Victorian upper middle-class life, bearing him thirteen children during the fourteen years which followed their marriage, the last of whom sadly died five months after his birth.

Two more died in tragic circumstances, while the eldest daughter Emily returned to Germany, where she married and settled down. In 1893, while his wife was staying with Emily to assist with the birth of her first child, Karl Russ died at the age of fifty-one. His health had been deteriorating for three years, and it became necessary to sell the business.

The head of the family was now Patrick's father Charles, his father's eldest son, who was only seventeen at the time of the bereavement. In common with many of their more enterprising compatriots, the Russ family had by now become effortlessly absorbed into middle-class English society.[1] There being nothing particularly Teutonic about 'Russ', it had not even been thought expedient (as with many other immigrant families) for Karl Russ or his sons to anglicise their surname. This attitude was confirmed by the family's immunity from the hysterical outburst of Germanophobia which erupted in Britain at the outset of the Great War, when patriotic citizens expressed defiance of the enemy by flinging stones at dachshunds in the streets.[2] In February 1917, as the British army prepared for its bloody assault at Arras, a schoolfriend presented Patrick's elder brother Victor with an instructive work entitled 'The History of the Hun'. Clearly it did not occur to either that a Russ could be anything but a patriotic Briton.

Karl Russ's eight sons had been educated at a reputable minor public school, Shebbear College in North Devon, to which his son Charles in turn

[1] A large and respectable German community existed in London in the later nineteenth century. After 1870 the German Club took over a public garden at Acton, and 'transformed it into a veritable summer *Biergarten* with the biggest dancing platform in this country, where German is chiefly spoken' (Christopher Trent, *Greater London: Its Growth and Development through Two Thousand Years* (London, 1965), p. 183).

[2] Cf. Arthur Marwick, *The Deluge: British Society and the First World War* (Boston, 1965), pp. 37–38. By the autumn of 1914, 500 German residents in Britain (later including the Royal Family) had formally anglicised their names (Hew Strachan, *The First World War* (Oxford, 2000–), i, p. 108). Even the celebrated snuff and cigar shop of Fribourg and Treyer in the Haymarket, whose eighteenth-century founder was of Swiss origin, felt obliged to trade temporarily under the name Evans & Evans (John Arlott, *The Snuff Shop* (London, 1974), p. 21).

sent two of Patrick's elder brothers. One of the major purposes of the English public school system as it evolved in Queen Victoria's reign was to produce a homogeneous class of gentlemanly administrators, qualified by classical education, probity of character, and physical prowess to administer a burgeoning economy and ever-expanding Empire. While this system was by nature highly élitist, within its enclosed and unselfconscious world distinctions of class and wealth were largely eschewed as 'bad form', and respect was primarily gained by status within the school hierarchy, above all through prowess on the playing-field.

There was consequently nothing in Patrick's family background to provide him with rational cause for embarrassment. Nor is there any reason to suppose that self-consciousness over his German ancestry played any part in his dramatic decision years later to sever himself from his roots. None of his brothers and sisters is recorded as having suffered any disquiet on this score: on the contrary, his inexplicable decision to abjure the family name provoked surprise and offence. They were justifiably proud of their grandfather's remarkable achievement, and Patrick's elder brothers Victor and Bernard were at pains to ensure that his grave in the family vault at Hampstead Cemetery was kept in good repair.

Both Charles Russ and his younger brother Sidney used their inheritance to put themselves through medical school. Of the two, it was Sidney who prospered. Before obtaining his doctorate in physics in 1909, he spent his early postgraduate years as a demonstrator in Manchester, where he studied under Lord Rutherford. He also worked with Röntgen in Germany, and returned to England to become a pioneer in understanding of radioactive material. In due course he was appointed Emeritus Professor of Physics at Middlesex Hospital Medical School, received numerous prestigious acknowledgements of his outstanding authority in his field, and was author of a number of scholarly books. He collaborated with medical colleagues in pursuing research on the effects of radiation on human tissues, specialising principally in the treatment of cancer. For his achievement in the field of radium work he was awarded the CBE in 1931.[1] Many years later Patrick, who admired his uncle's achievements, received the same honour from the King's granddaughter.

Though he too was endowed with considerable talent and energy, Sidney's elder brother Charles was to prove erratic – not to say eccentric – in his scientific pursuits and achievements. Ultimately his career would prove a failure – as the evidence suggests, an embittered one – but all that lay in the future.

[1] Highly laudatory obituaries of Professor Sidney Russ were published on 10 August 1963 in the *British Medical Journal* and the *Lancet*.

Charles married in 1902, a year before he qualified at St Mary's Hospital, Paddington. His bride, Jessie Goddard, was accounted by all who knew her a beautiful, intelligent, and sweet-natured girl. He was thirty-six and she twenty-four, an age difference by no means unusual for married couples at the time. Their marriage appears to have been one of unalloyed happiness. Jessie came of good family, but suffered the misfortune of being orphaned in childhood and brought up in fosterage. However she was well educated and a gifted painter. Patrick's brother Victor understood that his mother had been a fashion artist before her marriage.

Jessie bore her uxorious husband nine children in fifteen years. After living for some time in successive London homes, in 1908 Charles established his growing family in a handsome country house situated in what was then an unspoiled rural backwater in the valley of the little River Misbourn, between Chalfont St Peter and Gerrards Cross in south-east Buckinghamshire. Its extensive grounds and fine trees had led a previous owner to name it 'Walden', after Thoreau's famous wilderness retreat. The interior of the house reflected much of the splendour of grandfather Karl's house in St John's Wood, with ponderous family furniture, portraits, and silver laid out in lavish display.

It was an idyllic spot for young children to grow up, and the young Russes were fortunate in being numerous enough to organise their own complex and imaginative games in the grounds. The oldest was Godfrey, who was born just over nine months after his parents' marriage. Next came Victor, followed by their first daughter Olive. In 1909 a third son Michael arrived, who was succeeded in the following year by twin daughters Nora and Connie, and a further son Bernard in 1912. Patrick, the subject of this biography, was born at the end of the momentous year 1914. Christened Richard Patrick, he was known throughout his life as Patrick.

For the ever-increasing tribe of young Russ children, Walden was a self-sufficient magical world. Each child was known by a nickname. Some were customary abbreviations such as 'Olly' for Olive or 'Mike' for Michael, while others were more arcane. Godfrey was known as 'Roguey', Victor as 'Bew', Nora as 'Bish' (supposedly from a preference for using her bishop at chess), while Bernard was 'Bun' – a diminutive by which Patrick knew him throughout his life. Little Patrick became simply 'Pat'.

The atmosphere at Walden was overwhelmingly secure and happy. Uncle Sidney, who joined the family as a permanent resident, was popular with the children, in whose games he frequently joined. Jessie Russ was devoted to her family. An active gardener, she also retained her skill and enthusiasm for painting. Bernard later recalled how 'Mother loved gardening, and I remember her setting up her easel on the lawn and creating lovely watercolours of her beloved flowers', while Victor 'remembered her painting a flower picture for their Fathers birthday . . . [he] attributed his love of gardening to his Mothers influence'. Jessie Russ was always present as a focus of comfort and security to her youthful tribe, as they tirelessly romped around the house and its spacious grounds.

During the week the children saw little of their father, who travelled each day with his brother from nearby Denham railway station to his work in London. From 1906 until 1912 he worked as senior assistant at the Clinical Laboratory of Pathology and Public Health in Queen Anne Street off Cavendish Square, under the direction of a distinguished pathologist, Dr Thomas Eastes. In 1907 Eastes moved his laboratory to 38 New Cavendish Street. It was probably because he devoted excessive time to his own absorbing researches that Dr Russ was eventually discharged by his employer. Always intensely independent, he appears to have been gratified at setting up on his own, and promptly established himself in private practice nearby in Marylebone at 25 Beaumont Street. Dr Eastes claimed that the proximity violated a restrictive clause in their covenant. A bitter legal action ensued, which went before the Court of Appeal before being resolved in Charles's favour. Although he was later to become an irascible character, at the time he had a sunny and equable nature, and was in any case adjudged to have acted perfectly properly.

Despite this, his career as general practitioner was never very successful or remunerative, and he spent most of his time absorbed in researches in a laboratory he established on the premises. Although he published discoveries which received considerable acclaim at the time, his standing within the medical profession may already have become somewhat equivocal. At any rate when in 1915 he applied to work as a volunteer in the X-ray section (then known as the Electrical Department) at the Middlesex Hospital, the Medical Sub-Committee agreed to accept his services, but he was unable subsequently to obtain a paid post as assistant in the Department.

None of this meant anything to his young offspring, in whose eyes he enjoyed that semi-omnipotent status which young children normally accord their fathers. His eternal inventiveness and enthusiasm for every venture he pursued were qualities particularly appealing to children. To these were added the material advantage of an imposing physical presence. Well over six feet tall, he was a strikingly handsome figure of a man. Throughout the years of his marriage to Jessie he proved an affectionate and energetic father, who inspired and participated in his children's activities, especially those of the boys.

Bernard recalled how, 'when we were sick, Daddy would always come home with little extra presents for us, hidden in his medical bag. It made being ill almost worthwhile! I remember one day watching from the window when he arrived. He had bought us a little tricycle! Solemnly, this great, jolly, 6′4½″ giant put down his bag, mounted the little machine, and carefully pedalled his way up the drive, much to our delight.'

Among Charles Russ's multifarious enthusiasms was a delight in motoring. Initially he bought a motorcycle with sidecar, in which he would take Jessie for picnics in the surrounding countryside. His enthusiasm for all things mechanical was matched only by their propensity to go wrong. Victor remembered how he and Godfrey were regularly employed to hand their father his tools, sometimes in bitterly cold weather, while he tinkered away at the works of his motor bicycle. From this he graduated to buying a Wolseley motor car known to the family as the 'Globe', a magnificent machine with great brass carriage lamps on each side of the windscreen, which Bernard remembered as 'large enough to take the entire family, which was more like a charabanc or bus than a motor vehicle, for party purposes'. Unfortunately their father could not resist attempting to repair the car himself, generally with unhappy consequences.

So long as he possessed means to indulge his hobby, Charles Russ found it all but impossible to avoid the temptation of a new car. Victor's diary for 1919 shows that Charles added a Morgan, a three-wheeler, to the 'Globe'. The Morgan provided an exciting challenge, but since Charles was a giant and Jessie fairly diminutive as often as not the car tipped over when taking corners at speed. By good fortune no one suffered injury, and on the frequent occasion of a breakdown Jessie would sit good-naturedly watching her husband feverishly wrestling away beneath the vehicle's hood.[1]

Patrick was too young to participate in these adventures. He was born on 12 December 1914, the penultimate child in a succession of nine brothers and sisters. His brother Bun, at the time nearly three years old, remembered his appearance in the world.

> Patrick arrived when I was about three, the last of the children to be born at 'Walden'. I recall being with Mother in the big upstairs back bedroom before the event and clutching hard to her hand as a huge and noisy bird flew right over the house – the first aeroplane I had ever seen. Afterwards, allowed back into the room, I duly inspected my new brother and was put to work crawling about on the floor, smoothing out large sheets of brown paper. My infant mind led me to believe that these were the wrappings for the new baby, although I could not for the life of me understand why such a large parcel was to be made out of such a small infant![2]

[1] A.B. Russ, *Lady Day Prodigal* (Victoria, BC, 1989), pp. 9, 10–11.
[2] Ibid., p. 9.

It was an appropriately dramatic moment for Patrick's arrival in the world. That summer Britain had been precipitated into the bloodiest and hardest-fought war in her history.

On 2 August the British Government warned Germany that she would stand by her guarantee to uphold Belgian neutrality. When Germany declined to back down and declared war on Britain's ally France the next day, Britain lost no time in declaring war on Germany on 4 August. As German divisions poured across the Belgian frontier, public opinion was solidly united behind the Liberal Government, accepting that national honour required the country to fulfil its commitment to protect plucky little Belgium.

By Christmas it had become clear to the general staffs of all belligerent countries that a bitter struggle of uncertain duration lay ahead.[1] So far as the Russ family was concerned, however, the terrible conflict had little if any material effect on their lives. The family's German origin was an ancestral memory, and they followed with patriotic enthusiasm newspaper accounts of the gallantry with which the British army was fighting the hated Huns and Turks, and shared public confidence that, however hard and long the struggle, the British Empire would emerge triumphant.

As a medical practitioner Charles was exempt from military service, and was troubled on occasion by patriotic women who presented him with white feathers in the streets. Bun assumed that he was of a pacifist inclination, but one wonders whether he was reluctant to fight against his father's compatriots, who included cousins still living in Germany. On the other hand Bun remembered the excitement when their Uncle William called at Walden on leave from his artillery regiment at the Front. He 'came riding by on his cavalry mount and Mike was allowed to hold the reins while the horse cropped the back lawn and I remember sitting with Mother in the dining-room, having a feast of bread and blackcurrant jam.'

As the conflict ground to a bloody impasse, dramatic new methods of waging war emerged, ranging from the mass deployment of submarines, aeroplanes, long-range heavy artillery, and high explosive shells,[2] to tanks, motorised transport, machine-guns, poison gas, barbed wire and wireless telegraphy.

In the autumn of 1916 the Russ children had a dramatic glimpse of one of these novel aspects of the conflict. At the beginning of the previous year the

[1] The subsequently reviled Kitchener was among the few Allied commanders and statesmen who understood from the outset the inevitability of protracted total war.

[2] In 1918 German 'Big Bertha' howitzers bombarded Paris from a range of 76 miles with 264lb shells, whose trajectory ascended 24 miles above the earth.

Germans had launched a succession of alarmingly successful bombing raids on England, sending giant Zeppelins cruising silently through the night sky to drop bombs with lethal effect on towns as far inland as Shrewsbury. London was the prime target, suffering severe fire damage and numerous fatalities. Damaging as this was, it not unnaturally provoked disproportionate alarm in a country which had had no direct experience of warfare since the Dutch invasion of 1688. The fear excited by these raids was greatly exacerbated by the relative impunity with which the airships survived attacks by anti-aircraft fire and British aeroplanes.

On 2 September 1916 London was attacked by a fleet of fourteen Zeppelins. Though they were lit up by searchlights and fired upon from below, anti-aircraft shells exploded and tracer bullets passed by them without effect. It seemed they would return to Germany without loss, when RFC pilot Lieutenant William Leefe Robinson, flying his BE2 C fighter on anti-Zeppelin patrol, came upon a Schutte-Lanz SL11 airship at 11,500 feet over north-east London. Approaching within 500 feet of the monster, he raked it with machine-gun fire, but without effect. By now the airships had moved out of range of searchlights and anti-aircraft fire, and Robinson circled in a third time to attack the SL11 from below. He had barely finished firing one drum of his machine-gun when the rear of the airship burst into flame. As he swiftly took evasive action, the Zeppelin burst into a gigantic ball of fire which illuminated the countryside around and was watched by the population of London. For this feat Lieutenant Robinson received the VC, and though German air raids continued until the last summer of the war from this time onwards their airships suffered increasing losses.

The wreckage came down near Cuffley in Hertfordshire.[1] This was some twenty miles from the Russ family home, but the terrific blaze was clearly visible on the skyline. Two or three days later the family drove over to join crowds flocking to view the scene of the catastrophe. The wreckage was cordoned off; still, the children were greatly excited at receiving small fragments of aluminium tied with red, white, and blue ribbons, which were sold by the Red Cross to raise money for the war effort.[2]

[1] Cf. Nigel Steel and Peter Hart, *Tumult in the Clouds* (London, 1997), pp. 167–69. I am indebted to Dr Christopher Dowling of the Imperial War Museum for this reference.

[2] *Lady Day Prodigal*, p. 13. At the time he was compiling his memoir Bernard told his sister: 'Nora remembers well that Connie and I were in the pram whereas she had to trudge along and the result was that she wet her pants!' This cannot be right, since in the autumn of 1916 Connie and Bernard were aged six and four respectively. Doubtless Nora (who was living with Bernard at the time) and Bernard recognised the mistake before his book went to press. In addition Bernard antedated this event by two years when he came to recollect it in old age in his privately printed memoir, and was further mistaken in stating that the airship was shot

In old age Bernard published a memoir for the family's benefit, which includes these memories of life at Walden. However, as he was only five when the family left the house, they constitute a succession of lively flashbacks rather than a coherent whole. A more immediate glimpse of life as it appeared to the children at the time survives in the form of a schoolboy diary kept by his elder brother Victor during the first months of 1917.

Victor was born on 2 January 1905, and the journal begins with his twelfth birthday party: 'I had six presents, and cake . . . we had cards, musical bumps, and Keeping up the Zeppelin' – a topical game presumably involving preventing a balloon from touching the ground. During the Christmas festive season there was a magic lantern show, a family outing to see a pantomime of 'Cinderella' at the London Opera House, the erection of a snowman on the front lawn, and skating on a local pond. There was no dearth of amusements in that pre-television age. Brothers and sisters joined with enthusiasm in games of 'doctors', 'grocers', and 'spies'. Everyone collected stamps, and with his Meccano set Victor constructed a model clutch, an extending ladder on wheels, and a motor van. Lead soldiers garrisoned a fort and paraded about the playroom floor, while a fine electric train ran around its perimeter. This appealed to the inventive Dr Russ, who could regularly be found stretched out on the floor, as he toiled away at the box containing the engine's accumulator and rectifier, adjusted the track's points, or mounted the rails on boards.

Sadly the Russ family's lavish lifestyle at Walden was to come to an end before Patrick was old enough to enjoy the pleasures the fine house and garden afforded his elder brothers and sisters. At the end of 1916 Charles Russ withdrew his two oldest sons Godfrey and Victor from their boarding-school, Dean Close School, near Cheltenham. Bun recalled long afterwards: 'The incumbent Headmaster, father of the well-known poet James Elroy Flecker, was apprehended and charged with shoplifting. He had stolen a can of sardines!' It seems likely that this foolish scandal was seized upon by their father as a pretext for his removal of the boys from school. In reality his extravagant lifestyle was beginning to take its toll on the family's finances.

Next year his brother Sidney ('Uncle Beaney') married, and departed to set up his own home. If, as seems likely, he was part-owner of the house, this may account for Charles's sale of Walden that year and move to a considerably more modest house in Harrow.

down over Harrow Hill. The latter error may well have arisen from the fact that Robinson's home was at Harrow Weald, where a public house was named in his honour. Conceivably it was this too which led Bernard to misplace the episode at the time when the family had moved to Harrow.

It was unfortunate that Charles, accustomed to the opulence of his father's household, had found himself unexpectedly obliged to assume responsibility for his financial affairs at the age of seventeen. Though Karl Russ had been a wealthy man, his children came into a considerably reduced inheritance. Their father bequeathed half his fortune to his widow, while the remainder was divided between ten brothers and sisters. Accustomed to self-indulgence, and with his impractical and over-sanguine nature, Charles was to spend much of his life lurching from one financial crisis to another.

An unwitting indication of his declining fortune is provided by an entry in Victor's diary for St Valentine's Day 1917. 'The man who gave Daddy a dozen eggs at Wycombe on Sunday 28th of January, gave Mummy a chicken and another dozen eggs . . . Daddy had the chicken for supper.' Dr Russ's medical practice had been in decline for some time, and increasingly he found himself obliged to accept payment in kind from his less affluent patients. On 11 March Victor further innocently noted: 'Daddy and Rogue [Godfrey] went to Willesden in the Morgan to see one of his patients, and he gave Daddy t[w]o bottles of wine.'

On 26 January appears the ominous record: 'Daddy came home after dinner and Mr and Mrs Taylor came to look over the house.' By the second week of February packing cases arrived, 'Daddy took up the carpets in the Drawing Room and the linoleum and also the carpet and underfelt in the study', and 'I packed my soldiers in my tuck box'. The house and even garden were stripped of virtually everything that was removable. All the electric fittings were transferred to their new home, so that packing had to be conducted by the light of candles and paraffin lamps. That Jessie's beloved bulbs and other plants were raised and potted for transferral to their new garden was understandable, but the dismantling and removal of a summer house (nicknamed 'Boodle') appears a little excessive.

The melancholy time for departure from the family's beloved Walden finally arrived on 22 February 1917. That day Victor recorded in his diary: 'We moved to 10 College Road, Harrow. There were three vans and they did not take all the things. Daddy, Rogue and I took down curtain rings. We had dinner in the nursery. Mummy, Pat & Daddy went in the Morgan, the rest of us by train.'

It was his task to take up his mother's plants and replant them in their modest new setting, for which he was paid a welcome two shillings. Meanwhile Charles and the boys laboured at putting up curtains, laying linoleum and carpets, and installing the electricity. On St David's Day Jessie took her two youngest boys, Bernard and Patrick, to visit their paternal grandmother who lived conveniently nearby at 60 Lowlands Road. While their new home at Harrow bore no comparison with the splendours of Walden, some compensation for Charles Russ lay in its greater proximity to his elderly mother's home and his London laboratory. In those days Harrow was situated in a pleasantly rural landscape, its hill dominated by the impressive buildings of the celebrated public school attended by Lord Byron and Winston Churchill.

On 16 January Victor had recorded: 'We began doing lessons with Mummy, Roguey, Victor, Olive, Michael, Con., Nora, because Dean Close School began then.' This was presumably to compensate for the fact that Godfrey and Victor had been withdrawn from the school, while none of the others had begun their education. How capable a teacher Mrs Russ might have proved was never discovered, since from that day onwards there is no record of the experiment's being repeated. However great her enthusiasm, she must at once have discovered the impossibility of attempting to teach a group of children whose age and knowledge ranged from those of two well-educated public schoolboys to the six-year-old twins Connie and Nora. That Jessie and her husband even contemplated the project suggests considerable naïvety, and helps to explain much that went wrong with the family in ensuing years. Significantly, while Charles Russ found ample time to drive about the countryside in his smart Morgan, visit friends, and attend the theatre with his wife in London, he evidently saw no pressing need to arrange the continuation of his two eldest sons' education.

It was not until the autumn that Godfrey and Victor resumed their schooling, almost a year after leaving Dean Close, and Michael (aged eight) joined them in April 1918. As Bun explained: 'The three older boys were . . . away at day school – the John Lyon School for Boys, founded by Elizabeth I, and next door to the great Harrow school at the top of the Hill. They all had bikes, Godfrey even having saved for one of the new Sturmey-Archer Three Speeds, and were free to come and go as they pleased, but for the rest of us it was a different story.'

The children took their move for granted, and do not appear greatly to have missed Walden. Their number had been increased by the withdrawal of Godfrey and Victor from boarding-school, and the novelty of the situation provided its own appeal. The girls went shopping with their mother in London and joined her on visits to their grandmother. There were outings to the cinema and happy hours watching trains go by. Once Victor recorded a noteworthy occasion when he and Godfrey devoted themselves to counting 'the people passing our gate between 5.45 pm and 6.30 pm'.

At this time Patrick was still the baby of the family. On a blank page of Victor's diary for 1917 one of the children drew a charming little pencil sketch of him.[1] He was a sickly child, and long afterwards recalled suffering from regular bouts of an unspecified ailment which confined him to bed for prolonged periods. In 1987 his brother Bernard wrote: 'Nora and I noted that it was Pat's birthday – his 73rd – on Saturday, 12th December. It is amazing to think that he has survived so long, considering his frail health and weak chest, bronchitis etc. in early life.' When Patrick as a young man came to write his novel *Hussein*, his description of the effects of cholera upon the hero reads much as if it reflects bitter experience: 'He lay on a string bed, his body distorted with the furious pain; it wracked him so that he could scarcely breathe the heavy air that seemed to weigh down on him like a stifling blanket.'

The decline in the material fortunes of the Russ family does not appear to have affected Charles's good spirits for the first year of their move to Harrow. As before, he frequently took Jessie and the children for drives in the Morgan, Kew Gardens being a regular destination in consideration of Jessie's great interest in flowers and gardening. Victor noted that 'Daddy took Michael and me to Wandsworth 3rd London Hospital', where he presumably worked in addition to the Middlesex Hospital. Before long little Pat was allowed to join in these family jaunts.

At home Charles busied himself cheerfully about the house and garden, engaging the assistance of Godfrey and Victor, who received modest but welcome payment for their labours. As at Walden, he applied himself to the children's train set. 'Daddy came home early and made the electric engine go with the accumulators and he began to charge them,' Victor recorded contentedly. 'We had supper in the Nursery because the electric railway was in the dining-room. Daddy brought home Rum & Wine' – probably further payment in kind from one of his diminishing band of patients. Other entries confirm that there had been no diminution in the treats which brightened their lives. 'Daddy came home after tea and put up the electric railway, and tried to make the engine go from the mains. Daddy gave Rogue and I a slab of Hume's Nut Milk Chocolate each.'

Meanwhile across the Channel the war pursued its relentless course, with the prospect of victory apparently no nearer in sight. The older children daily scanned with avidity maps published in the newspapers of the fluctuating front lines, and shortly after their arrival at Harrow Victor recorded in his diary two exciting events occurring on the same day: 'I went for a ride on our

[1] Sixty years later Patrick recorded in his diary: 'A civil letter . . . from Bun [Bernard, then living in Canada] with an oddly touching photocopied p fr Vic's diary of January 1919 showing me in bed.'

new bike. British troops in Mesopotamia capture Bagdad.' A few days later, on St Patrick's Day 1917, Victor and Olive patriotically spent a penny on Irish flags to wear in honour of the Irish regiments (all of whose men were volunteers) fighting gallantly on the Western Front.

The struggle was to drag on for another year and a half of unrelenting carnage and destruction: 1917 merged into 1918, with hopes of victory seemingly ever diminishing. In March 1918 Lenin signed a peace treaty with Germany at Brest-Litovsk, which surrendered the richest regions of European Russia to the enemy. Not only was Germany now in possession of untold material resources with which to prosecute the war, but she was free to concentrate all her forces on the Western Front. Millions had died and were yet to die, and the lives of innumerable survivors would be irretrievably scarred by the slaughter.

Although the tragedy which struck the Russ family early that spring had no connection with the war, it was no less uniquely terrible in its effect. A month after the birth of her youngest child Joan in July 1917 in their home in Harrow, Jessie Russ had to undergo a severe operation for an abdominal ailment. It appears that she was suffering from cancer, but whether the surgery proved unsuccessful or she experienced a fresh attack remains unclear. Whatever the cause, she died quite suddenly on 30 March 1918 at the age of forty-one. The effect of the loss was devastating on the entire family, above all on her unhappy husband.

Until the end of his days Bun could not rid himself of the memory of that dreadful day.

> When she was about to die, Dad and I think Uncle Sidney or Beany, as we called him and whoever was the attending physician were gathered around her bed and each of the children was brought in and lifted up to kiss Mother goodbye although we did not know it at the time, she was on the verge of death, I believe by cancer. But I do remember that when the funeral occurred, I strolled upstairs and went to look in her bedroom and to my horror saw it empty and little blue candle flames on each corner of the wire mattress. It was a horrifying sight for a youngster and I shall never forget it. Of course somebody should have locked the door, but that is what happened. I also remember the night she died, the lady we called Aunty Mason and Godfrey called Hauntie Mason, a great friend and companion of our Mother, came to our bedsides weeping and hugging us and having to tell us that she had indeed left this earth. I remember her as a sweet and lovely presence. I cannot remember any[thing] unpleasant or unkind about her.

Patrick is unlikely to have remembered anything of the spacious glories of

Walden, which he had left two months after his third birthday, so 10 College Road, Harrow was the first home of which he would retain any distinct recollection. Though he was just three when his mother died, the gulf which suddenly opened up before him became entrenched in his consciousness as an unbearably painful memory, and exerted an ineradicable effect upon him for the remainder of his life.

At the time he appears to have suffered from a confused *mélange* of emotions, being too small to understand the reality of what was happening around him. In his novel *The Catalans*, written in 1952, Patrick placed these words in the mouth of Xavier (an unmistakable self-portrait):

> When I was a really small boy I loved my stepmother[1] . . . I loved her, and I thought about things for her and how when I grew up I would do this, that, and the other to give her pleasure: and when they took her away I was so desolate – desolate. But even then, at its tenderest, my power of affection must have been of a feeble growth, for when they told me that she had died . . . I was more concerned with acting, tasting the importance of tragedy, than with genuine regret. Yet it is unfair to say that: I was only a very little boy . . . a year is such a long period in a child's life.[2]

This passage occurs in a lengthy confession recounted by Xavier to his cousin Alain, the overall burden of which is his anguished realisation that he believes himself to have lost since childhood the capacity to feel emotional concern for a fellow being. Since there is no doubt that Patrick retained from infancy an irreparable sense of loss at his mother's death, it is hard not to believe that his tendency to excessive self-analysis gradually induced an irrational sense of being found wanting at the moment of crisis, when he experienced a covert sensation of importance on finding himself at the centre of a tragedy, which increased his innate fear that he lacked natural affection. Both Dickens (in *David Copperfield*) and Tolstoy (in *Childhood*, written from personal experience) vividly describe the manner in which children experience sensations of egoism embarrassingly obtruding themselves into occasions of profound grief. The two great writers appreciated the extent to which this seemingly incongruous self-regard may come to haunt those who experience it in early childhood.

[1] It is clear that in the novel Patrick has substituted 'stepmother' for 'mother', very likely from considerations of discretion. Earlier Xavier explains that he had only known his stepmother for a year, which approximates to Patrick's relationship with a mother of whom he had preserved but a faint impression. In contrast, he knew his stepmother Zoe for over forty years.
[2] *The Catalans*, pp. 101–02.

Unlike the gregarious and self-confident Dickens and Tolstoy, both of whom were fortunate in enjoying a happy childhood, Patrick was an exceptionally introverted and isolated boy. Combined mischances of character and circumstances led him to confuse a natural childish weakness with reprehensible lack of humanity, and a conviction instilled at so tender an age that he had been insufficiently affected by his mother's death added to the guilt, self-doubt, and vulnerability which assailed him throughout his life.

Jessie's death left her bereaved husband all but incapacitated by grief. His daughter Connie recalled 'how fond of his wife Charles Russ was, constantly following her about'. However, Connie was very critical of all the pregnancies her mother had. Victor believed that his father was reduced to such a state of distress that he was unable to work for three years. Although this was broadly true of his medical practice, which had been in serious decline for some time before his wife's death, he now took to absenting himself for the greater part of each week from a home which bore such painful associations in order to immerse himself in his clinical researches.

In the previous year Charles Russ had begun working at the Male Lock Hospital, at 91 Dean Street in Soho. (Whether he continued his voluntary employment at the X-ray department at the Middlesex Hospital is unknown.) The Male Lock specialised in treatment of venereal diseases, which by the time of his arrival there in 1917 had reached epidemic proportions following the catastrophic breakdown in moral standards brought about by the Great War.[1] It is not hard to picture the unhappy widower seeking to alleviate his desolation during his daily round at the hospital and in private researches in his Beaumont Street laboratory, only to become plunged again into painful memories during brief weekend visits to his home and family.

In later life his youngest daughter Joan jotted down this brief reflection on her life.

> In 1917 I was born on what may have been a sunny day, July 10th. I know not. Three weeks later Mother was dead, and I, the youngest of 9 children, was wheeled out of my home to a local aunt. My father had been married quite young, I believe, so he was accordingly bewildered by being the only parent to 5 boys and four girls. His answer to this was to become a near hermit commuting between home and his surgery, having planted all the children in boarding schools, or foster homes of some sort.

[1] Cf. Marwick, *The Deluge*, pp. 109–10.

Although three or four years were to pass before any of the children attended boarding-school, and Joan alone was sent to a 'foster home', overall her summary provides a fair impression of the disastrous effect of the bereavement on the Russ household.

Baby Joan was in fact nine months old when her mother died and left home some nine months after that, when she was sent to live with her affectionate Aunt Bertha (Charles's sister) and Uncle Frank Welch at their home in Pinner in Middlesex. It does not appear that her father ever troubled to tell her the reason for this summary expulsion from the family home, which is hard to explain and still more to justify. To the end of her days she retained a guilty delusion that her birth was the cause of her mother's death. Sixty years later she jotted down this 'memory': 'A dark Vict. bedroom. a baby born. bringing death to the Mother [–] the exodus'. In 1973 she published a poem invoking her dead mother:

> Grim, grudging the day of my entrance,
> A burden, and worse, causing death.
> Away beyond Earth and World's distance,
> Went Mother, my first, her last breath.

In *Lady Day Prodigal*, his privately published memoir, Bernard Russ wrote: 'Our lives now changed drastically . . . A succession of great-aunts and nannies ensued, each less convinced than the last of their ability to control all nine of us. Father, quite shattered by Jessie's death, was of little help in domestic matters, and I am not sure what suffered the most; his practice or his family.'

Still the war dragged on, and ironically it was at this late stage that the family came closest to experiencing its direct effects. From the end of 1917 a fresh threat manifested itself with the appearance over English skies of German aeroplanes, whose 300kg. bombs devastated buildings and inflicted extensive casualties. On 19 May 1918 the Germans made their final desperate effort of the air war, when a fleet of Gotha heavy bombers attacked London. Though thirty-four people were killed and ninety-eight injured and much damage was inflicted on buildings, seven aircraft were brought down by the greatly improved air defences, and no further attempt was made to attack the capital.

It was presumably this occasion which Bernard recalled in old age. 'When we were at Harrow, shortly before Mother died there, we had air raids and if we were out in the garden, we were hurried into the cellar with a lantern. The German Air Force decided to make a final stand by bombing London,' he wrote, going on to record a childhood impression of seeing shadows of aeroplanes crossing their garden. Though this cannot in fact have occurred, the alarm was real enough to imprint itself on his mind, and he recollected that 'I was holding on to the side of Joan and Pat's perambulator at the time, and we were quickly issued into the house to take refuge in the cellar . . .'[1] Nora, with whom he discussed the episode, also remembered the momentous occasion, which caused her to wet her pants in agitation.

Germany was beaten. After the failure of Ludendorff's last offensive in the early summer, the Allies struck back in a campaign of masterly strategy which left the exhausted enemy with no option but to sue for peace and sign the Armistice on 11 November. No record survives of their reaction, but the young Russes must have shared the jubilation and relief which gripped the nation at the long-anticipated conclusion of 'the war to end all wars'.

For the bereaved Charles Russ, however, there was no consolation. Unable to cope with life in a home redolent with memories of his adored Jessie, he decided the time had come to leave. The household was again uprooted, and this time transferred to 276 Willesden Lane in Willesden Green, a suburban location closer still to Charles's work in London. The house, a relatively new one, was sufficiently substantial to provide room for the large family. Set back from the road behind a privet hedge and small front lawn, it also possessed a respectably sized back garden. With little Joan now living with Aunt Bertha and Uncle Frank Welch in Middlesex, four-year-old Patrick was the 'baby' of the nine brothers and sisters.

Unhappily the move did nothing to mitigate the acute distress of the bereaved widower, who could not escape fond memories of a happy past beyond recovery. As his son Bernard recalled, for the second time: 'In endeavouring to leave memories of Mother behind and start a new life, Father found he could not bear to abandon all her plants, and the flowers which she had so much loved, so Victor and his bike were commissioned to move and replant as much of the garden as was feasible.'

Not long after the family had settled in, Patrick became acquainted with a figure who, it is hard to avoid concluding, exerted a lasting effect upon his life. The family was visited by Leonard Morse Goddard, Jessie's younger brother, known as 'Uncle Morse', who called to condole with his brother-in-law. The inadvertently confused account provided in Bun's *Lady Day Prodigal* suggests that Uncle Morse lodged at this time next door with 'Aunt Grace'.

Their uncle was a sailor and had arrived from Canada to take up a post on

[1] Russ, *Lady Day Prodigal*, p. 13.

the new liner *Empress of Canada*, which had just been constructed on Tyneside. He moved into the house next door. To the younger Russ children he not unnaturally appeared an exotic stranger.[1]

Bernard vividly remembered the excitement with which he and his brothers and sisters listened to their sailor uncle's exotic yarns. Like so many Victorian boys, he would go down to the docks to admire the ships, and indulge in dreams of sailing the Seven Seas. Before long he became apprenticed to a Scottish merchant line, and being a strong and resolute lad found the rough but adventurous life as much to his liking as his romantic imaginings had led him to anticipate. As Bun later recalled,

> Uncle Morse would fascinate us with long yarns of his days at sea, and we would sit enthralled in his study – which he insisted on calling his cabin – looking at his apprenticeship papers, which showed that as a young cabin-boy, he was entitled to one a shilling a month and his laundry. He had gone round Cape Horn in a wind-jammer, and when standing watch at the wheel, had learned to fill his tall seaboots with seawater to insulate his feet against the perishing winds of the Southern Ocean. Gradually, he worked his way up through the ranks until he was a Captain, sailing through the pirates of the China Sea.[2]

While Uncle Morse's charismatic personality and picaresque career would have inspired any high-spirited lad of the time, it is clear that they exerted an electrifying effect on the hypersensitive imagination of the youngest member of his audience. The youthful hero of Patrick's children's novel *The Road to Samarcand* (1954), which opens in a pirate-infested China Sea, is an orphan adopted by a kindly uncle who enrols him as a hand aboard his schooner, in which together they sail the high seas encountering perilous adventures.

From time to time in later life, when his fame as a nautical novelist was established, Patrick laid claim to having sailed in various types of square-rigged ships in his youth. While it will be shown that it is not impossible that he did so, his reminiscences of life spent before the mast were at the least exaggerated. His most lapidary utterance upon his formative years, as he came to reconstruct them for the benefit of the outside world, was included in his preface to a collection of essays published by the British Library in

[1] The relevant volumes of *Kelly's Directory* show that no one named Goddard lived next to 276 Willesden Lane at the time. Most likely Uncle Morse lodged there during his short visit, the Russ home being fully occupied by its large family and housekeeper.
[2] *Lady Day Prodigal*, p. 14.

1994 as a tribute to his literary achievement.[1] Passing briefly and cryptically over his childhood, he wrote: 'One of the compensations I have spoken about was the sea. The disease that racked my bosom every now and then did not much affect my strength and when it left me in peace (for there were long remissions) sea-air and sea-voyages were recommended. An uncle had a two-ton sloop and several friends had boats, which was fine . . .'

Although it is uncertain whether this seagoing episode really occurred, it seems likely that at the very least it was coloured by the stories Patrick heard from his seafaring uncle *par excellence*, and despite the fact that he never sailed with him it is revealing that when discussing his own experience of sailing Patrick implicitly associated it with Uncle Morse.

One may picture the shy little boy seated silent among his elder brothers and sisters, his imaginative powers leading him to picture himself as enactor of his inspiring uncle's dramatic exploits. The appeal would not have been confined to the colourful adventures which set this wonderful man apart from ordinary mortals condemned to dwell in suburban Willesden Green. Uncle Morse's exploits were those of a homeless boy who had ventured forth upon the high road to adventure, where he gained the highest pinnacles of youthful aspirational glory. Forever losing and regaining shipboard comrades aboard successive vessels, the wandering hero remained an essentially solitary figure roaming the empty oceans: an Odysseus 'of many wiles', single-handedly surmounting daunting dangers through exercise of innate wit and courage.

In their new home a fresh phase of existence was beginning for the family, with dramatic implications for the infant Patrick. As Bernard recalled of the period following their mother's death: 'The days at Willesden Green, while still plagued by a succession of nannies and domestic staff to none of whom we paid much heed, were much more bearable now that we had real family close at hand.' In fact one of his 'real family' was nothing of the kind, but their next-door neighbour whom they affectionately dubbed 'Aunt' Grace. 'Aunt Grace had a wonderful way of smoothing down the tangled emotions and usual disputes of our somewhat complex household, and shortly after our move to Willesden Green, persuaded Daddy that I really should by now have started school.' Bernard was accordingly sent to kindergarten at the nearby Maria Grey day school in Willesden, which was also attended by his three sisters.

Bernard, ever at pains to play down in his memoir any suggestion of family

[1] A.F. Cunningham (ed.), *Patrick O'Brian: Critical Appreciations and a Bibliography* (Boston Spa, Wetherby, 1994).

strife or unhappiness, continued cryptically: 'We had not been a very close family, emotionally, perhaps because of my mother's early death and the subsequent preponderance of housekeepers coupled with my father's active mind but failing physical health . . .' The first of these to stay for any length of time was a formidable lady named Mrs Newton, who had been a colonel in the Women's Auxiliary Army Corps 'and wore an ample display of ribbons and medals upon her equally ample bosom'. Eventually she fell out with her employer, and on his birthday at the beginning of 1919 Victor noted in his diary that 'Mrs. Ashbrook came "on approval" to tea'. An attractive widow, she took up her situation in the household four days later. Bernard recalled that 'after Hanty Mason, she was our most favourite of all the housekeepers, and proved a good friend as well as mentor'. It was not only the children who found her delightful. Ten days later fourteen-year-old Victor laconically recorded in his diary: 'Uncle Willie came home from France. He stayed with us for a few days. He looked at Mrs. Ashbrook.'

But nothing came of Uncle Willie's admiring glances, and before long Mrs Ashbrook left the household. As ever, the children were afforded no explanation for her departure, but Bernard believed that it resulted from her having set her cap at the handsome but inconsolable widower who was master of the household.

The influence of 'Aunt Grace' on the family's affairs, benevolent and constructive as it clearly was, was necessitated by Charles Russ's neglect of his family and household. That it required her intervention to arrange so fundamental a step as Bun's enrolment at kindergarten speaks for itself, as does his father's inability to keep a housekeeper or governess for long. Victor's diary records his father's visits to the household, but his stays were sufficiently brief and intermittent for Victor to feel it worthy of note one Sunday that 'Daddy was at home all day'.

Charles Russ found himself emotionally and practically incapable of managing the responsibilities of his large household, seeking solace by immersing himself in his researches. Wholly persuaded of the efficacy of the fashionable belief in electrical treatment as a cure for numerous ailments, he devised an endless succession of ingenious but largely ineffective and even frightening remedies for afflictions ranging from gonorrhoea to myopia. Bun was particularly impressed by 'the eye ray':

> I remember him working in his study at weekends for a long time with various models of the instrument which eventually satisfied him. The item is perfectly useless as far as I can see, but is interesting and simply comprises a cylinder bound with copper wire and suspended above a vessel of water with lead shot at the bed of it. The person who gazes at the cylinder will find it turning and

depending I suppose, on the strength of the eyesight of the beholder, the more the cylinder would revolve. It is quite uncanny to see it happen . . .

Another of his ingenious devices, which might at least have worked but was fortunately never put to the test, was a self-locking apparatus designed for telephone boxes, which sealed their doors automatically if anyone telephoned the fire or ambulance services. Though its public-spirited purpose was to trap perpetrators of hoax calls, it was rejected by an unimaginative Post Office. Among his other hobby-horses was a devout belief in the efficacy of carbon tablets, which he considered good for the blood, and his refusal to throw away burnt toast which supposedly served the same function.

Although Dr Russ's career was to suffer protracted decline and ultimate failure, he was a wayward genius. Bernard recalled 'his telling me that when the late King George V was unwell, the Royal Physician, Lord Dawson of Penn, sent a specimen to my father for analysis and shortly after the specimen arrived, Lord Dawson was on the phone to my father, asking for a verdict. My father says that he answered that he had just received the specimen and that the question he was putting to my father lay on the very boundaries of scientific knowledge. Immediately Lord Dawson responded and said "Russ, that is where I live".' For the most part his children had a lifelong admiration for his professional achievements. In an interview conducted late in his life, Patrick mentioned his family's scientific bent: 'One relative was a bacteriologist, another a physicist who worked on radium with Rutherford and Louis de Broglie, another a geologist.'[1] That he coupled his father (the 'bacteriologist') with his Uncles Sidney (the 'physicist') and William (the 'geologist'), who were genuinely distinguished in their fields, suggests that he shared something of his brothers' and sisters' respect for their father's professional talent. Something of his tireless energy and undaunted inventiveness must have communicated itself to the growing Patrick, whose facility in matters mechanical veered similarly between surprising skill and ludicrous failure.

The successive housekeepers that Charles Russ employed to manage his bachelor household were also supposed to act as governesses to the children. Left behind while his brothers and sisters were away at school or kindergarten, for much of the year Patrick found himself confined to his own company during the greater part of each week. It is not surprising that he became an intensely introspective boy. Throughout his childhood and adolescence there is no indication that he ever possessed a single friend

[1] Stephen Becker, 'Patrick O'Brian: The Art of Fiction CXLII', in George Plimpton et al. (eds), *The Paris Review* (New York, 1995), p. 116.

outside his family. Even among his numerous brothers and sisters, the only ones with whom he was to enjoy protracted intimacy were those nearest to him in age, Bun and Joan. But throughout the time the family lived at Willesden Green, Joan was away with her aunt and uncle at Pinner.

While Jessie was alive, Charles Russ participated in his children's games. That era however was a departed world of which Patrick had been too young to retain more than faint recollection. Following their mother's death, the children's father tended to be absent throughout most of the week, returning home only late at night or at the weekend. His enthusiasm for electric trains appears to have waned at just the time when Patrick might be expected to have appreciated them, and such spare time as he allowed himself with his family was largely devoted to his cars.

It is hard to avoid concluding that Dr Russ was more than a little selfish. However precarious the family's financial situation, he never failed to indulge his hobbies, however extravagant they might be. For example, he owned no fewer than twenty-three cameras! Seven months after his wife died he lost his mother. To the dismay and justified indignation of her children, she was found to have bequeathed the whole of her half-share in their father's estate to her sisters. All Charles inherited from her was a modest sum of money and her house at Harrow, which he promptly sold. Though he ransacked the building with his usual thoroughness, even taking Godfrey and Victor to assist in removing coal from the coalshed, this accession to his financial resources did not improve the family's lot in any perceptible way, and appears to have been swiftly dissipated. It would be understandable if his general bitterness was increased by resentment at his mother's unnatural diversion of his legitimate inheritance.

For a while at least Charles Russ maintained two cars, with whose repair and maintenance Godfrey and Victor assisted. They received sixpence a week pocket money, to which their father regularly added sums (entered as 'wages' in Victor's Cash Account) for working on his cars, extending the bicycle shed to make an improvised garage, and conducting other useful tasks.

While it would be unjust to suggest that the younger children were completely neglected, apart from being permitted to join their father in an occasional drive to visit a relative or the theatre (of which he was very fond), or while away an hour with him at a game of chess, it does not appear that he displayed much interest in them. He markedly preferred the company of his eldest sons, evidently on account of the company they afforded him in pursuit of his hobbies, and their usefulness as assistants. Still, he did not entirely ignore more juvenile pursuits. 'I transferred my Meccano crane from the nursery to my room. Daddy admired it,' noted Victor. Another entry in his diary strikes a poignant note: 'I heard Daddy singing in the eve.' Such cheerfulness was evidently rare enough to appear worthy of record.

During these early years, Patrick suffered severely from a bronchial ailment. On 15 January 1919 Victor noted laconically in his diary: 'Mrs. Ashbrook took the children to Mariah Greys school. I packed up my books and cleaned my boots. Pat was very bad.' A week later he noted in passing 'I had a game with Pat'. Shortly afterwards illness obliged Victor himself to remain at home for a week. 'I completed my Meccano model,' he recorded. 'Pat was with me all day. I told him fairy stories and played at Policemen. We had Bovril, sweets & oranges for lunch . . . We had a game in the dark.' Next day, no doubt to Patrick's delight, 'I still remained at [home] and did not go to school until Tuesday. I played with Pat and told him fairy stories.'

This pleasurable occasion was a rarity, at least in term time. His three older brothers continued to attend the John Lyon School at Harrow, which involved catching a daily train throughout the week, including Saturdays. Quite often they returned late in the evening after Patrick had gone to bed, and so for two-thirds of the year he saw them only at relatively short intervals. The girls and Bernard were also away at school for most of the day, while the latter in addition was occupied for much of his free time with the local Boy Scout troop.

Protracted confinement in the house in Willesden Lane must have appeared an unhappy void. Only in the holidays was the house suddenly filled with lively spirits. Patrick participated in their games, of which the most memorable were elaborate set-piece battles waged upon the playroom floor. The opposed armies were manned by the beautifully crafted lead soldiers made by the firm of Britains, which afforded unforgettable delight to generations of boys. Not for them the drab khaki of the Great War, from whose horrors the country had just emerged. The main body of infantry, equipped with the spiked helmets of the line or the furred busbies of the Guards, advanced in line or column wearing the scarlet coats of the army of the great Queen-Empress. Beside them marched gallant levies from every part of the British Empire: sepoys from India, Gurkhas from Nepal, askaris from West Africa. On their flanks trotted gaily uniformed lancers, hussars, and dragoons. Still more fascinating to manœuvre and operate was the horse artillery, with guns and limbers drawn by harnessed teams of six horses. Their limbers housed twin rows of tiny shells, which were discharged from the guns with the aid of an explosive cap. Equally enticing were the mule-gun teams, with their four mules bearing the detachable wheels, carriage, and gun barrel, together with ammunition rolled up in an elastic band. Battles could continue for days or even weeks. Victor remembered in later years how he acted as commandant of the field hospital (casualties being gratifyingly extensive), while Patrick as the youngest was content to fulfil whatever subordinate role his seniors assigned him.

The boys were avid collectors of stamps and cigarette cards ('fag cards'), which involved much mutual swapping and purchasing. In the garden at the back of the house there was enough space for each child to maintain a plot, whose produce was studied with eager rivalry. From time to time a slow-growing vegetable was dug up to check its progress, with predictably destructive consequences. Michael and Victor built a hen coop, which housed a batch of bantams brought back one day by their father from a patient in lieu of fee. This time it was the architecture which proved unsound: the chickens escaped, inflicting such damage on the garden that it was decided to eat them rather than their eggs. However, as Nora later recalled, their father 'was curiously absent from any of these plans'.

Life, then, had its ups and downs for Patrick at the house in Willesden Lane, but it was the latter which prevailed. He could barely recollect his mother, while his father effectively abandoned his responsibilities to Mrs Newton and her successors. For three years Patrick spent wearisome hours of each day in a house empty save for a succession of housekeepers. His recollection was that 'upon the whole it was a very lonely childhood'. Small wonder that he became deeply introverted from an early age, unconsciously devising mental techniques for coping with loneliness and tedium. He further described himself as 'pre-adolescent: a sort of elderly child', expressing a conviction that 'he was certainly not very popular among his brothers and sisters'.

It is hard to credit this last assertion. A chance record of Victor's affectionate concern for his young brother when he was sick was noted earlier. On another occasion Victor mentioned that 'We had our half-term holiday . . . and I had a game of pulling children round on carpet'.[1] Nothing suggests that any of Patrick's brothers or sisters disliked him during their childhood, nor indeed is it easy to conceive why a shy little boy very much the infant of the family might have provoked their resentment. His brother Bun, his closest in age and companionship, displayed affection for him, especially when they came to attend school together. Patrick remained fast friends with his sister Joan until he left home at the age of nineteen. He seems

[1] Victor's widow Saidie informed me that Patrick maintained regular contact with her husband until his death: 'Victor and Pat used to exchange letters every Christmas. One year Pat sent him some lily seeds . . . Pat wrote to us at the time Victor died saying he was disappointed that I hadn't let him know and that he might have come over for the funeral. He wrote [that] Victor was a very good brother to me – much better than I was to him.'

from an early age to have developed a carapace of self-sufficiency setting him emotionally apart from those around him, and it was perhaps this quality which led him in later years to imagine that he had been disliked by his elders.

In Patrick's novel *The Catalans*, a chapter is devoted to a lengthy confession by Xavier. In the course of a remarkably frank revelation of this fear, he has this to say of its origin: 'Somehow between that time [his stepmother's death] and this I had turned from a normal affectionate child, or at least a child loving enough to hate fiercely for another's sake, into a man so abnormal that he had not the power to feel any sorrow for his wife's death.'

There is good reason to believe that Patrick was unduly harsh with himself, and that his real problem in this respect lay in his fundamental fear and mistrust of others. In reality he was capable of intense affection and kindness. Tragically, his obsessive conviction that he was surrounded on every side by hostility and malice caused him to erect elaborate psychological defences designed to protect him against the remotest possibility of betrayal. Given this deep-rooted malaise, together with his awareness that his psychological isolation originated from the circumstances of his childhood, it seems likely that Patrick's belief that his brothers and sisters disliked him as a child was a creation of neurotic fancy.

From the ages of three to six, Patrick was but one of the little horde of Russ brothers and sisters placed in the custody of what his brother Bernard termed the 'succession of nannies and domestic staff to none of whom we paid much heed'. Lacking a parental presence to uphold their authority, these unfortunate women could exercise no more than a minimum of discipline over the turbulent young household. There is no special reason to suppose that Patrick found their rule particularly oppressive. Doubtless they were for the most part only too relieved to see the backs of the unruly youngsters, and to leave the placid little boy to his own pursuits. Only towards the conclusion of his time at Willesden Green is there evidence that Patrick was subjected to the unchecked authority of a governess whom he heartily detested as a domestic tyrant.

Many children who have experienced an unhappy childhood have managed to survive more or less unscathed. However for a boy of Patrick's preternaturally sensitive and vulnerable character the sensation of abandonment in a hostile world was so strong that in later life he could come to precarious terms with it only by expunging or adapting his early life to accord with his emotional requirements. Thus his biographer is presented with formidable obstacles when attempting to reconstruct this decisive period of his life, which he went to such pains to suppress or reinvent.

Fortunately there exists a body of evidence which, provided it be treated with due care, can be utilised to cast a remarkably revealing light on Patrick's childhood. His change of name in 1945 and invention of an alternative upbringing were intended to erect a formal barrier, behind which his real past could be consigned to oblivion. Yet his past survived in the one place from which it was most necessary to banish it: his own mind.

Given his inborn talent as a writer, it was virtually inevitable that he would remould his life in fictional form. Much of his earlier literary output, culminating in the novel *Richard Temple* (1962), is broadly autobiographical. Needless to say, these works do not provide a factually accurate account of Patrick's life (although they include much that demonstrably is), but rather represent a sustained exercise in moral justification and recasting of those aspects of his adolescence which he found repugnant. However, if treated objectively and checked against independent evidence, aspects of Patrick's early writings provide invaluable source material for this vitally formative period of his life.

Richard Temple describes the unrelieved monotony of the hero's life as a boy at home: '. . . he never ran about voluntarily, at least not when he was alone, as he always was in the holidays . . . In intervals of drawing he was happiest (when he was at liberty) in mooning vaguely, counting his slow, lethargic steps in the disused stable-yard, carefully walking on the cracks, or staring for a pattern or a face in the crazed roughcast of the wall.'[1]

This description is closely echoed in *The Yellow Admiral* (1997), where we learn that Jack Aubrey's father's irresponsible conduct had 'at times so oppressed his naturally cheerful boyhood that even now this house cast a gloom upon his spirits – and he was never cordially happy there except in the parts behind, the stable courts, the walled garden and the far garden with its grotto'.[2]

Patrick's direct references in later life to his childhood and adolescence are scanty and allusive, and significantly almost always relate to places rather than people. Among them is a tantalising allusion to a vivid childhood memory. In 1946 he mentioned in his journal: 'The smell of the wood instantly reminded me of the pile with rats in at Hampden, twenty five years ago.' His memory had flashed back to 1921, when he was six years old and living at Willesden Green. At the time Joan was living with their Aunt Bertha and Uncle Frank in nearby Pinner. Their daughter Christine, who was about the same age, remembers occasional visits from Patrick, with whom she and her sister Margaret played games of 'touch' and hide-and-seek in the garden, and tended their pet rabbits. She recalls her cousin as a lively, sporting little lad, though his father appeared an awesomely forbidding figure, with his

[1] *Richard Temple*, p. 25.

[2] *The Yellow Admiral*, p. 21

giant height and beetling eyebrows. From time to time the children were taken for picnics on Little Hampden Common, some twenty miles away in the Chiltern Hills. Aunt Bertha was an observant naturalist of thorough Victorian type, and it may have been during these exhilarating outings that Patrick acquired his abiding love of the natural world.

The formation of his character as a solitary dreamer, increasingly seeking refuge within the world of his imagination, almost certainly originated during his days at Willesden Green. At the same time, his life there was not unredeemedly grim. At weekends and holidays he must willy-nilly have been drawn into his brothers' and sisters' games and been distracted in other ways. According to Bernard, during the time that she remained as their housekeeper, Mrs Ashbrook 'proved a good friend as well as mentor', 'Aunt Grace' next door was solicitous for the children's welfare, and 'Aunty' Mason, their much-loved nanny from Walden days, arrived occasionally from her home in Devonshire to stay.

In his formal autobiographical sketch, published in the 1994 British Library tribute, Patrick recounted of his childhood: 'much of the time I was ill, which was not only disagreeable in itself but which also did away with much in the way of regular education and companionship. Fortunately there was a governess, dear Miss O'Mara . . .' That neither he on any other occasion nor anyone else in the family referred to this Miss O'Mara does not prove her non-existence, but I am inclined to believe that Patrick had his stepmother (whom his father married when Patrick was eight, and of whom he became very fond) in mind. Mentioned in *The Letter of Marque* (1988), *The Thirteen-Gun Salute* (1989) and *The Wine-Dark Sea* (1993), she is described as 'Miss O'Mara, the daughter of an officer killed at the Nile'. Patrick's stepmother's first husband was a naval officer who was killed at Gallipoli, and he could well have been aware that O'Mara means 'child of the sea' in Irish.

TWO

Nooks and Corners

> A lover of nooks and retired corners, I was as a child in the habit of fleeing from society, and of sitting for hours together with my head on my breast. What I was thinking about, it would be difficult to say at this distance of time; I remember perfectly well, however, being ever conscious of a peculiar heaviness within me, and at times of a strange sensation of fear, which occasionally amounted to horror, and for which I could assign no real cause whatever.
>
> (George Borrow, *Lavengro*)

Life continued on this uneven course for nearly three years during the Russ family's stay at 276 Willesden Lane. Bun returned home for a spell after his time at kindergarten came to an end, since he was not sent to primary school but 'taught at home' – whatever that meant. Then the children's circumstances changed dramatically. After completing his schooling at the end of the summer term of 1919, Godfrey began a degree course in engineering at Northampton Polytechnic Institute. His departure from the family home was followed by that of Victor, who was sent to work in a bank. Finally, at the beginning of 1921, when Patrick was just six, all his remaining brothers and sisters suddenly departed the family home. Bun and Mike were enrolled at their father's old school at Shebbear College in North Devon, while the sisters Olive, Connie, and Nora went to Edgehill College, a Methodist girls' boarding-school some fifteen miles from Shebbear.

In the same year that Charles Russ sent two of his sons and all three daughters remaining at home to boarding-school he sold the family home at Willesden Green. The two moves were very likely interrelated, the reduction in his circumstances presumably resulting from the considerable expense required to meet increased school fees. However, he appears to have made sufficient profit from the sale to purchase the house next to his premises in Marylebone. Henceforth the only property he owned consisted of the adjacent houses at 25 and 27 Beaumont Street, which served him both as residence and professional practice.

Since there no longer existed a separate family home, Dr Russ arranged for the five children at boarding-school to spend their school holidays lodging in North Devon. They were regularly sent to live with three kindly spinster sisters, the Misses Hill, who lived not far from the two schools. London Lodge was in the grounds of Clovelly Court, an eighteenth-century mansion occupying a magnificent situation on the cliffs overlooking the Severn Sea. These were happy occasions, even for Nora who recalled her schooldays with bitter dislike.

The five Russ children remembered their warm-hearted hosts with affection. Twenty years later Ethie and Trixie Hill came to visit Olive and her children, who were then living at Ilminster, and three weeks before his tragic death in action in 1943 Michael travelled down to stay at London Lodge, where he spent a fine spring day sawing and splitting logs for the sisters.

It was a curious chance which brought the Russ children to this spot. Mrs Hamlyn, the Dame of Clovelly Court, was a neighbour and friend of my maternal grandparents Howard and Frieda Wicksteed, who lived at the neighbouring fishing village of Appledore. When Patrick's brothers and sisters were playing in the garden of London Lodge, they may well from time to time have glimpsed a car passing up the drive, in which sat a little girl who would one day transform their brother's life and work.

In his memoir Bun mentions in passing that his Uncle Emil (younger brother of his father) owned 'a large house in South London with more than enough room for our brood during school holidays, and where we were always welcome'. His daughter Betty remembered its 'huge garden', where the children enjoyed playing.[1]

So the brothers and sisters at school were absent from home for all or virtually all the year. At Christmas 1923 Bun remarked that 'the whole family was united for the first time for many years'.

With the sale of the house at Willesden Green Patrick suddenly found himself immured in a town house with no companion, and deprived of the relative freedom of the sizeable house and garden in Willesden Lane. It is hard to believe that he did not suffer from sensations of envy and

[1] *Lady Day Prodigal*, p. 4. Uncle Emil, like many of the Russes, had enjoyed a highly picaresque career. After leaving Shebbear College he decided not to enter the family fur business, but took himself off to India, where he established his own business making military uniforms in Quetta. In 1918 he won an enormous sum on the Calcutta Sweep, which enabled him to retire to England.

deprivation when contrasting his confined existence with the happy freedom enjoyed at school and in the holidays by his brothers and sisters. His isolation had become permanent, and for nearly three years he rarely saw his brothers and sisters. In addition the move to his father's bachelor establishment in Beaumont Street largely deprived him of the consolations of privacy in which he had taken increasing refuge in the house in Willesden Lane. Now was the period of his early childhood when he must have felt all but abandoned.

Given the enormous influence which he undoubtedly exerted on Patrick throughout the latter's childhood and adolescence, it is frustrating that so little is known of Charles Russ's personal history in the years immediately following the death of Jessie. Bernard Russ's words convey an impression that Jessie's death may have caused him to suffer from some form of mental breakdown, from which it may be that he never fully recovered. Formerly an affectionate father, he became increasingly remote from his children, until after three years he effectively expelled them from his household.

Bernard's son Charles, who came in later life to know his Aunt Nora well, informed me: 'From Nora's real remembrances, which was [*sic*] so different from Father's, she admitted that her Father had treated her very badly, and she didn't have many fond memories at all.' This coldness extended to the next generation, and young Charles and his sister Elizabeth never received even token affection from their grandfather: '. . . there was a lot of letter writing to Grandfather and [his second wife] Zoe, but not a thing ever came back to Canada from them, for any of us, grandchildren though we were . . . I know I wrote to them several times but never received any answers. We didn't exist as far as Charles senior or Zoe were concerned. We didn't ever know what it was like to have grandparents.'

It is unfortunate that Bun did not elaborate on the tantalisingly brief reference to his father that it 'took him many years to recover and the repercussions are still with us today'. In fact his memoir suppresses more than it reveals. His son Charles in Canada recently sent me this revealing glimpse of his father's real state of mind:

> While I am penning thoughts, I thought I should share a couple of quotes from this summer [2003] that came my way. The first is a long conversation I had with the long time housekeeper for Dad and Fifi [Bernard's widow]. I had 'phoned over to be in touch with Fifi, and because she was out at the time, I spent a good half hour (long distance!) chatting with Jane. One of the things she related to me was an occasion when she happened into Father's study while he was starting to work on the L.D.P. [*Lady Day Prodigal*] book

> and was dealing with his early years. She somehow interrupted his thoughts about his own Father, and much to Jane's surprise, he blurted out that he HATED him more than anything else he could imagine. The inference was that that was also the sentiment that all of the younger ones shared. I had never heard anything of this strength of feeling concerning his Father before now.

Charles further told me that Bernard 'was incapable of having any male friendships ever. I know this better than anyone else who ever knew him, believe me! The only types of connections might have been if the other was willing to listen a lot and smile or laugh at the right places. Father was the pontificating type who was able to talk but seldom listen effectively for any length of time. A one way connection was all that was allowed. Perhaps there is a parallel with Patrick?'

Altogether there is every indication that after the death of his first wife Charles Russ became inordinately selfish, authoritarian, and possibly sadistic, and that his cold or harsh treatment of his children blighted several of their lives in greater or lesser measure. When at the age of seventeen Bun joined his elder brother Mike in Australia, the latter reported to their sister Olive that eight months in the bush 'did knock some of the shyness & awkwardness out of him'. But where did the shyness and awkwardness come from? Charles Russ's expulsion from home of his baby daughter Joan, and later of Olive as a teenager, to live with their uncle and aunt suggests a grossly unfeeling character. He also failed to attend the same two daughters' weddings.

While a general picture of the Doctor's character can be gained from these fleeting vignettes, Patrick himself provided a remarkably explicit memoir of this early period of his life in his short story 'The Thermometer'. The plot is simple. A small boy arrives to visit for the first time a relative, 'Cousin Carew'. Carew is portrayed as a giant, forbidding figure, cold and detached, possessing no understanding of children, and puzzled to know how to treat this particular specimen.

> They had nothing whatever to say to one another, and between them the silence grew so massive that it could almost be seen . . . The boy saw a vast column of authority on the other side, omnipotent and grey. Grey the vague clothing that draped the massive form, grey the enormous trousers, untidily folded like an elephant; and the huge stone face, expressionless and everlasting, was also grey.

After a brief strained exchange, during which Carew awkwardly takes out his watch from his waistcoat pocket and replaces it, he explains cursorily that he is obliged to go out for several hours. He leads the boy from his study into his laboratory beyond, where he instructs him to remain until his return. To occupy the intervening hours, he provides the child with a copy of *The Times*. As he leaves, the man turns back to remark, 'with an artificial lightness and certainty, "Of course I need not say that I am sure that nothing will be touched".'

Intrigued by the panoply of exotic objects with which the room is filled, the child eventually cannot resist exploring the multifarious array of bottles, retorts, and instruments. His confidence fortified by his isolation from the outside world, he pauses before a mirror to indulge in defiant mockery of his caretaker, Mrs Clapp, whom he heartily detests for her officiousness and vulgarity, mimicking her and scoffing at her tedious injunctions. Growing increasingly bold, he turns to subject the various instruments by which he is surrounded to closer examination.

Eventually his attention is directed to the thermometer of the story's title, and he observes with fascination how the position of its mercury may be altered by manœuvring it beside the flame of a Bunsen burner. Gradually he moves the thermometer closer until the mercury satisfactorily expands to fill the entire tube. But at this point disaster unexpectedly strikes: the boy seeks to reduce the expansion by dipping the instrument into cold water, which instantly causes it to shatter into fragments. Seized with terror, he frantically engages in hopeless attempts to repair the damage.

The horror of the situation becomes ever more desperate as the recession of afternoon daylight gradually plunges the room into darkness. Just as the boy's fear is becoming unbearable, the tension is shattered by the clarion ring of a telephone in a corner. The boy, standing paralysed in the centre of the room, hears the swift approach of heavy footsteps. The door and its masking curtain are swept aside, and the huge threatening figure of his cousin looms in the entrance. Striding to the telephone and lifting the receiver, he asks the boy to switch on the light. In a brief and cleverly exercised denouement, Carew notices the broken thermometer on the floor – only to remark casually to his unidentified interlocutor that he must have knocked it to the ground with his coat on entering the darkened room.

The interest of the story lies not in the incident which gives it its title, which is deliberately anticlimactic, but in the vivid insight it provides into the succession of complex emotions passing through the child's mind during his protracted spell in his alien surroundings.

Suggestively, Patrick was at conscious pains to mask the identity of the two characters. The boy remains nameless throughout, until at the very end his cousin addresses him in passing as 'Philip'.[1] Contrived concern is still more clearly evinced to distance the relationship between boy and man. In the manuscript Carew is described as being at once 'his cousin once removed' and 'his paternal grandfather's brother'. This discrepancy survived into proof stage, where Carew continues to feature at different points as both cousin and great-uncle. Presumably an observant proof-reader corrected this contradiction in time for the published version, where Cousin Carew becomes son of the boy's great-uncle.

The story contains other unexplained anomalies clearly reflecting considerations extraneous to the tale. No reason is provided for the boy's visit to his cousin, to whom he is evidently a stranger, beyond that of having 'a talk over the future'. Despite the fact that his little cousin's arrival had involved a 'journey', and must presumably have been arranged in advance, Cousin Carew exchanges a mere couple of sentences with him before abruptly announcing his departure for 'the Institute', from which he would not return until four o'clock.

However ignorant Carew may have been of the ways of children, it beggars belief that he would have left an unknown small boy alone and unoccupied throughout much of a day with ready access to the complex range of artefacts which he employed in his researches. As the narrator observes:

> the incubator held cultures and living tissues that were the fruits of long months of preparation – a hand playing with the long rod of the thermostatic control, or even idly fondling its shining counterpoise, might falsify the results of a whole series of experiments – and apart from the incubator there were scores of appliances, instruments, switches, dials and complicated arrangements of glass, all functioning and all vulnerable: it was decidedly unsuitable in every way.

The confinement of the boy in the laboratory is as needless as it is unexplained. His introduction to his cousin takes place in a spacious study,

[1] This was the name Patrick used in the original manuscript version, where it is misspelled 'Phillip'. However, in the proof copy he crossed out Philip, replacing it with 'Charles' – only to revert to Philip in the published version. It seems not unlikely that Patrick took the name Philip from Somerset Maugham's *Of Human Bondage*, which he read at least twice, and which was also a favourite of his sister Joan. A note he jotted down in 1942 remarks striking parallels to his perception of his own existence: 'it is a big, strong book. Two things – as isolated bits – strike me: one of Philip's early reading – thus providing himself with a refuge from all the distresses of life – creating for himself an unreal world which would make the real world of everyday a source of bitter disappointment. And again (which appears to me closely connected) – how wide a country, arid and precipitous, must be crossed before the traveller through life comes to an acceptance of reality.'

which would provide an appropriate place for the child to wait. Instead the scientist leads him into his laboratory. Clearly Patrick's primary concern was to confine the small boy for a prolonged period within the laboratory, whose atmosphere and contents beset him with sensations of intense curiosity and liberating introspection, combined with unnerving fear.

'The Thermometer' was included among a series of short stories published in Britain by Rupert Hart-Davis in 1956, under the title *Lying in the Sun*. There is no need to indulge in surmise regarding its fundamentally autobiographical character, since Patrick privately acknowledged as much. Among his preparatory notes he jotted down these words: 'But would it be any good? I am afraid of self-pity or at least self-quaintery, own head on one side, creeping in.' On 15 January 1955 he noted in his pocket diary: 'I finished a story – broken thermometer – 5000 [words] nearly – very heavy going. It felt dubious – a little embarrassing; self-quaintery is always to be feared in anything at all autobiographical about childhood – approving self-quaintery – own head on one side – oh so unconscious simper – poor one.'

In view of this admission, it is hard to overrate the significance of the story for an understanding of Patrick's childhood. For a start, there cannot be any doubt that the setting is described from life. The walls of the study in which the small boy first confronts his elderly cousin are lined with photographs of grimly authoritarian figures: 'Koch, Pasteur, Ehrlich, Creighton, Beale[1] and Müller, in frock coats, beards and steel-rimmed spectacles, dignified, hairy and inhuman . . .' That their forbidding appearance added to the daunting atmosphere of the room is understandable, but the catalogue of names is dramatically discrepant. No small child could be expected to have identified this array of celebrated bacteriologists of a previous generation. Yet the primary intention of the tale – implicit in the published version, explicit in Patrick's preparatory notes – was that everything 'Should be seen only through the child's eyes'.

This disparity becomes yet more evident when the child finds himself alone in the laboratory beyond.

> It was not a room into which a man accustomed to children would have introduced the little boy. Cradled in its basket under the main laboratory bench stood a carboy of sulphuric acid, ten gallons of brimming vitriol, while above it nitric, hydrocyanic, oxalic, hydrochloric, malic, formic and hydrofluoric offered the possibilities of fuming experiment and sudden death in a neat range of Winchester quarts. On a shelf to the right of the bench a large jar of caustic

[1] Patrick owned a copy of Beale's work *On Slight Ailments* (1896), which had probably belonged to his father.

soda in cigarette-like sticks provided the same end by a different means: the strychnine was on the top of the cupboard, however, and almost out of reach.

As implausible as the implicit ascription of this arcane catalogue to the mind of a small boy is the likelihood of a professional scientist's leaving a strange child alone for hours in a laboratory affording unrestricted opportunity for irreparable damage, more still endangering his life. As so often in the story, Patrick unconsciously wavers between the boy's perspective and that of informed adult narrator. That this did not result from oversight is indicated by the careful list which he drew up when planning his story: 'Thermometer. Gerards ureometer. Basic fuchsin. Bunsen burners pilot light. Microscope – eyepiece – stage, vernier. Test-tubes in a rack [one of which is reproduced as a drawing]. Cultures. Incubator. Chemist's balance.'

These notes confirm the indications that Patrick was recalling apparatus in a real laboratory with which he had been exceptionally familiar. This is further indicated by the description of the room's unusual proportions: 'It was a five-sided room with the couch flanked by glass-fronted bookshelves along one wall.' That its topography should be represented with precise accuracy was evidently of significance to Patrick, since he sketched a little plan of the room and its furniture in his notebook.

'The Thermometer' almost certainly relates to the occasion when Patrick was first informed that he was to live alone with his father in Marylebone. The boy in the story travels to town from a home where he has been in the sole care of a governess. On arrival he is ushered into the presence of a tall and forbidding relative, a virtual stranger who nevertheless possesses total authority over him. The purpose of the visit is to talk about the child's 'future', which by implication will involve a major change in his life. Patrick was six at the time when he would have undergone this experience, which accords with indications of the boy's age in 'The Thermometer'.

Both the story itself and Patrick's preparatory jottings suggest that his pen portrait of Mrs Clapp (the 'Loathesome caretaking woman' of his notes), with her tiresome catch-phrases and irrational rulings, represents a real figure assigned responsibility for the household at Willesden Green. Bernard recalled in his memoir that Mrs Ashbrook was succeeded by 'Scotch Annie', who 'took her place in our affections'. However Bernard's memoir tends to view everything through rose-tinted spectacles, and his childhood experience was besides very different from Patrick's. 'Scotch Annie' was not a woman of education like Mrs Ashbrook, but 'one of the domestic staff, and supposed to be in charge of the marketing – which she hated to do'.[1] This corresponds

[1] *Lady Day Prodigal*, p. 17.

with Patrick's reference to his domestic tyrant as a 'caretaking woman', rather than housekeeper or governess.

That 'Cousin Carew' is a portrait of Patrick's father is indisputable. He is described as 'much larger than even Mrs Clapp's most spiteful predictions had foretold, so bodily vast and spiritually overwhelming'. Dr Russ towered at nearly six feet five inches. Like Dr Russ, Carew is a bacteriologist, and both are in addition specialists in urology.[1] When at the close of the story Cousin Carew suddenly notices the broken thermometer, he reassures his interlocutor on the telephone that it is 'Nothing of any importance. I was afraid it might have been the ureometer . . . No. No. It was only a thermometer.' In the proof copy Patrick made the allusion more specific: 'the ureometer, my Gerard's ureometer'. However, in the published edition he omitted the technical description.[2]

Carew features as an awesome and unapproachable figure, who finds the boy about as comprehensible as one of his laboratory specimens. Yet there are indications that Patrick had originally been undecided what function the relative should play. At one point he considered making him a largely otiose figure, or even removing him altogether. Preparing his outline, Patrick pondered: 'Should I supprime the old man['s] reflections, in order to intensify the child's alarm – or rather, the reader's share in it and in the subsequent relief.' He concluded by considering whether he should not 'Supprime the entirety of Mr Carew?'

Though ultimately Patrick settled on his representation of Carew as a broadly unsympathetic figure, he continued until a late stage of composition to treat him with some ambivalence. On the first page of his outline Patrick briefly indicates the absence of rapport between man and boy. The next line however contains a fragmentary sentence: 'The impersonal and ready indignity of the good old' – at which point he frustratingly cut off the remainder of the page. Sizeable sections of the preparatory notes have been neatly cut off, while another page has been torn out altogether. It was unusual for Patrick to do this, and one cannot help suspecting that it was the intensely personal nature of this particular story that led him to destroy some of his more explicit allusions to his father.

Patrick's notes indicate that he wavered between portraying his father as passively cold and insensitive or an actively harsh oppressor. 'Or of course the whole thing could hinge not on their relationship at all but on the child's

[1] Could the 'Institute' to which Carew betakes himself for the day have been the Courtauld Institute, which *inter alia* specialised in research into urological diseases?

[2] Conceivably his decision (possibly influenced by my mother) to omit the reference reflected awareness that it would make the identification of Cousin Carew with his father too explicit.

fortuitous escape from rebuke – the man treads on the pieces, blames himself – child dribbles quicksilver into its handkerchief . . . In this case the more alarming the man the better. There is no point in making him either human or sympathetic . . . Should be seen only through the child's eyes.'

On the other hand he squeezed this little note between two paragraphs of his manuscript: 'The matches [with which he had lit the Bunsen burner], blackened head and tail betrayed him in the morning, and he was whipped.' This passage was however omitted from the published version, possibly again through tactful concern to avoid too close identification with an actual incident.

Cousin Carew is a forbidding figure arousing general dread in his young visitor, but the active villain of the story is the detested Mrs Clapp. Patrick included in his notes this drastic abjuration, which in the event he omitted: 'He had ceased to believe in God when he had learnt that He had made Mrs Clapp – ceased to believe in Him, that is, as an interesting being or as one who could possibly be on his side.'

A still more instructive exclusion is indicated in Patrick's original composition. He marked it with a wavy line in the margin, presumably to indicate uncertainty about its appropriateness for inclusion. After a catalogue of what the fastidious boy regarded as distasteful expressions repeatedly uttered by his governess ('the bowels must be kept open'; 'keep our fingers from picking and stealing'; 'Mrs Clapp called a chamber-pot the article'), there follows this paragraph:

> Yet he did not wish her away. He feared her and when she whipped him he hated her with incandescent rage; but she was one of the few constants in his life, and he would rather have had an unhealthy, loveless constant than none at all. Furthermore, he knew that she was afraid of Mr Carew, which made Mr Carew very terrible – he had always been represented as an irascible creature of enormous power ('Let Mr Carew catch you telling a wicked falsehood like that, and he'll soon send you packing off to Someone below.' 'I'll report you to Mr Carew.' 'Mr Carew shall hear of this') and his appearance, his strong smell and his prodigious silence at their recent interview had done nothing to belie her words.

Once again one cannot help wondering whether Patrick omitted this brief passage because it approached closer to reality than was acceptable. The reflection on Mrs Clapp reveals almost everything about the relationship between the child and the two adults who wield authority over him. While the sensitive child feels justified in regarding his governess as stupid and vulgar, he instinctively appreciates that her tyranny primarily reflects ignorant fear inspired in a vulnerable servant by her absent employer. The discarded parenthetical mention that she whipped him appears to be no more than a momentary attempt to justify his hatred for her. His description of Mrs Clapp's relationship to Mr Carew as 'deferential to him and smooth' is inapplicable to the child of the story, who has never seen them together, and can only reflect retrospective understanding of the relationship between his father and a caretaker employed at his house in Willesden Lane.

Overall it appears that Patrick felt impelled to recreate that grimmest of moments in a generally wretched childhood, when his brothers and sisters simultaneously left home without any foreseeable prospect of return, leaving him alone under the arbitrary control of an ignorant and interfering servant. Shortly afterwards he was removed from the only home he had really known to live in a London house with a frighteningly distant father who was virtually a stranger to him: 'How old are you? – But he had already asked the question.'

The apprehension with which he regards Cousin Carew reflects the child's perception of the adult world generally. The primary function of that unfeeling race was to impose innumerable rules, whose capricious and irrational nature made it almost impossible to avoid breaking them and incurring punishment. Their authority was unconfined, and if the whim took them they could flout or alter the rules.

In the absence of any other effective protection, deception and hypocrisy provided legitimate defensive measures: 'one did not live with Mrs Clapp for long without becoming tolerably sly'. So accustomed had he become to the necessity that he practised it even in private. During his inspection of the laboratory (the passage is omitted in the published version), 'he sauntered in the general direction of the burner, with his eyebrows somewhat raised and a false expression on his face'.

The safest course was to avoid the company of adults together. In a household destitute of companions of his own age, this meant withdrawal into solitude: a condition he had long come to relish for the freedom it conferred. The northward-facing window and heavy curtain masking the door of the laboratory 'gave the inside of the room and everything that went on inside it, a very special feeling of insulation – a deaf and inner world . . . he saw at once that it possessed extraordinary attractions', providing as it did 'that feeling of total privacy that was essential for glee in him'.

Insulated from the hostile world, Philip indulges in gratifying if impotent defiance of the oppressor. Communing with his reflection in a little mirror, he mocks Mrs Clapp with every forbidden word and gesture he can recall. He concludes his exorcism of the governess with a string of shocking oaths

('Damn, belly, dung, Devil, bloody') – only to be struck with fear on recalling that the last two verged on being blasphemous. Even in the apparent security of a deserted room in an empty house, he could never feel wholly safe. At any moment heavy footsteps might approach, and the door to his refuge be abruptly flung open. Defence and escape being alike impossible, he was left with but one means of dealing with the crisis: '. . . he span until he was dizzy – the best way he knew of changing an unwelcome flow of thoughts and averting the evil chance'.

A far more alarming situation arises with the fatal shattering of the thermometer. After frantic unavailing attempts to repair the damage, 'he understood that the catastrophe was whole and real, and that his attempt at piecing together the fragments could never succeed. He accepted this dully . . .' Momentarily he believed he might succeed in persuading himself that the disaster had not really occurred, 'but there was no hope of that now'. Escape was impossible. 'He was feeling sick. He was going to be sick. For a long time he hung over the sink with the tap running: he took a drink in his cupped hands. Now he was very cold and his desperate apprehension seemed to have been swallowed up in the misery of being sick . . .'

A significant omission from the published version was a paragraph in which the child contemplates committing suicide:

> If he swallowed the quicksilver he would die. Quicksilver was poison: everybody knew that. He poured it from the beaker into the palm of his hand and returned to the couch where he sat swilling the little heavy pool of metal round and round in his hand. There had been no sound for some time, and he was beginning to escape from reality again when with an appalling suddenness a telephone bell exploded & shrieked out somewhere in the room.[1]

On each occasion that the child is gripped by panic, his reaction is similar. Fearful of the consequences of blaspheming before the mirror, he spins himself round *in a deliberate attempt to make himself giddy*. Faced by the far more frightening shattering of the thermometer, he goes to the sink and *tries to make himself sick*.[2] Finally there is the suppressed episode of his *contemplating or unsuccessfully attempting suicide*. Attempts to induce illness or invite death represent classic symptoms of the psychology of children who, feeling themselves neglected and threatened, resort to desperate measures in

[1] Earlier Patrick contemplated making the boy actually swallow the mercury, but apparently survive unscathed: 'Child swallows m persuaded of deadly quality.'

[2] It is unclear whether he was actually sick or not, and in the manuscript Patrick deleted a sentence: 'Hanging over the sink he found that he would probably not be sick.'

order to gain sympathy by placing themselves in the situation of vulnerable or mourned victims.[1]

A poignant revelation of the source of Patrick's transparently portrayed feelings of inadequacy and fear is found in a single telling alteration to the original text of 'The Thermometer'. As the dreaded moment of his cousin's return fast approaches, the boy stands in the middle of the room, frozen with terror:

> Shut away in that darkening room, sealed from the rest of the world, he felt that it had gone wrong, as it sometimes had before – time had gone wrong when he had been lost, and once in a waiting-room.

So runs the text published in *Lying in the Sun*. When Patrick first wrote it, the sentence appeared in this form:

> Shut away in that darkening room, sealed from the rest of the world, he felt that it had gone wrong, as it sometimes had before, when he had been lost *and at the funeral.* [italics inserted]

Whose funeral? Nothing in the story indicates that anyone has died. It appears that at this point of his confessedly autobiographical tale Patrick had momentarily reverted in memory to being once again the small boy abandoned in his father's gloomy laboratory. For once there had been a real funeral at which he had indeed been lost. Long years later Patrick's brother Bernard recalled the dreadful moment in the spring of 1918: 'Looking back now, I suppose my father must have known for some time that Mother was dying of cancer . . . but we were not really prepared . . . I knew she was going away, but at the age of six it was hard to understand. Joan, Pat and I were considered too young to attend the funeral . . .'.[2]

It was while the family was absent from the house that Bernard ventured into his mother's empty bedroom, leaving three-year-old Patrick alone in the nursery with his baby sister Joan. Despite his tender age there is no reason why that terrifying moment should not have imprinted itself ineradicably on his consciousness. The fact that he referred to the funeral, rather than directly to his mother's death, is suggestive. Like Bun, he possessed no understanding of the impending tragedy, and their mother's unexplained departure made the occasion of the funeral, when they found

[1] Cf. Alfred Adler, *The Neurotic Constitution: Outlines of a Comparative Individualistic Psychology and Psychotherapy* (London, 1921), p. 208.
[2] Russ, *Lady Day Prodigal*, p. 12.

themselves alone in the silent deserted house, the event which could never be forgotten.[1]

'The Thermometer' undoubtedly had especial significance for Patrick. The passage quoted earlier from his diary, in which he recorded his completion of the story on 15 January 1955, concludes with these telling words: 'M[ary] did not like it. This makes me hate her, which is monstrously unfair. Dread of losing grip.' In her own diary my mother wrote: 'P. wrote boy & thermometer tale & I got so depressed.' This disapproval was extraordinarily uncharacteristic, as was Patrick's expressed resentment. Her consistent role (as will be seen, a vital one) was that of all but uncritical admirer of Patrick's literary talent. I have little doubt that it was the autobiographical aspect of the tale which made her so frank in her expression of distaste. The likely cause of her objection was a tragic event unfolding at that very time in distant England.

Just over a month after Patrick completed his story, on 26 February 1955 his father died of pneumonia at his home in Ealing. That he was gravely ill, if not dying, must presumably have been known to Patrick at the time he wrote the story, since he was in close touch with his stepmother and brother Bun, who had flown over from his home in Canada to be with them. It is hard to believe that the two events were unconnected. Was it the imminent departure of his father from this world that impelled Patrick to set down in permanent form the darkest hour of his childhood?

'The Thermometer' is unique among Patrick's literary works in his overt acknowledgement of its autobiographical character. However, other early short stories and novels also contain thinly disguised accounts of his early life as he recalled it. Episodes in his novel *Richard Temple* unmistakably reflect the years which followed the dissolution of the family household at Willesden Green. The eponymous Richard's recollection of his lethargic and introverted existence is not one of unremitting misery. Solitude affords him refuge from the company of his grim and unsuccessful father. Acknowledging that he had been an idle and unambitious child, Temple justifies himself by asserting that he had possessed 'a very delicate sense of honour; and in those days he had a great deal of affection in his heart, affection for the asking'.

The intensity and inescapability of his solitude induced in the boy a state of resignation which supplied the place of positive contentment. Regularly left alone in his bedroom, 'He had an excellent temperament for that mild

[1] In *The Road to Samarcand* (1954), the young hero's uncle explains to him: '"When you joined us in Wang Pu after. . ." He paused. He didn't like to say "after your mother and father died" . . . He coughed and went on, ". . . after the funeral . . ."'

confinement, a solitary, idle and unfretting mind; and there was never a pleasanter place of apprenticeship than this room'. Within his private stronghold, Richard obtained solace by mental wanderings along time-devouring byways in a miasmatic state of contented passivity, discovering and rediscovering variations in patterns in the wallpaper, or conducting protracted undemanding mathematical calculations. Patrick's acute sensation of lack of parameters and purpose in his childhood existence appears to have induced a compensatory fascination with structured order: a quality he carried forward into his literary career.

Preparatory notes for his early stories frequently include factual details drawn from his own experience, and Temple's minutely exact description of the wallpaper in his bedroom suggests imagery imprinted in Patrick's memory: 'There were thirty-nine bands of lyres and roses on the wall that ran from the door to the window.' That the young Patrick sought diversion and found comfort in repetitive exercises such as those he ascribed to his *alter ego* is confirmed by a reflection jotted down years later: 'order gives pleasure / order alone? think of / the perfectly ordered / repetitive patterns common on linoleum / and 'stained glass' [here he added: 'particularly in our childhood'] / but perhaps the orderliness / of these marks set out in / order are less disagreeable / than they would be in / promiscuous confusion.'[1]

The oddly intrusive inverted commas placed about 'stained glass' apply to a singular detail in *Richard Temple* so aptly as virtually to exclude the possibility of coincidence. Here is the description of Richard's father's study, as the boy enters: 'He hurried down, his face composed in an expression of dutiful worry, and stood lumpishly in the accepted place, on the edge of the black hairy rug. It was a brown room, yet cold, and the two north-facing windows on his left, *with their lower panes covered with translucent paper lozenges* [italics inserted], gave on to a scraped grass-plot. One was further obscured by a monkey-puzzle tree made of blue-black metal . . .'

Among the tasks to which young Richard Temple applies himself when whiling away the tedium of his existence is that of converting the succession of roses on his wallpaper into a calendar.

> He began to count off the days . . . starting from the roses that marked the present date. The progression of weeks ran up and up, and on a Wednesday . . . they ran under a picture, to emerge on Thursday week.

[1] Richard Temple, languishing in a Nazi gaol, spends his time counting, re-counting, and measuring the tiles of his cell (*Richard Temple*, p. 5). Earlier in his life he expresses fascination with the kaleidoscope: 'In the small illuminated round there were these brilliant particles, existing in some other space and light, invested with some other significance, perpetually changing and perpetually almost apprehended' (ibid., p. 95).

His reconciliation to the tedium of enforced isolation by devoting hours to detection of patterns in wallpaper or carpets, engaging in repetitive calculations, imaginatively exploring the interior of a house in a painting, and undertaking similar ploys for passing the time away are familiar symptoms of the mentality of long-term prisoners, who seek to fill the mental vacuum through absorption in meaningless abstract exercises, endlessly protracted by ingenious variations, which substitute an introspective realm of dreaming for the inaccessible world of reality. A day may come, however, when these elaborately constructed defences are turned around into menacing siege-works. After years of self-induced conditioning, on his eventual release the prisoner finds the outside world an unstructured mental wilderness: a state not infrequently resulting in emotional turmoil from which complete recovery may prove difficult or impossible.[1]

The paradigm of isolated child as prisoner receives marked emphasis in *Richard Temple*, where the hero relives his previous life while incarcerated in a Nazi gaol in Occupied France. He utilises the self-discipline developed by the unnatural constraints of his childhood to persuade his tormentors that they are dealing with a weak, foolish, and cowardly victim. They are too obtuse to realise that his childhood years of failure and psychological withdrawal have endowed him with resources of inner strength and cunning sufficient to defy and ultimately outwit the most ruthless and omnipotent of persecutors.

Temple provides a clear exposition of the debility which assailed him. Lying in his darkened cell, he finds his spirit all but crushed by the numbing effect of endless solitude: 'And when he had said and repeated to himself all that he had to say, then there was the huge and overwhelming boredom. The man would be living on the shore of nothing: he would have nothing to do or say; he would see nothing; but still he would be alive. He would have to live interminably, with no sequence of events.'[2]

In fact, however, the hideous ordeal unexpectedly engenders hidden strengths of which Richard had been hitherto unaware.

[1] Confined to a protracted spell in the punishment cell of a Soviet gaol, Vladimir Bukovsky preserved his mental equilibrium by imaginatively 'constructing a castle in every detail: from the foundations, floors, walls, staircases and secret passages right up to the pointed roofs and turrets'. On his eventual release he found the contrasted chaos of real life almost unbearable: 'This noisy world won't tolerate the uninvolved – it pushes you, pulls you, orders you about, makes demands on you, threatens you and tells you to be careful. What do you want of me? Leave me in peace, let me alone. Don't touch me. I want to squat right here, alone and stare into space, seeing nothing' (*To Build a Castle* (London, 1978), pp. 22–24, 177–78).
[2] *Richard Temple*, p. 15.

> Prison had acted like a forcing-house on his intelligence and cunning: he had been comparatively stupid, slow, unthinking, before he had been caught . . . The man that went in . . . was barely recognisable as the man that lay there now. He was barely recognisable to himself and sometimes he looked back with a cold furious contempt at the old weak time-wasting life-eating submissive slob Temple – unbelievably weak, submissive, and silly, *silly*; and sometimes survivors from the past looked at the present hard, competent animal with dismay and even horror.[1]

In an effort to appreciate the distance he had travelled, the prisoner retraces in imagination his days of childhood. His principal recollection is that of regular beatings at the hands of his tyrannical father, customarily followed by lengthy periods of confinement to his room. However, the boy found the isolation strangely congenial. 'He had an excellent temperament for that mild confinement, a solitary, idle and unfretting mind . . .' Temple's reveries betray an element of self-hatred, a failing by which Patrick was himself continually tormented.

The question of beating represents an unpleasant factor which is impossible to avoid addressing. For much of the five years stretching between the break-up of the family home at Willesden Green and his first attendance at school it seems likely that Patrick suffered from more than debilitating boredom and inadequate instruction. In 'The Thermometer' the boy revealingly flinches from an anticipated blow as 'Cousin Carew' raises his arm to pull aside the laboratory curtain. Constitutionally unsuited to the role of parent, still less that of teacher which he spasmodically attempted, there is reason to believe that his father was wont without much reflection or discrimination to resort to corporal punishment.

Everything known of Charles Russ suggests that he would be likely to inflict his punishments on as erratic and irrational a basis as he conducted himself generally as a parent. There was the awesomely intimidating effect of his gigantic stature, described so vividly by Patrick in the opening paragraphs of 'The Thermometer'. In *Richard Temple* Patrick's hero as a child undergoes repeated beatings at his father's hands, and the same theme is developed in another plainly autobiographical passage contained in his earlier novel *The Catalans* (1953), where he describes the brutal father of the central character, Xavier.

Xavier explains of his father that 'he beat me, you know, with no justification at all, or on a trumped-up charge neither of us believed in . . . I

[1] *Richard Temple*, pp. 22–23.

had suffered so much from bullying – from mental assault much more than from beating, which I took as it came . . . the atmosphere of domestic tyranny when I was a boy.' His father 'was an evil-tempered man, powerful, domineering, and restless; a ferocious domestic bully', who had become 'sour, bitter, harsh, and overbearing'. 'There seemed to be no tenderness in Hercule [Xavier's father], none at all. He was quite unloving, at least as far as his son was concerned: but he would not leave him alone, whatever the boy did.'[1]

Making every allowance for Patrick's tendency to judge the world from his own viewpoint, there exists sufficient independent evidence to justify the broad outlines of this description. Faced with similar treatment, another child might have reacted very differently, falling into violent rages or seeking escape by one means or another. Patrick in contrast evolved a capacity for detachment from reality over lengthy periods, subsiding on occasion into induced lassitude.

The profound loneliness and neglect experienced by Patrick led him to school himself against dependence on human relationships. His bronchial complaint may have served to exacerbate this condition, but I do not believe it played that decisive part in his upbringing which he later ascribed it. Furthermore there are clear indications that, as he effectively confessed in 'The Thermometer', he deployed sickness (whether real or fancied) on occasion as a stratagem for self-protection. Finally, as solace for his loneliness and perhaps as compensation for the inadequate state of his education, he was drawn to extensive reading, much of it among branches of literature alien to most boys of his age. This afforded exciting sensations of voyaging in exotic regions unknown to his contemporaries, as well as compensatory consciousness of intellectual superiority.

In summary, if his later assertions and hints of Irish origins and upbringing be removed, Patrick's account of his childhood days is broadly consistent with what is independently attested by other sources. He suffered from persistent bronchial attacks, his schooling was exceptionally curtailed, as a child and adolescent he experienced prolonged periods of enforced solitude, and he was largely self-taught through voracious bouts of reading. Deprived at a vulnerable age of contact with other children, he developed an exceptionally sensitive and vulnerable nature. The loss of his mother in early childhood greatly increased his lack of self-confidence, and there is every indication that nearly five critical years intervening between the tragedy and his father's remarriage afflicted him with a suppressed psychic wound incurable as that of Philoctetes. As one of the principal characters in *The Catalans* reflects, 'I wonder how much every man's heart hardens as he goes

[1] *The Catalans*, pp. 86.

farther and farther from his boyhood.'[1] But the time of suffering and deprivation was far from having reached its term, and Patrick might have emerged into manhood with a more secure personality had his circumstances during the ensuing decade been more happily arranged.

The shadowy figure of the mother he had barely known exerted particular fascination for Patrick.[2] It was doubtless his contrasted perception of his parents which led him to adopt a notion that there was something discreditable about his paternal background, and to identify himself with the families of his mother or stepmother, the two becoming to some extent fused in his imagination. Jessie's forebears the Goddards were an old armigerous family, one cousin being Lord Goddard, a notoriously harsh and prejudiced Lord Chief Justice of England from 1946 to 1958. Her successor Zoe not only vaunted her gracious upbringing at Horton Rectory, but was not averse (as members of the family recall) to providing the family with 'constant reminders that they were living in her houses and on her money'.

Patrick's revulsion against his father and attachment to his vanished mother manifested itself in other ways. His elder brother Victor once queried whether Patrick might not have been illegitimate, while in 1988 Bun wrote cryptically to his sister Joan: 'One of these days when we are face to face, I will discuss with you the change of name which Mike made [he assumed the name O'Brien for a while in Australia] and Pat copied. It happens that I have Pat's birth certificate and we know full well that he is indeed the child and youngest son of our parents.' In the following year he stated still more emphatically: 'I really think he thinks he is not my brother . . . but I have his birth certificate anyway and whether he likes it or not, I claim him as my brother.' Bun reverted to the theme in yet another letter, noting that 'Mike changed back to Russ when he joined the Air Force, but whether Pat really thinks he is not a Russ, I do not know'. There is more than a suggestion that Patrick genuinely doubted that Charles was his true father. While in reality his paternity is not in doubt, it is easy to conceive how misgivings might have arisen in his imaginative fancy. In *Richard Temple* he makes his agitated hero overhear a conversation in which a group of acquaintances assert emphatically that he is a bastard: 'He told me he was

[1] *The Catalans*, p. 125.

[2] A similar situation occurred in the case of Leo Tolstoy, whose mother died when he was eighteen months old. He retained an idealised image of her, and wrote in later life: 'She appeared to me a creature so elevated, pure, and spiritual, that often in the middle period of my life, during my struggles with overwhelming temptations, I prayed to her, begging her to aid me; and such prayer always helped me much' (Aylmer Maude, *The Life of Tolstoy: First Fifty Year* (London, 1908), pp. 8–9).

the illegitimate son of somebody or other, but it was a great secret, and not to be known.'[1]

As he grew into maturity Patrick became haunted by an obsessive fear that he and his forebears on the paternal side might be socially not quite *comme il faut*. He was a child alone, vulnerable and fragile, before whom the void might open at any moment. His deep personal insecurity made him long to enjoy the romantic and secure status of a gentleman, in the sense that the term was understood at the time. Patrick justified his detestation of his father by deprecating his family's background in trade. Describing Richard Temple's reflections as a child, he included this telling passage:

> He [Lloyd George] was Welsh and he was common. Yet Richard's father was a Welshman; and Richard was his father's son. Was there some unavoidable taint in this? Or did he perhaps belong to his mother's side? He had always assumed that in the nature of things he was one of the better sort – he would have flung a handful of gold to the respectful peasantry before galloping on to the aid of the king. It was an assumption that he hardly questioned openly, for he was feeling little more than a hint of the immense force of English social pressures and he had only a vague suspicion about how they were to impinge upon him, only the most cloudy doubts about where he fitted in. He scarcely questioned the assumption; but now he would be glad to be confirmed in it, for underlying all this there was the remotely glimpsed possibility that he might be found to belong to the other side, that his mother might learn of this and cast him off. And then what constituted a gentleman?[2]

Such compensatory fantasies evolved gradually during Patrick's unhappy adolescence. Meanwhile in the latter part of 1922, by which time he had been living alone with his father at Beaumont Street for nearly two years, there occurred an event which wrought a dramatic transformation in the Russ household generally and Patrick's life in particular. After nearly five years of mourning his beloved Jessie, Charles Russ fell in love again, and on

[1] Similarly Stephen Maturin, while both illegitimate and sensitive about the fact (*HMS Surprise*, p. 301; *The Fortune of War*, p. 160), enjoys romantically aristocratic paternity (*HMS Surprise*, p. 73). Of an illegitimate son of the Duke of Clarence serving aboard Jack Aubrey's ship, he makes this curious observation: 'as a fellow-bastard he was well acquainted with the temptation to prattle, and its remarkable strength' (*Blue at the Mizzen*, p. 142). Is he suggesting that it is tempting for bastards of high birth to boast of the fact? It is curious that C.S. Forester also suffered from an 'acute fear of bastardy', and like Patrick changed his name, which was originally Cecil Smith (John Forester, *Novelist and Story-Teller: The Life of C.S. Forester* (Lemon Grove, CA), 2000, pp. 64–65).

[2] *Richard Temple*, pp. 29–30.

20 December 1922, a week after Patrick's eighth birthday, he remarried. His bride, Zoe Center, was an attractive widow, a year younger than him. Her husband William Rudolf Center had been a surgeon in the Royal Navy, who died in the Allies' ill-fated attempt to seize the Dardanelles. His ship HMS *Russell* sank after striking a mine on 27 April 1916, with the loss of 199 officers. Fleet Surgeon Center died from severe burns on the following day in the Naval Hospital at Malta, aged forty-five.

Precisely when and where Charles met Zoe is not known, and all Bernard recollected was that 'During our sojourn at Marylebone, Father met and married a wonderful lady.'[1] It seems that Charles pursued a fairly heady social life,[2] while she was undoubtedly a good catch. At the time Zoe was living in a smart house overlooking Hyde Park at 96 Knightsbridge. She appears also to have possessed a considerable inheritance in her own right, and her husband had been a man of independent means.[3] Although it is doubtful whether Charles ever fully recovered from the death of his first wife, the marriage was to prove a happy one. The couple were wed at St Paul's Church in Knightsbridge, where Charles's eldest son Godfrey, then a nineteen-year-old student at Northampton Polytechnic College, was a witness.

The newlyweds' honeymoon was spent in Malta, where they visited the tomb of Zoe's first husband in the Capuccini Naval Cemetery. While it is clear that Charles Russ's second marriage was a genuine love match, his combination of straitened circumstances and extravagant lifestyle cannot but have made her respectable financial status exceedingly welcome. Zoe appears likewise to have been devoted to her handsome and sociable husband. Bun recalled years later in a letter to Joan: 'I once ventured to tell her how remarkable I thought her courage in tackling the task of nine stepchildren. She chuckled and said "I wasn't *brave*: I was *ignorant*!"' Joan likewise recorded that her stepmother 'always maintained that she knew nothing of these nine children till after the honeymoon'. Since Zoe certainly met Godfrey and possibly Victor (who was two years younger, and had also left

[1] Russ, *Lady Day Prodigal*, p. 24. The wedding certificate of the middle-aged couple shows that Zoe discreetly deducted two years from her age, and Charles one.

[2] He was among other things an active freemason, eventually becoming Grand Master of a Lodge. His daughter Joan remembered his setting out in his regalia to attend evening sessions.

[3] In addition to their family home her husband left her the not inconsiderable sum of £9,502 ('The Probate Register of the High Court of Justice in England, 1916'; cf. *The Times*, 5 August 1916). Dean King's assertion (*Patrick O'Brian*, p. 31) that Zoe initially arrived in the Russ household as governess to Patrick cannot be correct. Setting aside her wealth and position, he was unaware of the fact that by 1922 Dr Russ had abandoned his house in Willesden Lane, and the installation of an attractive widow of his own class in the bachelor household at 25 Beaumont Street would have been highly improper.

school) this cannot be literally true, but presumably applied to the seven children of school age and below.

Following her marriage to Charles, in 1923 Zoe purchased a home in the country.[1] Melbury Lodge, a charming Victorian country house, is situated in the picturesque village of Kempsey, on the banks of the Severn four miles south of Worcester. If the story of Zoe's being kept in ignorance of the children be true, Patrick must have been tucked discreetly out of the way during his father's courtship. Now he was introduced to his new stepmother, who seems to have taken to him at once and treated him thereafter as a firm favourite.

Patrick's reaction to the sudden appearance of a new mother after so many years of isolation is unrecorded. While his situation must have appeared materially improved, it is likely that so sensitive a child found the novel situation disturbing. Fifty years later he wrote in his diary: 'Early bed & absurdly Freudian dream – parents being married – intense jealousy on my part (yet observed by my present me).'

Before long Patrick was joined at Melbury Lodge by Joan, whom he had only known as a little girl with whom he played during rare visits to Aunt Bertha and Uncle Frank at Pinner. Now aged five, she arrived at the family home which her father's remarriage enabled him to provide. Sadly, the move was to have a disastrous effect upon her for the remainder of her life. Her Aunt Bertha and Uncle Frank had become very fond of her, and even proposed to adopt her as their daughter. Her father declined the offer, a refusal which in later years Joan came to resent. She received little kindness or affection from her father and stepmother, whereas at Myrtle Lodge the kindly Welches would have provided her with that happy home and proper education which she was largely denied. Her father's insistence on her return home may have arisen from jealousy of his brother-in-law's prosperity, a weakness to which on occasion he gave expression.

In 1991, Bun, who appears to have been besotted with his stepmother ('how very blessed we were during her time, and again when that wonderful lady took us on,' he recalled in 1969), informed an astonished Joan of the circumstances in which he had been informed she left Myrtle Lodge: 'I well remember hearing of your being rescued by dear Stepmother from Auntie Bertha and Frank Welch, Margaret and Christine, where you being kept in the servants quarters or released were having your meals with the skivvies and I still feel indignant about it, because the rescue by our Stepmother was

[1] So Joan recalled, but Bernard believed his stepmother 'inherited a house in the village of Kempsey'.

timely and effective.' Joan's response has not survived, but this account of her 'rescue' must represent a fantasy concocted by her stepmother. Indeed, it could provide a fair description of the treatment she herself meted out to Joan in coming years.

Joan's daughter Gwen informs me that Joan 'always spoke well of Aunt Bertha and Uncle Frank and was grateful to them for taking her in. I wish she had kept her little rag doll Pansy which the cook had made for her and which she afterwards hugged or took her frustrations out on. She felt guilty ever after about how she'd treated Pansy!' Christine Welch remembers that her cousin Joan was treated as one of the family, and photographs of the three cousins in her family album include one of them on the beach enjoying a holiday in Cornwall. Although Joan's father occasionally called on the Welches while she lived with them, she was never permitted to come home throughout those five years. Bun recalled that when they met at Kempsey in 1923, 'I had not seen you since our mother died, I think, unless perhaps when Mike and I went to the Pinner home of Uncle Frank and Aunty Bertha where you were living with Margaret and Christine.' Indeed, so perfunctory were her links with her family during her five years' absence from home, that on being introduced to her stepmother at Melbury Lodge she exclaimed to her father: 'where have you been keeping my Mummy all this time?'

At first Patrick and Joan were the only children in the house. Presumably Zoe felt there was a limit to the number of undeclared stepchildren she was prepared to receive at the outset of her marriage, and in consequence the two little children were thrown together and swiftly became particular friends. This they remained until late middle age, when sadly they fell out in consequence of what appears to have been a mutual misunderstanding.

For two years, ever since his five older brothers and sisters departed to boarding-school, Patrick had eked out a dreary existence in his father's bachelor establishment at Beaumont Street. He was eight years old, and had still not been to school. It was the most wretched period of an unhappy childhood, and it is not difficult to picture his joy on finding himself removed from the dingy and relatively cramped quarters of his father's house in Marylebone to the spacious grounds of Melbury Lodge. In addition he now enjoyed a congenial companion in the form of his young sister Joan, a cheerful tomboy who happily shared his imaginative adventures around the rambling home and extensive garden. As Bun recalled in an unpublished memoir which he compiled over the winter of 1989 to 1990, it was hard to imagine a more ideal setting for children: 'The house at Kempsey was large and had obviously been a handsome mansion at one time. There were stables, outhouses, and the usual appurtenances to a massive mansion. Also there were some very fine large trees. My youngest sister has written lately saying that she drove by there and regretted to see that the trees had come down.' It was here, for an all too brief space of time, that Patrick at the impressionable ages of eight and nine was first enabled to enjoy to the full the active pleasures of boyhood.

Over half a century later Joan wrote to him: 'An hour will get you to the beautiful Malvern hills and Worcester. Remember Kempsey? I've often passed that house (in much better shape than it was) on my way to our week-end striding the Malvern Range.'

Although Patrick had for long years become distanced from his family, he promptly responded with nostalgic enthusiasm:

> You speak of Kempsey: yes, I have a fragmentary recollection of the house, some details being very sharp and clear (old Pugh,[1] the cellars where I found some glue and piles of damp, unbound Gentleman's Magazines of the early nineteenth century, a robin's nest in the ivy-covered wall and Daddy telling me not to feed the fledglings, a Christmas with snow on the ground) but the general picture is extremely vague. Melbury Lodge the place was called: and if you should ever pass that way again, please would you photograph it for me?

These vivid memories indicate the manner in which Patrick later occasionally modified the circumstances of his early life. Describing his childhood to a sympathetic interviewer, he had this to say: '"I was a sadly sickly little boy . . . I spent a lot of time in bed in a great house. In the cellar was a chest full of *Gentlemans Magazine* . . . All in very sound condition. And I read in their entirety the reports that slowly came through and then the aunts [? accounts] that followed of Anson's noble voyage."' From this the writer not unreasonably concluded: 'The seeds for Aubrey and Maturin were sown in the mid-50s when O'Brian wrote two linked novels about Anson's 1740s circumnavigation of the globe, featuring a prototype of their friendship. *His interest in that voyage began in childhood . . .*' (italics inserted).[2]

But Patrick specified to Joan that the volumes he discovered in the cellar belonged to the nineteenth century – *not* the eighteenth. This was not the sort of detail he was likely to mistake, and in fact many years were to pass before he discovered Anson's voyage, which he put to such effective literary use in his novels *The Golden Ocean* and *The Unknown Shore*. On St Valentine's Day 1945, when he was thirty, my mother gave him the three volumes of the

[1] Who 'old Pugh' was I have been unable to discover. It seems he made a lasting impression on Patrick, who used his name for the protagonist of his autobiographical novel *Three Bear Witness*.

[2] Peter Guttridge, 'A landlubber beneath the stuns'l boom iron', *Independent*, 3 July 1993.

Gentleman's Magazine for 1743, 1744, and 1745 which contain the accounts of Anson's triumphant circumnavigation of the globe. Patrick began reading them at once, noting: 'Masses of information, both solid and (what is more in some ways) ephemeral. Handsome panelled calf. Vilely printed – hard to realise that any verse can be good in such a dress.' He was still dipping into them three months later, and it is evident from his comments that this was the first occasion he encountered them.

How much he read and understood of the volumes he found at Melbury Lodge is impossible to tell. What surely provoked the excitement of the inquisitive eight-year-old was his discovery of mysterious piles of ancient tomes in a dark subterranean chamber, bearing all the connotations of hidden treasure. The feeling of being the sole discoverer of esoteric lore would have borne particular appeal to the neglected child, whose sole avenue to freedom had long lain in the resources of his imagination.

Patrick's ability to extract pleasure from enforced isolation is an emotion recalled by Stephen Maturin when 'he lapsed back into that contented solitude of an only child, going his own way, in silence, without reference to anyone at all. It was a natural way of life and it suited him very well . . . He therefore wandered alone, much as he had done when he was a boy, peering into the water-shrew's domain . . . and making a rough inventory of the resident birds: he also read a great deal in Woolcombe's noble but utterly neglected library, where a first folio Shakespeare stood next to Baker's *Chronicle* . . .'[1]

In the interview cited earlier Patrick declared himself to have been 'a sadly sickly little boy', implicitly singling out the days at Melbury Lodge as a time when he spent 'a lot of time in bed'. However the extent of his ill health remains tantalisingly difficult to establish. It has been seen that he suffered from a severe bronchial ailment in early days, but nothing suggests that he was a reclusive invalid during his time at Melbury Lodge. Had he been, he would surely have recalled the fact in his letter to his sister. It seems more likely that he indulged in idling and introspective dreaming, a propensity arising from the prolonged spells of isolation to which he had been subjected. He subsequently came to regard inactivity as a weakness of which he did not wish the world to become aware, and adopted measures to expunge it from the record. These bouts of inertia continued to exert a malign effect upon him well into early middle age, and he overcame them only by the rigorous exercise of self-discipline.

[1] *The Yellow Admiral*, p. 49. Patrick possessed a folio copy of Sir Richard Baker's *A Chronicle of the Kings of England From the Time of yᵉ Romans Government unto the Death of King James* (London, 1696).

Another fleeting glimpse of those carefree days survives in a solemn contract, drawn up in what appears to be Patrick's handwriting on a blank page of a diary which Victor had kept during the first months of 1917. Patrick's blithe acceptance of the vague terms of the exchange suggests that his inability to cope with legal transactions began at an early age: 'This diary was given to Victor Russ, who gave it to Pat Russ, who gave it to Nora Russ for something else.

{signed, N. Russ.
{witnessed by P. Russ.'

Before the diary passed into Nora's possession, Patrick pencilled in a couple of random notes suggesting that he already possessed that eccentric humour which was one of his prevailing characteristics as man and writer. Taking up his pencil, he solemnly recorded:

'Wednesday April 11th 1924.
'nobody has a birthday today in our family.'

While true the reflection may have appeared a little lacking in significance, and at the end of the year he added this calculation:

'Patrick Russ.

'10 on December 12th	1924
on which	10
they say he was born →	1914.'

In 1923 Victor's Christmas present to Patrick was a copy of *William Again*, most recent in the immensely popular series by Richmal Crompton. In every chapter William cheerfully engages in and generally escapes the consequences of misdeeds which, if perpetrated by Patrick, would have provoked a terrifying onset of parental wrath. The final story, 'William Gets Wrecked', must surely have touched a personal chord.

> William laid aside 'Robinson Crusoe' with a sigh. His dreams of pirate-king and robber-chief vanished. The desire of his heart now was to be shipwrecked on a desert island . . . He decided to set out on a voyage . . . To a casual observer William looked only a small boy walking slowly down a road, frowning, with his hands in his pockets. He was really an intrepid mariner sailing across an uncharted sea.
>
> 'Hello, William.'
>
> William had a weak spot in his heart for Joan. He rather liked her dimples and dark curls. In his softer moments he had contemplated Joan actually reigning by his side as pirate-queen or robber-chieftainess. Now he felt that her presence might enliven a somewhat lonely voyage.

'I'm an explorer,' he said, 'sailin' along an' lookin' for new lands.'

'Oh, William,' Joan pleaded, 'may I come with you?'

He considered the matter with a judicial frown.

'All right,' he said at last. 'Will you come in my ship or will you have a ship of your own?'

'I'd rather come in your ship, please.'

'All right,' he said. 'Well, you're in my ship. Come on.'

It was a strange chance that at this very time Patrick first enjoyed the company of his own Joan, with whom he engaged in exploits comparable to those of the fictional William. Indeed, a misadventure which led Patrick into trouble at the time reflected one of the incorrigible William's exploits remarkably closely. In 'Just William's Luck', another story in the same book, an aunt rashly allows him access to her archery set, which she recovers only after discovering damage inflicted on the landing window, her cat, and the next-door gardener. Patrick's sister Joan recalled an unfortunate accident, likewise involving a bow and arrow, in the garden of Melbury Lodge. The weapon was probably somewhat primitive, as more than twenty years later Patrick was to reflect wistfully: 'how I would have loved a proper arrow that would have flown true when I was a youngling'. This may explain why he once discharged a shaft which accidentally struck Joan close to her eye.

Patrick was given a sound thrashing, which was probably not the first and certainly not the last he received at his father's hands. On the likely assumption that his attitude towards parental chastisement in his autobiographical novel *Richard Temple* reflects his own feelings, he resented physical punishment as a malevolent and degrading ordeal, which he unhesitatingly ascribed to latent sadism.

In this instance the punishment would have appeared more than a little unfair, in view of the fact that he had himself been the victim of sustained target practice at his brothers' hands. Bun recalled that 'On one occasion, my stepmother was alarmed by the fact that my youngest brother was tied to one of these trees and senior members of the family took pot shots at him with arrows, although these were quite harmless, it was a test of the little fellow's pluck – he did not whimper or cry and felt he was quite a hero and a martyr, like St Sebastian.'

Nora remembered 'that Patrick had been Zoe's particular favourite, whilst he was young'. The affection was reciprocated, and Patrick retained throughout his life strong affection for his 'mother', as he invariably described her. Regrettably her arrival in his life failed to overcome the profound psychological damage he had suffered during the previous five years. Moreover his father's combination of indifference towards his children, and irascibility continued to create problems.

Autobiographical passages in Patrick's early novels indicate that he regarded his father as a tyrant, while his stepmother fulfilled the role of a sympathetic but (in his estimation) culpably impotent protector. Nora's memory confirmed that, although little Patrick was Zoe's favourite among her stepchildren, she appears to have had little success in protecting him from his father.

In *The Catalans*, Xavier reminisces: 'When I was a really small boy I loved my stepmother, you know, and when they quarrelled I hated my father. I loved her, and I thought about things for her and how when I grew up I would do this, that, and the other to give her pleasure . . .' In *Richard Temple* Patrick is more specific about the cause of their quarrelling, at least so far as it related to him. Waiting in his bedroom to be summoned for yet another beating, the boy Richard overhears his father and stepmother arguing in the study below, the latter apparently pleading with her husband to relent. Eventually however she succumbs, leading Richard to the bitter conclusion that 'she was really on his side against the common enemy'.

Whether or not Charles Russ had really concealed the existence of his numerous offspring from Zoe until after their marriage, he was initially careful to restrict the number whom he invited to their family home. The two eldest, Godfrey and Victor, had already left to follow their careers. It was not until the Christmas holiday of 1923 that the entire family gathered under the same roof. It was the first time since that melancholy day in 1918 when Dr Russ sent away his baby Joan. It proved to be a happy occasion. As Bun recalled to Joan more than forty years later: 'Whenever I write to you I think of you opening the door at Kempsey when Step-Mother whom Mike and I had met for the first time at Worcester railway station, arrived. I had not seen you since the days when you were with Aunty Bertha and I always remember that particular Christmas with great delight, because we had snow, we had carol singers, the village band, mince pies from the local bakery, Godfrey and Victor rode up on their bikes from London and the whole family was united for the first time for many years.'

Following this belated introduction to the full brood of her newly acquired stepchildren, it seems that Zoe was prepared to receive them during part at least of the holidays while she and Charles continued to live at Melbury Lodge.

Bernard remembered that their father had not lost his eccentric fascination with ingenious devices:

> . . . it was found that the greenhouse included a pond with a fountain and this

> intrigued my father, because it was stagnant and unsightly, so he thought he would drain it and as he was rather keen to show that it could be done by means other than taking a bucket or two and emptying them outside the greenhouse, he took a hose and arranged for it to siphon the water out of the fountain area. One of my brothers [Mike] was impatient of this because he had to go every now and then and take a fresh bucket and take the full bucket out, so he thought he would cut short the procedure by taking it out bucket by bucket and never mind the siphoning. This really annoyed my father and made an impression on me, showing his concern to demonstrate to those of us who are ignorant, the principle of siphoning liquid from one place to another and that is how I learned about that.

Patrick later borrowed the name for Melbury Lodge, the 'neat gentleman's residence' that Jack Aubrey leases in the novel *Post Captain* (1972). Still more significant are the circumstances in which the house features in Patrick's story. Jack Aubrey's Melbury Lodge is transferred from Worcestershire to a locality in Sussex, which is described in glowing colours reflecting the countryside around Lewes where Patrick would experience his other period of childhood happiness. It is not difficult to detect the application to Patrick's own experience, when he represents Jack as renting the house in order to avoid living with his irresponsible and impoverished father, his mother having died some years earlier. Although in Patrick's case his father lived at home at least part of the time, the presence of his stepmother and Joan, together with the freedom from supervision in the large house and garden, gave him for the first time a happy refuge from the oppressive presence.

A still more revealing allusion appears in *The Yellow Admiral*. Towards the beginning of the novel Jack Aubrey breaks the dreadful news to his wife Sophie of the failure of a great lawsuit in which he was involved: a disaster which spelt his financial ruin.

> She digested this. It was the wreck of their cherished, accumulated hopes as far as that particular case was concerned. 'We shall have to sell Ashgrove,' she said after a pause. 'The creditors will not wait.'
>
> Jack cast her a loving glance. What she said was true; the only evident solution, since Woolcombe [his own house] was entailed; yet it was scarcely one that he could have proposed. Ashgrove was her own, and could neither be sold nor mortgaged by him, very much her own, and even legally so, by settlement – a rambling house they had planned together, piece by piece, but of course carried out almost entirely by her, with Jack being so long at sea.

Jack Aubrey's ruinous legal action drew much upon my own battle in the courts against Lord Aldington in 1989, in which Patrick took a keenly sympathetic interest. However, Sophie's selfless offer must reflect a much earlier episode in his life. In the summer of 1924, having been the family home for little more than a year, Melbury Lodge had to be sold to meet Charles Russ's debts. His reduced circumstances after 1921 had not inhibited his penchant for flamboyant new cars,[1] and although financial profligacy was undoubtedly the cause of his having to remove his children from their schools not long afterwards, it appears from Bernard's account that he advanced failing health (for which there appears to be not a trace of evidence) as his pretext for the disaster.[2] Privately even the outwardly loyal Bun was compelled to acknowledge his father's incorrigible self-indulgence: 'The extravagant habits which undoubtedly my father developed from early manhood were hard to discard and showed even in his later days, after he had gone through bankruptcy proceedings and had had to discontinue private schooling for four of five of the children. He would still go to the theatre with my stepmother quite often and would dine out. I am not reproaching his memory in bringing these matters up, but simply taking it that the habits of a lifetime are not likely to be interrupted in a notable manner.'

Given her devotion to her husband, Zoe appears to have accepted the sacrifice without repining, and would not have betrayed misgivings or resentment before the children. As her personal property, Melbury Lodge was not affected by her husband's debts, and doubtless was sold by her to save him from total financial disaster. The parallel with Sophie's sweet-natured gesture in *The Yellow Admiral* is surely too close to be coincidental. In any case, the significance lies not in the actual circumstances but how they were perceived by Patrick.

The sudden loss of his temporary paradise after the previous years of deprivation must have come as a dreadful blow to him. His happy refuge, after all, had been recently gained and as unexpectedly snatched away. It is likely that the loss considerably exacerbated his resentment of a father whose irresponsibility and extravagance had inflicted such disaster upon the family. These characteristics are a recurrent theme in Jack Aubrey's relationship with his father.

Charles was obliged to effect drastic retrenchments, which even the sale of his wife's house was unable to prevent. Unquestionably the most damaging effect of the crisis was that which it inflicted on his talented children. The only one to escape was Godfrey, who graduated at the end of the year with a

[1] While Bernard was at Shebbear College, 'Father came down to fetch us in his latest car' (*Lady Day Prodigal*, p. 21).

[2] Ibid., pp. 21, 66.

BA in Engineering from London University.[1] He fulfilled the early scientific bent he had displayed as expert repairer of the children's train set by becoming an electrical engineer at Westrex Ltd, with responsibility for installing and repairing the newly invented sound system equipment used in cinemas throughout the eastern part of the country. Victor had been compelled to abandon the prospect of further education, and found uncongenial employment in a bank. As his widow Saidie recalled: 'When I asked Victor once why he came to go into a bank, he said "I think Dad thought 'I've got the other boys settled so what can I do with Victor – he better just go into a bank.'" So he did but he was much more suited to do something more academic. Before the war he was studying French and Old English.'

Victor's explanation of his father's professed cause for his decision was charitable. Charles Russ was careful not to allude to the true reason why his son had been unable to attend university, namely his own inability or refusal to provide the necessary funding, nor would he do anything to assist his other sons to find employment appropriate to their tastes and talents. There can be no doubt that Victor possessed a first-class brain, and among other gifts his childhood enthusiasm for chess eventually led to his becoming a talented player, who competed at Hastings and even played on occasion against the celebrated Grand Masters Capablanca and Alekhine. An even-tempered soul, he literally made the best of a bad job.

Olive and Michael, who had achieved excellent results in the examinations for Oxford and Cambridge respectively, were likewise denied opportunity for higher education, while Bernard and the twins Connie and Nora were withdrawn prematurely from their schools at the end of the summer term of 1924. The Shebbear College register laconically records the reason for Michael's and Bernard's departure as 'Financial stress'.

Charles and Zoe Russ returned with their family to London, where they initially lived in Charles's house at 25 Beaumont Street. However, by the autumn he was obliged to sell the house and move his practice to 63 Wimpole Street, which he shared with five other practitioners. As this provided no room for the family, Zoe rented a flat at 146 Kenilworth Court, a handsome brick mansion block in Lower Richmond Road, on the south bank of the Thames in Putney. Although the block overlooked the tree-lined river, the Russes' flat was at the back. The spacious house and garden at Kempsey had been replaced by quarters providing cramped space for a sizeable family. Godfrey and Victor, of course, no longer lived at home. Michael gained menial employment at a surveyor's estate office in the City, but whether or

[1] Although he conducted his studies at Northampton Polytechnic, the degree was awarded by London University.

how long he continued living at home I have been unable to establish.[1] Of the flat's four rooms and bathroom, one was used as the Russ parents' bedroom and another would have been the sitting-room. This left two bedrooms, the smaller of which was presumably occupied by Pat and Bun, leaving the four girls to occupy a single room.

Olive was accorded the thankless task of acting as unpaid governess to the smaller children. There was friction at times between her and the twins Connie and Nora, which Connie ascribed to their birth having deprived Olive of her position as the sole girl of the household. Patrick and Joan were largely left to their own devices. It appears that Bun was enrolled for the last year of his primary education at a London preparatory school.

Bernard later claimed that 'Zoe performed marvels in the household, which soon became a much happier and lively place, and everyone came to love and depend on her'. This rosy view was not shared by his sisters. Bernard's son Charles tells me that his Aunt Nora had very unhappy memories of this time: 'Nora and Olive had to regularly scrub potatoes and boil meat, and produce meals, to keep the house fed. No help from the boys! Connie was disabled [she had been crippled at birth with muscular dystrophy], and so she and Pat were relegated to being looked after, by the stronger ones (mostly Nora).' Joan's son Harry also recalls: 'My mother made many references to her stepmother, all of them disparaging. She was unhappy about what she saw as her stepmother's favouritism towards her stepsons. I heard similar opinions from Connie and Olive.'

Joan later expressed the view that her father had married Zoe for her money. Whilst allowance must be made for her feeling of resentment at the neglect and ill treatment she suffered at the hands of her stepmother, Charles's incorrigible extravagance may suggest that the accusation contained at least an element of truth. It could further be that Zoe's otherwise inexplicable hostility towards her stepdaughters sprang from jealous awareness of his attachment to the memory of Jessie. It was understood by the children that their stepmother had suffered one or more miscarriages during her first marriage, which if true may also account for her hostility towards her husband's daughters by his extremely fecund first wife.

Reminiscing to her children in later years, Joan described her new life in London as dreary and restricted in the extreme after the carefree days at

[1] Their final reports from Shebbear record that Mike and Bun were 'Staying at home when last heard of', their address being given as 25 Beaumont Street. In 1939 Mike remarked in a letter to Olive from Australia that 'all city dwellers are pretty much alike whichever suburb they belong to whether Putney or Wooloomooloo', which may reflect a memory of life in Lower Richmond Road.

Melbury Lodge. As always when living in London, the Russ parents were generally out enjoying a full social life, and the girls at least did not regard their absence as a deprivation. There was a private courtyard below for use by the occupants of Kenilworth Mansions, and in the safe atmosphere of pre-war London the children were generally free to wander in the streets outside, but as they had little or no pocket money and not much to do, their existence must have been tedious.

Joan's son Harry learned that his 'mother's relationship with Patrick according to her testimony was close when they were very young'. Nevertheless, 'it does seem that they [the children at home] suffered both emotionally and materially. I dimly remember her saying that at one point Pat had no shoes. She had a lifelong fear of being enclosed which gives some evidence of her claim to have been shut in cupboards when she was young.' Joan further recalled to her daughter Gwen an occasion when she and Patrick were playing beside the Thames at low tide, when he cheekily taught her to draw circular 'bums' in the mud. For Patrick the covert defiance of adult authority would have provided an appeal beyond the innate delight in vulgarity characteristic of small boys. Unfortunately the mischievous children were caught in the act and reproved by the eighteen-year-old Olive, who was supervising her little sister.

At the time Joan considered Olive 'very bossy', but in so far as this reflected reality it was most likely a consequence of her elder sister's own deeply unhappy predicament. Not only had she been denied that opportunity for higher education which her hard work at school had earned her, but she was treated with gratuitous unkindness by her father and stepmother. Her father was for some reason positively cruel to her. Although Nora regarded her sudden removal from school as a deliverance, having detested her days at Edgehill College, in old age she told her nephew Charles how she twice ran away from home with the intention of becoming a nun. Eventually, Olive plucked up courage to leave home.

The family lived in Kenilworth Court for some two years. There was a flurry of excitement in the spring of 1925 when they watched the start of the Oxford and Cambridge Boat Race from the windows of a neighbour's flat, but Charles Russ's finances resumed their disastrous descent, and shortly afterwards he was humiliatingly declared bankrupt, owing the then substantial sum of £4,000. Once again his extravagant lifestyle had made the temporary recovery accruing from the sale of Melbury Lodge merely a postponement of downfall. After this it appears that the family became permanently dependent on his wife's money.

THREE

Strange Schooldays

Nor was my life an unsuitable preparation for my future, in that it demanded constant wariness, the habit of observation, and attendance on moods and tempers; the noting of discrepancies between speech and action; a certain reserve of demeanour; and automatic suspicion of sudden favours.

(Rudyard Kipling, *Something of Myself*)

One of the most astonishing aspects of Patrick's achievement lies in the fact that his education comprised a total of four years' schooling, during which time he passed not a single examination. The tragedy is that, so far from feeling pride in becoming one of the world's most acclaimed authors despite this severe handicap, he remained so deeply ashamed of his lack of academic qualification that he kept it a profound secret even from his closest friends. Only now can the true story be recounted: one which I believe redounds remarkably to his credit.

In 1926 the family moved from Putney to a house at 54 Sutherland Avenue in Maida Vale, which was to remain their London home for the next six years. This represented for the girls the most unhappy period of their lives. How far the domestic tensions affected the eleven-year-old Patrick is unknown. As his stepmother's favourite, he possibly escaped the worst consequences of an increasingly miserable household. Unlike his sisters, he attended school for the first year and lived in the country for the next three.

An evocative glimpse of Patrick's warm relationship with his stepmother appears in his novel *Richard Temple*. Describing the tedium of hours spent alone in his bedroom, Temple conjures up memory of a picture hanging on the wall.

This picture was a little watercolour of Colpoys rectory, where his mother had

> been born; he had never been there, but he knew it exceedingly well from his mother's descriptions of her life there, and he could go confidently through the door under the Regency porch and know that if he went along the hall to the left of the stairs he would come to a door leading to a walled garden with a peacock in it. He was standing on an immense stretch of lawn running his finger down the iridescent sheen of the kind peacock's throat when the sound of a door opening below made him jerk.[1]

There is reason to believe that this represents a real picture at which Patrick himself frequently gazed with imaginative fascination. Never having known his mother, he always addressed his stepmother Zoe as 'mother'. Her father, the Reverend Bennett Blakeway, had for forty years been vicar of Horton near Leek in Staffordshire, where she was born. According to members of the Russ family, she was wont to assert her social standing as a 'daughter of the manse', and Horton Rectory is indeed a handsome Georgian building set in an unspoiled rural landscape.

Built in 1753 by John Wedgwood, a wealthy local landowner, its warm red brick walls and parapeted Macclesfield stone roof appear as imposingly elegant as its interior is gracious. The spacious rooms were adorned with oak-beamed ceilings, shuttered windows, and fine fireplaces. The servant's facilities included a butler's pantry, while steps led from the entrance hall down to extensive cellars equipped with stone wine-racks and a well. At the rear of the house beside the courtyard stood a substantial coach-house built to house five horses and a carriage.

Not only does the exterior of the house in the painting described in *Richard Temple* correspond to that of Horton Rectory, but the walled garden beyond and 'immense stretch of lawn' were likewise to be found at Zoe Russ's family home. Since these could not have been visible in the painting, it seems that Patrick similarly 'knew it exceedingly well from his [step]mother's descriptions of her life there'. One may readily imagine him pondering the inviting façade in the picture, which conjured up an enchanted maternal refuge lying beyond. The fact that this paradisal retreat was located in his stepmother's house, entrance to which lay through the portals of an elegant Georgian house, requires no emphasis in the content of Patrick's subsequent imaginative absorption into the world of late Georgian England.

Time and again Patrick made the hero of his stories 'a child of the manse', and it may well have been wondering reflections as his stepmother expatiated on the grandeur of her family home which first led him to become entranced by Georgian England. Indeed, it seems not unlikely that

[1] *Richard Temple*, pp. 26–27.

Horton Rectory provided the basis for Jack Aubrey's ancestral 'Woolcombe House':

> The walled garden was . . . unchanged . . . the same exact rows of vegetables, bean-poles, gooseberry-bushes, currants, the same cucumber and melon frames, so vulnerable to a flying ball, and the same smelly box-hedges, while on the red-brick walls themselves apricots and peaches were changing colour. Indeed the whole back of the house, stable-yard, laundry, coach-house, all the unimproved part was infinitely familiar, reaching back to the firth things Jack had ever known, as familiar as cock-crow . . .[1]

As yet Patrick had received no formal education. Since he was nine when the family fortunes plunged to their nadir in 1924, there could be no question of his attending public school. The sole published source for this formative period of Patrick's life remains his brother Bun's privately printed autobiographical memoir. Unfortunately for the biographer, it is a work which suffers from serious deficiencies. It was in old age that he set himself to recall his childhood memories, which were liable either to have been misconceived at the time of their occurrence, or confused after an interval of some seven decades. Still more serious distortion resulted from his concern to minimise family dissensions: above all, his suppression of anything detrimental to his father's memory.

News of Bun's project greatly alarmed Patrick, who had long sought to distance himself publicly from his family. Angered and alarmed at the prospect of having his early life placed on public record even in so obscure a publication, he raised strong objection to his inclusion in the work. Consequently Bun tactfully repressed any allusion in *Lady Day Prodigal* which might enable an outside reader to recognise in his brother 'Pat' the author Patrick O'Brian. This consideration led Bun to reduce to a minimum any mention of their shared childhood experiences.

In a rare public comment on his schooling, Patrick told a journalist of his 'strong memories of prep school in Torbay'.[2] Dean King suggests that 'Zoe might . . . have funded Patrick's early education by sending him for a time to prep school in Torbay, where he came to know the coast of Devon'.[3] This

[1] *The Letter of Marque*, pp. 225–26. Cf *The Yellow Admiral*, pp. 21, 25, 26.

[2] Peter Guttridge, the *Independent*, 3 July 1993. Patrick also referred to his time 'at prep-school in Devon' in an interview with Keith Wheatley, 'The Long Life of O'Brian', *Financial Times*, 11–12 January 1997.

[3] King, *Patrick O'Brian*, p. 34. 'Tor Bay, in the vicinity of Paignton, where Patrick O'Brian once attended prep school' (idem, *Harbors and High Seas: An Atlas and Geographical Guide to the Aubrey–Maturin Novels of Patrick O'Brian* (New York, 1999), p. 34).

however represents double conjecture of very dubious value, and there are strong reasons for discounting Patrick's claim to have attended preparatory school.

When called upon to give a speech of thanks on the splendid occasion of his receipt of the Heywood Hill Literary Prize at Chatsworth in 1995, he touchingly confessed that the only other prize he had ever received had been when he was at preparatory school at Paignton, when his headmaster awarded him a double-bladed penknife for 'trying hard' in a race. Patrick was consumed with nerves at public appearances, and this was one of the most demanding he had ever faced. In his diary he wrote: 'I launched into my ¼ prepared anecdote, which went quite well (though I left out the main or only point).'

Perhaps the most telling indication that Patrick never in reality attended a preparatory school is the fact that there was no good reason for him to do so. His brother Bun was sent to Shebbear 'when I had reached the grand old age of eight!' (actually nine). Seven or eight was the customary age for entry to preparatory school, and if Patrick was sent to boarding-school it is hard to conceive why he would not have joined his brothers at the school attended by two generations of the Russ family. (At the time Shebbear accepted boys aged seven to nine, who were placed in Form 2.) None of his four elder brothers attended preparatory school. The great advantage to Charles Russ of sending his three daughters to Edgehill College lay in its proximity to Shebbear, and it seems highly improbable that he should have elected to send his youngest son to a third school on the far side of the county. And if Patrick did attend a school in Devonshire at the same time as his brothers and sisters, why did he never join them during their school holidays at Clovelly?[1]

In *Richard Temple*, Patrick dispatches his eponymous hero to preparatory school. In marked contrast to the vivid portrayal of life at the grammar school which he subsequently attends, its atmosphere is very indistinctly conveyed, comprising little more than a couple of unconvincingly adult conversations with a self-confident fellow-pupil, Gay, whom he encounters in later life little changed in speech or manner. Apart from this, Temple's preparatory school experience (normally five or six unforgettable years of a boy's life) is confined to an account of his sitting the scholarship examination for a public school: a measure necessitated by the inadequacy of his father's straitened means. In the event he fails, and is obliged to attend a grammar school. Much

[1] In view of his evident concern to magnify the woefully inadequate extent of his education, it is significant that Patrick provided no reference to primary school education in the *curriculum vitæ* he submitted when applying to join the Royal Air Force in 1934.

is made of the resultant social humiliation to which the sensitive boy feels himself permanently consigned: 'everybody went to public school: it was part of the process and nothing else was thinkable . . . Only cads went to common schools – indeed, they were called cads' schools.'[1]

I find it implausible that anyone who had actually attended a preparatory school would have encountered the subtle discussion of class stratification which plays so prominent a part in this episode of *Richard Temple*. Preparatory schools comprised hierarchies owing little or nothing to the outside world, bounded by the prefectorial system and differentiations between boarders and day-boys, and respective dormitories and classes. Altogether these self-sufficient communities resembled little neo-feudal societies, whose power structures were demarcated by age, physical strength, prowess at games, or personal qualities of leadership and imaginative ingenuity. In such an atmosphere the social or professional status of a boy's parents was a matter of negligible concern. Furthermore, preparatory school boys tended to be little concerned with the standing of the schools they would subsequently attend, which more often than not they had never seen and of which they possessed the haziest conception. Gay's exposition to Temple of the arcane niceties of the English class system carries scant conviction as a topic likely to concern a couple of twelve-year-olds, and reads rather as the ruminations of an insecure adult projected into childhood.[2]

The first certain fact known of Patrick's education is that he was sent to grammar school at the age of ten. To have been accepted, he must have attained at least elementary proficiency in reading, writing, and basic knowledge of required subjects. But if, as appears to be the case, he never attended primary school, how had he acquired this knowledge?

His accounts of his early upbringing are tantalisingly brief. In his introductory essay included in the collection of *Critical Appreciations* published by the British Library in 1994, he devoted a single paragraph to his early years.

> I shall not deal with my childhood and youth in any detail, however: although the period had its compensations it is not one that I look back upon with much pleasure, partly because my home fell to pieces when my mother died a little

[1] *Richard Temple*, p. 32.

[1] It is intriguing to note that the discussion occurs in 'a place beyond the cricket pitches called Starve-Acre . . . Richard was carving a lump of chalk into the likeness of the school porter.' Did Patrick have in mind Hangman's Acre just behind Lewes Grammar School (which he attended), whose soil is chalk? If so, this would indicate that the brief and unconvincing preparatory school episode in *Richard Temple* represents an extrapolation from Patrick's memories of his schooldays at Lewes.

> after the end of the 1914–1918 War . . . and partly because much of the time I was ill, which was not only disagreeable in itself but which also did away with much in the way of regular education and companionship. Fortunately there . . . [were] some tutors whom I shall always remember with gratitude: even more fortunately most of these long stays in bed were spent within reach of books, and I read endlessly. Not that I was a chronically bedridden invalid or anything like it – I did go to school from time to time but upon the whole it was a very lonely childhood.[1]

Regrettably this bears only partial relation to reality. There is no reason to suppose that ill health played any part in depriving him of formal education, his concession that 'I did go to school from time to time' seems excessively dismissive of his four consecutive years of attendance at grammar schools, and there is reason to believe that he was never instructed by 'tutors'.

Nevertheless the account is 'psychologically true', to the extent that it reflects Patrick's idiosyncratic perception of his early years. In particular he felt impelled to suppress experiences so distressing that he found it impossible to confront them directly. These arose largely from his deeply troubled relationship with his father. In this miniature autobiography Charles Russ has effectively been removed from the picture. In avoiding direct reference to his formal education Patrick attributes his haphazard schooling solely to sickness, claiming also that it was supplemented by private tutors, which might be regarded as an acceptable alternative for a gentleman's son at the time. The family's ever-increasing poverty remained a source of deep embarrassment to Patrick, which he ascribed to the Wall Street Crash and the Depression of the 1930s. While the account is misleading, it is nevertheless true that Patrick suffered from recurrent bouts of illness, was a poor pupil who gained little from his schooling, and who acquired the greater part of his knowledge and understanding from private reading and observation, assisted by intermittent informal instruction at home.

When and how Patrick first learned to read is unrecorded, but it is likely that he acquired the facility at an early age. Sporadic instruction and help by those who surrounded him in the house at Willesden Green – successive governesses, 'Aunt Grace', his elder brothers and sisters – could have sufficed to enable so intelligent and curious a boy to read by the age of four or five. Long years later he recalled the delight of reading by torchlight beneath the bedclothes at night. One work in particular gripped his imagination.

[1] A.E. Cunningham (ed.), *Patrick O'Brian: Critical Appreciations and a Bibliography* (Boston Spa, Wetherby, 1994), p. 16. Though Patrick's allusions to his education are hazy, it is again worth noting that they include no reference to attendance at preparatory school.

'And when he was very young,' Patrick reminisced in 1999 of his earlier self, 'his stepmother, the kindest of women, took him to see her sister,[1] who gave him the Rev Mr Wood's *Natural History*, a mid-nineteenth-century edition illustrated with a fair number of engravings. Since he was already something of a naturalist (an admired, much older brother had practically invented birds),[2] the boy devoured the book, which was written by a sensible, well-informed, scholarly man.'

Patrick's copy lies before me as I write, its battered condition attesting to the extent to which it was lovingly perused during those long-departed years. It is possibly the only book (certainly one of very few) which he preserved into later life from his childhood, indicating how much it meant to him. It imbued him with a lifelong fascination with natural history, and had he not devoted his talents to writing novels he could certainly have become a naturalist of distinction.

Patrick described himself as an inveterately studious reader from a very early age. As well as reading the inimitable 'Just William' stories, he doubtless shared his brothers' excitement when the *Boy's Own Paper* made its weekly appearance in the bookstalls. His own earlier ventures into writing fiction strongly suggest that, like most of his youthful contemporaries, he succumbed to the spell of the thrilling novels of Percy F. Westerman, G.H. Henty, Captain Charles Gilson, and other celebrated boys' writers of the period. In January 1919 Victor read Gilson's *The Mystery of Ah Jin*, whose title evokes those exotic realms of Oriental conspiracy and intrigue which provided a major source of inspiration for Patrick's early literary career. His brothers subscribed to local public libraries, so there can have been no shortage of reading material appealing to a boy of his age.

In Patrick's case his solitary existence induced in him such exceptional pleasure from reading that almost any subject excited his curiosity. It has been seen with what precocious avidity he perused the mouldering volumes of the *Gentleman's Magazine* he discovered in the cellar of Melbury Lodge at the age of eight or nine.

Speculation with regard to Patrick's educational upbringing becomes supererogatory in 1925, when he and his brother Bernard were sent to Marylebone Grammar School. The school has a long and distinguished

[1] Unfortunately I have been unable to discover anything about this sister, beyond the fact that she is recorded (though not named) in the 1901 Census as living with her sister Zoe and parents at Horton Vicarage. I am grateful to Dr Michael Harte for providing me with this information.

[2] This may have been Victor, an entry in whose diary at the age of twelve suggests a precocious interest in natural history.

history, and at the time of the boys' enrolment had a high reputation. Established in 1792 as a charitable foundation under the name of the Philological School, in 1901 it became the St Marylebone Grammar School for Boys. (Its old boys continue to be known as Old Philologians.) In view of Patrick's subsequent passion for the Royal Navy during the Napoleonic Wars, it is interesting to note that his school's original patron was Thomas Collingwood, nephew of the great admiral who was Nelson's principal brother-in-arms.

In 1856–57 a fine Victorian Gothic building was erected by public subscription, its opening being presided over by the Archbishop of Canterbury. Queen Victoria was the school's first Patron, being succeeded in turn by her son Edward VII and grandson George V. The school's reputation and fortunes fluctuated in late Victorian and Edwardian times, but by the end of the Great War it was in a flourishing state. In 1923 a temporary crisis arose when the unfortunate Headmaster, whose mind had become disturbed in consequence of harrowing wartime experiences, flung his three-year-old daughter from the balcony of their flat and jumped after her. The poor little girl died, but her father survived and was sentenced to a spell in Broadmoor.

By the time Patrick and Bernard arrived a young and energetic new Headmaster, Philip Wayne, had introduced a vigorous programme of improved educational standards and enlargement of the school buildings and grounds. Masters wore gowns in class, the excellent facilities included a fine chemistry laboratory, and a satisfactory proportion of the boys gained university places. The fees were £15 per annum.[1]

Charles Russ must have become familiar with the school's reputation during the many years he had lived and worked in the neighbourhood. Possibly his move from Putney to nearby Maida Vale shortly before the boys began their first term there was influenced by the decision to send his two youngest sons there, since Sutherland Avenue lay a short bus ride from Marylebone Grammar School.

Patrick arrived for the Michaelmas term of 1925. In view of his lack of formal education, he was fortunate in qualifying for entry. However, he was widely read and intelligent, and had possibly received some instruction from his father. Perhaps the school made allowances for the fact that he had no prior education, especially if this were explained on grounds of illness. Then again, Bernard was clearly a promising pupil with good reports from Shebbear, and the school may have been persuaded to relax its entry qualification to accommodate his young brother.

[1] I am grateful to Mr Edward McNeal, formerly Deputy Headmaster, for providing me with information about the school, and also for presenting me with a copy of his invaluable monograph, *St Marylebone Grammar School: A Brief History till 1954* (London, 1979).

At the time there were only 160 boys on the school roll, with one class in each year, which helped to make the atmosphere less intimidating. Patrick was also lucky to have the companionship and protection of his elder brother, who precociously became a member of the cricket First Eleven, which made him quite a lion at the school. Bun recalled their schooldays at Marylebone: 'Off Patrick and I went as day boys to Grammar School. Having attended Shebbear, I considered myself quite the man of the world, more than capable of lending a hand with Pat's homework as he struggled to master the intricacies of English Language and Literature, but he has long since turned the tables on me, having an established literary career.'

That Patrick required assistance in the one subject in which he might be expected to have been proficient serves to confirm the haphazard nature of his previous studies. While it appears that he had read widely for several years before his arrival at Marylebone, and probably possessed a broader range of knowledge than most of his contemporaries, his belated introduction to school life made him resentful of discipline and poor in application. Throughout his adult life he remained prone to perpetrating odd spelling mistakes.

Patrick acknowledged his idleness at school. When in 1946 poverty compelled him to withdraw his own son Richard from preparatory school, despite his unhappy experience he decided to act as his tutor. Angered by what he took to be the boy's obtuseness, he confessed in his diary: 'He will only sit vacantly in form (as I did in maths) learning nothing', noting further that 'he can say the multiplication table in five minutes (which, by the way, is more than I could ever do)'.[1]

The indications that he was fundamentally lazy as a child, and prone to prolonged periods of inactivity, will surprise those who knew Patrick during the long decades after he and my mother had established their home in France. There he eventually became a model of self-discipline and industry, applying himself with exceptional rigour to his writing on a daily basis. However, in the earlier years of his adult life he devoted years to the pursuit of diversionary interests, and experienced protracted dark periods when he despairingly resigned himself to the prospect of abandoning his literary ambitions permanently. That he was able single-handedly to overcome bouts

[1] Patrick wrote of the hero of his most autobiographical of novels that 'he was useless with sums' (*Richard Temple*, p. 25). The theme recurs throughout his writing. Jack Aubrey 'had been a stupid boy at figures in his time, badly taught' (*HMS Surprise*, p. 28), and 'had suffered much from his own lack of education' (*The Reverse of the Medal*, p. 68). Even Stephen Maturin's 'arithmetic had always been slow hesitant and poor' (*The Far Side of the World*, p. 159; cf. *The Letter of Marque*, p. 15).

of lassitude and distraction so deeply ingrained during his early years was not the least of his achievements.

Patrick's consciousness of superior knowledge probably made him impatient of the humdrum repetitive tasks required of a schoolboy. An additional cause of his failure to succeed at school arose from his instinctive aversion to authority and consequent disinclination to accept instruction. These were certainly among his most marked characteristics in later life. On the other hand, he was an obedient child with a keen interest in those branches of learning which appealed to him. Ron Welford, who sat in the same class with him, recently recalled that he was 'of average height, stocky build and with light brown hair, slightly wavy. He was not a games player but rather a student type.' It is interesting to note that at this stage of his life there is no suggestion of his appearing diminutive or sickly, as has been asserted.

Despite the difficulties he encountered with the academic programme, there is no reason to suppose that Patrick's time at Marylebone Grammar School was unhappy. The brothers enjoyed a similar sense of humour, and Bun described in his memoir their shared delight in a lecture given by Jerome K. Jerome, a celebrated Old Boy of the school best known as the author of *Three Men in a Boat*. At the age of eighty-eight, Ron Welford wrote of his

> vivid recollection of JKJ giving his talk in the old theatre. He wore a large black coat, partly hiding a distinct embonpoint. He had a roundish face with a benign expression throughout his talk, of which I have no recollection what it was about but strange to relate, I can remember after all these years, two of the jokes he told us. 'A charlady was visiting her doctor for a vaccination. The doctor suggested her arm. "O no doctor – I'm always using my arms but I seldom sit down." ' The other joke concerned a gentleman who concerned himself with comparing the behaviour of monkeys compared with the behaviour of ourselves. He shut a young monkey in the room and intended to observe his behaviour by spying through the keyhole. Unfortunately he was thwarted! The monkey had exactly the same idea!

Patrick entertained pleasant recollections of the school: this is suggested by a laconic note jotted down during a brief visit he made to London in June 1949: 'Pilgrimage to George Street and Marylebone Lane.' Thirty-five years later he made the same nostalgic tour with his brother: 'Bun & I looked at George St & Marylebone Lane – Rothes was still there, almost exactly the same.'[1]

[1] Mr Ted McNeal has kindly identified Rothe's as a café at 35 Marylebone Lane. Three years after his 'pilgrimage' with Patrick, Bernard paid a visit to their old school which he was saddened to find 'boarded up and shown as for sale. I don't know whether it fell victim to the efforts of Mrs. Shirley Williams' – an Education Minister bitterly hostile to grammar schools.

Pat and Bun spent only a year at Marylebone Grammar School, and left at the end of the academic year of 1926. It was the summer of the General Strike, when throughout the country volunteers flocked to assist in keeping essential public services running. Their eldest brother Godfrey employed the skills provided by his training as an electrical engineer to shunt railway engines, while Michael worked at the London Docks unloading refrigerated meat. Though big and strong for his seventeen years, on one occasion he had to run for his life pursued by an angry crowd of striking dockers. What presented the Government with a grave constitutional crisis appeared an exciting adventure for many young men of the middle classes, who delighted in situations requiring the sort of courage and resource for which their public school training made them eminently qualified. Though too young to be directly involved, Bun and Pat participated in the intense public concern, and the former recalled being 'most amused one day to see an old gentleman in top hat and spats riding to his office in the City on an antique penny-farthing machine!'[1]

The crisis was broadly resolved in the traditional British spirit of compromise, but there were those who feared the influence of extreme socialism, or even detected behind the strikers the sinister hand of Bolshevik Russia. While Patrick remained throughout his life a consistently moderate and largely apolitical conservative, one wonders whether his deep-rooted fear of crowds may not have been reinforced by memories imprinted at an impressionable age of those turbulent months when sections of the press and public voiced wild fears of a revolutionary uprising.

In the second half of 1926 Zoe Russ, accompanied by her two youngest stepchildren, left London to live in the country. Their new home was at Lewes in Sussex. Far from crowded and turbulent London, Lewes is a peaceful picturesque old hilltop town, whose tile-hung timbered houses are dominated by the magnificent ruins of its medieval castle. It contains many ancient and beautiful buildings, including a handsome Tudor house occupied by the unfortunate Anne of Cleves after her callous rejection by Henry VIII. Many of the town's narrow medieval streets survive, together with numerous fine churches, imposing Georgian public buildings, elegant private houses, and antique hostelries.

The new home of the Russ household was a terraced house at 10 Priory Crescent. This pleasant Regency row is situated close to the ancient parish church of St John the Baptist in Southover, a quiet quarter with a distinctive

[1] *Lady Day Prodigal*, p. 25. In old age Bernard misplaced his memories of the General Strike as occurring after his time at Lewes Grammar School.

character of its own located at the foot of the hill upon which the town is set. Immediately behind Priory Crescent lie the impressive ruins of the Cluniac monastery of St Pancras, set amidst extensive wooded grounds. It was there that King Henry III was compelled to accede to his barons' demand for limitations on the royal power, following his defeat by Simon de Montfort at the celebrated battle of Lewes in 1264.

The atmosphere of a thousand years of history which hung about the town exercised a potent effect on the young Russ brothers. Bun, who joined the household shortly afterwards, later recollected: 'The new house was next door to the church housing the remains of a niece of William the Conqueror . . . We [he and Patrick] transferred to the local Grammar School, founded by Henry VIII in 1509, and next door to the castle. It is hardly surprising that history became one of my favourite subjects!'

It was not large, but the Russes' house presented in every way a pleasing contrast to their London home. It shared a handsome walled garden with its immediate neighbours, while magnificent views were obtained on both sides from the upper windows. To the north the castle keep frowned haughtily over trees and houses, while to the south the crest of the Downs stretched away beyond the monastic park, its undulating flanks shifting in colour and aspect beneath coasting clouds. Buzzards floated and larks sang above the grassy slopes of Mount Caburn, an impressive height crowned by the coiled ramparts of an Iron Age hill-fort. Caburn afforded long views across the broad vale below the town where the meandering Ouse pursues its way to the sea. Indeed the Sussex countryside, so close beyond the lofty rampart of the Downs, resembled the sea in its freedom and the opportunity it afforded for an imaginative spirit to soar bird-like over hills and woods, marshes and fields. In *Richard Temple* Patrick recalled 'those days full of limpid air, when white clouds passed across the sky, and the light changes'.

A family photograph shows Patrick about this time as a cheerful little boy in shorts, much closer to Richmal Crompton's William Brown than the sickly invalid of his own and others' imagining. It is impossible to detect whether the badge on his school blazer bears the beehive crest of Marylebone Grammar School, or the emblem of Lewes Grammar School. The latter seems likely, in view of the fact that the photograph was taken on a grassy hill. A London boy would be unlikely to wear his school uniform on a trip to the countryside, and we are probably safe in envisaging a proud eleven-year-old Patrick posing in his new school uniform in September 1926 shortly before the commencement of his first term at Lewes Grammar School.

The reason for this move is unrecorded. It seems unlikely that it had anything to do with the state of Patrick's physical health. He had after all lived for most of the previous five or six years in London without recorded ill effect, and after completing his schooling at Lewes his parents brought him back to live with them again in the city. If his medical father considered country air essential to his health, why did he initially send him to school in London? It should again be emphasised that the fragility of Patrick's health at this stage of his life has been grossly overstated.

The decision cannot have been lightly taken. The brothers' transfer after only one year at the excellent academy at Marylebone might naturally be expected to have at least a temporarily damaging effect on their academic progress. In addition the move imposed considerable additional financial burden on the family's (i.e. Zoe's) strained resources. To the Russes' family house in London was now added a second in Lewes. All in all, it seems that some unanticipated significant factor instigated the move. Since the family's stay in Lewes coincided with the three years of Patrick's attendance at the Grammar School, after which they returned to London, the most likely explanation is that it related to his education.

Patrick had arrived at Marylebone Grammar School with no previous schooling, so it is hardly surprising that the year he spent there proved both educationally inadequate and emotionally damaging. We know from his own confession and Bernard Russ's memoir that he was a backward and idle pupil, and it is likely that his school reports were unpromising.

There is little reason to suppose that Charles Russ would have paid much sympathetic heed to his son's plight, but his stepmother had formed a close bond with him. If Zoe found her attempts to protect her young stepson from his father's worst excesses largely ineffectual, she may have concluded that he required a complete break with the household in Sutherland Avenue while his education was completed, and tactfully persuaded her husband to accept the new arrangement. There was no reason for him to object: he may have been relieved at the prospect of ridding himself of the playful prattle of his three youngest children in the evenings at his home in Sutherland Avenue, and in any case Zoe would pay for the house at Lewes. By the same token she had no reason to regret leaving behind Olive and the teenage twins Nora and Connie. Connie's daughter Linda recalls her mother saying that they were known as 'the Russes of Sutherland Avenue', after the famously down-trodden Victorian daughters in 'The Barretts of Wimpole Street'.

An alternative possibility is that Marylebone Grammar School found Patrick's performance so inadequate that his father was asked to remove him at the end of the year.

As so often, *Richard Temple* offers valuable clues to Patrick's perspective on events. Shortly after his failure to gain a scholarship to public school,

Temple's father dies. No reason is given for his sudden demise, nor is the reader given more than the barest glimpse of the boy's emotional reaction to so momentous and unexpected a loss. Since his father was a vicar, Richard and his mother are promptly obliged to vacate the rectory and move to a new home close to the town of 'Easton Colborough', where he enrols at the local grammar school.

The inconsequential and dramatically inept introduction of the father's death probably reflects a facet of Patrick's elaborate psychological doctoring of his own past. The humiliation of being a 'mere' grammar-school product is expatiated upon at length in *Richard Temple*, and throughout his adult life Patrick rigorously hid the fact that such had been his own upbringing. In the novel Temple's father comes from a relatively humble social background, and his poverty is accounted an 'unavoidable taint'. A recurrent theme in Patrick's early fiction is that of annihilation inflicted on those who seek to visit harm upon the heroes of his tales, whether animal or human. Though Charles Russ paid regular visits to Zoe's new home in the country, this was the first occasion in Patrick's life when he found himself largely freed from his father's forbidding presence. The arbitrary linkage of the death of Richard Temple's father to his son's enrolment at grammar school suggests an authorial 'slaying' of his own father, from whose frightening presence he unexpectedly found himself liberated.

As ever, Bernard's memoir is frustratingly reticent in its references to his young brother at this time. Although this was partly in deference to Patrick's wishes, Bun may well not have remembered much. He was at Lewes for only the first of the three years, during which he spent all or most of the school holidays engaged as unpaid assistant to his father at his laboratory in London. It is fortunate therefore that *Richard Temple* includes a thinly disguised account of Patrick's time at Lewes Grammar School.

The description of Easton Colborough in the novel matches Lewes so closely as to make them unmistakably one and the same:

> He went up one of the steep lanes that lead towards the High Street . . . He turned into the broad, mild splendour of the High Street . . . on the left was the barbican [of Lewes Castle], then the pink brick and white stone court-house with its curving flight of steps and the royal arms in its pediment, then a long row of bow-fronted shops; on the right the Harp and Crown with its enormous sign, the Palladian corn-exchange and the little Regency theatre, followed by a recessed line of the grander houses of the town, with white steps, green doors and brass knockers.[1]

[1] *Richard Temple*, p. 40.

Any visitor to Lewes ascending St Martins Lane from Southover and turning right into the High Street will at once recognise the description.[1]

Given the fictional Richard's acute sensitivity to social status, and his bitter disappointment at failing his public school scholarship examination, dramatic consistency might lead one to expect him to find his attendance at grammar school depressing and distasteful. In fact, for a while at least, the boy remains remarkably happy. In view of Patrick's lifelong concern to disown the embarrassing fact that he had attended grammar school, his hero's unexpected contentment suggests that he himself largely enjoyed his time at Lewes Grammar School.

The school lay within easy walking distance of Priory Crescent. Passing the handsome Tudor mansion of Southover Grange in its walled garden on their right, Bun, Pat, and Joan daily climbed a steep shaded street, whose broad brick pavements flanked a flint-cobbled watercourse. Even by Lewes standards Keere Street is a particularly charming passage, and Patrick clearly relished the picturesque old houses ascending in stepped succession on either side of the umbrageous tree-lined alley. Many pleasing Georgian and Victorian features would have appealed to his curious eye, such as the recessed cast-iron shoe-scrapers set beside doorways. Gaining the summit, the boys passed by a fine timbered fifteenth-century house, crossed the busy High Street where Joan left them to attend her little school near the castle gate, and entered the doors of the handsome flint and brick-dressed gabled building which housed the Grammar School.

Patrick appears to have believed that this was where the school had been established four centuries earlier. Given its archaic appearance this was understandable, though in reality the house is a neo-Tudor structure erected in 1851, to which the school had been transferred in 1885 from Southover at the bottom of the hill. His estimate of the educational standards provided by Lewes Grammar School was not high:

> The school at Easton had remained very much what it was when it was founded, some four hundred years before, a place of instruction for the boys of the town and the immediate countryside. Its meagre endowment had tempted no man's cupidity, and it had neither become a minor public school nor part of the state's

[1] There was however no 'little Regency theatre' nor 'Harp and Crown'. The latter might be the Crown, or alternatively the more prominent White Hart, but neither bore 'an enormous sign'. There is no means of telling whether these minor additions reflect faulty memory or dramatic modifications. Plimpton Rectory, where the Temple family lived before moving to Easton Colborough, is described as 'isolated – no neighbours except the Hall'. Patrick must surely have had in mind the tiny village of Plumpton to the west of Lewes, which in his day consisted of little more than a small church in a field and a moated Elizabethan manor house.

> system of education. It was a grammar school: the chief subject was grammar, Latin grammar, and the boys bawled their way through *hic haec hoc* as their predecessors had always done. The great part of the school was housed in one vast barn-like hall which had three classes in it, three separate classes with three masters and three distinguishable pandemoniums; the noise in this hall seemed to be quite chaotic, but somewhere in the din there would always be a pack of boys going through their *hic haec hoc*. The cobwebs in the bare rafters had stirred to this noise for centuries,[1] and it was not likely that the school would change its ways now: in all these years it had never turned out a classical scholar of any reputation, but perhaps that had never been its intention . . .

While the description of the physical setting is accurate, Patrick's condemnation of the school's scholastic achievements was unjustified. If anything the opposite was the case, as his brother Bun's experience proved: 'The school was small but the teaching standards very high. In fact, the highest pass in University Entrance exams in all of England was obtained by one of our fellow students . . . At the end of my first year, I graduated with my Oxford Junior First Class Certificate with Honours in History and English, my passport to university.'[2]

However, it is likely that Patrick was a poor scholar, and unwilling to accept that this might reflect inadequacy on his part. It has been seen that he was confessedly idle, and had difficulty in keeping up with his fellow pupils at Marylebone. In the event he left Lewes Grammar School without passing his matriculation.

Though Patrick was in many ways an unusually clever and imaginative boy, a combination of lack of early schooling, resentment of formal instruction, and sense of intellectual superiority may have combined to make him find classwork difficult and repugnant. In fact he possessed a natural aptitude for mathematics, and his indolence probably arose from his reluctance to acknowledge his ignorance, and an innate aversion to instruction. He would have resented competing with boys whom he regarded as of lower intelligence, who were nevertheless enabled by their advantages of previous schooling and more equable character to outdistance him in class.

[1] At the time of the Civil War a veteran soldier suffered a recurrent nightmare thirty years after leaving school that 'he is there at the hic, haec, hoc with fear and trembling' (David Tylden-Wright, *John Aubrey: A Life* (London, 1991), p. 24).

[2] Russ, *Lady Day Prodigal*, p. 24. The school's pupils included the celebrated diarist and polymath John Evelyn, who wrote: 'I was put to schoole . . . in 1630 . . . to the Free-schole at Southover neere the town, of which one Agnes Morley had been the foundresse, and now Edward Snatt was the master, under whom I remained till I was sent to the University.'

Nevertheless Richard Temple finds his fellow pupils surprisingly congenial:

> They were far more tolerant than the boys of Grafton [his implausibly snobbish preparatory school], and they received him without any of the inquisition or ill-treatment that he had dreaded. They formed an almost classless society, in which parents' status was accidental and of little importance; and in this society accent counted for nothing – some of the country boys spoke broad and some of the town boys spoke with a nasal whine, but it made no odds: after a week it was imperceptible.
>
> In its way it was a very restful school. There were no games at all except those which the boys played by themselves for fun, and with scarcely a sigh Richard . . . took to the ancient, common, childish games of marbles (called alleys here), conquerors[1] and tops. He had never spun a top in his life before, but presently he learnt, being taught by a broad-faced, kind, hoarse boy . . .

This section has the ring of authenticity. Temple's excessive sensitivity to the nuances of social ranking, combined with his resentment of the parental irresponsibility which deprived him of the opportunity of public school education, might easily have led Patrick to depict his spell at grammar school as an ordeal of humiliation and frustration. Yet he is represented as looking back on it as a happy interlude in an otherwise deeply troubled life.

Patrick's delight shines through the memory he ascribes to Richard Temple. His terrifying father was away for most of the time at his laboratory in London. Just as it appears to have been Zoe who decided that her favourite stepson needed opportunity to develop away from the constraints of their London home, so it is likely that it was she who now urged upon her husband the urgent necessity of considering Patrick's future.

There is good reason to believe that Patrick attempted and failed a decisive entry examination at this time. In old age he was asked by a journalist:

> Had he not wished for a career at sea? 'What I wanted was either sail or the Royal Navy,' O'Brian admitted. 'I was too sickly to go to Dartmouth. I tried because I had the support of some admiral relations but I had not enough teeth, an inferior heart, rotten spine and brain not much cop.'[2]

At that time the normal age for entry to the Royal Naval College at Dartmouth was thirteen. Neither then nor later in his youth was Patrick in

[1] A game involving 'conquerors' and 'conquered', or the traditional autumnal activity of 'conkers'? 'Alleys' are mentioned in Elizabeth Gaskell's *Ruth* (1853).

[2] Keith Wheatley, 'The Long Life of O'Brian', *Financial Times*, 11–12 January 1997.

the debilitated physical state he described, but 'brain not much cop' would be a fair description of his academic standing. When I first read this interview I confess I assumed that Patrick's claim might represent characteristic romancing, but recently discovered legal documents relating to custody proceedings over his son indicate that the assertion was true. In an affidavit submitted in 1949, he testified: 'I had at first hoped that Richard would try (as I did) for Dartmouth . . .'[1]

The advantages promised by success could not be underestimated. Graduation from the college provided professional and social advantages comparable to those bestowed by a university degree. Although there was an annual fee of £75, it was considerably less than that required for a public school.[2]

Reference was made earlier to Patrick's claim to 'strong memories of prep school in Torbay'. However he overlooked the fact that he could not have attended a school '*in* Torbay', which is not a town or village but an inlet of the sea between Torquay and Brixham. That consideration apart, it may be wondered why he should have fastened on South Devon. A likely clue lies in what he had to say in the interview about his fanciful preparatory school: 'The Atlantic Fleet used to gather and King George would come down to review them. The destroyers would tear along. Four funnels they had, with black smoke streaming from them.'

Although candidates sat the examination at the schools they attended and were interviewed in London, one wonders whether Charles and Zoe Russ may not have taken Patrick to visit the college beforehand. If so, the magnificent view from its frontage could have been that which afforded him the exciting prospect of warships plying up and down the Channel. Dread of public exposure prevented his locating the preparatory school in Dartmouth itself, and so he selected Torbay across the headland to the north-west. However, unlike Dartmouth, Torbay had no association at the time with the Royal Navy.[3]

[1] It seems certain that Patrick was being truthful on this occasion. Not only would it have been entirely contrary to his character needlessly to volunteer an implicit confession of failure, but any false assertion was likely to be challenged in court by his wife Elizabeth. Furthermore the parenthesis was accessible only to the handful of people involved in the closed court hearing.

[2] For conditions at Dartmouth at the time, cf. Jane Harrold and Richard Porter, *Britannia Royal Naval College 1905–2005: One Hundred Years of Officer Training at Dartmouth* (Dartmouth, 2005).

[3] We may have here an illustration of the extent to which Patrick found himself more at home in the early nineteenth century than the twentieth. Until the Napoleonic Wars the British fleet regularly used Torbay for its Channel anchorage, but thereafter the construction of a massive breakwater at Plymouth provided the Navy with an Atlantic harbour comparable in extent to Portsmouth (W.G. Hoskins, *Devon* (London, 1954), pp. 456, 459–60, 500). In *The Yellow Admiral* (p. 82) Patrick paints a vivid picture of shipping gathered in the bay during the blockade of Brest.

Patrick's grievous disappointment at failing the entrance examination to Dartmouth further explains his subsequent sense of inadequacy at not having attended public school. Such a setback would have deeply undermined the self-esteem of so naturally gifted but poorly educated and overly sensitive a child. His father's and his own anticipatory confidence in his unusual talents could only have exacerbated the blow.

Patrick's bitterness is mirrored by Richard Temple's disappointment at failing 'a scholarship examination': 'He did not win any scholarship, not even the smallest; the recollection of this time arose cold and dark in his mind [Temple is recalling the event in middle age] – the first adult, whole and irremediable unhappiness.' The boy's father proves unexpectedly sympathetic. His reaction to his son's failure strikes an oddly discordant note, in view of his otherwise unremittingly harsh and insensitive attitude: 'Llewelyn Temple had been kind when the news came. "Well, I'm sorry, Richard bâch, but there it is. Perhaps it is all for the best. We must try not to be too disappointed." It was the kindest thing he had ever said, and the sudden spurt of generous affection that Richard had felt then had not died away in twenty years.'

Clearly judgement here must be subjective, but the father's uncharacteristic display of humanity bears a ring of reality. Charles Russ was capable of the occasional display of sympathy towards his children,[1] and in this case there was good reason for him to adopt an understanding attitude. He must have known that the crushing disappointment resulted from his gross neglect of his son's education.

On the other hand the project of sending Patrick to the Naval College is likely to have originated with his stepmother. It was she who withdrew Patrick to Lewes in order to further his education, and almost certainly she who paid the fees. The fact that her late husband had been an officer in the Royal Navy made Dartmouth an obvious choice to fasten on for her stepson.[2]

[1] Joan's daughter Mary recalls that her mother remembered her father as cold and unfeeling, but she nevertheless cherished the memory of one or two occasions when he displayed momentary kindness towards her.

[2] Although Patrick did not as he claimed possess any 'admiral relations', his stepmother may well have acquired influential connections during her marriage to Fleet-Surgeon William Center.

FOUR

A Literary Prodigy

> It is whimsical enough that as soon as I left Magdalen College, my taste for books began to revive; but it was the same blind and boyish taste for the pursuit of exotic history. Unprovided with original learning, unformed in the habits of thinking, unskilled in the arts of composition, I resolved – to write a book.
>
> (Edward Gibbon, *Memoirs of my Life and Writings*)

Patrick's failure to gain a place at Dartmouth in 1927 is linked to a decisive turning point in his life, for which the Royal Navy has reason to be grateful. It was at this time that he took a radical step beyond living through works written by others, and boldly decided that he would himself write a book. This was his juvenile first novel *Cæsar*, which was published in October 1930. It would be natural to assume that the book was written shortly before its submission to the publisher, but this is irreconcilable with the evidence.

In his brief introduction to the new edition of *Cæsar* published by the British Library in 1999 Patrick recalled the circumstances in which he came to write the book. He began: 'I doubt if my present self would have liked the twelve-year-old boy who wrote this tale . . .' Patrick was twelve in 1927. Though not averse to modifying reality when necessary, in this case there was no reason for him to do so. His introduction to the new edition was the outcome of prolonged and delicate discussions with its sympathetic editor, Arthur Cunningham, and he devoted considerable time and thought to composing his preface. It was written in the aftermath of sensationalist press revelations about his hidden past published in the previous autumn, and (unlike his earlier preface to the British Library's *Critical Appreciations* published in 1994) includes nothing that is demonstrably untrue, save the claim that illness was the basic cause of his inadequate education. Since the occasion of his describing the circumstances of his writing his first book was its reissue some seventy years later, he had particular reason to bear in mind the original date of publication. Had he been concerned to reassign its composition to an earlier period in order (say) to account for its literary immaturity or exaggerate his precocity, it is hard to believe that it would not have occurred to him to provide some explanation for the three or four years' interval before the book appeared in print.[1]

Nor is a simple error likely, since he describes himself as being at the time of writing a 'little creature' and 'pre-adolescent: a sort of elderly child' – descriptions appropriate to a twelve-year-old boy, but scarcely applicable to a sturdy youth of fifteen who had completed his education.[2] Furthermore, Patrick's notebooks include many instances of his pedantic precision when calculating the dates of past events in his life. Frequently his concern to establish a correct year is indicated by a subtraction sum entered in the margin of his notes. Thus in 1970 he noted in his diary 'I read Waley's Analects (after all these yrs – 25 plus)', a reckoning which is accurate to the year. Two years later he recorded in a journal he kept of a visit to Dublin: 'my window looks straight on to the corner of Stephen's Green, diagonally across from the dear Miss Spains of 35 years ago'. As ever his recollection was precise, since it was indeed in 1937 that he stayed in Dublin when completing his second novel, *Hussein*.

Again, Patrick remarked self-deprecatingly that at the time he 'was certainly not very popular among his brothers and sisters'. While nothing suggests that this was ever really the case, it would be entirely inappropriate following his return to London in 1929 after three years' absence, when all his brothers and his elder sister Olive had left home to pursue their careers. There is no evidence and little likelihood that Connie and Nora resented their young brother.[3] The only sibling with whom he was in close contact at the time was his younger sister Joan, who adored him.

Patrick continued his account with a paragraph explaining the circumstances in which he wrote *Cæsar*:

> The boy [i.e. Patrick himself] was also something of an invalid, which

[1] Patrick's date of birth in 1914 had been widely noted in press articles, while *Cæsar*'s original date of publication is printed on the copyright page of the new edition.

[2] Patrick wrote in his diary on 24 October 1998: 'I read most of Cæsar . . . almost entirely forgotten: it is rather silly, *childish* & moderately dull, but not downright discreditable or embarrassing' (italics inserted).

[3] I have been unable to establish when the twins Connie and Nora left home. As Connie's daughter Linda has explained to me, Bernard was wrong in implying that she entered a nursing college in or about 1924 (*Lady Day Prodigal*, p. 23). If one may judge by her appearance in an unpublished story Patrick wrote in the 1950s, he remembered Nora with affection.

> interfered with his education and worried his father, a bacteriologist in the early days of vaccines and electrical treatment: the young fellow . . . therefore spent long sessions in the incubator room, sitting at a glass-topped metal table and doing the simple tasks set by his tutor. But the tasks left a good deal of time unoccupied, and since it was obviously unthinkable to bring a book to read, the boy, by some mental process that I can no longer recall, decided to write one for himself, thus discovering an extraordinary joy which has never left him – that of both reading and writing at the same time.[1]

As with Patrick's other brief accounts of his childhood, while the overall tenor is substantially correct, component details are not. Although he had as a small boy been 'something of an invalid', this was not the cause of his inadequate education.

By 1925–26 Charles Russ's reduced financial circumstances had compelled him to leave his substantial practice in Wimpole Street for rented rooms at 50 George Street. Bun recalled: 'The handsome rooms he once occupied in Beaumont Street and Wimpole Street were far superior to those in which he eventually went in George Street, close to Baker Street. I suppose that with the dwindling of his practice, it did not warrant his having any spacious or gracious suite of rooms and he simply had one main room or office, which acted also as a waiting room[,] and then his separate consulting room. In school vacations it was my job to keep the premises tidy and clean and particularly, to wash out glass vessels and other materials which he used in the course of his bacteriological work.'

It was in these cramped quarters that Dr Russ worked throughout Patrick's schooldays.

As with his purported attendance at preparatory school, Patrick's account includes a number of revealing incongruities. How could a tutor have instructed him in his father's consulting or waiting room? Is it likely that so impractical an arrangement was even considered, when during daytime hours lessons might have been conducted in the family's successive homes in Putney and Maida Vale? Again, why was the boy obliged to remain at the table long after his task was completed? Why should it have been 'obviously unthinkable to bring a book to read'? Only the tutor would have been in a position to determine whether his pupil had completed his previous day's tasks adequately. And if for some inexplicable reason Patrick was required to remain at his place for a fixed period, what objection could there be to his perusing a suitably instructive book, rather than idle his time away? Besides, after the tutor's departure how was his father to know that the book his son

[1] Patrick O'Brian, *Cæsar: The Life Story of a Panda Leopard*, p. 5.

chose to read did not constitute part of his coursework? Again, Dr Russ strongly objected to having his children in close proximity when it did not suit him, and was generally indifferent to their activities, scholastic and otherwise. Last and not least, for what purpose might Patrick have required tutoring in 1929–30, when he had left school and was not contemplating further education?

Only one explanation reconciles this succession of anomalies. The sole person with reason to impose the curious regime undergone by Patrick was his father, and it must have been he who set his son tasks to complete within a set space of time. This would explain why the boy had to travel each day to his father's office, why it was his father who determined the length of time required for his homework, and why it was he who decided whether or not his son might read when his task was completed. Conscious of the fact that to declare his work finished would invite the danger of being set more, Patrick acted as would any self-respecting small boy placed in his situation: he eked out the remainder of his time doodling or daydreaming – occupations which in his younger days he found congenial.[1] He could not bring a book to read for pleasure, since that would inevitably be discovered. One day, during this tedious round, he hit upon the happy idea of liberating himself from the gloomy confines of the laboratory by transforming himself into a wild animal in distant India. The sight of his small son writing earnestly in his exercise book would deflect his father's suspicion. Such, I suggest, were the real circumstances of the genesis of *Cæsar*.[2] A literal reading of the passage under examination accords perfectly with this interpretation:

> The boy was also something of an invalid, which interfered with *his education* and *worried his father* . . . the young fellow . . . *therefore spent long sessions in the incubator room*, sitting at a glass-topped metal table and doing the simple tasks set by his tutor.

What can be the significance of the adverb when we read that, in consequence of his father's concern over his education, 'the young fellow . . . *therefore*

[1] Patrick's early notebooks are studded with complex skilfully executed doodles.

[2] The dust-jacket of the original publication states that 'Patrick Russ is sixteen . . . He began this story when he was fourteen [in 1929] and finished it in March of this year [1930]. "I did it mostly in my bedroom and a little when I should have been doing homework."' This was however written under his father's eye, and presumably represents what he wished him to believe. He was plainly concerned to locate the composition at Lewes, since he would have ceased all homework after leaving the Grammar School in July 1929, and the burden of this version is to explain how the writing came to be conducted unknown to his father.

spent long sessions in the incubator room' – unless his father were himself the tutor?

The leitmotif of 'The Thermometer' is the extent to which Patrick regarded his time in the laboratory as a form of imprisonment. His brother Victor understood 'that when Pat was writing his first book his Father used to lock him in his room to make him get on with it'. While unlikely to be literally true, this may well reflect how Patrick regarded the circumstances.

Patrick's memoir indicates that his tutoring was conducted in just such a haphazard manner as might be expected were his father his teacher. Instruction may constantly have been interrupted by Dr Russ's turning to his studies at his laboratory table, when the boy was left to continue working on his own. This approach was not conducive to great exertion on his part, particularly given his acknowledged idleness. His instruction at the hands of an awesome and generally abstracted and impatient father probably had psychologically disturbing effects, one of whose most striking symptoms was Patrick's propensity for years afterwards to periods of mental inertia. The attendant stress conceivably exacerbated his propensity to asthmatic attacks. What is certain is that throughout his youth he remained exceptionally introspective, asocial, and resistant to instruction: personality problems which were to affect him throughout his life.

Why did Dr Russ feel impelled to tutor his son? Given his preoccupation with his own researches, it seems reasonable to suppose that he undertook the task for a specific purpose. Indeed, Patrick (who had no feeling of recognition, nor reason for feeling any recognition, of his father's contribution to his education) explains that the state of 'his education . . . worried his father', and that it was this that led to his receiving lessons in the laboratory.

All this, as the reader has probably already appreciated, points to one conclusion. Charles Russ was so little concerned with his son's education generally as not to trouble to send him to school before the age of ten, following which he removed him at the minimum legal age of fourteen.

But if Patrick wrote *Cæsar* in the summer of 1927, how was it that nearly three years passed before its publication? The most likely explanation is consistent with the reconstruction provided here. If Patrick's father was in fact the unidentified tutor alluded to in his preface to *Cæsar*, for reasons which his own account makes clear the boy could not reveal that he secretly neglected his preparation in order to write a book. While living in Lewes it appears that he saw relatively little of his father, and their relationship became even more distant. But when Patrick returned to London in the latter part of 1929 with his education completed, there was no longer any reason to conceal the fact that he had written a book. He could readily have claimed to have written it at Lewes.

Thus we may picture the meek little boy in shorts seated at the glass-topped metal table in the laboratory, while his father moved about his microscopes, retorts, and ureometers on the far side of the room. The moment Patrick had completed whatever task his father imposed upon him, he surreptitiously drew his exercise book from beneath the pile and resumed the adventures of the free and noble 'Panda Leopard'.

'First you must understand that I am a panda-leopard. My father was a giant panda and my mother a snow-leopard.' So the novel opens, and in the brief foreword which he provided for the published edition Patrick's father noted mock-seriously: 'If a giant panda and a snow-leopard become the parents of a wild animal such as Cæsar, the character which it will possess can only be surmised.' Of course such a creature does not exist in the natural world; Cæsar's panda parentage is effectively discarded after the initial description, and he features throughout the story as a normal leopard. When he meets his wife, he observes that she is 'a snow leopard nearly as big as myself', while she in turn 'admired my spots'. (The book's illustrator, Harry Rountree, portrayed Cæsar as a normally spotted leopard.)

The fleeting and supererogatory introduction of the 'panda factor' may have derived from a childish misapprehension. In his introduction to the 1999 edition Patrick describes the pleasure gained from his copy of Wood's *Natural History*, given to him 'when he was very young'. The engraving which accompanies Wood's account of the leopard bears the subtitle 'the *Leopard*, or *Panther*', and he goes on to note that 'The Leopard and Panther are considered as the same animal, on the authority of Mr. Gray.' One may perhaps picture Patrick as a small child confusing the 'Leopard-Panther' or 'Panther-Leopard' with a 'panda-leopard': a sobriquet affectionately retained when he came to write the novel.[1]

Certainly there are indications that Patrick at an early age became fascinated by the agility, ferocity, and strength of the leopard, and there is much to suggest that it was from Wood's account that the story of *Cæsar* germinated. One of the most vivid episodes in the novel is the friendship which develops between Cæsar and a white hunter. Wood relates of the leopard: 'It is easily tamed, and expresses great fondness for its keeper, and will play with him like a cat.' He goes on to recount an anecdote of a beautiful specimen in Wombwell's Menagerie which 'was exceedingly fond of playing with the tuft at the extremity of a lion's tail, and from the familiar manner in which he patted and bit it, he evidently considered it as manufactured for his own particular entertainment'. Cæsar in captivity is suddenly awakened by a

[1] The panda is unaccountably omitted from the Reverend Mr Wood's work: may this perhaps further explain the infant Patrick's confusion?

sharp pain in his tail, to find an ape in the neighbouring cage playfully tugging it.

A poem composed by Patrick in the early 1960s evokes an image of a small boy wandering along London streets, lost in dreams of ferocious wild beasts.

> If I could go back into my dream
> I should see the cheetahs again & the leopards & the unknown
> sharp-faced brute in the abandoned houses off Pall Mall
> And I should know those sharp exactly-pointed things I said (& wrote.)
> for the dream was also that in print – transparencies . . .
> running head-on round a corner in a street
> inhabited by independent polar bears
> And suddenly you know that this is it
> of course: the plain, self evident essential truth.

Cæsar describes the natural life of a wild beast with considerable skill and marked absence of anthropomorphism. Nevertheless it is excessive to suggest that 'few would attempt a story in which the narrator is an animal, let alone a predator'.[1] From Anna Sewell's autobiographical representation of a horse's life in *Black Beauty* (1877) and Jack London's vivid biography of a wolf, *White Fang* (1906) to Kipling's *Thy Servant a Dog* (1930), and their innumerable epigones writing specifically for children, authors have repeatedly utilised the theme.

Cæsar is a well-written imaginative tale, but what primarily distinguishes it from others of its genre is the author's extreme youth. It was to this factor that Patrick's father proudly drew his readers' attention, and Patrick himself regarded it as a piece of not discreditable juvenilia. Dr Russ suggested in his introduction that 'the author's immaturity of literary style and method – which are quite unspoiled by any senior pen – may also contribute to its favourable reception'. However it is hard, indeed impossible, to accept literally the claim that Patrick's original manuscript was published unaltered. There must surely have been some revision, if only to eliminate grammatical and spelling errors when (as is likely to have been the case) the text was polished at the beginning of 1930. By then Patrick's literary tastes were both varied and advanced for his age. It was in that year, for example, that he read George Borrow's *Lavengro* with intense pleasure.

Certain motifs in the story provide poignant echoes of Patrick's character and upbringing. Cæsar's father makes a very fleeting appearance, and no explanation is provided for his banishment from the story. 'Of my father I remember little, except a hazy recollection of a very large shape which

[1] King, *Patrick O'Brian*, p. 49.

brought food to my mother in the first few days of the opening of my eyes.' The inadequacy of the father was a recurrent theme in Patrick's writing almost to the end of his days.

Cæsar's mother is in striking contrast a figure of central importance to the family. She and her cubs are constantly compelled to move from one home to another, while she devotes herself to providing for them, frequently at the risk of her own life. Eventually she is killed while trying to save Cæsar's brother from a forest fire. Thus he is deprived of his mother at an early age, and becomes an orphan, since for a reason which remains unexplained his elder brother 'had run away a long time before'. The growing panda-leopard is unable to forget his loving parent, especially when he feels threatened. After being captured and incarcerated by a party of huntsmen, 'I did not sleep at all well, however, and I dreamt of elephants and guns in which my mother seemed mixed up'.

Much later, when fully grown, Cæsar experiences a further vision of maternal protection. Awakening from sleep, he is startled to find a huge python preparing to attack him.

> I jumped up, and either my eyes were deceiving me or something, for between me and the terrible snake I clearly saw my mother. She looked pale and smoky, but perhaps that was the sleep in my eyes, and I thought I saw her baring her teeth in a snarl at the snake. The snake glided out of the door, which was slightly ajar. Then the thought that perhaps she had lived through the fire flashed through my mind, and I started forward with a purr of delight to meet her, but to my horror and amazement there was nothing there. I had gone right through her.[1]

After many dramatic adventures Cæsar meets a beautiful leopardess, who establishes a home with him in a snug cave where she bears him a brood of handsome cubs. The story concludes tragically, when Cæsar is killed by a ferocious band of wolves from whom he is valiantly protecting his family. He lies mortally wounded, 'while my wife . . . licked me frantically, trying to stop the blood, which poured from scores of my wounds. The light seemed to be fading, though I knew it was only afternoon, and I felt curiously aloof from my body and felt no pain . . . my strength was ebbing fast, and I was weak like a little cub again. I looked at my wife, but I could not see her so clearly . . . I looked at her again, and she seemed very far off and misty, like my mother was when I saw her in the hut years before.'

Another theme bearing marked resonance with Patrick's early life is that

[1] *Cæsar*, pp. 61–62.

of the rigours of his imprisonment after being captured by the hunters. 'Can you imagine the utter dreariness of the long hours between the times when my master came and fed me in the night? If so, you will be able to understand my intense hatred for all men, except my master and a few others.' Noteworthy too is the extraordinary number of animals and humans savagely killed by Cæsar, and the gruesome nature of many of their deaths. Clearly this may be in part assignable to the delight in portrayal of violence characteristic of boys of Patrick's age at the time of writing. However, it is tempting to recognise another enduring trait of his character. When he believed himself injured by another, a fear to which he was excessively prone, more often than not that person was summarily eradicated from his life, becoming unmentionable and effectively 'dead'.

For the present, however, the manuscript of *Cæsar* (possibly uncompleted) was set aside, and Patrick returned to school at Lewes. Disappointment over his failure at Dartmouth appears to have faded quite swiftly, and he continued with one of the happiest periods in his life.

Patrick's memories of his childhood spell in Lewes continued to haunt him during the ensuing years. In 1952, after they had settled in France, Patrick noted when my mother was away on a visit to her parents in England: 'In the afternoon a card from M, obscurely in Lewes: and I was dreaming of it last night – the morning before, was it? – Keere Street and little Coote's sister.'[1] The dream is tantalisingly suggestive. Coote may have been a fellow pupil at the Grammar School – perhaps a scion of the family of F.H. Coote, the well-established men's outfitters at number 28 in the High Street. More intriguingly, could the vivid evocation of 'little Coote's sister' indicate that a precociously amorous chord was struck in Patrick's youthful breast?[2] There are indications that this may have been the case.

In *Richard Temple* Patrick makes his hero, at a time when his existence appears particularly low, abruptly cast his mind back to a poignant episode in his childhood. At the age of twelve he had experienced an unforgettable relationship with a little girl named Diana.

[1] By a remarkable chance the picture on the card was of Keere Street! Mr Coote of the High Street shop was remembered as 'a very interesting man and . . . very interested in the arts' (*Lewes Remembers: Shops and Shopping* (Lewes, 1999), p. 53).

[2] Writing long afterwards of Jack Aubrey, Patrick evoked the poignancy of juvenile love: 'Riding down into the village he passed the dame's school he had attended as a very little boy, a school where he had first learned to love, if little else: for at that time the dame had a niece to help her, a fresh girl quite pretty, though freckled as a thrush, and the infant Jack had lost his heart to her – followed her about like a puppy, brought her stolen fruit' (*The Surgeon's Mate*, p. 118).

> . . . she was quite exceptional: exceptional not only in that their relationship was 'pure' but also in that he knew her very well – it would be difficult to define love in any way that did not come very near his feelings for her. And when they were separated by an ugly, unscrupulous piece of parental blackmail which neither of them were old enough or hard enough to resist, they thought they would part in a place that had been particularly kind to them, far up the river . . . They mismanaged the parting – butchered it, indeed – and instead of one going one way and one the other they went to and fro, so that it was drawn out in an exquisitely painful manner. But it came to an end somehow and he set off to walk back to London . . .[1]

In the novel Patrick locates this unhappy scene by the Thames at Kew. However it can scarcely have escaped his mind when writing the book that Richard Temple never goes near London during his childhood. Patrick specifies that the incident took place when he was twelve, at which time he would have been a pupil at the Grammar School at Easton Colborough. It was at the same age that Patrick attended the Grammar School at Lewes, on his way to school daily ascending Keere Street, where the encounter with 'little Coote's sister' became entrenched in his memory. It is unlikely that the geographical mislocation in the novel arose from a clumsy error, and it is equally strange that so momentous a rite of passage was not included at the appropriate juncture of Temple's schooldays at Easton Colborough. A likely explanation is that Patrick felt under compulsion to distance his childhood romance from its real location. In the novel Temple's parents place a squalid interpretation on the juvenile *amour*, which could explain Patrick's concern that no reflection of reality be detectable. The river of the children's anguished final parting must have been one flowing past Easton Colborough, i.e. Lewes: in which case it was Patrick's favoured haunt, the Sussex Ouse. Could it have been chance that led him to choose 'Diana' as the name of the love of Stephen Maturin's life?

As ever in Richard's life there was a serpent in his Eden. 'Yet quite suddenly and with no clear warning his life went bad: in those days he could not see why it was so nor tell exactly how it began, yet now as he looked backwards the division was as sharp as that between light and dark.' In due course Richard Temple was promoted to the Headmaster's class. 'Old Mott had the usual schoolmaster's perversion and he was an ugly man with a cane; Richard was a fine juicy boy, which was provocation enough, but his ignorance of Latin was also a real, almost legitimate, offence to Mott, who, with a dirty gleam in his eye, began to call him out almost every day. There

[1] *Richard Temple*, p. 82.

had always been a great deal of beating at school, but up to that time Richard had escaped . . .'

That the Headmaster of Lewes Grammar school was prone to resort to corporal punishment is attested by Bernard Russ in his memoir: 'The Headmaster, the Rev. Griffith, was also Vicar of Glynde . . . and well-known for his use of the cane.' How frequently Bun suffered chastisement he does not mention. For him, as with most boys at a time when beating represented accepted and regular punishment, it provided a momentarily unpleasant but otherwise unremarkable experience, to which he had become accustomed during his years at Shebbear. Indeed, he provides in the margin a humorous sketch of the Headmaster preparing to apply his rod to the upraised bottoms of a row of small boys, accompanied by a light-hearted limerick:

> I am the Vicar of Glynde
> For a change, it is pleasant, I find,
> In my school, full of noise,
> To chastise the boys
> By dusting them well behind.[1]

In *Master and Commander* Jack Aubrey recalls his hopelessness at Latin when at school, laughingly telling Stephen Maturin 'how old Pagan used to flog me'. In *The Thirteen-Gun Salute* he again compared floggings dispassionately administered by bosuns' mates with those of 'old Pagan, my schoolmaster. Plagoso Orbilio, we used to call him.'[2] Jack cheerfully dismissed his punishment as a harsh but inevitable factor in the maintenance of discipline. However he speaks in character, which provides no suggestion that Patrick's memory of his own sufferings at the hands of Mr Griffith ever mellowed.

Whether the Headmaster at Lewes Grammar School was really sadistically inclined is impossible to tell, and remains beside the point in the present context. Unlike Bun, a child as emotionally vulnerable as Patrick would have found the punishment as humiliating as it was painful. Bun had left school at the end of his first year, so that Patrick was on his own for the next two years.

As his treatment of his own son Richard in later years indicates, he did not regard corporal punishment as morally reprehensible *per se*. This confirms that he interpreted the beatings he received as unjustifiable personal assaults. Richard Temple's selection as prime victim of the Headmaster's vindictiveness leads to his wholesale ostracism by his fellow-pupils. However the general prevalence of beating at the school makes their reaction not a little

[1] Russ, *Lady Day Prodigal*, pp. 22, 24.

[2] *Plagoso orbilio*, 'fond of flogging': a quotation from Horace.

improbable. Rather it would seem to illustrate Patrick's lifelong propensity to detect slights where none existed, and his concomitant anticipation of general antipathy among those around him.

In 1945 Patrick adopted the drastic measure of repudiating his earlier life: a rejection which involved the extreme steps of changing his name and reinventing his past. He was to maintain this precarious pretence until his death over half a century later. Though he was astonishingly successful in deluding all but a small and diminishing group of family and intimate friends who had known him before he came to assume his fresh identity, there remained the far more difficult problem of reconciling himself to a past he regarded with such revulsion. Thus a fundamental aspect of his early 'autobiographical' novels and stories was a thorough exorcism of unacceptable aspects of his formal life. This therapeutic process necessitated subtle restructurings of reality, since excessive invention or distortion would have been inadequate to afford him the requisite degree of conviction. This translation of fact into fiction had the further advantage of transferring events to a plane where art transcended venial lapses in conventional morality.

From earliest childhood Patrick was by his own admission an exceptionally sensitive boy, excessively prone to believing himself injuriously treated. Many years later he jotted down this random collection, which provides a revealing example of this characteristic:

> When I was about 13 or 14 I was a prurient little creature and one day when my [step]mother asked me to go upstairs to her room and fetch something I noticed the Bible open upon the table and it happened to be open at the account of Susanah and the elders. This, whose lewd content I perceived instantly, could not be forgone and I lingered to read it all.
>
> I was scolded when I went down: but I was scolded on the grounds of having looked at her letters; and the idea that such a thing could be believed of me, the impossibility of combating the incredulous look that met my protestations and the feeling of total estrangement set up a frustration that I can taste at this moment – atrabilious.
>
> That such a thing can be believed of me . . . I was not a pure boy nor particularly honest; but I was perfectly honourable in that respect. And the most complete rogue will go scarlet with indignation at being accused of the one or two crimes that offer no temptation to him.

That he should have been provoked both at the time and years later to such an extremity of indignation over so trifling an incident says much for the thinness of his skin. He had after all misbehaved, the delay in his return provoked understandable suspicion, his stepmother's reproof was mild, and he must surely have understood that the reproaches directed at him reflected simple misunderstanding.

Still, overall Patrick's three years at Lewes Grammar School represented a happy interlude during an otherwise dreary childhood, marred only sporadically by the pain and indignity of school beatings. There were evenings, weekends, and long holidays to enjoy in the glorious surroundings of the Sussex Downs, with Joan beside him throughout as loyal friend and playmate. His 1981 letter to her, mentioned earlier, displays a deep sense of nostalgia for their childhood days together: 'The photographs . . . sent me back a great way: to Priory Crescent among other places. There was a fig-tree in that walk behind where I nearly put out your eye, and sometimes when I smell fig-leaves here the whole place comes into mind with singular vividness. I remember, for example, that while your wound was being dressed and I was waiting in the drawing-room for execution I read, or rather looked into, a big quarto edition of Don Quixote with sombre illustrations by Gustave Doré.'[1]

Joan was a shy little girl – not surprisingly in view of the fact that she had arrived at the age of six as a stranger amongst her family, where she was accorded scant affection or kindness by her stepmother. On her first arrival at infant school, she appeared in so shabby and dishevelled a state that she was subjected to a public washing before the class. This shameful exposure humiliated her to an extent which she never overcame, and throughout her life she would not allow members of her own family even to witness her combing her hair.

As compensation, the lack of confidence which she shared with Patrick increased the natural affinity between the two children, who were thrown close together even during their first year at Lewes, when Bun also lived with them at Priory Crescent. The academically able Bun would not have been slow in making friends of his own age at the Grammar School, and it does not appear that he participated much in the activities of his young brother and sister during his relatively brief spell at Lewes. He returned to London during school holidays to assist his father, and writing to Joan in later years all his recollection was that 'I did not see much of you before my return from Australia in 1938'.

From time to time the children were taken by their stepmother to the seaside, which lay a short train ride from Lewes beyond the Downs. Seaford, then a pleasant little red-brick town on the Sussex coast not half an hour from

[1] It appears a curious coincidence that Patrick accidentally injured Joan's eye on two distinct occasions in their childhood. However Joan remembered the occasion at Melbury Lodge as vividly as did Patrick that at Lewes.

Lewes, afforded access to the broad strand stretching from Newhaven to Beachy Head beneath the chalk cliffs of the Seven Sisters, which soar to more than 500 feet above the rocky foreshore. The huge expanse of sea, sand, and sky made a profound impression on Patrick's imagination, and there he was able to indulge his all-absorbing interest in nature: exploring rock-pools, investigating marine detritus left by the receding tide upon the wet strand, and straining his gaze upwards at gulls tossed high aloft in the salty breeze. Many years later Joan paid a nostalgic trip to Lewes, where she visited their old home at Priory Crescent, walked up a gratifyingly unchanged Keere Street, and gazed upon her old school. After that, she recorded: 'Went on to Seaford which looked as white and sea-clean as when Pat & I had to play on it all day. V. lucky with a magnificently fine day singing sunshine brilliant on the azure sea and the chalk-headland, start of the Seven Sisters . . .'

In his short story 'The Walker', written in 1953, Patrick describes a stroll along the cliffs on what are recognisably the northern outskirts of Collioure, the small French town where he and my mother had settled four years earlier. Noting that it was more of a scramble than a walk, the fictional narrator recalls:

> When I was a little boy I lived for a time in a place where there was an immense stretch of sand, hard, pounded sand upon which you could walk for miles and miles. You never had to watch your feet on the level sand: walking was effortless, and the rhythm of your steps and the half-heard incessant thunder of the sea induced that trance in which one can go on and on forever, singing perhaps, or talking to the air. There were shells, too, far better than the shells are here, delicately stranded at the watermark, and all kinds of sea-wrecked things, trawlers' floats, kelp, sea purses, spindrift, tarred or whitened planks of wood.[1]

Patrick clearly had in mind the beach at Seaford. Twenty years after his time at Lewes, visiting the seaside with my mother at Morfa Bychan in North Wales, he noted: 'I found a pipe fish which reminded me of the one I found at Seaford long ago.'

In childhood and adolescence Patrick escaped from unpalatable reality into the world of natural history, of which he became a meticulous observer. A favourite excursion during his time at Lewes was to the aquarium at Brighton, where he would stand delightedly gazing at a wide variety of exotic fish and even seals and dolphins. His earliest fiction afforded him opportunity to transform himself, shaman-like, into bird or beast. One of his

[1] *Lying in the Sun*, pp. 82–83.

early short stories, 'A Tale about a Peregrine Falcon', paints a vivid picture of the grandeur of the coastline between Seaford and Beachy Head. It provides a valuable insight into the mind of the solemn little boy, with his preternaturally observant eye for nature and landscape. The story itself is simple. A female falcon, who has hatched a clutch of two eggs in her clifftop eyrie, flies off in search of food, repels a rival trespassing upon her territory, captures a pigeon, and saves her nest from the depredation of an egg-collector. Without a trace of anthropomorphism, the author views everything from the perspective of the predator, whose world is portrayed with accuracy – a description deriving without question from first-hand observation.[1]

The bird's 'wonderful eyes' survey the vast expanse of land and sea from Newhaven to Pevensey in its variegated entirety: 'she mounted higher in wide circles until the marshes appeared as a flat mud-patch below her, and the downs which surrounded them like green hillocks stretching away to the sea in the south and the weald in the north'. Nothing was concealed from her: with a glance she detected a water-rat feeding by the banks of the Ouse, where the river meandered through marshes towards the sea. Soaring inland over the Downs, the falcon's all-seeing eye espies a pigeon flying fast above Mount Caburn, whose steep slopes Patrick himself frequently ascended to gaze from its grassy ramparts over Lewes and the levels far below.

Having circled the Downs and Weald in successful search of prey, on returning to her nest the falcon is startled to hear harsh screams from her male companion, the tiercel. Flying closer, she discovers him fluttering and shrieking angrily about a man who has descended by a rope from the clifftop in order to steal her precious eggs. Though the tiercel flaps furiously about the man's head, he is unable to distract the marauder. It is the female falcon who mounts high in the air above, stooping suddenly with fearful speed to set her talons fast in the robber's face. With a despairing cry he loses his hold, and drops to his death upon the rocks far below.

A number of significant factors distinguish 'A Tale about a Peregrine Falcon' from Patrick's other animal tales. With a single exception, the twelve stories of *Beasts Royal* occur in exotic parts of the world, known only

[1] Patrick's account is completely true to nature. The Reverend F.O. Morris, an eminent Victorian ornithologist, observed of the peregrine that 'it still breeds on Newhaven cliff, and the high cliffs which form Beachy Head, in Sussex. A pair have been in the habit of building there for the last quarter of a century . . .' He recounts the method, so graphically portrayed by Patrick, whereby the falcon stoops with terrifying speed upon its prey, and describes the respective roles of male and female in their spirited defence of their nests (*A History of British Birds* (London, 1851–57), i, pp. 88–99).

to Patrick from his extensive reading. 'Old Cronk', an account of a heron's day fishing, is evidently set somewhere in Britain, but nothing in the narrative indicates a specific location. In marked contrast 'A Tale about A Peregrine Falcon' is set in a geographically identified landscape, with which Patrick was so familiar.[1]

Uniquely among his early short stories involving beasts of the wild, the protagonist remains nameless, with the subliminal effect of identifying her perspective with that of both author and reader. The landscape of the Downs and stretch of coastline between Newhaven and Beachy Head is viewed at a single sweep, as one removed from the scene might contemplate it in the mind's eye. It is surely not fanciful to identify the falcon's perspective with that of Patrick, the eternal outsider, observing the world from his external vantage point. Significantly it is a world void of human beings – save at the highly charged moment of its conclusion, when the valiant intervention of the mother falcon frustrates the rapacious nest-robber from taking her clutch. The narrative is redolent not only of profound nostalgia for the open sea and sky, but also of fierce resentment of the man who violates the idyll.

Patrick wrote the story after his home had once again been uprooted and returned to London. Now he had greater reason than ever to detest his renewed claustrophobic confinement in his father's urban house. A deep love of the open countryside had become one of his prevailing instincts, and his three years at Lewes unquestionably represented an idyllic interlude in a life racked by deep-rooted feelings of inadequacy, loneliness, and guilt. In the interval he had grown from a child to an adolescent capable of articulating (at least to himself) his sensations of frustration and resentment.

A striking indication of the extent to which Patrick cherished his time at Lewes is given by an expedition he made to the town the moment the war ended in 1945. Three days after VE Day, he noted in his pocket diary: 'In the Lewes train I read Congreve's Old Bachelor amusing farce, but what an incredibly savage, inhuman set of lechers.' It is hard to conceive of any reason for his undertaking the journey, save that of seizing convenient opportunity to pay a nostalgic visit to the scenes of his boyhood.

During a visit to England in January 1967, Patrick drove with my mother to walk again about the Lewes levels, where he vividly recaptured carefree days forty years earlier, when a small boy searched for newts and elvers on the

[1] The story was first published in March 1933 in *Great-Heart: The Church of Scotland Magazine – for Boys and Girls*. When it came to be included in *Beasts Royal* Patrick inserted a few minor alterations, two of which are concerned with identifying the setting more specifically with the coast of Seaford and Newhaven.

banks of the Ouse. In 1978 he again found opportunity to return to the town, where he searched in vain for 'old Mr Bedford's stuffed birds'. Three years later he described his visit to Joan:

> When I was in England some years ago I too went on a sentimental pilgrimage to Sussex. Some changes I found in Lewes – the stuffed bird museum in the castle-gate had vanished so entirely that nobody even remembered its existence; our marsh was horribly overgrown; and the way up past the great quarry and the golf-club to Caburn was closed – but the High Street looked much the same and Keere Street was as steep as ever and the downs still had their familiar shape.

Apart from his dimly recalled stay at Kempsey the time he spent at Lewes there was the only period of Patrick's early life for which he expressed nostalgia.[1] Some thirty years after their departure he jotted down these lines:

> How I loved drawing out those blankets of
> matted weed in order to catch newts
> the marshy smell
> the bold terrae filii
> elvers
> idyllic banks ignorance.

The likely location for this nostalgic reverie must surely be the banks of the sluggish Ouse, or the water meadows of its tributary brook the Winterbourne stream which passed by the Russ home in Priory Crescent. In a short story written in the summer of 1949 Patrick recalled a vivid moment on the banks of the Ouse during his last summer at Lewes, when he first became aware of a sensation of standing apart from life: an alienation which grew stronger over the ensuing years. 'And always, from the very first time that he had known it, a boy walking along the tow-path, a summer's evening in the shadow of the heavy, dusty green of the trees, twenty years ago, always there had been something of anticipation in it.'[2]

As the years passed by he found those dreamy days of anticipation increasingly painful to contemplate. At the end of an enforced stay at nearby Eastbourne in 1977 he noted in his diary: 'A last, rather sad look at Lewes, Southover & the deathly Ouse.'

However, there is no mistaking the loving evocation of the countryside around Lewes which appears at the beginning of *Post Captain*. There Jack

[1] In a brief note addressed to her long-dead mother on the sixtieth anniversary of her death, Joan likewise recalled 'the country sweetnesses of Lewes and Kempsey'.
[2] 'The little Death', in *The Last Pool*, p. 211.

Aubrey establishes himself in a house which Patrick named Melbury Lodge after his stepmother's home in Gloucestershire. The building is however removed to a more familiar setting.

> Polcary Down and the cold sky over it; a searching air from the north breathing over the water-meadows, up across the plough, up and up to this great sweep of open turf, the down . . . and far away below them on the middle slope a ploughman standing at the end of his furrow, motionless behind his team of Sussex oxen . . . the river winding through its patchwork of fields, the towers or steeples of Hither, Middle, Nether, and Savile Champflower, the six or seven big houses scattered along the valley, the whale-backed downs one behind the other, and far away the lead-coloured sea.

Enchanted days on the great stretch of sand at Seaford were not forgotten either. In *The Letter of Marque* Stephen Maturin spends a few days exploring a cliff by the English Channel, while Jack Aubrey trains his men for a cutting-out attack on an enemy frigate. After a beautifully observed description of the grassy slope leading down to the rocky seaside and 'the immeasurably vast calm sea', Stephen's 'eye wandered out over the sea and the lanes that showed upon its prodigious surface, apparently following no pattern and leading nowhere, and he felt rising in his heart that happiness he had quite often known as a boy, and even now at long intervals, particularly at dawn: the nacreous blue of the sea was not the source (though he rejoiced in it) nor the thousand other circumstances he could name, but something wholly gratuitous. A corner of his mind urged him to enquire into the nature of this feeling, but he was most unwilling to do so, partly from a dread of blasphemy . . . but even more from a wish to do nothing to disturb it.'

As Stephen ponders these fleeting moments of unclouded happiness, which lie for the most part in the distant past, they are abruptly dispelled. 'This importunity had hardly arisen before it was gone. A rock-dove, gliding placidly along before him, abruptly swerved, flying very fast northwards; a peregrine, stooping from high above with the sound of a rocket, struck a cloud of feathers from the dove and bore it off to the mainland cliff, beyond the *Surprise*.'

Patrick retained his passion for natural history throughout his life. In addition his delight in other ever-widening fields of knowledge increased rapidly during his early adolescent years at Lewes. However indolent he might be in class, out of school he read whatever he could lay hands on. His curiosity was unrestricted, and it does not appear that he pursued any particular course beyond delight in exploratory novelty. Unfortunately only occasional glimpses are preserved of specific books he enjoyed during his childhood. One author whom he remembered as having given him especial pleasure was Jules Verne. In 1976 he decided to try the works of 'dear Verne' again, and obtained copies from the London Library. 'J Verne, the amiable but rather foolish creature,' he wrote in his diary: 'In the 50 odd intervening years I had forgotten every detail but the left-handed shell and the enormous pearl.' It was characteristic of him to have remembered such trifling but exotic details. A consolation of the disagreeable circumstances of his childhood was afforded by a plenitude of books in the successive homes where he lived. He retained long afterwards a vivid recollection of the magnificent illustrations to *Don Quixote* by Gustave Doré. In the late 1950s he drafted an opening sentence for a story: 'The public library at Lewes, dark & dark brown: it was in a harsh 1880 building down by the slow river.' Regrettably the project progressed no further, but we are left with the impression of an earnest little boy scanning the shelves in search of arcane items of knowledge.

It was not only an enduring love of the rolling landscape and open sea which gripped Patrick during his intensely formative stay in Lewes. In the 1920s the town and countryside around had largely escaped the remorseless advance of time, and a sense of security and profundity of experience which derives from continuity with a past era appealed strongly to him. Motorised vehicles were rarely seen, almost all transport still being horse-drawn. Life had changed little since the previous century. Few cottages possessed electricity or running water, shepherds on the Downs bore crooks and wore traditional embroidered smocks, and ploughs and wagons could occasionally be seen being drawn by teams of the local oxen with their characteristic huge curved horns. A Lewes inhabitant recalled how even after the Second World War, 'really genuine peasants would occasionally come in the afternoons, people with huge boots, trousers kept up by leather straps, who would bring in cabbages, rabbits, and mushrooms'.[1] The broad Sussex dialect was universally spoken in farms and villages, and widely in the town.

Although the cataclysm of the Great War had shattered the foundations of English society, in the countryside and county towns the old order continued to outward appearance little altered. Relations between the classes had changed little. Most people lived and worked where their forefathers had done before them, and old customs did not change overnight. Good manners and mutual respect ensured close, often cordial, relations between people of widely differing social backgrounds. The principal great house of the neighbourhood was Stanmer Park, seat of the Earl of Chichester. Shopkeepers in Lewes High Street mentally rubbed their hands as they saw His Lordship's car draw up outside. Generally it

[1] *Lewes Remembers*, p. 14.

was the chauffeur who came to purchase goods, but on occasion the tinkle of the doorbell heralded the entry of the Countess in person.[1]

The evocative descriptions in *Richard Temple* show that the town's Georgian and Regency elegance captivated Patrick, whose hero later recalls 'the Venetian light that bathed Easton Colborough's corn-exchange'. While there existed many picturesque reminders of the town's more ancient past, from the Castle and Priory to Anne of Cleves's house, it is the ordered perfection of Georgian building that evokes Richard's admiration.

Patrick's own attraction to history began no later than his discovery of the *Gentleman's Magazine* in the cellar at Melbury Lodge at the age of ten, and his early unpublished ventures into fiction include jejune essays at historical romance, which, whatever their literary defects, manifest pronounced relish in the colourful resonances of the distant past. The publication presented obvious appeal to so lonely and introspective a child. In the course of correspondence conducted in 1994 with the American writer Stephen Becker, he responded to the question 'What is it like to fall into the past?' with words that recognisably spring from the heart:

> The sensation of falling into the past is not unlike that of coming home for the holidays from a new, strenuous, unpleasant school, and finding oneself back in wholly familiar surroundings with kind, gentle people and dogs – inconveniences of course, such as candlelight in one's bedroom (hard to read by) but nothing that one was not deeply used to.[2]

From an early age he learned to relish odd little circumstantial items of information about past eras, which convey a sense of period more immediately than chronicles of great events. A glimpse of the eclectic extent of his reading at this time is afforded by his purchase of an odd volume of *The Justice of the Peace, and Parish Officer* (London, 1776), a guide to statute law in the reign of King George III compiled by John Burn, justice of the peace for Westmorland and Cumberland.

Patrick's enthusiasm for the world of Georgian England appears to have been first aroused by tales told by his stepmother about her upbringing in her father's beautiful rectory at Horton. Later he plunged himself into that imagined world by extensive reading in literature of the period. It has not been possible to establish when he first began to read Jane

[1] *Lewes Remembers: Shops and Shopping* (Lewes, 1999), pp. 75–76. 'The hearse-like Daimler from Plimpton Hall came winding through the narrow lanes from time to time' (*Richard Temple*, p. 49).
[2] *Paris Review* (1995), p. 123.

Austen,[1] but a reflection entered in his diary in 1974 indicates the appeal the Regency period exerted on his imagination: 'Complete idleness on my part. I finished Mansfield Park & with it all JA's works – such a refuge, that comfortable stable world, in spite of its sometimes (I think) false values & cant.'

Lewes was not only remarkable for the comfortable elegance of its Georgian buildings; despite its modest status as a market town it could boast association with many of the more exotic characters of that gracious era. Its proximity to Brighton and fine racecourse attracted regular visits from no less a personification of the age than George, Prince of Wales, later Prince Regent, who was generally accompanied by a number of his more raffish companions, ranging from his secret wife Mrs Fitzherbert and the inveterate gambler Charles James Fox, to wild rakes like Lord Barrymore and Sir John Lade, whose wife Letty retained the profane language of her earlier career as a highwayman's mistress. Though Patrick is unlikely to have been aware of the fact at the time, it is fitting in view of his enduring devotion to Jane Austen that she used the Star in Lewes High Street as the setting for the ball in her unfinished novel, *The Watsons*.[2]

On a less elevated literary level, it was during Patrick's time in Lewes that the popular Sussex novelist Jeffrey Farnol, whose books he would have seen prominently displayed in bookshop windows, could regularly be observed taking a pint of ale in his accustomed seat in the nearby White Hart: a hostelry affectionately portrayed in several of his romances.[3] His rollicking tales of Regency bucks, highwaymen, Jacobites, prizefighters, one-legged sailors, smugglers, and aristocratic beauties posing as farmers' daughters, their setting as often as not his beloved native Sussex, gave the youthful Patrick much escapist delight.

Patrick's short story 'The Trap', published in *The Last Pool*, recounts an adventure involving a high-spirited young poacher, a wicked squire, his

[1] A reference to his reading *Emma* in 1945 is the earliest of which I have record, but as he constantly re-read her novels there is no reason to suppose that was the first occasion.

[2] For an excellent account of social life in late Georgian Lewes, see Colin Brent, *Georgian Lewes 1714–1830: The Heyday of a County Town* (Lewes, 1993), pp. 129–48. 'Lewes . . . is a large and populous town, distant eight miles from *Brighton*, and is frequently visited by company in their morning rides' (*A Guide to all the Watering and Sea-Bathing Places; with a Description of the Lakes; A Sketch of A Tour in Wales; and Itineraries* (London, 1805), p. 93).

[3] In November 1977 Patrick visited Lewes, where he called at the White Hart: 'Pub much changed. I cd scarcely see much because of the furious traffic: but what a gt deal there is that I never saw at all, long ago.' It is the more interesting that he *did* remember the White Hart so clearly – not a place intrinsically likely to interest a small schoolboy.

brutal gamekeeper, and the genial landlord of a tavern named after a prizefighter – all fundamental ingredients of Farnol's stories. Again, Stephen Maturin's encounter with the eccentric author 'Blue Breeches' in *The Letter of Marque* reads in style and treatment like pure Farnol.[1] Naturally Patrick did not directly imitate Farnol's work, since apart from other considerations he did not retain any of his books, but the influence seems clear.[2]

That Patrick should have succumbed to so cheerfully robust an influence at an impressionable age is perfectly understandable – but it was certainly not one he would have acknowledged. Closely related to his deep sense of irrational shame at having been deprived of adequate educational opportunities was a persistent waking nightmare that his learning and literary skills might at any time become exposed as inadequate: a near-paranoiac fear which all too often led him into needless exaggeration, invention, or withholding of material facts.

One manifestation of this was careful concealment of anything which might appear to detract from the originality of his writing. While he was more than happy to acknowledge debts owed to literary giants such as Samuel Johnson and Jane Austen, and his familiarity with obscure eighteenth-century works, he was preternaturally apprehensive lest anyone suppose he might have been influenced by any book he regarded either as of inferior quality, or similar enough in style or content to his own to invite the imputation of imitation. Such authors were dismissed with a contemptuous smile ('we don't read *that* trash!'), and shortly after he died I was amused to discover the volume of *Hornblower* stories which he bought during the war stuffed into a sack along with other condemned works at the back of the rocky recess behind his study.[3]

If Patrick relished the novels of Jeffrey Farnol during his years in Lewes

[1] Cf. Jeffrey Farnol, *Peregrine's Progress*, ch. iii, 'An Extraordinary Tinker'; *The Broad Highway*, ch. xxii, 'A Literary Tinker', etc.

[2] Nevertheless his short story 'No Pirates Nowadays', written ten years after leaving Lewes, includes what looks uncommonly like a direct reflection of Farnol. The story features a laconic Scotsman named Ross, who is regularly given to exclaiming 'Mphm' and 'Hmph' – ejaculations surely rarely uttered by an actual Scot. The tale concludes: '"Mphm," said Ross, winking at Derrick.' Farnol's novel *Sir John Dering*, which is set in and around Lewes, likewise features a comical but heroic Scotsman, and the story concludes on a strikingly similar note: 'Sir Hector emitted that sound to which no one but a true-born Scot may give utterance, and which, so far as poor words go, may be roughly translated thus: "Umph-humph!" quoth Sir Hector Lauchlan MacLean.'

[3] The irrationality of Patrick's apprehension is illustrated by the fact that his naval stories were demonstrably *not* influenced by *Hornblower*, but by what he termed 'the real thing': i.e. naval memoirs, contemporary technical handbooks, and other primary sources.

and they originated that lifelong absorption which amounted to his virtual relocation in the eighteenth-century and Regency eras, I have little doubt that he would have taken pains to suppress the fact and discard any copies he may have possessed.

Many of Farnol's novels are set in the period when Britain was at war with Revolutionary and Napoleonic France. When the Emperor assembled his Grand Army at Boulogne for the invasion of England, Kent and Sussex had special reason to fear a landing. Each time Patrick travelled to Seaford, he would have passed a material reminder of those dangerous times, in the form of one of the seventy-four Martello towers constructed by the Government of William Pitt along the threatened coasts. In the event its howitzer and swivel-guns proved needless. So long as the ships of Admiral Lord Keith's fleet kept watch and ward along the Channel, even Napoleon dared not attempt a crossing of Britain's impregnable moat.

In the early decades of the twentieth century the past of Lewes was not confined to architecture, history books, and literature, but survived in many ways as a living entity. The most remarkable instance was the famous Lewes Guy Fawkes celebration. This festival had been celebrated annually for some two centuries before the Russ family arrived in the town, and continues as the most elaborate and splendid in the country. Different societies or gangs known as 'Bonfire Boys' parade through the streets, attired in an extravagant array of varied fancy dress, and headed by leaders attired as bishops. Fireworks are discharged in all directions, tar barrels set ablaze, and an effigy of the Pope burned on an enormous bonfire. The whole town becomes wild with jubilation, not a little liquor is consumed, and every opportunity for pranks and witticisms indulged. As an old Sussex adage quaintly held: 'The herrings come to see the bonfires on Guy Fawkes's day.'[1]

Half a century later Bun vividly recalled in a letter to Joan the excitement which the occasion afforded the three Russ children on 5 November 1926: 'I expect you will remember Guy Fawkes' Day in Lewes and the parish parades with bands, costumes and so forth converging on the dripping pan and then the tossing of the effigy of the Pope over the bridge across the Ouz [*sic*] down below the main part of the town.' As Jack Aubrey gleefully expresses it in *Master and Commander*: 'Lord, how we used to keep up the Fifth of November.'

The Dripping Pan to which Bun referred is a large sunken rectangular piece of ground surrounded by earthen banks a few hundred yards along the road to the east of Priory Crescent, which is thought to have been a medieval saltpan. It provided an ideal open-air amphitheatre for public events, and

[1] A.R. Wright and T.E. Lones, *British Calendar Customs* (London, 1936–40), iii, pp. 155–56.

made a lasting impression on Patrick, who transferred it to Dorset in his novel *The Yellow Admiral* as the setting for the boxing match between Jack Aubrey's coxswain Barrett Bonden and Black Evans the gamekeeper.

Bun was present at another crowded occasion in the Dripping Pan, when Lloyd George delivered a speech there. All he could recollect in old age was gazing from the fringes of the crowd upon 'the wide open space . . . where he was giving his oration, waving his white locks about and if I understood what he was saying, I certainly do not remember it now'. He recalled that the speech, 'as far as I know, was well received in our Sussex area'. Pat probably accompanied Bun to this lively scene in the sleepy Sussex town, and the excitement aroused by the visit of the great Liberal statesman affected the household at Priory Crescent. In *Richard Temple* the hero describes his father as 'a passionate admirer of Lloyd George', but goes on to assert that 'in the opinion of the Hall and of almost everybody else in the vicinity Lloyd George was a hateful person, untrustworthy and unscrupulous, envious, mean and glib; he was a dirty little Welshman, a vulgar, jumped-up attorney overflowing with jealousy and spite, bent on England's ruin. *A common little man*: the final damnation.'

From this it is a reasonable guess that Charles Russ was a Liberal, and it was probably he who took the children to attend the rally. Whether it was then or later that Patrick overheard disparaging references to Lloyd George, notorious *bête noire* of the upper classes in the early twentieth century, his father's political views may have confirmed his fear that his paternal ancestry was tainted and inferior.

Richard Temple includes a lovingly detailed description of Lewes cattle market, which was held every Monday at the old Tanyard near the railway station, a stone's throw from the Russ family home. A swarm of enterprising hucksters set up stalls proffering wildly variegated fare, which exerted magnetic attraction on an impressionable child. Long years afterwards, Temple recalls how 'the week-long desert was cram-packed with sheep, pigs, cattle, poultry, bright red ploughs, blue harrows, pedlars, hucksters, bone-setters and respectable long-established stalls that sold harness, saddles, brasses, girths, curry-combs and plaited whips . . . On the right there was a flimsy trestle set out with cards of celluloid studs and cuff-links, brilliantly striped, penknives with many blades, patent glasscutters and frail inventions for slicing beans . . .' Richard and his schoolfriends

> moved on, lingering past a man who wished to sell them a gold watch wrapped in a ten-shilling note for sixpence, providing they could tell the right packet from the packets full of chaff, and dawdle through the penetrating reek of swine to the herbalist's, where a grave, attentive crowd looked at a picture of a

> transparent man, or rather of a partially transparent man, for where none of his vitals were concerned he was solid enough: only here and there his purple liver, his spleen and bowels showed through. His bearded face, however, with its serious and evangelical expression was scarcely one that could rightly belong to an undressed body, far less to a transparent one; it floated on another plane, surrounded by pinned-up shrivelled plants, a dusty halo; and there were other bunches round the body below, with ribbons leading from them to the parts they healed, and with a wand the herbalist pointed them out as he described the diseases. Rising of the lights; strangury; horseshoehead and headmouldshot; dropsy, marthambles, the strong fives and the moon-pall; stone; gravel; pox . . . the herbalist would not stop or spare them anything; in a high, unfriendly, didactic voice he went right on through cancer, consumption, bloody flux, the quinsy and worms.[1]

The exotic range of ailments and cures intrigued and amused Patrick, and it may well have been here that the seeds were sown which would one day provide Stephen Maturin with his professional expertise.

Years later Patrick's sister Joan jotted down this joyous memory of their shared Sussex days: 'I have had many homes, but home to me will always be Lewes. The old castle on the steep hill among black and white timbered houses, looking out over the South Downs to the sea. Our house outside the ancient city wall of flints with sturdy flowers in the crevices. The road, chalky and bordered with wildflowers, as it wound its way to Newhaven over the marshes. The great ring of downland, from Mt Caburn scarred with R.[oman] Encamp[ment]s. to File Beacon, distant in hazy blue with a glint of the sea at its feet. But the warm quietness turf scented, up on the downs, with heady perfume of gorse in the sun, alive with the blue frittilias has more than home to it.

'It seems to me to be England's heart.'

This harmonious and picturesque world must have appeared congenial to Patrick. Intense personal insecurity combined with increasing perception of his father's fluctuating and generally declining position and social status induced agonised doubts regarding his family's profession in the social hierarchy. He had no desire to become a duke and achieve superiority over others: rather he wished to enjoy the comfortable confidence and sense of place attainable by being *a gentleman*. The realms into which he withdrew existed in his imagination and to satisfy his penetrating intelligence it was essential that they be as richly real as that harsh world into which he had had

[1] *Richard Temple*, pp. 38–40. Sadly Lewes cattle market was closed in 1992 (Helen Poole, *Lewes Past* (Chichester, 2000), pp. 91–93).

the misfortune to be born. Almost certainly it was during his halcyon three years in Lewes that the seeds germinated which ultimately blossomed into his brilliant literary re-creation of the Georgian world.

The Russ family finally returned to London some time after the end of the summer term of 1929. Patrick was now fourteen and, having attained the statutory age requirement, his relatively brief period of formal education came to an end. His withdrawal from school and the abandonment of the family residence at Lewes was probably occasioned by yet another plunge in the family fortunes. He left Lewes Grammar School without obtaining his matriculation. Though the indications are that he was generally happy during his time at the school, his scholastic progress remained decidedly inadequate. This disappointing record presented a marked contrast to his brother Bun's success, and Patrick later came to ascribe inordinate significance to high academic qualification.

FIVE

In the Doldrums

Into this Universe, and *Why* not knowing
Now *Whence*, like Water willy-nilly flowing;
And out of it, as Wind along the Waste,
I know not *Whither*, willy-nilly blowing.
(Edward Fitzgerald, *The Rubaiyat of Omar Khayyám*)

When Patrick and Joan returned with their stepmother to 54 Sutherland Avenue in the summer of 1929, it was to a household where much had changed. The once-numerous family was now greatly depleted. Godfrey and Victor had long departed the family home to pursue their careers, and for some time Olive, now twenty-three, had found life increasingly intolerable at home. Charles Russ was frequently harsh and tactless in his treatment of his eldest daughter. As her sister-in-law Saidie Russ told me: 'Their Father objected to Olive wearing high heels so he cut the heels off her shoes.' Furthermore, 'Victor said "Dad used to scold Olive for not eating enough when she was trying to get slim". When I asked what she did about it, he said "Oh, she just wept and carried on slimming".' Ill feeling was apparently mutual and, as another of Victor's memories suggests, may have originated when the sixteen-year-old Olive found herself rudely ousted as 'mother' of the family after her father's marriage to Zoe Center. Olive told her sister-in-law 'how their Step-Mother wouldn't let her pour her Father's coffee in the morning – and I knew exactly how he liked it'.

Eventually Olive had become unable to continue suffering such indignities and privations and departed to live with her kindly Uncle Frank Welch and Aunt Bertha at their new home, a handsome country house set in five acres of grounds outside Pinner. It was they who had looked after little Joan until her father's remarriage, and now they provided Olive with a happy refuge. Charles Russ does not appear to have raised objection to the move, and perhaps welcomed the modest saving in household expenditure resulting from his daughter's departure. Margaret Welch told me she recalled Olive's sulkiness when things did not go as she wished, but her moodiness may reflect the long years of repression in her father's home.

According to her younger sister Joan, their father's unnatural coldness towards Olive was exacerbated by the influence of his wife. Joan described how her father wished to give Olive as an engagement present a silver fox fur coat (obtained at reduced price from the former family firm), but Zoe managed to dissuade him from even this grudging gesture. Henceforward a total rift opened up between father and daughter. Contact was never resumed, until long afterwards Olive's Uncle Sidney persuaded her to visit her father on his deathbed. He greeted his eldest daughter with the exclamation: 'Who is this nice lady who has come to see me?'

Although Mike and Bun had passed their matriculation with flying colours, entitling them to a place at university, as in the case of Victor their father's impecuniosity denied them the reward of their hard work. Both appear to have remained remarkably unembittered by this. As Bun tactfully put it: 'Mike had . . . foregone his university studies in favour of employment in a surveyor's real estate office in the City of London. University was expensive, and Father had done all for us that he could . . .'

By the time Bun returned to London in the summer of 1927 after his final year's schooling at Lewes, Mike had moved to the other side of the world. He had discovered the existence of an Australian Government financed project known as the Dreadnought Scheme, which provided assistance to young men wishing to emigrate. In June 1927 he embarked for New South Wales, and launched into a peripatetic existence for which his fine physique and resourcefulness well fitted him.

Now the only boy living at Sutherland Avenue, Bun proved an enterprising lad prepared to accept whatever life offered.

> I, too, was on my own and found a job in the city. Part of my job was to collect rents in the tenements and slums of the East End. It was depressing and often boring, but at least I was making a small financial contribution towards my keep. And how small it seems by today's standards! Fifteen shillings a week . . .![1]

Though he made no complaint, it says little for his father that he was prepared to exact rent from his son's weekly pittance in return for a bed in the family home.

Even Bun set aside his rose-tinted spectacles when in later years he reluctantly contemplated family life at Sutherland Avenue. In 1988 he

[1] *Lady Day Prodigal*, pp. 24, 26.

acknowledged in a letter to his sister Joan: 'I prefer not to think much about the days in London for that was an unhappy abode and particularly so, I think, for the twins.' Given that Bun provoked Joan's express irritation by his consistent lauding of Zoe, it seems likely that their stepmother rarely visited the household at Sutherland Avenue during the time she lived at Lewes from 1926 to 1929.

By the time Bun was seventeen he had experienced more than enough of tedium and deprivation, and became increasingly disturbed by his employment, which required him not merely to witness but exacerbate the degraded condition of those impoverished tenants from whom he was required to collect rent in some of the poorest parts of London. Eventually he made enquiries, and found that the Dreadnought Scheme was still in operation. Mike was by now well established in Australia, where his letters home told of an enviably free and exciting existence. Shortly after Patrick's return from Lewes to London in the latter part of 1929, Bun sailed for Australia in the company of fifteen or twenty other young men of assorted backgrounds, who like him sought a new life beyond the confines of a Britain which was beginning to suffer the effects of the worldwide stock market crash, and offered constricted opportunities. On 28 November Mike informed Olive that 'Bun arrived in Sydney last Thursday O.K.'

Patrick must have longed to join his brothers, who were living an existence that he could experience only in imagination. Mike sent home vivid descriptions of life in the bush, where he encountered such exotic creatures as the tree-climbing kangaroo, which 'lives in the top of the highest trees & eats leaves, it somewhat resembles a kangaroo, hopping on its hind legs when on the ground, but its tail is longer & its ears much shorter', and the beautiful cassowary 'all bright blue neck & breast [,] black wings with vermilion bugles hanging from its neck, but very timid & rare'. But apart from any other consideration Patrick was too young to follow his brothers' example.

In 1929 the household at Sutherland Avenue had dwindled dramatically since they last lived there three years earlier. The once-flourishing tribe of children was reduced to the twins Connie and Nora, who were now joined by Patrick and Joan. With their house at Lewes sold, Charles and Zoe were more frequently at home. The family was to remain at Sutherland Avenue for another three years. Unfortunately we now enter on a period of Patrick's life whose events are only intermittently recorded, leaving much that must remain conjectural or altogether unknown. When he had last lived at close quarters with his father, Patrick had been a cowed and unformed child. Now, however, he had finished his schooldays and was approaching the age of fifteen.

Subsequently he provided a formal description of his occupation during the years between his completing his schooling and leaving home as 'Author & Secretarial Work for father'. Although he never expatiated on the nature of this 'secretarial work', it is hard to imagine that his father's reduced practice required much assistance in the way of correspondence and similar duties. As Joan vividly recalled, the greater part of their time together at that time constituted idling about the house and pursuing such desultory amusements as lay to hand.

However, Patrick was probably not entirely abandoned to his own devices. In earlier years Charles Russ had drawn his three elder sons into assisting him with those ingenious projects in which he engaged with childlike delight, such as repairing his cars and motor bicycle or installing electrical lighting. He enjoyed their companionship as fellow-enthusiasts in his hobbies. As the only boy of the household, Patrick enjoyed consolations denied his sisters. In the summer of 1929 Charles Russ had taken Bun with him to the Exhibition of Inventions, where they demonstrated a device for preventing car radiators from freezing, and there are indications that Patrick participated in experiments in the laboratory at George Street, which his father's infectious enthusiasm and his own consuming curiosity would have made pleasurable occasions.

In later life Patrick was much taken with Edmund Gosse's autobiography *Father and Son* (1907), in which Gosse describes his repressed childhood at the hands of a father who was a gifted pioneer naturalist, but whose sectarian fundamentalism prevented his coming to terms with the revolution in natural sciences which followed on the publication of Darwin's *Origin of Species*. Though the book culminates with young Gosse's departure from home and his wholesale rejection of his father's views, he cannot help retaining a touching measure of respect and affection for his errant parent.

Ruminating in later years on how strangely distant appear the past stages of one's life, Patrick reflected on 'the ring (particularly for the young) of, say, 1929': 'Remember Scaliger and how he was destroyed by his father's romancing, sucked in with his earliest milk and truer than any subsequently-learnt fact.'

The reference provides a unique insight into how Patrick came to regard his adolescent upbringing. The source for his knowledge of Scaliger was D'Israeli's *Curiosities of Literature*, a late eighteenth-century miscellany which from an early age afforded him much pleasure and instruction: 'Joseph Scaliger', wrote D'Israeli, 'inherited from his father, with an ardent love for study, the most ridiculous vanity, with a most caustic and most insufferable humour.' In 1594 he published an extravagant encomium of his father Julius's supposedly unsurpassed achievements in almost every field of learning, and endorsed his claim to illustrious descent from the ancient princes of Verona. This cornucopia of talents and hereditary grandeur was afterwards demolished in a virulent attack by a rival scholar, who compiled a merciless exposure of Joseph's self-promotional tribute to his father, in which he painstakingly catalogued 499 lies. Among numerous impostures, he revealed that the elder Scaliger bore no connection to the princes of Verona, having been in reality a man of plebeian origin born in the shop of a gilder. After fruitlessly attempting a succession of ignoble employments, Julius eventually succeeded in fraudulently passing himself off as a physician with a degree from the University of Paris.

Although Joseph espoused his father's conceit and arrogance in full measure, he 'possessed a finer taste: his style is more flowing and easy . . .' However, 'His writings, like those of the father, breathe singular haughtiness and malignity . . . he was incapable of thinking or speaking favourable of any person.' Despite his undoubted learning, like his father he frequently succumbed to gross error. All in all 'Scaliger, the father, was . . . an illustrious impostor', whose lifelong pretences to profound learning and high birth were not merely absorbed by the son but uncritically embellished by him. So committed had been Joseph's identification with his father, and so devastating the effect of his exposure, that they brought the wretched son to a premature death.[1]

The close parallel which Patrick detected in his own adolescent relationship with his father is illuminating. The reference to the younger Scaliger's destruction by 'his father's romancing' surely reflects the combination of awe and fear with which Patrick regarded his parent on his return from Lewes to London. In 1929 Charles Russ continued to sustain delusions of imminent acclaim by the scientific world,[2] which his sixteen-year-old son had no reason to doubt. Eventually he ascribed his own worst faults and weaknesses to those he came to detect in his father.

Charles Russ's sudden burst of collaborative enthusiasm for Patrick's achievement in writing and publishing *Cæsar* initiated an illusory period of relative warmth between them. Unlike Mike and Bun, Pat was not driven out to gain an uncongenial and unremunerative living. While he experienced much neglect, this was meliorated by the genuine enthusiasm with which his father regarded his literary endeavours, and his continuing

[1] Isaac D'Israeli, *Curiosities of Literature* (London, 1793), pp. 180–88. Despite their failings, both Scaligers were in reality profound scholars, which however is beside the present issue.

[2] Bernard recalled his father's disappointment at failing to make his fortune from a device for preventing car radiators from freezing. He also proudly declared himself the inventor of 'magnetic spectacles for ptosis' – a drooping of the eyelid from muscular failure. Presumably they were designed to draw back the errant lid.

faith in his father's professional talent. The sudden accession of approval from so awe-inspiring and distant a parent, combined with the natural lassitude which his grim upbringing had induced in him, enabled him to survive the ensuing years of virtual confinement at home with some degree of equanimity.

However this is not to suppose that relations between father and son were ever entirely easy. As a child Patrick had instinctively discovered means of coming to terms with or evading his father's tyranny, and as a youth on the verge of manhood he adapted himself to altered circumstances. In *Richard Temple*, which revolves around the confinement of its hero in a Nazi gaol, just as the prison provides a symbolic representation of the homes in which Patrick was effectively confined, so the ageing interrogator represents an appropriate model for his father at this stage of his life:

> Reinecke was looking tired and dispirited, and suddenly very much older. Temple, from behind his moron's face, watched him with a more eager intensity than a lover: for this Reinecke was God for him – Jehovah. He was the Almighty, and Temple had been in the hollow of his hand all these horribly counted days. He was Reinecke's priest and sacrifice: he had learnt, oh so quickly, how to predict Reinecke's shifting moods, how to propitiate his wrath and how to be as sparing of his sacrifice as possible: for Temple's own body was the sacrifice.

Just as in 'The Thermometer' the child 'automatically dodged his head' when Carew raises his hand to move the curtain, so as Reinecke 'passed staring, Temple flinched – an involuntary flinch, of course, an unwilling tribute'.[1]

A more explicit insight relating directly to the period of Patrick's late adolescence is found in his novel *The Catalans*. No one who knew him well could doubt that this passage represents a description of his relationship with his own father:

> Xavier's father was an evil-tempered man, powerful, domineering, and restless; a ferocious domestic bully. It was not that Alain blamed his Uncle Hercule [Xavier's father] then; he accepted him as a force of nature and hated him without forming any judgment; but he was sorry for Xavier . . . There was something very moving, in those days, in the sight of that proud, cold young man being humiliated and bully-ragged, and bearing it with a pale, masked fortitude.

[1] *Richard Temple*, pp. 6, 8.

In another telling passage Xavier, i.e. Patrick, delivers this bitter tirade against his father's profession:

> I don't wish to be extreme: I dare say that bacteriologists as a class do think very kindly of mankind as a whole when it occurs to them to think of it at all; but I think their guiding motive is curiosity rather than humanity. And I know that with regard to their fellow men as individuals they are neither much better nor much worse than the rest of the world: they certainly do not conspicuously overflow with love for their neighbors or their colleagues. And I am sure of this, that the popular idea of bacteriologists as wise white-coated angels yearning day and night is so much nonsense: many of them are disagreeable men, some not even of average intelligence. And any bacteriologist who gives countenance to this 'dedicated servant' notion is guilty of abominable cant. I hate cant.[1]

Fear was an intrinsic component of Patrick's relationship with his father, to which he had learned to accommodate himself from a very early age. His comparison of his predicament on returning to London in 1929 with Julius Scaliger's infatuated acceptance of his father's authority and self-delusion suggests that he continued to regard him as awesomely omniscient and omnipotent. Subsequent realisation that his father's pretensions to eminence as a scientist were hollow, and his pre-eminence at home far from reflecting the prestige which his young son had unreflectingly taken for granted, were to become an ever-increasing source of resentment as the years passed by. Ultimately it is likely that they contributed to Patrick's dramatic decision to sever himself from his past by changing his name in an attempt to begin his life entirely anew.

Patrick's description of himself as 'author' reflected the one true and lasting benefit of the desultory course of his adolescent life. Periods of confinement as an invalid in early childhood, followed by prolonged isolation in the houses at Harrow and Willesden Green, led him at an early age to discover solace in extensive reading. This eventually drew him to compile adventures of his own, when he voyaged in imagination under different guises far afield in exotic lands. In a BBC interview in 1998, he recalled that as a child he had attempted writing 'rather fanciful things of a person of my own age making surprising voyages and so on' – projects which he candidly acknowledged to have represented 'wish-fulfilment'.

Absorbed in his imaginary world, a lonely boy readily succumbs to the influence of books encountered at that impressionable age. Patrick speedily

[1] *The Catalans*, pp. 86, 93–94.

developed a powerful predilection on the one hand for tales of voyages and accounts of distant lands, and on the other for history. Both genres of literature provide ideal avenues for escape: the one transposed in space, the other in time. They facilitate the reader's removal into a world of visionary enchantment, where he communes with people and places endowed with a fascination and variety transcending his constricted circumstances. He had succeeded in entering that secret garden of enchantments which lay beyond the portals of the Georgian rectory in the painting on his bedroom wall.

Reasons have been given for believing that Patrick surreptitiously wrote his novel *Cæsar* during periods of enforced idleness while being tutored by his father in his laboratory during a school holiday in 1927. He returned to London with his stepmother and sister Joan after finishing his education at Lewes Grammar School after the end of the summer term of 1929, and it was probably then that he first showed his father the manuscript of his novel, claiming to have written it in Lewes and on his return to town. Charles Russ was not backward in responding with enthusiasm to any constructive achievement by his sons. He recognised at once the merits of the adventures of the panda-leopard, and set about finding a publisher. Although at the time his own publications had been of an exclusively scientific nature, he nurtured literary ambitions and was familiar with the procedure of dealing with publishers.

In May 1930 Dr Russ approached the reputable publishing house of G.P. Putnam's Sons, and at a meeting with the editor Geoffrey Lackstead signed a contract on his son's behalf. Patrick received an advance of £10, and the book was published in October that year, with a foreword written by his father in quaintly pedantic but unmistakably proud terms.

While Patrick must have been gratified by his father's approval and support, it was 'To Zoe Clara Russ' that he dedicated his book. Bun later recalled that 'Stepmother . . . was very well read, I think more than Dad'. Dean King suggests that Patrick's youthful 'fervour for India' originated 'perhaps through Uncle Emil's tales of his years there, and certainly [was] deepened by Kipling's writing'.[1] While the latter is undoubtedly true, there is no evidence that he ever met Uncle Emil. Although it has been seen that his elder brothers and sisters stayed with their uncle on occasion during the school holidays, Emil's daughter Betty, only a year younger than Patrick, had no recollection of him. If we are to look beyond literary influences for his passion, a more likely source would be his stepmother, whose first husband William Center was born in Hindustan and spent the first ten years of his life there.

[1] King, *Patrick O'Brian*, p. 51.

In the Russ family Patrick's precocious achievement was regarded with admiration, and at the end of the year Mike wrote from Australia to his sister Olive: 'While Im on the subject of writing I must say young Pat seems to be on the right track; its a pity he wasn't out here & he could write all the animal stories he wished at first hand. I have not read the book yet but its coming from Bun this week.'

Like most children's novels written by a first-time author, the book attracted few review notices, but those that did appear were broadly favourable. Across the Atlantic a mild criticism voiced in the *New York Herald Tribune* that '*Cæsar* may be too human – or boylike – in his reactions for complete plausibility' seems unjustified. This muted recognition is unlikely to have affected Patrick's rapturous discovery at finding himself a published author, and for all the grievous setbacks he was to encounter during his literary career his goal in life was now firmly established.

In the following July he proudly presented Joan with a copy on her birthday, inscribed 'To Joan from Pat Jul 10th/31'. Despite Dean King's comment that 'Love was not a topic to be mentioned' and his suggestion that the 'dry' wording confirms the family's lack of 'ability to display emotions', Patrick's laconic phraseology is unlikely to have reflected more than the general aversion of boys to any display of sentimentality. Ample evidence attests to the extent to which Patrick remained fast friends with his young sister as long as they shared the family home.

Patrick's remarkable achievement in becoming a published author at the age of fifteen gave him the confidence he had previously lacked, not least on account of the approbation it gained him from his father. Though he continued to find his existence within the family home unbearably tedious, that was after all a condition to which he had become long accustomed and largely resigned himself to accepting.

Joan, on the other hand, enjoyed no such compensations. At the age of thirteen she had been withdrawn from her school at Lewes, and was to wait five long years before she could resume her education. Inclined though she was in old age to reminisce about her early days, she avoided dwelling on this period of her life, confining herself to a laconic allusion to 'The Victorian bits & pieces. The crude discomforts of S[utherland]. Ave.'

From every account it appears that Zoe was far from maternally inclined. Her stepdaughters recalled that she was rarely at home. Victor's wife Saidie remembered that 'Olive . . . Mentions that Step-Mother had *twelve* evening dresses in her wardrobe. She was a sea captains widow.' She and Charles clearly enjoyed the full social round she had doubtless known as a wealthy widow in Knightsbridge.

Number 54 Sutherland Avenue remained the family home for another two years. It appears to have been the spartan conditions in which the children were living at this time to which Patrick briefly alluded in his preface to the tribute published by the British Library in 1994: 'But by this time the Wall Street crash had come and gone; we were in the great depression of the Thirties, and people were learning sometimes successfully, how to live and even entertain without servants to wait at table, cook, wash up, make beds: a civilisation that had never been known before and one that spread a certain gloom.'[1]

Characteristically Patrick ascribed his family's depressed condition to the general economic decline of the middle and upper classes. Privately, however, he recognised that the 'depression' and 'gloom' reflected less the condition of society at large than the prevailing atmosphere in the household of Charles Russ. Three years after writing this account, he noted in his diary: 'Ill-temper, general gloom & by night remorse of conscience reaching back nearly 70 years.'

In the summer of 1931 Dr Russ, a lifelong devotee of the theatre and music hall, arranged public performance of a play he had written. Most likely this represented a long-term ambition, although he may have been spurred to creative activity by the previous autumn's publication of *Cæsar*. The opening night was on 9 July. Entitled *Hidden Power*, the drama centred on a murder perpetrated by an anæsthetist during an operation, and attention principally focused on medical issues of a specialist nature. What it lacked in well-contrived plot and dramatic realisation of character was compensated by concentration on professionally correct medical terminology and equipment, while much of the dialogue constituted protracted exchanges relating to abstruse aspects of hypnosis, psychological analysis, anaesthetics, and related issues of more concern to Harley Street practitioners than dramatic critics. It is not altogether surprising to find that the play's principal (possibly sole) review appeared in Britain's leading medical journal, the *Lancet*.

The production, which ran for two months, was a privately funded venture involving *inter alia* engagement of a repertory company, hire of King George's Hall in Great Russell Street, renting costumes and props, and printing advertisements and programmes. While it is hard not to empathise with the Doctor's obsessive pursuit of literary creativity, there is something profoundly distasteful about the attitude of a father who was happily prepared to fund so expensive a hobby-horse, while remaining unwilling to pay to keep his youngest daughter at school.

Meanwhile Patrick had been working on a fresh literary production, and in

[1] Cunningham (ed.), *Patrick O'Brian*, p. 17.

October he published a short story in the popular boys' magazine *Chums*. Entitled 'Skogula – The Sperm Whale', it followed the pattern established by *Cæsar* of recounting the adventures of a mammal viewed (in this case, implicitly) from the perspective of the creature itself. As with all Patrick's stories, his narrative approach was dramatic while remaining unsentimentally realistic. He had clearly conducted some research into the natural history of the whale, and his story recounts the adventures of Skogula, a young bull, as he accompanies the wanderings of a school of whales through the Atlantic and Indian Oceans. A succession of dramatic incidents, such as readers of *Chums* would appreciate, follow in swift succession. Skogula is attacked by harpooners, witnesses a fearful combat between his father and a rival bull in which the former is defeated and disappears, and twice emerges successfully from attacks by giant swordfish. Finally he engages in a ferocious battle with a rival whale over 'an attractive young cow called Miska'. Just as his strength is failing from a succession of grievous wounds, Skogula is saved when his antagonist is blown up by a fortuitous collision with a mine.

'Skogula' was probably inspired by Kipling's story 'The White Seal' in *The Jungle Book*, while the description of the battle with the swordfish may have derived from Wood's mention in his *Illustrated Natural History* that 'the whale is an object of particular enmity to the Sword-fish'. However, the literary style is entirely Patrick's own, his stark and even brutal realism differing markedly from the half-humorous approach adopted by Kipling.

The story contains many lively descriptive vignettes, testifying to Patrick's striking imaginative powers at such an early age. Although the imagery is at times grim, it is rarely gratuitously ghoulish. Thus at the outset, Skogula pursues an octopus:

> His quarry, however, saw him and ejected a black cloud, disappearing into the ripped-up side of a sunken ocean-going tramp lying on the sea-bed under many fathoms of water. The decks harboured hundreds of crabs and shellfish which had come for the dead bodies of the crew years before, and because of the great quantities of crabs, the octopi lived both in and around the ship in great numbers.
>
> As the whale passed a few feet above the deck, looking for the octopus, the skeleton of a man lashed to the wheel shifted in the current, and the skull rolled down the sloping deck, dislodging some crabs who lived inside.[1]

A further trait which Patrick shared with Kipling was an absorbing interest in the mechanics and application of technical operations. Describing the

[1] *Beasts Royal*, p. 13.

attack on Skogula, he explains how 'the harpooner seized his first harpoon and stood up in the bows. He was poised for the cast when a clumsy hand at tub oar fouled the whale rope. This spoilt the harpooner's cast, and his iron, which lodged just above Skogula's left fin, had no force in it. Then the whale dived. The harpooner darted an angry glance at the clumsy hand, and seized the second harpoon, which was lashed to the first by only a short length of rope; he threw it overboard, as the whale was already under the surface.'

Patrick's concern for accurate representation of procedural niceties probably owed much to collaboration with his father in experiments in the George Street laboratory. It has been seen with what minute exactitude he was able to describe its contents when many years later he came to write 'The Thermometer',[1] and throughout his adult life he threw himself with unbounded enthusiasm alike into the theory and practical application of activities ranging from beekeeping to astronomy.

In 1932 Charles and Zoe Russ decided to move from Sutherland Avenue to a larger and smarter house close to Regent's Park, at 144 Albany Street.[2] Although the teenage brother and sister remained as neglected as ever, the household at Sutherland Avenue bore such grim associations that the transfer to a larger house appears to have made life appear rather more tolerable. The rooms where Dr Russ received his patients were divided from the remainder of the house by double green baize doors. Although Joan (and presumably Patrick) was employed from time to time in cleaning the retorts and other apparatus of the laboratory, at all other times access was rigorously prohibited. Joan never forgot the sinister atmosphere evoked by the double doors and forbidden territory lying beyond. The children were aware that many of the patients who surreptitiously visited their father's premises suffered from venereal ailments, which conferred an atmosphere of revulsion on the excluded region.

Joan often spoke to her family about her days with Patrick at Albany Street, and she and her brother derived much consolation from each other's company. Most of the time they were left to their own devices, wandering about the deserted rooms of the house. They were assigned duties such as clearing the table and washing up after breakfast, which in the absence of their parents were frequently neglected and only hurriedly completed just before their return in the evening.

[1] In *Richard Temple* (pp. 32–33) the protagonist as a boy abstracts small items of especial fascination from his preparatory school laboratory, which few possessed in the 1920s. This may reflect temptations Patrick occasionally found himself unable to resist in his father's laboratory.

[2] The house and virtually the whole of the formerly elegant street have since been destroyed by developers.

This monotonous regime continued for years with very little variation. Patrick and Joan, both gifted with exceptionally vivid imaginations, devised numerous distractions which enabled them to while away the time with some degree of contentment. Fortunately the house was full of books, which they devoured regardless of subject-matter. They played a great deal of chess, and the popular board game halma which the family had enjoyed as children. The latter now belongs to Joan's daughter Gwen: 'The board's playing surface is yellowed but in good condition otherwise, though the back has been scribbled on over the years. I have them [the pieces] in the rather battered tin Mom and Pat kept them in – a faded souvenir of the Coronation of George V and Queen Mary.' Of that strange period in her mother's life, she further recalls:

> In his teenage years Mom said Pat became concerned with style and something of a poser. He liked the Noel Coward image and began to go about the house in the type of silk dressing gowns and cravats Coward wore. He also used a cigarette holder. Pat also developed a taste for all things Oriental. I know from reading about it that there was a general surge of interest at this time in Oriental matters. Mom remembered Pat had a hookah pipe and used it. He also introduced her to Fitzgerald's translation of the 'Rubaiyat of Omar Khayyam' which she always loved and we had 3 or 4 verses read over her grave at the funeral. Mom always spoke of her early years alongside Pat with great affection. They were good companions to each other at a very confusing time.

Gwen's sister Mary adds that her mother's and Patrick's favourite reading included the *Strand Magazine* (in which the Sherlock Holmes stories originally appeared), Somerset Maugham's novels, and the pseudo-Oriental works of Ernest Bramah. To this their brother Harry adds that 'She admired . . . O. Henry. She had a particular fondness for Jerome K Jerome', whose anecdotes had delighted Patrick and Bun at Marylebone Grammar School. Patrick became infatuated with everything relating to the exotic East, and in addition to smoking his hookah and burning joss sticks assumed the role of a connoisseur of teas. He taught Joan to smoke: a habit she retained throughout her life, as did Patrick erratically until he eventually succeeded in giving it up altogether. He gave Joan a Chinese mirror and other Oriental objects, which she preserved to the end of her days. They shared an admiration for the celebrated Austrian tenor Richard Tauber, and were fortunate enough before leaving Sutherland Avenue to attend one of his concerts at the Albert Hall. It was a memorable occasion: King George V and Queen Mary were present, while Tauber sang many of his popular renderings of songs by Puccini and Lehár. A particular favourite of Patrick's at this time was Borodin's Polovtsian Dances from

Prince Igor, but when in old age he waited to hear a performance on the radio he 'did not like them when they came'.

How either of the children would have fared alone does not bear contemplation. They made perfect foils for each other, each being highly intelligent, imaginative, and strong-willed. As a boy and the elder of the pair, Patrick naturally tended to act as the initiator of ideas and projects. In view of his unduly sensitive and competitive nature this was fortunate, since otherwise their happy relationship might have been marred by those quarrels and coldnesses in which Patrick frequently became involved in later life. Nevertheless, Joan contributed as much as she received from their partnership, and the value of the loyal and stimulating comradeship during Patrick's vulnerable teenage years can scarcely be overestimated. Joan herself displayed indications of budding talent as a writer, and though circumstances prevented its ever attaining fruition, her later letters, journals, and jotted memories of early days are remarkable for their fluency and liveliness. In 1973 she privately published a small collection of poetry.

As often occurred in Dr Russ's peripatetic existence, a change of residence stimulated other initiatives. Patrick, who was seventeen at the time of the move to Albany Street, had received no formal education since his withdrawal from Lewes Grammar School three years earlier. Now, however, he was enrolled for a course of evening classes at Birkbeck, a college of London University situated in Malet Street in Bloomsbury. Charles Russ appears belatedly to have realised that his son could not remain for ever kicking his heels at home. Patrick had left school without passing a single examination, and it was essential that he acquire some formal qualification to have any opportunity of gaining employment.

This initiative presents marked contrast to Dr Russ's treatment of his other sons, who were driven to earn their own living the moment they left school. Mike and Bun were obliged to seek unpleasantly menial occupations, and it has been seen that rent was demanded from the latter for the privilege of living at home. It seems that for a time Patrick was regarded with approbation by his parents. Zoe favoured him above her other stepchildren, and Charles had been enthusiastic over the publication of *Cæsar*. However Patrick subsequently sensed that his father's bouts of approval and support stemmed rather from self-indulgence than affection. In much the same way he had enjoyed the company of Godfrey and Victor, when they were of an age to participate in his passion for motorcars.

The fees at Birkbeck College were £5 a term, and Patrick began his studies there in the autumn of 1932. The purpose of the course was to gain the matriculation, which required a pass in five subjects. A restricted choice was permitted, from which Patrick selected mathematics, Latin, French, English, and English history. Though nothing is known of his approach to his studies, it is probable that his character was sufficiently developed to induce him to apply himself seriously to his work.

Joan's recollection of the years she and Patrick spent immured in the large Victorian house, fending off the pervasive tedium, surely represents a realistic picture of their time together. Such an atmosphere is generally not conducive to creativity, and it appears that Patrick found himself only intermittently motivated to summon up sufficient self-discipline to continue the success he had achieved with the publication of *Cæsar*. But it is important to recall how sparse is the available evidence for these years of his life. Thus in old age he recalled a visit to Chester in 1933 where he admired the celebrated 'Rows', but nothing is known of the occasion of his being there.

At the age of eighteen Patrick published two more short stories. In March his 'A Tale about a Peregrine Falcon' was published. An editorial note on 'Our Contributors' noted that 'R.P. Russ has made a name for himself by Nature stories, although he is not much older than *Great-Heart* readers'. This story was examined in the previous chapter for the light it throws on Patrick's experiences during his time at Lewes.

In the same year a second story, entitled 'Wang Khan of the Elephants', was published in *The Oxford Annual for Scouts*. As with its predecessor 'Skogula', 'Wang Khan' owes its inspiration to Kipling's *Jungle Book*: in this case 'Toomai of the Elephants'. In Kipling's tale Toomai's adventure is recounted at some length: challenged by his mocking elders to attend the secret dance of the elephants which no one in recorded memory had witnessed, he rides out into the jungle, observes the astonishing ritual, and returns triumphant to the universal approbation and respect of his fellow mahouts.

Like Toomai, Patrick's hero Little Moti is a cheerful, self-confident urchin ('Lift me up, fat pig,' he urges the elephant), son and grandson of respected mahouts, who is entrusted with the handling of his father Moti Lal's favourite elephant, Wang Khan. Beyond this, there is little resemblance between the two stories. Patrick's tale comprises a sparse four and a half pages. His elephants work for the Amalgamated Teak Company. Moti Lal accompanies Wang Khan, wisest and strongest of the great beasts, to a point in the river where logs are being sorted and floated downstream. Returning from their midday siesta to gather newly felled timber, the elephant team discovers a huge and dangerous log jam blocking the river. The English overseer orders Wang Khan, with Moti Lal on his back, to enter the water and remove a large log at the apex of the obstruction. During this dangerous operation Little Moti falls into the river, where he and his father (who plunges into the water to rescue him) are saved from being crushed to death only by the heroic efforts of Wang Khan, who sacrifices his own life to save his beloved master and his child. Employing his mighty strength to hold back the heaving body of moving logs just long enough to enable father and son to gain the bank, the great elephant is finally swept away and crushed to death far downstream.

The insouciant impudence of Kipling's dauntless child exercised an understandable appeal for Patrick, who had long learned to practise in private mockery of his feared elders. Despite the obvious literary debt, Patrick's fluent prose does not appear a mere pastiche of the master, and his account of the practical aspects of teak-gathering and his representation of Indian dialogue are convincing. In two major respects the treatment differs radically from that of Kipling. In 'Toomai of the Elephants' the English overseer, Petersen, is portrayed (no doubt realistically) as a figure of immense experience and profound understanding of the ways of elephants. He is the first to recognise and acclaim Toomai's extraordinary achievement, and displays strong paternal concern for his well-being when he is injured. As was seen, the story ends on a triumphant note.

In Patrick's story the white superintendent is in contrast a brash and inexperienced young man. He 'rejoiced in the name of Smith . . . and considered himself above taking advice from a native'. It is due to his incompetent handling that the tragedy occurs, and as the log jam grows perilous, 'Smith strode up and down the bank, very scared, and bawling for Wang Kahn'. It is not without significance that Patrick chose to substitute an arrogant and incompetent tyro for Kipling's benign father-figure.

The tragic ending of 'Wang Khan' is likewise characteristic. More often than not Patrick's stories of creatures of the wild conclude either with the brutal death of the protagonist, generally at the hands of a human, or with the creature's savagely avenging himself on his human persecutor.

Patrick wrote the story at the time when he was enthusing Joan with his relish in everything emanating from the gorgeous East, a world of distant glamour which contrasted markedly with the drabness of their solitary London existence. His budding talent was confirmed by the high quality of these stories, which were followed by 'The White Cobra', published in *The Oxford Annual for Boys* in 1934. Once again it is scarcely possible to doubt his debt to Kipling, whose story 'The King's Ankus' in *The Second Jungle Book* includes a majestic white cobra called 'White Hood'. However, it appears to be the idea alone which Patrick borrowed, as his story is entirely original and represents a new development in his literary progress.

The white cobra of Patrick's story is Vakrishna, a serpent venerated by the local Punjabis for its exceptional colour, and regarded as an incarnation of the god Krishna. A wily Muslim snake-charmer named Hussein makes his way to the village near to which lies the serpent's lair, gains the confidence of its inhabitants by his skill at snake-charming, and at night abducts the coveted Vakrishna, substituting one of his own cobras which he had painted white. Exulting over his valuable acquisition, Hussein departs in haste. However at his first halt he is rudely awakened when he is ferociously beaten by the furious villagers, who had pursued him on discovering the loss of their totem.

This is the first of Patrick's stories to feature a well-drawn human figure. Hussein is an adept trickster, who derives infectious pleasure from the skill with which he practises his deceptions. His exploit is recounted in a style imbued with light-hearted cynicism, and its conclusion displays a sardonic humour of which Patrick was to make increasingly effective use in subsequent works. The startled Hussein's unpleasant awakening is explained as follows:

> The priest, apparently more compassionate than the rest, stayed to revive him, and when he came to his senses, Hussein asked him how they had found out his crime.
>
> 'A little before sundown,' said the Brahmin, 'when all the village was assembled, your snake came out, and before our eyes he cast his skin, and I, taking it up in its entirety, clearly perceived the fraud, as the paint flaked off.' And with this the compassionate man beat Hussein more grievously than the others, leaving him for dead.[1]

It is tempting to ascribe Patrick's growing delight in irony to defensive measures evolved during his vulnerable childhood. As a helpless small boy, the only safe means of expressing defiance of oppressive adult authority lay in private mockery of his persecutors, covertly indulged in early days and later shared with his sister Joan. As an adult Patrick tended to shy away from direct confrontation when he felt himself affronted, preferring cold resentment, sarcasm, or bitter allusions in his diary as safer and more satisfying alternatives. Unfortunately this proved as often as not unsatisfactory or even counter-productive, since it tended to irritate or provoke the victim whom it was intended to crush, leaving Patrick little more confident than before – however bold the front he assumed.

This may explain a strange remark in a letter his brother Bun wrote from Canada to Joan in 1989: 'You comment about Pat having a sadistic streak. I did not know that he had subjected you to various forms of torture and bullying, so I am rather disappointed.' Joan's letter has not survived, but

[1] *Beasts Royal*, p. 66.

since it was written at a time when she had come to feel slighted by Patrick it is hard to take the accusation (for which no other evidence exists) seriously. Most likely it represented an intemperately exaggerated reference to times in early years when Patrick had exercised his caustic wit at her expense. It is possible to envisage him as a boy occasionally taking advantage of his superior age and intelligence to mock her relative ignorance, but nothing suggests that he intended real malice at the time, or that she took lasting offence. The tedium of life in Albany Street must have led to minor squabbles and outbursts of mutual irritation.

Taking into consideration the nature of his childhood and adolescence, it is unsurprising that Patrick should have developed a self-absorption amounting almost to solipsism, which could appear to others as insufferable conceit. In one of many revealingly autobiographical passages contained in his novel *The Catalans*, Patrick acknowledged this: 'Upon my word I am not very fond of myself. But I certainly was when I was an adolescent. I passed through my period of mysticism then. Even then I was frightened of damnation; and I was told (and thoroughly believed) that a man's first duty was to save his soul – his primary, imperative need. There may be a more selfish doctrine, but I do not think that I have ever met with one.'[1]

Only through his writing was he able to provide a satisfying corrective to faults and weaknesses of which he was all too painfully conscious. There uncharitable or petulant sarcasm could be transmuted into gently humorous irony, underhand deceptions become wily pranks, and defensive withdrawal courageous defiance.

The year 1934, the third that he and Joan spent in Albany Street, began on a promising note. In January, having completed the two-year course at Birkbeck College, Patrick passed his matriculation. He never alluded to it in later life, instead insinuating or even asserting that he had attended an ancient university. His reticence is understandable in view of the fact that he was nineteen when he took the examination, which his brothers and sisters had passed at the normal age of fourteen or fifteen. On the other hand, he reaped considerable benefit from his belated serious application to the subjects included in his curriculum. Despite his subsequent deprecatory self-assessment of his ability at mathematics, he continued to apply himself to aspects of the discipline, which retained its appeal throughout his life. In particular, after developing an enthusiastic interest in astronomy in the early 1970s, he covered reams of paper with abstruse calculations relating to the positioning of stars observed through his telescope. Researches which he

[1] *The Catalans*, p. 97–98.

conducted in the British Museum a few years after he left home indicate that he had acquired considerable proficiency in French[1] and Latin. With regard to English, by the time he attended Birkbeck he had read widely if eclectically, and can have encountered little difficulty with the subject. Yet he must have gained considerably from a formal course of instruction, which would have introduced him to much worthwhile literature. Similarly, formal study of English history would have gone far to entrench his fascination with the past absorbed during his days at Lewes.

With his examination result satisfactorily achieved, Patrick threw himself energetically into preparation of his second book, which was published that September. It constituted a collection of eleven short stories, including the four he had already published in children's magazines, to which he now added seven others describing adventurous passages in the lives of creatures of the wild. Entitled *Beasts Royal*, the book was handsomely produced with fine illustrations on the dust-jacket and in the text by Charles Tunnicliffe, the gifted wildlife painter.

All the tales are characterised by Patrick's vigorous prose style and realistic depiction of natural history. The additional stories included two adventures involving his scapegrace young hero Hussein, who had made his first appearance in 'The White Cobra'. The first concerns his companionship and exploits with an elephant named Jehangir, successor to the gallant but tragically fated Wang Khan. In the next, Hussein reverts to his professional occupation as a snake-charmer. In a witty variation on Kipling's famous Rikki-tikki-tavi, Patrick makes Hussein secrete a number of snakes about a British political officer's house, which before a gratified audience he induces by his piping to emerge and safely inserts in a sack. However, just as Hussein is concluding his deception, he unexpectedly entices forth 'a great hamadryad cobra, one of the most venomous of snakes' from its hiding place within a drainpipe. A fierce and dangerous battle rages between the noxious creature and Hussein's pet mongoose Jellaludin,[2] who eventually kills and eats the reptile.

Patrick's indebtedness to Kipling in many of these stories is transparent, but his narrative style was too confidently fluent and his originality so patent

[1] A bitter attack on Patrick published after his death included the allegation that 'O'Brian preferred to attribute his mastery of French to his governess and his French-speaking mother – who, it turned out, had died when he was an infant' (*Daily Mail*, 3 October 2003). I very much doubt that Patrick ever advanced such a claim (for which no evidence is cited), particularly since he had publicly declared nearly a decade earlier that 'my mother died a little after the end of the 1914–1918 War' (Cunningham, ed., *Patrick O'Brian*, p. 16).

[1] Jehangir and Jellaludin were named after two early emperors of the Mughal dynasty, in which Patrick evidently took an interest.

that it does not appear to have occurred to anyone to accuse him of attempting a pastiche of the master's work. Nor does he appear at the time to have been concerned that his merit as a writer might be called in question on such a score. Years later, however, he repudiated the author whose works he had once so deeply admired, and to whom he owed so much.

In *Richard Temple* Patrick denounced Kipling through the mouth of his hero as a crude racist. By the time the book was published in 1962 the Indian Empire had vanished, and the mass of English literati united in condemning Kipling as an outmoded imperialist. Concerned not to be seen to espouse reactionary views, Patrick shifted his estimate accordingly. Privately, however, he continued to acknowledge Kipling's rare talent and influence on his own writing. In 1974 he noted in his diary: 'RK a deeply vulgar fascisant essentially false brute but with such ability & more than ability – How well I know that from 40+ years ago: & what a wretched influence on a silly false romantic boy.'

At the time Patrick wrote his early Indian tales he not only entertained unfettered enthusiasm for Kipling, but also shared contemporary admiration for British achievements in India. Although in 'Wang Khan of the Elephants' the white Sahib is a self-important youth, both in *Cæsar* and Hussein's successive adventures English officers and supervisors tend to feature as the masterful, sympathetic characters portrayed by Kipling. Among the books Patrick clearly enjoyed at this time was *Bengal Lancer*, the autobiography of Major F. Yeats-Brown. Published in 1930, the popular memoir recounted in dashing style the author's youthful adventures and exploration of Hindu mysticism during his service with one of the élite cavalry regiments of the Indian army. It was presumably from *Bengal Lancer* that Patrick took the name of the mahout in his 'Wang Khan of the Elephants', Moti Lal being an elephant ridden by Yeats-Brown on an exciting pig-sticking expedition.[1]

In particular, boys placed in such a predicament tend to envisage themselves as beasts or birds of prey – tigers, eagles, and the like – whose literally superhuman strength and ferocity confer on them powers immeasurably superior to those of the most daunting of adult men.[2] Certain

[1] Hussein's fortunate discovery of a gold mohur among the copper coinage given him by the Rajah's dishonest treasurer (*Hussein*, p. 178) echoes an exchange between Yeats-Brown and a guru at the Taj Mahal: 'Take your gold mohur, Sahib. These two rupees will feed me for two weeks' (F. Yeats-Brown, *Bengal Lancer*, London, 1930, p. 115). Subsequently Yeats-Brown appears to have been cast with Kipling into Patrick's mental oubliette, for it is surely he who is intended by a contemptuous reference to 'theosophistic retired Indian Army officers' in an unpublished short story Patrick wrote at the beginning of 1955. In his memoir Yeats-Brown describes an audience with Mrs Annie Besant, high priestess of theosophy.

[2] Cf. Alfred Adler, *Problems of Neurosis: A Book of Case-Histories* (London, 1929), pp. 150–51.

revealing motifs recur throughout Patrick's animal stories. For a start, the protagonist is without exception a formidable predator or possessed of overwhelming strength. As the dust-jacket description of *Beasts Royal* observed: 'His animals have regal qualities; they are the kings of the beasts. There is Wang Khan the elephant, chief of his herd; Shark 206, the terror of the pearl fishers; Vakrishna, the white cobra. Other mighty animals in his pages are leopard, gorilla, condor and rhinoceros. Each is the hero of a life and death adventure.' In all but one story Patrick's creature overcomes a formidable adversary in a ferocious struggle. Not infrequently the hero's bloody victory is followed by his own death, inflicted by a fresh adversary while he is in a vulnerably stricken state. As often as not the enemy is a man, who only manages to overcome his naturally more powerful opponent by inequitable use of harpoon, gun, or bow.

Patrick unconsciously sought to endow himself with the powers of a wild beast, whose strength and aggression offered protection in a hostile world. Despite this, many of his protagonists come to a gruesome but heroic end. In *Richard Temple* the hero is portrayed as a mild self-effacing character, who nevertheless when provoked to physical combat displays a violent ferocity which daunts his adversaries. However when he is nearly killed in a car crash, a traumatic experience described in terms suggesting that it is effectively intended as his 'death', the chapter concludes with the words: '. . . he lay quiet in a welling pool of blood and a thick close crowd gathered to watch him die, pressing closer about the dark blood'.

That Patrick envisaged death as an ever-present possibility is suggested by a cryptic entry in my mother's diary for 20 October 1951, written not long before he began work on *Richard Temple*: 'P. wrote his death dream.' It must have been about the same time that he wrote a brief reflection entitled 'The Soul', in which he pondered the disturbing implications of death and its impenetrable aftermath.[1]

The implications of Patrick's symbiotic projection into the animal kingdom become clearer still when the outcome of his near-death experience in *Richard Temple* is compared with the concluding passage of *Cæsar*. The panda-leopard lies dying from wounds sustained defending his wife and cubs from a pack of wolves:

> My strength was ebbing fast, and I was weak like a little cub again. I looked at my wife, but I could not see her so clearly . . . I glanced up for the sun, forgetting where I was.

[1] *Lying in the Sun and Other Stories* (London, 1956), pp. 115–16. The setting is the cemetery at Collioure, where Patrick now lies.

> I looked at her again, and she seemed very far off and misty, like my mother was when I saw her in the hut years before.
>
> Then a terrible pain shot through me, and when it died away I could only just feel her licking, and I sank into a wonderful dream, in which everything seemed far off, and I thought I saw my master, and then –[1]

When Richard Temple awakes in hospital, 'propped up in the attitude of pneumoniac[2] death, with rubber tubes in his nostrils, stuck by adhesive plaster; he was not suffering in any way, for not only was he somewhat apart from his body but his body too was below suffering now; and he knew that if he chose to make no effort he could die – that death (at least this death) was not what he had expected or feared, and that it was in fact rather friendly than otherwise, a profound quiet'.

It is not just Richard's acceptance of the inevitability of death as a peaceful sleep affording escape from life's harsh rigours which parallels Cæsar's end. Just as Cæsar feels himself melting away into a warm vision of his wife and mother, Richard Temple awakes in his hospital bed to find a beautiful stranger sitting beside him. She proves to be the heroine of the story, Philippa Brett – a barely fictionalised representation of my mother, Patrick's lifelong companion and supporter. It seems that for Patrick death represented complex alternatives of boding menace and contented relapse into a haven of feminine protectiveness.

[1] *Cæsar*, p. 88.

[2] The adjective is inappropriate to the context, and inevitably recalls Patrick's recurrent respiratory problems.

SIX

Bohemian Days

> When we came upon Highgate hill and had a view of London, I was all life and joy. I repeated Cato's soliloquy on the immortality of the soul, and my soul bounded forth to a certain prospect of happy futurity. I sung all manner of songs, and began to make one about an amorous meeting with a pretty girl, the burthen of which was as follows:
>
> She gave me this, I gave her that;
> And tell me, had she not tit for tat?
>
> I gave three huzzas and we went briskly in.
>
> (James Boswell, *Journal*, 19 November 1762)

In 1934 Patrick was nineteen. Although the dreary time in Albany Street had not improved his relationship with his father, the passing of years introduced a subtle difference into their relationship. While he remained in many respects as vulnerable as ever and his father's authority as unchallengeable, each was moving towards a fresh stage in his life.

The time finally arrived when Charles Russ (very likely prompted by Zoe) accepted that his son must enter upon a career. In 1927 inadequate schooling and lack of self-discipline had prevented his entering Dartmouth, denying him the opportunity of becoming an officer in the Royal Navy. However, he and his father remained attached to the idea of his pursuing a career in the armed services, and the purpose of his belated undertaking of the matriculation at Birkbeck College was presumably to qualify him for the profession for which he applied that summer.

By 1934 Hitler had been Chancellor of Germany for over a year, and concern was voiced in Britain and France at the threat presented by German rearmament. Widespread public faith in the efficacy of the League of Nations and similar panaceas for maintenance of world peace greatly impeded the British Government's efforts to build up the country's military resources. On 20 July 1934 a programme was introduced in the House of Commons for increasing the strength of the RAF over the coming years. Although its inadequacy was vigorously denounced by Winston Churchill, who was privately apprised of the true extent of Germany's alarming progress in aircraft production, even this half-hearted measure was strongly opposed by the Socialist and Liberal parties, committed as they were to policies of appeasement.

While nothing suggests that Patrick entertained particular interest in politics at this time (it was not a sphere which ever concerned him deeply), the idea of joining the armed services presented obvious appeal. Even his father could not have persuaded himself that the boy was likely to adapt himself to the humdrum careers into which his two eldest brothers had been conveniently steered, and the indications are that he was impressed by his youngest son's precocious talent. While military service did not require high academic qualifications, the glamour and prestige associated with officer rank would undoubtedly have appealed to Charles Russ's class-conscious outlook. However modest and tardily achieved, Patrick's matriculation qualified him for acceptance by the Army or Air Force. He chose the Royal Air Force.

Any suggestion that Patrick suffered from serious ill health at this time of his life is irrefutably invalidated by this career move. He could not have been accepted as a recruit had he really suffered from the ailments to which he later alluded, and on 7 May his medical examination passed him 'Fit as Pilot'. Though unfortunately his medical report has not survived among RAF records, the examination would certainly have been rigorous.

Having passed his interview and medical examination, he was accepted as an acting pilot officer on a probational six-year commission. On 14 September he arrived with other young recruits at the RAF Inland Area Depot at Uxbridge, Middlesex. There he was issued with his uniform and other equipment, and a fortnight later he and his companions were posted to No. 5 Flying Training School at Sealand, five miles north-west of Chester.

There the recruits began a course of intensive training, which involved a rigorous daily round of practical instruction, parade-ground drill, PT, rugby, boxing, and rifle-shooting on the range. Much classroom work was also required, some idea of its scope being indicated by Patrick's official RAF Pocket Book. Its contents cover multitudinous topics ranging from aircraft maintenance and recognition to night flying procedure, protection from gas attack, camouflage skills, and methods of erecting temporary aeroplane hangars. It further included a daunting range of esoteric information, including knot-tying, butchering, camp cooking, and the most efficacious mode of constructing field latrines. Though such ingenious and varied activities would normally have appealed to Patrick, they were less acceptable when administered under conditions of military discipline.

A characteristic indication of the unreality of the times was the manual's omission of Germany from the illustrated catalogue of International Aircraft Markings, presumably on the grounds that Germany was not supposed to have an air force at that period. Reminders of Britain's worldwide imperial responsibilities were reflected in instructions dealing with 'Salvaging Aero Engines by Camel Transport', 'Examples of Native Daily Rations', or 'Characteristics of an Arab Raiding Party'. Other entries could have come straight from Patrick's adventure stories:

> 316. The Akhwan, or villagers of Ibn Saud, may be distinguished from the Bedouins by the white kerchiefs worn round their heads like turbans instead of 'Agals.' These should be distinguishable from a thousand feet.
>
> 319. Kurdish Tribes. – Kurds live only in the hills and on the lower spurs, and are distinguished from Arabs by their loose, baggy trousers. They may be roughly grouped into nomads (called Kochar), semi-nomads, and settled cultivators. Sheep form the chief wealth of Kurds.

However, Patrick encountered little that was romantic among the barracks and hangars of the unlovely RAF station at Sealand, set as it was in an isolated location beside the desolate mudflats of the estuary of the Dee. Abruptly he was plunged into an existence for which his character and experience could scarcely have been more unsuited.

One aspect of the training of officers, upon which great emphasis was laid, was their abrupt initiation into the arcane practices of service life. They had to learn to accept unquestioningly whatever duties were imposed upon them, however unpleasant or pointless they might appear, and accommodate themselves to the rough-and-tumble of barracks life and time-honoured etiquette of the officers' mess. These activities ranged from mastering the abstruse niceties of hierarchical relations between ranks to the robust and often violent horseplay which traditionally plays a major part in the life of junior officers in all branches of the armed forces.

All this presented little problem to young men who had just come down from public school, to whom it was little more than an extension of a life to which they were fully accustomed: strict discipline, subtle gradations of status, close companionship, and emphasis on physical prowess on and off the games field. In addition most had experienced a foretaste of military discipline in their school's OTC (Officers' Training Corps). Many of their parents had served in the Great War, their experience and attitude making the rigours of military service appear an accepted way of life to their juniors.

None of these considerations bore remote application to Patrick. His father's age had precluded his serving in the War. Whereas most of his fellows arrived straight from school, he had left Lewes Grammar School five years previously. He had never attended a boarding-school, nor enjoyed the companionship of a friend, nor even owned a pet. It would be easy but uncharitable to mock the pretension of Patrick's reply to a journalist, who questioned him about the emphasis laid on friendship in the Aubrey–Maturin novels: '"One's friends at school and university were very, very dear and life just drives you apart . . . ."'[1] Patrick was always conscious of the fact that in reality he had neither possessed any schoolfriends nor attended university.

For years his sole close companion had been his younger sister, while the Russ household was characterised by an almost total absence of discipline and order. Patrick's thin-skinned character was such that he found the stringent discipline and boisterous camaraderie to which he was now exposed equally repugnant. His sensitive and introspective nature made him prone to resent authority and swift to take offence, while he was wholly inexperienced in establishing relationships with people of any age – least of all those robust and carefree young men with whom he was now compelled to spend every moment of the day and night.

Patrick's new comrades are unlikely to have found him a congenial companion. Not without justification, Patrick held a high opinion of his own intellectual talents. When he applied to join the RAF, he must have felt conscious pride in his description of his 'Prior Occupation' as 'Author & Secretarial Work for father'. The very month of his arrival at the Uxbridge depot saw the publication of *Beasts Royal*: the latest success in a literary career which included the appearance of a highly praised novel and a succession of short stories.

Patrick must have entertained high expectations of the prestige he might enjoy among a set of companions fresh from school, and he would not have been slow to let them know what sort of figure had arrived among them. However he was received initially, it cannot have been long before he became regarded as a bumptious young prig who needed taking down a peg or two. His natural reaction would have been withdrawal into a pose of lofty indifference, punctuated by expressions of disdainful sarcasm in face of provocations.

Dean King, whose description of Patrick's brief spell in the RAF reflects imaginative reconstruction from accounts by others trained at No. 5 Flying Training School, suggests that: 'The school held boxing and rugby matches

[1] *Financial Times*, 11–12 January 1997.

in which the airmen proved their grit. These were undoubtedly tough on Patrick, who was among the smallest in his class and physically weak . . .'[1]

This appears unwarranted. When he joined up, Patrick included among his previous attainments 'Cricket, football, boxing': sports which he may well have practised during his four years at grammar schools. After leaving he enjoyed no further opportunity to engage in field games, and it is unlikely that he continued boxing. However there is no reason to suppose that he was 'among the smallest in his class' (he was of average height), and he was emphatically not 'physically weak'. On the contrary, unless there occurred some revolutionary improvement in his constitution over the next decade, he was unusually lithe and strong.

Unfortunately physical strength and courage alone would not have sufficed to afford Patrick protection against sustained baiting or maltreatment by combined adversaries, and a situation in which he found himself surrounded by real or fancied persecutors would have appeared insupportable. Though he occasionally mentioned to me his early enthusiasm for boxing, he never referred to his brief service in the RAF. However there are passages in his fiction which reflect his attitude towards his experience.

The central figure of Patrick's short story 'The Happy Despatch' is unmistakably autobiographical. Written fourteen years after the time of his service in the RAF, it recounts a sinister event experienced by a man named Woollen, who has retired from an unsuccessful career in the British Army to a remote corner of Ireland, where he enters upon an equally hopeless attempt to maintain himself on a small farm – as was eventually to be Patrick's own experience.

Reminiscing to himself about the successive disasters which had plagued his life, Woollen pondered this dismal recollection of his military service:

> With neither connections nor abilities, he had found his way into one of the nastiest of infantry regiments, and he had passed several unenviable years in association with a number of third-rate subalterns who, sensing his timidity, had from the first used him ill. He had been their butt, and they had shown an ape-like ingenuity in making him wretched. Some of them had traded on the kindness of his stupid heart.[2]

Tobias Barrow, the absent-minded but erudite young surgeon's mate in Patrick's early naval novel *The Unknown Shore*, is an obvious prototype of Stephen Maturin; each of them in varying degree personified Patrick

[1] King, *Patrick O'Brian*, p. 62.
[2] *The Last Pool*, p. 49.

himself. Tobias's amiable otherworldliness makes him the butt of two loutish fellow-members of the midshipmen's mess, who subject him to a number of unpleasant practical jokes. On one occasion he dislodges a bucket of water which his persecutors had balanced over a door, which to his acute distress destroys precious drawings representing hours of careful labour. His robust friend Jack Byron 'had told him many and many a time that it was only a joke, that they meant no harm, and that one must take a laugh against oneself', and Tobias set about gathering up his ruined work, reflecting resignedly that doubtless he would be able to complete it again in due course. 'The need for putting up with barbarity was something he could not understand, however. He took Jack's repeated assurances that it was so, but he had never been to school nor mixed with people of his own age, and the whole thing remained incomprehensible and sad.'[1]

Tobias survives his time of travail, and under Admiral Anson's command rounds the Horn in HMS *Wager* and returns home triumphant with the gold of the Spanish Indies. His creator's fate was less happy. On arrival at Sealand, Patrick and his companions began their flying training. Initially this involved instruction on the ground, followed by lessons conducted in the RAF's standard training aeroplane, the Avro Tutor. However in Patrick's case it is unlikely that his experience extended beyond classroom instruction and practice on the ground. In *Richard Temple* he makes his hero recall 'the parachute-tower from which you were dropped with the thing already open, but you were always supposed to go through the motions of pulling the rip-cord and if you did not (you wished them all to hell) the fat man in charge would cry, *it isn't cricket, Temple*, in real distress'.[2]

Patrick's active training lasted barely three weeks. Having begun on 1 October, he was withdrawn on the 25th. A month later he was formally discharged from the RAF, and on 4 December this announcement appeared in the *London Gazette*:

> Royal Air Force: The short service commissions of the undermentioned Acting Pilot Officers in probation are terminated on cessation of duty – 29th November 1934: William Ocock Pridham, Douglas George Scott; 1st December 1934: Basil Stuart Francis, Richard Patrick Russ, Thomas Brisbane Yule.

A number of conjectures have been advanced as to the cause of Patrick's

[1] *The Unknown Shore*, p. 109.

[2] *Richard Temple*, pp. 279–80. In Wales Patrick described to Edgar Williams the safe way of jumping from a cart, explaining that it was based on the landing technique employed by parachutists.

being dismissed the service, the most extreme of which was his brother Bun's belief that he had crashed an aeroplane on one or more occasions.[1] In reality his dismissal arose from nothing so melodramatic. He neither crashed nor suffered any injury, and the abrupt termination of his military service did not relate in any way to his state of health.

The true reason is clearly set out in his RAF record, in which he is disparagingly described as a 'Very backward pupil who appears to be temperamentally unsuitable. Unlikely to make an efficient service pilot.' Precisely what this implied is not specified, but not hard to infer. It was less his ability to handle the controls of an aeroplane which was called in question, than the fact that he was, in time-honoured military parlance, 'not officer material'. He distanced himself from his fellows, whom he regarded with disdain as immature noisy boors: an attitude which in turn provoked derision and antagonism. Much more seriously, he would have found it difficult to accept superior orders with good grace.

Unable to rid himself of his mistrustful attitude towards the world ingrained in him during his formative years, Patrick never succeeded in overcoming his apprehension and discomfort in company. He generally found almost any sort of instruction (real or fancied) intolerable, interpreting it as patronising and implying inadequacy on his part.

Apart from being pre-eminently unsuited to a military career, there are hints that Patrick's discharge may have been provoked by some form of nervous breakdown. While it is important to avoid unwarranted speculation, it is not unlikely that Patrick's constitutional inability to bear the combination of authoritarian discipline and social disorder required by his military training could have brought on a nervous crisis. The unfortunate loss of his RAF medical record prevents one from learning whether some incongruous references in *Richard Temple* to an incendiary attempt reflect a frantic action perpetrated by Patrick at Sealand.

Though I do not believe he ever alluded publicly to it, he retained pride and residual affection for his brief service with the Royal Air Force. He carefully preserved his RAF Pocket Book and the 'wings' from his uniform cap as mementoes, and many years later wrote to my mother when she was staying in London asking her to buy him an RAF tie. This suggests that he enlisted with high expectations, and that his summary dismissal imbued him with increased sensations of disappointment and failure.

[1] In 1989 Bun wrote to Joan: 'I think he was invalided out of the Air Force or was just let go, because I think he had smashed a couple of aeroplanes in the course of his training.' Dean King believes that 'some accident did occur during Patrick's RAF training (he would complain of a bad back)' (King, *Patrick O'Brian*, p. 70).

Following his departure from the RAF, he returned home to enter upon a period of his life which is as crucial to understanding his complex character as his early upbringing. Frustratingly, however, the ensuing five years of Patrick's life are sparsely chronicled, fitful light being thrown only where chance has preserved records of varying significance and reliability.

About the time that Patrick entered the RAF his father, who was now fifty-eight, decided to retire from a medical practice which had ceased to function in much more than name. Evidently reluctant to acknowledge his implicit failure, he continued to list his surgery in the rooms he rented at 50 George Street in the *Medical Directory* for a further three years. Whether he maintained premises there is not known. Whatever the situation, by 1939 even this charade was dropped and his entry reduced to a laconic 'address uncommunicated'.

In the winter of 1934–35 Charles and Zoe Russ left London with their sole remaining child Joan to live at Crowborough in Sussex. Patrick had no alternative after his discharge on Christmas Day 1934 but to rejoin them in the new family home. It is not hard to imagine his shame and disappointment, but the nature of his reception is not known – unless the spluttering indignation of Canon Harler in *Richard Temple* reflects a measure of reality.

It seems that Patrick and his father had been on reasonably cordial terms before he took the train to Uxbridge with such high hopes in September. *Beasts Royal* was dedicated 'To my Father'. It is likely that Dr Russ was as enthusiastic a supporter of this literary venture as he had been for the publication of *Cæsar* four years earlier. Presumably he (or at any rate Zoe) paid for Patrick's two years' evening classes at Birkbeck College, which again suggests a generally supportive attitude. Whatever long-term plan was contemplated when Patrick began the course, by the time he came to take his matriculation it must have been regarded as his passport to a full-time career as a Royal Air Force officer. As the services are discreet about their reasons for rejecting recruits, Patrick may have been able to ascribe his dismissal to ill health or some other acceptable cause.

Overall it does not appear that relations between the insensitive self-absorbed father and his touchy, introspective son ever extended much beyond outward show of mutual respect as Patrick entered manhood. Zoe, who regarded Patrick with affection, probably sympathised with his disappointment, and this would have mitigated the unhappy consequences of her stepson's failure. Certainly the loyal Joan will have commiserated with him: indeed, she cannot but have welcomed his unexpected return. Following what had been assumed to be his permanent departure, she faced the prospect of remaining immured for the indefinite future with her father and stepmother in their remote country retreat.

Although far from spacious, so far as the two youngsters were concerned Ford Field Cottage possessed many advantages over the larger house at Albany Street. Whereas in London they had little to occupy themselves save read, play board games, and indulge in shared imaginative fantasies, they were now free to explore the beautiful countryside around Crowborough. The cottage was situated in an isolated location in Ashdown Forest, where Patrick could indulge his long-standing enthusiasm for natural history. While no contemporary account has survived of the time he spent there, both he and Joan subsequently attested to the warmth of their recollection of the cottage and surrounding landscape.

On 8 January 1967 Patrick made an expedition with my mother to revisit the house. Though it was a bitterly cold day with snow on the ground, old memories came flooding back, afflicting him with profound nostalgia. He described the visit in a letter he wrote to Joan in 1979, and it is clear that after twelve years the emotional experience had not dimmed. Possibly inspired by this, Joan herself travelled to the cottage in September of the following year.

In a further letter to Joan in 1981, Patrick wrote:

> When I was in England some years ago I too went on a sentimental pilgrimage to Sussex . . . I went to Crowborough, which I hardly recognized until I reached Smugglers' Lane – no alteration there until I was down at the far end, and there was the Cottage, even smaller than I had remembered it – Lord, to think that we could live in that box, even with the wooden sheds! But alas it was empty at that time, and abandoned and the garage that Daddy had put up a little farther down was falling to pieces. It fairly went to my heart, and I did not go down the leafy lane into Ashdown Forest as I had intended but turned the car and drove away into the present as fast as ever I could.

The situation of the leafy retreat, with its 'Smugglers' Lane', is reminiscent of the setting of many a scene in Jeffrey Farnol's Sussex novels.[1] Whether or not this contributed to its appeal, the cherished memories which the sight of their old home aroused in brother and sister were associated with the romantic locality, and had little to do with their relationship to their parents. Throughout his life Patrick was wont to record lasting attachment to places, but only rarely to people.

[1] When Jack Aubrey and Stephen Maturin ride through Ashdown Forest, Jack warns Stephen to check the flints of his pistols since they are entering a haunt of highwaymen (*Post Captain*, pp. 52–53).

It is apparent from their descriptions that while living in the cottage at Crowborough in 1935, brother and sister spent much time wandering in the forest, and the impression is that they projected on to it a visionary landscape of their own devising. However, his settled life at Ford Field Cottage cannot have lasted more than a few months, and certainly did not exceed a year. He later returned to his parents' home from time to time, and that he was treated as a welcome visitor is indicated by the fact that four years later they invited him to stay in order to recuperate from a bout of illness.

It was probably during the months he lived at Crowborough that Patrick wrote two further short stories. Though he was now twenty he continued writing for children, albeit at a sophisticated level. In 1935 *The Oxford Annual for Scouts* published 'The Snow Leopard', a hunting story set in Nepal. During its climactic episode, the boy hero of the tale panics while he and a Gurkha officer, Major Chetwynd, are engaged in scaling a precipitous cliff. The kindly Major helps him to a safer spot and arouses the boy's profound gratitude when, describing their adventure to his father, he says nothing of the boy's momentary terror and instead emphasises the danger of the ascent. Is it too much to detect here Patrick's own longing for recognition from a father, from whom he had belatedly received a modicum of support and approval? Or more specifically, could it reflect understanding acceptance by his father of his failure to make the grade in the RAF?

His second story that year, published in *The Oxford Annual for Boys*, recounts a further adventure in the life of the wily and cynical Hussein, for whom Patrick and his readers entertained understandable affection. In 'Cheetah' the talented young man bribes Yussuf, an initially reluctant elderly trainer of cheetahs, with opium to allow him to handle the hunting animals. During a hunt staged before the Rajah who owns the cheetahs, a leopard charges on to the ground and attacks Yussuf. Hussein valiantly flings himself on to the fierce beast in an attempt to save the old man, and after a desperate struggle the Rajah succeeds in shooting the animal. Overcome with gratitude, Yussuf adopts Hussein as his blood-brother, and is richly rewarded by the Rajah. Here again we encounter the motif of a boy's engaging the affection and respect of a father-figure.

Unfortunately this throws no light on the circumstances of Patrick's life at the cottage in Sussex, particularly as the stories may have been written before his brief term of service in the RAF. However Patrick's dedication to *Beasts Royal* does indicate paternal approval of his work which is likely to have extended to his further literary endeavours, and it seems that his father extended towards him at this time at least a measure of tolerance and even goodwill.

Generally speaking, however, numerous members of the present generation of the Russ family attest to parental memories of their grandfather's indifference and neglect of his children, not infrequently extending to brutal unkindness. It seems unlikely that Patrick's lasting resentment would have occurred had relations between them been actively affectionate during the final years he spent at home after leaving school.

Dr and Mrs Russ had never concerned themselves unduly with the maintenance of their successive family homes, and conditions in the household deteriorated radically now that they were living in reduced circumstances far from former acquaintances. Although there was adequate room in the house, Joan was obliged to sleep in an outhouse and attend effectively as a servant on her father and stepmother. Joan's daughter Gwen points out that 'Mom's schooling was very haphazard, and it seems she hardly went to school at all between the ages of 9 and 16'. On their arrival at Crowborough her parents belatedly decided to grant her a residual measure of schooling. Initially this presented problems that were distressing to the unhappy girl. She had mistakenly come to believe that her birth had been the cause of her mother's death, but whether this delusion originated with her father is unclear. Her stepmother appears to have regarded the four girls with more or less equal resentment, but as the one who lived alone with her parents long after all the others had departed, Joan's suffering was the most acute.

Given her sisters' confirmation of their stepmother's cruelty there is no reason to believe she exaggerated the extent of her maltreatment. One horrific occasion occurred when Joan experienced her first menstruation. It was an event for which she was totally unprepared. Frightened on discovering her sheets inexplicably stained with blood, she ran to inform her stepmother – whose reaction was to punch her savagely in the stomach.

Before long the ramshackle state of the cottage at Crowborough became notorious in the neighbourhood, and the Russes gained a reputation for squalid bohemianism. When Joan was first taken to be enrolled at a nearby school, she was rejected on the grounds that no one could expect a respectable establishment to accept a pupil from that house 'up on the hill'. Fortunately she was admitted to Tunbridge Wells High School. It says much for her intelligence that, despite the extended gap in her prior education, it was not long before she flourished at the High School. In 1936 she won the Upper Fifth Form Prize, a copy of *The Approach to Librarianism* by Henry A. Sharp. The book was chosen at her suggestion, since for some time her love of literature led her to nurture the ambition of becoming a librarian.

However this was not to be, and after leaving school she worked first as a student teacher, and then as secretary for an insurance office in Tunbridge Wells. She continued living at home, presumably because the small salary paid at that time of acute unemployment left her no choice in the matter. Despite the fact that she was now a working adult, she continued to be subjected to a regime little less repressive than before. Even modest use of make-up and lipstick was harshly forbidden by her stepmother. Joan accordingly resigned herself to remaining something of a gawky tomboy. Once when her elder brother Victor came to stay, he was told by his father and stepmother that they had tried to persuade Joan to join the local tennis club to meet young people, but she refused on the grounds of shyness. Since she was an exceptionally strong-minded girl, a more likely explanation was shame at her lack of decent clothing and equipment.

Long before any of this occurred Patrick had left his family for good and departed to seek his fortune in London. This major step took place in 1935, the year following his rejection by the RAF. There is a tantalising indication that he underwent a significant experience in Oxford some time that year. In his diary on 26 May 1985 he records: 'I took . . . bus to Oxford – to the middle of Oxford, first by Worcester [College]. I went first by Univ[ersity College] (wch I hardly recognized, & the [?] are largely gone) to Magdalen bridge, retracing my 1st steps 50 years ago . . . I grew sad & weary.'

Given Patrick's accuracy in such reckonings, this would place the previous visit he clearly found so memorable in 1935. Could it be that he attempted the entrance examination to one of the colleges that summer? Once when his friend Richard Ollard, innocently leaving him no opportunity for evasion, happened to ask him where he was at university he replied 'University College, Oxford'. (Richard later learned from a girl working at the college that it possessed no record of his attendance.) When for Christmas 1983 I sent Patrick an anthology on the university, he commented in his diary: 'reading . . . N's book on Oxford, wch has some fine things in it wch makes me v sad.' It looks as though he may have tried and failed the examination for Oxford that summer.

In 1985 he noted 'A letter fr the secretary of Brooks's saying that I was elected on 19 XII. It wd have been humiliating to be refused, & horribly public.' Few surely would regard such a rebuff as particularly humiliating, and a rejection would not have been made public at all. When he could feel so sensitive about so relatively trifling a matter as membership of a club, the extent of Patrick's shame at having failed to enter university is understandable.

With his arrival in London begins the most ill-documented and mysterious period of Patrick's life. I have been unable to discover for certain the circumstances of his leaving home, the expectations which instigated so decisive a move, where exactly he lived on arrival, nor how he maintained and occupied himself on a day-to-day basis. Occasional isolated matters of significance can be established on reliable evidence, but the rest remains tantalisingly uncertain and in large part irrecoverable. While frankly conceding that 'There is little documentary evidence of events during this part of his life', Dean King unfortunately sought to bridge the gulf by introducing a discursive account of Dylan Thomas's picaresque life in Chelsea at the time. However, no reliable evidence exists that Patrick ever experienced any contact, direct or indirect, with Thomas,[1] and it is necessary to search elsewhere to recover something of the turbulent and decisive period of Patrick's life in London during the pre-war years.

Material facts which can be established with certainty are so sparse as effectively to be summarised in a brief paragraph. Patrick, who was now aged twenty, left home to live in London, where he settled in Chelsea. Shortly after his arrival he married, and subsequently his wife bore him a son and daughter. During this time he travelled to Ireland and spent a summer in Italy – in each case, possibly more than once. He published three short stories and a book, and engaged in research for a further work which he never completed.

However there exists one valuable source which, if employed with discretion, goes far to illumine the obscurity of Patrick's life between 1935 and 1940. This is his novel *Richard Temple*, to which extensive reference has already been made in relation to his schooldays at Lewes. The idea of the story came to him suddenly on 12 March 1953. Although at times he encountered severe difficulties in its composition, thanks to my mother's enthusiastic encouragement he completed the book on 16 January of the following year. His American publisher Harcourt Brace displayed initial interest on being sent the first chapter and a synopsis, but subsequently changed their mind, and it was not until after extensive rewriting and further attempts to interest publishers that the book finally made its belated appearance in 1962.

Richard Temple is unique among Patrick's books, not only for the protracted delay in its publication but in that it was originally written as a quite different story. Whereas in the published version the eponymous central character engages in minute examination of his earlier life while incarcerated in a German gaol in Occupied France in 1944, its predecessor focused entirely on Temple's adventures after he was dropped as a British agent behind enemy lines in southern France, and only culminated with his

[1] In 1975 he read the biography of Dylan Thomas by Constantine FitzGibbon, on which he made several observations in his diary. Had he had any direct acquaintance with the poet, I strongly doubt he would have withheld reference to it.

capture by the Germans. For some reason Patrick became dissatisfied with this work and some four months later informed my mother of his plan to recast it entirely in the form of what he described as his 'Chelsea novel'.

Significantly, Patrick altered the name of his protagonist from William in the earlier version to his own first name, Richard, in the second. It has been seen how closely the account of Richard Temple's childhood and relationship with his father followed Patrick's own youthful experience, while the description of his schooldays at 'Easton Colborough' represents an almost entirely factual account of the three largely contented years he spent at Lewes. It will be further shown how closely the concluding biographical section describing Richard's romantic attachment to the beautiful Philippa Brett reflects the opening stages of Patrick's relationship with my mother.

As Patrick's informal title 'Chelsea novel' indicates, the greater part of the book recounts his hero's experience as a young man eking out a bohemian existence in pre-war Chelsea. This section likewise contains much that is autobiographical, but the paucity of confirmatory evidence makes it requisite to employ considerable caution when taking it as a basis for reconstruction of Patrick's own life.

Richard, a talented artist, arrives all but penniless in Chelsea to study at art school. His existence is punctuated by what he acknowledges to have been a series of squalid sexual affairs, for the most part conducted with promiscuous girls of widely ranging social background and limited education, or married women eager for titillation to enliven their humdrum bourgeois existence. Much of the narrative is taken up with discussions, part-intelligent and part-pretentious, concerning art, the meaning of life, and topics of similarly profound concern to imaginative young men enjoying their first years of freedom from the constraints of boyhood. Temple is represented as part anti-hero, part contemptuous observer of the foibles and deceits of the shallow and mercenary society into which he is thrown. His account is broadly cast in the form of a confessional, in which he is woundingly honest about humiliating experiences he has undergone.

Considerable emphasis is laid throughout on Temple's deficiencies: the mortification inflicted upon him by his poverty, the regularity with which he allows himself to be seduced by women for whom he entertains neither respect nor liking, his awkwardness in company, his snobbish regard for class and status and corresponding weakness in permitting himself to be patronised and manipulated by people of superior social background, and his abject fear of authority. At the same time his stoical refusal to succumb to the barbaric treatment meted out by his German interrogators leads to his spiritual redemption, and the novel concludes on a strongly symbolic note with his last-minute rescue by the forces of the French Resistance.

Thus, with all his innumerable faults, Richard is portrayed as an ultimately virtuous figure engaged in a Sisyphean struggle to triumph over burdensome handicaps inflicted upon him by an unkind fate. The leitmotif is Richard's valiant resistance to the cruelty of his sadistic Nazi captors, who are bent on extracting the names of his contacts in the French Resistance. He emerges triumphant, having skilfully used his former weakness to outwit the remorseless cunning of his persecutors.

Richard's cover story is that he is a small-time black-market racketeer, which accounts for his secretive behaviour and initial reluctance to explain his activities. To this end he creates what he terms his 'pseudo-Temple', a figure conjured up from his earlier self. This ploy provides ingenious means for Patrick to describe and dissect the vagaries of his own youth. It was a period of his life which he wished to forget: a time of inadequacy and failure, culminating in events he had reason to regard with shame. Significantly the crisis itself (which will be recorded in due course) does not feature in the novel, at least not in anything approaching realistic terms. There was a sharp limit even to Patrick's self-laceration.

Autobiographical in character as this section of the novel undoubtedly is, it is after all a novel. Some of its characters are clearly invented, while others drawn from life are introduced from later periods in Patrick's life. To take but one example which happens to be known to me: not long after his arrival in London Richard meets and resumes his friendship with Charles Gay, his friend at preparatory school. Their paths since had diverged widely, Gay having become a diplomat after passing effortlessly through Winchester and New College, Oxford. When not posted abroad, he lives in a large 'flat behind Victoria lent him by an absent colleague'. This unusually sympathetic figure is a portrayal of Charles de Salis, a diplomat friend who had a flat at 3^F, Morpeth Terrace behind Victoria Station. However, their acquaintance began about 1951, long after the period covered by *Richard Temple.*

It is reasonable to assume that other characters were based at least in part on real people, most long forgotten and unidentifiable. It also seems likely that an episode in which Temple lives rough in the East End was based on the experiences of Patrick's brothers Mike and Bun before they departed for Australia in the 1920s, rather than anything Patrick himself encountered. Again, as I shall show, a melodramatic section in which Temple becomes involved with a gang of upper-class criminals was inspired by a sensational incident widely reported in contemporary newspapers.

In the darkness of his prison cell Temple reflects upon the purpose and origin of the personality he seeks to project to his German captors, and the irony of its representing the man he once had to some extent really been.

> Pseudo-Temple was a little, silly unclean man with skins of pretence that Reinecke had peeled off one by one to reveal the vague shape of the abettor of shady deals, the man of no country but a café table, the minor blackmarketeer, the perpetual underling, who had made a stupid failure of his one independent commission.[1] He was a convincing creature: he was also a sort of general confession, for he represented some aspect of every mean, dishonest, ungenerous, discreditable act or thought or even temptation in Temple's life – a life not wanting in materials.

Temple's ploy was ingenious, since it required the minimum amount of falsehood that might endanger his cover story in face of persistent interrogation. It was effective, too, from Patrick's point of view as the novelist, since it enabled him to examine his earlier failings as a means of consigning them irrevocably into the past.

Ruminating on the events of his early life, Temple recalls how after leaving school at Easton Colborough (Lewes Grammar School) he had been sent to work as a resident pupil at the studio of an artist in the south of France. Patrick himself never enjoyed such an experience, and the details of this imaginative interlude plainly draw for their inspiration upon his and my mother's life after their move to France in 1949.

This episode concludes obscurely with reference to 'a letter that told him that his days in France were done', and in the next chapter we find Richard installed in Chelsea, where he has gained a scholarship to the 'Reynolds' art college. By this Patrick intended the Royal Academy, of which Sir Joshua Reynolds was elected first President at its foundation in 1768.[2] However, given his concern in the novel to utilise the actual topography of London, the absence of any reference to Richard's journeying from Chelsea to the Academy in Piccadilly, or description of its building and conduct of its classes, makes it virtually certain that Patrick himself never had any connection with the Academy.

While Patrick's motive for making Temple an artist rather than a writer may reflect nothing more than concern to avoid drawing too obvious a parallel with his own career, it is nevertheless not inconceivable that he did actually attempt to establish himself as an artist. Not only was he ardently enthusiastic and extremely well informed about painting (qualities demonstrated *inter alia* in *Richard Temple* and his biography of Picasso), but two years after his arrival in Chelsea he described himself to a girl he met on

[1] Could this be an allusion to Patrick's abortive attempt to become an RAF officer?

[2] 'It was the best school, in that it was the oldest and that it had the most prestige; it had Academicians as lecturers . . .' (*Richard Temple*, p. 72).

holiday as 'an artist', and offered to make a mask of her face. Numerous surviving sketches in his notebooks indicate that he was a careful draughtsman with a singular aptitude for caricature: a specialised skill which is ascribed in the novel to Richard Temple.

Patrick may have managed to escape the isolation of his family home in Sussex by persuading his father and stepmother to allow him to study as a painter in Chelsea. If so, the most likely school he would have attended was the Polytechnic in Manresa Road, which boasted an art school of high repute.[1] In *Richard Temple*, following his father's death and his mother's lapse into alcoholism, Richard's maternal uncle becomes unofficial guardian to the adolescent youth. A philistine snob, Canon Harler regards his nephew with scant sympathy or affection. Despite this, he advances him £78 per annum to maintain him at the 'Reynolds'. Regrettably Richard, despite his portrayal as a brilliant artist, proves a far from diligent pupil: 'He had hardly been near the school in those last terms except to keep himself enrolled, and he had completely abandoned figurative painting: he declared . . . that he would not be judged by a reactionary crew, a gang of Academicians . . .'

In the event his failure to gain his diploma results not from idleness but his defiant submission of a 'Last Judgment' whose figures were instantly recognisable as the examining Academicians, whom Temple had adorned with 'cuckold's horns and blubber lips', while their wives were exposed stark naked alongside them.

This extravagantly defiant gesture is clearly fanciful,[2] and if Patrick himself undertook a course in art the absence from classes ascribed to his *alter ego* is a more likely cause of failure.[3] It would have been characteristic for him to have entered on such a course with enthusiasm, only to become disgusted when required to accept the mandatory regular attendance and rigorous discipline. In addition there were the dangerous distractions of Chelsea's heady social life.

All this is confessedly guesswork. It may be that Patrick never enrolled for any course, and drew for Richard Temple's experiences as a painter on his

[1] When he called on Clough Williams-Ellis at his home in 1945, Patrick noted that 'Miss W-E. was at Chelsea Pol.'. This was Williams-Ellis's daughter Susan, who was about the same age as Patrick. Could it be significant that he bothered to note such a detail for my mother's benefit? Unfortunately attendance records for the period are incomplete, so there is no means of establishing the question either way.

[2] One is reminded of the private mockery and obscenities with which the child Patrick relieves his feelings in 'The Thermometer'.

[3] In this context I cannot help recalling the remarkable equanimity with which Patrick accepted my comparable failure to complete a Ph.D. at London University, whose fees he had generously met.

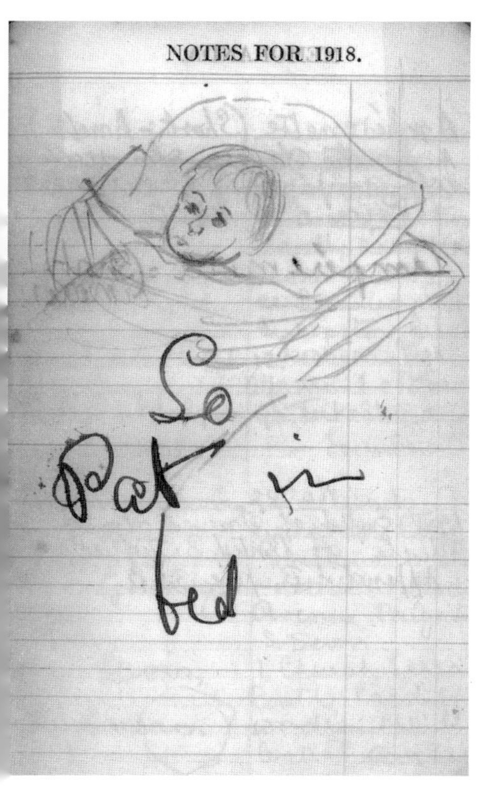

Patrick as a baby, sketched in his elder brother Victor's diary *c.* 1917

Patrick O'Brian, a formal portrait most likely taken for a publisher's promotional purposes

Charles Russ and family (minus Joan, then living in Pinner) after the death of Jessie; photograph taken in front of the Russ home in Willesden around 1920. *Seated* (*left to right*): Nora, Barney (Bun), Connie, Dr Russ, Patrick. *Standing*: Olive, Godfrey, Michael, Victor

Visit of Dr Russ to see Joan at Pinner in 1920. *Left to right*: Godfrey, Joan, Charles Russ, Aunt Bertha (Welch), Christine Welch, Uncle Frank (Welch). Patrick was presumably not taken on this visit. The angle of the camera suggests that the photograph was taken by Margaret

Welch family holiday in Cornwall 1919: Joan (held by nanny), with her cousins Margaret and Christine

Patrick and his cousin Christine Welch, *c.* 1919

Aunt Bertha (Goddard) with (*left to right*) Christine, Joan, and Margaret, *c.* 1920

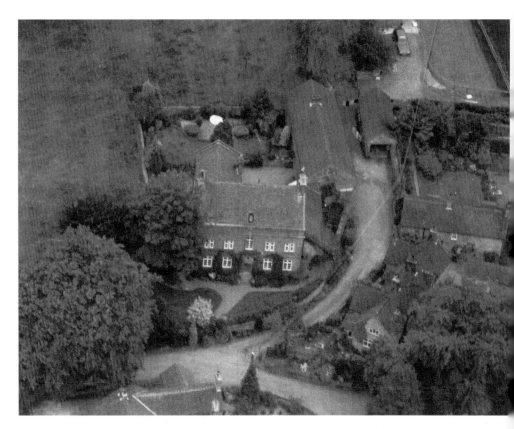

Horton Rectory, Staffordshire, home of Patrick's stepmother Zoe. Her descriptions of the house first inspired Patrick as a boy with his enduring love of Georgian England

The mid-nineteenth century edition of *Wood's Illustrated Natural History* given to Patrick by his stepmother's sister, which exercised considerable influence on his early writing

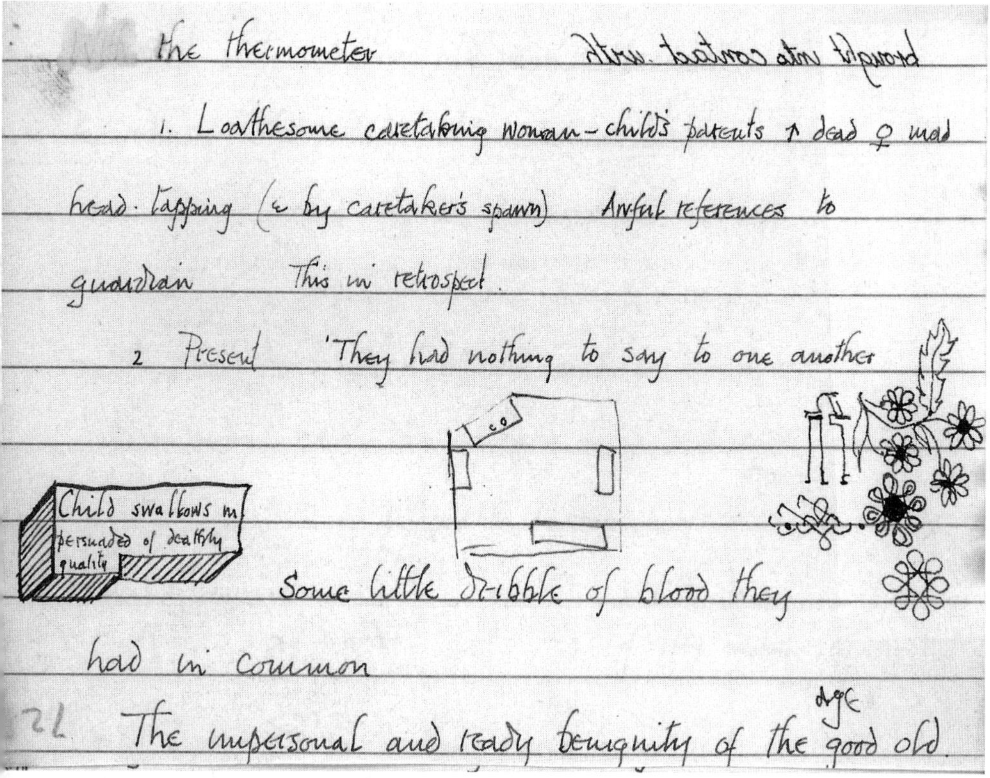

The Thermometer brought into contact with

1. Loathesome caretaking woman – child's parents ♂ dead ♀ mad head-tapping (& by caretaker's spawn) Awful references to guardian This in retrospect.

2 Present 'They had nothing to say to one another

Child swallows m persuaded of deathly quality

Some little dribble of blood they had in common

2L The impersonal and ready benignity of the good old age

Notes for 'The Thermometer', Patrick's remarkably explicit autobiographical short story (written in 1955) describing a dramatic moment in his childhood, showing a plan of his father's laboratory

Entrapment of the unicorn – an illumination copied by Patrick from a manuscript in the British Museum *c.* 1937, when working on a book of bestiaries

(*Above*) Keere Street, Lewes, up which Patrick walked daily during his three years' attendance at Lewes Grammar School

(*Below*) 10, Priory Crescent, Lewes, where Zoe Russ lived from 1926 to 1929 with Patrick and Joan whilst Charles generally stayed in London

(*Above*) Patrick when he first attended Lewes Grammar School in 1926, aged eleven

Oxen at work in Sussex, showing the unchanged character of rural life in Lewes at the time Patrick lived there. Ox-teams like this feature in the opening chapter of *Post Captain*

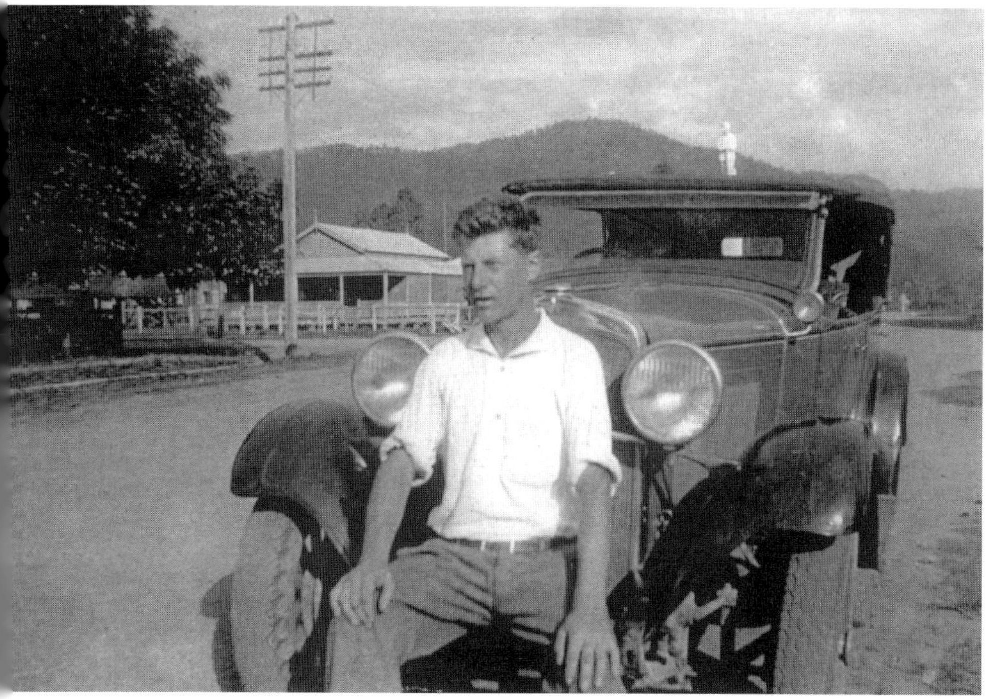

Patrick's elder brother Mike, in Australia. Having emigrated in 1927 to New South Wales as part of the Dreadnought Scheme to encourage young men to move out to the dominion, Mike led an adventurous existence in the outback

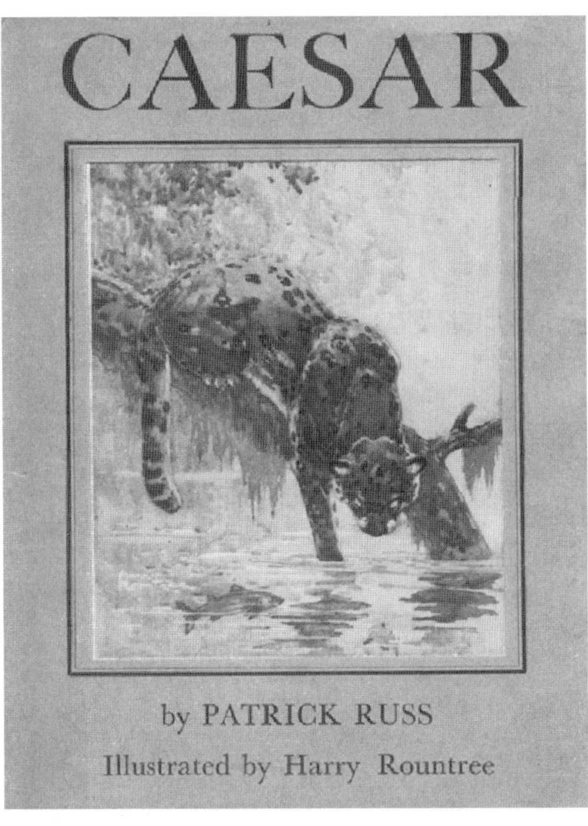

Cæsar, published in 1930. Patrick's first published book, which he wrote at the age of twelve in 1927 while being coached by his father for admission to the Dartmouth Naval College. He later considered it 'rather silly, *childish* and moderately dull, but not downright discreditable or embarrassing'

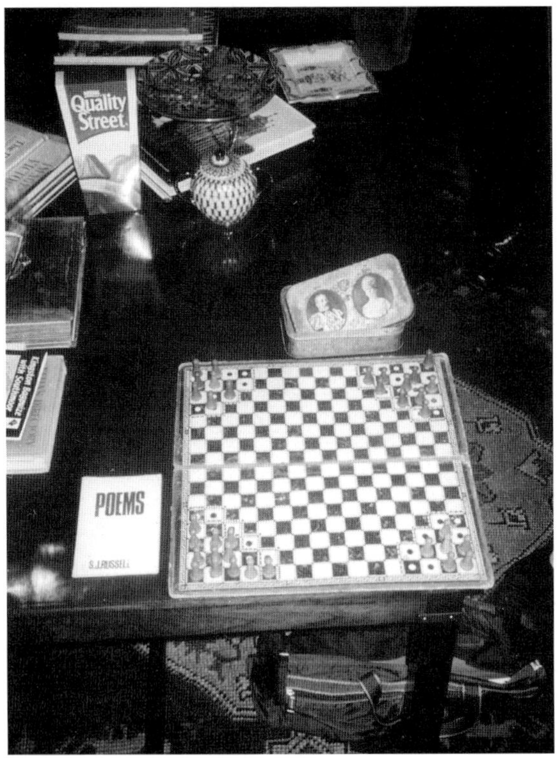

Halma game used by Patrick and Joan at 144, Albany Street, 1932-34. Patrick and Joan took much consolation in each other's company during these years of boredom and neglect in the large house in which Dr Russ conducted his practice

own interest in art, combined with an extensive acquaintance with artists' studios acquired during his bohemian days in Chelsea. Equally, poverty-stricken as he was, he must have had *some* source of income, and the specific allowance of £78 (dispatched by his uncle's bank in weekly instalments of 30 shillings) granted Richard by the mean-minded parent-figure in the novel bears a certain ring of reality. Dr Russ is unlikely to have agreed to subsidise his son's enjoyment of a life of idleness in London unless it were for the purpose of enabling him to pursue a worthwhile career. He had been supportive of his son's successes as a novelist, and may have thought that he might succeed as a painter. It was clear that he was unsuited to a career in the professions.

At the time a young man could survive on an income of 30 shillings a week. A studio in Redcliffe Road could be rented for precisely that sum, while fees at the Chelsea Polytechnic amounted to a mere 12 shillings a term. Before ultimately attaining success as a professional artist, Richard is represented as living in considerably more constricted quarters than a spacious studio, and manages for a time to feed himself on 7s. 3d. a week.

The novel is also valuable for the evidence it provides for the topographical basis of Patrick's life during his years in Chelsea. It is striking to what extent he was, like Thomas Hardy, concerned to establish his fiction in the context of actual locations, which he relished describing in evocative detail. Numerous examples, often privately acknowledged, scattered across his works over the years serve to confirm this predilection. In addition it is important to recall that he was living in Chelsea when he completed the book in 1960, and had frequent occasion to pass streets and houses bearing poignant memories of that earlier existence he sought to evoke in his 'Chelsea novel'.

At the outside of the Chelsea section of *Richard Temple*, Patrick catalogued the places where Richard had lived before the war. '. . . in an attempt at putting order into his thoughts he tried to recall the sequence of his rooms, from that first enchanted den with a window on the Thames to the house with the pigeon-loft on the King's Road which saw the last days of his protracted adolescence. He remembered . . . Dovehouse Street; Smith Terrace with its monstrous bugs, immune to sulphur-fumes; the World's End; the lower end of Redcliffe Road.'[1]

This introductory summary is oddly at variance with Temple's account of his successive homes in the narrative proper. Only the first and last (in reverse order) correspond: the attic room in the King's Road, and his lodging in Redcliffe Road. In the story each of his moves is clearly described, one

[1] *Richard Temple*, p. 65.

succeeding another in circumstances which leave no scope for any intervening residence. Thus, following his departure from Redcliffe Road, there is no reference whatever to the homes at the World's End, Dovehouse Street, and Smith Terrace listed in the prefatory catalogue. Instead Richard stays in the studio of an artist named Gobbo, while the latter is absent in Cornwall. On Gobbo's return, Richard moves directly to 'the pigeon-loft on the King's Road'.

The descriptions themselves also include a number of discrepancies. Thus Temple, looking down from the window of Gobbo's studio, sees a friend passing 'just where Pamela Grandison had walked' by a pillar-box on the other side of the street. Yet a bare fifteen pages earlier this incident is located outside his subsequent residence in King's Road. This is one of many instances suggesting that Patrick became so absorbed in the autobiographical aspect of *Richard Temple* as to allow his own experiences unwittingly to obtrude to such an extent as to bring about a succession of dramatic inconsistencies, whose value lies in the extent to which more often than not they betray the reality lying behind the fiction.

Whether or not Patrick occupied a 'first enchanted den on the Embankment' is unknown. However the detailed description of Temple's lodgings in an unspecified house at 'the lower end of Redcliffe Road' smacks of reality. Redcliffe Road was at the time a haunt of avant-garde artists and intellectuals, many of whose houses contained studios to rent,[1] and the description is so detailed and specific as to suggest a vivid recollection of his own lodgings at the outset of his stay in Chelsea.

> At the lower end of Redcliffe Road there was a cat-haunted landing: in front of him there was a cupboard and directly to his right the door of a room with a tea-party going on in it. There came back to him the nature of the dim, unfiltered light on the landing, the shadowy colour of the door, the smell of that London staircase in the winter and the sound of the tea-party, to which they had asked him. He was rather late, in so far as it was possible to be late for one of these indefinite meetings, which took place at night: later, at any rate, than he intended; for in that rabbit-warren of a house, now abandoned to a multitude of people with one room apiece, the servants' staircase forked into three, and dark passages wandered here and there among the cisterns, promising shortcuts.[2]

Richard is attending a party shortly after his arrival in London. About to open the door, he overhears a mention of his name and pauses to eavesdrop.

[1] Cf. Joan Wyndham, *Love Lessons: A Wartime Diary* (London, 1985), pp. 41, 42–43, 140–41.
[2] *Richard Temple*, pp. 65–66.

What he hears is neither complimentary nor encouraging. After contemptuous mockery of his claim to be the illegitimate son of a nobleman, Richard finds his character being dissected in coldly analytical terms.

> 'He has, I am afraid, no settled system of any sort . . . so that his conduct must not be strictly scrutinised. His affections are social and generous, perhaps; but his desire for imaginary consequence predominates over his attention to truth.'
>
> 'He is also a frightful snob.'[1]

Temple's reaction to these unpleasant truths reflects a deep-rooted fear which his creator entertained throughout his life: 'He had suspected for some time that people often spoke about him like this behind his back.' While the fear was largely fanciful, Richard repeatedly acknowledges the justice of such malicious comments, confessing at one point that 'indeed he must have been a monster at that stage'. He freely accepted his social ineptitude, finding himself obliged 'to depart from his natural solitude and dread the loneliness that he had always accepted: he was a natural solitary, and he had little social talent or discrimination'. He admits that he 'does not understand the wider sense of the common social rules but clings to them as arbitrary formulæ'. Indeed, his deep sense of insecurity makes him conscious of the niceties of social status, and accentuates his fear that his paternity and upbringing provide inadequate status for a real gentleman. 'However immovable Richard might have become in painting he was still acutely sensitive to common worldly status': a sensitivity which provokes him on one occasion into violent over-reaction to a sneer at his lack of public school education.

Lacking that careless ease which he vainly longed to acquire, Richard admonished himself: 'Always remain aloof, correct and professional, impassible.'[2] Yet no matter how determined his effort to practise these precepts, he remained desperately ill at ease in company. How could it be otherwise, when he freely acknowledged himself to be a 'vapid creature whose feelings were mostly froth, and who was, for nearly all the time, a most appalling bore'? A characteristic instance of his sensation of inadequacy occurs during a solitary visit to a crowded pub:

> It was indeed very much like being in a sea, sitting at the bottom while it soughed and boomed: he had come just for this immersion, but now his mood was dropping, and he wished he had not. He thought that perhaps the beer would improve this state, and as a preliminary to fetching it he began to move the empty glasses in front of him; but his hands were so shaking and uncertain

[1] *Richard Temple*, p. 67.

[2] Patrick recorded similarly strict self-advice in his notebooks.

> that he was afraid he would knock them over and he stopped. He deliberately relaxed the tension in his stomach and with studied calmness he gazed mildly about.[3]

The raucous hubbub of broken conversation at once unnerves and disgusts Richard. Nervously fiddling with his empty beer glass, he surveys the company with a combination of resentment and fear, from which the exaggerated savagery of his reflections provides private relief: 'They were loud-mouthed pub-men . . . nasty businessmen in suits who are often seen there, but even more often in drinking-clubs later on – middle-aged roaring laughter, a kind of obligatory booming . . . the worst of hangers-on, comparatively rich, confident, brutally ignorant. Good sports, out for a lark; sly, treacherous and mean.'

How often have I heard Patrick give vent to comparable distaste even after attending a comparatively mild social occasion. The origins of his lifelong detestation and fear of the multitude ('apes') surely lie in his isolated and asocial upbringing. His father's daunting presence and irrational rage and violence had ingrained in him instinctive terror lest at any moment his modest tranquillity be brutally violated. Nor can it be doubted that his principal source of confidence lay in the medium of his art, which enabled him to create a world of which he was the ultimate controller.

In a passage set during his stay in France between leaving Easton Colborough and arriving in Chelsea, Patrick describes in elaborate detail Richard's composition of a painting of the martyrdom of St Sebastian: '. . . in the bottom right-hand corner he had already painted three crossbowmen, very close to the observer and crowded together, pointing their bows at the saint, who was tied to a low cross on the left of the picture and who had already received a great many arrows, or bolts . . . The saint stared back at them with a harsh fortitude . . .'[2]

The Saint's proletarian persecutors are 'a villainous set of brutes', on whom the artist conveys features recognisable as those of real people in the locality. The contrast could not be more explicitly rendered: mindless thugs dominate the foreground in order to launch murderous missiles against the defiantly heroic victim, helplessly withdrawn into what he might have hoped to be discreet obscurity.

When he wrote this, did Patrick's mind fly back to those distant days at Kempsey Lodge, when he was eight years old? There he had been used as the butt of his brothers' bows and arrows, and as Bun recalled long afterwards he

[1] *Richard Temple*, p. 120.

[2] *Richard Temple*, pp. 56–57.

'did not whimper or cry and felt he was quite a hero and a martyr, like St. Sebastian'.

Not surprisingly Richard becomes at once fascinated and alarmed by the bohemian society in which he finds himself, whose self-conscious disregard of the norms of social behaviour appears as daunting as it is enticing to the hitherto sheltered recluse.

> The world in which he lived, it is true, was concerned more with things of the spirit than was the Stock Exchange; but this did not make it all of a piece nor prevent it from being pretty phoney in a great many of its aspects – there were the inevitable hordes of silly and dirty people in search of a literary justification for silliness and dirt, the uncircumcised Jews and the white Negroes, as well as the lechers – and there was a strong sense of class distinction, which ran, apart from a few obvious inversions, upon exactly the same lines as those which divided Easton Colborough into its unnumbered castes.[1]

Anyone who doubts the accuracy and sardonic perceptiveness of Patrick's description of the pre-war Chelsea artistic set will find them portrayed to a nicety in the diaries of Joan Wyndham, published in 1985 under the title *Love Lessons*. A middle-class teenager fresh from boarding-school, Wyndham found liberated Chelsea almost too intoxicating for words. Eagerly plunging herself into the round of studio parties, she daringly downed gin, shared wicked books with arty characters ('Ulysses, Henry Miller, all the bad books you've never read' – 'Rupert [whose beard identified him as an artist] went on reading *Madame Bovray* [*sic*]'), waxed ecstatic over glimpses of real or assumed 'pansies' & 'lezzies' ('Soho is a scream'), swore ostentatiously ('that famous word again – the one beginning with b!'), and prided herself on her intimacy with artistic geniuses who dazzled her with their 'latest eccentricity', including such wildly hilarious excesses as naming a cat 'Henry Miller'.

Acknowledging that 'I'm not decadent at all really, I only wish I was', Wyndham did not lack determination to achieve her ambition. 'Of course I long for someone young and vital and idealistic – but do such creatures exist?' Desperately seeking her ideal idealist, she rushed from bedsit to studio, flirted with Communism, mocking alike the dreary working classes and boring elderly folk and trying fearfully hard to get drunk.

Patrick knew and despised the Joan Wyndhams who flocked around Chelsea and Fulham, dismissing them in *Richard Temple* as 'those skinny unwashed girls with their Joyce and Eliot and no more foundation of

[1] *Richard Temple*, pp. 69–70.

literature than The Madcap of St. Bede's: and all their talk about sex, based on nothing more than a little furtive grappling among themselves'.

Much of this contempt doubtless represents hindsight and Patrick's unremitting scorn for his earlier self, but as a detached and introverted observer he was probably conscious of the vacuity and pretentiousness of much of the society in which he found himself. His learning, though as yet fragmentary, was exceptional in being as genuine as was his thirst for knowledge. Clever conversation posed few attractions for him – both its frivolity and the consciousness that it was not his forte repelled him. No doubt on occasion he met people who interested him at least for a time, and there must have been moments when he fancied himself shining amid the throng. But disillusionment was ever swift to recover its sway over his fragile personality.

To those who met him in later life, Patrick appeared excessively defensive and often insufferably arrogant. Clearly no single explanation can suffice for so complex a character, but one undoubted factor lay in the candour with which he analysed his own personality and motives. Young, shy, and possessed of lofty ambitions he frequently felt despondently incapable of realising, it is likely that he suffered from constant bouts of low esteem throughout his early twenties.

Although his gaucheness and deep-rooted sense of inadequacy made him uncomfortable in company, one form of social encounter could at times provide him with momentary relief. Patrick (it is really pointless to distinguish him from Richard Temple in the context) had grown into a good-looking young man, and the combination of shyness and intellectual desire which consumed him made him attractive to the protective instincts of women. Until his arrival in Chelsea his sole companion and friend had been his sister Joan, which had at least accustomed him to intimate relationship with the opposite sex.

Deprived of his mother at an age he could barely remember, and becoming thereafter a virtual exile from humanity, it would be surprising had his emergence into the world not made him more than usually susceptible to the vagaries of love which beset most young men. Richard Temple looks back on his early affairs with a mixture of contempt and disgust. However it is likely that this cynical view reflects his later dissatisfaction with his youthful self rather than an entirely realistic reconstruction of his emotions at the time. He was in desperate need of a kindred spirit, and the disillusionment which so often swiftly follows on youthful infatuation would have appeared the more acute in his case because of the significance with which he sought to endow each encounter.

Given the widely available opportunity afforded by the bohemian society of Chelsea, it can scarcely be doubted that Patrick's description drew on his own experience. In fact he told me once that he had enjoyed many sexual encounters in his youth, though it will be seen shortly that a material circumstance in his own life makes it highly unlikely that such activities occurred on anything like so promiscuous a scale as those he ascribed to Richard Temple. Elsewhere in the novel he explains that in the retreat of night Temple could lower his daytime guard. Agonising in his German prison over the shameful wastefulness and puerile pretences of his early life, he believes his nocturnal monologues represented further contemptible displays of weakness: 'It was a rather subhuman activity: but most of these grapplings had another end as well – at this period he was a great talker, and his loquacity suffered from a night alone. How much he talked, and what balls; and when mendacity sickened him, he fell into the other extreme of candour; but he never would be quiet or continent.'[1]

The 'balls' doubtless represented an opinionated babble of unformed opinions on art, literature, and life, which in daylight hours he either blurted out in a manner which he was conscious of being confused or wrong-headed, or found himself too diffident to articulate. As for 'the other extreme of candour', that can only have been remorseful confession of all that he found inadequate and reprehensible about himself. Nagging apprehensions of worthlessness and failure nudged at his elbow throughout the day, and he resolutely strove to conceal them from the outside world. Yet here he was, time and again abandoning his best resolutions, exposing his nakedness physically and metaphorically in the presence of some foolish slut whose antagonism he doubtless provoked by dropping her as quickly as he had picked her up.

[1] *Richard Temple*, p. 71.

SEVEN

First Love

> What you mention of your private feelings on an interesting subject, is indeed distressing; but assure yourself that scarce one person out of twenty marries his first love, and scarce one out of twenty of the remainder has cause to rejoice at having done so. What we love in those early days is generally rather a fanciful creation of our own than a reality. We build statues of snow, and weep when they melt.
>
> (Sir Walter Scott to G.H. Gordon, 12 June 1820)

Appropriately enough, it is within the 'rabbit-warren' where he lodged at Redcliffe Road that Richard Temple experiences the first of his many sexual relationships: one he recalled with what appears unjustifiable bitterness.

> . . . at quite an early stage he had thrown away his sacred first commission for love or rather out of kindness for such a disagreeable young woman, a frigid shrew at heart, who was not even pretty.
>
> She lived down the corridor in that house in Redcliffe Road, and nearness, opportunity and a lingering amiability in her were enough to bring them into a very close connection. Doris was her name, and she was employed in a decorating firm: she was unlike most of his acquaintance in being self-supporting, clean, neat and efficient; she was also pathologically jealous and sexually inept, but until they were lovers he did not know that and it was in the earlier days that she was particularly kind to him and used her contacts to get him a commission. Later on he exploited women's kindness in a most odious and deliberate way, but he never had it so good as this first time, when his approach was entirely disinterested and ingenuous.[1]

Richard's denigration of Doris appears so unwarranted as to intimate an

[1] *Richard Temple*, p. 74–75.

emotional outburst reflecting an episode in Patrick's own life. In fact it is clear that 'Doris' represents a rancorous portrait of his first wife, Elizabeth Jones. Richard's affair with Doris begins shortly after his arrival in London, which must also have been the case with Patrick and Elizabeth. He had lived sufficiently long at his parents' home at Crowborough in 1935 to cherish fond memories of the locality, and married Elizabeth in February of the following year. The time available for him to move to London in the summer or autumn of 1935,[1] meet Elizabeth, and develop a relationship leading to their marriage at the beginning of 1936, cannot have exceeded more than a few months.

Elizabeth Jones was an attractive twenty-four-year-old, who was born in the little village of Pen-y-cae near the mining town of Rhosslanerchrugog in north-east Wales, where her father worked as a collier. Tragically she lost both her parents in early childhood, and found herself an orphan at the age of seven. Her education had been rudimentary, and Welsh was her first language. Naturally intelligent and enterprising, as a teenager she departed to seek her fortune in London, where she gained employment as a domestic servant and then a seamstress.

At the time of their marriage Elizabeth was twenty-five, and Patrick just twenty-one. On the basis of my interpretation of this section of *Richard Temple*, they met as fellow-lodgers in the house at the bottom of Redcliffe Road. Whether she had been chaste prior to their meeting is unknown, but there is a suggestion of reality in Richard Temple's account of their being friends before they became lovers, during which time 'she was particularly kind to him'. Elizabeth was gentle and pretty, and her fluency in the ancient language of her forebears would have appealed to Patrick's proclivity for the arcane and exotic generally, and the study of languages in particular. That she was four years older than him mattered little in the context of their shared youth. Indeed the added confidence this gave her, together with her familiarity with the world into which he found himself so abruptly propelled, may well have added to the appeal she exerted on the impressionable and inexperienced Patrick.

We can picture the excitement and sense of freedom which gripped him on finding himself the recipient of affectionate devotion from an attractive young woman. After the stifling atmosphere of Albany Street and Crowborough (to say nothing of his brief disastrous exposure to the rigours of military life), the hedonistic atmosphere of intellectual Chelsea society must have appeared liberating almost beyond belief. For her part, the kindly and protective Elizabeth found the good-looking and intense young Patrick

[1] In addition there is the likelihood that he attempted to gain entry to Oxford that summer.

deeply attractive, with his gentlemanly (despite his own misgivings) air, enthusiastic flood of knowledge, precocious achievement as a writer, and boundless ambition to make a name for himself in the arts.

Although Patrick later went to great lengths to decry Elizabeth and depreciate the nature of their relationship, he was unable wholly to suppress his memory of his first rapturous furtive discovery of love in the crowded house in Redcliffe Road. Whilst Elizabeth resurfaces in the novel thinly disguised as Richard's drunken and insane mother, the brief section describing his relationship with Doris makes clear the 'amiability' which made her 'particularly kind to him', her concern to help him with his work, her industry in keeping their tiny nest orderly and clean, and his inescapable reasons to be grateful to her.

A curious little factor in Patrick's subsequent writing suggests that, despite the disaster and bitter years of recrimination that followed, his first experience of love retained an ineradicable hold on his memory. Richard Temple lives for some time in a garret room in the King's Road. Squalid though his quarters are, 'this early period included the highest days of his life and a more pure happiness than any man could ask for or expect'. At one point he is obliged to live for a while elsewhere, and on his return discovers that 'his old place no longer existed. It did not surprise him to find that the house had been pulled down . . . in the open space where the house had been there was a faint mist of green. It did not surprise him much to find that most of his things had been taken . . .'[1]

Though it has earlier been mentioned that 'its ultimate landlords were going to pull it down', the episode appears in many ways surreal. While it is unclear precisely how long Richard had been absent, it is hard to believe that a house containing several tenants paying quarterly rents could have been demolished in a relatively short space of time without reasonable notice. Nor is it likely that the landlord would have allowed a tenant's property to be stolen simply because he happened to be away from home at the time (we learn that his belongings, which included several large paintings, were openly removed under the gaze of his neighbours). That Patrick himself was confused when dealing with this odd incident is evinced by his making Richard walk off 'down the mean streets of Fulham to the King's Road' – when the house is itself situated in the King's Road. Odder still, when Richard later comes to be installed in a flat in Pimlico, he wanders one night in a daze 'until after a long passage of darkness he found himself standing silently in front of the door of his old lodgings in Chelsea'. Patrick had clearly forgotten that both lodgings and door had been demolished some time earlier!

[1] *Richard Temple*, p. 135.

Examples have been and will be given illustrating Patrick's tendency to obtrude passages from his own life into his novels, and the extent to which this is made apparent by inconsistencies in the narrative. The theme of a character's returning to a London house where he had known exceptional happiness, only to discover it entirely demolished, clearly assumed a particular significance. In *The Reverse of the Medal*, published in 1986, on returning to London Stephen Maturin discovers that his old home at the Grapes has disappeared.

> His mind was far away, and the shock was therefore all the greater when, having turned the corner to the inn, he looked up and saw nothing but a blackened hole railed off from the street, with rain-water shining in its cellars, a few charred beams showing where the floors had been, and grass and ferns growing in the niches that had once been cupboards . . .
>
> A wound, and a strangely unexpected one, thought Stephen, walking north. He had no idea how much that quiet haven meant to him . . .

Apart from the obviously striking resemblance between the two incidents, a common detail of just the type that Patrick would be likely to observe lies in the 'ferns growing in the niches'. While living in his King's Road room, Richard Temple likewise observes 'a little dark fern-like plant' growing in his window frame, while others 'also grew in the leaf-choked gutters'.[1]

The most likely explanation of Patrick's recurrent attachment to the curious motif of the vanished house is that it reflected some searing incident in his own life. The sole appropriate circumstance of which I am aware was the devastation wrought by German bombs on Redcliffe Road in the autumn of 1940. On 11 September number 34 was blown up, and in the middle of the following month successive raids destroyed seven further houses and inflicted appalling damage on others. As Joan Wyndham noted in her diary, 'Redcliffe Road is like a street of the dead.'[2] While we do not know the number of the house in which (assuming my reconstruction correct) Patrick and Elizabeth lived during the early part of the winter of 1935–36, it could well have been among those destroyed in 1940.

During the Blitz Patrick was based at a nearby ambulance station, where he would certainly have been made immediately aware of the effects of these German raids, and as likely as not called upon to attend this particular scene of devastation. Confirmation of this suggestion appears in the description of

[1] *Richard Temple*, pp. 84, 135, 137, 276; *The Reverse of the Medal*, pp. 123–24.
[2] Wyndham, *Love Lessons*, pp. 118–19, 121, 135–36; Winston G. Ramsey (ed.), *The Blitz: Then and Now* (London, 1987–90), ii, pp. 183, 187.

Richard Temple's arrival at the site of his vanished home, which includes a curious reference to 'the shattered branches of the tree [in front of the house], so broken as to look chewed when he stared close'. While it seems unlikely that such damage would be inflicted during a builders' demolition, the heavily scarred trunk is precisely what might be expected from the detonation of a high-explosive bomb.

When Patrick wrote *Richard Temple* he had long been at great pains to eradicate every trace of his earlier life. Despite this, it looks as though the physical destruction of the house where he underwent his first experience of love was capable of inflicting upon him that deep 'wound' he ascribed to Stephen Maturin.

In 1935 the love affair between Patrick and Elizabeth progressed swiftly: so much so, that they were married on 27 February of the following year at Chelsea Register Office. Dean King is surely right in suggesting that 'The marriage could not have pleased Patrick's class-conscious, financially struggling parents'.[1] Charles and Zoe Russ were inordinate snobs, who refused to attend the marriages or even acknowledge the spouses of those of his offspring whom they regarded as belonging to an inferior class, and it does not appear that they troubled to attend the brief and colourless ceremony.

Nor does it seem that Elizabeth was ever invited to Crowborough, since whenever Patrick stayed with his parents he communicated with her through affectionate letters and poems posted to their London dwelling. In *Richard Temple* the hero's father is said to have 'cut up very ugly, very rough, when he found that he had a whore in the family'. Though the reference in the novel is to Richard's mother, the stricture is conflated with condemnation of Richard's own conduct, and there can be little doubt that Patrick combined the character of Temple's mother with that of his wife Elizabeth. Victor Russ's widow Saidie recalled that his sister 'Olive remarked that Step-Mother had liked Patrick's first wife Elizabeth'. If so, her affection did not amount to much. When Elizabeth fell on hard times, neither Zoe nor Charles appears ever to have lifted a finger to help her.

At the time of their marriage the young couple were registered as living together in a basement flat at 2a Oakley Street, at the corner of King's Road. The witnesses are named on the certificate as José Birt and E.H. Taaffe. Nothing is known of the former, but Edward Taaffe was a young Irishman whom Patrick described as 'my particular friend'. Ten years later he dedicated to him a short story, 'The Dawn Flighting'. It is clear that he retained fond memories of Taaffe. In *The Commodore* (1994) he has Diana

[1] King, *Patrick O'Brian*, p. 68.

Villiers riding with 'Ned Taaffe's hounds' in Ireland, and again in *The Yellow Admiral* we hear of her driving a coach and six 'once or twice in Ireland – Ned Taaffe's machine'.[1] In 1980 Patrick recorded a vivid dream of his old friend, with whom he had long lost touch. '. . . so home & to an early bed where I dreamt so sadly of Taafe & Kathy. The Chelsea of 40 years ago was much the same but we were our now age: he wd not take the 1st step twds me, nor did he seem really pleased when I did so . . . They neither of them had their own faces, but their identities wr the same.'

Given the isolation of his existence prior to sudden immersion in London's most sociable quarter, Patrick presumably acquired these and other friends soon after his arrival. He possessed considerable natural charm, and among a set whose artistic pretensions often reflected self-esteem rather than achievement his position as an established author must have conferred a cachet of prestige and apparent self-confidence. Nor would his youthful conceit and didacticism have appeared excessively *outré*.

In May 1936, three months after their marriage, Elizabeth became pregnant, and about the same time they moved from Oakley Street to 24 Gertrude Street behind St Stephen's Hospital in Fulham Road,[2] a couple of streets away from that house in Redcliffe Road which probably provided the scene of their first meeting in the previous year. Since they shared the three-storeyed house with another couple and three further people, they are unlikely to have occupied more than a single room. However, they were young and resilient, possessed a circle of friends, and it appears that Patrick anticipated the prospect of becoming a father with pride.

Here it is necessary to pause in the sparsely attested narrative of Patrick's married life to consider an episode which, if it occurred, was to prove of lasting significance in his career. In view of his life's major achievement, the question has been frequently raised whether Patrick himself ever experienced life at sea under sail. In later years he asserted on a number of occasions that he had done so as a young man. His fullest account appeared in the British Library collection of essays of appreciation, published in 1994:

> One of the compensations I have spoken about was the sea. The disease that racked my bosom every now and then did not much affect my strength and when it left me in peace (for there were long remissions) sea-air and sea-voyages

[1] *The Last Pool*, p. 175; *The Commodore*, pp. 280–81; *The Yellow Admiral*, p. 73.

[2] This may well be the house at the World's End listed at the outset in *Richard Temple* as the last of those inhabited by Temple in pre-war Chelsea. Gertrude Street lies a stone's throw from World's End.

> were recommended. An uncle had a two-ton sloop and several friends had boats, which was fine; but what was even better was that my particular friend Edward, who shared a tutor with me, had a cousin who possessed an ocean-going yacht, a converted barque-rigged merchantman, that he used to crew with undergraduates and fair-sized boys, together with some real seamen, and sail far off into the Atlantic. The young are wonderfully resilient, and although I never became much of a topman, after a while I could hand, reef and steer without disgrace, which allowed more ambitious sailoring later on . . .[1]

Citing a sceptical comment made in his latter years by Bernard Russ, Dean King expressed cautious reservation: 'Perhaps Patrick did have such an experience, or perhaps it was a convenient invention when some claim to square-rigged sailing expertise was desirable.'[2]

The issue seems too important to be left to vague or arbitrary judgements so long as opportunity exists to verify Patrick's claim in light of independent evidence. On a couple of occasions he let fall intriguing allusions to the specific vessel in which he claimed to have sailed. In an interview on French television in June 1994 he described how as a young man he had a friend of the same age, whose cousin Arthur possessed a large sailing ship on which he (Patrick) sailed on voyages extending to Morocco and out into the Atlantic. In the same year, Patrick told *Le Figaro Magazine* that 'J'ai découvert la navigation sur un trois-mâts de mon oncle, qui avait appartenu au duc de Westminster'.

Combining these allusions with the account which he provided for the British Library *Festschrift*, we learn the following:

1. It was thanks to his 'particular friend Edward, who . . . had a cousin who possessed an ocean-going yacht, a converted barque-rigged merchantman, that he used to . . . sail far off into the Atlantic'.
2. It was a three-masted yacht, which had previously belonged to the Duke of Westminster.
3. Edward's cousin who owned the vessel was named Arthur.

[1] Cunningham (ed.), *Patrick O'Brian*, p. 16. Patrick provided similar accounts in interviews with Mark Horowitz (*New York Times Magazine*, 16 May 1993), Peter Guttridge (*Independent*, 3 July 1993), Richard Luckett (*Daily Telegraph*, 23 June 1993), and Keith Wheatley (*Financial Times*, 11–12 January 1997).

[2] King, *Patrick O'Brian*, p. 48. King's further comment that 'Such an experience was never mentioned in any of the biographical sketches accompanying Patrick's early stories or sea books' is scarcely relevant, since most of his early books, including the two 'sea stories' *The Golden Ocean* and *The Unknown Shore*, are not accompanied by biographical sketches, while those that are (such as *The Catalans*) comprise only brief allusions to his previous publications and home in the south of France.

There is one vessel to which all these details apply, and I am grateful to Dr Richard Luckett, Pepys Librarian at Magdalene College, Cambridge, who managed to track down the perfect match. As he wrote to me on 18 November 2001: 'I have no doubt that *Fantome II* was the vessel P.O'B. described, particularly as I know from other sources that Arthur Guinness would take her out and sail for perhaps two hundred miles and return, without having gone anywhere, except for the sail.'

Fantome II was a magnificent 611-ton barque-rigged French merchantman, built at Nantes in 1896 and originally christened the *Belem*. After being employed for several years in the nitrate trade sailing to the west coast of South America, she was bought and converted into a yacht by the Duke of Westminster. The Duke in turn sold her to Colonel the Hon. Arthur Guinness, who renamed her *Fantome II*.[1]

The consistency of these details, and the fact that Patrick provided some on one occasion and some on another, led me for some time to share Dr Luckett's belief that he had sailed on board Colonel Guinness's yacht. Eventually however I was dismayed to discover irrefutable evidence in his later diaries that this cannot have been the case. One afternoon in October 1991, while walking with my mother on the ridge above their house at Collioure, Patrick observed on the far side a magnificent vessel in the harbour of Port-Vendres. Full of curiosity, they hurried down the hill and examined the yacht from the quayside. Patrick made a note on the spot, from which he recorded that evening that it was 'the barque Belem, built at Nantes in 1898 . . . sold to D of W 1914 then to Sir A.E. Guinness ocean-going yacht until 52 . . . 12 staysails & jibs 10 square sails can make 12k[nots] under sail'. On enquiry he learned that the *Belem* was due to depart next morning. Early on the following day he and my mother crossed the hill into Port-Vendres, where they

> Checked the Belem's measurements & contemplated her rigging. Then we went a little before 11 & she was making ready – people gathered but not too many – & almost on time she cast off & motored towards the jetty. We had scarcely hoped to see her set any sail, but a slight N breeze had sprung up & as she passed out of the port she did so with 3 fine staysails. We could not tell her direction but at all hazards hurried up the devilish Béar road: & there suddenly she was far below, heading SE under courses, topsails & most fore & aft sails, looking perfectly lovely, the staysails white interrupted curved Δs catching the sun between the square sails – lovely proportions – an entity. We moved farther

[1] *Fantome II* is described in John Scott Hughes, *Famous Yachts* (London, 1928), pp. 132–37. I am further grateful to Dr Luckett for providing this reference.

> up; she moved farther out, setting the topgallants & eventually remarkably broad & deep royals. Her course was erratic at 1st . . . but eventually she settled for I suppose Cap Creus & sailed gently (3 or 4k?) into the blue. Such joy. (& in such a horrible, horrible world).

This was definitely Patrick's first contact with the *Belem* (evidently a new owner had restored her original name), which within a couple of years he identified as the yacht on which he had sailed before the war. I feel unhappy at being compelled to expose Patrick's fanciful assertion, and confess to having momentarily contemplated omitting any discussion of his claims to sailing experience. Still, it would not surprise me if his introspective imagination might not after a time have persuaded him that he had actually sailed in the vessel which had so profoundly captured his emotions – just as years earlier he and my mother somehow came to believe that Ireland really was 'his' country. On belatedly becoming an internationally acclaimed public figure during the last decade of his life, he found himself constantly under pressure to do something which he detested from the bottom of his heart: namely, discuss his past life. In particular he was thrown on the defensive on being recurrently posed the tediously obvious question whether he had any practical experience of seafaring. A year before his enraptured contemplation of the *Belem* he had been irritated by the woman who handled his affairs at his literary agents, who 'was indiscreetly pressing me on my sea-going experience'.

That Patrick never sailed on the Duke of Westminster's yacht is now certain, and since it is inextricably linked to this factor there is no longer reason to believe in a connection between Edward and Colonel Arthur Guinness.[1]

However, this revelation does not necessarily refute Patrick's claim to familiarity with the sea *in toto*: 'I knew the element tolerably well, having sailed in most rigs.'[2] There are indications that, while his claim (or conviction?) that he sailed in Colonel Guinness's yacht was false, he had nevertheless gained practical experience of service before the mast on a more modest vessel or vessels. One of the drawbacks of public exposure of Patrick's embroidery of his past life is that it has sometimes led to unjustified scepticism regarding events or experiences which were in fact true. To take but one example, the discovery that he was not born or brought up in Ireland

[1] I undertook much fruitless research in this direction, which would have been avoided had the existence of Patrick's valuable diaries not been unaccountably concealed from his heirs by the Executors of his Estate until challenged nearly two and a half years after his death (cf. *Private Eye*, 11–24 June 2004, p. 24).

[2] 'Just a phase I'm going through?', *Daily Telegraph*, 27 August 1994.

misled Dean King into doubting whether he wrote his early novel *Hussein* in that country.

Could it be that Patrick experienced a voyage such as he described – but not in the *Belem*? Might the enchanted vision gliding away beyond Cap Béar into the wine-dark sea have substituted itself in his imagination for a ship on board which he really sailed more than half a century before?[1] This might appear an argument of desperation, but for pertinent factors which are not easily dismissed.

In the first place there exist independent indications that Patrick had experience of manning a ship at sea. In March 1946, when living with my mother in North Wales, he wrote in his journal: 'Some time ago there was an account of a whaling expedition to the Antarctic that would set off soon. It would be immense fun to go, and it would give material for writing. Typically I have not written to the United Whalers of St. Mary Ave yet, although I have drafted a note: it would be rather stunning to be taken at my word and told to report in a week's time.' Patrick duly dispatched his application, and although he was disappointed there was a consolatory factor: 'A pleasanter letter was that from the United Whalers, who very civilly say that they are sorry there is no spare room in their ships, but if I would like a job as one of the crew would I write again in September.'

For some reason he did not pursue the project, but it seems unlikely that his application would have been taken as seriously had he not been able to provide some evidence of appropriate experience. Whaling was a specialised occupation, and whalers were normally crewed by no more than a dozen men. There can have been little call for a volunteer who had not been to sea – above all at a time when there was a glut of men with extensive seagoing experience. By the end of the war the Royal Navy and merchant marine together employed nearly a million men, and following the close of hostilities many were seeking fresh employment. At the same time Britain's whaling fleet was seriously depleted in consequence of the sinking of numerous vessels during the war.

Notes and sketches compiled shortly after his arrival in France show that Patrick had an intimate understanding of the workings of sailing vessels, long before he contemplated writing anything about the sea. On 17 May 1950 he

[1] The graceful image remained imprinted in Patrick's imagination, and not long after he wrote to the American writer Stephen Becker: 'How true it is that a ship under sail has a beauty entirely of its own; & the intensity of the emotion is quite particular too. About a fortnight ago I was in Port-Vendres, full down the way when one was casting off from the quay: her staysails just enabled her to weather the jetty & then she put before the wind, a tramontane, set course, upper & lower topsails, topgallants, then remarkably deep & broad royals & so away & away out into the haze of Cape Creus for Barcelona. She would have lifted your heart.'

walked from Collioure to Port-Vendres to view a fleet of fifteen or sixteen Spanish schooners which had put in bearing cargoes of oranges. It was surely not an inexperienced eye which singled out (for example) 'the Cruz del Sur, a topmast schooner is the term, I think – bow quite different from the usual clipper line of the others. She looked as if she really *sailed* the deep sea, instead of coasting along with an auxiliary and one sail. I could not see how the staysails worked. Her masts were wood (the moulding of one metal) and were wonderfully tall – the height of the mizzen (the tallest) was, I think, greater than the ship's length.' Patrick's account is accompanied by detailed sketches and descriptive notes concerning the vessels and their equipment, indicating a remarkable degree of technical understanding.

Returning to his specific claim, in one of the fullest of his rare references to his seagoing experience he provided the journalist Keith Wheatley with a version which differs in emphasis from those he provided on other occasions. '"I shipped in a small vessel, rigged as a barque. The idea was to restore my health. It gave me a tolerably accurate knowledge, particularly of the upper rigging," he recalled. "In the very early 1930s one was still surrounded by shellbacks, sailors brought up from childhood under sail and they formed the crew of a yacht owned by the guardian of a young man who shared a tutor with me. We were very close friends indeed. This man just loved to sail. Not to get anywhere, just to sail. Oh dear, I loved that. I did absorb an awful lot of sea lore . . ."'[1]

This time, although Patrick alludes to the great yacht, he makes no direct claim to have sailed aboard her, and if his seagoing experience represented pure invention, what was the point of constantly introducing the 'two-ton sloop' when he might have confined himself to the magnificent *Belem*?[2]

Patrick never dated his sailing experience with any precision. In his interview with Keith Wheatley he assigned it to 'the very early 1930s', and his memoir for the British Library publication also locates it during his early adolescence, when 'we were in the great depression of the Thirties': i.e. 1929–33. This chronology is hard to accept. Setting aside the difficulty in envisaging what useful part a teenage invalid might have played on board a large sailing vessel, had Patrick enjoyed such an adventure while living at home in Sutherland Avenue it would have been impossible for Joan not to have known and recalled it. Yet neither she nor Patrick made any allusion to it when reminiscing about their shared childhood experiences. In 1989 Bun wrote to Joan *à propos* Patrick's fame as a naval novelist:

[1] 'The Long Life of O'Brian', *Financial Times*, 11–12 January 1997.

[2] I have not found any reference made by Patrick to the sloop prior to his inspecting the *Belem* in 1991. Had he done so, he might have felt obliged to retain it to ensure consistency – but this does not appear to be the case.

> His apparent knowledge of seamanship under sail and the naval terminology never ceases to amaze me. As far as I know, he has never been to sea in a tall ship or any other for any distance, but he must have just lived in the Greenwich Museum, swotting away at the terminology or having had much more experience in the Mediterranean near his home, than I had ever dreamed about.

Although Joan's replies have not survived, one would expect Bun's subsequent correspondence to have mentioned so momentous a revelation had she been able to correct him.[1]

Furthermore Patrick stated more than once that his friend Edward who introduced him to sailing 'shared a tutor with me'. Yet it has been shown that Patrick almost certainly never had a tutor other than his father, and nothing required him to have one after leaving school in 1929. Three years later, when his father accepted that he needed formal educational qualification, he sent him to evening classes at Birkbeck College. Joan, who was with him throughout that time, recalled only long and lonely days confined with her brother in an otherwise empty home. Had Patrick then possessed a 'particular friend Edward', she would surely have remembered him.

All this indicates that if Patrick's early sailing had any basis in reality, it must have occurred after he left Crowborough for Chelsea in or about the autumn of 1935, and before his departure from London early in 1939. This is confirmed by the likelihood that it was not until his arrival in Chelsea that he came to know the 'Edward' who facilitated his voyage. This can only have been Edward Taaffe, who was living in Chelsea at the time of Patrick's arrival, and acted as a witness at his wedding in February 1936. Taaffe is an Irish name, so it is not unlikely that he had relatives and friends in Ireland. It is interesting to note that Patrick identified his friend by his Christian name only, although an Irish surname would have increased the plausibility of his story.

After Elizabeth became pregnant in May 1936 nothing is recorded of Patrick's activities for the remainder of the year until its conclusion, when the Christmas edition of *The Oxford Annual for Boys* published a fresh short story by him entitled 'Noughts and Crosses'. Presumably written earlier that year, it represented a striking departure from the genres he had previously pursued, shifting from animal tales and stories of India to his first seafaring

[1] Bernard himself could have had no direct knowledge of Patrick's activities, since he was in Australia throughout the relevant period. A newspaper attack on Patrick's reputation attributed Bernard's comment 'to O'Brian's younger sister' (*Daily Mail*, 3 November 2003), thus according the comment an authority it entirely lacks.

adventure. Its heroes Sullivan and Ross, whose idiosyncratic personalities provoke clashes from time to time, comprise a resourceful pair who in this and subsequent stories survive a succession of dangerous adventures.

The setting of the story is the smoking-room of a gentleman's club, where Sullivan is recounting his experience of a dangerous shipwreck on the Great Barrier Reef. Together with his friend Ross he was sailing on a whaler which, after surviving a fierce storm, experienced an attack by a school of sharks frenziedly attracted by the smell of a tank on board which had contained oil from sharks' livers. Unfortunately Ross, ignoring the pleas of his fellow-sailors, insisted on continuing fishing, with the disastrous consequence that the sharks attack and sink the ship, devouring all the crew save him and Sullivan, who escape by mounting the floating tank. In this precarious situation they while away the time playing noughts and crosses until at last they are rescued. The tale concluded, Ross reveals himself to be present among the auditors and frankly acknowledges the truth of the story.

Both Patrick and his editor were clearly pleased with this new departure in his writing, and the next issue of *The Oxford Annual for Boys* in 1937 contained a further adventure of Sullivan and Ross, entitled 'Two's Company'. This time premonitions of Aubrey and Maturin are clearly detectable. Sullivan plays the violin and keeps a pet sea eagle, while Ross plays the bagpipes and converses with a pet skua. Confined together in a lighthouse by the rotting carcass of a stranded whale,[1] the two friends eventually find the isolation preying upon their nerves to such an extent that a fierce fight breaks out between them. Despite this outburst, and the fact that apologies are neither offered nor invited, their friendship endures.

There are indications that Sullivan and Ross owe their inspiration to the friendship between Patrick and Edward Taaffe.[2] Taaffe, like Sullivan, was an Irishman, while Patrick at one time adopted the Scottish surname Ross. Like Ross, Patrick was eccentric, wilful, frequently impractical, and prone to quarrel with his closest friends. In view of this, may not the maritime setting of the tales also have arisen from their shared experiences? Of the two, Sullivan is the more equable and experienced sailor, while Ross displays at times disarming professional incompetence and feckless irresponsibility. One is reminded of Patrick's own erratic handling of intricate manual tasks,

[1] This curiously repellent factor is reminiscent of the incident in *HMS Surprise*, when Stephen Maturin is marooned on an island covered in excrement and survives only by drinking 'birds' shit'.

[2] It is tempting to infer that the combination of names was suggested by that of Somerville and Ross, whose humorous tales of rural life and hunting in Ireland at the beginning of the century would have appealed to Patrick.

and Stephen Maturin's obdurate inability to understand seamanship.[1]

If indeed Edward Taaffe took Patrick with him on a vessel belonging to a friend or relative, it is reasonable to suppose that he was the experienced sailor Patrick declared him to have been. On the other hand, just as Patrick proved unable to cope with discipline during his brief service with the RAF, one may readily imagine his perpetrating continual blunders aboard ship and resenting instruction or reproof. The unusual emphasis on repellent filth and disgusting stench encountered at sea by Sullivan and Ross recalls Patrick's own visceral distaste for dirt and disorder. Finally, it is more than likely that he would have found enforced proximity even to so close a friend profoundly trying, and the relationship could at times have suffered a severe strain.[2]

Although the case remains at present unproved, 'Noughts and Crosses' may have owed its inspiration to a sailing expedition Patrick undertook with Taaffe in the summer or autumn of 1936. Perhaps the smoking-room reconciliation between Sullivan and Ross was paralleled in real life by a release of tension felt by Patrick once the two young men returned to the pubs of Chelsea. He is likely to have accepted with good humour his friend's anecdotes among mutual friends of his blundering attempts to master the rudiments of seamanship.

A fundamental running theme of the Aubrey–Maturin relationship is that of deep friendship surviving constant threats of rupture, largely owing to the bluff Jack Aubrey's ability to overlook or ride out stormy passages provoked by Stephen Maturin's sensitive nature and sardonic wit. Patrick described Edward Taaffe as his 'particular friend', and particular friends were a rare commodity in Patrick's life.

Another of Patrick's works strengthens the impression that his assertions reflected reality. In 1955 he wrote his first naval novel, *The Golden Ocean*, whose young Irish hero Peter Palafox sails with Anson during his famous circumnavigation of the globe. Travelling to find a ship at Queenstown, Peter and his friend Sean O'Mara make friends with an impulsive, generous-hearted young man of the same age named Peregrine FitzGerald, whose wayward father had 'ruined himself by pursuing three law-suits at once about a right of way through his demesne'. As a consequence he obtained a posting

[1] Patrick mentions in passing that Sullivan and Ross 'were both educated men . . . at one time they had owned a small tramp steamer . . .'

[2] At one point Stephen Maturin confesses of Jack Aubrey: 'I love him as much as I have loved any man, but often these last months I have wondered whether we can stay in the same ship without fighting. I am no longer what small comfort I was to him, but a present irritation and a constraint – our friendship is constrained. And the tension, cooped up in a little small ship day after day, is very great – covert words, the risk of misunderstanding, watching the things we say and even sing' (*Post Captain*, 1972, pp. 274–75).

in the Royal Navy for his impoverished son, who 'began to read voyages' in preparation for his career.

Quarrelsome and prone to violence when he fancies himself provoked, FitzGerald has to be sharply called to order by his superiors on board ship, and proves entirely unsuited to a career at sea. Unlike Peter and Sean, who take everything in their stride, FitzGerald expresses disgust on being shown his 'horrible booth' of a cabin, and succumbs to a severe bout of seasickness. Much worse ensues when he fails to obey an order sufficiently promptly, and when punished by being 'mast-headed' suffers an acute attack of vertigo. The agony he experiences is portrayed by Patrick with painful realism: 'FitzGerald was up there, gripped by some awful horror that Peter could see but not entirely understand: he was physically helpless . . . helpless and exhausted, yet his courage was not destroyed, nor his pride.'

When FitzGerald leaves the ship at its next landfall, Peter takes the opportunity of sending a letter to his father, which begins: 'I embrace this Opportunity of sending you my Love and Duty by the Hands of Mr FitzGerald who is my particular Friend and who is leaving the Ship and going Home in an Indiaman. He is a prodigious good Fellow and a very Fine Gentleman, but is not quite suited for a Life at Sea. He is to have a Pair of Colours in the Company's India service, but vows he will go there by Land, for the Sea-passage would make him pule into a Lethergy [*sic*].'

Parallels between FitzGerald and Patrick are surely too close to be coincidental. FitzGerald is obliged to seek a career in the Navy on account of his eccentric father's inability to manage his financial affairs. Like the youthful Patrick, he devoured books of voyages. Swift to take offence and react with violence to a perceived insult, he is nonetheless a generous-hearted soul. He resents receiving orders, and encounters difficulty in mastering the practical duties and jargon of the service. While Taaffe was Patrick's 'particular friend Edward', Peter Palafox describes FitzGerald as 'my particular Friend'.

FitzGerald bears in addition two attributes Patrick subsequently accorded Stephen Maturin, whose character unquestionably reflected his own. Maturin is a FitzGerald, though born on the wrong side of the blanket. Patrick remarks of him at the outset of *Master and Commander*: 'It was difficult to tell his age, for not only had he that kind of face that does not give anything away, but he was wearing a wig, a grizzled wig, apparently made of wire, and quite devoid of powder: he might have been anything between twenty and sixty.' Similarly when Peter Palafox meets FitzGerald, he finds him 'nothing like what he had expected: for one thing . . . he was very much older. And yet on closer inspection he was not so ancient in fact: he wore his own hair (which was red), but it was powdered, and powdered hair, like a wig, made a person appear of an indeterminate age.' Patrick, who was profoundly conscious of not having enjoyed a normal boyhood and had difficulty in maintaining equable relations with young men of his own age, described his earlier self as 'a sort of elderly child'.

Possibly the most significant factor in Patrick's partial self-portrayal as FitzGerald in *The Golden Ocean* is his painfully convincing description of the young man's paralysing attack of vertigo. Patrick similarly suffered from fear of heights, although like FitzGerald he courageously struggled to overcome it. Six months before he began writing the novel he and my mother picnicked on a beach near their home in France. It was a happy occasion until, as she recorded that night in her diary, 'P. got stuck though, climbing up the cliff to go home, & I got Tomassier & four other men with huge rope.'

The climb is not a very difficult one, and Patrick's inability to move arose from an attack of vertigo. Not long after, when beginning *The Golden Ocean*, he recorded a vivid dream. He, my mother, and his son Richard were seated on the edge of a sheer chalk cliff. Suddenly, without warning, my mother began sliding over the edge. 'She did not look round but in the last moment she said "I'm sorry, P., I'm afraid I'm slipping . . ."' Patrick and Richard watched as her body gathered speed until it plummeted into the sea far below.

> Between the time that I saw her and the time she spoke I did nothing. I was afraid of the edge and the height and as I did not know officially I was able to do nothing.
>
> I think I looked away momentarily – 'not having seen anything.' (not *my* fault) I was angry (or rather, *sour*): but then in the last second I was intolerably moved by her voice . . .
>
> I could not have done anything. We were sitting rather far apart and I think my legs were already over the edge: there were a great many reasons why . . .
>
> Apart from that one tearing moment I hardly felt anything: it was all instantly covered by refusal to feel (or denial of feeling) – a refusal that works for the moment in almost any circumstances: that is, it suppresses the symptoms. But while I was on my way down the path I had already formed and elaborated a fantasy in which I had not only done something, but had done it effectively – I had held her and pulled her up.

One source of vertigo (as opposed to rational fear of dangerous heights) lies in an insecure childhood, which leads the growing infant to be assailed by unconscious terror that at any moment everything sustaining his existence may dissolve without warning. Forty years later Patrick recorded another dream, in which he found himself standing on a castle wall above 'a sheer drop of perhaps 1000′ to an estuary . . . a voice telling me about it in the silence – *the horror of the void*' (italics inserted).

FitzGerald's nightmare experience could well reflect Patrick's unexpected terror on ascending the rigging. Like FitzGerald he would have striven to overcome and conceal his failing. In one of his few brief accounts of his sailing experience he mentioned that 'I hurried up the rigging as briskly as I could and was encouraged to go more briskly'. He likewise ascribed Stephen Maturin 'an indifferent head for heights and the upper yards of even a frigate filled him with paralysing dread, scarcely to be overcome by the strongest effort of will'.[1]

There is something a little incongruous about the regularity with which Patrick introduced the two-ton converted sloop as prefatory to the grand 611-ton *Fantome II*. Although he described Colonel Guinness's yacht and its activities in some detail, he never expatiated on his own services aboard. In contrast he explained with some precision that its modest predecessor was 'a small vessel, rigged as a barque', and that 'it gave me a tolerably accurate knowledge, particularly of the upper rigging [*n.b.*]'.

All in all, I am inclined to think that Patrick may have been taken by Edward Taaffe on a sailing venture off the Irish coast. The indications are, however, that the boat or ship in question was a relatively modest vessel, and the voyage or voyages in which he participated not necessarily very extensive. In *The Golden Ocean* FitzGerald asks Peter:

> 'You are a great sailor, I dare say?'
>
> 'No,' said Peter, shaking his head. 'Not at all. I have played about in our boat, and in the fishermen's curraghs, but I have never set foot in a ship – a brig was the biggest I ever sailed in.'
>
> 'Is a brig not a ship?' said FitzGerald with a smile.[2]

It may be that Patrick's brig became a ship.

A newspaper attack published a fortnight after Patrick's death remarked sarcastically: 'He had no personal naval experience, other than overlooking the Mediterranean.'[3] Ironically, dread of sour comments of this nature tended to provoke Patrick to enhance reality, despite the fact that his literary achievement would be the greater had he *not* been to sea.

[1] Jessica Mann, 'A Man from a Better Age', *Sunday Telegraph*, 15 December 1996; *The Nutmeg of Consolation*, p. 15.
[2] *The Golden Ocean*, p. 31.
[3] *Mail on Sunday*, 16 January 2000.

All in all, considering the enormous gaps in information regarding Patrick's youth, it would be unjust to assume that his claims to sailing experience represent pure fabrication.[1] Apart from the possibilities already discussed, he had further extensive opportunity during the four years after the war when he was living with my mother in Wales close to the sea. On his first arrival their landlord Clough Williams-Ellis 'said that if we got a dinghy we were welcome to keep it at Portmerion [*sic*]'. Williams-Ellis, himself a keen amateur sailor, made frequent expeditions along the rugged Welsh coast in his 15-ton Loch Fyne ketch *Scott*, on occasion rounding Land's End and cruising to the English and French Channel coasts.[2] Williams-Ellis was generous and hospitable, and could easily have invited the young couple for trips on board his boat.

Finally, it may be asked why Patrick seems to have transferred the experience back to his late childhood, and why he never mentioned it publicly until the last decade of his life. There is a consideration which may provide satisfactory answers to both questions.

It has been seen that Patrick married at the end of February 1936, and that his wife Elizabeth became pregnant in May. Nothing is recorded of his activities during the remainder of that year. In 1945 Elizabeth testified on oath that 'before the war . . . [Patrick] spent most of his time abroad on business'. Since he obtained his first passport in June 1937, wherever he travelled during the first half of their time together in London, it cannot have been the Continent. The only foreign country he could have visited without a passport was the Irish Free State.

Given indications that 1936 was the year Patrick was most likely to have accompanied Taaffe on a sailing trip, could it be that he misled Elizabeth into

[1] Recently (16 August 2004) BBC journalist James Landale published an article about Patrick announcing that 'fresh evidence suggests the legendary writer couldn't even sail'. The 'fresh evidence' is in fact a reprinted summary of reminiscences originally published in the American sailing magazine *Latitude 38* in August 2000 by Tom Perkins. Perkins, an admirer of Patrick's work, invited him and my mother to join him on a cruise aboard his magnificent yacht *Andromeda* in the Mediterranean in May 1995. In the course of his interesting and sympathetic article, Perkins mentioned: 'I introduced him to the helm, but he seemed to have no feeling for the wind and the course, and frequently I had to intervene to prevent a full standing gybe. I began to suspect that his autobiographical references to his months at sea as a youth were fanciful.' With due respect to Mr Perkins, whose friendship Patrick valued, the suspicion seems unwarranted. Patrick was eighty years old at the time, and could scarcely be expected to demonstrate facility in handling a large modern yacht on the basis of having sailed as a deck hand on very different types of vessel nearly sixty years earlier.

[2] Jonah Jones, *Clough Williams-Ellis: The Architect of Portmeirion* (Bridgend, 1996), pp. 120–21. Soon after his arrival in Wales in 1945 Patrick was gratified to discover on enquiring in Portmadoc that a dinghy could be bought for £10.

believing on both occasions that he was 'abroad on business'? Throughout his life he intensely disliked having to account for his movements, and this time there was reason for him to be evasive. No young wife would have been pleased at seeing her husband disappear to enjoy a lengthy bachelor holiday, above all when she was pregnant and they were living in poverty. As will shortly be seen, Patrick certainly visited Ireland in the following spring. Since he possessed barely sufficient financial resources for day-to-day survival, it seems that someone must have funded his trip or trips. And who more likely than Ned Taaffe, at once his 'particular friend' and sole Irish connection?

In the little household in Gertrude Street, as Patrick and Elizabeth struggled to make ends meet in their new home the unhappy differences within the Russ family were exacerbated when news broke that Patrick's sister Nora had converted and become a Roman Catholic nun. On 29 November 1936 she entered the Convent of the Franciscan Sisters at Mill Hill, adopting the religious name Sister Mary Francis. This enraged her father, who professed the Lutheran tradition of his family. However, it seems likely that his indignation stemmed from self-justification rather than piety. As Nora's brother Mike wrote in a letter from Australia to their sister Olive four years later: 'It is a pity that Nora is going RC crazy but if Father writes those Catholic plays what can one say?' The allusion was to the eccentric theatrical pieces whose performance Charles Russ continued to produce at his own expense.

On 2 February 1937 the long-awaited event in Patrick's household arrived, and Elizabeth gave birth to a boy in St Mary Abbots Hospital in Kensington. He was given the names Richard Francis Tudor: Richard after his father, Francis from that of a friend Francis Cox, an artist living in the King's Road, and Tudor in romantically royal recognition of Elizabeth's Christian name and Welsh ancestry. The carefully chosen names suggest that Patrick anticipated the arrival of his child with pride and pleasure. The last name suggests affectionate regard for his wife.

Patrick was after all only twenty-two, an age when the prospect of parenthood generally represents a dramatic statement to the world. Moreover his son would be the first of the next generation of the Russ family. Though he had enjoyed no opportunity in adult life for direct contact with children, his writing for an appreciative juvenile readership gave him particular reason to relish the prospect of bringing up his own child.

Whatever his feelings before the arrival of Richard, it seems that Patrick was dismayed at discovering the reality of parenthood little to his taste. Indeed, the indications are that his first visit to his wife and infant son in the hospital came as a profound unexpected shock. As ever, he expressed his feelings through his fiction. The scene is described with virtually no attempt at disguise in *The Catalans*, written sixteen years later. The speaker Xavier confesses:

> When Dédé was born . . . I was disappointed to find that I did not experience those raptures that are supposed to arise in a man seeing his wife with their first child. I did not find the child a sympathetic object, but indeed rather a disgusting one; and the sight of Georgette, radiant, worn and animal, suckling it, made my gorge rise. So then I made no pretence at conventional transports . . .'[1]

In *Richard Temple* this visceral disgust is expressed in a succession of violent diatribes. Pondering why he had not married, Richard reflects: 'He had started out so sentimental and tender-hearted that he might easily at this time have been surrounded by the smell of rancid babies.' Stephen Maturin is similarly repelled by infants, describing them as 'poor mewling little larval victims', and marvels on hearing of a colleague's longing to have a daughter: 'Strange, strange: it is a passion to which I cannot find the least echo, when I peer into my breast.' A sailor on board the *Surprise* lists 'Chamber-pots, pap-boats, swaddling clouts drying in the kitchen' among the more repellent aspects of having a small child in the home.[2]

The acute revulsion towards infants ascribed by Patrick to figures who more often than not unmistakably personify himself is ascribed particularly to their insanitary smell and dirt. That he was extremely fastidious by nature, especially in respect of matters relating to sex or excreta, is very clear. A memorandum apparently written during a stay in hospital in the 1950s expresses his anguish at public exposure of his most intimate activities. 'The ghastly thing about this place is the utter lack of privacy . . . they are grouped about the lavatory, clustered next to it in silence – impossible. Impossible, too, to prepare lotion, boil kettle, without being seen.'[3]

A phobia so extreme as to make Patrick find it intolerable to remain in the same room as a baby may have originated in circumstances relating to his own infancy. It may plausibly be supposed that so neglected a child would have

[1] *The Catalans*, p. 99.

[2] *The Catalans*, p. 99; *Richard Temple*, p. 97; *The Mauritius Command*, pp. 256, 257; *The Surgeon's Mate*, p. 275; *The Nutmeg of Consolation*, pp. 212, 224–25. To Lady Clifford's explanation that 'children are my husband's aversion, his absolute aversion: he cannot bear them', Maturin calmly replies: 'I am told that it is often the case with men' (*The Hundred Days*, p. 220).

[3] Patrick's nephew Harry Russell informs me that his mother Joan similarly 'absolutely abhorred nudity especially female nudity'.

been prone to bedwetting, a predicament perhaps exacerbated by insensitive treatment at the hands of one or more of the inexperienced caretakers who replaced his dead mother. Listing salient characteristics of the abominated 'Mrs Clapp' when preparing his short story 'The Thermometer', Patrick singled out her constant emphasis on bodily parts such as 'crutch' and 'armpits', and her concern with his 'habits' on 'the article' (chamberpot). Dirt and disorder are closely associated, and disorder was something which alarmed Patrick above all things.[1]

Whatever its origin, the inordinate revulsion which babies aroused in Patrick was undoubtedly instinctive and uncontrollable. Returning to the occasion of the birth of his son Richard, it is noteworthy that the description of the event in *The Catalans* includes an acknowledgement that '*I was disappointed to find* that I did not experience those raptures that are supposed to arise in a man seeing his wife with their first child' (italics inserted). This suggests that up to the moment of his arrival in the hospital ward Patrick shared Elizabeth's excited anticipation, and that his recoil came as a shock.

Accustomed as she was to Patrick's wayward and introverted character, and given his tendency to be guarded in his expression of emotion, Elizabeth probably noticed nothing especially untoward in his muted reaction. Furthermore, despite his constitutional inability to be a fond father to a small child, Patrick nurtured a rigorous sense of paternal duty, and as will be seen was scrupulous in fulfilling what he regarded as his obligations.

[1] 'As we know, dirt is essentially disorder. There is no such thing as absolute dirt: it exists in the eye of the beholder. If we shun dirt, it is not because of craven fear, still less dread or holy terror. Nor do our ideas about disease account for the range of our behaviour in cleaning or avoiding dirt. Dirt offends against order. Eliminating it is not a negative movement, but a positive effort to organise the environment' (Mary Douglas, *Purity and Danger: An analysis of concepts of pollution and taboo* (London, 1966), p. 2).

EIGHT

Troubled Times

> Our conscience which is a great Ledgier booke, wherein are written all our offences, a register to lay them vp, (which those Ægyptians in their Hieroglyphickes expressed by a mill, as well for the continuance, as for the torture of it) grindes our soules with the remembrance of some precedent sinnes, & makes vs reflect vpon, accuse & condemne our owne selues.
>
> (Robert Burton, *The Anatomy of Melancholy*)

When his juvenile works *Cæsar* and *Hussein* came to be reissued by the British Library in 1999, Patrick contributed a two-page introduction which included a paragraph describing the circumstances in which he came to write the second of the two books: 'I was living in Dublin at the time . . .' Dean King makes it clear that he regards this claim with suspicion:

> Since he married Elizabeth in London in February 1936 and Richard was born there in February 1937 and the book was published in April 1938, it is difficult to fit this into the chronology, unless he spent some time there soon after leaving the air force and nearly three years passed between the time he wrote the book and its publication, which is unlikely.[1]

Here we have a salutary reminder that each assertion advanced by Patrick about his early life must be considered independently, and the fact that he can be shown to have occasionally altered or coloured facts cannot be taken to bear general application. In this case, for example, however unlikely Patrick's account might appear, it happens to be true. Although he began writing the novel in London about the time of Richard's birth, shortly after

[1] King, *Patrick O'Brian*, p. 75.

registering the event at Kensington Register Office he departed to Ireland where he completed his second novel, *Hussein*.

Three years earlier Patrick had included in his collection of animal tales *Beasts Royal* three stories of which the youthful Indian Muslim Hussein was the engaging hero. Patrick's editor at Oxford University Press, Charles Kaberry, was a perceptive admirer of his work. It has been seen that following the publication of *Beasts Royal* Kaberry commissioned him in successive years to write stories for *The Oxford Annual for Boys*. 'Cheetah', which appeared in 1935, recounted Hussein's fourth adventure, which Patrick subsequently incorporated as a chapter of the novel.

It seems likely that Patrick's abrupt departure to live away from home for two or three months after registering Richard's birth arose from his inability to work in close proximity to his infant son. Even had he not found the spectacle and smell of small babies intolerable, constant nightly disturbances and lack of privacy would have made concentration impossible within the narrow confines of the single room in the basement flat in Oakley Street which constituted their family home.

While it is uncertain why he fastened on Ireland as his refuge, it has been seen that there is reason to believe he may have accompanied his friend Edward Taaffe on a visit there in the previous year. If so it would explain both his confidence that it would prove a congenial location for his work, and his access to means of funding a trip which far exceeded his financial resources.

Life cannot have been easy for Elizabeth during her husband's absence for the next two months or so, living as she was alone with her small baby in cramped quarters without any assistance, and dependent on very constricted financial resources. Despite this the indications are that she loyally supported her husband throughout his struggle to establish himself as an author.

Patrick's first destination after crossing the Irish Sea was Belfast. Where and why he stayed there is not known, and further suggests prior acquaintance with the country. What is certain is that he plunged himself into his work without remission. His assertion that he wrote *Hussein* at the rate of at least a thousand words a day is borne out by the appearance of the manuscript, which contains surprisingly few alterations and conveys every indication of polished fluency. So felicitous was the flow of the work that it required very little editing, and the published version approximates closely to Patrick's swiftly written original.

He calculated that the finished manuscript amounted to 82,000 words, which suggests that he began writing the book about February. The greater part of his work in Ireland was completed in Belfast, and it was only the last section that was written in Dublin. He moved there at the beginning of April, and there is no reason not to credit the account he wrote over sixty years later of his stay in the Irish capital.

> As for *Hussein* . . . I cannot remember its genesis with anything like the same clarity [as *Cæsar*], but I rather think that it derived from a tale I wrote for one of the Oxford annuals, to which I contributed fairly often: Mr Kaberry, an amiable man who ran the annual, said it would be a pity to publish no more than the abbreviated form I showed him, and suggested that I should expand it to a book. I was living in Dublin at the time, in a boarding house in Leeson Street kept by two very kind sisters from Tipperary and inhabited mostly by young men studying at the national university with a few from Trinity. What fun we had in the evenings: the Miss Spains from Tipperary danced countless Irish dances with wonderful grace, big-boned Séan from Derry sawing away at his fiddle and the others joining in as well as they could. On Sundays we would go to a church where, without impropriety, the priest could say his Mass in eighteen minutes; then we would ride [by tram] to Blackrock to swim; and all this time the book was flowing well, rarely less than 1000 words a day and sometimes much more. I finished it on a bench in Stephen's Green with a mixture of triumph and regret.[1]

The date was 29 April 1937. After concluding the last paragraph, Patrick pencilled with evident relish the postscript:

> 29.IV.37 Baile Aṫa Cliaṫ [the Irish name for Dublin] Finis + AD MAIOREM DEI ƷLORIAM. +.

Hussein is an admirable work, especially for so young an author: swift-moving, humorous, rich in language and exotic settings. In common with virtually all his works it includes autobiographical elements. Hussein's mother dies within a year of his birth, after which his father 'carried a sweet memory with him always'. An old Sikh called 'Hurri Singh' surely derived his name from Hurree Jamset Ram Singh, the Indian boy whose quaint speech memorably enlivened life at Greyfriars School in *Billy Bunter* –

[1] O'Brian, *Cæsar*, British Library republication, p. vi. That Patrick was consciously echoing Gibbon's mingled triumph and regret on completing *The Decline and Fall of the Roman Empire* (John, Lord Sherfield, ed., *The Miscellaneous Works of Edward Gibbon, Esq. With Memoirs of his Life and Writings Composed by Himself* (London, 1814), i, p. 255) does not of course detract from the authenticity of this description.

classic schoolboy fare of the pre-war era from which Patrick was subsequently concerned to distance himself.[1]

An American reviewer who described the book as a 'medley of Eastern folk-tales, assembled in the form of a novel' was perceptive in his assessment.[2] Episodes follow upon each other so swiftly and colourfully that one barely notices the joins. Patrick's febrile imagination was always ready to supply additional dramatic interludes. Towards the close of the novel Hussein, passing himself off as a professional storyteller, offers to tell some villagers 'the tale of the Maharajah of Oudh, and of the Maharani, who was a ghoul'. In the published edition we are told no more than that 'the tale was very well received', but in his manuscript Patrick noted: 'here the tale might follow, about 2,500 [words]'.

It is interesting to note again Patrick's favourable view of the Raj. At the outset of the story he describes the horrors of a major cholera epidemic: 'The dead were thrown into great pits, for there were so many. The Government did all that it could, and trains came from the south with food and doctors. It is said that men of the I.M.S. [Indian Medical Service] died from overwork and exhaustion and nothing else.' The father of his stepmother's first husband William Center had been a senior medical officer of the IMS in the Punjab, and it is not unlikely that she would have spoken of him to Patrick, since his passion for India began while they were living together at Lewes.

Years later Patrick told a journalist that if he 'hadn't been Catholic, [he] would surely have been a Communist in the thirties, believing the world could be changed'. The first claim is untrue, and the second unlikely. He was certainly not a Catholic in the 1930s or 1940s.[3] Although he later professed himself a member of the Church and defended its authority, I doubt whether he was ever a communicant. Certainly many young men of the day, who had suffered much less than he in the way of real or fancied deprivation and humiliation, channelled their frustration into vengeful feelings of class hatred and self-indulgent expressions of concern for the poor by joining the Party. Such indeed might have been the course adopted by Patrick, but here again his idiosyncratic character made him not as other men. Intellectually he was too intelligent to be taken in by political panaceas, and his intense individualism made him instinctively averse to following fashion.

[1] The Chinese character Li Han in Patrick's later Sullivan and Ross stories speaks a comical English reminiscent of that employed by Billy Bunter's Indian friend.

[2] *Saturday Review of Literature*, 9 July 1938.

[3] His wife Elizabeth declared on oath in 1949 that neither she nor her husband 'was a Catholic' (PRO J77/3990).

Over the winter of 1945–46 he observed the French political scene with some interest, expressing satisfaction when the Communists suffered reverses. His admiration for the Indian Empire confirms that he never flirted with left-wing notions current in the Chelsea of his day (which he would doubtless have found tiresomely affected), nor did his enthusiasm for Ireland and the Irish lead him at that time to espouse an anti-colonial viewpoint.

Many years later, on a further visit to Ireland in the autumn of 1972, he recorded in his journal: 'Shelbourne [Hotel] pleasant, & my window looks straight on to the corner of Stephen's Green, diagonally across from the dear Miss Spains of 35 years ago: a striking contrast & in some ways a sad one.'

It will be noted how exact was his remembrance of the date and circumstances of his earlier visit. The reflection clearly aroused strong feelings of nostalgia, and he observed further: 'Perhaps colour does not really mean a great deal to me, at least as far as visual memory is concerned: I always forget the strawberry-roan of Dublin brick.' During the last months of his life, when Patrick was living and writing at Trinity College, he saw much of our youngest daughter Xenia, who began her studies there. Walking with her through the streets, he would regularly pause to recount small incidents from his past which familiar spots unexpectedly dredged up from his memory.

It does not appear that Patrick returned to Dublin until twenty years after his completion of *Hussein*, when he flew from London to visit me when I was studying at Trinity College. Even so it is abundantly clear that he had fallen in love with Ireland at first sight. His memories of happy evenings at his lodgings in Leeson Street show how readily he took to the people, whose unaffected good manners, lack of excessive concern with social status, and spontaneity in conversation could not have presented a stronger contrast to everything he resented in English life. It must have been this visit which occasioned his later fanciful claims to an Irish connection, which in his twilight years was greeted with derision by a small clique of publicists unaware of the force imagination may exert upon an impressionable mind.

His time in Ireland also aroused a love of Irish literature. He developed particular enthusiasm for James Joyce, although this may have been coincidental, since *Ulysses* received its first general publication in Britain by the Bodley Head in 1936. Indeed it is unlikely that he read the book in Ireland, where it was generally unavailable.[1] What would have appealed to him were its efflorescent humour, luxuriant parade of learning, genial disrespect for authority and convention, fluidity of Anglo-Irish diction, and happy evocation of the then unchanged topography of Georgian Dublin. It is not possible to specify which if any other Irish authors he read at this time,

[1] Contrary to a widespread misconception, it was not banned in the Republic.

apart from Liam O'Flaherty's novel *Skerrett*, a copy of which he retained in his library.

Patrick had long been fascinated by languages. He had passed his matriculation in Latin and French three years earlier, and retained a creditable proficiency in both tongues. His novels set in India are permeated with native words and expressions, and not long afterwards he made a determined effort to master Chinese. His wife spoke Welsh as her first language, and it is scarcely surprising that Patrick took a keen interest in its cognate Celtic language across the Irish sea.

He also practised calligraphy, and his handwriting (which at this time constituted a hurried but not unattractive scrawl) was in due course to become notable for its elegance. The beauty of Irish script attracted his admiration, and it has been seen that he concluded the manuscript of *Hussein* with the Irish name and lettering of Dublin: *Baile Ata Cliat*. He also entered a facetious calculation in Irish script in a margin of the manuscript. He maintained this practice for a while, observing shortly after returning to London: 'I am bεri foηd of a loη3 peη', to which he added in mirror writing: 'it has, moreover, a fine nib'.[1]

The enchantment which the island of saints and scholars wrought upon Patrick's imagination is illustrated by two charming short stories included in his collection *The Last Pool*. The book was published in 1950, the year after he and my mother migrated from Wales to France. As will be shown, the dates of composition of these tales varied greatly. Throughout the war Patrick appears to have abandoned creative writing altogether, and during the four years which followed (when living in North Wales) he suffered from a prolonged and agonising bout of writer's block. Consequently, while most of the thirteen short stories were composed in Wales, two certainly and very likely a third were written a decade earlier, having lain fallow in manuscript throughout that time.

Almost all the stories in the collection are devoted to descriptions of sporting adventures: fishing, hunting, and shooting. The portrayals of nature and thrill of the chase are brilliantly evoked and the collection was justly praised on this account. Almost all are permeated by a settled sense of

[1] Oddly enough Patrick had been accustomed to using an Irish pen many years before his first visit to Ireland. A few weeks before his death he wrote this poignant little note: '21. X. 99 . . . How I wish I could find that close-written paper with my earlier thoughts: as I recall it had a fine liveliness. Is this a Cross pen? Cross of Ballinasloe. That is an odd attachment I have with an element of all least poetic truth going back to my adolescence or even childhood – at least 70 years – reinforced by Borrow & my Ballinasloe.'

pessimism and often culminate in grim disaster, undoubtedly reflecting Patrick's frame of mind at the time.

Two stories present so striking a contrast with the melancholy and tragedy of the others as to require some explanation. 'The Green Creature' and 'The Virtuous Peleg' belong to an entirely different genre. Delightful virtuoso gems, they are gently humorous pastiche adaptations of themes from Irish folklore and medieval literature. 'The Green Creature' tells of the monster of Lake Orbuidhe, a shape-shifting creature who elects to assume the form of a beautiful young woman. Her demon master dwelling in the neighbouring mountains persuades her that it was 'her nature to require the blood of men four times in every hundred years: it was so that if she could not come at it she would grow old and hideous, whereas she was exceedingly beautiful and desired above all things to remain so'. Daniel Colman, a handsome and athletic young seminarist, encounters her while out fishing on the shore of the lake. After a wrestling match so violent that it 'raised white-topped waves upon Orbuidhe', the pair call a truce and settle down in the green creature's cave over a shared meal of kippered trout to argue the toss on a rational basis. Daniel Colman, as clever as he is brave, succeeds in persuading the lady that she is deceived by her evil mentor and, wistfully abandoning his prospects for the priesthood, gains her hand in marriage.

'The Virtuous Peleg' is told with equal charm and deceptive skill. Peleg is a young monk possessed of great physical strength, but modestly conscious of his inadequacies as a man of the Church. Eventually he finds opportunity to redeem himself by accomplishing an expedition replete with wonderful adventures. After encountering an amiable but absent-minded angel, who puts him to the test in a wrestling match from which he very properly emerges master, Peleg receives guidance which enables him to survive unscathed a succession of cheerfully bizarre and perilous encounters by land and sea. At last he arrives at a cave inhabited by no less a person than 'the captain of the devils, a grand spotted one' grandiloquently squatting amid his impish following.

Seized and confined by these foes of God and man, honest Peleg manfully endures the most ingenious of torments and enticing of temptations. Finally he turns the tables on his captors and all ends well, with Peleg's guardian angel dispatching him on a mission of conversion 'to fourteen kings of the pagan shore to whom you must preach the faith, for now there is virtue and understanding in you. That is the message: and now we shall take a glass or two together, for I have a bottle conveniently near at hand, and it appears that I will not see you again until I stand with my trumpet to sound you in over the mossy walls of Paradise.'

Both tales owe their inspiration to a state of mind radically different from that which produced the carefully observed and finely written but more self-conscious literary stories collected in the same volume. And could it be that Patrick's description of the young monk setting out to sea with his companion St Kevin reflects his recollection of an Atlantic voyage in the previous year?

> Peleg sat on a thwart while the tide swept them out and away on the far, broad sea. For hours and hours Peleg sat there in a holy calm, regarding the beauty of the calm sea, for it was like a small pond in its calmness and there was the long path of the moon behind them. The air was warm and sweet like hay to smell and the curach slipped through the quiet water, creaking a little and the water making a little slip-slipping noise under it.
>
> Dawn came up with the glory of heaven and still Kevin slept. Peleg longed to wake him so that they could be speaking of the voyage . . . He stared wildly round the pale bowl of the sky, green and grey where it met the sea all round and no land, and no land at all; unending waters stretching away and away to the edge of the world and the sun glittering on them.[1]

It is impossible not to be struck by the discrete character of these two ebullient Irish stories, gleaming like emeralds amid their sombre fellows in *The Last Pool*, whose dark seam of pessimism and recurrent apprehension of catastrophe reflected the bleakly uncreative period which Patrick suffered during the immediate post-war years. What bright flash could have caused his joyous excursions into 'The Virtuous Peleg' and 'The Green Creature'? Nothing approaching their easy exuberance appears in any of Patrick's published or unpublished works during the seventeen years which passed between his completion of *Hussein* and composing *The Golden Ocean*.

One of the most striking characteristics of the two stories is the Anglo-Irish idiom which skilfully conflates contemporary Irish speech with the style of the early Irish heroic and ecclesiastical sagas, at least as they feature in translation. The achievement is remarkable on two counts. Generally speaking, Patrick did not possess great aptitude for memorising dialects with which he was not in direct contact. While his lower-deck characters in the Aubrey–Maturin series are realistically portrayed, their speech is generally represented by a sort of hybrid demotic, making little or no allowance for the medley of English dialects which would in reality have been heard aboard one of His Majesty's men-of-war. Scottish characters such as Lord Melville and Admiral Keith intermittently deliver themselves of a 'wheesht, man' or 'puir

[1] *The Last Pool*, p. 71.

laddie', but overall their speech is an unconvincing representation of the Doric spoken north of the Border.

A marked exception to this rule is found in the Anglo-Welsh diction of *Three Bear Witness*, which was written shortly after Patrick had lived for four years amid a rural community in Wales, saturating himself in the local idiom.[1] That 'The Virtuous Peleg' and 'The Green Creature' were written during or shortly after Patrick's stay in Ireland in 1937 may be further indicated by the fact that his ability to reproduce Irish speech was not retained for long. In his short story 'No Pirates Nowadays', written at the end of 1939, the Irishman Sullivan's brogue is confined to an occasional 'my boyo' or 'me boyo': a form of address the more incongruous because in every other respect his speech is rendered in conventional English. A few months later Patrick wrote the early part of his novel *The Road to Samarcand*, in which Sullivan and Ross reappeared as major characters. By this time Sullivan's hibernicisms had dwindled to a solitary 'not at all, at all'.

Always an avid haunter of second-hand bookshops, Patrick also used Irish literature. 'The Virtuous Peleg' owes much to translations of medieval Irish saints' lives, while 'The Green Creature' appears at least in part to owe its inspiration to the saga of Fergus mac Léidi, whose hero engages in a colourful combat with the underwater monstress (*sinech*) of Lochrury. Patrick's hero 'Daniel . . . held his wind until he was black in the face and his features were much disordered', while the breath of the monster encountered by Fergus in the saga 'turned him into a crooked and distorted squint-eyed being, with his mouth twisted round to his very poll'.[2]

However it may be that Patrick's knowledge was mediated through the works of writers such as Joyce and James Stephens rather than derived directly from translations of the medieval sagas, of which he possessed no copies and of which I never heard him claim any knowledge. Another likely source of his jocular yet fundamentally respectful pastiche treatment of early hagiography was Richard Garnett's collection of short stories *The Twilight of the Gods*, which first appeared in 1888, Patrick's copy being published in 1927. 'The Virtuous Peleg' has marked resonances with Garnett's delightful story 'The Bell of Saint Euschemon', although there is a strong contrast between Garnett's sceptical attitude towards early Christianity and Patrick's affectionate adaptation of quaint elements found in the lives of Irish saints.

'The Green Creature' and 'The Virtuous Peleg' were probably written

[1] Recently Edgar Williams, a native of the valley in which the story is set, remarked to me on the faithfulness of Patrick's dialogue to reality. It is also apparent from Philip Madoc's admirable recorded reading of the novel.

[2] Standish H. O'Grady (ed.), *Silva Gadelica: A Collection of Tales in Irish with Extracts Illustrating Persons and Places* (London, 1892), ii, pp. 283–85.

during or shortly after Patrick's visit to Ireland in 1937. The conclusion is not decisive, but this examination of what might appear a trifling issue seems justified by the extent to which it suggests that Patrick's stay in Ireland was a luminous interlude during a deeply troubled period in his life. It may further account for his otherwise unexplained assumption of Irish connections or origin: a claim which he is first recorded to have advanced later in the same year, while he was still in the first flush of infatuation with the country.[1]

The fact that the stories were not published at the time is no insuperable obstacle to this reconstruction. As has already been noted, other stories published in *The Last Pool* were written years before. At the Oxford University Press, Mr Kaberry may have felt sufficiently pleased with *Hussein*, while considering the two eccentric Irish stories inappropriate for the schoolboy annual he edited. They include blithely uninhibited sexual allusions inappropriate for the young readership of *The Oxford Annual for Boys*. More often than not a single rejection sufficed to deter Patrick from risking refusal at the hands of another publisher.[2]

It was probably not until early June that he returned from Dublin to his family in London.[3] It was no doubt in a state of apprehensive excitement that he despatched the typescript of *Hussein* to the Oxford University Press, but in the meantime his overwhelming concern was to find some means of maintaining the family in Gertrude Street. Before long he discovered opportunity of employment with the Workers' Travel Association. This was a semi-politicised travel agency, which arranged holidays for young tourists at Locarno in Switzerland.

The possibility of visiting the Continent for the first time must have appeared attractive to Patrick. Locarno was a romantic port and health resort, situated on the edge of Lake Maggiore at the foot of wooded cliffs surmounted by a picturesque group of monastic buildings clustered about the church of Madonna del Sasso – all mirrored in the still, clear water below. The language and ambience were Italian, and the setting idyllic. Although villas and houses had begun to spread beyond the town, little white chapels could still be glimpsed among surrounding vineyards and groves of oranges and lemons.

The Workers' Travel Association arranged for its customers to stay at the

[1] In Patrick's story 'Two's Company', which was written later in the year of his visit to Ireland, the name 'Cuchulainn' given to Sullivan's tame eagle suggests an interest in Irish legends.

[2] In June 1954 both his British and American publishers turned down his novel *Richard Temple*, which he promptly abandoned and did not take up again until five years later.

[3] Patrick was back in London on 23 June, and it would have been a hardy man who swam regularly at Blackrock much earlier in the year.

small Hotel Quisisana, where Patrick's duties involved arranging the visitors' reception, accompanying them on trips to neighbouring beauty spots and places of historic interest, and looking after them generally. On 23 June he obtained his first passport, so he did not stay long in Gertrude Street with Elizabeth and their baby Richard before setting off abroad once again.

This episode came to light only after the publication of Dean King's biography in the United States in 1999, when he was approached by two Englishwomen who had travelled as young girls on one of the Association's holidays at this time, but he was able to insert it in the UK edition the following year. The sisters Beryl and Joan Ainsworth were then aged twenty-one and eighteen respectively. The younger of the two was of a type familiar to Patrick from the world he frequented in Chelsea. As King describes her, 'Joan, a perky graduate of an arty private school in Ealing . . . was fond of the theatre and now had a job selling theatre tickets for Keith Prowse on Bond Street.'

They had led a sheltered middle-class existence, and found the worldly-wise Patrick an attractively exotic figure: 'He told them that he was Irish, and, according to Beryl, that he had been an RAF pilot until an accident with a propeller had sent him to the hospital, where, he said, the doctors had put a steel plate in his head. He also told them that he was an artist and that he had written a book of stories called *Beasts Royal*. He raved about James Joyce, and when Joan confessed that she had not read him, he playfully chastised her, saying that in that case she had not been educated at all.'[1]

Though the sisters only stayed at the Hotel Quisisana for a fortnight, in no time at all Joan was creeping downstairs each night to join Patrick in his bed. This episode would be barely worth mentioning were it not for the unique insight it provides into Patrick's state of mind at this time. Chatting confidentially with the sisters, he dramatically doctored the reason for his discharge from the RAF, laid claim to being Irish, and described himself as an artist who also wrote books.

While Patrick's infidelity to Elizabeth is not creditable, he should perhaps not be judged too harshly, given the girl's willingness and the near-impossibility of his wife's ever learning of the brief holiday affair. Moreover the fact that he made it clear from the outset that he was a married man and firmly refused to agree to Joan's suggestion that they continue the affair on his return to London (easy as that would have been), indicates the cursory and purely physical nature of his lapse. Since this affair came to light quite by chance, it inevitably raises questions concerning the state of Patrick's marriage to Elizabeth during the years they lived together. Much of the

[1] King, *Patrick O'Brian*, pp. 69–71.

principal section of *Richard Temple* is taken up with Richard's extensive sexual encounters, and as the novel reflects so much that is autobiographical it is impossible to avoid confronting the question of whether they may not in some degree have reflected reality.

Sexual laxity was the norm among much of the artistic community of Chelsea at that time. As a dazzled Joan Wyndham explained, the Chelsea élite regarded itself as enticingly exclusive, comprising as it did 'about 120 people who'd all been to bed with each other once and were wondering what to do next'. For a girl lacking pretension to genius the ready road to becoming a member of this tight little community was to join them in bed. As Wyndham's old school friend Thetis proudly declared: 'My dear . . . I've lost my virginity! It was marvellous, so simple and easy and natural.'

Released from virtual imprisonment in Albany Street and Crowborough, the temptation proffered by a promiscuous set of women may have appeared overwhelming to a socially naïve and sexually inexperienced young man like Patrick. In his novel, having broken off his initial brief relationship with Doris, Richard Temple engages in innumerable fleeting and unsatisfactory affairs. Patrick's firm refusal to continue his holiday affair back in London suggests that he avoided serious infidelity. But precisely what he might have regarded as 'serious' in the circumstances is impossible to know. In the 1960s, discussing a romance in my life, Patrick asserted that he had been quite a 'bull' in his youth. Given the presence of numerous Joan Ainsworths and Joan Wyndhams who regarded sex as their passport to the world of high art, it is not unlikely that he occasionally succumbed to temptation. In *Richard Temple* the disgust with which Temple describes his profligacy suggests the generally purgative purpose of the novel, a function which may also have led to exaggeration.[1]

Overall, there is no justification for supposing that Patrick was seriously unfaithful to Elizabeth during the early years of their marriage, at least not by the standards of the society in which they lived. Most of the grubby encounters ascribed to Temple in the novel are patently fictitious, and the novel's most radical departure from reality lies in the swift and total end to his initiatory romance with Doris (the model for Elizabeth). Patrick's own marriage, following as it did soon after his arrival in Chelsea, presented inhibitory practical and moral obstacles to loose conduct absent from the novel. I believe that the extreme fastidiousness which was one of his most

[1] Patrick's sister Joan informed her daughter Gwen that he once got a girl in the family way, and that his father arranged an illegal abortion for her. Dr Russ was certainly professionally in a position to undertake such an operation, but in the absence of corroboration it would be pointless to place weight on the story.

marked characteristics makes it unlikely that he emulated the lax behaviour of Richard Temple.[1]

In *Hussein*, which was written immediately prior to Patrick's stay in Switzerland, he laid strong emphasis on his hero's essential fidelity to his one true love, which however he did not regard as seriously violated by occasional lapses during his travels: 'Hussein was always faithful to Sashiya, for she was more important to him than anything else, and he always guarded her memory very close to his heart; but he was, like most men, faithful in his own way.' On being seduced by the 'remarkably pretty' Fatima, one of the four wives of an old Mohammedan, 'He was a little dismayed when she proved to be exceedingly amorous, but he closed his eyes, and saw Sashiya in her place.'[2] It would be interesting in this context to know more of the girl whose image flashed into Patrick's memory when watching a French television documentary in 1977: 'There was nothing on, apart from a quite good piece on parent/child communication . . . (speakerine v like Patricia 40 years ago).'

Many men, whether from nature or hypocrisy, tend to dismiss mutually consensual passing encounters as of small consequence within the context of marriage. 'Hussein's code was an elastic one, and it would stretch surprisingly on occasion'. It is not unlikely that Patrick's fundamental attitude was that of Richard Temple: 'in work, as in some of his dreams, he reverted to his old and habitual self (which was incidentally a sexless state); he was alone and happy in his solitude, unaware of himself and conscious of little but the slide of the brush on the plaster, the immediate technical problems of the continually changing surface'.

Hussein contains what appears an idealised self-portrait in the high-minded Prince of Kathiawar, a youth of consummate beauty, exquisite taste, and lofty principles. His superlative qualities led him to be pursued with equal ardour by his father the Maharajah's wicked homosexual *wazir* and his favourite concubine. 'But the young man disregarded all these matters, and applied himself still more to literature in all its forms, and to chess.'

Patrick's employment at Locarno continued until the autumn, when he returned to his family in Gertrude Street. Worryingly, months had gone by without the Oxford University Press indicating whether they intended to

[1] Harry Russell recalls of his mother Joan that: 'Her father was a consultant venerologist and I remember her telling me how she despised the patients coming to see her father. As mentioned earlier this attitude is of a piece with her general abhorrence of all things physical.' Patrick shared his sister's knowledge, and not improbably her viewpoint. If so, fear as well as fastidiousness could have influenced his attitude towards women.

[2] *Hussein*, pp. 212, 213.

accept *Hussein* for publication. He could not afford to let the grass grow under his feet, and began considering urgently what literary task he should undertake next. He would soon be twenty-three, and was growing ambitious to advance beyond his current status as literary entertainer. Obsessed with a desire to gain acceptance in the world of formal scholarship, in his eyes this represented an élite club, hedged about by esoteric qualifications of rank and precedence no less rigorously defined than those governing the social élite from which he likewise felt excluded. It was about this time that he determined to achieve a reputation as a serious scholar.

The topic upon which he fastened was one which exerted a natural appeal to his tastes and imagination. Since early childhood he had been fascinated by the world of natural history, and was also strongly attracted by information of a recherché character. Towards the end of 1937 he began intensive researches on medieval bestiaries, with a view to compiling a book on the subject.

Here again a contributory influence by Garnett's *Twilight of the Gods* seems likely. Garnett's stories are characterised not only by sardonic wit, swift-moving narrative flow, and adept manipulation of plot, but by the authentic erudition to be expected of the Director of the Reading Room at the British Museum. That he displayed his learning lightly and employed it languidly made its profundity no less apparent, and these it need hardly be said were to become among Patrick's more striking literary characteristics. As T.E. Lawrence observed in an introduction in the 1927 edition Patrick possessed:

> Dr Garnett was a very sure scholar, who had done the plain things and the big things and was tired of them. In this book lies his leisure, as much for our delight as his. It wants no learning to enjoy the *Twilight of the Gods*; but the more learning you have, the more odd corners and hidden delights you will find in it . . . His spells are real, his sorcery accurate, according to the best dark-age models . . . On the point of scholarship let us give the book a first-class. Ditto in magic, in alchemy, in toxicology; ditto in wit and humour.

It may also have been Lawrence's affectionate evocation of the magnificent Panizzi Reading Room, with its 'great ceiling covered so solemnly overhead', which first directed Patrick towards a 'province . . . wise, rich, sober, warm, decent (even dingy), industrious . . .' Lawrence's depiction of the building as a 'Temple', and its inmates as 'devotees' who 'live with the best materials of the past, studying them, endeavouring by every context of literature and history to understand them more fully, to see them more remarkably in the round', reflected just those factors which drew Patrick irresistibly towards scholarship.[1] 'For this select few on earth, Greece and Rome, Babylon and Egypt are not dead. These empires are . . . things of vital importance, growing daily larger and clearer, their bread-and-butter, their ideal, their study, the business of their working hours and the chosen pastime of their leisure.'

Such was likewise the appeal which abstruse regions of learned lore exerted on Patrick's imagination. Why should he not become one of the 'select few' who dwelt in those rich restricted realms?

Having obtained a reader's ticket, Patrick began regular journeys to the British Museum (a number 14 bus conveniently passed almost door to door from Gertrude Street), where he immersed himself with characteristic energy and diligence in a thorough examination of printed and manuscript sources.

The bestiary was a popular genre of medieval literature, one of whose major original sources was Book 12 (*De Animalibvs*) of the encyclopaedic *Etymologiæ* of the great seventh-century Spanish scholar Isidore of Seville. *De Animalibvs*, which in turn derived much of its information from classical lore, provided descriptions of the natural history of all known living creatures. While it contained a great deal of accurate information, it also included much that was legendary and fantastic. Authors in subsequent centuries embroidered and added to Isidore's catalogue, and to a medieval readership eager for marvels the more implausible the description, the greater its appeal.

Patrick delighted in the rich hoard of unintended humour provided by this bizarre branch of literature, and his meticulously compiled notes reveal the extent to which he relished quaint and curious items of imaginative zoology. Among the many manuscripts over which he pored, *Li Bestiaire de Philippe de Thaün* told him that for a reason not explained 'the flattened leg of the lion' provided a symbol of the coming of Christ. A further helpful attribute of the royal beast was his ability to capture his prey by making a track on the ground with his tail, which his simple-minded victims felt constrained to follow. The ass he found easy meat, since the foolish beast 'is by nature mad, as scripture says, he will stray from his road if he is not forced to it'. However, the lion was himself not immune from dangerous eccentricities. When 'angry he hangs himself by his feet; on the earth he will hang himself when he is furious'. Nevertheless as king of beasts he symbolises many aspects of God. His skill in covering his tracks by swishing his tail over the ground, for example, represents a sure sign of the Incarnation, which God (for a reason

[1] Could Patrick have taken the surname of his autobiographical hero from Lawrence's reference to the British Museum as a 'Temple' dedicated to recondite learning?

which Philippe does not fully explain) similarly preserved as a secret from men.

Philippe's allegorical interpretation extends further: 'And know another mark of the lion, it is that he sleeps with open eyes; and know that this signifies the Son of St. Mary; in his death waking, when, dying, he killed death.'

There exists a further remarkable manifestation of the lion as symbol of Christ: 'Know that the lioness bears her son dead, and so it remains until the lion comes, and he roars above it, so that it lives on the third day; you shall understand this figure.' All this Patrick painstakingly copied from the manuscript 'Bibl. Cott. Nero A. V., fol. 41 recto. – 82 verso'.

From *Li Bestiaires d'Amour de Mestre Richard de Fournival* Patrick transcribed this graphic account of the complex courting practice of the elephant:

> When the male wishes to beget upon his companion and his mate, they go away to the Orient, close to Paradise, where, on a mountain there grows the mandragore, of which we shall treat afterwards. Then the she-elephant goes to the herb and eats of it at once, then the male, – mark this well – eats, when he sees that she entices him to it. When they have both eaten it, with wantonness and play they come together, as beasts should do. The female conceives at once, and the young that she gets, she carries two years, as I have told you.

As ever, a Christian exemplar was detectable. Richard de Fournival explained that just as the lion provides an image of Christ, so the paradisal mating practice of the elephant and his wife corresponds to the companionship of Adam and Eve. The king of beasts is useful even in death, for the smell of his burning bones affords sure means of repelling serpents.

Powerful though the elephant is, it does not lack deadly foes. The female is obliged to bear her solitary offspring in water, in order to avoid its abduction by the dragon. The unicorn is capable of disembowelling the wretched creature with its hoof, which is 'as sharp as a scimitar'. However the unicorn in turn is readily captured by seating a virgin near its lair, upon which it is irresistibly drawn into laying its head in her lap. Maître Richard quotes the unicorn's explanation of its vulnerability: 'For I tell you that I have been taken by the perfume, and she holds me yet by the perfume. And my whole desire is to follow her and pursue her.'

Patrick carefully copied and coloured an illumination from the manuscript of this interesting scene. His reproduction displays considerable skill in draughtsmanship, and the gloating leer on the face of the warrior driving his spear into the unfortunate unicorn's flank and the voluptuous figure of the inviting naked virgin are rendered with sensual relish.

As his researches continued, he discovered the unicorn to have been but one of innumerable exotic bests encountered in distant parts of the earth (though Conrad Gesner in his *Historiae Animalium* recorded the discovery in 1520 of one of their horns in Switzerland). In Ethiopia, for example, there are ants the size of dogs who occupy their time in mining gold. However, they are regularly deprived of their wealth by a neighbouring people, who employ a complex deception involving hungry mares carrying beautiful shining boxes, which are driven across to graze the territory of the ants. The latter, who apparently lack suitable receptacles, delightedly rush to store their gold in the boxes. Their task completed, the mares are immediately lured back by the whinnying of their foals retained by their masters. Thus the men wallow in wealth, while the anguish of the ants (who are evidently incapable of learning from experience) is testified by a doleful wailing from beyond the river demarcating their frontier. This account gave Patrick particular pleasure, and he included both it and the means of entrapping unicorns in an unpublished story he wrote two years later.

It was his hope that the book when completed would be accepted by the Oxford University Press, which had after all published his work for children, so enabling him to achieve his ambition of becoming a scholar of serious repute. His researches were without question wide-ranging and thorough. He consulted an extensive list of manuscripts and early printed works, from which he copied and translated numerous passages in addition to those cited above from Latin, medieval French, and Middle English. His synopsis, entitled 'Beasts to be dealt with', covered twelve chapters on relatively conventional creatures (although including the unicorn) such as the tiger, ant, and whale, before moving on to others describing more exotic beasts ranging from the salamander, cockatrice, and basilisk to the phoenix and centaur.

How long Patrick toiled at these researches is not recorded, but they must certainly have required months of intensive reading before he suddenly abandoned the project in mid-flow. Since his synopsis remains uncompleted, it does not appear that he submitted his work to the Oxford University Press, so it is unlikely that it was ever rejected. The work he had already accomplished was impressive, and had he informally consulted an editor at this stage one would expect him to have received sufficient encouragement at least to complete his synopsis.

Patrick's principal motive for his work on bestiaries is clear. The autobiographical hero of his novel *Three Bear Witness* (1952), a university Fellow named Pugh, is engaged in work on a book on *The Bestiary before Isidore of Seville*. Pugh refers with rueful self-mockery to 'the small circle of palæographers who had read my articles',[1] and the reader is plainly invited to regard him as an unworldly Casaubon immersed in esoteric researches.

Throughout his life Patrick repeatedly drew attention to his research on bestiaries. As early as 1953 he provided this summary outline of his career for the dust-jacket of *The Catalans*: 'Patrick O'Brian was born in 1914, and started writing early. He produced four books before the war, and also worked for many years, in Oxford, Paris, and Italy, on a book on Bestiaries. Most of this valuable material was lost in the war.' Over forty years later he explained in his introduction to the tribute published by the British Library: 'in the late Thirties I was chiefly taken up with a book on Saint Isidore of Seville and the western bestiary, for which I had done a good deal of reading in the British Museum, at the Bodleian, at the Bibliothèque nationale, in Padua and at the Vatican'.

In a sympathetic interview, Jessica Mann learned that 'Patrick O'Brian has been a writer all his adult life, but his unpublished early fiction and a study of the medieval bestiary and St Isidore of Seville disappeared in 1940 when that bad man [Hitler] blew my house in Chelsea up with a bomb.' The assertion that his hard-won researches were destroyed in the Blitz is endorsed by Dean King, who goes so far as to specify 20 October 1940 as the date that 'his manuscript in progress, a non-fiction account of St Isidore and the Western bestiary, was destroyed' by an unexploded bomb which hit 24 Gertrude Street.[2]

Unfortunately much of this represents romancing on Patrick's part. While he did labour long and hard at the British Museum, he almost certainly never extended his researches to Paris, Padua, the Vatican, or even Oxford. Of his *alter ego* in *Richard Temple* it is stated that 'he had copied Baldovinetti and Luini in the Louvre', but on the other hand he overhears the unpleasant comment that 'He says that he has been at Munich, a fiction so easily detected that it is wonderful how he should have been so inconsiderate as to hazard it.' Given the confessional theme of the novel, this may indicate that he was both conscious of embroidering such claims and aware of the danger that incurred. So far as King's story is concerned, Patrick was not living in Gertrude Street

[1] *Three Bear Witness*, p. 10. The reference to 'palæographers' is a characteristic attempt at a display of arcane erudition, since there appears no reason why palæographers should be especially concerned with such a work. The name of Isidore of Seville also appears designed to conjure up an image of scholarly obscurity. (Patrick perpetrates a minor lapse in referring to 'The Bestiary *before* Isidore of Seville', whereas elsewhere he correctly alluded to the great Spanish scholar as effective founder of the genre.) Isidore's work had classical predecessors, such as the *De natura animalibus* of the second-century Claudius Aelianus, but nothing suggests that Patrick possessed any knowledge of that period.

[2] Cunningham (ed.), *Patrick O'Brian*, p. 17; *Sunday Telegraph*, 15 December 1996; King, *Patrick O'Brian*, p. 86.

in 1940, nor was his work destroyed during the war. Not only did his notes survive in what appear to be their entirety, but my mother recorded in her diary on 6 December 1952 that Patrick had briefly resumed the project: 'P. working hard on Bestiaries, his cold is gone.'

In reality his *métier* was not really that of scholarship pure and simple, and he was to apply his encyclopædic knowledge and intuitive feeling for history to other fruitful fields. Nevertheless it remains curious that Patrick did not continue his researches at least to the point of submitting his planned synopsis to the Oxford University Press. Since he appears to have begun his work in the autumn or winter of 1937, the extent of his researches at the British Museum suggests that they continued at least into the spring of 1938. Why he abandoned the planned book remains unknown. While it is not inconceivable that he eventually lost interest in a project insufficiently near to his heart, this seems unlikely in view of the advanced state of his synopsis and his pressing need for money. There is a likely reason, but because of its significance its discussion must be reserved for another chapter.

That is to look ahead, and in the meantime the little household must have been overjoyed when news finally arrived that the Oxford University Press had accepted *Hussein* for publication. On 17 December 1937 Patrick signed a contract with the publisher Sir Humphrey Milford, which provided a not inconsiderable advance of £50 payable on signature, and 10% royalty on British sales.

Overall, however, throughout the years Patrick lived in London with Elizabeth their financial circumstances remained direly straitened. As has been seen, the suggestion in *Richard Temple* that he received an extremely modest allowance from a relative may reflect reality, if only because it is hard to see how he could have survived otherwise. In the novel the hero is driven to live rough for a time on the streets, and the exigencies of making do on little or no money are depicted with squalid vividness. Although in reality Patrick and Elizabeth were at least able to maintain their little home in Gertrude Street until shortly before the time came for them to leave London, the young couple lived continually on the brink of financial crisis.

In the novel Richard is driven to occasional petty shoplifting, helping himself to the small amounts of paint required to pursue his career, and scavenging oranges at Covent Garden to supplement his meagre diet. Though he escapes the attention of the law on these accounts, he subsequently becomes involved in an unpleasant incident which further alienates him from his uncle and respectable people generally. One night he is driven to shelter from a heavy downpour in the porch of a house in Westminster, where wealthy people are holding a dinner party. The wind shifts, driving the rain into his haven, and he dashes for protection into a car parked beside the pavement. Fortunately it is not only unlocked but has its key left in the ignition. On a sudden whim he starts up the engine and drives away into the darkness on a mad joyride.

A sense of exhilaration grips him as he speeds through the darkness of empty streets towards the countryside, and somewhere beyond the Edgware Road he succeeds in shaking off a pursuing police car. However, after losing his way to such an extent that he finds himself mistakenly driving back into London, he finds the police chasing him again. On a wild impulse Richard steps on the accelerator, takes off at 'shocking speed', skids, and crashes the car. After being held overnight in a police cell, he is hauled up in court and heavily fined. Richard Temple's indignant reaction is that which Patrick would himself have adopted.

After this Temple becomes involved in serious crime. He is taken up by an older man named Torrance, a generous, charming, but wholly ruthless former public school boy, who regards himself as standing outside law and morality. The impressionable Richard is readily induced into forging paintings which are sold as genuine by his new patron, following which he joins Torrance and a couple of other upper-class criminals in perpetrating a series of burglaries in country houses with which their social contacts have made them familiar.

These episodes, realistically described, may have been partially inspired by a relatively trivial escapade. My maternal grandfather was led to believe that Patrick during his poverty-stricken days received a warning from the police for stealing bicycles. Whether he really did so, or merely borrowed them for convenience (in the traditional manner of contemporary undergraduates at Oxford and Cambridge) is unknown. Assuming there be any truth in the story, the latter explanation seems more likely if he merely received a warning. My grandfather's informant was probably Father de Zulueta, the Catholic priest of Chelsea, who knew Patrick and Elizabeth and subsequently became friendly with my grandparents when they lived in Chelsea.

To Patrick a stern police warning (particularly had it followed a night in a cell) would have borne excruciating resonances of the grim patriarchal oppression under which he had suffered for the greater part of his life. In *Richard Temple* he refers resentfully to the smug 'righteousness of being a keeper', and says bitterly of the police 'although it could not be said that they *framed* him in the full meaning of the word they certainly abused his confidence and distorted the course of justice to make it arrive at the conclusion that they thought just'.

The circumstances would have appeared not a little sordid as well as embarrassing, and in the story there are tell-tale hints that Patrick's humble bicycle may have been upgraded to a Rolls-Royce or Daimler. It is after all unlikely that such a car would have been left unlocked with its ignition key in place. No satisfactory reason is given for the high-speed police chase – and above all nothing in the story allows for Temple to have learned how to drive a car. That the episode long rankled in Patrick's mind is indicated to me at least by his occasional outbursts of exaggerated resentment against the British police. In May 1952 my mother provided this telling description of a film she and Patrick saw in their local French cinema: 'Horrible, righteous, brute-faced American police, armed & decked out – scores of them hunting down a rather nice thief who had all our sympathy.'

I have no doubt that Patrick was speaking from the heart when he made Richard Temple reflect that 'nothing in the world was so ugly as the sight of a man in the hands of his righteous enemies – that nothing was so ugly, miserable and boring as fear – that a man kept in a cage was liable to become an ugly beast, his soul having evaporated between the pages of the *Police Gazette* – that it was immoral to be treated as a thief'. Or, as his mentor Torrance put it: '"Power corrupts; and the spiritual corruption of the police is something inconceivable to people who do not know anything about it. It is not only that they are inverted criminals, but they never have the criminal's saving sense of sin", and Richard went right along with that.'[1]

This trifling lapse in Patrick's youth (assuming it really occurred) throws a revealing light on the extent to which his treatment at his father's hands coloured his perception of authority, and the manner in which he could contrive an extensive artistic superstructure on a slender foundation of fact. Richard Temple's involvement in major criminal activities had no basis in Patrick's own experience. It will be shown at the appropriate juncture that the character of Torrance was probably drawn from a man with whom Patrick became acquainted long years afterwards, while his gang's activities were undoubtedly based on an atrocious crime perpetrated by a group of young aristocrats which caused a sensation in the contemporary press. Having invited an unfortunate jeweller to an hotel bedroom on the pretext of examining some diamonds, in the process of robbing him they assaulted him so violently that he died. Among them was Lord Jermyn (afterwards Marquess of Bristol), who was sentenced to birching and a period of imprisonment. Patrick makes this all but explicit when he states of one member of the gang that he 'had taken up with a far more stupid, brutal and notorious set – the fellows (actually related to Crichton, as it happened) who had very nearly beaten an old jeweller to death'. Not only is the crime virtually the same, but Richard's friend Philippa Brett alludes to 'Avon's son'

[1] *Richard Temple*, pp. 186–87.

as being among the members of the gang. Lord Jermyn's father was the Marquess of Bristol, and Bristol is situated at the mouth of the Avon.

Apart from his work on bestiaries little is known of Patrick's activities in 1938. An exciting moment arrived when *Hussein* was published in April. It was after all the first of his works to be directed as much towards an adult readership as to children. Not only was it published by the Oxford University Press, but it was the first contemporary novel it had published since its foundation in 1585. The book's sales and reviews in Britain were satisfactory, and it gained the attention of the *Times Literary Supplement*, although the review itself was ponderously humourless. This muted reception was eclipsed when *Hussein* was published in the United States at the beginning of the following month, where it received glowing reviews in such prestigious newspapers as the *New York Times* and *New York Herald Tribune*. The former made favourable comparisons with Kipling and the *Arabian Nights*, and went on to describe *Hussein* as 'gorgeous entertainment not only in the story which it unfolds but also in the manner of the telling'. The *Tribune* was if anything yet more ecstatic in its praise: 'As the pages move by things become slightly plausible, then credible, then entirely believable. Finally they are living, factual events, and Hussein, in search of his Sashiya, is a hero as alive and human as Tom Jones seeking his Sophia.' The reviewer could scarcely have made a comparison more pleasing to Patrick, with his devotion to English literature of the eighteenth century.

Meanwhile the novel's fortunes appeared to be soaring. On 8 March Patrick received a further advance royalty of £17. The Press shipped out batches of copies to India and Australia, and at the end of June sent Patrick three guineas 'for reproduction of The Snow Leopard, & The First Story Teller's Tale, in certain Indian journals'. On 26 August a Polish publisher bought the translation rights to *Hussein*, followed by a similar purchase on 5 November by the German publisher Wilhelm Goldmann of Leipzig.[1]

Patrick had finally 'arrived' as a writer, and among those whose opinions mattered most to him his star must really have appeared to have risen. Although there exists no direct evidence of Charles Russ's reaction, a likely echo appears in *Richard Temple*, whose hero wins the highest prize at the Reynolds School of Art. 'When Richard won the Haydon, Canon Harler took him to the Café Royal instead of Lyons, and gave him a pound with less moral gesticulation than he usually employed over half a crown.'

[1] The rising threat of war and the war itself caused the German publication to be delayed until 1952, when Patrick received a royalty of £28/13/9d. I have been unable to discover what led Goldmann to fulfil its contract several years after the intervening cataclysm, by which time *Hussein* had been long forgotten in Britain and the USA.

Hussein bore the affectionate dedication in Welsh, *I fy ngwraig annwyl a fy mab bychan*, 'To my dear wife and little son'. Elizabeth was proud of her husband's success, and the inclusion of Richard in the dedication indicates genuine fondness for his son. While the dedication might be dismissed as a sop to convention, a clearer pledge of Patrick's affection was provided in the month after the book's publication in England, when Elizabeth became pregnant for the second time.

In so far as one may judge from the scanty evidence there is no reason to suppose that the little household at 24 Gertrude Street was other than united in mutual affection. That summer Patrick's brother Bun arrived in England, having spent nine years in Australia. He had worked his passage home as a steward on board the Canadian Pacific liner *Empress of Britain*. During the long voyage he became engaged to a girl called Violet Herbert, who had been working as a ship stewardess for several years. His father and stepmother journeyed to Southampton to meet them, while on their return his brothers Victor and Patrick (so Victor's widow Saidie recalls) 'wickedly planned to meet them and make their conversation consist of all the most abstruse and difficult words they could think of – to confuse Violet'. Such a game would certainly have appealed to Patrick, and it appears from this that he was at home in the autumn. Bun himself recalled meeting his nephew Richard during his visit, describing him as 'a little fellow'.

By a fortunate chance Bun's stay at Crowborough coincided with Joan's 21st birthday on 10 July 1938, when he and Victor clubbed together to present her with a fine Sunbeam bicycle which she cherished for the rest of her life. She was working at the time as a student teacher at a nearby school, where Bun gave the pupils an account of life in Australia. He had arrived with the patriotic intention of enlisting in the Army, but unfortunately failed the medical examination on account of an injury to his arm inflicted while castrating piglets in the outback. Greatly disappointed, he accepted an invitation from his Uncle Cecil (his mother Jessie's brother) and Aunt Gwen to come and stay at their home in Seattle. He crossed the Atlantic, arriving at Seattle in time for Christmas, where he and his fiancée received a most hospitable welcome. In March of the following year they were married. Violet had saved a substantial sum of money from her earnings, with which she and Bernard were able to establish themselves in Canada. She bore him two children, Elizabeth and Charles, but after a few years Bernard abandoned her.

Though financial exigencies represented a persistently nagging threat, later in the year a further short story by Patrick appeared in *The Oxford Annual for Boys*. Entitled 'One Arctic Summer', it branched into a novel theme. The story centres on a fierce conflict in Lapland between a saintly

Russian Orthodox priest, Father Sergei, and a clutch of fanatical Lapp shamans. Employing a combination of physical strength and moral authority, Father Sergei saves a wounded English airman from his barbaric enemies, and after seeing him transported to safety remains in the icy North to convert the heathen Lapps to Christianity.

In view of Elizabeth's statement that her husband regularly travelled abroad as a courier throughout their married life, it is possible that he returned to Locarno or undertook similar work during part of the summer of 1938. His marriage began to come under severe strain that autumn, but discussion of this momentous development must be reserved for the next chapter. On 8 February of the following year Elizabeth gave birth at St Mary Abbots Hospital in Kensington to a daughter, whom they named Jane Elizabeth Campaspe Tudor.

When the birth came to be registered at Kensington Register Office on 16 March, unlike the previous occasion this time it was Elizabeth who attended. She gave her address as '301 King's Road', while Patrick was described as 'Author of 24 Gertrude Street Chelsea'. Dean King suggests that 'something appears already to have been amiss between the Russes'. However, there is no reason to read anything significant in the distinct addresses, which was a purely temporary arrangement. Shortly afterwards Patrick himself left Gertrude Street for good to join Elizabeth at their new flat at 301 King's Road.

It could be that they separated temporarily because of Patrick's inability to conceal his revulsion at the birth of his first child. However, whatever distress Elizabeth suffered from her husband's peculiar aversion to childbirth and babies was now entirely eclipsed by a terrible tragedy. The newborn infant was diagnosed as suffering from the then incurable congenital defect of spina bifida: a condition in which the spine fails to close over, leaving a gap in the vertebral column. Any infection was likely to prove fatal, and early death was a virtually inescapable prospect.

The horror which babies aroused in Patrick was pathological. That his conscience remained deeply troubled by his treatment of his wife on this occasion is apparent once again from astonishing passages in *Richard Temple*. Calling on an absent neighbour, Richard unwillingly finds himself subjected to rambling explanations by the wife and the unwelcome attentions of her two infant children.

> Richard listened gloomily, while the watery children crawled silently about: they were dressed in thick, blubbered wool, and the one Richard thought of as the urine child kept trying to climb up on his knee . . . It was terribly depressing. But the needs of the other child obliged her to carry it out of the

room, and she came back at the moment when he gave his tormentor a strong push with his foot.[1]

On being discovered kicking the unfortunate infant into the fire, Richard departs fuming with resentment at the mother's indignant reproaches. He 'had seen Eunice arrive, and had seen her take up with Briggs when she was a fresh and lively girl who loved to dance; and now she was a yellow-faced,[2] long-nosed slut and her tiny mind was as strong as a horse and unalterable now. Ill-used; and so a shrew and righteous for ever after.'[3]

To Patrick, a woman's giving birth represented such a monstrous aberration as to destroy her good looks and character beyond recall (though the gross excess of language suggests some awareness of the irrationality of this reaction). The incident continues to prey on Richard's mind to such an extent that it leads him to repudiate the idea of living with a woman at all. Later on an artist calls on him,

> to hear his views on women – on concubinage, to be exact. 'Don't let them in,' said Richard, putting away the ultramarine. 'No,' he cried, 'never *live* with one – it will not do. Even if she can keep you . . . it would never do for you, you understand – you could not cope. There is a voice there, a person there, bawling about eat your pie now – drink – wash – just in the hours where you need everything in your hand. She is going to object if you bring other girls in or go away without saying anything – everything has to be arranged. Slopping pails of water – broom. No. It is convenient, I admit, but it will not do. Think of poor Dürer. Did you know a man called Briggs? No. They swell up directly: you look round, and there is a woman with a big belly, knitting, and the next thing you know there is a little Urine or a little Slime running up and down shrieking.'[4]

These splenetic outbursts appear wholly inappropriate to the context of the novel, given that Richard Temple does not marry, while his brief visit to Mrs Briggs provides his only contact with babies. His reaction is so extreme and

[1] Irritated by a small boy, Pugh the protagonist of Patrick's other autobiographical novel *Three Bear Witness*, ponders whether to 'give him an unseen slap when Bronwen [his mother] took him away' (p. 59).

[2] Patrick described Elizabeth as 'looking yellow and disagreeable' when he saw her after a long interval in 1949.

[3] Meek wives who become termagants provide a recurring theme in Patrick's writing. Tom Pullings's wife acquires 'a certain developing shrewishness (unimaginable to those who had only seen her as a timid country-mouse several years and four stout children ago)' (*The Thirteen-Gun Salute*, p. 26).

[4] *Richard Temple*, pp. 191–92.

his language so absurdly venomous as to indicate expression of some psychotic phobia on the part of Richard Patrick Russ rather than that of Richard Temple. On leaving her house, 'He came down the mean streets of Fulham to the King's Road and walked up to it.'

But for the tragic circumstances, it is amusing to observe Patrick yet again inadvertently substituting the circumstances of his own life for those of his fictional hero. Temple could scarcely have left her house and walked 'down the mean streets of Fulham to the King's Road', since Mrs Briggs herself lived in the King's Road. On the other hand that is precisely the route Patrick would have taken had he returned to Gertrude Street after visiting Elizabeth and their two infant children before he joined them at their new flat in King's Road.

Whatever Patrick's reaction to the birth of his daughter Jane in the early spring of 1939, he and Elizabeth were soon sharing their new marital home, their life together to all appearance little changed. Some time later Patrick apparently fell sick. Saidie Russ informed me that in 1939 Victor visited him in a London hospital, where he found him 'very ill'.[1] Victor cynically conjectured that 'his illness was caused by poverty and drinking too much'. Shortly afterwards he took Saidie down to Crowborough to introduce her to his father and stepmother as his prospective bride (they were to marry in the following year). Zoe Russ promptly declared that Patrick was welcome to come and convalesce with them. However he declined the offer, discharged himself prematurely from the hospital, and afterwards informed Victor that he had gone on a walking tour in the Welsh mountains to recover his health. This episode presumably occurred no later than the end of June 1939, since Patrick's brother Michael wrote from Australia on 31 July to his sister Olive: 'I am glad also to hear of Pat gradually improving . . .'[2]

On his return to Chelsea Godfrey and Victor charitably arranged for the poverty-stricken young family to leave London and live in a small semi-detached dwelling in the Suffolk countryside, which lay within reach of Godfrey's home at Thorpe-next-Norwich and whose rent they paid.[3] Gadds Cottage was small and its facilities primitive, with an outdoor lavatory and the sole water supply a pump in the garden. But although the location was remote and the surrounding landscape bleakly desolate in winter, Patrick appears to have enjoyed the freedom and challenge which their new existence

[1] It may have been Victor, who like his elder brother Godfrey was always generous to members of his family in financial difficulty, who paid for Patrick's stay in hospital.

[2] The time limit is confirmed by the fact that Saidie attended a Land Army course in Scotland in the autumn of 1939, so her visit to Crowborough must have occurred earlier.

[3] The village has long since been engulfed by Norwich city.

offered him. He had a lifelong yearning for total independence, however straitened the circumstances, and relished the concept of being as nearly self-sufficient as possible. He kept ducks on a little pond in the garden for their eggs, a goat for milk, grew vegetables, engaged enthusiastically in handiwork about the house and garden, and collected firewood from the countryside around. Not long after their arrival he acquired a single-barrelled smallbore shotgun, with which he roamed the fields in search of rabbits, pigeons, and the occasional illicit pheasant. It was probably about this time that he acquired a copy of Colonel Hawker's *Instructions to Young Sportsmen in all that Relates to Guns and Shooting* (1839),[1] which suggests that his addiction to reliving the past through practical pursuits as well as in imagination had already begun. He also obtained a set of skis, on which he crossed the snow on his hunting expeditions during the harsh winter of 1939–40, and a fine tweed overcoat and winter clothing. How he could afford these may have puzzled Elizabeth, but she had long learned that nothing irritated her husband more than questioning.

Little is known of the Russ family's day-to-day life at Gadds Cottage. Such information as has survived derives almost exclusively from fleeting memories retained in later life by three-year-old Richard, together with a few family photographs. Conditions must have been harsh for Elizabeth, who had to make and mend for her young son and gravely sick baby daughter. A devoted mother, she was racked with concern for Jane, who required constant care.

Meanwhile in the greater world a storm was gathering which would bring chaos and tragedy to the lives of millions. Before a year was out a blast from the whirlwind gusted through the remote Suffolk household, bringing unimaginable changes to the Russ family.

Shortly before Patrick and Elizabeth left London, Hitler occupied Czechoslovakia. The invasion violated the express undertaking he had given Neville Chamberlain at Munich, and within a fortnight the Prime Minister issued a solemn guarantee in Parliament that Britain would come to the aid of Poland were she to be threatened by similar aggression. However, Hitler outwitted the Entente powers by entering into an alliance with the Soviet Union, for which Stalin had been secretly angling ever since the Nazis came to power in 1933. On 23 August the red flag and swastika fluttered side by side in Moscow, as Molotov and Ribbentrop signed the notorious pact whose secret clauses divided the northern world from the Rhine to the Bering Strait between the twin totalitarian powers.

Poland's bitter fate was sealed. On 1 September German forces crossed the

[1] He was certainly in possession of his copy in 1942.

frontier in overwhelming force, in defiance of an ultimatum issued by Chamberlain on the same day. Two days later the Prime Minister announced to the British people that the country was now at war with Germany. France followed suit, but despite valiant fighting by the Polish army and air force, any opportunity of continuing resistance ceased when on 17 September Hitler's Soviet ally invaded the country from the east.

How Patrick, living in his remote Suffolk cottage, reacted to the gathering crisis is not recorded. However the reaction of his *alter ego* Richard Temple, who remains indifferent to public events until the opening of the blitzkrieg on London, more likely than not reflects his own. Throughout his life Patrick displayed only transient interest in contemporary politics. His waking thoughts, it is strongly to be suspected, were primarily concerned with matters nearer home. The phoney war must have appeared unreal to a family living at near subsistence level in the gaunt snowbound landscape of freezing East Anglia.

Apart from the daily struggle for survival, which he faced with resourcefulness and even relish, with the arrival of long nights over the bitter winter of 1939–40 Patrick applied himself to resuscitating his literary career. It appears to have been in the spring of 1938 that he abandoned work on his projected book on medieval bestiaries, and his last piece of creative writing was the children's story 'One Arctic Summer' published at Christmas of the same year. Dean King suggests that Patrick's next published story 'No Pirates Nowadays' was written just 'Before war turned life on its head', and that the rigours of life at Gadds Cottage combined with wartime preoccupations to frustrate his writing for the space of a decade.[1] In reality it was precisely when war broke out that his literary inspiration suddenly took on a fresh lease of life.

Patrick completed 'No Pirates Nowadays' on 2 November 1939. Judging from the appearance of the manuscript it was written at a single stint; and since his count showed that it amounted to 7,400 words, it must have been begun shortly after the outbreak of war. The tale reintroduces the adventurers Ross and Sullivan, who had last appeared in 'Two's Company' in *The Oxford Annual for Boys* in 1937.

To these Patrick now added a fresh character in the form of Sullivan's nephew Derrick, who is, significantly, an orphan. The story, published in *The Oxford Annual for Boys* in the following month, is a colourful adventure tale likely to have appealed to boys of different ages. While the exotic locations, ranging from the opening scene in the wastes of the Sahara to

[1] King, *Patrick O'Brian*, p. 83.

distant islands in the North Pacific, are as ever vividly depicted from the resources of Patrick's imagination, the characters remain stock types of the schoolboy literature of the era. Sullivan is an impractical visionary Irishman, Ross a laconic Scotchman, and Derrick the youthful hero with whom young readers are invited to identify.

On laying down his pen Patrick's immediate reflection was: 'Pretty poor, I'm afraid, and I'll have to cut it to 5,000 at the most.' In the event he was relieved to find the publishers prepared to retain about 6,000 words, for which they paid him £6/16/6d. 'Hack's price', he reflected, 'but very acceptable.' Patrick's deprecatory comment should not be taken as indicating that he regarded the tale as a potboiler, nor that he was embarrassed to find himself still ploughing the field of children's literature. He clearly regarded the characters he had created with affection, since they were to reappear years later in his full-scale adventure novel *The Road to Samarcand*, at which he was to work fitfully over the next fourteen years.

As Patrick's note indicates, money was a very potent consideration. Without pausing, he swiftly set himself to writing a further short story of very different character. Wretched though his present existence must have appeared generally, his first return to country life since his happy boyhood days at Lewes afforded him genuine solace in the form of his acute love and perception of nature. His new tale, which he entitled 'The Return', seems to represent his first venture into descriptions of man's relationship with nature. The plot is simple enough, comprising as it does nothing more than an account of a day's trout-fishing. However, again apparently for the first time, Patrick's writing is characterised by delicate attention to detail and brilliant evocation of atmosphere. Long days spent stalking grouse and rabbits in open fields and plying his rod from river banks for trout or bream had drawn his deeply introspective nature into a fresh and rewarding literary genre.

He finished 'The Return' a mere five days after completing 'No Pirates Nowadays'. The story conveys the impression of having been written in a state of inspired enthusiasm. On 15 February 1940 he recorded with gratification and relief his success in selling the first serial rights of the story to *John O'London's Weekly* for the handsome sum of twelve guineas: 'just when funds had completely run out. Laus Deo et Domina Gloria: magnas ago gratias Tibi.'[1]

Now Patrick had the bit between his teeth. No sooner was this story completed, than he launched himself into a third. Each was entirely different from its predecessor in approach and subject-matter. He appears to have

[1] The story was published in the magazine on 10 May, under the title 'The Mayfly Rise'.

been driven by elation, eagerness to profit by his new-found ability to earn an income by his pen, and desire to explore fresh avenues. Yet there are also intimations of an underlying lack of self-confidence. The best of his stories which flowered briefly that winter were those drawn from his own experience: evocative accounts of the Suffolk landscape, unspoiled by artificially dramatic turns of language or plot. Nevertheless he constantly reverted to experimenting in a wide variety of genres, on the whole with little success.

His next tale, completed on 17 December 1939, was Patrick's first concession to the war fever gripping the country. Untitled, it told the story of a wealthy Jew, Moshe Ahrens, whose father's wealth and intrigues had gained him a commission in a crack regiment of the old Prussian army. Despite every effort, however humiliating, to ingratiate himself with his aristocratic fellow-officers, Ahrens continues to be regarded with coldness and disdain, the butt of crudely anti-Semitic jokes and insults. Eventually he finds himself falsely accused of betraying his country's secrets (a prince of high blood is the real culprit), and is provided with a revolver in his room to do the decent thing. Even then, his persecutors had not reached the limit of their malice: the gun proves to be loaded with a blank cartridge, and Ahrens is marched out to face the regiment's malicious contempt.

The story was never published, which was probably just as well. The snobbishness and malignity of the German officers are too unremitting (to say nothing of their historical implausibility), and the simplistic parallel with the Dreyfus case so obvious as to undermine what small originality the story contains. Even with Britain once again at war with Germany, such an uninspired tale was unlikely to make much impression on the reading public.

From a biographical point of view the story of a man desperate to join a class to which he does not belong, ultimately paying a terrible penalty for his doomed attempt, bears implications which it is needless to emphasise. But there is no indication that Patrick ever submitted the story to a publisher, and like its successor it seems likely that it represented nothing more than an experimental effort to move in a fresh direction.

His next endeavour was a colourful romance set in the high medieval period. In later years he must surely have chuckled on considering this, his first venture into the realm of historical fiction. 'And it befell as I had read,' as the fictional author remarks, and befall thus it did indeed, for the narrative is replete with high Victorian 'tushery'. Though Patrick had now turned twenty-six, published two books and a number of short stories of high quality, it seems that his continuing attraction to writing children's stories led him to set down on paper themes which had enraptured him in childhood and lain fallow for years after. It has been seen that there are indications that

Patrick was a boyhood admirer of the works of the popular historical novelist Jeffery Farnol, and his untitled crusading tale bears resonances of Farnol's *Beltane the Smith*, being similarly set in an imagined old England whose forests and castles are peopled with noble knights and lovely ladies, gallant archers, humorous hermits, and evil barons.

Patrick bestowed on his hero, Sir John of Bellesme, the same illustrious surname as the dispossessed Lord of Garthlaxton in *Beltane the Smith*. Although the flowery language and daring deeds reflect his literary source, Patrick unmistakably obtrudes himself into the story. Dismissed at the outset by his elder brothers as 'a stripling youth, pale with nosing into dead books', Sir John returns from the Crusade 'grown into a man bigger than themselves, and the dark, lean face under the helmet was that of their father and their famous warlike uncle, the bishop'. Recounting his high adventures in the great hall of the castle, Sir John tells how, after surviving many a fearsome fight in the Holy Land, 'we fell in with a caravan of merchants bound for the great silk marts of the East'.

Apart from the customary Ethiopian slave, his sole surviving companion is a valiant Irish knight Sir Padraig of Kerry, whose name evokes a small Lewes schoolboy brandishing his wooden sword in the garden behind 10 Priory Crescent. Together they arrive at a land 'on the borders of the kingdom of Prester John', bounded by a river which divides it from a realm inhabited by gold-gathering ants. After the courageous but rash Sir Padraig is devoured by the insects, our hero employs an ingenious ruse for tricking the ants of the treasure, which he had learned from 'an ancient book that I had read in the house of the monks of Winchester': i.e. the *Bestiaire Divin* of Guillaume le Clerc, which Patrick had carefully annotated in the British Museum three years earlier. His ensuing adventures, which include entrapment of a unicorn by the traditional method of luring it into laying its head in the lap of a beautiful virgin, likewise drew directly on Patrick's notes for his projected book on bestiaries. After wedding the Oriental beauty Lilith who entrapped the unicorn, Sir John returns home, after passing 'with a numerous train through the land of the anthropophagi, across the stoney desert to that country where the mandrake grows and where there are elephants, passing with great peril into the kingdom of the Great Cham'.

Home at last, in a scene reminiscent of Uncle Morse's sessions recounting his seafaring memories to the Russ children in his 'cabin' at Willesden Lane, our hero describes his adventures in the castle hall before a spellbound audience. This done, he deals summarily with the evil elder brothers who had plotted his death when they dispatched him on his travels, and implicitly lives happily ever after with the sultry Lilith. Behind his defensive carapace, Patrick remained an unabashed romantic at heart.

That this story and its predecessor were not accorded titles probably indicates that Patrick was aware of their failings, and explains why he does not appear to have submitted them to a publisher. The story of John of Bellesme and Padraig of Kerry was completed three days after the New Year of 1940. It was a fateful year for millions, and for Patrick was to prove the decisive turning point of his life.

A longer interval followed before he undertook his next literary work. Perhaps he realised that he had not as yet resolved his particular *métier* as a writer, and was casting about in his mind for a fresh opening. The freezing months of January and February required unremitting labour to keep the house warm and his family fed. Most days he fared forth with his shotgun in search of game for the pot, and it was the reflections and observations which accompanied these congenial expeditions which inspired his next tale.

The opening sentences of 'The Dawn Flighting' convey that atmospheric sense of place which was to prove one of Patrick's greatest strengths as a writer:

> The night was old, black, and full of cold, driving rain; the moon and the stars had already passed over the sky: they had been hidden since midnight by the torn spume. Dawn was still far away. In the mounting wind stronger gusts blew hard out of the dark east, carrying the thin rain flatways from the sea. Bent double, with the breath caught from his mouth, a man struggled against the rushing, living air: he walked on the top of the sea wall that guarded a reclaimed great marsh.[1]

The story is deceptively simple. An unnamed man sets out with his shotgun and dog before dawn in search of game, successfully brings down a brace of duck and a teal, and watches the pale, pure dawn approaching across the eastern sea.

> From far away there came a sound over the marsh on the still frozen air: he looked around, but he could see nothing. The sound grew stronger, a rhythmic beating, strangely musical, and he saw three wild swans. The light caught them from below; they flashed pure white against the cold blue. High up in the air their great singing wings carried the wild swans from the north: they flew straight and fast with the long necks stretched before them. The rhythm

[1] *The Last Pool*, p. 177.

changed, sighing and poignant, and a leaping exaltation filled the man as he gazed upon them, up away in the air.[1]

Gripped by the enchanted spectacle, the man continues to stand entranced long after the musical sound has passed away. 'Then he stirred, and hitched the bag higher on his shoulders. He plucked his feet from the mud, and went on. He was unreasonably happy now.'

It is impossible to doubt that all this is described from the life: indeed, I would be surprised if someone with local knowledge could not follow in the huntsman's tracks today. Patrick finished the story on 14 March, three days before his name-day, which throughout his life he always kept with due attention. Re-reading the manuscript, he noted hypercritically: 'Not so bad as far as it goes, but I meant it to be a good deal better than this. I was interrupted by threshing machine, M.S.[2] and sick-feeling. I have not conveyed the sound of swans flying at all well, nor the joy it is to hear them.'

This note confirms what a reader might infer, that the story reflected his own experience. Later he struck out the comment, reproving himself with the words 'Pompous ass'.

'The Return' and 'The Dawn Flighting' were later published in 1950, in a collection of thirteen short stories by Patrick entitled *The Last Pool.* Apart from the two clever parodies of Irish literature which I have suggested are linked to his visit to Ireland in 1937, all but one of the remaining stories are semi-autobiographical, mostly originating in hunting or fishing incidents experienced when he was living with my mother in Wales after the war. All these save one can be shown to have been composed while Patrick was living in Wales, and the exception was probably written during his time at Gadds Cottage.

'The Trap' differs markedly from the other tales contained in *The Last Pool*, which evoke themes of rural life and landscape with consummate skill. 'The Trap' in contrast is located in some unidentified corner of rural England. Its topography is commonplace and indeterminately envisaged, while the period is that vaguely defined late eighteenth-century-cum-Regency era beloved of historical novelists, when bold lads of humble origin dauntlessly defy and outwit oppressive excise officers, justices of the peace, or lascivious baronets. The name of the village inn, the Champion of Wales, evokes the robust and idyllic Old England portrayed in the novels of Jeffery

[1] *The Last Pool*, p. 186. The quotations are from the manuscript, which differs in some respects from the published version.

[2] It is hard to know what this represents, unless it be the accepted abbreviation of *memoriæ sacrum*, 'sacred to the memory of . . .' As will be seen in the next chapter, that is a distinct possibility.

Farnol. All the customary elements of Farnol's stories are present: the tiny cottage in which the impoverished hero dwells with his beautiful highborn wife and baby, the village inn with its genial landlord, the Big House where the tyrannical squire lords it over the neighbourhood, and the dark wood where daring poachers venture after his pheasants.

The young man, Luke Carpenter, driven by the need to support his young pregnant wife, steals out at night with his gun to poach a modest bird or two from the superfluity which the landowner and his friends slaughter in droves for idle entertainment. The squire, a retired admiral, employs a band of villainous gamekeepers who set lethal mantraps throughout his wood. Luke borrows a shotgun from the village innkeeper, and climbs over the admiral's park wall. Inside the preserve he discovers a mantrap and shifts it to another position nearby, after which he creeps into the thicket where he succeeds in shooting one pheasant and catching another. The report of the gun swiftly brings Yellow George, the most brutal of the gamekeepers, on to the scene. Luke makes an exciting escape, in the course of which his pursuer is predictably fatally gripped by the jaws of the mantrap.

Although the story is well told, the encounter in the wood being especially convincing, it is notably lacking in that meticulous evocation of period detail and atmosphere which provides so marked a characteristic of Patrick's historical novels. The conflict and characters of oppressor and oppressed are likewise stereotyped. So black is the character of the admiral that even his ship is named after the deranged Roman tyrant Caligula. At the conclusion of the story Luke is rewarded by the landlord for his brace of pheasants with a quart of beer laced with gin, together with a guinea discreetly left at the bottom of the tankard. It is surely not overly pedantic to suggest that no one possessed of any genuine historical knowledge could suppose this likely.[1] Such cavalier inaccuracy suggests the largesse and language of the romantic novel, in which golden guineas and foaming quarts of ale feature as standard adornments.

'The Trap' suggests a simplistic incursion into the field of historical romance, comparable in approach to the medieval heroics of Sir John of Bellesme. By the time Patrick came to settle in Wales, he had employed the intervening five years in extensive reading of eighteenth-century literature and history, after which it is hard to imagine his writing such a jejune narrative. As he observed acerbically of Goldsmith's *History of Rome* in his pocket diary for 1945: 'It is not history – hardly even chronicle. It seems to me that works like the Hammonds' English labourer are worth more than a

[1] On 13 September 1795 a friend of Parson Woodforde paid a shilling for 'a fine Cock Pheasant' (John Beresford, ed., *The Diary of a Country Parson: The Reverend James Woodforde* (London, 1924–31), iv, p. 227).

dozen such books, as far as inculcating an historical sense goes.'

There is a further indication that this story was among those which Patrick wrote in 1940, while he was living with Elizabeth in Suffolk. The four tales described earlier were written on the blank pages of an eighteenth-century ledger, which he had doubtless picked up in a second-hand bookshop. The original owner used the volume to record proceedings during the years 1768 to 1770 relating to an Essex enclosure act, which was inevitably passed in favour of the influential landowners who had drawn up the bill.[1] It is noteworthy that the only section of 'The Trap' which evinces any detailed knowledge of eighteenth-century social life is that relating to the expropriation of Luke's inherited common rights. Patrick accurately outlines the requisite legal proceedings, concluding with the meeting of the commissioners before whom Luke impotently seeks to assert his rights. All the information required to describe the procedures is found in the manuscript.

During the bleak winter of 1939–40 Patrick supplemented his family's sparse diet by shooting game on neighbouring land. This must regularly have involved trespass and poaching. His small folding shotgun was designed for concealment, and Patrick very likely drew on his own experience when he described Luke Carpenter setting out to poach game in the squire's covert, moving cautiously 'with a birding-piece held under his stiff arm, rigid down his side under his smock'.

Though the manuscript has not survived, it seems reasonable to conclude that Patrick wrote 'The Trap' soon after the middle of March 1940, when he had used up all the blank pages in the enclosure ledger. Although of marginal literary significance, from a biographical point of view the story casts light on the germination of Patrick's interest in the writing of historical fiction. That it remained unpublished for ten years was probably due to the fact that it was like all the adventure stories he composed at this time intended for children. If so, editors of children's magazines might well have considered it too violent for their young readers. When eventually he included it among the collection submitted to Martin Secker in 1949, it was considered appropriate to appear with other sporting tales in *The Last Pool.*

Throughout that eerie winter and spring, when Britain found herself committed to a war which was not being fought, Patrick passed his days in shooting, fishing, engaging in handiwork about the house and cultivating their little garden, writing his stories, and finally applied himself to writing a third novel. Of his family life at Gadds Cottage little beyond this is known. His son Richard was too young to remember anything of significance, and

[1] It is ironical that one of them was the Earl Waldegrave of the day, whose descendant, the Hon. William Waldegrave, is a prominent admirer of Patrick's works!

how relations stood between his mother and father remained hidden from him at that time. As will shortly appear, all was not well with their marriage. However, it was rare for Patrick to become involved in overt confrontation. If a situation arose which he found unacceptable, he would allow himself a withering sarcasm or malevolent glance, but otherwise ignored the offending party or left the room. Argument had been almost entirely suppressed throughout his childhood, and open confrontation became alien to his nature.[1] In fact nothing suggests that open friction existed between him and Elizabeth. Not long after, she herself declared on oath that their relationship continued cordial for a further three years.

However this may be, a day arrived in the late summer of 1940 when Patrick departed Gadds Cottage: as it proved, never to return. After his death, his son Richard provided this account of the event: 'O'Brian left, returned to London and lived alone in Chelsea where he drove ambulances during the war and continued with his writing,' he told a journalist. 'I was four [actually three] years old when he just got up and left without any warning or reason. I think he did it on the spur of the moment. It was a selfish thing to do. One of my uncles had to drive over and take my mother, my sister and me to his house and look after us . . . I think he couldn't cope with the grief and shame of having a disabled child. There was a stigma attached to it in those days. He took it as a reflection on himself.'

The reporter, who was clearly dependent on Richard for his information, adopted the hypothesis as fact: 'In one of his novels, for example, O'Brian has Captain Aubrey rescue a young autistic girl. When faced with a disabled girl himself, O'Brian fled.'[2]

In fact Patrick's departure had nothing to do with his daughter's dreadful illness, and it is untrue that he 'left without any warning or reason'. Jane had after all been born over a year before Patrick left his family, and her ailment was diagnosed at birth. That he was constitutionally ill equipped to be a good father is indisputable, but nothing suggests that the constant demands imposed by Jane's illness troubled him excessively. All the labour of physical care and (it is to be suspected) most of the emotional distress fell upon the baby's devoted mother. Finally, even were one to adopt the harshest view of the extent to which he might have been affected by Jane's sickness, it must be recalled that he was aware she was unlikely to survive long. In fact Jane lived on for a bare two years.

[1] His diary entry for 18 January 1980 is sincere, so far as overt displays of anger are concerned: 'Pepys as a domestic tyrant distresses me.' During more than fifty years of marriage to my mother I do not believe they ever engaged in overt quarrelling. Chill resentment on the part of either or both was the customary manner of expressing a difference.

[2] Peter Hillmore, *Mail on Sunday*, 16 January 2000.

The family moved to their refuge in Suffolk shortly after Jane's birth, when Patrick lived to all appearance contentedly in that remote backwater. By the summer of 1940 he had participated for more than a year in a near-subsistence existence, which differed little from that which he was to enjoy five years later with my mother in North Wales. His health was good, and for the first time he was able to enjoy that life close to nature which was enduringly dear to him: shooting, fishing, and observing wildlife. Poverty represented no novelty for him, and lack of concern for material prosperity was one of his most salient virtues.

Clearly nothing can justify Patrick's leaving his wife and small children, above all in the dire situation which it placed them. Nevertheless, Dean King's suggestion that he might have been affected by a superstitious fancy that spina bifida originated in 'the infirmities or wickedness of the parents' is too absurd to contemplate, nor is there any reason to suppose that tension over the baby's sickness 'exaggerated the personality differences between husband and wife and provided many reasons for resenting their current existence'.[1] Finally, so far from its being the case that 'Patrick's creative endeavours suffered', he had completed a succession of short stories over the winter and by the summer was in the full flow of writing a new novel.

It was about this time that Patrick began writing his third children's novel, *The Road to Samarcand*. At the end of 1945 he noted that 'I have just re-read that Samarcand tale. It is better than I had supposed, and it is well worth finishing. Suffers from want of central plot. It is hardly more than a series of incidents, more or less probable, fortuitously connected.' In fact he did not resume work on the story until 1954.[2] His reaction to what he considered the naïvety of his writing, combined with the virtual certainty that he abandoned all creative work throughout the war, indicate that the early section was compiled while he was living at Gadds

[1] King, *Patrick O'Brian*, p. 81. However, if it be true that Patrick's father had earlier arranged for Elizabeth to undergo an abortion, could it be that Patrick saw the birth of a crippled child as a form of retribution?

[2] After he had completed 6,000 words in 1954, my mother wrote in her diary that it 'is nearly half way'. Patrick generally estimated in advance the number of words he felt appropriate for the book on which he was working. The novel constitutes some 82,000 words, suggesting that when he resumed work he had completed the first six chapters. Chapter 7 begins with a vivid excoriation by Professor Ayrton of Chingis Khan and other great conquerors, which concludes with Sullivan's ringing endorsement that 'Aggressive war is the great crime of the world.' This reads like a post-war denunciation of Hitler. Before the war Patrick named Hussein's faithful elephants Jehangir and Jellaludin, successive 'world conquerors' after Chingis, which suggests that he then espoused a more romantic view of mighty warlords.

Cottage.[1] Equally, its cessation in mid-flow suggests that his departure from home was relatively sudden and unexpected.

Dean King concludes his description of Patrick's departure: 'When they learned what had happened, Patrick's oldest brother, Godfrey, and Connie, his wife, who were living in Thorpe-next-Norwich, drove out to Gadds Cottage and picked up Elizabeth and the two children.' The sole source for this and other widely publicised accounts of Patrick's leaving the family home is his son Richard, recalling events experienced as an infant some sixty years earlier. It is natural that at the time he can have understood little if anything of what was happening and as the years passed remembered still less, with the consequence that he inadvertently misinterpreted and telescoped events.

In the first place, Patrick did not simply disappear without explanation. Elizabeth had no more reason than thousands of other mothers at that stressful time to believe that separation from her husband meant their marriage had ended. On the contrary, clear evidence exists that she long continued to believe that all remained well between them. He wrote regularly to her over the next two years, and supported her financially. Nor was she taken away from Gadds Cottage by Godfrey and Connie the moment he left, but went some time afterwards to live with them when eventually she found herself unable to endure life as a single mother isolated in the countryside.

Throughout their wedded life Elizabeth had become accustomed to her husband's protracted disappearances, for which he often provided inadequate explanation, resignedly accepting them as characteristic of his eccentric ways and resulting from his need to earn money to support his family. On this occasion however it is more likely than not that Patrick explained his reason for leaving. At the beginning of September 1940 Hitler launched a massive air offensive against Britain, and London began to experience the horrors of the Blitz. Patrick volunteered to join the Ambulance Service, and left for London to perform his duty. Elizabeth cannot but have been distressed at being left on her own with two small children to care for, but at that time she was scarcely alone in suffering such a plight.

[1] Further confirmation of this lies in the extent to which the setting of the novel belongs to the pre-war period. The atmosphere is very much that of the Great Game, with Britain still firmly in control of her Indian Empire, Bolshevik agents from Soviet Russia stirring up tribes in Central Asia, and no intimation of the Second World War. Only at the end (i.e. when Patrick was writing in 1954) does a helicopter make an anachronistic appearance.

NINE

Broken Marriages

A single bad Act no more constitutes a Villain in Life, than a single bad Part on the Stage. The Passions, like the Managers of a Playhouse, often force Men upon Parts, without consulting their Judgment, and sometimes without any Regard to their Talents. Thus the Man, as well as the Player, may condemn what he himself acts; nay, it is common to see Vice sit as awkwardly on some Men, as the Character of Iago would on the honest Face of Mr. William Mills.

(Henry Fielding, *The History of Tom Jones, a Foundling*)

It is time to explain the part played by my mother in supporting Patrick's life and literary achievement. It was so decisive that it is impossible adequately to understand him and his work without a full account of her character and background. Though subordinate to her personal contribution, her family and upbringing exercised lasting effects both on the remarkable nature of their relationship and his career as a writer. The fact that Diana Villiers and Sophie Aubrey reflect varying perspectives of my mother is but one of several intriguing factors in an extraordinarily close and enduring love affair which lasted for over sixty years.

Dean King writes: 'Although Patrick often acknowledges that Mary was his most trusted reader, the extent to which they collaborated was a secret she took to the grave.'[1]

In view of his awareness that I was on the most intimate terms with them and lived with them off and on for nearly half a century, this seems an odd assertion. Others, such as Patrick's literary agent Richard Scott Simon and his successive editors Richard Ollard and Stuart Proffitt, are certainly aware of the extent of her labours on his behalf. In November 1980 Patrick remarked: 'M. having checked her figures, states that this is the 51st book of

[1] King, *Patrick O'Brian*, p. 389.

ours that she has typed. Strangely enough we had never counted them, or at least not for many, many years. Fifty books! I am amazed.' This was but one, and by no means the most important, of her contributions to his achievement.

King's incomprehension is justified to the extent that my mother's character and the nature of her marital relationship with Patrick remained elusive even to their few intimate friends. Visitors to their home invariably found her a charming and equable hostess, who often intervened to smooth over difficulties provoked by Patrick's hypersensitive nature. However, her character was infinitely more complex than might be deduced from such passing and oddly formal encounters. Indeed, I continue to find her more difficult to understand even than the introverted and at times self-deluding Patrick, whose pretensions paradoxically served as windows providing glimpses of underlying realities.

My mother was born on 4 November 1915 at 3 Bath Terrace, Instow, a little village on the River Torridge in North Devon, where she was christened 'Frieda Mary'. Though given her mother's name of Frieda, she was always known as Mary. The entry on her birth certificate for 'Rank or Profession of Father' describes her father Howard Wicksteed as 'Lieutenant First Sixth Devon Regiment Territorial (Gentleman of Independent Means)'. It was not the best of times for officers and gentlemen. My mother's godfather was her young uncle, George Hicking. Within eight months he and his brother Francis were dead, killed on the same day at the battle of the Somme. The effect on their parents when they received telegrams announcing the dual tragedy may be imagined. George and Francis were my grandmother's only brothers, and their deaths brought to an end the Hicking baronetcy.

My grandfather was born in 1883 at Axbridge in Somerset. Though his branch of the family had moved to the south of England in the eighteenth century, the Wicksteeds had been settled for centuries on the border of Shropshire and Cheshire, where their principal seat of Wicksted Hall gazed out over the Vale Royal of Chester, until it was destroyed in a fire at the end of the eighteenth century. They appear to have been a quarrelsome family. In the reign of Edward III William de Wykkested was slain by his enemies, those responsible being fined £100 by the Black Prince and required to find sureties for his two legitimate and seven illegitimate children. In the reign of Henry VI, a century later, his descendant John Wykstyd of Merbury was obliged to provide numerous recognisances to keep the peace.

My grandfather appears to have inherited this awkward streak, though his character was also affected by the tragic loss of his mother when still only a boy. He grew into a very handsome and athletic man, straight as an arrow with piercing blue eyes, utterly fearless, and independent to the point of eccentricity in his views and conduct.

His lack of concern for the opinion of the world made him somewhat wayward. He and his elder brother Francis were educated at Dulwich College (where they were contemporaries of P.G. Wodehouse), and afterwards at Pembroke College, Oxford. Though he retained throughout his life a good knowledge of classical languages, he spent the greater part of his university days playing rugger, hunting, and leading a full social life. He kept a much-loved terrier, which (dogs being forbidden in the college) he trained to climb into a basket lowered on a rope into the street, which was then drawn up to his bedroom. When he came to take his Finals, he recalled on the night before his Scripture examination that he had been too busy to prepare himself. In desperation he sat down and learned by heart a list of the kings of Israel. When next day he entered the Examination Hall and found no question in his paper to which this was pertinent, he firmly wrote below the first question: 'I am afraid I do not know the answer to this, but here is a list of the kings of Israel.'[1]

For a time he travelled with his best friend and future brother-in-law Chris Battersby in Canada, where they lived in the wilderness by Larder Lake, and afterwards bought a fruit farm near the Niagara Falls. Eventually he tired of this, sold his half share to Battersby, and returned to England. His only attempt to gain a living comprised a brief and uncongenial period of work for a brewery.

He married my grandmother, Frieda Mary Hicking, in June 1911. He was seven years older than her, and met her when she was a shy and pretty twenty-year-old. Just over a year after their marriage my grandmother gave birth to a son, named Howard after his father, but who became known thereafter in the family (not entirely to his pleasure) by his nanny's nickname of 'Binkie'. Though my grandparents' marriage was to prove one of almost unalloyed happiness, the golden age in which they had lived was approaching a grim and sudden end. Within three years Europe was convulsed in the horrors of universal conflict. My grandfather was commissioned into the 6th Battalion of the Devonshire Regiment before the outbreak of war in August 1914, and raised a platoon after the declaration. After the exceedingly raw recruits had received some rough and ready training and arming, the battalion was posted to India.

*

[1] My mother recounted this episode to Patrick, who included it in Jack Aubrey's education (*The Fortune of War*, p. 61).

The 6 Devons had been quartered at Lahore. At the time of their arrival in India many of the troops were still little more than uniformed civilians. On one occasion my grandfather, returning to cantonments, paused to speak to the sentry. As they chatted, he suddenly noticed a vicious-looking serpent gliding towards them. 'Kill that snake!' he ordered. Standing firmly to attention with his rifle and bayonet, the sturdy Devonian replied bluntly: 'Oi durzn't, zur.' My grandfather was obliged to break the creature's neck with his officer's cane, not (as he confessed to me) without considerable qualms.[1] However within a few months intensive training had transformed the battalion into an efficient fighting unit.

Not long afterwards my grandmother arrived to join my grandfather, leaving their son Binkie in the care of his devoted nurse Thursa. Early in the following year (1915) they were delighted to discover that my grandmother was expecting a second child, and she returned home to prepare for the delivery. On her arrival she went to live in North Devon, across the River Torridge from the little fishing village of Appledore where my grandfather's sister Wenna was married to the Rector, the jovial and rather unparsonical George Scholey. As mentioned earlier, my mother was born in November of that year.

Meanwhile in India, my grandfather's battalion had been transported to join forces assembled on the Tigris, which were preparing to relieve Townshend's beleaguered division in Kut. In the early spring of 1916 the British launched a major attack on the Dujailah Redoubt, which provided the major Turkish line of defence before the town.

The 6 Devons were in the forefront of the assault, which predictably resulted in a massacre. The British troops marched and countermarched across open country 'as flat as a billiard table', until they were finally ordered to charge and seize the enemy trenches at bayonet point. While all ranks advanced 'never faltering or hesitating', it was afterwards suggested that the officers were 'almost too brave', being picked off as they charged ahead of their men.

The battalion, which had conducted every manoeuvre with impeccable coolness, suffered appalling losses during this disastrously handled operation. Of 32 officers and 642 men who had landed at Basra two months earlier, 18 officers (including the Colonel) and 225 men were killed, missing, or wounded by the close of that bloody day. Among the more grievously wounded was my grandfather.

[1] Patrick was delighted with the story when I related it to him, and could not resist introducing variations on the response into his novels (e.g. *Post Captain*, p. 353; *The Fortune of War*, p. 10; *The Far Side of the World*, p. 222).

Surviving casualties were brought back to an encampment where there was a crippling shortage of surgeons, drugs, and dressings. The severely wounded, including my grandfather, were deposited untreated in a 'dying tent'. Fortunately the men of his platoon discovered him, and removed him to the 'lightly wounded' dressing station.[1]

My grandfather returned to India, where he was placed in hospital and lay for months in a very precarious state of health. The moment she learned of his plight, my grandmother (who was aware of the deficiencies of the medical services in India) made immediate arrangements to join him. Her newly born baby Mary was placed in the care of her devoted 'Nannie Scott', to whose home in Glasgow she was taken to live for the duration.

After the month-long voyage to India, my grandmother remained tending my grandfather until he could return to England. There he underwent protracted treatment and convalescence in hospitals at Bath and Folkestone. After his partial recovery he was assigned to light duties such as training recruits, until he was invalided out of the Army in 1917. Like so many others who had undergone similar experiences, my grandfather could never entirely drive the war from his mind. My uncle recalls him long afterwards sleep-walking about their house at night, shotgun in hand searching for Turks.

Once he was fully recovered, my grandfather bought a house at Appledore in order to be with his sister Wenna and her husband the Rector. Aunt Wenna was the kindest and most Christian of women, gentle and uncompromising in her faith. She horrified my grandfather by disposing of much of her portion of the family fortune. Unhappily it was invested in brewery shares, which she regarded as 'not at all nice to own'. She recommended a young woman as housemaid to my grandparents. One day our cook suggested that my grandfather look under her bed. There he found a tin box, full of household silver not in regular use. Aunt Wenna explained that although she knew the poor girl had been in prison, she was convinced that she had reformed. During the war she worked conscientiously as a Red Cross nurse at Instow across the river from seven in the morning until seven at night, being much in demand from the patients for her skill at playing the piano. One of her few recorded expressions of indignation occurred when she discovered that my grandfather had donned her uniform to pose for a photograph with my grandmother's brother-in-law Cyril Woolley.

Having established themselves in their new home, my grandparents sent

[1] For a graphic account of the Mesopotamian campaign, cf. R.E.R. Robinson and W.J.P. Aggett, *The Bloody Eleventh: History of The Devonshire Regiment* (Exeter, 1988–95), iii, pp. 32–41. My grandfather's personal experiences I learned from him and from my Uncle Binkie, who provided me with a detailed account.

for my mother from Scotland, and her elder brother Binkie was likewise retrieved from the care of his nanny. In later life my mother consistently asserted that her childhood had been uniformly wretched, from her exile in a squalid disease-ridden tenement of the Gorbals in Glasgow to her misery at boarding-school and neglect at the hands of her parents. In reality her Scotch nanny in her brother's words 'spoiled her rotten', and she cannot have recalled much of a place which she left at the age of two. I suspect it was because of consuming guilt arising from later circumstances that she persuaded herself she had suffered a deprived childhood. To quote her brother again: 'Actually my Sister was spoilt soft, could do nothing wrong in Pa's eyes until O'Brian came romping along. She had a wonderful home.'

Home was Staddon, a spacious house of Tudor origin with a Georgian wing, set on the hillside above Appledore. Its view extended over the church tower, visible among the trees at the bottom of the steeply sloping lawn, across the broad tidal sweep of the Torridge to the little village of Instow, and rolling green hills beyond.

Though Staddon was spacious and elegant, and enjoyed a setting of rare natural splendour, it could not be described as a grand house. However, the interior appeared particularly fine on account of my grandfather's magnificent collection of eighteenth-century satinwood furniture, porcelain and china, paintings, and other beautiful works of art for which he had a perceptive eye. So far as I was concerned, the most valuable objects were a carved paddle and executioner's club, whose round head was shaped like that of a bird with a skull-penetrating beak made of some adamantine stone.[1] These had been presented in the nineteenth century to my great-grandfather by the King of Fiji, and bore little silver plates dedicating them 'to my friend and helper, Dr Francis Wicksteed', who during his travels around the globe had afforded His Majesty vital medical aid.

The summit of the hill behind our house provided a spectacular view of the great arc of Barnstaple Bay. Northwards across the estuary the coast extended along the sand dunes of Braunton Burrows to Baggy Point, while to the west beyond the Northam Burrows lay the beach of Westward Ho! at the foot of soaring cliffs which provided the setting for Kipling's *Stalky & Co*. Far off on the north-western horizon loomed as a magical presence the whale-backed isle of Lundy, its craggy contours and

[1] Patrick undoubtedly had this formidable instrument in mind when in *The Far Side of the World* (p. 273) he provided Jack and Stephen's South Pacific amazonian captors with clubs 'topped with mother-of-pearl eyes on either side of an obsidian beak'. The King of Fiji also presented my great-grandfather with a canoe, which he profanely converted into a chicken hutch.

lighthouse at times plainly visible to the naked eye, at others withdrawn behind a cloak of fog.

At the time of my mother's childhood little in Appledore had changed for a century or more. The old shipyard below clattered to the sound of square-rigged sailing vessels under construction, an industry whose history stretched back long even before the port sent vessels to combat the Spanish Armada. In 1346 Appledore provided seven ships and 120 men for King Edward III's Crécy campaign. A beached wooden frigate still lay within the estuary, where it was used as an isolation hospital. An ancient cannon mounted guard upon the quayside, which my uncle vividly recalled being discharged on Armistice Day in 1918: 'the result was lethal and not repeated'. Amid the jubilation not only were bonfires lit up, but so apparently were all the villagers save Aunt Wenna, a firm teetotaller.

Appledorians were conservatives to a man. Fishermen still wore traditional gold earrings as they mended their nets on the cobbled quayside, while everywhere in the steep narrow streets could be heard the broad Devonian dialect in its pristine purity.

I have little doubt that Patrick based the 'Shelmerston' of the Aubrey–Maturin books, 'an out-of-the-way port with an awkward bar and a dangerous tide-race . . . much frequented by smugglers and privateers', on my mother's memories of Appledore. A Shelmerstonian serving under Jack's command on board the *Bellona*, Vaggers, is named after one of the Appledore ferrymen of whom my mother was very fond.[1]

Until the Second World War the West Country represented a world which had undergone no very marked physical or social change for a century or more. Outside the nearby market town and port of Bideford, the greater part of the population was engaged in fishing, farming, and shipbuilding. Then there were the gentry and clergy, who for the most part lived in large houses and employed numerous servants. Despite great distinctions in wealth and comfort, the relationship between these starkly contrasted classes was generally close and cordial. At Staddon the servants were treated as part of the family. Tom Fisher the head gardener was a taciturn figure, who had experienced the grim duty of serving for three years in a burial company on the Western Front.

Close relations were also enjoyed with the villagers, who in turn helped their neighbours to the best of their ability. The ancient houses in Meeting

[1] Shelmerston features in *The Letter of Marque*, pp. 7–9; *The Commodore*, pp. 23–26, 119–20; *Blue at the Mizzen*, pp. 69–70, 71–72. Vaggers appears in *The Commodore*, pp. 119–20, 122, 131. In the novels the village is transferred for narrative convenience from the north coast of Devon to the Channel.

Street, a steep cobbled lane below our house descending to the quay, received a free water supply from Staddon. Archaic customs survived which served to hold the community together. Staddon possessed what were termed potwalloper's rights and obligations on Northam Burrows. Once a year the potwallopers, accompanied by their families and a huge lunch to allow for entertaining casual helpers, crossed the Burrows. Their principal task was to replace stones on the Pebble Ridge which had been washed off by winter gales. In addition timbers from wrecks were recovered to provide winter fuel for cottagers and villagers who lacked trees.

Staddon was an idyllic spot for a child to grow up. My grandfather had originally bought thirty acres with the house, to which he added another fourteen bought from his close friends the Hon. Denys and Lilys Scott, so that the hill belonged to our house. With its surrounding forty-four acres of fields, it provided unrestricted opportunity for childhood adventures and explorations. Below the drive leading to the front of the house a steep lawn descended to the thicket and wall dividing my grandparents' property from the churchyard below. At the top was a tennis court set on a projecting terrace, where the exiled King Prajadhipok of Siam played when he leased the house in about 1931, and again in 1940. On one memorable occasion I managed to push the garden roller over the edge of its retaining wall, and gazed in awestruck rapture as it thudded to the ground below and raced with gathering speed to the bottom of the grassy slope, where it crashed through the bushes and wall to end up in the churchyard. I do not recall the consequences, but doubt whether they were too alarming as my grandparents could never bring themselves to be very severe.

My mother and uncle were fortunate indeed in their parents, friends, and household. My grandfather worked off his superabundant energies in the extensive garden. Totally indifferent to outward appearances, despite my grandmother's regular but futile protests he invariably wore a favoured threadbare jacket or venerable mackintosh. Once, toiling by the front gate, he was accosted by a passing tramp, who enquired whether 'the Guvnor is a generous bloke?' 'No,' replied my grandfather confidentially: 'he's a mean old bugger!'

My grandmother was somewhat shy and retiring, but possessed of a strong inner confidence, and was remarkable for her elegance, dignity, and gentle manners. While her education had been confined to that accorded girls of her class in late Victorian England, she had strong natural intelligence, and was extremely well read. Unfortunately the strained relations which arose when my mother introduced Patrick to her parents led him to introduce a grotesque travesty of her into his novels, where she features as Jack Aubrey's awful mother-in-law.

My mother was a very pretty little girl, with blue eyes and fair curly hair, and a forceful character inherited from her father. On one occasion a friend was collecting for charity, and mentioned that 'it is no good going to Mr So-and-so; he is such a horrid mean old man'. 'Oh no, he isn't,' exclaimed my mother, 'he is very nice and will give it to me!' Even the reputed miser proved unable to resist her charms. She and Binkie, two and a half years her senior, spent happy days playing in the garden and fields, stalking rabbits with his little .410 shotgun, or gazing from the mound on top of the hill (reputedly the site of a Civil War battery) through an old brass-bound naval telescope at the building of the Saunton Sands Hotel on the other side of the estuary. As the years went by Binkie acquired a motor bicycle, on whose pillion my mother eagerly joined him at every opportunity.

Next to Appledore, the place dearest in my mother's affections was the romantic island of Lundy in the midst of the Severn Sea, which belonged to the Harman family who were close friends of my grandparents. Martin King Harman, the owner, declared his island to be independent of Great Britain, and became in consequence known as 'King' Harman. He printed his own stamps and issued coinage, currency being reckoned in 'puffins' after the quaint-looking birds which colonised the sheer cliffs of Lundy. The British Government ignored the secession of Lundy, the coins being used in the island shop by those who chose to do so, while the stamps covered the cost of the voyage from the island to the mainland.

My mother was sent to a nearby school between Appledore and Bideford. Lively and game for any adventure, she was popular among her friends. She developed a crush on Douglas Fairbanks, whose anniversary she solemnly entered into her Christopher Robin Birthday Book. The school was attended by all the 'nice' girls of the neighbourhood, many of whom were similarly high-spirited daughters of her parents' friends.

Over the winter of 1927–28, when she was twelve, she was sent to school in Switzerland to recover from a bronchial complaint. She loved her stay there, when she first acquired that fluent French which was to stand her in such good stead in future years. From her bedroom window she enjoyed a magnificent view of the Dent du Midi mountain and a fine ancient castle. Despite her pleasure in the school and its surroundings, she constantly flew back in her imagination to old familiar scenes. After Christmas 1927 she wrote home: 'I hope you all had a very happy Xmas, I did, but I longed for you all to be with me, it is the first time in my life that we have not all been together for Xmas . . . Miss Clerke sent me a card of Clovelly with Lundy in the distance the other day.' Her mother came out to see her after Christmas, when my mother reported to her father: 'Mum is *very* brave, you should see her going down the hill at break-neck speed.' But her heart remained in

North Devon, and she wrote home: 'I am longing to come back to Dear Old Lundy, I have got a bad attack of "Lundy Itus" tonight.'

By the age of sixteen my mother, lively, daring, and beautiful, had become the toast of North Devon. She was presented at Court, and might be expected in due course to marry one of the heirs to a great estate in the West Country. Fate – or rather, Lundy – directed otherwise. In his memoir my old friend Mr Gade, Mr Harman's landagent, recalled my mother's arrival on the island for a longer visit than usual.

> The arrival on Lundy of Mary Wicksteed as storekeeper was a minor event, but deserving of mention because she made her mark upon Lundy although she was only resident for a few months. Mary was the only daughter of Mr. & Mrs. Howard Wicksteed of Appledore, and she was about seventeen years of age, and had just left school . . . it was not long before she became what one visitor named the belle of the trawler fleet. Mary was pleasant with all people and became a general favourite, not only with the trawlermen. In addition to her storekeeping duties, she became a constant companion of Ruth and Diana Harman when they were on Lundy for school holidays. In June of 1933 Count Dimitri Tolstoy Miloslavski asked permission to camp on Lundy with two friends, and that Dmitri and Mary early had an affinity for each other is sure. I remember Mary performing a little dance of delight before me when she announced that the Count had asked her to have tea with him and his friends at their camp.[1]

This was my father, at the time a twenty-year-old undergraduate at Trinity College, Cambridge. Born in Moscow in 1912, he had been smuggled out of Russia three years after the Revolution by his brave English nanny, who brought him to England. He found refuge at Bude Castle in North Cornwall, where his Aunt Maroussia was already living as the friend of Admiral Sir Douglas and Lady Nicholson. Before going on to Cambridge my father attended Wellington College, where he was Captain of Fencing.

Mr Gade was right: my mother and father had indeed fallen in love. They seemed ideally suited. My father was tall, handsome, intelligent, and fun-loving, and like my mother an enthusiast for walking and climbing. Indeed, it was from the cliffs above Bude that he had frequently gazed at Lundy on the northern horizon, memories of which led him to bring his university

[1] Also staying on the island at this time was a studious young man named George Turner (cf Felix W. Gade, *My Life on Lundy* (Cheltenham, 1997), pp. 153–54, 172, 181). He nurtured a secret passion for my mother, which he was far too shy to declare, but as will be seen many years later resumed his friendship with her long after she had married Patrick.

friends camping there in 1933. Invited to stay with her parents at Staddon, it was not long before he proposed to my mother in the garden, and was joyfully accepted. The match appeared ideal in every way, save for the couple's extreme youth. My grandparents entertained misgivings on that score, but their daughter's infatuation was not to be overridden.

The wedding took place in the following year on a beautiful June day at Appledore church. The streets of the village were festooned with flags, and the church bells and those of the neighbouring village of Northam pealed merrily throughout the afternoon. The wedding present that gave my mother most lasting pleasure was given to her by her brother Binkie: a dachshund puppy, whom she promptly christened 'Miss Potts'. As will be related, she was to enjoy an adventurous life with her mistress.

The happy occasion was crowned by the departure of the glamorous young couple in an aeroplane, which took off from Northam Burrows. As the *Western Morning News* excitedly reported: 'This was the first occasion of a North Devon bride flying to her honeymoon, and appropriately enough she flew in a machine known among aviators as "the honeymoon express" – a Desoutter cabin monoplane.'

My parents' honeymoon was spent in the Tyrol, and to the assembled family, friends, and well-wishers waving goodbye they appeared a golden couple flying away to a golden future. At first everything seemed to promise that this would indeed be the case. In the following year my father became President of the Cambridge Union, and gained his degree. Glittering prospects lay before the young couple. In 1985 I was invited by the Glasgow University Union to speak at a commemorative debate on the occasion of their centenary. During my visit I was presented with a history of the Union, from which I discovered that by a remarkable coincidence my father had been a guest speaker at their previous jubilee in 1935. 'The speech of the evening, as the Debate Report made clear, was undoubtedly that of Count Tolstoy-Miloslavsky, the President of the Cambridge Union, who closed the Debate in a speech of perfect assurance that was fully justified. Supreme excellence, oratorical, accentual, factual, and dialectic, made this the best effort of a good evening . . . We congratulate him, sincerely, on a really brilliant performance.'[1]

My parents settled down in a picturesque fifteenth-century farmhouse at Orpington in Kent, surrounded by four acres of apple and cherry orchards. Here I was born a year after their wedding. At the end of the following year, 1936, our family moved to London, where we lived in a comfortable flat occupying the ground floor and basement of 45 Courtfield Road in

[1] Gerald Warner, *Conquering by Degrees: Glasgow University Union* (Glasgow, 1985), p. 117.

Kensington. We were accompanied by my Austrian nanny Emma Selb, who arrived at Orpington not long after I was born. In April 1937 my sister Natasha was born, and in the same year my father was called to the Bar at Gray's Inn.

At Courtfield Road, in my childish eyes at least, my mother and father displayed great affection for each other. At all times they appeared devoted to each other and their children. Emma Selb, writing to me forty years later, had nothing but warm memories of her life with us.

However by the following year matters appear to have begun to deteriorate. Early in 1938 my father suffered a bout of pleurisy, and was told by his doctor that he needed mountain air to recuperate. Since Emma's beautiful old home in the Tyrol was kept by her family as a *Gasthaus*, it was decided that we should spend part of the summer there. We arrived at Feldkirch in the middle of May 1938, two months after Hitler occupied Austria.

A month later our party was joined by a friend, who chanced to catch a glimpse of an ominous crack in the edifice. Walter Greenway had been a contemporary of my father at Wellington and Cambridge, though he had not known him well at either. They chanced to meet in London, and Walter mentioned that he was looking for somewhere to live. My father suggested that he take up quarters at his flat in Courtfield Road. His room was beside the front door and he led an independent life, seeing my mother and father only intermittently.

In June 1938 my parents invited him to join us in Austria. On arrival he found that my father was obliged to spend most of the time confined to the house. Some Austrians were also staying in the house, one of whom was a Nazi but otherwise pleasant enough, and as everyone spoke German the company proved very congenial.

My mother regularly left my father with my sister and me under Emmie's care to go for long walks in the mountains with Walter and their Austrian guide, Toni Pflösler. One day Walter was startled when he unexpectedly came upon my mother and Toni kissing each other in a glade. Tactfully he stole away, and thought little about the matter until he became party to a dramatic development in the following year.

My mother, who had led a charmed and privileged life, and unquestionably married when far too young, was rather spoiled and irresponsible at this time. Wholly ignorant of politics and charmed by Austria and the Austrians, she even concluded postcards sent to England with an enthusiastic 'Heil Hitler!' This naïve flirtation with Nazism was brought to an abrupt halt on her return to England, when she rashly ventured a Nazi salute in my grandfather's presence. In that gruff voice which none dared gainsay, he barked: 'We'll have none of that stuff here!'

My father's outlook was also very different from that of his young wife, and possibly reflected something of the incompatibility which was clearly already arising between them. Observing a prominently displayed framed photograph of Hitler in a local restaurant, he promptly ordered the cowed proprietor to turn it face about to the wall. He had long taken a keen interest in current affairs, and at Cambridge aroused admiration for the skill with which he debated political issues in the Union. However, my mother may have come to appreciate that the situation was not quite as rosy in the new Reich as she had fancied in the mountains of the Tyrol, when our beloved Emmie sent a postcard to explain that she could not rejoin us at Courtfield Road, since she was unable to obtain the visa now required to permit her to leave 'Germany' – as she significantly emphasised.

It must have been during the autumn of 1938 that my mother first met Patrick. Exactly where and how it happened I have been unable to discover, but there are several indications that it was about this time. It seems unlikely that my mother would have engaged in her flirtation with the dashing Austrian guide Toni Pflösler during our summer holiday were she hankering at the time after Patrick. More indicative is the fact that on our return I was sent to my first school, the French Lycée in South Kensington.[1] However I spent only the Michaelmas term there, after which I was sent with my sister to live with our grandparents in Devonshire.

Patrick's story 'One Arctic Summer', which must have been written in the late summer or autumn of 1938, includes features unique to his *œuvre* in two striking respects. This was the only occasion that his literary muse concerned itself with Russia, while the Orthodox priest who is its principal character provides the sole example found in his writing of a worldly yet morally pure man. A curious aspect of the story lies in its anachronistic placing of a contemporary airman in a context implicitly suggesting Imperial Russia, which at the time Patrick wrote had vanished twenty years earlier. While the injured airman recalls Patrick's abortive term of service in the RAF and his claim to have been invalided out, one is left wondering what might have provoked so admiring a description of a Russian priest.

When my mother married my father she became converted to Russian Orthodoxy, a faith which she adopted with characteristic enthusiasm: so much so, that she retained nominal adherence and strong attraction to our Church after the embittered breakdown of her marriage. Over twenty years later Patrick and my mother were married at the Russian Orthodox church in

[1] Walter Greenway, recalling our holiday in the Tyrol, remembered that I was about to attend the Lycée: 'that was my last memory of you: this quadrilingual child aged five!' (actually three).

London, both being devoted to the priest who married them, Father George Cheremetiev. When Patrick visited Russia in 1963, he took care to attend divine service (a relatively infrequent occurrence for him), where he lit candles to my mother and me.

In 1938 a new priest had just arrived to administer to the spiritual needs of the Russian émigré community in London. Like Father Sergei in the story, Father Michael Polsky was a big man with a thick mane of grey hair and beard of corresponding length and fullness. His personality was as striking as his physical appearance, and his dynamism, charm, and holiness swiftly wrought a dramatic improvement in the church at Buckingham Palace Road, whose community had fallen into a state of some desuetude under his predecessor. A deeply spiritual figure, he troubled himself little with trifling matters of outward form. Thus it concerned him not at all when during the war young émigrés from Yugoslavia working in munitions factories attended Sunday services in overalls or trousers.

It was presumably Father Michael who cemented my mother's lifelong attachment to the Orthodox Church, and it is likely that she would have introduced Patrick to him – although unlikely that he would have been made aware of the relationship between them. Patrick's Father Sergei is the only real character in his tale, and he conveys a strong impression of being drawn from the life.

> It sounds most unpleasant, but he was easily the best man I have ever known, and I have met archbishops and cardinals: there was nothing obviously religious about him, he never asked anyone whether he was saved, or anything remotely resembling it . . . I think he must have been the nearest approach to the more robust kind of medieval saint that one could find.

If as seems likely Father Michael was the model for Patrick's Father Sergei, this affords further confirmation that Patrick's acquaintance with my mother began before 'One Arctic Summer' was published in the latter part of 1938. In February 1939 there occurred an event which suggests that their relationship had become permanent. When Patrick's second child was born in February 1939 she was named rather grandly Jane Elizabeth Campaspe Tudor. One of these names suggests a clue to Patrick's secret life at the time. 'Campaspe' is a strikingly unusual name. It was that of the favourite mistress of Alexander the Great, who arranged for her to be painted in the nude by Apelles, the greatest painter of antiquity. During sessions in his studio the artist fell in love with Campaspe. The conqueror eventually discovered their affair, but magnanimously conceded his mistress to Apelles. According to Pliny, Alexander talked a great deal of nonsense about art in Apelles' studio, until the painter politely suggested that he keep quiet concerning a subject about which the boys who ground his colours knew more. The moral appealed to ancient and modern writers alike, affirming as it did the enduring superiority of art over temporal power and grandeur.[1]

Patrick is unlikely to have fastened upon so peculiarly esoteric a name as Campaspe save in the context of this tale, which bore striking application to his own circumstances at the time. It was about the time of Jane Campaspe's birth that my mother, an admired society beauty, left her aristocratic husband for a humble but talented artist.[2] In *Richard Temple* Patrick portrayed himself as a poverty-stricken but brilliant painter obsessed with his lack of gentle birth. Whether or not he made any serious attempt to become an artist, he was certainly a clever and careful amateur draughtsman and extremely knowledgeable about painting. Hypersensitive with regard to what he felt to be his ignoble position in the social hierarchy, he cannot have failed to relish the implications of the story. In *Richard Temple* we find the hero making himself *persona grata* in a great country house through a display of encyclopædic knowledge of the ancestral paintings and furniture, concerning which their patrician owner understands little or nothing. In another episode the eponymous hero cuckolds the wealthy husband of a woman who spends sessions in his studio being painted in the nude.[3]

Where and how my mother first met Patrick is unlikely ever to be known. A chance meeting might readily have occurred at any time, since Patrick's home in Gertrude Street lay within ten minutes' walk of our flat in Courtfield Road. It is not difficult to imagine my mother's irresistible effect on Patrick. In addition to her personal qualities, she combined impeccably upper-class birth and social connections with marriage to a nobleman, whose name and title she bore. Enough has been seen of Patrick's early life and character to indicate how potent a factor such considerations would have represented. As he acknowledged in *Richard Temple*:

> There is not much to be done in the arts without instinct: no intellectual effort will paint a picture, but perhaps after years and years of anxious plodding a man

[1] *Plinii naturalis historiæ*, xxxv, 36, where the lady's name is however given as Pancaspe. It seems that Patrick did not discover Campaspe in classical literature, but from a derivative source such as the Elizabethan playwright John Lyly's play of that name (cf. E.K. Chambers, *The Elizabethan Stage* (Oxford, 1923), iii, pp. 413–14). He possessed a volume of Pliny edited by Ioannes de Laet, *C. Plinii secvndi historiæ naturalis libri XXXVII* (Leyden, 1636), which however is not that containing the tale of Apelles and Alexander.

[2] Patrick's novel *The Unknown Shore* concludes with his humble hero Tobias Barrow snatching the well-born beauty Georgiana from under the noses of 'the Duke of Lothian and Sir James Firebrace'.

[3] *Richard Temple*, pp. 180–81, 192–95, 197–201.

> might come to the point at which the true beginners start. Philippa and her kind, with their natural and highly developed sense of *how to behave* in an infinity of finely differentiated circumstances, were artists in living, and they had begun with an understanding of the fact that he was now reaching, with a mind appalled by its truth and significance.[1]

No doubt there will be those who condemn such an outlook as sadly pretentious. For my part it appears a harmless and in Patrick's case understandable desire. If it be considered laudable, or at least respectable, to seek material success in life, then what is especially wrong with wishing for other more intangible but nonetheless satisfying advantages? It was primarily the effortless ease and self-confidence of her class which appeared so desirable to Patrick, whose sense of insecurity verged at times on outright terror: 'He [Temple] was still afraid and on the stretch – afraid very much as a rat is afraid, of countless known and unknown pursuers; and the fear had many of the same effects, if a rat is indeed hard, untrustworthy, savage and full of hate.'

My mother was sufficiently her father's daughter not to affect airs and graces reflecting her social status. Nor in any case was such pretentiousness generally characteristic of her class at the time. As ever, *Richard Temple* reflects Patrick's acute observation of such subtleties.

> Many of his old suppositions had been backward, provincial, plainly mistaken, or (more often) based upon observation of the more careful middle class; Philippa's voice contained inadmissible vowels, and at Churleigh, in spite of its many points of identity with Easton Colborough, he had heard some criticisms of the royal family that would have made a republican stare. There were many things in which experience was challenging his earliest and sometimes painful – unnecessarily painful – tenets: *these* people did not give a damn whether you had been to a public school or not – they were less imprisoned by their caste, he observed . . .[2]

During their life together my mother's instinctive understanding of Patrick's character led her to subsume her wishes to his almost entirely. When for example he fretted over the 'proper' way of conducting himself in a given social situation, she was invariably careful not to instruct him, but to participate as a fellow enquirer in his hesitant analysis. Equally, she rarely spoke in company about her life in North Devon, and then as often as not

[1] *Richard Temple*, p. 248.
[2] *Richard Temple*, p. 255.

only to lament the fancied deprivations of her upbringing. I am sure she sensed that any allusion to her earlier life which even hinted at superiority would have made her situation *vis-à-vis* Patrick difficult or untenable. He, on the other hand, absorbed the advantages he believed they conferred by means of indirect enquiry, or through that process of osmosis with which he was peculiarly endowed.

It is more difficult to explain the overwhelming appeal Patrick exerted on my mother, which certainly baffled my father, her family, and most of her friends. That he was a young man of obscure origin, scant education, barely able to scrape a living, and no perceptible prospects, were not the greatest of his disadvantages in their eyes. Although good-looking, he did not present a very impressive figure. As his self-portrait in *Richard Temple* indicates, in company he generally appeared gauche, ineffectual, or clumsily pretentious. Nevertheless he could display considerable charm, above all when not overawed by an interlocutor. His appeal bore much of the 'little boy' character, which has a strong appeal upon a certain type of woman. Something of this is suggested in his self-portrait of the child Richard Temple, who 'had a great deal of affection in his heart, affection for the asking'.

I suspect that such factors appealed to the undeveloped maternal instinct in my mother. Visitors to their house at Collioure were often surprised and privately indignant at Patrick's occasionally crushing rudeness, to which she never voiced anything but the mildest dissent. To me, however, it became a matter of some interest to discover who was really in control. In the early years of my life in their successive homes at Collioure it seemed unquestionable that Patrick was 'the boss' (she regularly addressed him, only half-humorously, as 'sir'), and I like others wondered that my mother did not rebel against his scornful reproofs. Latterly my view became modified and I began to question whether my mother's seemingly abject compliance with Patrick's every opinion (sometimes extending to eager endorsement of successive self-contradictions) might not represent an unconsciously subtle form of control.

Patrick, whose self-analysis in *Richard Temple* is extremely frank, appears to have understood something of this. At one point he has two girls discuss the relationship between Richard and the beautiful and much-desired Philippa.

> 'Why is he sitting so very close to Philippa Brett?'
>
> 'Because he likes it, I suppose,' said Sally, pursing her lips. 'She picked him up in Piccadilly, and he has never been the same man since. She knocked him down and secured him when he was helpless; now he likes it . . . I think Philippa is quite fond of her prey.'

> 'He is really very good-looking.'
>
> 'She says he is wonderfully pure.'
>
> 'My God. He doesn't look it.'
>
> 'She says she can trust him absolutely anywhere.'
>
> 'Dear me.'
>
> 'She says it is great fun being with him, and you feel quite safe, like being with a eunuch.'[1]

The image of the creative artist had a potent effect on my mother's imagination. No intellectual, she was nevertheless tolerably well read, and as a girl had a sincere love of English literature, sharing Patrick's enthusiasm for Kipling. Her proximity to the colourful bohemian life of Chelsea facilitated contact with its artistic inhabitants, and made her attraction to a creative character all but inevitable. That said, it might be asked why she was not drawn to an established artist or writer, rather than one with so sparse a record of achievement as was Patrick's in 1938. But the outcome suggests that what she desired was not to be the mere appanage of a gifted creator (she appears to have gained little satisfaction from my father's burgeoning career as an ultimately highly successful barrister), but to play a decisive if vicarious role in the act of creation. Certainly it is no exaggeration to suggest that she did indeed go far towards 'creating' Patrick. He himself was invariably at pains to emphasise the extent to which she played a crucial, indeed decisive, role in his writing.

To this must be added my mother's heady love of adventure. Among characteristics she shared with Stephen Maturin's Diana Villiers was an almost total lack of fear, and corresponding determination to have her own way regardless of the risks. Both she and Patrick were to prove outstandingly resourceful and courageous in face of daunting reverses which fate constantly inflicted upon them, and relished encountering and overcoming setbacks which would have overwhelmed most people. Patrick's combination of present failure and destitution with vaulting ambition and unassailable confidence in his own genius presented the promise of a journey ahead for the two young people, which would be filled with just the type of excitement my mother craved and relished. Then again, the secrecy and impropriety of their intrigue was most likely attractive to my mother's at times self-indulgent and contradictory nature. Covert intrigues and even the scandal provoked by the liaison appeared deliciously exhilarating, while the position she had enjoyed as fortune's darling would have made her rashly careless of the consequences.

There are indications that Patrick suffered a variety of emotions during the

[1] *Richard Temple*, p. 271.

first year or so of his affair with my mother, ranging from trepidation to guilt and contrived attempts to cast my father in an ill light. In *Richard Temple* Philippa Brett's beauty, background, and personality all reflect his image of my mother. However the circumstances of their coming to know each other are reflected much more closely in Temple's prior affair with Valerie Hewer. 'A disgusting visceral pain and an extreme vileness came welling up to destroy the order of his mind,' he reflected, and experienced a shocking sense of sin. His mistress suffers from no such qualms: '"I have told Mr. Hewer about you," said Valerie, and at this news Richard's [cigar] ash fell in one solid piece. He had always understood Valerie's husband (she had a delicacy in naming him) to live somewhere in the murkier recesses of 1890, a roaring disciplinarian, who kept her very short of spending money . . .'[1]

Although Mr Hewer is portrayed as a vulgar businessman, Patrick obviously had my father in mind. In his short story 'Samphire' (1953), which depicts the relationship between my mother and father, the latter is represented as an insensitive authoritarian. While that charge may have been self-serving or exaggerated, it is regrettably true that my father's besetting weakness was an extreme parsimony (most likely originating in the terrifying insecurities of his early life), which had disturbed my mother as early as their honeymoon. Given her impetuous nature, it may be that she took little trouble to keep her relationship with Patrick secret, and might defiantly have acknowledged it if challenged.

Patrick's tendency to use his fiction to obliterate people for whom he nurtured hostility in real life features rather naïvely in the section of *The Road to Samarcand* which he wrote just before leaving Gadds Cottage in the summer of 1940. A Russian agent called Dimitri Mihailovitch has his villainous projects brought to an abrupt end when Patrick's hero Sullivan breaks his neck. It can scarcely be coincidence that this treacherous foe bears my father's Christian name and patronymic.[2] The extent to which Patrick's mingled feelings of guilt and resentment towards him remained entrenched in his unconscious mind is revealed by an entry in his diary for 2 December 1976: 'A remarkable dream of having murdered Dimitri, being judged by Nigel:[3] waiting for the sentence I asked M[ary] for poison.'

The first time I learned of Patrick's existence cannot have been long after he and my mother met. I had been sent to live at her parents' house at Appledore, and I recall sitting in the sun with her on a lawn in their garden,

[1] *Richard Temple*, pp. 193–94.

[2] I am grateful to Walter Greenway for pointing this out to me.

[3] Curtis-Raleigh, a friend who was a judge.

when she told me that she had a friend who was 'a writer'. Something of her emotion must have conveyed itself to my infant mind, for otherwise it is hard to imagine why her words should have remained permanently fixed in my memory. I gained the impression that 'a writer' was a very exciting person indeed, and afterwards pondered the matter deeply. My mother must have explained something of what the profession entailed, since I solemnly decided that I too would be a writer. I remember taking an exercise book, on whose cover after some thought I inscribed the title *The Lions*. After further reflection, I turned to the last page and compiled an index. That was as far as my first literary composition proceeded. When I told Patrick of this many years later, he smiled and remarked that it is the section in between which tends to be more difficult to accomplish.

This must have been in the spring or summer of 1939. By then my grandparents were aware that their daughter's marriage was on the rocks, and that she was conducting a passionate affair with a disreputable young married man. My grandmother warned her that if she continued on the path she was pursuing, she could well end up losing her children altogether.

Her brother Binkie was at home on leave in the summer of 1939 from the Sudan, where he was working for the Sudan Plantations Syndicate. As he recalled:

> An old friend William Coham-Fleming, of Coham House, Coham, Black Torrington . . . went [with him] to see Mary at the end of my leave in July 1939. She was already caught up with Patrick. We talked many hours and I hoped we had got her to accept your father's generous offer to give her custody of you and Nat[asha] – she was devoted to you both – and pay all her costs [of the divorce]. We were sadly wrong in our optimism. She was in those days very fit, a bit on the plump side (which suited her well) and very gay in the best sense of the ill used word . . . I liked your father more than somewhat and was distressed that he refused to see me. He was revolted to know Mary preferred Patrick to him. I agree with that sentiment.

This discussion occurred in early July at the family flat in Courtfield Road, where my mother was living after my father had departed in anger and disgust. Binkie returned to the Sudan, having received the impression that my mother accepted my father's terms, and would have nothing further to do with Patrick Russ. Shortly afterwards she left Courtfield Road, never to return.

Much later, in a rare outburst my father told me indignantly that she even took my Post Office Savings Book. I fear this could be true, as recently (14 February 2003) I discovered in a low dark corner of the bookshelves of my mother's house a copy of Edward Lear's *Nonsense Poems*, which bears an inscription to me from my Aunt Molly dated 1939. The flysheets had been torn out and reversed to conceal the fact, and my mother must have surreptitiously purloined the book. The overriding influence on her conduct at the time was her extreme wilfulness, then focused unreservedly upon 'her darling Patrick' – as her brother indignantly termed him.

An incident which occurred immediately after the discussion between my mother and her brother indicates how little intention she had of abiding by the agreement which she gave him to understand she had accepted. Walter Greenway had left Courtfield Road during the winter of 1938–39, and he had for some time thought little about the Tolstoy family until he received an unexpected telephone call at his home at Fleet in Hampshire: as he recalls, in July or August 1939. To his surprise the caller proved to be my mother, who asked him whether he had any knowledge of an affair she claimed my father had conducted with a girl-friend of hers, who had been a frequent visitor to their flat. Walter replied truthfully that he knew nothing whatever about the matter. Nor indeed had he any inkling until this moment that anything was wrong with my parents' marriage. In the climate of the time he regarded extramarital affairs and divorces as all but inconceivable in respectable society.

Not long afterwards he received a second telephone call from my mother, asking him urgently to come and see her where she was staying not far away at Burley in the New Forest. Walter promptly drove over to the house, where he found my mother in a state of high agitation. She explained that she had been compelled to leave the marital home in Courtfield Road, on account of her discovery that my father was conducting an affair with her best friend.

Walter had been profoundly startled by the news, but was bewildered to know what it could have to do with him. My mother now explained that matters had proceeded so far that there existed no alternative to a divorce, and asked Walter whether he would agree to appear as a witness to my father's infidelity. Embarrassed, Walter once more insisted that he had not the slightest knowledge of my parents' marital affairs, and so could not possibly play any part in a court hearing.[1] My mother, clearly disappointed, had no choice but to accept Walter's refusal.

[1] Dean King states that 'Greenway had been appalled at Tolstoy's treatment of Mary' (*Patrick O'Brian*, p. 98). As Walter explained to me, his indignation was confined to the terms of the divorce settlement as explained to him by my mother, and did not relate to anything he had himself witnessed. I would like to express my gratitude to King for putting me in touch with Walter Greenway, whom I had not seen since the age of three.

Whilst it is dangerous to judge of such matters at so distant and sparsely recorded a remove, it is hard to avoid concluding that my mother had no evidence of infidelity on my father's part, since she could find no better alternative to her desperate and futile attempt to secure damaging testimony from Walter Greenway. Nor was she able to provide evidence of his adultery during subsequent divorce proceedings.

Walter Greenway's interview with my mother was relatively brief, and conducted without anyone else present. Thus, despite the assurances she had given her brother a week or so earlier, my mother lost no time in seeking grounds for divorce which would establish my father as the guilty party, so enabling her to retain custody of my sister and me. Her brother Binkie had returned to the Sudan under the impression that all relations with Patrick Russ were severed, and that the divorce, unsavoury though it must be, would at least provide her with custody of her children. Clearly the fact that she did not establish an open liaison with Patrick until considerably later confirms that she successfully deceived her family (on whose behalf Binkie had visited her) and my father into believing that she had severed relations with her lover.

The dilemma my mother faced was both distressful and perplexing. The forces arrayed against her relationship with Patrick were formidable, to an extent she had insouciantly probably not anticipated. Her family and their friends were intractably opposed to the liaison, and regarded her shameless betrayal of her husband and abandonment of her children with disgust and shock. To leave my father and set up home with her lover would provoke a social scandal which, however little she might be concerned with the proprieties, must deprive her of access to virtually the whole world she had hitherto known. Nor could purely practical questions be altogether ignored. Where and how were she and Patrick to live? She possessed a financial endowment settled upon her by her father, which was however insufficient to enable a couple to live beyond humdrum domesticity. Were she to defy him, would he not deny her any financial support beyond her modest trust? He was a fond parent and the most generous of men, but could scarcely be expected to provide her with means of undertaking the shameful step he was so concerned to prevent. Last, but certainly not least, as her mother warned her, she would almost certainly find herself permanently deprived of access to her two young children.

Faced by these all but insurmountable obstacles my mother decided that for the present she had no alternative but to succumb outwardly to the pressures bearing upon her from every side. Equally, as the evidence will shortly show, she had no intention of abandoning Patrick, and continued to maintain secret communication with him. Following her brother's visit in

July 1939 there can be no doubt that she informed her lover immediately of the concession to which she had reluctantly felt compelled to accede.

Such was my mother's unhappy predicament. But meanwhile what of Patrick? It is certain that his wife Elizabeth knew nothing of the affair when he left her in the summer of 1940. Significantly, while in subsequent years she understandably spoke bitterly about Patrick, she never voiced any reflection on my mother. This she would surely have done had she had any reason to believe her involved in Patrick's betrayal.

Furthermore one would expect her to have informed members of the Russ family, who were generally sympathetic to her plight, of the circumstances. The fact that none of them appears to have had any idea why Patrick deserted his wife confirms not only that it eventually came as a total surprise to Elizabeth, but that neither she nor they ever discovered the reason. Finally, it is significant that, whereas my father cited 'Patrick Russ' as co-respondent in his divorce proceedings, when Elizabeth divorced Patrick no co-respondent was named. If, as everything suggests, she believed that Patrick did not meet my mother until two years or more after his leaving Gadds Cottage, she plainly could not hold her responsible for the break-up of her marriage.

It was seen in the previous chapter that in June or July of 1939 Patrick was admitted to hospital, and after discharging himself disappeared on what he told his family was a walking tour in Wales for the purpose of recovering his health. In reality, wherever he went after his discharge, it cannot have been Wales. When he travelled to the Principality six years later, his journal makes it plain that it was his first visit. Everything he saw represented a striking novelty. He recorded his excitement and pleasure on first glimpsing the Welsh mountains, gorges, and torrents, found it worthy of note that schoolchildren and farm workers talked Welsh in the train, and was amused by the fact that a porter in North Wales spoke 'in stage Welsh dialect'.

Almost certainly Patrick and my mother were enjoying a secret tryst at this time. My father had left the family flat in Courtfield Road before July 1939, my sister and I had gone to live with our grandparents in North Devon, and my mother was living on her own in London. She would certainly have learned at once of Patrick's illness, and hastened to visit him in hospital. His premature self-discharge and inability to provide a truthful explanation for his subsequent disappearance bear but one plausible explanation. What remains to be explained is what led Patrick to be confined in hospital. In his brief 1994 memoir, he wrote that 'between Munich and the outbreak of war my illness returned with greater severity. This time it left me in a sad way: my strength did not quickly return and I was rejected for active service.[1] The chronology tallies closely enough with his brother Victor's recollection of visiting him in hospital. Dean King asserts of this period in Patrick's life: 'Once again he would find himself in an unhappy house. Again his health would fail.' Conceding that photographs taken at Gadds Cottage 'show him looking fit and healthy', he nevertheless concludes: 'That is not to say that he did not experience an occasional flare-up of the tuberculosis or some other problem. He also complained of a bad back. Elizabeth told her son that there were lumps on his father's spine caused by a plane crash at flight school.'[2]

Whatever Elizabeth later told Richard, Patrick never suffered any injury to his back during his brief service in the RAF,[3] nor do I know of evidence that he suffered from tuberculosis. There were no lumps on his spine: at least, none that I noticed on the beach at Collioure when staying year after year with him and my mother. His brother Victor's sardonic conclusion that he was suffering from the effects of poverty and excessive alcohol suggests that the account the hospital provided of Patrick's ailment was inconclusive.

On the other hand, he would clearly not have been admitted unless doctors were persuaded that he was ill. The apparent inability of the hospital to explain the nature of his illness to Victor, coupled with his self-discharge when to all appearances he was still sick, invites the whimsical diagnosis that he was ill and yet not ill. Paradoxical though this may appear, there is reason to believe that this was indeed effectively the case.

Patrick's autobiographical short story 'The Thermometer' provides a graphic illustration of how the child, faced with a seriously distressing situation, sought to induce sickness as a means of inviting sympathy and evading responsibility. This gave him the double protection of placing him in the situation of a pitiable victim whom it would be illegitimate to punish, and of mentally detaching him from an unacceptable crisis.

As a child this stratagem doubtless evolved more or less unconsciously, but as he grew older he became overtly aware of the protective comforts enjoyed by an invalid. This is indicated, *inter alia*, in *Richard Temple*, whose hero discovers unwonted contentment during his confinement in hospital:

> Recovering fast from one disease, or complication of diseases, Richard fell directly into another, and in this case (like so many other sufferers) he loved to read about the symptoms, prognostics, other examples and history of his malady . . . Nothing could have been more idle than his life at this time. He was

[1] Cunningham (ed.), *Patrick O'Brian*, p. 17.

[2] King, *Patrick O'Brian*, pp. 47, 79.

[3] It is questionable whether he flew at all during his brief term of service.

> washed, fed, woken and told when to sleep by an impersonal authority; and his mind was idle in most of its aspects, for he was spiritually contained within the antiseptic walls of the ward – his remote and squalid room had only the smallest far-off existence . . . he did not envy anyone . . . but he was hailed a-pieces with love.

The beautiful Philippa Brett hastens to visit him in his ward, and on his release from hospital invites him to stay at Churleigh, her grand ancestral country pile.[1] She shows him to his bedroom, and departs with a promise to return and guide him through its endless maze of galleries and reception rooms. Until that moment he had been charmed and intrigued by the house, but the moment the door closed behind her he felt his confidence wane at the prospect of encountering her family in such a daunting setting.

> Yet anxiety filled the room as soon as she shut the door: he had felt it coming into the remoter parts of his mind as soon as they had left London, driving soberly towards Hampshire in Philippa's reined-in, frustrated car, and between moments of amazement at the brilliance of the world and at their airy passage through it, and in the few moments when they were not talking, he had realised the particular strength of feebleness. In his [hospital] bed he had been fortified behind his frail but invincible sheet: he could do nothing, he was responsible for nothing, and his existence was almost absolute and uncontingent – he had no antecedents; and if anything he was on his own ground.[2]

Nothing could be more explicit in general terms, but is there any justification for supposing that Patrick's confinement to hospital in July 1939 represented such an instance of psychosomatic sickness? An unpublished short story he wrote later throws revealing light on this question. Untitled, it concerns a young man named George, who finds himself experiencing listlessness and exhaustion. Visiting some old friends, the Wests, he grows increasingly exhausted, and momentarily falls asleep. He is woken before long by

[1] A strikingly similar scene occurs in *HMS Surprise* (pp. 299–300), when Diana Villiers visits Stephen Maturin on his sickbed.

[2] *Richard Temple*, pp. 221–22, 230–31. Philippa is represented as first meeting Richard in consequence of his being accidentally knocked down by her car. This is an obviously fictitious episode. Dean King describes my mother in 1940 as 'setting off to social functions in her sporty Jowett Jupiter' (*Patrick O'Brian*, p. 86), but provides no authority for the statement. My Uncle Binkie (her elder brother) informed me: 'I do not think that Mary had a sports car or any car come to that. She was a brave rather than a good driver and mostly used Pa's Vauxhall "12".'

murmuring, grave voices. '"He has pneumonia," said Dr Miller to them, secretly. "I will see about the ambulance."'

George falls to musing on his predicament.

> So he had pneumonia: how creditable. He was rather pleased. It removed all responsibility: though far down he felt an uneasiness, as if he were cheating and might be detected; it did not hurt – perhaps Dr Miller had been mistaken? They thought he was going to die, at the hospital, and sent to let his people know . . . they were wrong about his dying. He lived through March, through April, and in May he was alive and gaining. He slept nearly all the time, but he had finished with delirium, and it was real sleep; when he was awake his slow thoughts were his own. They rambled, wandered, spread abroad: he was hardly conscious of his body, had no desires – or desires so weak they scarcely counted – no duties, no decisions to make, no restlessness. It was a perfect state for vague wondering, reminiscence, like a long morning in bed protracted to beyond all measuring.

Lying in this passive, contented state, George recalls an outing with friends (the Wests and a couple named Holden) to a Cistercian priory.[1] The picnic and the weather had been perfect, but he had failed to shine in conversation, and felt put out. Turning for consolation to his companion Margaret, he is surprised to find her respond to his complaints with uncharacteristic lack of sympathy. 'Margaret's answers had grown reserved, something short of full agreement, when she declined to damn John Holden in all his aspects, he fell silent again, until they reached a bench. He felt ill-used, wretched, out of sorts.'

He tried a more successful tack.

> Starting from the subject of the cigarette that he lighted, he spoke about his health. He was, of course, a consumptive. She had not known? Oh, yes: they said he would probably live out the year. But he did not tell many people. He did not mind; only it was a little hard sometimes . . . When he thought of – but what did it matter? (A brave laugh, to show what depths there were, unrevealed). He coughed into his handkerchief.
>
> He enjoyed himself for the first time that day, quite carried away by his story and by a strong pity for himself, so truly felt that it made his voice husky.

[1]As ever, autobiographical allusions appear detectable. The ruins of a priory lay just behind the Russ home in Lewes, while an 'Easton Colborough' family named Holden features in *Richard Temple*, p. 233.

> Only once, when he saw Margaret's eyes fill with tears, did he feel a stir of compunction: for the lie itself he had no abhorrence, no regret even.

Although unstated, it is clear that George's relationship with Margaret is one of long standing: implicitly that of husband. Furthermore his deliberate deception of Margaret suggests that his sudden collapse may have been induced or even assumed.

Despite the success of his deception, George becomes troubled by his treatment of Margaret, and is concerned to justify his conduct towards her. Lying in his hospital bed, he

> tried to build up a vision of Margaret, but he could not get it together: it was a composite picture, a montage; Margaret in a blue coat jumping on to a bus, Margaret in profile looking unwell and disagreeable at a party – her nose was too long (she was feeling sick); Margaret's hands on the piano, her charming look when she threaded her way through the restaurant tables and saw him waiting for her. But it was never a satisfactory vision. He felt a deep movement, a revulsion, something uneasy about Margaret. They had never had any very close relationship, it had all been very immature: but was it not rather – ? If another man had done it, what would you have said? A solemn pompous bubble labelled Cad eddied about his unwilling thoughts until they were changed by the bustle and activity of nurses in the ward.

The unmistakable implication is that George had deceived and deserted Margaret, felt some compunction for having done so, and recognised that others would condemn his action as dishonourable. His guilt makes him take refuge in an illness which renders him an object of pity and protection.

The story concludes with a twist, which as in other of Patrick's tales is a purely literary device. A senior consultant inadvertently blurts out in front of George that, so far from being a malingerer, he really is a victim of an implicitly fatal tubercular disease.

Is it reading too much into this story to identify Margaret with Patrick's first wife Elizabeth? The parallels are striking. George is ascribed with surprising candour some of Patrick's most marked characteristics. Intellectually he is highly competitive (he actually concedes the term 'jealous'), seeking always to dominate the company in which he finds himself, and deeply resentful on feeling eclipsed by another. He expects his wife to endorse his every statement without reservation, and is so embittered by her uncharacteristic failure to do so that he permanently breaks off relations with her. According to Elizabeth, Patrick (falsely) claimed to have suffered a severe back injury during his RAF service, while George deceives Margaret by telling her he is suffering from tuberculosis.

George's feelings of guilt, shame, or a perceived need to justify himself in the eyes of the world, bring on an attack of sickness which appears partially psychosomatic and partially simulated. Though he acknowledges that he was sincerely in love with Margaret, he now decides that they had after all never been really close. Their relationship had been too 'immature'. It will be recalled that Patrick was just twenty-one at the time of his marriage to Elizabeth.

He wrote the story of 'George' ten or more years after his session in hospital in 1939 for inclusion in his collection of short stories published under the title *Lying in the Sun*, when he provisionally listed it as 'The Tubercular Wonder'. However in the event it was never published. Whether this was because his publishers rejected it, or he felt it to be too revealing, remains unknown.

This sequence of contingencies surely parallels Patrick's situation in July 1939 too closely to be coincidental. In that month my mother was visited at Courtfield Road by her brother and his friend, who urged her as forcefully as they were able to accept my father's offer to grant her custody of me and my sister, together with a respectable financial settlement, on condition she abandon her relationship with Patrick. She led them to believe that she had accepted their proposal, and thereafter persuaded her family that she had severed relations with her lover.

My father appears likewise to have been ignorant of the fact that she was surreptitiously continuing the liaison. Had he known, he would certainly have informed my grandparents. My parents' marriage was not dissolved until 1942, and the indications are that it was not long before then that my father and my mother's parents realised that they had been deceived. I lived with my grandparents from 1939 until 1942, when I recall my mother coming to see me during the first year or so, but towards the end not at all. Since my grandparents concurred with my father that she should have no access to me and my sister were she to resume her relationship with Patrick, this further suggests that there was an initial period when they were ignorant of its resumption.

Over the winter of 1939–40 my mother's open repudiation of the undertaking given to her brother lay in the unforeseen future. In July 1939 Patrick learned from my mother that she had reluctantly agreed to end their relationship. It is not difficult to imagine the devastating effect the news would have had on him. His resentment at my Uncle Binkie's intervention is reflected in the unflattering description of Philippa's brother in *Richard*

Temple: 'He was a tall, broad young man, with protuberant pale eyes and colourless or faintly yellow close-cropped hair over a florid face, and . . . his . . . lips were conspicuously thick . . . He brought obscene illustrated magazines.'[1]

In Patrick's story 'George', his hero's 'illness' is explicitly designed to deceive and elicit sympathy from Margaret (Patrick's own wife Elizabeth). It is implied that George has abandoned her, although no reason is given for the desertion. The story of the 'Tubercular Wonder' appears to combine two related aspects of Patrick's emotional crisis at this time: his deception and desertion of Elizabeth, and his desperate concern to regain my mother. Altogether it seems highly probable that the 'illness' which dispatched him to hospital in the same month that he learned of my mother's submission to her family represented an attack of some form of nervous hysteria, consciously or unconsciously induced in order to bring her to reconsider her shattering decision.

However, my mother's devotion to Patrick continued unabated, and it is clear that she remained in close contact with him until they eventually came to live together. In *Richard Temple* Philippa Brett visits Richard regularly in hospital, extricating him as soon as possible to bear him away to her home in the country. There can be little doubt that, as so often in the novel, this episode reflected reality. Indeed it is not unlikely that, unknown to Walter Greenway, Patrick was staying with her at the house at Burley where he visited her in the New Forest.[2]

Wherever it occurred, this 'honeymoon' could not be continued long, or suspicions would be aroused. After some weeks Patrick returned to Gadds Cottage, and though there are clear indications that secret communications and possibly occasional meetings persisted between him and my mother, he conducted himself to outward appearance as a dutiful husband and father. Most likely the account of Richard Temple's return to his squalid lodgings in Chelsea following his blissful stay with Philippa Brett in the country reflects his feelings at the time:

> His long holiday was over: his mind was filling fast with the confused fears and obscure hurrying associations that had before made it [his flat] so distinctive a

[1] *Richard Temple*, p. 224. I should make it clear that the description bears no resemblance to my uncle, whom Patrick did not meet at the time.

[2] In *Richard Temple* we learn in passing that Philippa's home Churleigh is situated in Hampshire, and that on their return to London she and Richard pass successively through Lyndhurst and Romsey. All this accords precisely with the situation of Burley – a name reminiscent of 'Churleigh'. Stephen Maturin's wife Diana, who is largely based on my mother as she appeared to Patrick in the early days of their acquaintance, lives in a 'vast great house' in Hampshire (*Clarissa Oakes*, p. 235).

> place for him; he would be obliged to deal with them, and with the new emotion that kept piercing up through them, which he supposed to be the remorse of conscience that he had heard of from time to time . . .
>
> For a very long time now he had divided his world: his world had been habitually divided (painting apart) into the sharps and flats, and by a somewhat different division, into the poor and the rich; he belonged to the sharps – he belonged with much more certainty to the poor; and the people on the other side of the barrier were his natural enemies, his natural prey. But there was no conceivable doubt about where Philippa stood; and there was no question about the mutual enmity of the two worlds.[1]

Not long after Patrick's return to his family in their run-down little cottage Britain declared war against Germany. Although he must have shared the *frisson* of fear and excitement which gripped the country, during the year which followed the combined Nazi and Soviet invasion of Poland the effects of the war had little impact in the remote Suffolk countryside. Patrick's placid round of shooting, fishing, and writing during the period of the phoney war has already been described.

To my mother in London, however, the struggle appeared real enough. Twenty-two years earlier a relatively small number of German air raids had inflicted heavy casualties on London, alarming the Russ family in distant Harrow. Since then the quality and number of military aircraft available to a belligerent power had increased beyond imagining, and in recent years the Spanish Civil War had demonstrated in the field the devastating effect of mass bombing raids, while Mussolini's invasion of Abyssinia illustrated the horrors inflicted by extensive use of poison gas. Leading scientists and public figures in Britain delivered wild and terrifying prognostications far exceeding the brutal reality. British preparations for protection of civilian lives in the event of bombing from the air had been set in motion well before the declaration of war, and now the Government launched a massive recruitment campaign for volunteers to act as drivers, fire wardens, firemen, and other personnel to deal with a horrific new form of warfare whose extent was impossible to anticipate.

In the capital one of the most significant roles was played by the London Auxiliary Ambulance Service (LAAS). Among those who volunteered for the service was my mother, who as a keen if erratic driver encountered no difficulty in obtaining a post. Fervently patriotic and fearless, she must have welcomed the danger and adventure which beckoned. Patrick described the scene in *Richard Temple*:

[1] *Richard Temple*, p. 246.

> London turned into a uniformed camp overnight and those who had no uniforms pinned arm-bands on themselves: Philippa had one as an ambulance driver, and she vanished into a fetid underground garage for twelve hours of the day or the night. It was a time of indescribable confusion, excitement and exaltation, and although nothing happened after those first unearthly, Martian sirens there was no sense of anticlimax: the general vitality of the people had been jerked up to extraordinary level, and it stayed there.[1]

LAAS records do not preserve details of individual personnel, but the description confirms the likelihood that my mother volunteered shortly after the declaration of war in September 1939. In common with numerous other upper-class girls and her fictional counterpart Philippa, she chose Chelsea as the district in which to work. There she was attached to Station No. 22 at 18 Danvers Street, where she was issued with a uniform, gas mask, and steel helmet, and paid £2 for a six-day week.

Whether and if so how often they were able to meet during the year of the phoney war is unknown, but my mother was constantly present in Patrick's thoughts at this time. Indeed, concrete evidence exists of the extent to which they remained in close contact throughout Patrick's year of exile in Norfolk. My mother nurtured a proprietory, almost maternal, concern for his well-being. In *Richard Temple* her counterpart Philippa Brett declares passionately to Richard on more than one occasion 'I could hurl money into your lap', while Valerie Hewer (whose affair partially reflects the circumstances of Patrick's relationship with my mother, though not her character) sends him a sapphire ring. In an episode which bears a suggestion of reality he attempts to pawn it, but on realising that the pawnbroker suspects him of having stolen it leaves the shop hurriedly and sells it instead in Bond Street for £100.[2]

Photographs taken at Gadds Cottage during the winter of 1939–40 show Patrick carrying the small .410 gun, with which as described earlier he hunted game to supplement his family's meagre larder. That gun could – indeed does – tell a tale. It originally belonged to my mother's brother, my Uncle Binkie, who had left it behind with all his other possessions when he returned to the Sudan after the termination of his leave in 1939. His father had given it to him in 1924, and though it lacked the power and twin barrels of a twelve-bore he greatly valued it, since as he explained to me 'it was a rare type of folding gun designed for lightness'. When war broke out that

[1] *Richard Temple*, p. 274.

[2] *Richard Temple*, pp. 209, 252, 267. I cannot help wondering whether this was the sapphire bracelet my mother received as a wedding present from her maternal grandparents, which she disposed of at some point after meeting Patrick.

September it became clear that he would be unable to return home for some considerable time, and when he eventually did so he discovered to his annoyance that my mother had appropriated the gun and bestowed it on Patrick.

Nor was this all. It was not until 1944 that Binkie returned home from Africa. While commanding an infantry company in the Camel Corps, he had been all but killed by the explosion of a hand grenade during close combat with Italian troops. After extensive treatment in hospital at Khartoum, he had been shipped back to England, where he stayed at Staddon to recuperate. His uniform had been ripped to shreds when he was wounded, and all he had to wear when he arrived home was the thin tropical clothing with which he had been issued in Khartoum. The English winter had arrived, but on searching his wardrobe Binkie discovered that all his warm clothing had vanished, save for his dinner-jacket and tails. 'Where was the rest? Mary had cleared the lot for dear Patrick O'B.' Thus the heavy overcoat, smart hat, and tweed jacket proudly sported by Patrick in photographs which Elizabeth took of him at Gadds Cottage came from Binkie's wardrobe. On the other hand the skis which he is shown using in another photograph taken at that time were almost certainly my mother's, brought back from her stay in Switzerland during the winter of 1927–28.

The momentous spring and summer of 1940 moved on, with the little family living to all appearance a life of exemplary contentment. They were poor, but largely owing to the generous assistance of Patrick's brothers Godfrey and Victor managed to survive. Only the constant suffering and concomitant worry resulting from baby Jane's terrible illness marred the peace of the household. So at any rate it appeared to the betrayed Elizabeth.

Finally there came the day, already described, when the German air raids began, and Patrick explained to his wife that he had decided to leave home to drive ambulances in London. It seems she accepted this as a natural move, and looked forward to his eventual return. She was a devoted mother, and at least had her two children as company. Inured since childhood to loneliness, poverty, and hard work, she was not one to complain about material conditions.

It is to be feared that Patrick's emotions were quite different. He was leaving to join the woman he loved, with the prospect for the first time of remaining close to her for the foreseeable future. Despite this, he was never entirely able to escape the reproaches of his conscience. Early in 1949 he jotted down this brief outline of a story, which in the event remained unwritten:

> The hard winter, with the lanes filled with drifted snow – the foam of snow driven hard through the thorn hedges – the waves curling over and the knife-

edged dunes to the lee of everything. And the strange birds (I could bring in those harriers, perhaps to keep the geese down). That starved pigeon. The crackling white ice whose Ox [?] puddles were – fretted – and suspended in the ditches.

Geese down in Queen's Penny Field. A boy with a .410. The open shards of spindle berries – their brighter seeds.

He could come out of the ditch suddenly too near them – the impossibility of getting one's gun up to a thing right at hand. The geese lift up and drift away a couple of fields to settle again . . .

The boy is the vicar's son – Christmas holidays – stained pine – .410 uncle's present – ~~huge guilty love for~~ conventional poverty.

The allusions are drawn from memory, and it seems that it was Patrick's intention to project his own experiences on to those of a child – either himself when young or his son Richard, who later regularly used the gun for shooting rabbits when staying with him in Wales. The words '.410 uncle's present' would no doubt have surprised my uncle in the distant Sudan. However it is the uncompleted phrase, afterwards struck out by Patrick, which throws the most revealing light on his memories of the exceptionally harsh winter of 1939–40.

TEN

Arms and the Man

For years the work of carnage did not cease,
And death's dire aspect daily he surveyed,
Death's minister; then came his glad release,
And hope returned, and pleasure fondly made
Her dwelling in his dreams.
(William Wordsworth, 'Guilt and Sorrow')

The fact that Patrick's departure from the family home in Suffolk brought his work on *The Road to Samarcand* to a halt in mid-flow suggests that it was unexpected. Almost certainly it was caused by a message from my mother urging him to join her. There can be little doubt that he would have leaped at the opportunity at any time during his year's stay at Gadds Cottage, but it took great and terrible events to bring them together.

My sister and I had been sent at the outbreak of war to live with our grandparents in Devon, and once my mother began working full-time for the ambulance service in London her opportunities for seeing us were restricted. I was four at the time, and recall her occasional visits. Staddon was the only home I knew, and I was beginning instinctively to regard my warm-hearted grandparents as parents. My mother was becoming something of an outsider in my life. As an alien my father was restricted in his freedom to travel, and since he was not permitted to come nearer Appledore than Exeter station, we were only able to meet him in the drab confines of the railway café.

In the summer of 1940 events suddenly placed my mother in a situation where she felt she could take the risk of establishing a full (though still secret) relationship with Patrick. Given the timing, it is not difficult to guess what enabled her to undertake this dramatic step. Throughout the first year of the war her hours of employment were long and training rigorous, but as yet she and her colleagues at the Danvers Street LAAS station were not called upon to put their skills to practical use.

The year-long unnatural lull of the phoney war, which in Western Europe constituted neither war nor peace, was abruptly shattered on 10 May 1940, when eighty-nine German divisions, backed by a reserve of a further forty-seven, burst into Holland, Belgium, and France. By the beginning of June the British expeditionary force had been driven into the sea at Dunkirk, and within weeks France surrendered. Britain now stood alone against the might of Nazi Germany, closely allied to Soviet Russia, and Hitler began preparations for the conquest of his remaining enemy.

Although it is improbable that the British armed forces would have been able to resist a landing of the *Wehrmacht* in strength, there remained the formidable obstacle of the Channel which no foreign invader had succeeded in crossing since 1688. Admiral Raeder warned his Führer that the German Navy would be unable to control the straits unless the *Luftwaffe* were to gain supremacy in the air. Massive preparations were promptly undertaken to achieve this end, and by August 2,669 operational aircraft were assembled in Belgium and northern France. On 5 August Hitler issued his Directive No. 17 authorising intensified air assault against the United Kingdom. Initially the principal targets were industrial sites and RAF aerodromes, but within a month resources were diverted from this pragmatic strategy to launching major bombing raids on London and other densely inhabited cities and towns. This shift in policy arose from Hitler's irrational rage when the RAF managed to inflict a couple of minor raids on the German capital. On 4 September, addressing an enthusiastic audience in the Sportspalast building in Berlin, he declared that as a consequence of Churchill's 'downright stupidity': 'If they proclaim they will attack our cities on a grand scale, we will *wipe their cities out*!'

A mere three days passed before Hitler's ferocious threat began to be put into effect. That evening German bombers of *Luftflotte* 2 inflicted devastating damage in the East End of London, principally on the London docks. During the night blazing fires lit up the sky, all but turning night into day. *Luftflotte* 2 departed after suffering some losses from anti-aircraft fire. Far worse was to come. Crossing the Channel from Belgium, a further 247 bombers of *Luftflotten* 2 and 3 droned over London for a leisurely seven hours, during which they dropped 330 tonnes of high explosive bombs and 440 incendiary bomb canisters, each of which contained 36 one-kilogram incendiaries. The inferno below enabled the predators to select their targets with precision, and by the end of that dreadful night widespread areas of the city lay in burning ruins. The worst damage was inflicted on the densely populated terraced houses of the East End, but across the river from where my mother was stationed Battersea Power Station received a direct hit. British ground defences proved inadequate to operate under night-fighting conditions, and the few available night fighter patrols of the RAF failed to down a single German aircraft.

This was but the preliminary to Hitler's determination to wipe London from the map, and by the end of October the *Luftwaffe* had killed 13,000 civilians and gravely injured 20,000. Defensive measures were progressively improved, but this brought little alleviation to the population generally, since it compelled the bombers to release their loads indiscriminately from a greater height. The Blitz had begun, and there was no knowing when or how it might end.

Although the precise date of Patrick's departure for London is not known, converging factors make this the most likely moment. Life in London in many ways had not altered radically from its pre-war course. There were sandbags and sentries in the streets, anti-aircraft guns in the parks, blackout and barrage balloons at night. Otherwise social life continued not so very differently from before. People came and went from the metropolis, visited their friends, and entertained – albeit on restricted rations. During the first year of the war my mother probably lived in a friend's house in Chelsea. In any case it would have been impossible to keep their relationship secret had Patrick then joined her in town, where they might be spotted in the streets at any time.

Suddenly everything changed dramatically. A week into the nightly bombing raids Joan Wyndham noted in her dairy: 'Everyone is leaving London now – Redcliffe Road is like a street of the dead.' Overnight lodgings became cheap and freely available, and my mother might have rented with her £2 LAAS weekly wage what before the war would have been considered a smart flat.[1] With the addition of her income from the trust provided by her father, she found herself for the first time in a situation of financial and domestic independence.

At the same time her life had become effectively cloaked in secrecy. No one could foresee how long the war would last, but few doubted that a long and hard struggle lay ahead. Overnight the nation became preoccupied with the terrible conflict, one consequence of which was that on every side social conventions were overlooked or abandoned. Most of her friends, above all those of her parents' generation, had departed to the country and rarely if at all visited London. The danger of discovery, provided reasonable discretion were exercised, was now diminished to an extent where the risks of being reunited with her lover appeared surmountable. My mother at last felt free to call Patrick to her side: a bidding which he obeyed with predictable alacrity.

[1] Wyndham, *Love Lessons*, p. 121; Theodora FitzGibbon, *With Love: An Autobiography 1938–1946* (London, 1982), pp. 53, 77.

In contrast to my mother's determination to further the patriotic cause, Patrick's attitude towards the war had hitherto been one of detachment, and he was principally concerned with completing *The Road to Samarcand*. As he explained in *Richard Temple*:

> Richard was extremely interested; he watched and listened with the closest attention; but he did not feel himself involved – he had no uniform. He had altered himself almost beyond recognition, but he had not completed the transformation and at that time he had no particular patriotism: indeed, he never felt the true stirrings of it until the fall of France. Just as formerly it had never occurred to him that he should work so now it did not occur to him that he should fight: he did not understand the issues involved, and at this time the fighting was very remote and theoretical, the authorities unbelievably inept and pompous.
>
> He had no uniform, and he might have stayed indefinitely on the sidelines if it had not been for Philippa. But there was never for a second the slightest ambiguity in her attitude. She and all her friends, all her kind, were entirely for the war, the bloody and total annihilation of the country's enemy. She could not conceive knowing anybody who had any reserves about the matter.[1]

Richard Temple is represented as responding to Philippa's call to arms by making determined attempts to enlist, but: 'The three services told him to go away, the third saying that he was wasting their valuable time, coming with a chest like that: he could pass no medical examination.' He himself explained in later years that 'between Munich and the outbreak of war my illness returned with greater severity. This time it left me in a sad way: my strength did not quickly return and I was rejected for active service.'[2]

It is difficult to reconcile this explanation with extensive evidence of Patrick's physical robustness. Two years earlier he had passed the rigorous medical examination required to join the RAF. Five years later, when detailed evidence for his private life first becomes available, his physical fitness and vigour were well above average.

In reality it is inconceivable that he would have contemplated undertaking a step whose consequence would have been an immediate posting far from my mother, with the prospect of not seeing her again for years, if at all. It is to be suspected that his later explanation reflected no more than Dr Johnson's consideration that 'Every man thinks meanly of himself for not having been a soldier, or not having been at sea'. Fortunately there existed an

[1] *Richard Temple*, p. 274.
[2] Cunningham (ed.), *Patrick O'Brian*, p. 17.

alternative course which was both honourable and acceptable to his private end, and my mother managed to arrange for Patrick to be enrolled at the same ambulance station as herself. Theirs was a reserved occupation, which excluded Patrick from the effects of the Royal Proclamation of 1 January 1940 making men from the ages of twenty-three to twenty-seven liable for military service. Although he acted for an ulterior purpose, he was certainly no coward. The service in which he was now engaged was fully as dangerous as anything he might have encountered in the armed forces.

It is unlikely that he knew how to drive on his arrival at Danvers Street, but sketches he made at the time of the workings of the internal combustion engine suggest that he received the regular rough-and-ready instruction. He and my mother were to remain throughout their lives fearless but highly dangerous drivers.

My mother's other overriding concern was to continue avoiding the discovery of her having broken her agreement with her parents and my father to keep away from Patrick. When he arrived in London they took the precaution of lodging discreetly at separate addresses. There was always the danger that my father, who had returned to his flat in nearby Courtfield Road after her departure in 1939, might at any moment discover the revival of their affair were it to be conducted openly. Friends from the time of their marriage remained in the neighbourhood, and it must have been one of them who informed my mother about this time that 'Dimitry is getting on well'.

Precisely where the couple lodged following Patrick's return to Chelsea I have been unable to establish with certainty. It was suggested in an earlier chapter that inconsistencies in Richard Temple's prefatory summary of the places where he lived in Chelsea throw a light on the question. On his arrival Temple carefully lists five places where he stayed during his early years in Chelsea. The first three are identifiable with successive houses in which Patrick himself lived throughout his time in London from 1935 to 1939. The catalogue however contains two further addresses to which the ensuing story makes no reference and allows no room. 'He remembered leather-aproned Hare, the removing man, who lived with Burke, his little horse, in a green triangular place, a hay- and stable-scented vestige of the rural village, near the sad walls of the workhouse, and how he had walked so many times by Hare's van: Dovehouse Street; Smith Terrace with its monstrous bugs, immune to sulphur-fumes.'

The apparently inexplicable inclusion of these two addresses which in the event not only play no part in *Richard Temple* but are incompatible with the story, together with the evocative allusions to the removal men and the squalid conditions in Smith Terrace, suggests they may have been streets where Patrick himself lodged after his return to Chelsea in

1940[1] The reference to his having at one time walked regularly past the house of the removal men is appropriate to a period of living in Dovehouse Street.[2] The firm he facetiously termed Burke and Hare was in reality an establishment named Burchett's, which occupied an old house in a picturesque corner of Glebe Place.[3] Had Patrick, like Richard Temple, lived near the workhouse in Dovehouse Street at this time, Glebe Place would have provided an attractive passage for his daily walk to the ambulance station in Danvers Street.

The first firm date which can be assigned to the start of their shared life is 4 November 1940, when Patrick and my mother celebrated her birthday together for the first time. In 1975 he noted in his diary: 'For the first time, I think, in 35 years I had nothing for M's birthday.' It can be seen how carefully he cherished his memories of their early days.

The young couple had much to occupy them beyond their first unfettered enjoyment of amorous bliss. The blitzkrieg on London continued from September over the winter and into the spring of 1941 with ever-increasing ferocity. The principal targets for the *Luftwaffe* were the London Docks, the City, government offices, and large factories. Night after night an eerie wailing of sirens heralded the droning approach of enemy bombers coming up the Thames. A lurid glow illumined the city as high-explosive and incendiary bombs rained down on the largely defenceless population, setting streets and public buildings ablaze as far as the eye could see. Searchlight beams swivelled erratically in the darkness above the rooftops, now flashing across the hundreds of barrage balloons floating overhead like great schools of whales, now darting to focus on the dark forms of German aeroplanes. The ear-splitting roar of anti-aircraft guns blazing back into the night from nearby batteries tended to be more effective in boosting civilian morale than inflicting casualties on the enemy.

Chelsea stood starkly in the firing line, as Battersea Power Station represented both a prime target and key navigational guide for *Luftwaffe* pilots flying upriver from the Thames estuary. The effect on the district was devastating. Barely a night passed without terrible damage to property and heavy casualties. Rows of houses were levelled in the course of a single night

[1] The novel makes no allowance for Patrick's year-long absence from London in 1939–40, passing seamlessly into his relationship with Philippa Brett (my mother).

[2] For the Dovehouse Street workhouse, cf. FitzGibbon, *With Love*, p. 159.

[3] Cf. Walter H. Godfrey, *The Parish of Chelsea (Part II.) Being the Fourth Volume of the Survey of London* (London, 1913), p. 77, plate 78. Richard Temple employs the firm to move his worldly goods in a horse-drawn cart to the 'pigeon-loft' in the King's Road (*Richard Temple*, pp. 106–07).

and entire streets set ablaze, their passage blocked by gaping chasms from which burst waterpipes spouted and severed gas mains flared. On the night of 27–28 September nearby Holland House was struck by a score of incendiary bombs, and in the early hours its Jacobean splendour was reduced to smoking ruins. On the evening of 12 November a direct hit by a high-explosive bomb smashed right through Sloane Square underground station, crushing a departing train, setting two gas mains ablaze, killing twenty-one people, injuring forty others, and leaving three unaccounted for. Nineteen patients were killed on the night of 18–19 February, when St Stephen's Hospital in Fulham Road received a direct hit, and a week later Chelsea bus station was badly damaged.

On 17 April the much-loved thirteenteenth-century Chelsea Old Church on the embankment, burial place of Sir Thomas More and Sir Hans Sloane, as well as Lawrences and Cheynes whose names also survive in familiar Chelsea streets, received a direct hit. A friend of my mother recalled the horrific scene.

'The nurses' home of the Cheyne Hospital for Children had the top floor blown off: and the nurses' bedroom, the ceiling light still shining, looked like a stage set. A warden perilously climbed up the bombed staircase and switched it off, although there was a flaming gas main burning around the corner which floodlit the entire area. The church was nothing but an immense heap of timber and stone, flames licking through it; a large vaulted tomb with a stone urn on top rose up undamaged in the front. The New Café Lombard and all the large and small houses at that end of Old Church Street had been flung together into a giant mountain of shale-like destruction, all lit by the fire and the gas main. Under that fantastic mountain were people, some still alive. Heavy stones were flung aside like pebbles: the local grocer of the street, Mr Cremonosi, put his hand down through a space and felt warm flesh. A naked unhurt woman was pulled up. An old lady appeared, staggering, from the far side of the mountain, having been flung at least thirty yards and then covered with glass, wood and bricks, from which she had extricated herself . . . A sixteen-year-old-girl, pinned, only her head showing, talked to a rescue worker: she was freed, but died several hours later.'[1]

Over that autumn and winter, month succeeded month with barely a night's respite from the hideous cacophony. Time and again my mother, Patrick, and their fellow-drivers at Station No. 22 leaped into their ambulances and negotiated rubble-strewn streets on their frenzied way to reach spectacles of blood and destruction. The injured were taken as fast as wrecked streets allowed to designated local hospitals: St Stephen's, St Mary

[1] FitzGibbon, *With Love*, pp. 71–75.

Abbots, and the Royal Orthopaedic Hospital. I remember my admiration when my mother, during one of her visits to Staddon, described to me how her dauntless dachshund Miss Potts (or 'Miss Pätz', as she had become known during our visit to Austria in 1938) invariably accompanied her, seated on her lap with paws firmly set on the steering wheel and sharp muzzle gazing ahead through the windscreen.[1]

So intense was the excitement that my mother recalled feeling little fear, since living on a nightly basis with the perpetual threat of imminent death made abnormality appear almost normal. Nor were she and her colleagues any safer while awaiting calls in their headquarters in Danvers Street. In October and November 1940, for example, LAAS reports recorded regular damage to the building: '12.10.40. "Pane of glass in garage roof broken by shell. Shrapnel through roof. 21.10.40. Ceiling damaged and glass broken"'; '29/10: 16 panes of glass broken in garage roof, 2 cars damaged'; '19.2.41 Number of Windows broken, burst water mains which flooded in our rooms. Bomb on adjoining premises caused damage to roof, glazing and asbestos sheeting'.[2]

However, there was a high spirit of camaraderie among the members of Station No. 22. Patrick put his literary talent to work, composing this rousing anthem to raise their spirits.

> Lines of unpredictable merit written on the back of Miss Patz, a rough-haired Dachshundin in the year of Grace a thousand nine hundred and forty-one, on Wednesday, the 8th (?) day of January, at about half after one in the afternoon, it being a cold day, dismal with half molten snow.
>
> The people of this station are disconsolate and rude,
> All English to the tonsils, and filled with British phlegm
> They blow their noses horribly, and between the blast is spewed
> A flux of ghastly small talk. Why God, did you make them?
> *¿Was other clay not handy?
> Was then nothing else to please?
> Oh Lord that gave us brandy
> And lamb and fresh green peas
> *¿Why did you turn Your Hand to these?

[1] Miss Potts was not always treated with the respect which was her due. She accompanied my mother everywhere, following without a lead. However on one occasion the doorman at a restaurant tried to stop her, and on her explaining that her dog always accompanied her, replied firmly: 'Don't give me that: that ain't a dog, it's a mongoose!' Fortunately, in the Second World War dachshunds escaped the patriotic hostility accorded their predecessors in 1914 (E. S. Turner, *The Phoney War on the Home Front*, (London, 1961), p. 114).
[2] London Metropolitan Archives, PH/WAR/3/74.

The last line is (I think) an Alexandrine, which is very clever indeed, probably.

*That is affected, I must admit. But am I inferior to a Spaniard? ¡No!'

The composition appears to have gone down well, since Patrick was inspired to provide a more polished version:

In dispraise of the Personnel of 22 St L.A.A.S.

The people of this station are disconsolate and rude
They are English to the tonsils, and with British phlegm embued
In proof of this opinion to their handkerchiefs I point
And not only to their kerchiefs, but oyster eyes and roomy joint,
But also to their tempers, habitually vile
The fruit of grave distemper and coagulated bile.
All wart-hogs in comparison are quite high-souled and mild
Which leads to the conclusion that the better beasts are wild.
This may be sung (though the notion is grim)
To the tune of a well-known American hymn.
viz., or vide licet, if you should prefer the word*
Mine eyes have seen the glory of the coming of the Lord.*

*you must say this as if it rhymed with Lord
*or 'Lord,' if you would have it so, as if it rhymed with word.

Amid the chaos and carnage my mother and Patrick derived enormous consolation from the excitement of their guilty love. It must have been after some minor tiff that Patrick addressed these light-hearted verses to her:

Pray, love, forgive me my sourness
Think of me
No uncharity
But have in gre
My love for thee,

And account not my dourness.

For heavy cheer
And loutish leer
All loathly gear
Comes not near

My love for thee.

Your P.

He addressed a number of similarly humorous and affectionate verses to her, which provide intriguing glimpses of their life together at this extraordinary period. One, recounting a nocturnal adventure in the life of Miss Potts, begins:

> Patz went out in the dead of the night,
> In the dead of the night went she.
> But first she carefully put out the light,
> And closed the door with a key.

Accompanying illustrations show Miss Pätz leaping for the light switch and letting herself out of the front door with a latchkey. Momentarily pondering in fluent German verse whether she might not go to a club, she decides instead on a pub, where the next illustration shows her seated at the bar.

> She went quite straight to the Lion called Black
> Tossed down a quick pint, and never looked back
> For a wicked old Owl, who took his dram raw
> Determined to try the truth of the saw –

A graphic illustration portrays Miss Potts standing at the bar receiving a pint from a handsome black lion, while being eyed up by a pipe-smoking owl wearing a steel helmet bearing the 'A' of the ambulance service. The Black Lion was a convivial pub nearby on the corner of Old Church Street and Paultons Street, frequently by members of the ambulance service.

The Owl, recalling Chaucer's advice on taking advantage of women when tipsy,

> . . . plied her with whisky, with gin and with rum
> And said that he wished she would instantly come
> To a very fine party to be held at a club
> So complacent and willing she then left the pub.
> At the club she encountered a motley crew
> Hard-drinking and raffish and lecherous too
> They drank bottles of whisky and magnums of gin
> Till Patz felt uncertain what state she was in.

The club was probably one of those frequented at this time by my mother's friend Theodora FitzGibbon, who remembered evenings spent at 'a basement drinking club called The Gateways in Bramerton Street . . . The Studio, next to the Town Hall, the Pheasantry, and one in a private house in Upper Cheyne Row called, appropriately, the Crater Club!'[1]

[1] *With Love*, p. 64.

At the club the Owl finds Miss Pätz an armchair, where she sits gazing up at him with a charming smile, cigarette in one hand and glass in the other.

> The owl thought, 'aha, now may I eat grass,
> But this is the time when I make the first pass.'
> And through his vile mind there passed devious shapes
> Of libidinous bitches and lecherous apes.

The tale concludes with a brief verse exchange between the two, alternating between German and French. The Owl invites his attractive companion to a drive in his car. 'Oh no, you old devil,' replies the dachshund in her native tongue, 'what can you be asking? That van belongs to the LCC!' The bystanders begin scoffing at the Owl, who promptly drains a bottle of wine and vows not to leave before he has *la chienne* in his arms.

Miss Pätz and the Owl in these teasing verses obviously represent my mother and Patrick. There is significant indication that they lived apart, and Miss Pätz's furtive departure from her home suggests the need to evade a vigilant landlady. Clearly they enjoyed more than a *frisson* of excitement from the secrecy with which they were obliged to conduct their romance.[1]

On 10 May 1941 the *Luftwaffe* launched what Churchill described as 'the most destructive attack of the whole night Blitz', whose swathe of devastation across London cost 3,000 lives and the destruction (among innumerable other buildings) of the House of Commons. However, as he further observed: 'This, though we did not know it, was the enemy's parting fling.' On 22 May Kesselring transferred his headquarters to Poland, where his air fleet followed him at the beginning of the next month in preparation for the German invasion of the Soviet Union on 22 June. Although air raids continued throughout the war, the hideous intensity of the Blitz was over.

A relative lull fell upon Station 22 of the LAAS, and Patrick began to look around for some more stimulating occupation. How he obtained his next posting is unrecorded, but once again it seems likely that *Richard Temple* provides a reliable guide. The beautiful Philippa seeks contacts among her and her father's influential friends, but in the end it proves to be Temple's old schoolfriend Charles Gay who 'had something to do with one of the many branches of intelligence but which or what naturally remained vague: he had taken Richard for an interview with some military and civilian people in

[1]On 28 April 1941 the Oxford University Press wrote to inform Patrick that *Hussein* was being withdrawn from print. However the only address they had was 301 King's Road, where Patrick had been living with Elizabeth a year before, and the 'letter [was] returned from this address by Post Office undelivered'.

Kilburn (a suburban house in the best tradition) and the interview had been conducted in French.' This proved fruitful, and he took 'a great oath of secrecy'.[1]

The character of Charles Gay was based on Patrick's and my mother's diplomat friend Charles de Salis, but since they did not come to know him until after the war it remains unknown who effected the introduction, unless de Salis were 'a friend of a friend' as yet unknown to Patrick. The reference to the interview at Kilburn bears a ring of reality.

In his brief introduction to the British Library's volume of appreciative essays published in 1994, Patrick wrote cryptically: 'Sometime after the blitz had died away I joined one of those intelligence organisations that flourished in the War, perpetually changing their initials and competing with one another. Our work had to do with France, and more than that I shall not say, since disclosing methods and stratagems that have deceived the enemy once and that may deceive him again seems to me foolish.'[2]

As he explained, a fluctuating succession of organisations concerned with countering Nazi propaganda and influencing public opinion throughout Occupied Europe culminated in the creation of the Political Warfare Executive (PWE). It was in the aftermath of the German invasion of the Soviet Union on 22 June that, following much ministerial and inter-departmental wrangling, the organisation was established to co-ordinate the ideological war against Nazism. Its remit ranged from monitoring BBC broadcasts, where the normal insistence was on accuracy and reliability, to 'black' propaganda involving anything from creation of imaginary resistance broadcasting stations on the Continent to concocting pornographic programmes designed to discredit Nazi and collaborationist leadership and authority.[3]

Patrick reported for duty at his new post on 26 September 1941, just six days after official notice had been circulated of the creation of the new organisation.[4] Its headquarters was then situated at 2 Fitzmaurice Place in the West End, and the organisation also maintained premises at Woburn Abbey, the palatial home of the Dukes of Bedford situated about forty miles from London.

An impression of Patrick's work, concerning which he remained extremely

[1] *Richard Temple*, pp. 274–75, 277.

[2] Cunningham ed., *Patrick O'Brian*, p. 17.

[3] The history of PWE is fully covered by Michael Stenton, *Radio London and Resistance in Occupied Europe: British Political Warfare 1939–1943* (Oxford, 2000) and David Garnett, *The Secret History of PWE: The Political Warfare Executive 1939–1945* (London, 2002).

[4] This would appear to confirm that Patrick obtained his posting through private contacts, since the existence of PWE remained officially secret.

reticent to the end of his life, will shortly be recounted from an account he wrote at the time. Meanwhile my mother continued working as an ambulance driver, and at the beginning of November took a formal course in first aid organised by the London County Council (LCC). On 4 November she entered in faulty Russian (which she had begun learning on marrying my father) this marginal jotting in her notes:

> Я такв лублу Пѣту ('I love Pat so much') / ПАТРИКЪ МАРИЯ ПАТСЪ ('Patrick Mary Patz') / 7 Redesdale St.

At the same time my mother wrote wistfully 'je voudrais un arbre de Noël pour Pat Il faut que je le lasse, alors': presumably there were none to be had in the shops. Just before Christmas Patrick gave her a watch, for which he painstakingly embroidered on a cloth patch the inscription: 'Patrick gave this watch to Mary his mistress V.XII.XLI.'[1] It appears that they had finally adopted the irrevocable step of living together, and that all three (naturally Miss Potts represented a most important member of the household) had moved into accommodation in Redesdale Street, round the corner from Smith Terrace where Patrick (accepting my interpretation of *Richard Temple*) had hitherto been living.

Now they discovered happiness beyond even that which they had experienced since Patrick's arrival in London in the summer of 1940. He had enthused my mother with his own love of old books, and she was delighted when he presented her with a first edition of Voltaire's *Candide*. Its brief inscription 'M. from P. 1942' conjures up with poignant immediacy those distant halcyon days, when their life together was beginning.[2] It was not long before she began to share his literary tastes. On 26 July 1944, for example, she bought a copy of Stephen Collet's *Relics of Literature* (1823) and two months later presented Patrick with Samuel Butler's mock epic *Hudibras* in an edition published in 1709.

The only clouds in an otherwise sunny sky arose from their former lives, which regularly returned to haunt them. My father somehow discovered that the couple were living together, and on 12 May 1942 he obtained a decree nisi in which Patrick was cited as co-respondent, the divorce being declared absolute in November.

Meanwhile it will be recalled that some time after Patrick left home in 1940

[1]Although open to the other interpretation, I feel sure Patrick intended the term 'mistress' in the sense defined by Dr Johnson: 'A woman beloved and courted'. It is in this sense that he describes Philippa Brett in *Richard Temple* (p. 241).

[2] The wording further illustrates the fallacy of drawing inferences from Patrick's equally laconic inscription in the copy of *Cæsar* he presented to his sister Joan in 1931.

his brother Godfrey and his wife Connie, who were devout Christians, provided a home for his wife Elizabeth and their two small children at their home outside Norwich. Godfrey, like the rest of his family, knew nothing of the true reason for Patrick's abrupt departure. While he displayed concern for the impoverished little family, he had no especial reason to regard Elizabeth's plight as different from that of innumerable other wives whose husbands were absent performing their duty to King and country.

Elizabeth and her children lived for some two years with Godfrey and Connie. Contrary to ill-natured accusations circulated after his death, Patrick did not abandon his family after leaving home. On the contrary, he was scrupulous in sending Elizabeth such financial support as he could afford. Although she later claimed in her divorce petition that 'the maintenance he sent me was most erratic and of . . . a small amount', she subsequently conceded that 'he provided me with three pounds per week' throughout the time of his absence. This comprised the whole of his weekly wage from the LAAS. Since he possessed no other financial resource, this left him and my mother dependent on the modest income of about £100 and wage of £2 a week that she received from her trust and her own smaller wage as an ambulance driver.

In addition Patrick maintained a regular and apparently cordial correspondence with his wife and son. In later custody proceedings Elizabeth submitted in evidence one of the letters he had written her during his absence in London. Most of it is missing from the file in the Public Record Office and all that survives are the opening words: 'Thank you for Richard's letter – he has written to me recently. There is no doubt at all that he must not come back to London [. . .]'.

Fortunately the description in Elizabeth's accompanying affidavit makes its import clear: 'I cannot recall the date when this was written but . . . At that time he had not begun to adopt the attitude of hostility he has since shown [after their divorce in 1945] and he was proposing that I should take a job as Matron at a Boys School; he regarded me as eminently suitable for such a position and pressed me to seek for such employment . . . The other side of the same piece of paper gives some clue as to our relations at that time before these unhappy circumstances arose' – the implication clearly being that, on paper at least, they continued amicable during the first year or so of his absence.[1]

It might be suggested that Patrick was only too content for Elizabeth to find permanent employment which would keep her at a safe distance from London. For some time after his arrival he took precautions to prevent her discovering his address, and she referred to a period 'when he was concealing

[1]PRO J77/3990.

his whereabouts under a British monomark' (a pre-stamped envelope which did not require a postmark).

However there is no reason to suppose that his concern for her welfare was not sincere (she evidently thought so), and life as a boarding-school matron would undoubtedly have been much more secure, lucrative (food and board were provided free with the salary) than her current situation as an unemployed woman. In addition it was normal practice for a school to accept the child of an employee as a pupil at no or greatly reduced cost.[1] Again, Patrick's concern that Richard should not return to London may well have arisen from the overriding consideration which led to hundreds of thousands of children being evacuated from the metropolis.[2] Their lives could be frightening enough even then, and the boy's mother subsequently testified that 'Richard . . . has been subject to nightmares and his chief nightmare, which has been a persistent one, is of Norwich being afire'. Fortunately Godfrey's home in the neighbouring village of Thorpe was as safe as could be expected in those dangerous days.

Richard recalled long years after: 'When I was five he sent me a present – a bottle of malt and cod liver oil, something no five-year-old would want. He also sent me a letter telling me to "look after our women folk".' On his next birthday Patrick sent a more appropriate gift, explaining that its predecessor had been intended as a joke. The 'joke' may have been feeble or the incident misrecalled from so young an age,[3] but whether Richard nurtured such bitter resentment at the time as he was to express more than half a century later seems a little unlikely.

Brought up an impoverished orphan, Elizabeth had received only a rudimentary education: a handicap after her move to London compounded by Welsh being her first language. During custody proceedings in 1949 she complained 'that my correspondence is objected to because I am said to be

[1] Elizabeth testified in an affidavit in 1945 that 'I had to live with his relations [Patrick's brother Godfrey and his wife Constance] when I had to apply for public assistance.' At the time this amounted to £1 a week and 6/- allowance for Richard.

[2] On 29 November 1940 the Minister of Health provided statistics showing that 759,500 children had been evacuated from London. The Ministry issued a poster showing a shadowy Hitler pointing in the direction of a smoking city and whispering in the ear of a mother gathered with her children under a tree: 'Take them back! Take them back! Take them back!' The exhortation beneath advises: 'DON'T do it, Mother – LEAVE THE CHILDREN WHERE THEY ARE' (Turner, *The Phoney War*, p. 87).

[3] Richard's memory was undoubtedly confused. The above account is taken from a newspaper interview in 2000. However, a year or so earlier he informed Dean King that he received the cod-liver oil on his fourth birthday, while the cited letter accompanied by a more appropriate present arrived on his fifth (King, *Patrick O'Brian*, p. 93). The version he gave King must surely be correct, since by the age of six he was living in London next door to his father.

illiterate'. If, as is likely, the drunken mother of *Richard Temple* represents Patrick's guilt-ridden image of Elizabeth, Temple's treatment of his mother's correspondence probably reflects something of Patrick's own reaction during the two years after he left her.

> He might even have been able to bar it out of his recollection if only every month, every Christmas, Easter and birthday had not brought a letter. At first the envelopes were typed by the people at the place where his mother was kept, but then they started coming in her hand, so completely unaltered that the sight of it made him tremble. He had opened them at first. They were odd, prim letters, obviously written under direction, impersonal and uninterested; and he had answered them in agony with trite phrases that concealed a burning prayer to be forgotten. But in time he left them unopened and answered with set phrases and a mechanical account of his progress, so far as it was acceptable.[1]

While his family was much better provided for at his brother's comfortable house and garden at 28 Thorpe Avenue, it is hard to believe that Patrick did not suffer more than a spasm of guilt on learning of the long-anticipated death of his little daughter Jane on 31 March 1942.[2]

Shortly after the tragedy Elizabeth returned to London with Richard. As she explained in an affidavit: 'At five Richard was sent by me to a little local school [in Norwich] for three months, but my daughter then died and as the bombardment of London had apparently ceased I decided to leave Norwich where I felt we were a burden and came to London with Richard to find employment. I then decided to send Richard to a Roman Catholic School . . . and I took this step because the educational system of London was disrupted at that time and the only other reasonable course open was to send him to a Council School which I did not then desire to do' – and she correctly assumed Patrick would likewise not approve.

[1] *Richard Temple*, p. 72. Eventually Richard stops opening the letters, but nevertheless preserves them in a cardboard box on his mantelpiece (ibid., p. 108). The ill-written letters are much more appropriate to those of the uneducated Elizabeth Russ, of which he actually complained, than Richard Temple's well-bred mother. As so often, confusion in Patrick's narrative betrays the fact that reality kept obtruding into his fiction. For how could Temple have 'answered with set phrases' her letters when 'he left them unopened'?!

[2] Although Stephen Maturin is given to expatiating on unpleasant aspects of infancy, he twice goes out of his way to adopt and protect abandoned children (*The Nutmeg of Consolation*, pp. 209–16; *The Hundred Days*, pp. 217–20, 222, 223–27, 229–30, 237, 239–40, 251–52). Still more significantly, he is racked with guilt on discovering that a generous gift of jewellery to the lively little girl Dil whom he befriends in Bombay proves the inadvertent cause of her murder (*HMS Surprise*, pp. 161, 163–64, 176–80, 181–83, 199–200).

Mother and son moved into a flat in 237 King's Road, immediately above another occupied by Francis Cox, their artist friend from before the war, and his wife. It was presumably in connection with Richard's attendance at his school, which was administered by the order of Servants of St Mary (Servites), that Elizabeth and Patrick came to know Father de Zulueta, the Catholic parish priest of Chelsea, a tall, distinguished, intelligent gentleman of aristocratic Spanish origin, who in ensuing years was to provide her with much spiritual solace and material assistance.[1] Richard remained at the Servite School until the end of the following year.

Elizabeth's life was not easy. Initially she worked on the assembly line of an electrical factory in Earls Court, and later obtained a job at a haberdasher's in the King's Road, where Richard remembered that she 'worked with four other women, doing repairs on ladies' stockings'. The pay was poor, but now that Patrick was receiving a good salary from the Foreign Office it is likely that he provided support in excess of the weekly sum he had previously paid from his wages as an ambulance driver. In addition Richard's kindly Uncle Godfrey called at the flat from time to time to check that all was well, when he also doubtless continued his contributions to the household budget.

At this time Elizabeth remained ignorant of the fact that her husband had recently been cited as co-respondent in my mother's divorce. More remarkably he succeeded in concealing his relationship from Elizabeth until September of the following year, despite the fact that they lived a mere five minutes' walk from each other. When she came to institute divorce proceedings against him in April 1944, she declared that he had been living and committing adultery with my mother since September 1943.

In court proceedings held in 1945 Elizabeth changed the year she understood Patrick to have begun living with my mother to 1942. That was the year when he was cited as co-respondent in my parents' divorce, and in view of what is now known of my father's private collaboration with Elizabeth over her custody proceedings, it can only have been he who informed her that Patrick and my mother had begun living together a year earlier than she had previously realised. Thus it is certain that throughout the time that she was living in East Anglia Elizabeth remained ignorant of Patrick's liaison. Not until 1943 did she become aware of his relationship

[1] Many years later Father de Zulueta, whom I came to know well, took me to visit Richard's mother, who was lying ill in a Chelsea hospital. Afterwards he muttered something to the effect that 'O'Brian is a strange fellow', and I received the impression that he did not entertain a very high opinion of him.

with my mother, and her subsequent knowledge never extended beyond a revised belief that it had begun in the previous year.[1]

Correspondingly from 1939 to 1942 Patrick and my mother managed to keep their relationship hidden from my father. When in the latter year he petitioned for divorce, the discovery that his wife was living with Patrick Russ must have come as a dreadful shock. Although my father remarried at the end of February in the following year, he changed dramatically from the boisterous and cheerful young man he had been at the time of his marriage to my mother into an increasingly melancholic recluse. Very likely the extent to which her betrayal wounded his sensitivities was exacerbated by the lasting effects of his loss of his mother when he was four, followed two years later by the terrifying time of his protracted concealment during the Russian Revolution. As though these harrowing experiences were not sufficient, he then suffered an unhappy upbringing at his adopted home in England. Despite the apparent success of his second marriage, which lasted for more than half a century, he remained so deeply embittered against my mother that he refused to attend my wedding in 1971 if she was to be present. Fortunately the problem was resolved by the necessity for successive Anglican and Orthodox ceremonies, which my parents attended independently.

The judgment in the divorce proceedings confirmed my mother's worst fears. In view of her desertion of her family and the fact that she was living in adultery with a married man, the judge pronounced her an unfit person to have access to her children. Although he granted her leave to apply for a review in three years' time, in the event she was not to see me again for another thirteen years, nor my sister until long after that. This deprivation caused my mother acute distress, from which she never fully recovered. Although she had unquestionably treated my father very badly, it seems excessively harsh that she was not permitted even to correspond with her children.

Elizabeth had never seen my mother, so provided she and Patrick were careful not to walk together in the neighbourhood they might expect to evade discovery outside their home. In the autumn of 1942 they moved into a house in Upper Cheyne Row which became their permanent home. They adopted the precaution of withholding their telephone number from the London directory, and must have been at remarkable pains to ensure they were not observed.

[1] In 1949 Elizabeth declared in an affidavit that her husband 'deserted me for another woman (with whom on his own confession he had been committing adultery while still living with me) when Richard was three years old'. Although true in fact, this claim must represent invention on Elizabeth's part. Not only is it inconceivable that Patrick would have volunteered such a confession at any time, but when she issued this declaration they had not met since her previous affirmation that he began living with my mother in 1942.

It is difficult at first sight to understand why he found this necessary. My mother's motive for secrecy had vanished with her divorce, which ended any present opportunity of establishing contact with her children. It could now make no difference to her whether Patrick's wife became aware of the situation or not. Evidently the continuing requirement for secrecy concerned Patrick alone, and the question arises as to what can have been his motive.

Inevitably it remains largely a matter for conjecture, but some inferences appear inescapable. Patrick was infatuated with my mother, and his dearest wish was to marry her. Now that she was divorced from my father, the sole remaining obstacle lay in his marriage to Elizabeth. Why then should he have gone to such lengths to conceal from his wife the affair which would give her immediate grounds for divorce?

My mother was as devoted to Patrick as he was to her. It was to remain the love affair of a lifetime. However, Patrick's isolated, erratic, and largely loveless upbringing imbued him with a sense of insecurity and excessive sensitivity which he could never shed. To one possessed of so exceptionally vulnerable a nature, the love of a woman endowed with every imaginable advantage of beauty, charm, and social position conferred great apprehension along with unimagined delight. Everything suggests that he remained scarcely able to credit his good fortune.

From the age of fifteen or so my mother had drawn men to her like a magnet. Her friend Diana Keast (née Harman), daughter of the owner of Lundy, recalls how girls on the island would descend to the quay to meet the daily paddle-steamer, privately hoping that the visitors might include presentable young men. My mother however put herself to no such trouble, since men inevitably clustered around her in no time after ascending the cliff path. She was flirtatiously charming, and the scant care she took to conceal her misbehaviour with the good-looking Austrian guide Toni Pflösler in 1938 suggests (as indeed I know) that it was not the only occasion of its kind. While her commitment to Patrick became total, it seems likely that there was an initial stage of their acquaintance when he was not the only man on the scene.

Richard Temple contains indications that when its eponymous hero first meets his Philippa he was not her first lover, and what he feared to be daunting rivals remained in the field. When Richard ('turning aside to hide the silly smile') tells his old schoolfriend Gay about his friendship with Philippa Brett, Gay expresses astonishment.

> 'You are flying pretty high, aren't you?'
> Richard laughed. 'I hope to marry her soon.'
> 'So do plenty of other people.'

Gay's scepticism proves justified, and just when he feels most confident of her affection Temple is devastated to find himself supplanted in Philippa's affections by a rival. Recollecting this shattering discovery in his German prison cell, Temple's autobiographical reminiscences conclude: 'With that recollection his mind went white . . .'

This episode probably reflects lively fears entertained by Patrick during the early years of his relationship with my mother. Philippa's social background is represented as grandest of the grand, and her manner of speech verges on a quaint travesty of upper-class insouciance. Major Brocas, Richard Temple's successful rival, is a 'splendid' army officer, whose 'Sam Browne, decorations, gleaming buttons here and there' cruelly outshine the civilian Temple. Inexorably she had been drawn back within the inaccessible ramparts of her class. In reality my mother eschewed any such inclination, and so far as I am aware completely abandoned conscious beguilement of other men once she had committed herself to Patrick. However, that could not prevent them from betraying their admiration, nor Patrick from perceiving it.

Patrick appears never to have been able to rid himself of his underlying fear that the prize he had gained against all reasonable odds might turn out to be too good to be true. In 1970, when they were both in their fifties, he went to stay for a while in Austria. There he suffered distress on failing at first to receive any communication from my mother beyond 'your one cold, dutiful note of the 22nd'. He sent her an anguished appeal:

> The lunch-tray came up just now, and when I realised that there was no letter on it I pushed the whole thing aside: all the more since yesterday was the only moderately cheerful evening I have spent for God knows how long . . . and since I spent this morning sending you a bauble for our silver wedding day. It seemed impossible that our minds should not have crossed.
>
> Sometimes you have said that I do not speak clearly, and it is true: I distrust words and I value indirection too highly. But I will say this as directly as can be – if you think my writing worth a straw, do not keep me in this state. While expostulations, harangues and pleading drift between me and my paper I can do nothing but hack work, and that only with a grinding, inefficient labour.
>
> Our relationship is vital to me. Write kindly if you have kindness left: tell me plainly if you have none.

Patrick's irrational but agonising early fears receive an echo in Jack Aubrey's dismay at failing to receiving letters in America from his equally faithful wife Sophie.[1] Still more to the point is the constant emphasis laid on Stephen

[1] *The Surgeon's Mate*, pp. 37–38.

Maturin's acceptance of Diana Villiers's cavalier attitude to chastity before their marriage, and his philosophical tolerance of her infidelities thereafter. Sophie and Diana unmistakably reflect different aspects of my mother as Patrick understood her, and I believe that Diana (whose character strongly resembles that of Philippa Brett in *Richard Temple*) represents *au fond* his awed and apprehensive perception of her at the time he first came to know her.

Reverting to Patrick's concealment of his affair from Elizabeth from 1942 to 1943, the only reasonable explanation is surely that he was concerned to avoid a divorce. How Patrick's marriage to Elizabeth might have fared had my mother never entered his life must remain matter for conjecture. They had after all continued living an apparently contented life in conditions of considerable privation and extreme solitude for some two years after he had fallen passionately in love with my mother. His introverted character made it impossible for him to sustain a sympathetic relationship with children, but the enduring concern he displayed to do the best he could for his son was genuine. Although he deserted his incurably sick daughter, before that he had remained beside her for well over a year in exceedingly cramped quarters under conditions which would have provoked stress in a far more equable character.

But for my mother's intrusion on the scene Patrick's marriage must have lasted longer than it did, and the possibility cannot be excluded that it might have continued for years, or conceivably endured altogether. Patrick was monogamous by nature, as his fidelity and devotion to my mother were to prove throughout more than fifty years of marriage. Although Elizabeth lacked my mother's beauty, education, and social status, she was attractive, kind, supportive of Patrick's literary aspirations, and quietly worked hard to provide him with a comfortable home. Given the obsessive compulsion with which my mother conducted her courtship with Patrick, it is to be feared that many men would have encountered difficulty in resisting the temptation for long.

This interpretation of Patrick's hopes and fears possibly receives support from an otherwise inexplicable anomaly which arose during a subsequent legal dispute between him and his wife. In 1945 Elizabeth testified on oath that 'From 1938 to 1942 he [Patrick] lived with me in Suffolk and was supported by me and his brother. In 1942 he left me and went to London . . .'[1] It is barely conceivable that so soon after the event she should have misplaced

[1]For what it is worth Richard also identified 1942 as the year of his father's abandonment of his mother, when he told a reporter: 'I was five when he left us' (*Guardian*, 27 November 2003).

the date of his departure by two years in a sworn legal document requiring careful consideration, above all when it would have been advantageous to her case to place Patrick's desertion earlier rather than later. The implication must surely be that she accepted her husband's absence as necessitated by his war work in London, but regarded their marriage and home as still intact up to the time he met my mother (as she thought) in 1942.

Patrick had consciously deserted and deceived his wife, but his deep-rooted guilt was not so readily shed. He frequently reverted to the topic in his fiction, seeking to banish his shame by ascribing faults to Elizabeth which were at the very least grossly exaggerated. The customary accusations included drunkenness, 'coarseness, insensitivity, sexual inadequacy', while elsewhere he attributed to her sins of vulgarity and poverty deriving from her 'Welsh background'. In fact he liked Welsh people, among whom he was to live for four years, and it was his wife alone who was subjected to this particular contumely.[1]

Guilt understandably represented an overriding factor with Patrick when contemplating his first marriage, and the indications are that it was only after its breakdown that he sought to salve his conscience by denigrating Elizabeth and casting around for pretexts to justify his betrayal.

Saidie Russ recalls that 'Victor told me that Pat had told him he only married Elizabeth because she was pregnant', and he explained to Joan Ainsworth (the girl with whom he conducted a brief affair in the summer of 1937) that his wife had tricked him into marriage by falsely claiming to be pregnant. The first claim cannot be true, since the marriage took place in February 1936 and their son Richard was born almost exactly a year later.[2] Clearly judgement must be suspended. Patrick was certainly very young and in all probability sexually inexperienced when he met Elizabeth Jones, and it may be that he came in time to persuade himself that he had been inveigled into marriage. As Stephen Maturin reminded Jack Aubrey in *The Surgeon's Mate*: 'you are to consider the possibility of there being no pregnancy at all,

[1] *Richard Temple*, pp. 28–29; *Three Bear Witness*, p. 11. There can be no mistaking who is intended in this passage: 'The back door opened, to display a square, red-faced woman, the spit of Mrs. Williams but for a cast in her left eye and, when she spoke, a shrill Welsh voice. She had her box on her shoulder. "Why, Bessie," cried Jack. "Where are you going? What are you about?"' (*The Mauritius Command*, p.7). Again, a few pages later Jack's mother-in-law Mrs Williams exclaims: 'Can you imagine such wickedness, Dr Maturin? To finger toadstools and then to touch my grandchildren's food with her nasty hands! There's a Welshwoman for you!' (p.10).

[2] Curiously Richard appears to have accepted the truth of his father's claim as reported by Victor. A lengthy interview he gave to the press shortly after Patrick's death declares (implicitly on his authority): 'In 1936 at Chelsea Register Office, the 21-year-old . . . Patrick Russ, married Sarah Elizabeth Jones, 26. Five months later they had a son, Richard . . .' (*Mail on Sunday*, 16 January 2000).

true or hysterical. The lady may deceive herself; or she may deceive you. You would not be the first man to be cozened so.'

Joan told her daughter Gwen that Patrick once made a Welsh girl pregnant, whereupon their father arranged through his contacts in the medical world for her to undergo an abortion. Joan was emphatic on the point, expressing indignation not at Patrick's misconduct, but her father's abuse of his social and professional position to arrange an illegal abortion. A story emanating from so close and normally reliable a source cannot be summarily dismissed. However, although the 'Welsh girl' can hardly have been other than Elizabeth, it is all but inconceivable that Patrick was the father. That would require him to have made Elizabeth pregnant and arrange for their child to be aborted – only to marry her shortly afterwards and become the proud father of a second child a year later. While it is unlikely that the truth of a story of this nature can ever be known, an explanation consistent with the circumstances could be that another man was the father, who seduced and abandoned Elizabeth in circumstances which aroused Patrick's sympathy and support.

It is impossible to tell what if any weight may be placed upon the accusation of drunkenness Patrick consistently levelled at figures intended to represent Elizabeth in *Richard Temple*. In the course of a bitter legal battle over custody of Richard in 1949, Patrick sought to restrict the boy's access to his mother among other reasons on the grounds that 'she drinks heavily, is often seen drunk'. Elizabeth indignantly retorted: 'The suggestion that . . . that I drink heavily is totally false. I have never been intoxicated in my life and I have only once been affected by drink which was at the age of 24 when I was introduced to intoxicating liquor by the Respondent for the first time, and it had an effect upon me owing to my complete inexperience.'

Patrick's attempts at literary exculpation cannot be taken literally. None of his readers could be expected to recognise their relevance to his own life, and it can only have been to allay tortured feelings of guilt that he constantly reverted to the topic. Reality could never be entirely banished from his mind, and at times he could be starkly honest with himself. For example in *The Catalans* Xavier (Patrick) explains to his cousin Alain:

> If you had been here more you would have gathered that it [his own] was an unexceptionable marriage, reasonably happy in a quiet, uneventful way: and you would have thought that the sudden breaking of it in a few years would have been terribly painful for me . . . well, it was not. The only pain I experienced was at the absence of my pain . . . I also felt relieved, and it was not

> without a real pleasure that I looked forward . . . to my quiet, solitary evenings again, and my walks in the country; the one without the consciousness of someone sitting there being quiet, and the other without having to walk slowly or choose suitable, easy paths. I cannot tell you how it shocked me to find that these were my feelings. It was a horrible shock. It could be said, in mitigation, that the marriage had not been a romantic one in the first place, not on my side, that is . . . And it could be said that on the physical side the marriage was not successful. But with every conceivable allowance it remained a horrible shock to look into my mind and find that it was so callous; so hideously callous. After all, nothing could change the fact that we have lived in the closest intimacy for years, that she had been a true and loving wife to me as far as she could, and that she was Dédé's mother.[1]

Overall Patrick seems to have been dismayed by the sudden dissolution of feelings of affection for the woman he had once undoubtedly loved: 'I had turned from a normal affectionate child . . . into a man so abnormal that he had not the power to feel any sorrow for his wife's death.'[2]

In addition he recurrently voiced gloomy reflections on the institution of marriage, to which he implicitly sought to attach blame for the breakdown of his own. 'The worst of marriage is its length, its cost, its dulness. Its secrecy, lack of candour lack of evident privacy . . .' he jotted in one of his notebooks. He was much taken with the expression 'The Sorrow and Woe',[3] and used it for the title of a short story about the discomforts of marriage. In it a character quotes Chaucer's mockery of

> . . . thilke doted fool that eft had lever
> Y-cheyned be than out of prisonn crepe.

Men weakly allowed themselves to be trapped into a union for which they were constitutionally unsuited. 'The animal sort of thing that most men

[1] *The Catalans*, pp. 98–99

[2] *Ibid*, pp. 98–100, 102, 115–16. Pugh in *Three Bear Witness* confesses to having been 'rather cold, lifeless and indifferent before, not inclined to sentiment at all: indeed, I had sometimes reproached myself for my lack of affection for others. It is a repulsive trait, and it usually goes with deep selfishness; but my life had not accustomed me to affection – I had no near relations, and in the common round of my adult life I had rarely met anyone who raised in me a feeling higher than tepid esteem' (p. 67). Richard Temple felt 'an incongruous guilty delight at the loss of Doris', and Patrick himself suffered from a persistent fear that he might lack genuine emotional feelings. In 1970 he wrote in his diary: 'Qu. do I really have much affection?'

[3] Cf. *The Yellow Admiral*, p. 87. Stephen Maturin provides a cynical view of a certain condition of marriage in *The Nutmeg of Consolation*, pp. 121–22.

marry because there is so little choice and because ils aiment ça [the sexual act] – at least for the moment,' reads another of Patrick's notes. This reflection is revealing on two levels, and it is surely not excessive to detect a lingering memory of his first rapturous encounter with Elizabeth in the house they shared at Redcliffe Road on his arrival in London.

Probably Patrick himself would have been hard put to it to account for his turbulent emotional state at this time. All in all, however, it is hard to account for his determination to keep Elizabeth in the dark other than by underlying concern to preserve a line of retreat should my mother leave his life as dramatically as she had entered it. In short, it seems that he could not wholly discount the possibility of returning to Elizabeth and Richard. Many facets of life took on a surreal aspect in wartime London. The outcome of the conflict appeared as remote as ever, but were peace to return might not much that appeared permissible in the heady atmosphere of the ravaged city revert to pre-war normality?

ELEVEN

The Secret War

> It seemed such an extraordinary thing to have Dora always there. It was so unaccountable not to be obliged to have to go out to see her, not to have any occasion to be tormenting myself about her, not to have to write to her, not to be scheming and devising opportunities of being alone with her. Sometimes of an evening, when I looked up from my writing, and saw her seated opposite, I would lean back in my chair, and think how queer it was that there we were, alone as a matter of course – nobody's business any more – all the romance of our engagement put away upon a shelf, to rust – no one to please but one another – one another to please, for life.
>
> (Charles Dickens, *David Copperfield*)

In March 1942 PWE had moved its headquarters from Fitzmaurice Place to Bush House in the Strand, where Patrick now spent his working week. Considerable speculation has been indulged regarding the nature of his wartime activity, much of it fuelled by his extreme reluctance to expatiate on the subject. It is unfortunate that a highly speculative and melodramatic account has been placed on permanent record, which represents both Patrick and my mother as engaging in amazing feats of derring-do behind enemy lines.[1]

[1]Despite conceding that 'There is no evidence that Patrick left the country during the war', Dean King goes on to imply that he was involved in cloak-and-dagger activities alongside the French Resistance. By the end of the war 'he had grown somewhat sickened by the service he had had to perform during the war. The secret services at times were forced to act ruthlessly to achieve their aims.' Finally, we learn that one reason for his decision to move in 1949 to a town in France at the foot of the Pyrenees was his 'deep emotional attachments to these hills from his war service'. To these heavy hints of active service in Occupied Europe, King adds a startling but incredible account of my mother's alleged participation in a covert operation in Vichy France during the summer of 1942 (*Patrick O'Brian*, pp. 89–92, 100–4, 155).

In reality my mother was not even working for PWE at the time when she is supposed to have been operating as a glamorous spy in France. I am in any case confident that had either of them experienced active service in Occupied Europe they would have let me know.[1]

Patrick was almost certainly expressing his own sentiments when, in an early unpublished version of *Richard Temple* (then named 'William Temple'), he wrote of his secret service hero: 'during his long period of service in the London office of the organisation to which he belonged he had often said how very much he would like to be sent on a mission; he had often pictured to himself William Temple as one of that great secret army that was being built up in France; not, perhaps, as a leading figure (he was a modest, unassuming character), but at least as an extra on that noble scene.'

Working often in close collaboration with Resistance fighters, it would be surprising had his perennially boyish imagination not led him at times wistfully to picture himself as a daring secret agent. In the manuscript of 'William Temple' he describes his hero as 'a man of about thirty, the son of a French mother and an English father, bilingual from his earliest days; he looked neither English nor French – an *average* looking man, neither tall nor short, good-looking nor ugly. He was perfectly suited for the work he was to do . . .' Save for the French mother, the prototype is not hard to recognise! In addition this appears to represent the first embryo appearance of Dr Maturin.

While Patrick's ambition to engage in active service was undoubtedly genuine, sadly it was never fulfilled. While it is probably true that his reluctance to talk about his wartime activity arose in part from the fact that he was denied such opportunity, it is unjust to assert that 'Following the war, he *eventually* clamped down tightly on the information in his book-jacket biographies' (italics inserted).[2] So far as I am aware his first post-war autobiographical notice appeared on the dust-jacket of his novel *Three Bear Witness*, which correctly states no more than that 'he joined the Political Intelligence Department of the Foreign Office'. Even this sparse information was supplied with reluctance, and I cannot find that he elaborated on it subsequently.[3]

[1]Although undercover operations of this nature normally fell within the remit of SOE, PWE was at times involved in infiltrating agents into Occupied Europe. An interesting example is to be found in file FO.898/90 at the Public Record Office.

[2] King, *Patrick O'Brian*, p. 100.

[3] A biographical note attached to his short story 'Not Liking to Pass the Road Again', which was published in *Irish Writing* in the same year, makes the same assertion. However, the information was not provided by Patrick, but apparently copied from the dust-jacket of his novel. My mother recorded in her diary that she was 'very surprised to find biographical notes after I'd refused them because P. doesn't like it'.

In contrast to this consistent reticence, not long ago a journalist claimed that 'Patrick told me he worked for Special Operations Executive, the undercover guerrilla/terrorist organisation set up by the British to subvert Nazi rule in Europe. Certainly, the heads of M15, M16, and Royal Naval Intelligence were present at the banquet [held in his honour at Greenwich in 1996] . . . Were they there merely to honour the author of the greatest series of novels to adorn the literature of the English language in the 20th century? Did they pay honour to a former colleague of great distinction? Or both, maybe?'[1] In fact this was but one of a number of erroneous reports published after Patrick's death, and the suggestion that he worked for SOE most likely reflects nothing more than confusion between that glamorous and well-known organisation and her largely forgotten sister, PWE. I greatly doubt whether Patrick ever made such a claim. Melodramatic speculation may have been unconsciously spurred by the obvious identification of Patrick with his creation Stephen Maturin, a master intelligence agent who frequently operates behind enemy lines.

The reality of Patrick's wartime service was very different, as is evident from a brief memoir which he compiled in his second year of work at Bush House. The danger of arguing from the general to the particular is especially evident in Patrick's case. On 24 November 1942, the day he completed his little autobiographical essay, British and American troops were engaged in fierce fighting with the enemy in North Africa. Operation Torch involved landings by Allied forces along the French-occupied coast from Casablanca to Algiers. Kesselring poured in crack airborne troops from Sicily to counter the invasion, and at the time Patrick was writing the success of this critical campaign hung precariously in the balance. While the world awaited the outcome with bated breath, Patrick reflected on issues which concerned him more nearly. His reverie is so characteristic that I cannot resist quoting it in full. It is written in fluent French, with a few minor errors.

'When I remain here, bored almost to death, I write, sometimes ponderous and clumsy futile comments – even *fulgineuse*,[2] if the word exists. But always that which I want to write about is restricted by my very sparse vocabulary, and I have to say what I can say, or rather I am obliged to say what I can.

[1] Kevin Myers, *Irish Times*, 8 July 2000. Speculative fancies may have been unintentionally fuelled by the comment of a Conservative Minister, William Waldegrave, who queried: 'What if Sir Dick White [successively head of M15 and M16] or some other modern successor to O'Brian's brilliant creation, Sir Joseph Blaine, had kept him in the intelligence world after the War?' (Cunningham, ed., *Patrick O'Brian*, p.10).

[2] *Fuligineux*, 'murky'.

Accordingly, speaking about anything, I always make use of phrases which I know well to be good French, like *tout à fait* or *merde alors*. Another difficulty for me is pronouncing words with "*an*" or "*am*" in them – the sounds come out of my mouth like "*in*" or "*im*".

'A sparrow wants to land at my window to obtain the crumbs which I have put there. But he sees me and he seems to me to be embarrassed – between hunger and fear. It is twenty past four. Forty minutes to go, and I will go home, *à la chaumière*. From ten o'clock in the morning until now I have only worked for half an hour; that makes five hours at least given up to the devil. I was a little bored, but with the help of the Times and the crosswords, breakfast, lunch, and tea, I have managed to kill time without too much trouble. And, what for me is quite enough, I have earned a pound, more or less.

'But if there were some other way of living, how happy I should be. I believe that I have learned how to appreciate my leisure, I flatter myself that I know how to live: a little boat, some books, enough cigarettes, a good sporting gun, several good friends to play bridge, or suitable for dining with from time to time, and three to four hundred pounds a year, there is my ample paradise. It goes without saying that the paradise contains M, and that I alone provide the money. But what is the use of dreaming? I can only see a tedious life, stretching over decades, and at the end a squalid existence deprived of all happiness, when I shall have lost health and desire for life – a desire at present less lively than it used to be two years ago.

'Now another day has started. Ten o'clock in the morning, and I have nothing to do, other than my cuttings – which will only occupy an hour. If I could read, it wouldn't be too bad, but there is not enough peace – *les* [illegible] *et les secondes* pass back and forth every five minutes, and at any moment may enter and catch me being idle. As I've said, the good Qg has just paid me a call to borrow some sugar: I heard nothing, and she came in and found me not working – if it had been C, perhaps I should have felt very embarrassed. He said yesterday that he thought that I did not have enough to do to keep me occupied, and that he would find me something more: good, but I certainly do not want it to be something of little importance, work which could easily be done by a young girl or an office boy, and I don't picture much else. Because in truth there is no room here for me: I am a supernumerary, and I do not have what is called position, and it's not even war. But I must wait: something good will doubtless turn up.

'Now the day is almost finished; there are only forty minutes left. I have bought a shirt, I have given crumbs to the sparrows, who have become a little tamer. I hope the day will come when they eat out of my hand. The good

Colonel Hawker[1] said that one should never look directly at creatures which one hunts, and he is right I know well. Evidently the maxim applies when one has tamed them and made them friends as well. There is always some unease in being looked at directly by strangers – even more, I imagine, when they're not of the same species.

'In my pharynx I can feel the beginning of flu: a certain dryness, a lack of something indefinable, rather than actual pain. Also my cigarettes don't provide me any more with pleasure or consolation. My poor M has already had hers for three days. How unfortunate she is, with her *aménorrhagie*, her parents, and everything.

'It didn't go too badly yesterday: boredom was kept at bay – why I don't know, because I lacked any useful occupation during seven of the eight hours, as usual. My cigarette lighter gives me much pleasure and a pretence of busyness with its little modulations[2] and the precision of its component parts. Also I walk up and down, papers in hand, with an expression of extreme preoccupation. I piss very often, and several times a day I wash my hands. Well, if that's my life I must accept it without too much discontent. It's only an idiot who always wants to cry out against inanimate objects, or against circumstances which cannot be altered.

'After all that, it is once again twenty past four and my 413th day here is practically over – but I have to account for 58 Sundays, and my fourteen days' holiday, and to add some ten, here or there, absences on grounds of health: that makes 321, less 58 Saturdays – half days. Let's say 301 full days at eight hours each. 2,408 hours. The first year I earned five pounds per week and since first October, six pounds – £42.

'Almost exactly one pound for each full day – or a half crown per hour. That doesn't take into account my wages, or rather gratuities, as a firewatcher which come to roughly £30. Accordingly up to today I have received £332 from the *maison Molyneux*,[3] the price of at least two thousand hours of boredom.

'If I had a strong enough will I would have saved about fifty pounds. But I haven't saved a halfpenny, in spite of my internal resolutions.

'Next year I must definitely economise to the extent of a hundred pounds should it prove possible. I have never owned a hundred pounds through saving in my life, and I believe that the feeling would be as gratifying as it would be novel. Sometimes I've observed in myself a certain miser's pleasure

[1]Lt.-Col. P. Hawker, *Instructions to Young Sportsmen in all that Relates to Guns and Shooting* (London, 1838).

[2]The lighter has grooved panels on each side.

[3]Presumably Bush House, though I have been unable to discover the significance of this sobriquet. PWE also occupied the nearby Ingersoll House.

when I have managed to preserve a sum of five or ten pounds in hand. I must guard myself against the craven and revoltingly sordid vice of avarice.'

Patrick concluded with an assessment of Somerset Maugham's novel *Of Human Bondage*, which he had evidently succeeded in re-reading despite the danger of discovery. Possibly this served to confirm his conviction that a novel was required to be deadly serious. Had Patrick then and for many years to come not been firmly convinced of the necessity to make his adult fiction gloomy and tragic, he might have profited from his service with PWE by writing a successfully ironical work adopting Evelyn Waugh's irreverent approach to discipline and officialdom.

This little memoir is of considerable interest, not only for the vivid glimpse it provides of Patrick's wartime activity (or rather lack of it, at any rate up to this time),[1] but also for the light it throws on other aspects of his life. The implication is clear that at the time of writing my mother had yet to join him at Bush House. His acknowledgement of his discomfiture when feeling himself stared at is revealing, as is his ability to subject to candid contemplation character failings which he would have gone to any lengths to conceal from others.

One may see to what extent his adult persona had become irrevocably affected by the strange circumstances of his upbringing. For what was Bush House but another Albany Street, with its endless succession of days of enforced tedium, compounded by the need to protect his idleness from detection by the authorities? He acknowledged his ability to come to terms with protracted inertia, but recognised also the extent to which it imbued him with a sense of worthlessness. Lastly his reference to *la chaumière* alludes to a dramatic development in his relationship with my mother.

The *chaumière* in question was not an imagined idyllic cottage in the country, but a beautiful Queen Anne house in Chelsea off Upper Cheyne Row, known as The Cottage. Its previous tenants vacated it some time after the outbreak of war, since when it had remained empty. The occupants might well have been unnerved by the terrible night of 14 September 1940, when a stick of bombs was dropped over the immediate vicinity. The damage

[1] Were Patrick's reflections on life at Bush House at all typical, they would confirm the sardonic estimate of no less a functionary than the Permanent Under-Secretary at the Foreign Office, who noted on 12 May 1944: 'P.W.E. . . . is a *scandal*. 1250 people in London, and 500 at Woburn, none of whom know what they are *supposed* to do' (David Dilks, ed., *The Diaries of Sir Alexander Cadogan*, London, 1971, p. 628). However, Cadogan exaggerated the number of personnel serving with PWE in London, which in fact amounted to 764 (Garnett, *The Secret History of PWE*, p. 394).

included total destruction of two immediately adjacent houses in Upper Cheyne Row, some five or more of whose inhabitants were left dead beneath the ruins. Although one of the houses adjoined The Cottage, the latter miraculously escaped damage and was left with a blank wall on its north side after its neighbour's demolition.

For long afterwards, as my mother's friend Theodora FitzGibbon found, it proved impossible to learn who was the owner. However in 1942 it was bought together with other properties in the neighbourhood by the Church Commissioners.[1] It seems that my mother somehow discovered (perhaps through a well-placed contact) that the tenancy would shortly become available, and arranged to obtain it for herself. The rent was a mere £70 a year, and the prospect of living for the first time in such a delightful house with her beloved Patrick proved too strong to resist.

While they were living in Redesdale Street (if my interpretation of my mother's mention of that address be correct), she and Patrick would have had frequent opportunity to observe this nearby handsome house lying empty. Later, in October 1945 my mother renewed her lease on a three-year basis, which confirms other indications that they first moved into the house about October 1942. The timing of the availability of the house was fortunate, since my father's institution of divorce proceedings earlier that year had removed any further need for my mother to conceal from him her liaison with Patrick.

Everything about the building appealed to Patrick's love of history, and his particular interest in the eighteenth-century age of elegance. As a report by the Chelsea Society described it: 'The Cottage, a very early 18th century structure, is approached by a passage way and stands in a large open space surrounded by a fringe of lean-to studios. It was probably one of the first buildings erected by Francis Cook on six acres of glebe land east of the houses in Cheyne Row, some of which he built. These six acres came to be known as Cook's ground. Occupants of The Cottage appear in the rate books from 1715.'[2]

I lived in The Cottage with my grandparents after 1945, and remember it well. Beneath its mellowed brick exterior it possessed an arched cellar, which according to local tradition at one time comprised a section of tunnel running to the Thames. An artist living in the studio next door, whom we knew as 'the Gnome', produced a drawing of it which he sold as a postcard, whose caption remarked darkly that this and other nearby passages were used

[1] I am grateful to the Archivist of the Church of England Record Centre for this information. Despite an intensive search, I have been unable to discover who owned the house before the Church Commissioners.

[2] *The Chelsea Society: Annual Report 1954* (London, 1954), p. 17. The house is described and illustrated in Godfrey, *The Parish of Chelsea (Part II)*, pp. 69–70, plate 68.

'for many gruesome and illicit purposes'. On the ground floor was a comfortable kitchen and elegant dining room (some years earlier the room to the left of the front door had been cut off and joined to the adjacent studio). The first floor contained a range of three fine panelled rooms: that on the left was used by Patrick and my mother as their bedroom, in the middle was the drawing-room (where Patrick engraved their initials on a window pane with my mother's diamond ring), and the one beyond housed Patrick's growing library. Upstairs beneath the eaves were two further bedrooms, at one time presumably occupied by servants, and a small bathroom.

Not long before moving into The Cottage, Patrick began work as a firewatcher. Men aged between sixteen and sixty were obliged to register for part-time fire prevention duties, limited to forty-eight hours a month. It seems Patrick derived pleasure from an experience which most found tedious. In later life he devoted himself to regular study of the stars, and there are intimations in *Richard Temple* that he found the sensation of sitting silent and alone above the darkened city conducive to contented meditation.

This is indicated by an incongruity associated with the lodging occupied by Temple on the borders of Pimlico and Chelsea. Much is made of the fact of his ability to escape the sordid confinement of his upstairs room 'by climbing on to the parapet outside the window . . . from which one could reach a blackened plateau, a plot of zinc some fifteen feet by ten . . .' On the first occasion he describes this refuge, Temple provides this careful account of the view from his 'plateau': 'It was bounded on three sides by sheer blank walls of yellow brick soaring blindly up and on the north by a sea of air – an ocean whose bottom was the uneven ancient higgledy-piggledy crowd of roofs, never meant to be seen, any more than the back of the huge advertisement away to the left, peopled by a host of chimneys, huge and portentous and all different . . .'[1]

However some 150 pages later the same view is unaccountably converted into an unrestricted panorama across the Thames to the south:

> He sat there on his sack, leaning against the trunk: the sky was lit here and there by the effulgence of some marshalling-yard or night-working factories south of the river, and by the power-station. There was also a factory away to the right: one of its chimneys could be seen, with the underneath of its smoke just tinged with crimson; and far over towards Battersea Bridge another sent up a plume that was in itself faintly luminous.[2]

[1] *Richard Temple*, p. 142.
[2] *Richard Temple*, p. 205.

It can be seen that the perspective from the rooftop has shifted by 180 degrees. Furthermore the walls of the first description have vanished, and the drab view of a confined range of roofs of private houses to the north is replaced by an unrestricted panorama southwards over the Thames.

As so often in the novel, the most likely explanation is that Patrick was describing places he knew, and in utilising them for the novel overlooked the fact that he had conflated two distinct locations. The details of the first are so inconsequential yet carefully depicted as to suggest a real rooftop site with which he had become familiar, which there appears no means of identifying. In the case of the second, however, the observer's situation is indicated with a fair degree of clarity. The 'power-station' can only be Battersea Power Station, which would make the 'marshalling-yard or night-working factories south of the river' the Southern Railway marshalling yards (and perhaps the Gas Light and Coke Company installations) between the power station and Chelsea Bridge. Since Temple is implicitly looking more or less directly across at Battersea Power Station, with Battersea Bridge lying at a considerable distance to the right, his rooftop observation post must have been situated somewhere in Pimlico, south or south-west of Victoria station.

'It was a warm, still night with no moon, overcast and as black as a London night can ever be, with the reflection of street lights and railways from the sky': so the prospect appeared to the reflective Temple – but it is precisely as a consequence of street lights that nights in Central London are *not* black, and it is scarcely possible to be 'sunk into the darkness' above a busy street in Pimlico. Only during the wartime blackout would such a site have been submerged in virtually complete darkness, and it seems probable that Patrick's graphic description of his hero's all-night vigil reflects his experience as a firewatcher, the second vantage post he describes being on a roof in Pimlico, possibly at the southern end of Ebury Street. It is easy to envisage Patrick, the natural solitary, enjoying night after night his lofty perspective of the sleeping city. The situation of outside observer, gazing over an unknowing world like the peregrine falcon of his early story, strongly appealed to him.

Such was the dreamy extent of Patrick's war, at least until the summer of 1942. That autumn a welcome visitor unexpectedly arrived in London, who brought with him more than a whiff of the real conflict. Patrick's brother Michael, who had emigrated to Australia in 1926, now returned to England for the first time. Following an adventurous career living rough in the outback, he volunteered in1941 to join the Royal Australian Air Force. It has been mentioned that for some unexplained reason he assumed for a time the surname O'Brien, but on enlisting to fight for his homeland reverted to his true name. Thus it was as Flying Officer Michael Russ that on 18 October he arrived with his squadron, which was stationed initially at Bournemouth.

Over the winter he travelled about England meeting every member of his large family, save his younger brother Bun who was still in Canada. He paid nostalgic visits to Shebbear College and the Misses Hill at Clovelly, with whom the younger Russes had been sent to lodge during their school holidays. On 18 March 1943 he wrote to his sister Olive, who had married and was living at Ilminster in Dorset, reporting that 'I have now at last met all my brothers and sisters in England and am glad to have found the time and opportunity to do so. Though I have had to live on trains & buses to do it.'

His travels included a visit to Patrick's wife Elizabeth and to his young nephew Richard, who never forgot his uncle's genially masterful personality and impressive appearance in uniform. Around the corner in Upper Cheyne Row he called on Patrick, who had last seen him as a gawky teenager. Now he was a tall, handsome figure, whose image lingered in Patrick's memory long years afterwards. In 1981 he wrote to his sister Joan, recalling that 'I remember Mike telling me that he had to have a special astrodome in his [Lancaster] to give him room to stand up when he was fixing the course by the stars'. Again, a year before his death Patrick wrote to Olive's son John Cole to say that 'Mike was certainly the brother I loved best, and his loss grieved me extremely though we had but a short meeting during the war'.

Losses to bomber crews over Germany were appalling, but Mike accepted the danger philosophically. On 29 April he told Olive: 'We lost a lot of planes from this Squadron while I was away on my delightful holiday in the West Country, alas some of my best pals were among them. The entire Squadron of us are moving next week over to Binbrook in Lincolnshire'; 'P.S. Have just been "briefed" for a trip tonight so just got time to scrawl this & post the letter.'

Mike returned safely from that mission, but a week later his Lancaster was shot down and he was reported missing, presumed dead. The loss had a shattering effect on the Russ brothers and sisters. Mike had appeared suddenly among them as a dashing warrior from the other side of the world, only to be snatched away like so many other young men at the height of his youth and vigour. In an interview with BBC television in 1998, Patrick told the director that he had modelled Jack Aubrey in part on a brother who had been shot down over Germany during the war. Footage followed insinuating that in reality he never had such a brother: a crude misrepresentation which grieved Patrick greatly.

Two and a half years after the terrible news of Michael's death my mother noted 'Mikes birthday (30th)', indicating the strong impression he had made on them during his fleeting visit. Patrick deeply lamented the tragedy. His brother's heroic death in action must also have accentuated his lasting regret that he himself never served in the armed forces: a regret which he was eventually able to sublimate through his unparalleled evocations of the qualities of Britain's fighting men during an earlier heroic conflict.

The war was now being taken to the enemy, and although German raids on London continued (eight people were killed across the river in a raid on Battersea during the night of 20–21 November) Patrick and my mother had settled into a relatively peaceful routine.

In due course she joined him at Bush House. Quite likely Patrick recommended her to his superiors, her fluency in French and German making her well qualified for the post.[1] They served together in the French Section, which was headed by Dr Leslie Beck, a scholar of French literature. Patrick entertained high regard for Beck, with whom he and my mother remained in touch after the war. Through him they received glimpses of the higher reaches of the Allied leadership. Writing in the 1990s to Admiral Johnson of the US Navy, an admirer of his Aubrey–Maturin *oeuvre*, Patrick recalled that 'During the war I was engaged in a form of intelligence, and my chief used to act as interpreter between Churchill and General de Gaulle in their sometimes acrimonious all-night sessions; and although the chief in question was himself no chicken he would come into our quarters the next day pale, shattered and scarcely able to work.'

The indications are that Patrick worked principally in London, although he was on occasion posted to Woburn. Once when extolling the virtues of venison to Arthur Cunningham (editor of the tribute published by the British Library in 1994), he recalled shooting deer in the park. He went on to describe how the catering staff misguidedly boiled the meat, which in consequence proved unpalatable. He and his colleagues lived largely on rabbits, which provided excellent fare. He also remembered the bitter cold of the great house.

Patrick followed the progress of the war with interest. He was constantly aware of infighting, not only between the various French political movements in London and France, but also between rival British intelligence organisations. Patrick drew on profound personal experience when he described 'the English tradition of independent intelligence agencies with

[1] Unfortunately the records of PWE in the Public Record Office do not include lists of personnel. All that can be assumed with confidence is that my mother had not joined Patrick at Bush House when he wrote his reflections at the end of November 1942. Her copy of Wessely's *A New Pocket Dictionary of the English and German Languages* is inscribed 'M. TOLSTOY/FRENCH SECTION'.

little or no communication between them . . . few of them could speak the language, few knew much about the history of the nation, and none could evaluate the claims of the different bodies that put themselves forward as the true representatives of the country's resistance'.[1]

He and my mother became close friends with a leading activist of the Resistance movement, Armand Goëau-Brissonnière, who was known by the sobriquet 'Renelière'.

Patrick obtained particular pleasure from the quirky and eccentric aspects of 'black' propaganda, which on numerous occasions he put to amusing as well as instructive use in his fiction. The hero of *Richard Temple*, reflecting on his wartime service in London, singles out 'The sleepy Levantine, who was supposed to drop pamphlets over North Africa, in the languages spoken there, and who was found to have dropped nothing but advertisements for his own green tea, and little samples of it'. After the war my mother gave her brother 'a block of French war time stamps which she said were printed in the U.K. and dished out in France to annoy the enemy', which he added to the family stamp collection. As a souvenir of her service my mother retained a leaflet which had doubtless been smuggled out of France by a member of the Resistance. Issued in Paris on 22 September 1941 by General von Stüpnagel, military commander of France, it provided a grim reminder that the war was not being fought for any light-hearted purpose: 'Any male person who helps, directly or indirectly enemy aeroplane crews who have come down by parachute, or who have made a forced landing, assists their flight, hides them or lends them assistance in any way, will be shot on the spot. Women who make themselves guilty of the same crime will be sent to concentration camps in Germany.'

On warm days Patrick and my mother took their lunch to eat on a bench in the garden of the Temple, whose splendid building had been destroyed in the Blitz. There they were less concerned to watch the silvery flights of Lancasters and Wellingtons crawling across the sky towards the Channel, than to observe 'the pair of black redstarts in the ruins of the Temple'.

There is no means of assessing how far Patrick's work altered as the war dragged remorselessly on. In the first half of 1944 the tasks assigned PWE intensified as Allied forces in Britain prepared for the gigantic gamble of D-Day. 130 million leaflets produced by the organisation were dropped on France in March alone, followed thereafter by an estimated 114 million every month. Plans were made for dropping some 2.75 million leaflets distributed by special bombs on D-Day itself. Apart from this the need to gather accurate

[1] *Post Captain*, p. 52.

intelligence became a matter of extreme urgency, as did timely triggering of Resistance activities in the enemy's rear in order to ensure that they assisted the Allied advance with maximum effectiveness.

One of Patrick's principal duties was compilation of detailed intelligence reports on conditions in France. They include typescript surveys of 'The Eastern Mediterranean Coast', a succession of reports of French regions compiled between September 1943 and May 1944, intelligence notes on French newspapers, and a report entitled '*REGIONAL CHARACTERISTICS OF FRANCE*. By Dr. Ross. 28th March, 1944'. Dr Beck evidently had a high regard for Patrick's talents and endorsed his report on 'Mediterranean France' with a covering note: 'To: Major Gerrard Here is an annexe on the Mediterranean coast of France, which I think contains a good deal of material in as short a form as possible. Dr. L.J. Beck A.D. (F) 15th May, 1944'. It is also likely that Patrick played a part in compiling some of the detailed zone handbooks on French cities and regions circulated by PWE, of which he retained a copy describing the city of Lyons.

One of his papers, entitled '*AGRICULTURE AND THE FRENCH PEASANT. Draft Notes Lecture by Dr. Ross on 24:3:44.*', was presumably among lectures delivered at the PWE training school at Brondesbury in north London.[1] Courses were conducted for the purpose of training recently joined members of PWE, as well as officers of the American Office of Strategic Services (OSS). Among the latter was an historian called Jack Christopher, with whom he became friends. Christopher was an amiable man, who accepted with equanimity a preliminary ordeal at the acerbic Patrick's hands. At least, I suspect he was the American who made the gaffe recalled by Walter Greenway: 'I remember particularly Pat's fury at being told by an American who worked in the same office that he (Pat) was wrong about some detail of Shakespeare. He told me that the man had said "You're WRONG".' Despite this normally unforgivable solecism they remained friends, and I met him when he was staying with Patrick and my mother some years later. By then he had learned not to contradict.

Patrick assumed the style and title of 'Dr Ross' at PWE. I imagine his doctorate was ascribed to the University of Padua (a claim he was to assert subsequently), which in wartime conditions would have the advantage of being difficult to check. 'Ross', a Caledonian version of 'Russ', recalls the character in his 'Sullivan and Ross' adventure stories.

Now that my mother was working beside him at Bush House, Patrick's circumstances were transformed. He revelled in her companionship for twenty-four hours a day as they travelled together on the underground from

[1] For the training school at Brondesbury cf. Garnett, *The Secret History of PWE*, pp. 397–403.

Sloane Square to the Temple and back, and shared work and office friends and politics. Their principal pleasure derived from the time they spent at The Cottage where a great attraction for Patrick was the garden. Throughout his adult life he derived intense pleasure from cultivating his own patch, and in the spring of 1943 he worked vigorously preparing soil and sowing vegetables. He was not the only one who enjoyed digging, as is indicated by a pleasing sketch he drew at the time showing the back of Miss Potts sticking out of a deep hole in the centre bed, from which she is frantically scrabbling out earth. The energetic dachshund is also portrayed engaged in various other activities, knocking at the front door, and running up a flag on a pole in the garden emblazoned 'WELCOME TO POTTO GRANGE'.[1]

After gallantly performing her duty to her country throughout the Blitz, Miss Potts sadly did not live to see the day of victory. Her place though not her memory was taken by an attractive guinea pig, who was accorded the original name of 'Miss Guinea'.

Much of my mother's best furniture remained safely stored at her parents' home but Patrick and she assembled sufficiently elegant fittings to set off the handsome interior of their Queen Anne residence. His fine collection of leather-bound books had now found an appropriate home. They included such precious rarities as the twenty-three volumes of abbé Prevost's *Histoire Generale des Voyages* (1746), Churchill's *Collection of Voyages and Travels* (1732), Anson's chaplain's account of the Admiral's historic voyage around the world (1762), and hefty folio editions such as Sir Richard Baker's *Chronicle of the Kings of England* (1696) and the delightfully entitled *The Famovs and Memorable Workes of Iosephus, A Man of Mvch Honovr and Learning among The Ievves. Faithfully translated out of the Latin, and French, by Tho. Lodge, Doctor in Physicke* (London, 1632). In addition Patrick was able to display his collection of samurai swords for the first time since buying them during his Oriental phase at Albany Street.

Shortly after Patrick and my mother moved into The Cottage her old friend Walter Greenway reappeared in her life. Now Major Greenway of the Anti-Aircraft Artillery, he was working for the Ministry of Supply at its headquarters in the Adelphi. In the late spring of 1943 he moved with his pregnant wife Susan into a house in Markham Square. It was not long before he discovered that my mother was living a few hundred yards down the King's Road, and their friendship was resumed. Walter and Patrick swiftly found they shared many interests, and the two couples spent contented

[1] The potto is a type of lemur. In view of her denunciation as a mongoose, Patrick's nickname for Miss Potts does not appear overly offensive. He later resuscitated my mother's beloved dachshund as the potto befriended by Stephen Maturin in *The Commodore* (pp. 235, 238, 239–41; cf. *Blue at the Mizzen*, pp. 62–63).

evenings and weekends together. When the Greenways' daughter Claire was born in July, my mother became her godmother.

Walter, who had gained a First in mathematics at Cambridge, shared Patrick's enthusiasm for all matters technical. Patrick had developed a fascination with old clocks, of which he had managed to obtain some fine specimens. Most were broken or deficient, but he derived great pleasure from attempting to repair them. What he lacked in training was amply compensated by persistence and patience, to which Walter now added his professional expertise. They spent long hours together, taking the clocks to pieces, constructing weights for their pulleys, and altogether having a fine time with their toys.

The two men also shared deep interest in naval history. Before the war Patrick had bought the six volumes of Robert Beatson's *Naval and Military Memoirs of Great Britain from 1727 to 1783* (1803), to which he added after the outbreak William James's *The Naval History of Great Britain, from the Declaration of War by France in 1793, to the Accession of George IV* (1837). This last work was to prove a treasure hoard from which he would continue drawing endless riches until the end of the century, long before which time the spines became so worn that he was obliged to replace them with canvas backings. James's skilfully executed plans of naval actions were now brought to life by the two amateur admirals. As Walter recollects, 'we had this wonderful battle: we fought the Battle of 1st of June [1794] in The Cottage in front of the fire, with matchsticks'. This took place in the drawing-room on the first floor. Such engagements frequently continued for days, and required much detailed discussion of tactics and seamanship.

Together they made expeditions to the second-hand bookshops of Charing Cross Road and Cecil Court, where they bought old books on naval history and other aspects of the eighteenth and early nineteenth centuries. Fine works bound in half or full calf could be bought for a shilling or so, and a set of half a dozen for a pound. However, as Walter reminds me, 'we didn't have that sort of money to throw around'.

Like almost everyone who came to know him, Walter found that Patrick could be difficult at times. He would pronounce an authoritative rebuke when he considered Walter wrong on some topic, and displayed resentment were it suggested that he might be in error. Walter's self-confidence enabled him to override such minor differences, and he was happy to be cast in the role of philistine. 'He was disappointed that I wasn't interested in abstract art,' he recalled. 'I was looked upon as being a failed intellectual! I managed to do this in a number of things, because, having done fairly well as a mathematician, I could be looked on as being intellectual enough to be a mathematician – but not in the real proper classics of English: Shakespeare and all that. So that I was looked on as the practical man . . . I did the mathematical part of building clocks, and that sort of thing!'

To do Patrick justice, I think he was generally aware when a companion consented to play the buffoon, and was humorously content to accept a charade which enabled him to avoid risk of serious confrontation. Although Walter was posted to Italy just before D-Day and afterwards to Egypt, they remained in touch and their friendship was renewed on his return to England in the autumn of 1945.

About the time Walter and Susan settled into Markham Square in the late spring of 1943, Patrick's wife Elizabeth and son Richard had returned to London from Norfolk and moved into a flat in King's Road. However elaborate the precautions Patrick adopted to conceal himself, Elizabeth's failure to discover his whereabouts over so lengthy a period appears astonishing. Wartime Chelsea bore no resemblance to its crowded and disorderly appearance today. For a decade or so after the war it retained much of its 'village' atmosphere, where most people were intimately acquainted with their neighbours, frequented the same grocery, newsagent, and other shops, and regularly encountered friends and acquaintances in the streets. During the war the population had become much reduced after many of its inhabitants abandoned their homes, and almost every street contained rubble-strewn spaces where houses had been destroyed by bombing. Today The Cottage lies snugly out of sight behind Upper Cheyne Row, but where the intervening houses now stand was at that time an empty bomb site, making the house and garden readily visible to any passer-by.

A likely explanation of this otherwise remarkable anomaly is that Elizabeth entertained no more pressing concern to renew contact with her errant husband than he with her. It was not until the autumn of 1943, well over a year after her return to Chelsea, that she discovered his address and that he was living with my mother. A Mrs Atterbury informed her that since 7 September she had observed someone answering to her husband's description 'living with the Countess Tolstoy at The Cottage, No. 1 Upper Cheyne Row, Chelsea'. Elizabeth showed the woman a copy of a photograph of Patrick taken during his stay in Italy in 1937, whom she identified as the man in question. Since Mrs Atterbury had no knowledge of Patrick's appearance before being shown his photograph, Elizabeth must already have been aware that her husband was living with my mother at The Cottage.

On 20 March 1944 she submitted a petition for the dissolution of her marriage. It was not contested by Patrick, and in due course a decree nisi was issued by the High Court on 18 December. Nothing suggests that the divorce was accompanied by hostile feelings on either side, and for more than a year and a half after Elizabeth began proceedings she and Patrick maintained harmonious if distant relations. She appears to have been as concerned as he that their marriage should be dissolved, and it seems that she wished to be free to remarry.

In the following summer Patrick noted in an affidavit that 'I was formerly under the belief that the Petitioner was going to re-marry after the making of the decree absolute, but I have recently been informed by her and believe that the man whom she was first proposing to marry has been killed, and that the man with whom she is now living in adultery cannot obtain a divorce.'

Much depends on how long she had known the first of these lovers. In her affidavit issued in response Elizabeth had no reason to mention him, but so far as the second man was concerned she acknowledged: 'I admit I am living with a man whom I cannot marry as he is not yet divorced. In previous holidays I have always been able to take the boy [Richard] away and not bring him into contact with this man . . .' Evidently the relationship was of fairly long standing, since the plural 'holidays' implies that it began at latest before December 1944.

That the attachment between Elizabeth and the first of her two lovers was strong and of some standing is suggested by the fact that they were awaiting the finalisation of her divorce in order to marry. On the charitable assumption that she did not take up living with another man for some time after her first lover's death, it seems reasonable to conclude that the earlier relationship began some considerable time before the end of 1944. More than this is impossible to say, but it does appear a distinct possibility that Elizabeth's belated petition for divorce from Patrick arose from her desire to remarry.

The fluctuating state of relations between Patrick and Elizabeth following his departure from Gadds Cottage in 1940 has been profoundly misunderstood and misinterpreted. This is understandable in view of the restricted range of evidence previously available, coupled with the fact that perception of the events became grossly distorted by the bitter ill-feeling which arose between the parties five years after their original separation.

The incriminatory evidence consists only of assertions made on oath by Elizabeth from June 1945, and virulent complaints she levelled against Patrick to her son Richard over the years to come. Dean King, who relied exclusively for his description on information supplied by Richard in interviews, explained that 'though she reviled Patrick in front of their son, she did not seek money because she knew he had little to spare but also, she told Richard, "for the sake of his art". But Patrick was certainly better off living with Mary than he had been, and this Richard could see if not fully understand.'[1] The

[1] King, *Patrick O'Brian*, pp. 97–8.

first claim was, as Elizabeth well knew, completely untrue. She repeatedly made vigorous attempts to extract funds from Patrick, who had already supported her for years on a weekly basis, paid for Richard's schooling, and thereafter continued sending her erratic payments until increasing penury finally prevented his continuing. By then she had remarried. Moreover Patrick was not, as implied, 'better off living with Mary than he had been' because of her money, but principally on account of his salary from the Foreign Office.

Characteristically, Patrick retreated into his shell. He does not appear ever to have criticised Elizabeth before Richard, and was scrupulous (if not always tactful) in insisting that he write to her regularly and assist her in other ways. Despite the mutual bitterness which ensued after July 1945, charges he raised against her in legal exchanges bore no concern with their past life, but related exclusively to current allegations of illiteracy, vulgarity, and drunkenness.

It must be emphasised that none of this should be interpreted as criticism of Richard, who plainly recounted as truthfully as he could what he remembered from the distant days of his early childhood.

Unless evidence can be produced to the contrary, it appears that Patrick and Elizabeth remained on harmonious speaking terms from the end of 1943 until the early summer of 1945. Her sole grounds for divorce was his proven adultery, and the judgment appears to have been obtained by mutual consent. She provided no obstacle to Patrick's regularly seeing his son, nor even to his receiving him in the house where he lived with my mother as his mistress. That autumn they arrived at an amicable agreement that he should cease paying her maintenance, and instead devote his resources to paying Richard's fees at boarding-school.

Now that matters were out in the open, throughout the coming year Patrick happily resumed contact with his son, whom he had last known as a three-year-old toddler at Gadds Cottage. Richard was now a sturdy boy of seven, who could barely remember his father. They had however remained in contact by correspondence, and despite Richard's subsequent acerbic comment about the ill-judged birthday present Patrick had considerable talent for writing sensibly and amusingly to children. Like most children the boy tended to accept without questioning whatever grown-ups chose to do in their remote and largely incomprehensible world. Long accustomed to his father's absence from home, it did not appear especially strange to find him now living in a separate house with another woman. London in wartime was not the most orderly of places in which to live.

He swiftly became very attached to my mother, who was equally devoted to him. He was not much younger than me, and her frustrated maternal affections at once found a focus in the likeable little boy. Unfortunately, as seen earlier, Patrick's attitude towards children was strangely contorted. He entertained a strong sense of duty – a little too strong, perhaps, since it frequently made his actions however generous appear to reflect obligation rather than affection. Richard remembered of that time:

> My father began to take me out occasionally on Saturdays . . . He made me a toy out of a wooden cotton reel and string . . . But he was always distant and uninterested. It was difficult to love my father – he was too cold and authoritarian a figure . . . I grew to love Mary more than my father. She was warm, friendly and nice to me. I rowed them both across the Round Pond.
>
> I have occasional memories of him taking me to Kensington Gardens around this time, and that is about it really. My relationship with him was cautious on my part. He was a bit of a stranger and I wasn't accustomed to him. I don't think he was accustomed to being with children either.[1]

Shortly after the astonishing news of the success of the D-Day landings, Patrick learned of a dramatic development in his own family. When he moved to London in 1935, he had left his sister Joan living with their parents at Crowborough. Following his departure she led a wretched existence, yet managed to achieve the necessary scholastic qualifications to obtain employment. After leaving school in 1936 she worked for three or four years as a student teacher, then in an insurance office in Tunbridge Wells, to which she bicycled daily on the handsome Sunbeam bicycle given her on her twenty-first birthday by Victor and Bun.

In 1942 Joan managed to escape from her stifling little cage when she joined the Women's Auxiliary Air Force, and was posted to Birmingham. She never forgot leaving home, when her father and stepmother declined even to come downstairs to say goodbye. Fortunately, not long after her arrival in Birmingham she became friends with a young man named Harold Russell, a precision engineer working in British Aerospace on the Rolls-Royce RB211 engine. A quiet, gentle man, his kindness and responsibility were greatly attractive to Joan after the loneliness of her previous life. In due course they were married on 17 June 1944. Harold Russell was a devout Roman Catholic, and before their marriage Joan converted to his faith. As her daughter Gwen told me: 'I think her taking up of Catholicism was a silent protest against her father in part, altho' it was a practicality she needed to go through in order to marry my dad who was a devout Catholic.' The marriage

[1] *Mail on Sunday*, 16 January 2000.

proved a lasting success, and Harold provided Joan with the calm and security she had always craved. Wartime conditions meant however that their wedding was a very low-key affair.

Charles and Zoe Russ declined to attend, having told Joan at the time of her engagement: 'if you want to marry that Birmingham man, you can do so without us'. Her father also raised objection to Harold's Roman Catholicism. While this possibly contributed to his refusal to have anything to do with his newly married daughter, it seems likely that his prime motives were snobbish consideration of class, to which he was throughout his life inordinately attached, and his tight-fisted dislike of spending money on anything not directly beneficial to himself. Understandably, Joan's children retain varying degrees of resentment towards a grandfather who excluded their mother and them from his life.

Joan's son Harry does not mince his words. As he wrote to me:

> I personally will not forgive the disgraceful rudeness, motivated by snobbery and religious bigotry, of the Russ family towards my father. He never did any of them any harm. He bore himself with a quiet dignity in the face of this appalling behaviour. He volunteered to join the RAF and on at least two occasions was severely burnt by incendiary bombs. He joined in 1938. It was typical of him that he did not bother to pick up his medals. He did a stint in South Africa. As a LAC servicing Lancasters and Spitfires amongst others he experienced a lot of bombing, airfields being prime targets. He was a devout Catholic all his life. He was a very unusual working class man in that he studied the faith not only the doctrines but the history as well. He did not just take it as read.

While Charles and Zoe cavalierly dismissed Joan from their lives, the absence of the rest of the family from the wedding was almost certainly due to the war. Joan maintained contacts with her brothers and sisters throughout their lives, and it is hard for example to envisage Nora entertaining objection to the match, given that she had herself flouted her father's wishes to become a Roman Catholic nun. What Joan had probably forgotten when she came to talk about the matter with her children was the fact that the weekend of her wedding was in Britain one of the most dangerous of the entire conflict.

Within days of the landing in Normandy, when Allied forces were desperately seeking to break out of their bridgehead, Hitler succeeded in striking back at Britain with monstrous weapons of long-range destruction. On the night before Joan's wedding 120 V1 pilotless aeroplanes (soon to be known as 'doodlebugs') descended unexpectedly on south-east England, mainly in the London area. During the first week of the onslaught civilian casualties totalled 756 deaths and 2,697 seriously injured, while extensive damage was inflicted on buildings ranging from docks to factories, hospitals, schools, and churches – to say nothing of private houses. On 18 June, Waterloo Day, a V1 scored a direct hit on the Guards chapel at Wellington Barracks during a parade service, killing 121 soldiers and civilians. The country prepared itself for a terrifying new form of attack.

Patrick and my mother regularly descended nightly to the cellar of The Cottage, where they had installed a steel shelter in which they could feel reasonably safe from anything save a direct or close hit, such as that which had destroyed the houses next door some years earlier. However, the danger continued, and the capital was shaken day and night by explosions. Once again Chelsea found itself in the firing line. On the flyleaf of my mother's Harrap's French Dictionary she wrote: 'This dictionary was blown across the room by a V1 during the 1939 war.'

In the second week of August the Germans began deploying the far more powerful and deadly V2 missile. This was a true rocket carrying a ton of high explosive, which ascended to an altitude of 50 or 60 miles at a speed of up to 3,600 m.p.h. and then dropped virtually without warning out of the sky, making any form of defence effectively impossible. Altogether the Germans successfully launched 1,115 V2s, of which about half landed on Greater London, killing a total of 2,642 people. On 3 January Chelsea was shaken again by a gigantic explosion which destroyed the east wing of the Royal Hospital, one of Sir Christopher Wren's masterpieces.

Alarming though the explosions in Chelsea must have been to Patrick and my mother, their most terrifying experience occurred at work on 30 June 1944. A cluster of flying bombs landed close to Bush House, one of which exploded immediately outside, causing extensive damage to the building and killing everyone in the nearby Aldwych post office, as well as the passengers of two buses which were reduced to charred and twisted frames. The tragedy occurred during the lunch hour, so no casualties were inflicted on personnel working for PWE and the BBC in Bush House.

If Londoners had not become altogether inured to danger, they were nevertheless accustomed to pursuing their daily round with relative calm. Theodora FitzGibbon provides this intriguing glimpse of life at The Cottage, which conveys the impression of having peacefully withdrawn from wartime chaos.

'House-hunting is always a depressing occupation, and in wartime London it was even worse, many of the "desirable residences" still being thick with the dust of bomb-blast. Then I remembered a pretty studio house, set back in a small cul-de-sac of Upper Cheyne Row, from the days of house-hunting with Peter after leaving Oakley Street. It was indeed desirable, but we could never find either who owned it or the agent. I went to see if it still existed. While strolling around the front garden the door opened and out came a friend, Mary Tolstoi, who was married to a grandson of the writer.[1]

'"How nice to see you," she said. "Have you come to call? I do hope so." I didn't like to give my actual purpose, but followed her in. It was a late autumn afternoon and the glowing fire was burning in the comfortable sitting-room.

'"Let's have some tea and make toast over the fire."

'A delightful idea, and during the course of that I told her how I had found the house empty a few years ago, but could never find its owners. I was so completely at home there, I felt it really should have been mine. But I didn't say so. Anyway it would probably have been far too expensive for us then, and this I did say.

'"Oh no, it's only £50 a year," she replied. "I got it from the agents at Harrods."

'That was the last place I would have gone to look for a house or flat, which made it seem more elusive and less "mine".

'"But why so cheap? It's quite large and so very liveable-in."

'"Quite simple," Mary answered. "It's haunted, you see. But they are enchanting ghosts, so friendly and happy. Maybe if we're lucky they might be here today: a little later is their usual time. But it doesn't happen every day."

'Well used to Celtic tales, I didn't for one moment doubt what she was saying and more or less dismissed it from my mind. We went on talking until darkness fell, which was fairly early at this time of year. A very delicate chiming clock sounded, which reminded me I should be going. I looked up to the mantelshelf but there was no clock there and I looked round the room.

'"Sh-sh," she whispered, "they will come any moment now. That's not my clock, for mine doesn't chime."

'I sat staring at the clockless shelf above the fire; then there was the sound of people chatting and skirts rustling. Once a small dog gave a yapping bark. The noise got louder as though a small party of people were going upstairs in the next room. There was light laughter and the happy buzz of conversation. They were obviously looking forward to a pleasant evening. Gradually it faded away as they reached wherever they were going. The whole thing took only a few minutes but seemed an age.

'"Mary, it's extraordinary, but what's the other side of this wall?"

[1]My father was in fact heir to the senior line of the Tolstoy family, and consequently a distant cousin of the famous writer.

'We went out and I saw there was nothing, just a small path to the back of the house. It was a charming experience. Mary had been right: they were delightful and happy and induced that feeling in their listeners.'[1]

Another visitor who retains vivid memories of The Cottage is my Uncle Ivan, who had stayed with my mother and father at their house in Kent when I was born, and afterwards at Staddon, my grandparents' home in North Devon. He and his elder brother Paul were trapped in France during the Occupation and only able to escape to England after the Allied invasion in 1944.

'I must have been eighteen when I first met Patrick O'Brian, in Mary's old house in Chelsea, probably in 1944 or early 45. It was winter all right. The house was chilly and his and Mary's last words to me every morning before leaving for the Ministry were always the same: "Be sure the fire doesn't go out in the sitting-room."

'I had the run of the house. A wide staircase led up to spacious bedrooms with high ceilings. The windows were dimmed by overgrown branches. Silence and stillness reigned in and out of doors but on windy, draughty days, things knocked and bumped, loose fittings rattled and doors creaked.

'Below there was the sitting-room and beside it the library which had a wide, wall-to-wall bookcase up to the ceiling. I would choose a number of books and return to my corner by the fireside.

'Mary, my sister-in-law, had been married to my half-brother.[2] I knew her from before the marriage when, long ago as a boy, I lived with her and her parents in their home in North Devon. But in those Chelsea days, Patrick, as far as I was concerned, was a newcomer in my life, and I in his. His name was Patrick Russ. He changed it later to O'Brian. Since there was common consent between them to live under the same roof, I did not venture any queries. To me he seemed a self-absorbed man, aloof and entrenched in a keep of his own, – not the warmly outgoing partner I would have expected for her. He wore tweeds, comfortable, informal dress, yet always my vision of him was in a lab-coat, actively analysing something or other. Should I

[1] FitzGibbon, *With Love*, pp. 152–53. Mrs FitzGibbon was not the only person to encounter The Cottage ghosts, of which I often heard my mother and Patrick speak. In 1957 Patrick's son Richard wrote to him: 'Once, several years back, you and Mary told me a great deal about the ghosts at The Cottage. Recently I was talking to someone who moved out because of the uncomfortable atmosphere she felt at The Cottage in particular you talked about the ghost of a dog, which sounds extraordinary. Can you remember much about it?' The unidentified woman must have lived at The Cottage before Patrick and my mother, as my grandparents were still living there in 1957. Neither they nor I encountered the ghostly presence.

[2] Ivan was born in 1926, and was consequently a child at the time of my parents' wedding. He kindly provided me with this account shortly after Patrick's death.

venture a remark that stirred his interest, he would train his eyes on me with a cool, global stare that made me feel he was eyeing me in a test-tube, a notion that made me extra reticent and inarticulate.

'Patrick had no reason to relish my presence in the house, especially when I had not announced any fixed dates or duration. Besides, my ties with Mary were a living reminder of a once happy existence with another man and the two children she bore him, a past in which he had no rôle. Despite these tacit strains on our rapport, I was nevertheless always impatient to see them both return from work.

'They were days without TVs and computers. The fireside hearth was the natural family focus for talk and relaxation. Apart from run-of-the-mill household matters, there were always the news. Wireless broadcasts invariably had an urgency about them. We were still at war.

'I never knew if Patrick's tales [i.e. the 'ghosts'] about the house were true. He might have been mounting a façade to speed my departure but that Mary, in whom I had complete faith, should concur with his words, I found bewildering to say the least. In short what he told me was this:

'The unexplained upstairs and downstairs noises I had alluded to and queried, were of no significance. They were the doings of the other occupants. Small stones not big enough to crack window panes were of no consequence. Bumps or thuds might be due to tension or strain in the woodwork. True, the tramp of many footsteps up and down the stairway could be unsettling but only if loud and persistent. Anyway, whoever they were, they were friends not foes. Firm action was rarely called for. The time they flung the bookcase full length down on the floor scattering the contents in all directions, was exceptional. A vicious reprimand at the top of his voice had effectively reduced them to respectful silence and inertia for a good two months. He said he and Mary had begun to feel remorse and to miss their company. The house had been on the market several times but word had got around and the price was adjusted downwards. The last clients were two RAF servicemen who loaned the house a short time but pulled out of the deal.

'After all these casual revelations, the moment for parting in the morning with: "Bye-bye, keep the fire in" was no longer the cheerful affair it had been before. The old house became heavy and its stillness oppressively audible. I do not remember which caused me most concern, the cellar or the bedroom.

'If I cared little for the cellar before, I cared still less for it now. The descent down the wooden steps with coal scuttle in one hand and torch in the other was perilous, visibility near nil, and the periphery of the area void of contours. I knew the old house was credited with an escape tunnel leading to the Embankment. If there was a bricked-up doorway I could see no signs of it. Once the scuttle filled, I had only one desire – to return to the upper regions as quickly as possible.

'The antiquated hinges, latch and handle on my bedroom door disconcerted me. There were no lock and key and the only way to keep the door firmly shut at night was to improvise a paper wedge. Should it become dislodged during the night, draught or no draught, the door was sure to sway open very slowly by itself, making a creaking noise as it went.

'I suffered several more nights under the protection of my flimsy sheets and eventually bid a genuinely rueful goodbye to my kind hosts, aware of some ill-defined premonition that it would be years, perhaps decades, before our paths would cross again. My suitcase with its heavy expandable metal clasps was a gift from my sister-in-law. It had M T-M [Mary Tolstoy-Miloslavsky] inscribed on it, her initials as they were before she married Patrick. For years it served to remind me of those quiet enigmatic days and nights I spent in their old home in Chelsea.'

The dramatic and dangerous year of 1944 closed with Patrick's formal severance from an aspect of his past he had long been anxious to place permanently behind him, but which at the same time presented him with new and vexatious problems. On 18 December a decree nisi was granted to Elizabeth Russ. The judge awarded her custody of Richard, allowing Patrick drastically restricted access to his son: 'Three to four days during the Christmas holidays, Two days during the Easter holidays, and One day at school during each school term all such access to be during the daytime only.' These draconian conditions not only reflected the fact that Patrick was living with a woman who was not his wife, but the fact that my mother had been denied access to her own children was taken as evidence that she was an unfit person to have care of a child. The terms appear the more harsh, since up to that time Patrick and my mother appear to have seen Richard relatively frequently.[1]

Despite the fact that he would now barely see his son from one year's end to another, Patrick's concern for Richard's education led him to commit himself to the financial sacrifice of sending him to boarding preparatory school. Seven was generally the age when boys were sent away to school, and Richard would be eight in February. Southey Hall was situated in the countryside near Exeter. The fees amounted to 45 guineas a term, with additional expenses required for travel, clothing, equipment, and pocket

[1]I am greatly indebted to Mr Ben Fenton for directing me to the important documentation relating to Patrick's divorce and custody proceedings, by what appears to be fortunate chance preserved in file J77/3990 in the Public Record Office. He discovered and first drew attention to their existence in an article published in the *Daily Telegraph* on 26 November 2003.

money. The Michaelmas term of 1944 was the last that Richard spent at the Servite School, and on 16 January 1945 he set off from Waterloo station with his new companions to begin a fresh life at Southey Hall.

Patrick's introverted character may not have made him a very congenial father, but he was a very concerned one. Not only was he determined to put his son through preparatory school for the next five years, but following that he intended to send him to public school. In 1945 he entered Richard for Wellington College, with a view to his eventually pursuing a career in the Army should he prove so inclined. The college was founded in 1854 as a memorial to the great Duke, and preparation of boys for military service represented one of its primary functions.

Since Wellington was the school attended by my father, where I was also to go in my turn, Patrick's choice may appear curious. My father later told me that my mother hoped by this means to gain opportunity of resuming contact with me. Although it was not certain in 1945 that I would go to Wellington, it is likely that my father put my name down at birth for his old school, and my mother could have been aware of this. On the other hand Patrick's choice could have been influenced by the fact that their friend Walter Greenway was an Old Wellingtonian and serving army officer. Walter became fond of Richard on meeting him after his return to England in the autumn of 1945, and Richard came to know him as 'Uncle Walter'. It was natural for Patrick to wish his son to adopt a military career, as a respectable profession which unlike most others did not require financial assistance he would be unlikely to be able to afford. Possibly he also unconsciously viewed it as vicarious compensation for his own abortive attempt to become an RAF officer.

CHAPTER TWELVE

Trouble and Strife

> But of all others, there are none perhaps, who are more obliged to the imagination for their ideal happiness, than the fraternity of which I am an unworthy member. There is no set of people, who are more ambitious to appear grand in the world, and yet have less means, than those gentlemen whom the world has stiled Authors. Wit and pride as often go hand in hand together, as wit and poverty: but though the generality of writers are by the frowns of fortune debarred from possessing a profuse share of the good things of this world, they are abundantly recompensed by enjoying them in speculation. They indulge in golden dreams, at the time that they have not sixpence in their pockets . . .
>
> (Bonnell Thornton and George Colman, *The Connoisseur. By Mr. Town, Critic and Censor-General* (1761))

By the beginning of February 1945 the Allied armies stood poised on the Rhine in the West and the Oder in the East for the final inexorable advance which would leave the Third Reich in smoking ruins. Although France and Belgium were now liberated, the French Section of the Political Warfare Executive continued regular broadcasting. But with the enemy's days numbered, it was clear that it could not be long before the organisation had served its purpose. Patrick's work became increasingly leisurely, and he appears to have found little difficulty in taking days off, enabling him to devote contented hours to literature. Little specific is known of what he read before 1945, but fortunately that January he began keeping a record.

Over the New Year he read Jane Austen's letters for the first time, with great attention, and then turned to Henry James. He found *What Maisie Knew* 'a very odd mixture of ½^{d} novelette, insane intensity and very able writing. Can't make anything of the latter part of his "The Cage" at all, but "The Pupil" went down very well indeed.' Returning to his favourite eighteenth century, he read Fanny Burney's *Evelina* with mixed feelings:

'Began Miss Burney's Evelina. It does not promise . . . Madly unreal Joseph, clumsy construction, total lack of humour, much wallowing in forced sentimentality. I would not have stopped before the end for anything, nevertheless.'

Patrick's childhood enthusiasm for exotic travel tales had not diminished, and a few days later he bought an Everyman edition of the medieval voyages of Sir John Mandeville, whose work constitutes a marvellously imaginative compendium of weird and wonderful beasts and kingdoms. Patrick was greatly pleased with Mandeville, noting that 'Sir J. is fine, very, but his editor is a castrated ape.' Despite Patrick's extensive knowledge of medieval bestiaries, nothing in John Ashton's preface appears to justify so extreme an excoriation. Probably it reflects no more than Patrick's general dislike of exegesis, arising from an aversion to anything which appeared to come between the original text and its reader. Then again, there was his underlying apprehension that his amateur approach to learning was deficient in comparison to that of professional scholars. This failing was occasioned less by jealousy, than from inherent conviction that academic learning represented a mystery to which he was denied access by an invisible barrier.[1]

Patrick turned from Mandeville's extravagances to the very different world of Anthony Trollope, which he found less satisfying. 'I wish he had kept the level down a bit. Lords, dukes and such are all very well in their way, no doubt, but they are difficult to bring to life in a novel, and a surfeit of them does give a novelettish air to the whole thing, which takes away from one's enjoyment.' However, Patrick conceded, 'There's some pure Dickens in A.T.'

His reading was eclectic, and by the end of the month he was alternating Anstey's *Vice Versa* ('very funny indeed') with Bagehot's study of the British constitution. His reflections on the latter confirm the impression that his political views, never particularly strong, were *au fond* moderately conservative:

> He is unfair on kings, I think. George III was too close to him. Kings are, after all, carefully bred, and they spring from men who won their crowns by ability. But then my bowels are Tory, if my head is Whig. Bagehot had no bowels.

He jotted down Clemenceau's sardonic aphorism: 'La démocratie? Savez vous ce que c'est? Le pouvoir pour les poux de manger les lions' ('Democracy? Do you know what it is? Power for fleas to eat lions').

[1] The protagonist of Patrick's novel *Three Bear Witness* engages in an argument with the local schoolmaster, in which 'I was able to knock his degree of Bachelor of Divinity on the head with my doctorates . . . He was eternally jealous of my different education and standing' (p.144).

The second-hand bookshops of Charing Cross Road and Cecil Court continued to act as an irresistible magnet. On St Valentine's Day 'I fell from my high economic resolutions, and bought the Tatler 4 vols 12mo. 1737 (McLeish is re-labelling them) for 12/6. calf for M[ary].[1] The Trial of James Stewart (the basis of RLS's Kidnapped, 8vo calf. 1753)'. He further purchased for 7s.6d. a curious little eighteenth-century novel, 'Pompey the Little',[2] which he presented to my mother as a Valentine's Day present, 'while M. very civilly gave me the Gentleman's Magazine 1743–4–5'. (The last volume contains an inscription in my mother's handwriting: 'A Valentine for P. Esteem the Giver'.) These volumes, which include accounts of Anson's voyage around the world which he was later to put to good use in his fiction, materially added both to Patrick's accruing interest in the eighteenth century, and to his understanding of the extent to which the immediacy of the past could be recovered by immersion in primary sources. 'Masses of information,' he noted: 'both solid and (what is more in some ways) ephemeral.'

In the volume for 1744 he followed the scandalous career of James Annesley: 'Wicked uncle, kidnapped heir, bastards, sudden death. Very gratifying: it makes the eighteenth century novel seemed far less tawdry & unreal.' He found the forgotten details and backstairs aspects of history especially fascinating. In *Pompey*, for example, he recorded the adjuration 'You are bloody complaisant, Sir', and observed that 'there is "tester" for bed, which I thought went out with the Tudors'. On 10 August he bought for half a crown a five-volume set of Henry Brooke's novel *The Fool of Quality* (1767), on which he commented:

> Extraordinary cross of housemaid & man of letters. Servant predominating. This brings what I have always considered mid-Victorianism to about 1750. When I read Richardson I shall probably find it is earlier still. The stock idea of the 18th C. as reasonable and unenthusiastic is only very partially true. When did the flow of soul start? Allied to pastorals?[3]

Patrick was unconsciously ploughing furrows whose harvest would take years to come to fruition. His extensive familiarity with authors of earlier centuries led him to an understanding of the radical distinction between past and

[1] [Sir Richard Steele (ed.)], [*The Tatler*] *The Lucubrations of Isaac Bickerstaff, Esq;* (London, 1737).

[2] *The History of Pompey the Little. Or, The Life and Adventures of a Lap-dog* (London, 1761).

[3] Pastoral romances and plays, with an idealised bucolic setting graced by articulate ladies and gentlemen, which flowered in the sixteenth and seventeenth centuries. Among the most prominent were Sidney's *Arcadia*, Shakespeare's *As You Like It*, and Milton's *Comus*.

present and to awareness of the absolute necessity of envisaging men and women within the context of their own era. Goldsmith's *History of Rome*[1] irritated him for its naïve failure to address itself to this fundamental task. 'One gets the impression that the Romans were an appallingly bloody-minded lot – true maybe – but what is far worse and quite false, is the impression that they were modern men (insofar as they were men, and not names) acting in an incomprehensible way in a vacuum. It is not history – hardly even chronicle.' Empathy and vivid sense of period were everything, and after finishing *The Trial of James Stewart*[2] he observed admiringly: 'It is impossible to see it objectively, having read Kidnapped but I am sure I could never have made such a tale of it.'

Despite his increasing fascination with the eighteenth century, several years were to pass before it dawned on Patrick that he might make use of his carefully garnered hoard of knowledge to write an historical novel of his own. The long years spent exploring the eighteenth century for private pleasure enabled him when the time came to write his historical novels with an effortless flow of instinctive realism.

It appears to have been during the war years that Patrick developed his interest in real history. The short stories he wrote and planned over the winter of 1939 to 1940 during his exile in Norfolk display a naïve view of the past, owing more to the popular historical novels which he had enjoyed as a boy than the real thing.

Absorption in the history and literature of the 'long' eighteenth century extending from Queen Anne's reign to the Regency provided him with an alternative course to those adopted by many young men disenchanted with their situation in life and society. The solitude of his childhood had accustomed to him to internalise his emotions, seeking escape from unbearable reality through exercise of an exceptionally developed imagination. As he savoured the delights of history, he was exhilarated to discover a richer, and in many ways more real, world into which he might withdraw at will. There he could commune with Johnson, Sterne, Swift, and Congreve, enjoying an equality with the most gifted men of the age. Wherever possible he preferred to read their works in contemporary editions, whose evocative appearance and smell contributed greatly to his feeling of direct participation in past eras.

This was the happy land into which he escaped. No momentary or

[1] *Dr Goldsmith's Roman History: Abridged by himself for the Use of Schools* (London, 1782).

[2] *The Trial of James Stewart in Aucharn in Duror of Appin, for the Murder of Colin Campbell, Esq* (Edinburgh, 1753). Knowing of my infatuation with the history of the Scottish Highlands, Patrick generously gave me the book ten years later.

frivolous form of escapism could have satisfied him: it was the *real* eighteenth century to which he withdrew, in all its rococo reality, material and spiritual. Like his great predecessors Walter Scott and Robert Louis Stevenson, he found forgotten humdrum details and unanticipated oddities more intriguing than the deeds of great men and the fate of nations. His great gift as an historical novelist, simple enough in concept but rarely effected in practice, was the ability to adopt a stance set firmly in the past. Furthermore, that past could be subtly adapted to provide him with a more comfortable world. Jack Aubrey is no grandson of a furrier, but the son of a general of old county stock, while Stephen Maturin although romantically illegitimate is 'a man of high breeding', acquainted with many grand people.

Patrick enjoyed the sequel to *Kidnapped* ('Catriona is quite good fun'), noting in particular that 'R.L.S. was very fond of the revolting father idea'. Had he read the same author's *Weir of Hermiston* (which, so far as I know, he never did), he would have found a theme close to his sensitivities yet more perceptively portrayed. Of Stevenson's other works he found 'Jekyll & Hyde improves on acquaintance – far far better than the broadcast – an excellent *hidden* horror. The Bodysnatchers seemed to me just vulgar, kitchen horror. For the real shiver there must be something (preferably hairy) round the corner. Dr James,[1] for example.' In due course Patrick himself was to make effective use of this technique in such stories as 'The Drawing of the Curranwood Badgers' and 'The Happy Despatch'.

Among the few twentieth-century works he read was one which did not impress him greatly.

> Forester's The Commodore is, I think, the first new novel I have ever bought. It seems much more extravagant than paying a guinea for, say, the learned job. It's a good tale, but not as satisfying as the other Hornblower stories. Smacks a little of formula and wants design. Also, it has not a great deal of meat, or if it has, a greater length is required to give it body.

Moving from Forester to Conrad, while admiring *Youth* and *Heart of Darkness* he complained: 'I like him very well when he is content to tell a story, but when he and his people are crammed with extraordinary feelings – very highly wrought – which I don't share (and don't believe in really) I get rather tired.'

Patrick was impressed by Professor Brogan's *American Problem*, which he confessed 'explains some American characteristics that I had previously attributed to innate vulgarity'. Throughout his life Patrick was given to occasional humorous disparagement of American arts and manners, but this

[1]M.R. James, *Ghost Stories of an Antiquary*.

largely reflected his adoption of the attitude of a late eighteenth-century Tory. In serious mood he would express high admiration for American writers and critics whose works he approved. I remember how eagerly when living in France he would await arrival of the *New Yorker*, which he pronounced the best journal of its kind, far superior to anything comparable published in Britain.

As the Allied armies delivered their final crushing blows to what remained of Hitler's vaunted Thousand Year Reich, Patrick and my mother enjoyed a relaxed and sociable time. On 12 January they took Richard to the pantomime. Afterwards they attended a party given by a friend, where my mother was intrigued by the Turkish naval attaché, Captain Ulusan. On Shrove Tuesday she provided Patrick with a supper of 'Admirable pancakes'. There were regular dinners and bridge parties with friends ('Dinner & bridge with Beryl. Very pleasant. We lost a shilling a piece, but made a small slam'), and a visit to the theatre as an occasional treat: 'Love in Idleness at the Lyric. A trifling comedy – good 1st act, degenerating into rather poor farce. The whole more than redeemed, however, by the extraordinary ability of the Lunts.'[1] With the coming of spring there was much to be done outside at The Cottage, and on 3 March Patrick declared triumphantly: 'I have been furiously active on the garden this last fortnight. The almond is out.'

Save for the rigorous restrictions which permitted him minimal opportunity to see his son, life generally appeared exceedingly pleasant. Patrick lived with his beautiful aristocratic mistress in a graceful Queen Anne town house, surrounded by well-appointed furniture, and boasting a fine library of rare old books. He appears to have been more than content with his lot, and only sporadically toyed with the idea of resuming creative writing. Reading *Emma* at the beginning of the year in his armchair beside the drawing-room fire, he conceived the notion of converting the novel into a detective story, to be entitled 'The Event of the 26th ult.'. The complex plot revolved around young Churchill's poisoning of his unpleasant aunt, in order to inherit the fortune he required to marry Jane Fairfax.

This however never extended beyond a bare outline, and he appears at this time to have been so little concerned to apply himself to the labour of writing a novel of his own that the next scheme he contemplated was that of compiling a volume of trivia, which would include a collection of suggested plots. Only one of these was completed. This was an outline of a gloriously melodramatic tale set in the reign of Edward III, concerning the pursuit of an alchemist named Thomas Cary by a sinister secret international organisation.

[1]A well-known married actor and actress, much loved and admired in their day.

'If I were to do it, I should plump for the Hanseatic League as the international villains; they were foreign – Ach! Himmel! So! – rich, monopolistic, an anonymous trust, combine or cartel of powerful and unscrupulous foreigners.'

Yet again it is intriguing to note the extent to which Patrick's approach to historical fiction remained embedded in the stage where he had left off in 1939–40, when he wrote 'No Pirates Nowadays' and his unpublished account of the exploits of a crusading knight. Indeed, his imagination appears to have reverted to the world of *Boy's Own* adventures which had afforded him such pleasure in boyhood and brought him precocious success in pre-war days. In the projected Thomas Cary story, he noted, 'Dumb Chinaman and express trains would have to be sacrificed to period . . .' A comic Chinaman features in 'No Pirates Nowadays'.

Either the notion simply did not occur to him, or if it did he lacked confidence to pursue it, but the idea of making literary use of the profound knowledge he was acquiring of eighteenth-century history and literature does not seem to have entered his head. In that field he could envisage no more imaginative project than compiling anthologies of amusing and out-of-the-way items encountered during his armchair explorations. His happy existence at The Cottage with my mother, combined with their daytime employment at Bush House, appears to have removed the spur to his ambition to become a creative writer.

The only cloud on this otherwise sunny scene was caused by a bout of ill health. In February Patrick paid repeated visits to Dr Hancock of 47 Queen Anne Street, who prescribed 'Aquamarine' and other remedies.[1] On the 10th Patrick recorded: 'Anointed last night and this morning: one pill & a draught at breakfast. A perceptible, but hardly significant, improvement.' Two days later there was some little further improvement: 'The applications, inward and outward, diminish sweating by about 20% I suppose – though it is hard to guage [*sic*]. It is not good enough, anyhow.' No visits are recorded for March, but by April Patrick again required medical attention, this time from a Dr Smithers. It might appear that he was dissatisfied with the limited success of Dr Hancock's treatment, but we find Smithers likewise prescribing Aquamarine. Though it is hard to be certain from these cryptic allusions, it

[1]Dr Philip Rizzo, a distinguished specialist in the field, kindly advises me: 'It may be that Aquamarine referred to a seawater-based solution useful to respiratory ailments, either as a spray or in some other form. If a pill, it could mean either what is being suggested, or – as you mention – the color of the pill.' He further observed: 'There is – it turns out – a good reason for P. O'B's twice underlining aquamarine. It probably is a product prepared out of beryllium.'

seems likely that Patrick was suffering from a recurrence of the bronchial ailment from which he had periodically suffered as a child.

Earlier, on 2 February (his son Richard's eighth birthday), Patrick had been sufficiently alarmed to arrange for a blood test and attend a cancer hospital to be X-rayed. This must have proved a false alarm since nothing more is heard of it, but may indicate that whatever ailed him was persistent or unpleasant. On the other hand there is nothing to suggest why Patrick should have felt he had reason to fear cancer, and his visit to the hospital may have been provoked primarily by the hypochondria to which he was occasionally subject. However this may be, from 18 May he ceased seeking medical assistance, from which one can only presume that his health (or outlook) took a sudden turn for the better.

It may tentatively be conjectured that Patrick's asthmatic attacks were caused in part at least by psychosomatic factors.[1] Whilst his allusions to pleasant spells of reading and visits to friends suggest a life of unalloyed contentment, developments had arisen which caused him anxiety. In the spring of 1945 it was impossible to avoid increasing concern with the fact that the Political Warfare Executive would before very long have served its purpose, the inevitable consequence being that Patrick and my mother would be abruptly deprived of their principal source of income.

Equally, it is of interest that it was precisely on 18 May, the last occasion in 1945 of Patrick's visit to a doctor, that he and my mother settled upon a project which kept them fully occupied until the autumn, after which their lives were to take another, more absorbing turn. Having spent the first months of the year reading solely for pleasure, Patrick's consciousness of the looming financial crisis is indicated by the fact that ten days after VE Day he suddenly decided to write a book. On the following Friday he paid a nostalgic visit to a place of which he retained happy childhood memories. 'In the Lewes train I read Congreve's Old Bachelor amusing farce, but what an incredibly savage, inhuman set of lechers.'[1] On his return he noted further in his pocket diary: 'I am starting to select stuff for a book of voyages – am a little vague about its eventual form.'

This was a topic in which Patrick was already well versed, and he had built up a small but select collection of rare early editions of books by travellers.

[1] Dr Rizzo confirms that 'asthma can be aided and abetted in its damaging effects by the emotions as well as pathogens, allergens, and other -gens, including a distressing sense of what you call vulnerability. It made him react defensively against real and imagined hostile forces, from boyhood on.' Dr Rizzo was one of a number of specialists in respiratory illnesses who addressed a seminar on Patrick's health arranged at the Smithsonian Institute by Patrick's friend Ken Ringle on 24 November 2000.

[2] *The Dramatic Works of William Congreve, Esq.* (Glasgow, 1761), i, pp. 17–96.

When as a boy he sought release from his solitary existence by roaming in his imagination to remote regions of the earth, he developed a gift for identifying passages remarkable for their colour, excitement, or humour. Earlier in the year he had noted down a number of 'Good things in Harris, vol. I': an allusion to his handsome six-volume folio edition of John Harris (ed.), *Navigantium atque Itinerantium Bibliotheca: or, a Compleat Collection of Voyages and Travels* (London, 1704). The context suggests that at that time he merely copied the extracts from private interest.

The time was inexorably approaching when he must end his indulgence in armchair dreaming, and apply himself once more to earning money by his pen. He and my mother set to work on their compilation, to which Patrick assigned the provisional title 'Other Men's Voyages'.[1] However there was no prospect of its providing an immediate solution to their impending financial crisis, nor could they realistically expect this or any comparable project to provide an income nearly commensurate with their needs once their employment ceased. Finally, the impression is conveyed that Patrick had become too long accustomed to leisurely reading to focus single-mindedly on writing and completing a book as swiftly as possible. Earlier in the year he had contemplated and dropped a succession of fanciful projects, and that he eventually fastened on an anthology rather than a creative work of his own does not suggest that his muse was functioning at full stretch.

His dreamy outlook is illustrated by the fact that while he shared the nationwide jubilation which greeted the Allied victory on 8 May, he was preoccupied with the downfall of a greater and more distant Empire. As the Third Reich eked out its final shameful days, he immersed himself in Gibbon's *Decline and Fall of the Roman Empire*: 'A very great man. Has he not set about clearing his mind of cant with too great a zeal? I am reading him slowly, with an atlas, dictionary & quantities of reflection & back-reference.' His sole recorded reference to the end of the war is an amused note of a report in the French newspaper *L'Aurore* three days before: 'London lives in feverish anticipation of the day following victory, *le Victory Day, le V.D. comme on dit là-bas.*'

However much Patrick was able to distance himself from harsh reality, my mother at least possessed a markedly realistic attitude towards their finances. The couple faced the prospect of becoming entirely dependent on her private income, which with tax rebate would barely cover the rent, rates, and running

[1] He toyed with further choices: 'I had thought of whimsy alliterative, or derivative titles, like "Painful Peregrinations" or "A Cento of Journeys" or "Vicarious Venture".'

costs of The Cottage. Their continued residence there and financial survival could be achieved only by one of two stark alternatives. Either Patrick must find fresh employment or there would be no alternative to effecting some radical alteration in their circumstances.

In 1993 Patrick told the American journalist Mark Horowitz that about this time 'I rejected the suggestion of becoming third secretary in the Paris embassy and determined to go back to writing.' Dean King expatiates on this:

> The Foreign Office, desperately short of staff, needed qualified personnel to fill embassy positions in liberated nations. It turned to the PWE, an organisation that would be phased out, for candidates. Patrick was offered the post of a third secretary in the Paris Embassy, an indication of the high regard in which he was held as a section leader in the PWE and the strong relationships he and Mary had forged with the likes of Goëau-Brissonnière. He turned down the post, probably owing to a combination of factors: to take such a position required personal wealth; self-sufficiency was a requisite. Even with Mary's help, Patrick O'Brian did not have the money. Though it needed a bit of resuscitation, Patrick still possessed a passion for writing. And lastly, no matter how essential the cause, he had grown somewhat sickened by the service he had had to perform during the war. The section services at times were forced to act ruthlessly to achieve their aims.[1]

On the whole I am disinclined to believe in the reality of this 'offer'.[2] Not only would such a position enable him to maintain his income at something approaching its current level, but it was not unlikely that my mother with her fluent French would find means of earning additional money. Nor can it be doubted that Patrick would have relished the prestige attached to work in the diplomatic service.

I suspect a more likely explanation is that he applied for the post but failed to obtain it. That December he noted: 'It was amusing to see in yesterday's Times an advertisement for a man to be director of FORD [Foreign Office

[1] *New York Times Magazine* (16 May 1993); King, *Patrick O'Brian*, pp. 103–04.

[2] So far from the Foreign Office's being 'desperately short of staff', it was in a position to take its pick from personnel hitherto seconded to other wartime duties. A third secretaryship was far from providing the lofty status which King suggests, and would in normal circumstances be awarded to a junior official rising within the service. Financial 'self-sufficiency' was not a requisite for the post. A third secretary at a British embassy began with an income of £300. Though this represented half the salary Patrick received at PWE, there was an additional Representation Allowance ranging from £150 to £650, and a House Rent Allowance of between £150 and £262, variations depending upon the requirements of the post.

Records Department]. They are combining the post of FO librarian with it. I wish it may not be gammon [humbug].' Not too much may be read into this, but the concluding sentence, together with the fact that Patrick was evidently given to studying the appointments column of the newspaper, suggests that he would have been glad of securing such a post.

The financial predicament he and my mother faced after the termination of their employment at PWE was catastrophic. Their income would be reduced to a sixth of its present amount. At the same time, with thousands of other well-qualified people similarly compelled to seek fresh careers, the chance of finding available employment was decidedly inauspicious.

Patrick himself possessed no alternative source of funding. No prospect of employment presented itself, nor could he expect any assistance from his family. His father and stepmother were now by no means well off, and besides notoriously close with their money. My mother's position appeared considerably more promising. Her father was a relatively wealthy man, and she was one of two children.

Faced by the impossibility of their being able to continue living at The Cottage, the young couple turned their thoughts to the enticing prospect of a refuge in the countryside, where they could grow their own vegetables and fruit and live as much as possible off the land. My mother obtained particulars of a cottage with an orchard near Ilfracombe, close to her parents' home in North Devon, and of a house and smallholding in the Wye Valley. Unfortunately the freehold price of the first was £550, and the second £1,595. Since their disposable financial assets at the time amounted to the unimpressive total of £15/4/4d the only possibility of purchasing a property lay in my mother's gaining access to the capital invested in the trust settled on her by her father.

She had little doubt of her ability to persuade him to agree to this. Regarding the house near Ilfracombe, she noted 'Mama should ask Braddick' – probably a local estate agent. Nevertheless, with so much hanging on the decision, she appreciated that it was essential to leave nothing to chance. Conscious of her parents' disapproval of her liaison with Patrick, she decided that the surest method would be to approach them in person. The three days from 4 to 6 June 1945 are marked in Patrick's pocket diary 'Go away', which I believe must refer to the journey he and my mother made to her parents' home in North Devon.

My grandmother described to me how my mother arrived at Appledore on the pillion of Patrick's motorcycle. She and my grandfather were scandalised. Everyone in the little village knew and respected our family, and for Mary Wicksteed to arrive flaunting her illicit relationship in this blatant manner must have appeared gratuitous rubbing of salt into the wound. My grandfather had been distressed beyond measure by his daughter's misconduct. Her living openly with a married man for five years was shameful enough.[1] Far worse in his eyes (he was no prude) was what he considered her heartless abandonment of my sister and me, to whom he and our grandmother were devoted. As if all this was not enough, he regarded Patrick as a seedy and unprincipled wastrel with an unsavoury past and no settled future.

It is clear that Patrick's arrival was unexpected. My grandfather flatly refused to allow him into the house. He was obliged to descend to the village, where he lingered on the cobbled quay in a state of embarrassment beside his motorcycle. For once he was probably right in imagining himself the cynosure of every coldly curious eye, while my mother remained closeted with her agitated parents in the big house on the hill above, employing every wile at her disposal to persuade them to agree to her request. Given Patrick's inordinate sense of social inadequacy, his summary exclusion must have appeared a humiliating realisation of his deepest fears.

He nurtured no levelling desire to drag down the class which the Wicksteeds personified. Their very invulnerability to material considerations represented its most enticing quality. Let a gentleman lose all his money: he retained his ancestry, arms, education, and ineffable sense of *savoir-faire*. An impoverished gentleman remained a gentleman, whatever his worldly condition. Patrick was consumed by romantic longing to belong to the ranks of this seemingly impregnable order. Had his father been born a gentleman, his professional and financial failures would have brought distress upon his family, but there would not have been the same shame attached to their reduced circumstances. At least, so it appeared to the anguished outsider.

What could have induced my mother to adopt this rash and thoughtless approach to her parents? She must have been confident of inducing my grandfather to release the capital from her trust. Long the apple of her parents' eye, and infatuated as she was with her lover, she had doubtless persuaded herself that his shining talents and unassuming charm would win over her parents. A marked factor in my mother's character was an inability to perceive matters from any viewpoint but her own.

[1]Richard Russ, interviewed by Dean King (*Patrick O'Brian*, p. 98), claimed to recall meeting my mother's parents at The Cottage in Chelsea during the war. I find it all but incredible that they stayed there while Patrick and my mother remained an unmarried couple. However, in view of the numerous chronological errors in Richard's recollection of isolated events from his childhood it seems almost certain that his recollection related to one of numerous occasions when he visited The Cottage after my grandparents went to live there at the end of 1945. A likely occasion was in the middle of January 1946, when he stayed there with his father and my mother before going to school in Devonshire.

Her proposal was doomed from the outset. Having experienced the devastating effects of the slump of 1929 and its aftermath, my grandfather was governed by an overriding fear that unfettered capital was almost certain to be swiftly dissipated. As her brother informed me: 'He doubted my Sister's care of capital and so only gave her the interest for life. That infuriated her.'[1] Though I am sure her father would have explained the reasons for his decision as kindly as possible, the expedition could not have been more misconceived, and succeeded only in antagonising her parents yet more strongly against Patrick. Eventually my mother re-emerged from her home, and descended the hill to bring him the crushing news. The errant couple disconsolately mounted his faithful motorcycle 'Panther', and set off dispiritedly on the long and dreary journey back to London.

While I doubt whether any circumstances would have induced my grandfather to comply with my mother's request, the chance of his assenting was assuredly not improved by her misguided decision to bring Patrick with her: above all, while they remained as yet unmarried. It seems surprising that she did not wait until their relationship had been properly formalised (which it would be, within a month).

This condign public humiliation may have had a long-term traumatic effect upon Patrick, and further explain factors peculiar to his character and writing. Of course the rejection could not have had lasting effect unless he were predisposed to suffer it, but it must have appeared a horrifying actualisation of his deepest fears. In early adolescence he had developed an irrational conviction that the Russ family generally, and his father in particular, were 'not quite respectable'. This can only have been exacerbated by his father's continuing descent in the financial scale, and corresponding inability to provide him with an adequate education.

After his marriage to my mother, her parents saw him quite frequently, when they did their best to conceal their continuing disapproval of their undesirable new son-in-law. Regrettably my grandfather possessed too forthright a character to be adept at disguising his feelings, of which my

[1]An embittered passage of Patrick's autobiographical novel *Richard Temple* (p.48) is unmistakably intended to connect my mother's subsequent poverty-stricken exile in North Wales with her father's refusal 'to let her touch the capital of her little trust-fund'. Some years later, speaking of my grandparents' class, he remarked that they 'worshipped capital'. At the time I had no idea to what he was referring, since I had never heard them speak about such matters. Another consideration which undoubtedly affected my grandfather's decision was the fact that he had tied my mother's trust through to her children. Elsewhere in *Richard Temple* (p. 173) a character 'would . . . have had a great deal of available money if he had not locked it all up in a trust fund for his wife and children (his father-in-law's prophetic soul)'.

mother and Patrick were all too aware. In his presence Patrick invariably conducted himself with unwonted awe and trepidation, and appears to have regarded him as an embodiment of the finest element of the English upper class (which indeed I would say he was). When he alluded to the Wicksteed family, it was always in terms of profound respect, as though they occupied a unique niche among the gentry. Sadly, my grandfather could not get over the anguish inflicted by his beloved daughter's misbehaviour. Conceivably relations might have improved as years passed by, but Patrick's awkwardly deferential manner in his presence served only to embarrass and irritate my grandfather, whose robust nature could not have differed more greatly from Patrick's.

This uncomfortable relationship is reflected in *Richard Temple*. Richard's failure to gain a diploma at an art college and inability to find a job at a time when millions of men were unemployed and seeking work, 'made the earth shift and creep beneath him'. On learning of his failure, his uncle, Canon Harler declares bluntly at their meeting that '*Richard would not get a brass farthing out of him*'. However, he concludes by relenting somewhat, indicating that if things were ever to become very bad, he need not wholly despair of assistance.[1] This is much how my grandfather might be expected to have reacted to any suggestion of breaking into capital. Although not prepared to accept dissipation of the modest nest-egg he had settled upon my mother, he was to prove consistently generous to the couple in years to come.

It was I believe his acute distress over his daughter's association with Patrick, above all their proposal to settle in the neighbourhood, which led her father to put his beloved Staddon up for sale in the late summer of 1945. This impetuous decision led to the beautiful house at Appledore, together with its surrounding glorious forty-four acres, being sold for a derisory £10,000. Many valuable and cherished articles in the house were sold at the same time. All this greatly upset my uncle, who had returned to work for the cotton industry in the Sudan. Like the rest of the family, he loved the house, and had assumed that on his eventual return it would provide a home for him and his family.

This precipitate action was characteristic of my grandfather, whose strong personality concealed a deeply emotional strain. The extent of his distress seems to have prevented his acting with proper consideration of the circumstances. Although he never discussed the matter, it is not hard to guess his reaction. He and my grandmother had provided a wonderful home

[1] *Richard Temple*, pp. 88–89. In general Canon Harler represents Patrick's father, but the promise of assistance in emergency is more applicable to my grandfather.

for us at Staddon. At the end of 1942 my father arranged for my sister and me to be sent to boarding-school, and after his remarriage in the following year we spent the greater part of our school holidays with him and our stepmother. For a short time our home was a flat in Queen's Gate, London, and thereafter a house by the Thames near Windsor. Though I still spent part of each holiday at Staddon until my father told me the sad news of its being sold, my grandparents necessarily saw far less of me than hitherto.

When, in the summer of 1945, my grandfather made his impetuous decision, it seems likely that it was instigated by my mother's sudden proposal to establish herself and Patrick in the neighbourhood. He would certainly have regarded with dismay the prospect of receiving his unwelcome new son-in-law in his home, and perforce introducing him to friends a bare decade after they had attended her popular wedding to my father.

Now however, as they worked long hours together in the British Museum researching their proposed book on voyages, my mother and Patrick's union finally received formal recognition. Although my father had divorced my mother at the end of 1942, Patrick continued officially married until Elizabeth was granted her decree nisi at the end of 1944. In June 1945, following the requisite six months' interval, the decree absolute was issued.

In his novel *The Catalans* Patrick placed this description of divorce proceedings in the mouth of a character by whom he plainly intended himself:

> in this case everything is quite straightforward – a simple desertion with adultery and certified avowal – and really there is nothing to prevent it from going through as quickly as possible. When these simple cases are delayed you will usually find that it is either a lack of diligence on the part of the lawyer or hunger for additional fees: occasionally there may be obstructive tactics on the other side . . .[1]

On this occasion the divorce proceedings were entirely straightforward, but no sooner had Patrick noted laconically in his diary on 25 June 'Divorced' than he found himself unexpectedly embroiled in protracted acrimonious exchanges with Elizabeth.

Within five days of obtaining the divorce, Patrick noted in his diary: 'Extreme difficulty with opp[osition]', the term he now employed with

[1] *The Catalans*, p. 147. Elsewhere Patrick refers to the 'interminable process' of divorce proceedings (*Richard Temple*, p. 173).

reference to Elizabeth.[1] He had some justification for feeling aggrieved. Elizabeth had agreed not to claim maintenance, and her present demand represented an entirely unexpected violation of that agreement. For more than a year and a half relations between them appear to have been maintained on as equable a basis as might be expected. The divorce proceedings had been conducted by mutual consent. Throughout 1944 and the first half of 1945 Elizabeth (in her own words) 'never put any difficulties in the way of [Patrick's] . . . seeing his son whenever he wanted to', entered 'by mutual agreement' (again her own words) into acceptable arrangements regarding both Richard's education and her maintenance, and had even been on sufficiently intimate terms to discuss her marital plans with him. Now however he found himself hounded for the financial support she had renounced more than half a year earlier.

What must also have rankled was that Elizabeth as a registered 'poor person' was represented gratis by solicitors appointed by the Crown while Patrick, who was on the point of losing his employment, was obliged to fret continually over meeting the fees of his solicitors, Messrs Baddeley Wardlaw & Co. of 77 Leadenhall Street.

What could have brought about this dramatic change in Elizabeth's attitude? Everything suggests that it was the cause rather than consequence of the lasting bitterness which arose between them. Some change in her outlook must have arisen to instigate her action, since nothing had occurred on Patrick's side to provoke it. Unfortunately her motive is unlikely ever to be known. The fact that her demand followed immediately on Patrick's marriage to my mother may be relevant, particularly in view of her apparent belief that my mother possessed money far beyond what was really the case. The stark contrast between The Cottage, with its elegant panelled rooms and fine furniture, and Elizabeth's little flat was later remarked by Richard, as was the assumption that his father's gracious lifestyle was sustained by my mother's financial resources.

On 16 July Patrick responded by providing the court with detailed accounts of his income and expenditure, which his private records show to be accurate. However, within a fortnight he received notice that his employment would terminate on 20 September. Despite this, he received constant demands for money from Elizabeth's solicitors over the coming winter. He responded to these fitfully when inclined, occasionally sending small sums, but when it eventually became apparent that his indigence was genuine her solicitors abandoned further attempts to extract money from him.

However, within a week or so of Patrick's marriage to my mother on 4 July

[1]In his 1945 pocket diary Elizabeth's address is entered simply as 'Opp. 237 Kings Rd.'.

1945, he obtained unexpected news which enabled him to return to court and challenge the terms of the decree. It seems that Elizabeth had overreached herself when she began demanding money immediately after the grant of the decree absolute on 25 June. His financial predicament being precarious, it became a matter of pressing concern to Patrick to learn the extent to which her domestic circumstances justified her application for maintenance. What he discovered must have astonished him, since it all but reversed the state of affairs as he had hitherto understood it, and enabled him to carry the battle to the enemy camp.

On 3 August Patrick submitted a formal application to have the December 1944 judgment awarding custody of his son to Elizabeth overturned. After pointing out the great expense and sacrifice to which he was putting himself to keep his son at preparatory school, he went on to explain that the considerations on which the 1944 custody award had been grounded were now effectively reversed. Then it had been his illicit relationship with my mother that made their home an unsuitable place for his son to stay, but this irregular situation had now been ended by his marriage.

He then moved on to produce evidence that it was now Elizabeth who was living in adultery. Although it was unnecessary in the affidavit to go beyond demonstrating the point, it reveals a remarkable degree of duplicity on Elizabeth's part. By this time she had been living with a man named Le Mee Power for at least nine months, and was covertly conducting the affair at the time the decree nisi was granted.

It can only be guessed how Patrick managed to learn about her affair. Perhaps incensed and alarmed by her unreasonable financial demands, he decided for the first time to discover something of her private conduct, and swiftly obtained evidence so damning as to be impossible to deny. Even then Elizabeth appears to have concealed the fact that their affair was of long standing, and in a later affidavit claimed that it was not until or about August 1945 that she had 'begun to live with Mr. John Cowper Le Mee-Power . . .'

Patrick's affidavit concluded: 'The Petitioner is a person of little education and is not a person likely to be able properly to supervise the education and upbringing of my said son . . .'

On 20 August Elizabeth responded with a defensive affidavit which set out a stinging catalogue of Patrick's alleged misdeeds. When they lived in Suffolk, he 'was supported by me and his brother'. While it is true that Godfrey was generous in his support, since Elizabeth was living in the country with no transport and two small children (one very sick) to care for she was in no position to earn money, nor is there any evidence that she did. After Patrick's departure to London, 'the maintenance he sent me was most erratic and of such a small amount that I had to give up my home and live with his relations'. But four years later she conceded that throughout that period 'he provided me with three pounds per week to maintain myself' and the children.[1] It cannot have been lack of funds that compelled her to leave Gadds Cottage, since in addition to this modest but sufficient income Godfrey was always at hand to provide assistance.

Finally, she declared that Patrick 'has never taken any great interest in our son and he is a violent and erratic man. Nevertheless I should raise no objection to the boy staying with him for part of his holidays . . .' The first allegation appears extraordinary in view of Patrick's vigorous objection to the custody award, and assumption of financial responsibility for Richard's schooling. That he was erratic was true enough, but Elizabeth provided no evidence for the alleged violence, a charge she appears never to have advanced on any other occasion and, given Patrick's character, appears intrinsically unlikely.

Divorce settlements naturally tend to be acrimonious, with fierce allegations flung by each side against the other, but Elizabeth's unabashed doctoring of factual issues so basic as dates and places calls in question the validity of her testimony generally. It is noteworthy that this appears to be the first occasion on which she laid any serious claim of harsh treatment at her former husband's door. The sole offence cited in her divorce petition was his adultery during the preceding three months. Nearly two years later it appeared all at once that there was almost no misdeed he had not perpetrated, and might not yet.

Whether Patrick rebutted these charges at the court hearing which followed is not recorded, but appears likely since the judge accepted his submission that he and his wife could now provide his son with a suitable family home, while it was Elizabeth's irregular domestic relations which appeared undesirable. The judge ordered that custody should be transferred to the father, and that the boy should spend half of each school holiday with either parent. Elizabeth was required to provide an undertaking that Richard should not be brought into contact with her adulterous lover.

All 'revelations' about Patrick's relationship and desertion of his first wife have been predicated on a very limited range of assumptions. The charges to which he was publicly subjected at the end of his life and afterwards amount to the following:

[1] On 26 April 1949 Elizabeth submitted to a court that she was earning 'between £3. 10. 0. and £4. 0. 0. a week', 'and am, therefore, in a position to take full personal charge of Richard'. This was for the expenses required to live in a comfortable flat in central London, and clearly her financial needs were considerably less when renting part of a remote country cottage.

1. Patrick abandoned his wife and family because he found himself unable to cope with living with a severely handicapped child.
2. He left home abruptly without explanation.
3. He showed no concern for his wife's consequent plight, and did nothing to assist her. Indeed he displayed nothing but bitterness and unkindness towards her.
4. Eventually she was obliged to divorce him on account of his relationship with my mother. Four years later she married again.

It can be seen that none of these accusations bears the smallest relation to reality. The circumstances of Patrick's leaving home have already been explained. His departure had nothing to do with little Jane's sickness, and there is reason to suppose that he gave what appeared good reason for his wishing to undertake war work in London. Having done so, he remained on amicable if physically distant relations with his family, and supported them financially to the best of his capacity throughout his absence. On available evidence it seems likely that Elizabeth divorced Patrick less (or not at all) in consequence of discovering that he was living in adultery, than in order to marry another man. The divorce was obtained by mutual consent, and prior to July 1945 affairs of common concern were discussed on amicable terms in and out of court.

Finally, Elizabeth later attested that even their exchange of mutually accusatory affidavits in July and August had not so far as she was aware provoked Patrick unduly. Her wild allegations had if anything served to strengthen his case at the custody hearing, and though he was provoked by her continuing demands for money over the following winter, it was not until the next year that relations between them became embittered on account of a novel and unrelated issue. Not only is this borne out by the evidence, but it receives explicit confirmation from an affidavit submitted by Elizabeth in 1949. In it she alluded to the letter Patrick wrote her in 1941 or 1942, in which he suggested that she find work as a school matron, and continued:

> At that time he had not begun to adopt the attitude of hostility he has since shown . . . The other side of the same piece of paper gives some clue to our relations at that time before these unhappy difficulties arose . . . the Respondent [Patrick] made this suggestion which I respectfully submit indicates his true estimate of my character, before his mind became inflamed against me as a result of my disclosing his address, quite innocently, to the husband of Mrs. O'Brian.

The episode in question occurred in February 1946, when Elizabeth secretly collaborated with my father on the eve of a court hearing at which my mother applied for access to her children. She lost the case, and this vindictive betrayal (as they regarded it) greatly angered Patrick and my mother, who made their indignation known through their solicitor's correspondence.

CHAPTER THIRTEEN

A New Beginning

Grant me, kind Heaven, to find some happier place,
Where honesty and sense are no disgrace;
Some pleasing bank where verdant osiers play,
Some peaceful vale with Nature's paintings gay;
Where once the harass'd Briton found repose,
And safe in poverty defy'd his foes;
Some secret cell, ye Pow'rs, indulgent give,
Let —— live here, for —— has learn'd to live.
(Samuel Johnson, 'London: A Poem')

On 4 July 1945 Patrick married my mother, and it was at the time when these unpleasant exchanges began that he moved to effect a further transformation of his status: one so seemingly inexplicable as to have remained a mystery for which even now a wholly satisfactory explanation cannot be provided. Given the effect it was to have on his life to the end of his days, and the extensive speculation which it understandably aroused when eventually made public, it is necessary to consider it in some detail.

Patrick's literary agent Spencer Curtis Brown acted as witness to his application on 14 August, and he changed his name on 20 August by deed poll from Richard Patrick Russ to Richard Patrick O'Brian. Thus my mother in the space of a month changed her name from Countess Mary Tolstoy to Mrs Russ and now Mrs Patrick O'Brian – the name she was to retain until her death half a century later.

My mother's change of name followed naturally with the deed poll, but Patrick adopted the additional measure of extending the new surname to his son. This came as a total surprise to Richard, who many years later decided to resent the change and revert to his original surname. In a newspaper interview he described the disturbing manner in which he was first made aware of his new name: 'Richard remembers that at the age of 11 [actually eight], "my headmaster suddenly called me into his study and told me my name was now O'Brian. Just like that. My father never explained to me why he had done this. He was too cold and reserved for me to ask. My mother had said it was just him 'being silly.'" '[1]

Two related questions arise from this unusual move. What was it that induced Patrick to change his name? And why did he choose that of O'Brian?

Dean King provides this reconstruction of Patrick's thoughts: 'Russ was canny enough to sense that this turning point in world history [the defeat of Germany] cleared the path for a break in his own history . . . What the name change signified was this: Farewell, Richard Patrick Russ. You bore your pain. You made your mistakes. You served your country. Now, thank God, the madness is over.'

In fact nothing suggests that Patrick had borne pain, believed himself to have made mistakes in serving his country, or suffered any traumatic emotion in consequence of the war's ending. On the contrary, everything indicates that he had enjoyed life at The Cottage, and the sole regret he felt at ending his employment with PWE was the loss of salary which that entailed. King's hypothesis also leaves unexplained the remarkable fact that Patrick did not change his name until *after* his marriage to my mother. Since she had also to adopt the name O'Brian, would it not have been logical to register the change prior to the ceremony?

This suggests that Patrick's action represented an unanticipated afterthought. In the previous month he and my mother had had their hopes of gaining access to her capital dashed, and found themselves with no alternative to leaving London to live in rented accommodation in some remote part of the country. An affidavit Patrick signed on 16 July indicates that he was as yet unaware how long his employment with the Foreign Office might continue, but another dated 3 August declares that it would 'cease on the 20th September next'. Since it was on 20 July that he applied to change his name, it may well have been then that he received formal notice of termination of his employment.

Everything suggests that Patrick's abrupt decision to change his name was

[1]*Mail on Sunday*, 16 January 2000. Patrick had presumably asked the headmaster to explain the situation to Richard immediately on his arrival at Southey Hall for the Michaelmas term. On 19 September, the latter wrote home: 'Dear Daddy and Marie. I have arrived safely. With love From Richard.' The postcard is addressed in an adult hand to 'P. O'Brian Esq.'. At the time Richard appears to have accepted his father's eccentric ways without question, and it was his mother rather than he who objected to the change of name. On 23 October 1945 Patrick noted irritably: 'Today's [post] had . . . a letter from Richard – he is obviously not writing to his mother, probably because she won't write to him in his proper name.'

directly related to the sudden crisis in their financial affairs. Unable to purchase a property with my mother's capital, and with their income on the point of being reduced to a sixth of its current level, he was faced with the prospect of living in a distant community where he would be a complete stranger. Patrick grasped the opportunity of making a formal move symbolically consigning his early life – above all his wretchedly unhappy childhood and distressing first marriage – to the past.

It is hard to think of a convincing alternative to this explanation. The damaging accusation that his change of name was motivated by shameful concern to conceal his abandonment of his first wife and children[1] has only to be considered to be rejected. It fails to explain why he waited five years before adopting the precautionary measure, and ignores the obvious fact that it was precisely those who had a motive for exposing 'his dreadful secret' who remained aware of his true identity. As things were, Elizabeth herself dismissed his action as no more than 'silly', and few others knew or cared about defects in Patrick's marital conduct. Indeed, had such been his motive, it must surely have occurred to him that a change of name would more than likely be derided as acknowledgement of guilt.

As the years rolled by Patrick gradually took to modest reinvention of his life before 1945. However, at the time the decision to change his name almost certainly arose from nothing more than discovering unexpected opportunity to reject his Russ heritage. While working for PWE he modified his name to 'Ross', and the fact that he used two distinct surnames at the same time (he was still employed by PWE when he changed his name to O'Brian) suggests that concern to shed the name Russ was his primary motive, while the choice of substitute represented a secondary consideration.

Confirmation of this hypothesis may be indicated by the fact that it appears to have been at this time that he adopted the drastic measure of disposing of copies of every book and story he had written under the name of Patrick Russ. He remained justifiably proud of his early works, to which he made discreet allusion on the dust-jackets of subsequent publications, and was gratified when towards the end of his life the British Library republished *Cæsar* and *Hussein* under the name of Patrick O'Brian. However after his death I found he had dumped books he regarded as in some way inadequate in a sack at the back of his cellar – but not a copy of *Cæsar*, *Beasts Royal*, or *Hussein* was to be found anywhere in the house. It is hard to resist the conclusion that this reflected a past decision that 'Patrick Russ' should be consigned to oblivion, and his adoption of a new

[1]Kevin Myers, *Sunday Telegraph*, 20 January 2002.

name on removing to a spot far from family and acquaintance is by far the most likely moment for such a dramatic gesture.[1]

The protagonist of Patrick's second intensely autobiographical novel *Three Bear Witness*, which is based on his life in North Wales, is a university professor who (like Patrick) has been preparing a book on bestiaries, and who (like Patrick) retires for a period of recuperation to a remote valley in North Wales. Introducing himself, he explains:

> My great-grandfather (from whom I have my name of Pugh) had come from Wales before he had established himself as a draper in Liverpool, and I believe there was quite a strong Welsh tradition in our family as late as my father's time. He, poor man, had been left a genteel competence by his draper grandfather; it had descended to him through his un-draper father, who had married a lady of very good family and dealt in large mercantile transactions, far from the counter. My father, a social man, living in a time of acute social distinctions, felt the Liverpool-Welsh side of his ancestry keenly. He dropped all Welsh contacts and added his mother's name, Aubrey, to ours. He had never cared for me to ask him about it . . .[2]

These fictional transferences provide the flimsiest of veils for Patrick's deepest personal concerns. A grandson abjures his unacceptable descent from a grandfather of alien race, who suffered the additional social stigma of being engaged in trade. He sets himself up as a gentleman and adopts a name more appropriate to his improved status, concerning which he resents being questioned. His choice of the gentlemanly-sounding 'Aubrey' bears an application to Patrick's future work which require no comment.

None of the above accounts for his fastening on 'O'Brian' in particular. Why, for example, did he not retain the surname 'Ross' by which he had been known at work for the past four years? Following his emigration to Australia, Patrick's brother Michael, having deserted his wife a month after the birth of their son in 1930, had assumed for a few years the name O'Brien. Years later their brother Bernard became convinced that Patrick had adopted his new name in imitation of his elder brother. He complained more than once about

[1] The only other decisive point was at the time of his move to France in 1949, but it is hard to see why he should have delayed until then to discard his early works (he took the rest of his substantial library with him), nor what might have induced him to adopt such a measure on moving to a country where no one could have heard of Patrick Russ. He did not have copies of his early novels when I first stayed with him and my mother in 1955, which in their restricted quarters I could not have avoided seeing.

[2] *Three Bear Witness*, pp. 10–11.

this to his sister Joan, to whom he wrote in 1988: 'I do wish he would think of himself as a part of our family and that he had not copied Mike in taking the name of O'Brian . . . However, there is no point in arguing about it, it would only create ill will.'

Shortly afterwards he returned to the theme:

> He simply copied Mike's name but he does not know why Mike changed his. I do and I have not been talking about it. It was not an honourable business at all.[1] I know one of our uncles [Ernest] changed his name from Russ to Russell during the First War, supposing Russ to be a very German name which it is and I believe the family simply regarded him as an outcast because of it. Perhaps we should have done the same with Pat. I don't think anybody would have done so with Mike because by the time he arrived in England in Air Force uniform he was a Russ again.

In a television interview broadcast in 1998 Patrick asserted that the character of Jack Aubrey was partially inspired by a brother who had been killed in the war. The allusion was of course to Michael, who had been shot down over Germany in 1943. So far as I am aware this was the first occasion Patrick made this claim, and previously he had declared on different occasions that Aubrey's career, and to a limited extent his personality, derived from that of the celebrated Lord Cochrane of the Napoleonic Wars.

Patrick's own attempt to pursue a career in the RAF had proved brief and inglorious, and that his genial and dashing war hero of a brother should have excited his affectionate admiration is unsurprising. It was seen in the previous chapter that nearly forty years later Patrick retained a vivid memory of the jovial authoritative giant recounting how he directed his formidable fighting craft by the stars. It is likely enough that the figure of Pilot Officer Michael Russ did contribute, at least in part, to that of Captain Jack Aubrey. The Royal Navy of Nelson's day had enjoyed a role in public imagination comparable to that of the RAF in the Second World War, and no fictional transformation could exaggerate the resourcefulness and courage of those who fought in either service. As Patrick emphasised in his introductory note to *The Mauritius Command*, it was needless 'to gild the lily by adding in any way to the Royal Navy's pugnacious resourcefulness in time of adversity'.

Yet Patrick's claim towards the end of his life that 'Mike was certainly the brother I loved best' surely represents imaginative exaggeration. After the age of five he saw little of his elder brother, who was away at boarding-school

[1] The allusion is to a fleeting affair which resulted in the birth of an illegitimate son. However, there is no indication that this was the reason for Mike's change of name.

in the West Country and rarely returned home during the holidays. He emigrated to Australia at a time when Patrick had been living away from home with his stepmother in Sussex for a year, and the brief call Mike paid him in Chelsea in 1943 was the only occasion they ever met again. The fact that Mike had for a few years on the other side of the world assumed a name similar to that which Patrick subsequently adopted appears very inadequate explanation for his selection of the distinct surname 'O'Brian' two years after Mike's death. As Bun's letter indicates, Mike's change of name provoked little interest at the time among his family at home, to whom he remained simply 'Mike'. There is in fact no certainty that in 1945 Patrick was even aware of his brother's temporary change of name. As Bun observed, when Mike arrived in England in 1943 it was as Michael Russ, since he had reverted to his true name on enrolling in the Australian Air Force two years earlier. Finally, for two years after Mike's arrival in England Patrick continued using the name 'Ross' – not 'O'Brian'.

Bun himself acknowledged on one occasion that 'I do not know why he took on the name of O'Brian'.[1] Nothing suggests that Patrick was impressed by Mike's change of name. Writing in 1998 to his nephew John Cole (son of his sister Olive), he drew attention to the difference in spelling, sharply pointing out that while Mike had irregularly adopted his version of the name for a time in the wilds of Queensland, in contrast his own change had been legally effected by deed poll.

There is in addition the curious question why Patrick adopted the unusual spelling 'O'Brian'. While attending Trinity College Dublin in the 1950s, out of curiosity I once scanned the Irish telephone directory, where I found only one or two O'Brians among hundreds of O'Briens. Walter Greenway recalls Patrick's emphasis at the time he registered the change on the rarity of the spelling 'O'Brian'. What could have induced him to fasten on a variant so unusual as to invite precisely the sort of embarrassing enquiry he was to spend a liftetime seeking to avoid?

In fact it appears that he happened upon the name by chance not long before he adopted it, in a context strongly appealing to his imagination. At some point during the winter of 1944–45, almost certainly no later than

[1] A running theme of Bun's correspondence with his sister Joan is Patrick's lack of communicability, and his consequent ignorance of Patrick's affairs. As late as April 1989 his knowledge of Patrick's domestic background amounted to no more than this: 'I do recall by his first marriage, he had a son, Richard, who must be now in his fifties, because he was a little fellow when I came back from Australia in 1938. I have no idea what became of his mother, Elizabeth, but understand that a divorce did occur and that Pat subsequently married this lady who had been married to one of the Tolstoy family. Perhaps you know more about it than I.'

January, Patrick transcribed a nineteenth-century commission of insurance subscribed by one 'P. O'Brian', which covered his 'good ship or vessel called the Regular Steamer and (?) Cowes or by whatever other Name or Names the same Ship is or shall be named or called', against all hazards she might encounter. It concludes with a catalogue of risks accepted by the policy, whose appeal to Patrick is obvious:

> Touching the Adventures and Perils which the said Company is contented to bear, and does take upon itself in this Voyage; they are of Seas, Men of War, Fire, Enemies, Pirates, Rovers, Thieves, Jettisons, Letters of Mart and Counter-Mart, Surprisals, Takings at Sea, Arrests, Restraints and detainments of all Kings, Princes and Peoples, of what Nation, Condition, or Qualities soever, Barratry of the Master and Mariners, and of all other Perils, Losses, and Misfortunes that have or shall come to the Hurt, Detriment or Damage of the subject matter of this Assurance.[1]

There are a number of textual indications that Patrick was copying an original document. Thus he inserts a question mark beside what was evidently an uncertain reading of the ship's alternative name, a dash for the illegible name of a port, and substitutes for a presumably tedious list the summary description 'Personal effects – household goods'. In fact there can be no doubt of the authenticity of the original document, whose phraseology follows precisely the format employed in nineteenth-century marine insurance certificates.[2]

Poised some months later on the brink of an adventure whose outcome was impossible to foretell, what more appropriate role model could Patrick find than that of this intrepid sailor embarking on a voyage encompassed by such a catalogue of glamorous perils? They read almost as a summary of those real-life adventures of his Uncle Morse which had so enthralled him twenty years

[1]Mr Frank Bland has kindly drawn my attention to a letter by David Greenwood, published in the *Nelson Despatch* (July 2001, p. 494). During a visit to Guernsey, Mr Greenwood visited the grave of the heroic Admiral Saumarez, one of Nelson's 'band of brothers'. He was surprised to discover a grave nearby bearing an inscription which includes the words: 'Patrick O'Brian who was a faithful and most trustworthy servant in the . . . family for 56 years'. By a yet more remarkable coincidence, O'Brian's wife, who shares his tomb, was named Mary! However I assume this must indeed represent no more than coincidence, since Patrick never to my knowledge visited Guernsey, while Admiral Saumarez's servant can scarcely have undertaken the responsibilities of the 'P. O'Brian' of the document Patrick copied.

[2]I am indebted to Dr Roy Clare, Director of the National Maritime Museum, for providing me with specimen copies of such insurance certificates. He could find no record in the Lloyd's Registers of a vessel named 'Cowes', but Patrick's question mark suggests that he may have misread the name.

before. The Irish surname may have provided additional appeal, given the affection Patrick developed for Ireland following his stay there in 1937. All in all, the hasty and unforeseen circumstances in which he adopted his new name suggest that he did so with little prior reflection, and that he happened fortuitously upon that which he adopted.

On 24 October 1998 a British newspaper published a lengthy feature article under the lurid headline: 'The secret life of Patrick O'Brian, Master of the maritime adventure'. This provided the first public revelation of his change of name, together with a detailed résumé of his background as a member of the Russ family, and an extremely partial account of his first marriage. His claims to Irish birth and upbringing were shown without difficulty to be untrue. The piece provoked much adverse critical comment on the public perception of Patrick as an Irish novelist. Even a close mutual friend confided to me that he felt 'betrayed'.

This reaction was surely grossly disproportionate and largely unjust. While Patrick's claim to be Irish was undeniably false, it was not a matter on which he laid anything approaching the emphasis ascribed to him, nor is there much to suggest that it ever bore great significance in his eyes. To assert that at this time he 'transformed himself into Patrick O'Brian, Irishman'[1] is a crude exaggeration, and manifests profound misunderstanding of Patrick's idiosyncratic mentality.

In the first place, manifestly all his acquaintance at the time of his change of name knew full well that his real name was not O'Brian, and that he was not Irish. Even Patrick's capacity for self-delusion could scarcely have led him to believe he could credibly transform himself into an Irishman. Since he found himself obliged to move to a part of the country where he would not be known, it would of course have been possible to elaborate a charade among new acquaintances. However after their move he and my mother evinced little desire to make friends locally, preferring to retain contact with their small circle of intimate friends from London, some of whom came from time to time to stay with them in their new home. Though a chance remark might at any moment have exposed Patrick's 'transformation' to his neighbours, he never once requested a friend (such as Walter Greenway, who stayed twice) to exercise tact on the subject. Dean King asserts that on his arrival at their new home, 'Patrick took on the persona of an Irish country gentleman. He could speak some Gaelic, and the people were gullible.' In fact he could not speak Gaelic, the people of the valley were far from gullible, and nothing more is recorded of Patrick's claim to 'Irishness' than a passing assertion to a

[1] Kevin Myers, *Sunday Telegraph*, 20 January 2002.

shepherd boy that he had worked on a stud farm in Ireland.[1] He occasionally expressed interest in related Irish and Welsh words, a curiosity which sprang naturally from his long-standing amateur interest in linguistics.[2] In what way he might have adopted the manner of a 'country gentleman' is beyond my comprehension, while the 'Irish' aspect does not appear to have extended beyond the implication of his adopted surname. In any case there was no reason to suppose that the people of the remote Welsh valley where he settled would regard Irish origin as any more impressive or congenial than English.[3]

An entry in the journal Patrick kept during his early months in Wales throws revealing light on his supposed design of persuading people that he was an Irishman named O'Brian. On 5 July 1946 he bought a bicycle from a man in Portmadoc who proved to be an author. Recounting their discussion of shared interests and experiences, Patrick mentioned in passing that 'he knew of me'. This would not have been possible unless Patrick had explained that all his books written up to that time were published under the authorship of 'R.P. Russ'.

So far as I am aware, the first recorded identification of Patrick as an Irishman was not advanced by himself, but by the Irish writer Lord Dunsany, who in a review of Patrick's collection of short stories *The Last Pool* published in 1950 described it as 'This charming book by an Irish

[1] It cannot be said for certain that he did not do so, since little is known of his activities in Ireland in 1937, and it is possible that he went there more than once before the war.

[2] Here, as elsewhere, I am greatly beholden to my good friend Edgar Williams for recounting to me his memories of Patrick's stay in Cwm Croesor.

[3] Welsh nationalism was and is strong in Wales generally and Cwm Croesor in particular, with some corresponding hostility towards England. The latter is occasionally manifested on a personal level, but almost always in response to real or perceived English arrogance or tactlessness. Strange as it may appear, identification with (or even interest in) Irish nationalism has always been of scant concern in the Prinicipality, save among a handful of scholars or political extremists. Historically there has never been any sense of ethnic affiliation between the Irish and Welsh. It was not until the sixteenth century that specialist scholars first became aware of the common Celtic origin of the Irish and Welsh languages. It is rare for a Welshman to hear an Irishman speaking his native tongue in Wales, and were he to do so it would appear as incomprehensible and alien as French or German. Irish (Catholic) nationalism at its height in the nineteenth and early twentieth centuries aroused little direct sympathy among the Nonconformist Welsh, and it was largely the Nonconformist lobby in England and Wales which brought about the downfall of the Irish nationalist leader Charles Stewart Parnell in 1890 (Richard Shannon, *Gladstone: Heroic Minister 1865–1898* (London, 1999), p. 497).

[4] *Observer*, 29 October 1950. One wonders on what grounds Patrick condemned 'the damned silly review Dunsany produced for the Observer' in a letter to his editor at Secker and Warburg. Could he have been annoyed or embarrassed by the uninvited ascription of Irish origin?

sportsman'.[4] Since neither the book nor its dust-jacket provided any biographical information about the author, Dunsany presumably inferred Patrick's origin from his surname. This explanation seems the more likely in that he does not appear to have read the book with great attention, describing it as 'a genuine collection of tales of the Irish countryside', when in fact only four of its thirteen stories are set in Ireland.

Inevitably Patrick's adoption of the name O'Brian led to an assumption among those who knew nothing of his background that he was of Irish origin. So far as he himself was concerned, he tended rather to accept than assert the identification, and then only rarely and almost invariably reluctantly.[1] It does not appear that any English edition of his books contains a claim to being Irish. Indeed, almost all his books published in England omit the brief biographical notice customary on dust-jackets. This reticence was generally at his own insistence, since he detested providing information of a personal nature. In March 1952 the magazine *Irish Writing* published Patrick's short story 'Not Liking to Pass the Road Again'. When a copy arrived from the publishers, my mother was 'very surprised to find biographical notes after I'd refused them because P. doesn't like it'.

His first books published under the name of Patrick O'Brian, *A Book of Voyages* (1947) and *The Last Pool* (1950) contain no biographical information, either in the books or on their dust-jackets. Despite his publisher's insistently requesting a notice, Patrick somehow managed to avoid doing so. The first book to include any personal information at all was *The Catalans* (1953), whose dust-jacket told no more than that the author 'was born in 1914', 'produced four books before the war', 'worked for many years . . . on a book on Bestiaries', and 'has lived for some years in Collioure'. When in 1956 Rupert Hart-Davis requested a brief biographical résumé for his collection of short stories *Lying in the Sun*, Patrick adroitly produced the following:

> As to the personal side, the *Spectator* for March 1st 1710 begins, 'I have observed, that a Reader seldom peruses a Book with Pleasure, till he knows whether the Writer of it be a black or a fair man, of a mild or cholerick Disposition, Married or a Batchelor, with other particulars of the like Nature, that conduce very much to the right understanding of an Author.' To gratify this curiosity, which is so natural to a reader, we may state that Mr O'Brian is a black man, choleric, and married.

However Patrick's concern to protect his privacy proved impossible to

[1] At the age of seventy-nine he was asked innocently by a neighbour at the dining-table in his club: 'Were you born in Ireland?' His reply is not recorded, but his diary entry makes it clear that he resented the question.

sustain when dealing with publishers in the United States, where some account of the author is regarded as *de rigueur*. In 1952 a brief biographical notice attached to 'The Green Creature' in *Harper's Bazaar* declared him to have been born 'in the west of Ireland'. King castigates the 'error, perpetuated by the author, that would continually reappear in reviews and even on the back of one of his subsequent books'. He might have mitigated the harshness of his criticism had he been aware that the description was published at the insistence of the editor, who sent Patrick a telegram with the peremptory demand: 'please send air mail biographical data and a photo immediately'. In view of his desperate need to establish himself as a writer in the United States, Patrick did not feel in a position to refuse. On 17 September my mother recorded in her diary: 'P. sent personal data & horrible Patau photograph to H.B.'

Although it might be assumed that the assertion of Irish birth was included in this 'personal data', it seems not unlikely that his reluctant and doubtless laconic response was subjected to editorial embroidery. 'The Green Creature' is an Irish tale written in convincingly Anglo-Irish prose, and if Patrick sent no more than the bland summary he provided in the following year for the jacket of *The Catalans*, *Harper's Bazaar* might well have considered it desirable to paraphrase Lord Dunsany's description of Patrick as 'an Irish sportsman' in his flattering review, which his literary agent[1] would undoubtedly have included with the book when submitting it to the magazine. That Patrick and my mother were annoyed by the notice is suggested by the fact that she omitted it when cutting out the article for inclusion in her collection of Patrick's published writings.

So far as I am aware, the sole assertion of his being Irish included in any of his books appears in a brief notice on the dust-jacket of his biography of Picasso published by Putnam's of New York in 1976. There he is described as 'An Irishman by birth', which might appear to provide irrefutable evidence of his alleged imposture. Significantly it does not. On 13 October 1975 his editor William Targ wrote to ask 'can you supply a photo of yourself and a biographical sketch for use on the jacket? I'll need some background material on you for publicity, etc.' On 24 October Patrick sent Targ two photographs (which in the event were not used), and a lengthy account of himself and his absorption with Picasso. *It contains no mention of his being born in Ireland, nor any other reference to the country beyond a passing allusion to his*

[1] Although I have been unable to find any evidence relating to Patrick's engaging Curtis Brown as his agent, it must presumably have occurred about the time he began compiling his anthology of voyages – his first book since the publication of *Hussein* in 1938, for which he did not employ a literary agent.

having known Dublin in the thirties – which of course he did. Patrick wrote to me at the time that 'Putnam hurried this edition of the Picasso book through the press at such a pace that I never had time to put in several valuable pieces of late-come information'. The words 'An Irishman by birth' must have been added by a well-intentioned editor.

Of course even tacit acceptance amounts to a degree of deception, but so sparse a catalogue as exists scarcely constitutes the 'reinvention' ascribed to him by malevolent critics. It is true that during the last decade of his life Patrick indulged in occasional claims to be an Irishman. Such imaginative lapses may be put down to a combination of old age, the increasing sickness and finally death of my mother (who tended to check some of his wilder fancies), and the long-postponed acclaim he received from readers, lecture audiences, and journalists happy to accept the master's *obiter dicta*. A year before my mother died, he wrote in his diary: 'A day memorable only for sadness & a profound depression, caused I think by . . . a flow, in an all too familiar voice, of false reminiscence.'

A singular example of such romancing is said to have occurred in 1993, when he was visited at his home by Mark Horowitz of the *New York Times*. It was rare for Patrick to agree to be interviewed, but he was persuaded by his American publisher that the article would greatly promote sales of his books in the USA. He regarded the interview with apprehension, and was very much on edge throughout Horowitz's stay in Collioure. His extreme sensitivity regarding his private life led to friction and *froideurs*. Although he had been warned in advance that 'I should be very happy to see you here . . . to talk about books and writing – Starling Lawrence [Patrick's editor at Norton] has I am sure told you about my dislike for personalities', as a good journalist Horowitz hoped to prise out something of the private man.

Dinner on his arrival at a restaurant in the town proved something of a disaster, with Patrick at his most didactic. Indeed, the atmosphere grew sufficiently strained for my mother to make her apologies and withdraw, and Patrick himself acknowledged in his dairy 'I was odious'. The next day dinner in their home proved equally tense. As Patrick described it: 'In the evening I brought him up to dinner: unhappily too much wine was poured & he displayed some of those inhuman rudenesses peculiar to his kind. M had to retire.' The 'inhuman rudenesses' represented attempts by the frustrated Horowitz to draw him out on his personal life. As a concession, Patrick allowed him to read a draft copy of the biographical notice he had written for the forthcoming British Library tribute. Although it was very brief and reserved, Horowitz seized with delight upon its sparse details, salient items from which he scattered in paraphrase through his article. Some minor fictions included an imaginative claim to childhood connection with Ireland (though not that he was born there), but little emphasis was laid on the matter.

Next day the journalist conducted his interview proper, which from Patrick's point of view went better than their previous discussions.

> Horowitz to tea, more amiable but oh so loquacious – amazed by BL piece – more than he had ever thought he cd prise out of me – I explained once agn that it showed the limits of what I chose to make public – he nodded & at once sd 'Can I say you wr born in Ireland?' This was the level of our understanding in the subsequent flood of literary theory, wch did however show that he knew the books better than I did. He was much civiller to M as well . . .

Patrick firmly declined to answer the question about his birthplace (the exchange incidentally illustrates the extent to which journalists sought to place words in his mouth), and when Horowitz concluded his visit on the following day by inviting him and my mother to dinner Patrick was relieved to feel that it had concluded on a cordial note: 'Pleasant meal . . . & we talked in an ordinary communicative manner: he sd pretty things on parting. I am glad it ended so well.'

In the event Patrick was greatly angered by the resultant article, not because it betrayed any small confidences he might have imparted, but on account of sceptical comments Horowitz ascribed to unidentified friends and colleagues. In July he described it to Erik Burns (who had earlier worked for his US publisher Norton) as 'that truly odious NY Times piece, as dishonourable a betrayal of hospitality and of confidence as I have ever experienced'. The article is highly laudatory of Patrick's work, and overall presents him in a discerning and not unsympathetic light, but his acute sensitivity to criticism must have been greatly exacerbated by the quoted criticisms. 'One longtime acquaintance put it . . . bluntly: "Patrick can be a bit of a snob, socially and intellectually."' Still more disturbing was this caveat: 'Reliable facts about his early life are not easy to come by. The only source is O'Brian himself, and over the years, says one friend, the story has varied a bit.'

Horowitz had courteously sent for comment and correction a draft of their discussions which Patrick approved, making only minor alterations. Since the sparse biographical details given in the article derive almost exclusively from Patrick's outline compiled for the forthcoming British Library publication, it contained little or nothing to which he could object on that score.

Later, however, Horowitz provided Dean King with details not included in his article, one or two of which related to Patrick's supposed Irish background. 'When Horowitz asked O'Brian if he should be called an Irish writer, he said, "Of course," acting amused that Horowitz would ask. Later, for good measure, he disclosed that he was from the west of Ireland and described the breathtaking cliffs plummeting to the sea there . . . "My childhood was coloured by the Irish Troubles, the Irish Civil War," he told Horowitz.' He went on to express support for a unified Ireland, whose Protestant population could choose between remaining in the Republic or leaving the country. 'But none of this was to be mentioned in the article, O'Brian cautioned the journalist. He feared that the IRA might target him or his family for reprisals. After all, he was an Irishman who had worked for the hated British Intelligence. O'Brian played this card to perfection, disarming Horowitz and casting his Irishness in stone.'[1]

As this appears to be upheld as the crowning instance of Patrick's 'reinvention as an Irishman', it is noteworthy how remarkably little it amounts to. First of all, the little he did vouchsafe was in reluctant response to what King himself acknowledges was a persistent bombardment of 'casual, leading lines [which] led the inquisitor nowhere'. Patrick, who at the time had rarely if ever allowed himself to be interviewed by journalists, became profoundly agitated at finding himself for the first time entertaining one of the breed in his home. Hence his abrupt shifts of mood, ranging from the vinous didacticism of the first evening, which he himself exceptionally acknowledged to have been 'odious', to the cordial atmosphere of their final dinner.

Despite this he appears to have succeeded in adhering to his refusal to disclose more of his personal life than was contained in the outline he provided. Even the journalist's continual professional probing could extract only the trifling additions mentioned above. In view of his concern to preserve his adopted surname, Patrick could hardly reply that he was *not* an Irish writer, but given his refusal to be drawn on whether he was born in the country it ought to have been clear that the definition was qualified. Rather than having 'disclosed that he was from the west of Ireland,' from my own experience I strongly suspect that Patrick evaded any direct response by expatiating impersonally on the glories of the west coast of Ireland, with which he was indeed familiar.[2] Finally, his injunction that 'none of this was

[1] King, *Patrick O'Brian*, p. 350.

[2] To provide but one example, on 9 April 1970 he recorded a visit to 'Dingle – a long drive in lovely weather. Then after a pause out to view the Blaskets; splendid. Such primroses, violets. Currachs. Curlews by night.' Next day he journeyed to the magnificent cliffs of Moher, where with clouds of herring-gulls screaming overhead he gazed awestruck across the heaving ocean to the Aran Islands.

to be mentioned in the article' appears to relate to his dislike of having his extreme solution to the Irish problem made public.[1] His supposed fear of IRA reprisals (for expressing an extreme Nationalist viewpoint!) was either a joke, or intended to reaffirm his concern that Horowitz should avoid reference to Irish antecedents.

Thus, so far from 'casting his Irishness in stone', Patrick made strenuous efforts to avoid the topic altogether. In the following year the British Library published its tribute to Patrick's life and work, to which the editor Arthur Cunningham invited Patrick to contribute. On 9 September 1991 he had replied that 'I would be quite happy to speak of writing, my life as a writer, my approach to creative writing . . . in considerable detail: but I should have little to say of my private life and nothing at all of a confidential nature'. In this brief piece, which was what he showed Horowitz, the Irish connection barely features. Although a claim to have been sent after his mother's death 'to live with more or less willing relatives in Connemara and the County Clare' was untrue, its implication is that he was *not* born in Ireland. The only other allusion, an assertion that 'it was Ireland and France that educated and formed me', was effectively true. His visit to Ireland in 1937 began a lifelong love affair with the country.

When news broke of Patrick's English birth and change of name Kevin Myers, an Irish journalist, initially displayed a good sense which English critics would have done well to follow: 'It is more than possible that he is an O'Brian but it is more than possible, one would gather, that he is not. It doesn't interest me greatly. I don't care what his name is. He is the man he is.'[2]

In 1996 Myers had written a lengthy feature article in the *Irish Times* (23 March 1996) extolling Patrick's exceptional gifts as a writer, in which he explained: 'Patrick O'Brian is from Galway. His first language was Irish. I trust the omission [of Patrick] in *The Oxford Companion to Irish Literature* will be rectified in its next edition.' If Patrick provided Myers with this information it was of course delusive. However, Myers may have been repeating misinformation published elsewhere. In the 1970s the *Irish Press* printed a number of poems and other pieces by Patrick, each of which was accompanied by an identical four-line description of the author, beginning: 'Born Co. Galway . . .' I have no idea how this error originated. In view of his extreme reticence elsewhere, it seems *prima facie* unlikely

[1] He once advanced the same extravagant policy to me, to which I voiced strong objection.
[2] *Sunday Times*, 27 September 1998.

that Patrick would have advanced such a claim in the one country where he might expect it to be checked.[1]

Doubtless additions could be made to this short (effectively non-existent) catalogue of Patrick's public claims to Irish origin, but I doubt that they would greatly modify its overall tenuousness. As script for a 'charade' lasting for more than half a century, it appears singularly insubstantial. Above all it must be recalled how deeply Patrick was concerned to abjure his early life. In order to sustain the mask, he had little choice when pressed but to provide an alternative version.

No evidence of which I am aware suggests that Patrick ever set much store by his public image as an Irishman. Besides, if he really had been seriously concerned to reinvent himself as one, why did he choose in 1945 to live in rural Wales when he might as readily have found a comparable cabin in Ireland? In 1954, when he and my mother engaged in a flurry of abortive attempts to discover a more congenial home than the cramped quarters they occupied in Collioure, he briefly contemplated doing just that. However, the project was lightly abandoned, and my mother's diary shows that so far as he was concerned a suitable cottage in England or France was as acceptable as one in Ireland.

Finally, any assumption that Patrick decided upon becoming 'Irish' in order to acquire a romantic and colourful background ignores the timing of his change of name. In the summer of 1945 the Republic of Ireland was not the most popular nation in British eyes. There was widespread public resentment of the advantage Germany had gained from Irish neutrality, and the IRA's eager collaboration with the Nazis was notorious in informed political circles among which Patrick moved. A bare three months before he came to register his change of name, President de Valera had paid a formal visit to the German Embassy in Dublin to express his condolences on the death of Chancellor Hitler.

In 1945 Patrick's public reputation was modest, but he had already published three books and numerous short stories, and was preparing a fresh work for publication. Like every writer, he lived in constant hope and expectation of public recognition. Whatever the reality, he must have regarded public interest in his affairs as a real possibility, and had concealment (rather than banishment) of his past life been his motive he would have realised how fragile the pretence might prove. His long-term editor at Collins, Richard

[1] The moment Patrick was dead Myers abandoned his previously positive attitude to him and published a succession of articles on the 'imposture' of Patrick's Irishness, culminating in a piece published in the *Sunday Telegraph* (20 January 2002).

Ollard, recalls receiving a letter from a woman claiming to be Patrick's sister, in which he was denounced as a fraud who had changed his name. Richard dismissed the matter as none of his affair, and thought the writer as likely as not 'a nutter'.[1] In fact the correspondent was clearly well informed, and it is astonishing that Patrick succeeded in retaining his secret until the end of the century. He himself was acutely conscious of its vulnerability, and consistently at pains to avoid public assertions about his private life.

Paradoxically, the extent to which Patrick internalised his emotions or expressed them through his fiction could at times lead to a belief, or half-belief, that his inventions reflected reality. The indications are that the aesthetic impact of the stately *Belem* sailing round Cap Creus in 1991 led to his believing it to be the ship on which he had sailed in his youth. That he never stated as much in round terms, and merely dropped allusions intelligible to no one but himself, appears to confirm the likelihood. As William St Clair suggests in his biography of Edward Trelawny, an acquaintance of Byron in Greece and incurable romancer: 'During his earlier years Trelawny knew he was being untruthful and he lived in fear of being found out, but for his later years it is hard to be sure . . . Over the decades his romanticism had eaten away at his discriminatory faculties like some slow-working disease until he could no longer distinguish genuine memory from fantasy.'[2]

Once adopted, such a deception is not easily abandoned, nor is it likely to remain static. A combination of general acceptance with the passing of time may bring about genuine delusion. In Patrick's case the tendency was greatly exacerbated by his isolated life, ingrained mistrust of his fellow beings, and my mother's almost unfailing endorsement even of his most contradictory utterances.

A prime example of Patrick's exceptional capacity for self-delusion is provided by a message my mother sent him in May 1961, when she flew to Ireland to hear me give a lecture to the Irish Historical Society during my last term at Trinity College. It being her first visit, she took the opportunity to

[1]The only conceivable sister is Joan, who in consequence of a mutual misunderstanding nurtured resentment against Patrick for some years. However, such an action seems much out of character for her, and Richard may have been mistaken in his memory, or the writer have misrepresented her status. Could she have been his first wife Elizabeth, who undoubtedly nurtured bitter resentment against him? She did not die until 1998.

[2]'The mask which he initially put on as a protection of disguise became his true face. Early in life he adopted a view of his own character which he then proceeded to live out in practice. As his view of himself changed, so did his behaviour. Shadow and reality chased one another until no one – not even Trelawny – could distinguish the two' (William St Clair, *Trelawny: The Incurable Romancer* (London, 1977), pp. 1, 182; cf. pp. 128, 143). I gave Patrick a copy of this book for Christmas 1980, on which he commented: 'I read some of W. St Clair's Trelawney Nikolai's present with limited approval – immense research but little literary talent.'

tour the Irish countryside. A postcard she sent Patrick from County Wexford enthused over the beauty of everything she saw, and concluded: 'Votre pays est merveilleux.' But both she and he knew better than anyone that his sole connection with Ireland comprised no more (or little more) than a visit undertaken nearly twenty years earlier, and another to see me at Trinity! Clearly such a remark, confined as it was to the two of them, could reflect no conscious pretence, and illustrates the extent to which they had come to collude in his self-deception.

His isolated childhood had long inured Patrick to internalising his emotions, which he found himself only able to express effectively through his writing. He experienced profound difficulty in establishing uninhibited rapport with anyone except my mother, so that his thoughts and actions were primarily directed towards his own sustenance. The enraptured effect of his first visit in 1937 led to the creation of an Ireland of the imagination, and he was singularly unconcerned to establish (as he so readily might have done) physical links with that Ireland which lay so accessible across the sea from the home where he lived in North Wales for four years after 1945. All in all, there can be little doubt that Patrick's Ireland provided him with a Happy Otherworld which his deprived childhood had denied him. In 1976 he recorded wistfully in his diary how he 'read in the Shell guide to Ireland, longing for that almost non-existent country'.

The real cruelty which the brutal attacks launched by his enemies inflicted on Patrick from 1998 arose much less from his denunciation as a purported liar, than from the destruction of a fragile fabric essential to his self-preservation. Even when discussing with me in the privacy of the rooms he then occupied in Trinity College Dublin how best to respond to the malicious campaign, he avoided direct allusion to the matter of the polemic, though he knew I must have known the truth from the outset and could feel confident of my unqualified support in the predicament in which he found himself.

Altogether the exaggerated concern over Patrick's change of name appears not a little ludicrous. As a neighbour in Collioure, the wife of a fisherman, remarked to me after it was proclaimed in headlines: 'What are the English so excited about? Did Voltaire write under his own name, or Molière?' Patrick himself might have quoted one of his favourite authors: 'If this irritability of genius be a malady which has raged even among philosophers, we must not be surprised at the temperament of poets. These last have abandoned their country; they have changed their name; they have punished themselves with exile in the rage of their disorder . . . Even the reasoning HUME once proposed to change his name and his country.'[1]

[1] I. D'Israeli, *Miscellanies of Literature* (London, 1840), p. 401.

*

His adoption of a new name and apparent shift in nationality have attracted such public interest that it appeared proper to digress from the narrative to consider its implications. Returning to the summer of 1945, when he could escape stresses arising from his continuing marital problems Patrick applied himself to work on his planned book of voyages. On 23 June he noted: 'I have read little recently: we are working quite steadily on our compilation.' The distinction drawn between 'reading' and 'working' is revealing. Reading not undertaken for a specific literary purpose he regarded purely as entertainment. This reflects a fundamental aspect of Patrick's approach to writing. Until about the age of thirty he devoted himself for prolonged periods of time to exploring branches of knowledge which intrigued him, apparently without any settled intent of putting them to a practical purpose. It was enough for him, at least in the first half of the 1940s, to conduct adventures purely of the mind. In the second half of the decade he was to become increasingly aware that his studies were serving no practical function, and suffered much agony of mind in consequence. However, throughout this time the accruing body of lore burgeoned slowly but steadily within his memory until it reached a point when inspiration began gaining a hold upon him, which enabled him to reap a harvest much the richer for being garnered in the deepest recesses of his mind.

The projected work was belatedly published in the autumn of 1947 under the title *A Book of Voyages*. It is a slim but entertaining volume, conveying little impression of deep learning. This is deceptive, reflecting as it does severe cuts inflicted by the publisher, who was concerned to produce a book accessible to a popular readership. In fact Patrick and my mother conducted extensive researches during the three months that they remained in London. They toiled in libraries, making detailed notes on obscure works, only a handful of which have survived in the published book. Patrick returned to his old haunt the British Museum, where among other primary sources he consulted the manuscript correspondence of Lady Craven.[1] Their labours grew the more intensive as the time approached when they would be obliged to leave London permanently and be deprived of access to scholarly libraries. It was literally a labour of love. Into one of the great volumes of his *Collection of voyages and Travels* by Awnsham and John Churchill (1732) my mother slipped a sheet of paper on which she had painstakingly inscribed a line of

[1]'Letters of the Lady C BM Add. MSS 55535 f. 327'. Patrick possessed a copy of *A Journey through the Crimea to Constantinople. In a Series of Letters from the Right Honourable Elizabeth Lady Craven, to His Serene Highness the Margrave of Brandebourg, Anspach and Bareith. Written in the Year MDCCLXXXVI* (London, 1789).

exotic script, with an accompanying translation: 'This, in the Malabar language, says that Mary loves Patrick. She does, too.'

Patrick had found an excellent literary agent, Spencer Curtis Brown of 6 Henrietta Street, Covent Garden, who was prepared to market the book. Less than three months after embarking on the project, Patrick noted joyfully: 'Our book of voyages is almost ready now. Secretly I am rather hopeful: it has some first rate stuff in it.' However it was now August, and Patrick had just received the long-dreaded notice from the Foreign Office that his temporary employment would cease on the 20th of the next month.

The financial crisis that this would cause threatened to overwhelm Patrick and my mother. With a month to go before his salary would come to an abrupt end, they had to act with frantic haste to resolve their desperate predicament. In the event they were forced to act so precipitately that his son Richard only became aware of their move after it had happened. The day before their final departure from The Cottage, he wrote from his preparatory school: 'When are you going to move to Fron Wen and where is it?'

Shortly after registration of their change of name, Patrick and my mother had somehow established contact with a wealthy landowner in North Wales, Clough Williams-Ellis, who owned a number of cottages on his extensive estates which he let to selected tenants. Williams-Ellis was a remarkable man: imaginative architect, profound scholar, and pioneer conservationist, who saved many of the most beautiful parts of Snowdonia from despoliation by electricity pylons, holiday homes and retirement bungalows. He was also a generous patron of the arts, and many of his properties were leased to painters and writers. Possibly a benevolent mutual acquaintance arranged an introduction. At any rate, opportunity suddenly presented itself for them to begin their lives anew.

On 19 September Patrick rose early to begin the long journey to inspect one of Williams-Ellis's cottages which appeared suitable, cheap rent being its principal attraction. Patrick had prepared a list of points to check on arrival: 'Hens? Ducks?'; 'Ask Mr W-E abt security of tenure at the end of 3 years – possibility of buying'; 'Do the local people speak English'. After all but missing the 9.10 train from Paddington, Patrick's day-long journey was punctuated by fears of finding himself on the wrong train or missing a change. He received a momentary fright when faced by 'horrifying "All out" crisis at Gob-something', from which he was saved by a pair of kindly women. Later on he mistakenly leaped out at Machynlleth, but fortunately 'error pointed out by kind porter in stage Welsh dialect'.

Such mishaps customarily befell Patrick when let loose in the wide world. His fellow-passengers proved consistently helpful and friendly. A particularly interesting companion was a naval officer, who in the course of conversation remarked that in early life he had served under sail, while his grandfather had been First Lieutenant of the *Implacable* during the Napoleonic Wars. Patrick made a mental note to check in James's *Naval History* whether the *Implacable* had fought at Trafalgar.

It turned out that the friendly Captain knew Williams-Ellis, of whom he disapproved and 'advises care'. He described Portmeirion, where Patrick was to stay overnight, as 'a fine old house (not village) bought by W-E, who has added mad châlets, campanile, sculpture & runs place as hotel'. Unfortunately this exchange concluded by Patrick's becoming 'hideously embarrassed' when the amicable Captain offered to exchange cards. Lacking one of his own, he was awkwardly obliged to 'announce name verbally'. The peril of perpetrating a social gaffe appeared omnipresent. Though he longed to eat the sandwiches and pear with which my mother had provided him, he could not bring himself to do so in front of other passengers.

Despite these minor worries the journey proved a pleasurable experience, and Patrick became entranced as the train crossed the Severn. 'Hills commence – 1,000 ft peaks at hand. Grow excited – wish for M. Country blotted out by drifting rain . . . Wales visible from time to time – gorges – torrents – am gratified.' Only that morning he had been travelling on a 49 bus up Oakley Street and Gloucester Road, and here he was passing through a wild terrain of mountains and forests. Outside in the corridor he could hear schoolchildren and farm workers speaking in Welsh, and passing beside the Dovey estuary his sharp eye observed a cormorant flying over the trees. Just after eight o'clock in the evening the train passed Harlech, where he observed standing on the platform a figure whom he marked down as the original 'Man of H[arlech]': actually the stationmaster.

His destination, the little railway station of Penrhyndeudraeth, presented a marked contrast to crowded Paddington.

> No one there. Cause pretty ticket collector (in pinafore) to get cab. Pretty t-c 'phones in Welsh. Ask if I can send wire. (For M., comfort of). No. Cab arrives. Wild (? drunken) driver – alarmed, but comforted by thoughts of insurance. Reach Port M. through sudden, half seen maze of old buildings. Find swagger type [smart] pub. Secretly alarmed. Am expected. Taken to cottage in grounds. Pleasant room. Fantastic view of estuary with lights – quite dark. Lose way back to house.

Portmeirion was Williams-Ellis's most exotic architectural achievement: a complete town constructed in a wild variety of architectural styles. Though it may be offensive to the taste of modernists, the overall effect is picturesque, and confirms the general rule that unified vision is one of the prime prerequisites of artistic achievement. Portmeirion is unlike anywhere else in the world, resembling nothing so much as a fantasy Mediterranean town brought to life from a painting by Rex Whistler.

Patrick managed to make his way back, and discovered the dining-room. 'Dinner – cool, but good. Have baseless suspicion that place is haunted by rich lechers – many cars parked. Coffee. Alarming crowd in lounge stares. Get cigarettes. Retire, but lose room. Find it. Eat pear. Bed. Write to and think of M. Empty bed in room alas. God bless xxx.'

After breakfast Patrick telephoned Mr Williams-Ellis, who arranged to receive him at 11.30. Having risen unnecessarily early, Patrick killed time by leafing through copies of the *Spectator* and *New Statesman*. In the latter he found an article critical of the Foreign Office and Ministry of Economic Warfare, which advocated the establishment of a permanent Political Intelligence Department. He guessed that the author must be 'obviously someone inside' – but how very remote now appeared that world of intrigue which had preoccupied him over much of the past four years.

The cab appeared and took him to Williams-Ellis's picturesque old manor house, Plas Brondanw. The interview began rather strangely. 'Ringing the bell produced little result, but I was let in finally by a vague young man, who ushered me into the presence. C. W-E was sitting with his back to the room – did not turn round, only muttered. A friendly hairy sort of a dog was welcoming, but this palled after a while, and I fell to inspecting the spines of books – some rather fine – he has written a good deal on architecture and such. At last he got up and exclaimed; I think he quite genuinely had not seen me. He was apologetic and civil. He is 60, tall, rather [illegible] hair, something after the style of Ld Russel [Bertrand Russell], a gentleman, but a terrific (and I mean terrific) highbrow. Wears curious garments. Lent me a macintosh cape. He drove me furiously a good way over some alarming roads, up into a fantastic valley, pointing out the houses of writers all the way. They breed in these parts.' Among them Williams-Ellis mentioned Bertrand Russell himself, who was contemplating renting a house, 'R[ichard]. Hughes over the way. Bard in village. Playwright further down. Hungarian over the pass.'[1]

The valley was wild and remote beyond conception, especially to one who had spent the past five years in war-torn London. Far from being daunted by the prospect of exile in this far-flung wilderness, at every turn Patrick felt mounting excitement. The setting was of a grandeur and magnificence beyond anything he had anticipated, and the reality of the adventure upon

[1]For exotic characters living or staying in the neighbourhood, cf. Michael Byrne, *Turned Towards the Sun: An Autobiography* (Norwich 2003), pp. 168–70.

which he and my mother were embarking now dawned upon him. In his autobiographical novel *Three Bear Witness*, Patrick vividly recalled his initial impression of Cwm Croesor.

> It was September when I first came into the valley: the top of it was hidden in fine rain, and the enclosing ridges on either side merged into a grey, formless cloud. There was no hint of the two peaks that were shown on the map, high and steep on each side of the valley's head. This I saw from the windows of the station cab as it brought me up the mountainous road from the plains, a road so narrow that in places the car could barely run between the stone walls. All the way I had been leaning forward in my seat, excited and eager to be impressed: at another time the precipices that appeared so frequently on the left hand would have made me uneasy, but now they were proofs of a strange and wilder land, and I was exhilarated.

They arrived at the end of the inhabited part of the valley. The car mounted a steep lane on the right, and drew to a halt before the garden gate of a tiny white cottage. There was too much for him to jot down in his notebook, and he reserved a full description for his return to Chelsea. Though the cottage and its setting remain unchanged after more than half a century, Patrick's own description cannot be bettered.

> I did not expect my cottage when the car stopped [explains Pugh (i.e. Patrick) in the novel]: 'indeed, I thought that the driver had pulled up again to open a cattle-gate. We had been climbing steadily the whole length of the road and now as I got out of the car the cloud grew cold and damp in wisps on my face. The cottage stood on the mountain-side, square and on a little dug-in plateau that almost undermined the road. It was the smallest habitation I had ever seen; a white front with a green door between two windows, and a grey roof the size of a sheet.[1]

Though the house was tinier even than Patrick had anticipated, his spirits soared as he gazed about him. The spectacle was magnificent, and is beautifully and accurately accorded its due in his novel.

'. . . I was not prepared for the splendour that stood high all round when I came out for my walk. The cloud had gone and there was the soaring mass of the Saeth leaping up into the clear sky. It was a mountain as a child draws a mountain, a sharp, stabbing triangle. I had studied the maps, but the

[1] *Three Bear Witness*, p. 8.

contours and figures, particularly the figures, had deceived me; I had expected hills, little more, and here was a mountain. Its height in figures meant nothing: there was the majesty, the serene isolation, that you expect (if Switzerland is your criterion) only from ten thousand feet and more. Indeed, I have seen many quite well-known peaks, high above the snow-line, without a tenth part of the Saeth's nobility.

'There was no snow on the Saeth, of course, but there was something very nearly as striking – great runs of shale, beds of it tilted up to ferocious slopes, and the lines of its fall.

'The strong impression of grandeur never faded; the more I saw the mountain the finer I thought it. It was incredibly changeable: on some days it would be a savage menacing dark mountain, a sombre weight – I had almost said a threat – in the sky. Then in the evening, some evenings, when each rock on the skyline was etched hard and distinct against the sky, the Saeth took on a quality of remoteness, almost of unreality. The Saeth in the moonlight, like something out of El Greco's mind; the Saeth with snow; the hard triangular peak of the Saeth ripping through the tearing driven clouds from the sea – with a mountain like that outside your window, you are not lonely.

'The rest of the valley was in proportion. It lay deep, wide and smooth between its long enclosing ridges and the stream wound through the brilliant green of the water meadows. There was the bottom of the valley, green, and with a narrow long strip of fields; then the gentle slopes, still green but with more brown mixed in the colour, a long, horizontal wall and then the slopes rose faster, more and more barren, to boulders, shale and at last to the barbarity of naked rock. Everywhere there were walls, dry-stone walls criss-crossing, walls of enormous length, running up impossible slopes. The whitish spots that I saw on the far slopes, peppered the length and breadth of it, right up to the top, were sheep; they could be heard, if one stopped to listen, and their voices came from every quarter, drifting on the wind.

'There were the farms, with neat squares of wall by them and a few trees: the one I had been to last night was just under me – absurd to have mistaken the way. They had dove-grey roofs that blended with the outcropping rock; one at least I stared at for several minutes before I saw it at all.

'Then there was the huge extent of air. I do not know how it is, but this feeling of the air as a thing with dimensions is peculiar to mountainous countries. Between me and the dark curved ridge that closed the top of the valley there was perhaps three miles of air, perfectly clear, but somehow evident. It was keen, fine air, a pleasure to breathe.'[1]

[1] *Three Bear Witness*, pp. 8–9, 17–19.

*

Anyone who visits Cwn Croesor today will recognise the accuracy of Patrick's description: the only change being his substitution of the name 'Saeth' for that of the Cnicht, whose soaring peak frowns across the valley towards the massive height of Moelwyn Mawr on the opposite side of the valley, at whose foot nestles the little white cottage, Fron Wen.[1]

Williams-Ellis waited patiently while Patrick conducted a minute inspection of the interior of the house. It consisted of two small rooms to the left and right of the front door, with a low storeroom at the back in the space where the roof sloped down to the ground. Immediately inside the door a ladder-like wooden stair afforded access to a low loft. Not for nothing was Patrick a devotee of *Robinson Crusoe* and *Treasure Island*. He drew a careful plan of the interior, downstairs and upstairs, with all measurements carefully noted, and specified details of such basic facilities as it contained. The house was not only tiny, but lacked every modern facility. There was neither electricity, running water, nor telephone. Far from being daunted, he regarded these deficiencies as a challenge. He noted with satisfaction that the roof had been newly repaired, and that the inside was 'quite spotless'.

His inspection of the interior completed, he conducted a circuit of the ground outside, compiling a rough map of the land about the house from the road passing just above to the River Croesor below. Finally he made a cursory sketch of the upper end of the valley, identifying scattered cottages, waterfalls, and the distant quarry to which the road ascended. On his return, Williams-Ellis told him that he could acquire the use of further land by arrangement with Mr Roberts, who held the tenancy of the farm immediately below. Potatoes and milk could also be bought there. No problem was envisaged regarding rough shooting on the mountain slopes, though he believed there was little to be found beyond hares and some grouse.

They then drove back to Williams-Ellis's house near the entrance to the valley, where Patrick was given an excellent scrap lunch. Afterwards he was shown round the place, which 'has some wonderful things. I should think he must be pretty rich.' He was also introduced to some of the family, but 'didn't like them'. Throughout his visit Patrick conducted himself much as he was to make Richard Temple behave during his stay at the grand house of Churleigh. 'All this time I had been showing off madly in the highbrow way, and I think I managed to keep my end up . . . I flattered him a lot.'

Altogether the expedition had proved a brilliant success. The lease was agreed, and Patrick gave Williams-Ellis a year's rent – the princely sum of

[1] Not the least of Williams-Ellis's public-spirited acts was the purchase of both mountains to protect them from potential spoilation (Jones, *Clough Williams-Ellis*, p. 45).

£8. Evidently he had made a good impression, for his host showed him a letter from another prospective tenant who had enclosed the rent in advance. 'We have been very lucky indeed,' he reflected.

Returned to his lodgings in Portmeirion, Patrick dined and set about compiling a meticulous inventory of household goods they would need to bring. Its contents illustrate the subsistence level of existence which lay before them. Necessities ranged from chamberpots, hurricane lamp, candles, lantern '(for M.)', tin bath, and flatiron, to '2 Primuses – meths.', 'Elsan fluid or whatever it is', 'clothes pegs & line', and 'spade, mattock, hoe, hook, axe (small)'. Last came the essential 'Packing cases for books, china etc.'

Poverty was both a curse and source of great embarrassment for Patrick. But the worry it caused him was entirely subsumed by his love for my mother, romantic excitement at the challenge which lay before them, and a conviction that together they could overcome every obstacle. Just before going to sleep, he addressed this touching note to her:

> As I shall go early in the morning I arranged to pay my bill tonight, to be called, and to have a cab by eight. But Oh M., the bill was £3.17.3 and I only had £4 and some silver – 10/- left now, and I don't know whether the cab is paid for, or my packed lunch, and there are the tips. Why wasn't I bold with cheque-book? But it is so dreadful to have one refused. Time, of course, will pass, and these things will cope with themselves, but just now they are a little horrid.
>
> I am going to put out the light now, dear M. I do wish you were here – have wished all day, for long periods at a stretch. Will you meet me, M.? Telegram with time [of the train's arrival at Paddington] was a powerful hint.
>
> M., I doubt whether our gurt [Devonian for 'great'] bed will get into Fron Wen.
>
> I am growing sentimental, you perceive. God bless. xxx.

FOURTEEN

'The smallest habitation I had ever seen'

> I cannot express what Satisfaction it was to me, to come into my old Hutch, and lie down on my Hammock-bed: This little wandering Journey, without a settled Place of Abode, had been so unpleasant to me, that my own House, as I called it to myself, was a perfect Settlement to me, compared to that; and it rendered everything about me so comfortable, that I resolved I would never go a great way from it again, while it should be my Lot to stay on the Island.
>
> (Daniel Defoe, *Robinson Crusoe*)

Their great adventure had begun. Patrick and my mother had little choice in the matter of their departure, and behind them lay a chapter of their lives marked by distressing circumstances from which they were determined to escape. At the age of thirty they accepted this dramatic relaunching of their lives as the adventure it was to prove, and left The Cottage with few regrets. Sadly some treasured possessions had to be abandoned. Ten years later, Patrick told me that he sold his precious collection of Samurai swords at the end of the war in consequence of his revulsion against Japanese war crimes. It is hard to see why this discovery occurred at so late a stage of the conflict, and a more likely motive lay in their desperate need to raise money.[1]

The day of their departure proved somewhat chaotic and lively. A further indication that the move represented a dramatic fresh start in his life is the fact that Patrick, for what appears to have been the first time in his life, began keeping a journal. A week after their arrival at Fron Wen, he recalled the confusion of that momentous day:

> *The move was something of a nightmare: it began with a rather vague packing about*

[1] He had after all bought them at a time when Japanese atrocities in China were arousing worldwide outrage, though it is true that he was then very young.

the first of the month, and reached a crescendo on the evening of the fifth. On Saturday [6 October 1945] *morning at eight, Burchett's men arrived with the van. There were three of them, one large stout elderly man – Charles, the foreman, one old frail man who packed the china beautifully, complaining most of the time, and a young, cocky, rather familiar fellow who did not care for work much. After a strenuous morning's work everything was stowed away very skillfully, two armchairs were fixed on the back for us, and Mrs. Guinea* [their pet guinea pig] *was put into a covered basket.*

We were given an hour for lunch, and we pottered about The Cottage, locking the powder closet and fastening the windows. Then we went to the Good Intent [a public house in Lombard Street], *which fed us on fiery curry, then from there to Burchett's yard* [in Glebe Place]. *The van was not quite ready, so we wandered down Old Church Street, nearly bought an unusually fine copper kettle for £2, and wandered back. They put us in the back of the van (rather like cattle) and we set out just after 2 o'c.*

The unbought kettle adds a poignant touch, indicating at once the couple's poverty and their romantic plans for self-sufficiency in wild Wales. What was to prove a decisive embarkation in Patrick's literary odyssey had begun, and he and my mother regarded the prospect with delectable anticipation. Accompanied by their trusty guinea pig, they greeted every stage of the journey with gleeful curiosity.

From the very first it was wildly bumpy. Mrs G's basket was hung on to Mary's chair's arm, for safety. When we had left High Barnet the country began to show, and we cheered up – not that we were feeling low about The Cottage, because we do not feel we have really left it, what with the P[arent]*s and its being in my name: besides, we had been feeling so keyed up about the move ever since Burchett said he would do it that the actual movement was uncommonly exhilerating* [sic].

Having sold their house in Devonshire, following the departure my grandparents took over the lease of The Cottage from Patrick although he continued for some time as the tenant in name. I never learned the reason for their making this choice, but suspect that, partially estranged as they were from their daughter and with their son working permanently in the Sudan, they wished to have ready access to my sister and me, my father's home in the country lying within easy access of London. We regularly travelled up to stay with them, when they treated us to visits to museums, pantomimes, theatres, and other delights.

Meanwhile Patrick and my mother continued on their journey:

We passed some lovely villages strung along the road in Hertfordshire: many of them seemed made for [Jane Austen's] *Emma, but there was one – a small town whose name I forget – that filled the bill almost exactly.*

Time went on quickly enough, but the jolting continued, and we got very tired of people grinning at us from cars behind. I suppose that our huge tin bath aroused their mirth. As it grew dark busloads of working people came along behind us; their headlights were unpleasant and the apelike hootings (silent in the din, but obvious) and gesticulations were worse. M. minded less, but I seethed, feeling as undemocratic as possible.

Here as so often Patrick quaintly betrayed his lifelong fear and dislike of the unruly crowd. The irrationality is patent, for how could he have detected 'apelike hootings' which were 'silent in the din'?! At the same time the reader should make considerable allowance for the sardonic humour and self-mockery which pervades his journals and letters. Nevertheless throughout his life he felt intensely vulnerable among strangers, and instinctively feared the unpredictable reactions of what he considered the rough insensitive masses. In his eyes they possessed the same disconcerting unpredictability and lack of control which alarmed him in children. Though he had been living in London for some years, the atmosphere in Chelsea at that time was very much that of a sleepy village, and The Cottage, set back from the quiet street with its delightful little garden, effectively lived up to its bucolic name.

My parents' stop for the night was at a town whose literary associations nurtured particular appeal for Patrick, a lifelong devotee of the hugely learned and robustly self-confident Dr Johnson: 'We came to Lichfield by nightfall. Charles enquired for rooms for us, but found nothing, so we went off by ourselves. The Goat's Head would have none of us, nor would the Angel – we had left our luggage in the van.'

The atmosphere of romantic adventure was enhanced by the evident suspicion that they were an unmarried couple.

At last we found the policeman in the market square we [who] *directed us to some pub or other, and in looking for it we chanced across the George, which took us in, a little doubtfully at first, but more wholeheartedly when it found out that we did not mind his single rooms. They gave us quite a good dinner – excellent beer, from Burton, only a few miles away. We went early to bed, whispering in each other's room, and feeling quite unmarried and furtive.*[1]

[1]When Maturin established himself in an independent residence after his marriage to Diana Villiers, 'there were also times when it added a certain not wholly disagreeable air of intrigue to the connection' (*The Ionian Mission*, p. 11).

Right early in the morning we got up – Charles had said that he wanted to start by eight – and ran down to breakfast. It was not ready, so we walked about the city for a little while. Dr J's house – a wonderful saddler's shop, several admirable 18th c. houses – but the Cathedral, which I had seen plainly from my window, was not to be found.

Breakfast was quite extraordinarily fine. An amiable, pretty wench gave us porridge, eggs and bacon, hot rolls, toast and marmalade, and ample butter: she apologized for there being only tea. The night before I had thought the bill a little high – £1.17.3 – but the breakfast alone was worth it.

Excellent inn, the George, plainly the best in Lichfield, and staffed with good, kindly people. What an immense difference civility in an inn does make. The George, we noticed, has a grand Assembly room. Very Miss Austen-ish.

As ever, Patrick found security in the eighteenth-century refuge which he had discovered during his vulnerable adolescence.

The van started at 8.30 (breakfast had made us a little late) and the jolting began again – rather worse this time.

We passed Shrewsbury, saw the Wrekin (I'm not sure which the Wrekin was, but there were several uncommon hills) and reached Llangollen. Going into Wales that way you see the change between the countries suddenly and most decidedly – gratifying. Then we walked about looking for lunch, but neither the Hand nor the Royal would feed us before 1.30, so, having admired the bridge and the Dee, we went back to the van and picnicked.

From Llangollen to Bala, there turning off for Ffestiniog. Bala looked horrible, and its inhabitants worse. The road grew rougher, and Charles more uncertain of the way. We took a turning that led us over an abominable road under Arenig: we were jerked hither and yon, smothered with dust and fumes. M. began to look pale. At last we came down a hill, began to stop, and then we at the back heard an ugly crash. Charles' foot had slipped off the brake on to the accelerator and we had gone through a slate tombstone wall outside a cottage. Hubbub in Welsh – pleasant young man – avaricious old woman – fuss in general. Started again. Charles went fifty yards and glided firmly into a stone wall. Despair mingled with relief at being able to stretch our legs and gape at the mountains around Snowdon. The fine young man (soldier on leave) helped with the repairs, brought enormous tea – farm butter, cakes in profusion – refused all payment, alleging similar kindness from people in London. Opinion of the Welsh character rises 100%.

This was the first of a succession of bizarre incidents which punctuated the journey: a curious prefiguration of numerous occasions when my parents were to prove dangerously vulnerable to motoring accidents which nearly brought their lives to a premature close. However, they felt confident of spending the night in their new home, as the van journeyed smoothly along the road which winds through the beautiful wooded Vale of Ffestiniog. Eventually they arrived at the little village of Penrhyndeudraeth, where they turned north towards the forbidding heights of Snowdonia. After a few miles they reached a point where a side road led to their ultimate destination. The entrance to the valley of Cwm Croesor proved to be blocked by a romantic if impractical pseudo-medieval gatehouse, through which Patrick had earlier passed on his journey to visit the home of their landlord, Clough Williams-Ellis. Typically he had failed to register the obstacle it might present to a larger vehicle.

This gatehouse (today the road regrettably skirts round it) epitomised Williams-Ellis's fondness for erecting picturesque follies: artificial ruins, towers, and extensions to existing buildings, carefully constructed from local stone and slate in order to blend successfully into earlier structures. While providing an appropriately mock-feudal entry to his wild domain lying beyond, it was also intended to deny entrance to vehicles of more than moderate size. Unfortunately this placed the O'Brians' removal van in the uncomfortable situation of the camel attempting to thread the needle's eye, so that they found themselves, their guinea pig, and all their worldly goods firmly jammed within the arch. After every effort to extricate the van in either direction had proved vain, Patrick trudged off two miles to the nearby village of Llanfrothen, where he found a telephone box and made a series of vain attempts to contact Pierce, the local taxi-owner.

After this frustrating failure he returned to the little group forlornly gathered about the trapped vehicle. Darkness was drawing on, and it was essential to find somewhere to spend the night. From the back of the van they lifted down Patrick's trusty motorcycle Panther, and with my mother on the pillion they set off on 'a horrifying voyage' in darkness down the winding narrow road, with its high banks and walls, to Penrhyndeudraeth in order to track down the elusive Pierce. He was nowhere to be found, and the village proved a distinctly unpromising source of assistance, comprising as it did a few scattered houses, no hotel, and an empty police station.

After a while, however, the policeman appeared, and helpfully arranged for a car to drive my parents to Portmeirion on the coast. Patrick had as we know already stayed there, but for my mother the visit was a novel experience. My parents' spirits were cheered. As Patrick noted, 'PortMeirion [*sic*] was quite good fun: it was looking particularly well, and dinner was good.'

Next day found their troubles not yet over. Patrick having characteristically forgotten to order a car for the morning, he and my mother were obliged to endure a tedious wait until noon, when a taxi eventually appeared to take them back to the Cwm Croesor gatehouse (the motorcycle had to be left behind for later collection). There they were delighted to find that Pierce had arranged for a lorry to be driven up to the far side of the gate, into which as they arrived they found their possessions being transferred from the trapped van. The removal men were not in the most cheerful of moods, having slept all night in their vehicle, and manifested evident suspicion that Patrick had somehow anticipated from the outset the successive hazards of their journey.

Pierce had further thoughtfully arranged for a car to transport my parents on the last leg of their journey to their new home, which enabled them to escape the ill-concealed rancour of Charles and his contumacious aides.[1] Their spirits became elated with every mile that brought them further up the long wild valley. On either side the hills increased in height and grandeur until their summits merged into a ceiling of mist, and the fugitive couple felt themselves to be entering a word as remote as might be imagined from the distressing travails and recriminations they had left behind in London. It would not be long before every crag and scree of the broad valley became as familiar to them as the shops and houses of King's Road from Oakley Street to Sloane Square.

At last they came to the point where a small side road ascends the hillside to the right, and drove up to the gate of Fron Wen. The impression conveyed by Patrick's *alter ego* Pugh in *Three Bear Witness* is throughout one of melancholy introspection. During this period of his life Patrick made only occasional literary use of the infectious humour which pervades his great Aubrey–Maturin series. Fortunately 'cheerfulness was always breaking in' upon the real Patrick, and the succession of part-comical, part-distressing accidents which had bedevilled the journey continued to afford him a mixture of frustration and amusement. Having apparently overlooked the useful precaution of arranging for collection of a key to the front door, the problem of entry was resolved by the agility of their driver, who scrambled on to the low roof, climbed through a skylight, and reappeared shortly after, having unbolted the side door. For once Patrick's epithet 'apelike' for working people proved appropriate and complimentary.

Passing into the darkness within, Patrick ruefully discovered that 'I had very much underestimated the value of Fron, and I had got my plan all wrong'. A vivid and accurate description of the interior as it appeared on his first arrival is provided in his novel.

[1] In *Three Bear Witness*, Patrick describes the driver of the car that takes him to the cottage as 'a bull of a man and silent'. Edgar Williams, who was living in the valley at the time, recognises this as a description of Giff Roberts, owner of the garage at Garreg.

> I stared about for a minute and then with a curious flutter of anticipation I walked up the path and in at the green door . . . I found a match and the lamp. The golden light spreading as the lamp warmed showed beams and a wooden ceiling a few inches above my head; the floor was made of huge slate flags, and the moisture stood on them in tiny drops that flattened into wet footprints as I walked. Still with the same odd excitement I took the lamp and explored my dwelling: I found a much better room on the left of the front door – two windows and a boarded floor, a comfortable chair and a Turkey rug by the stove. The house was built with stone walls of great thickness and this gave the window-sills a depth and a value in a small room I would not have expected. The far window looked straight out over the valley . . .
>
> Up the ladder-like stairs – I had to hold the treads with one hand while I went up – up the nine flat rungs of this staircase were two A-shaped lofts, made by the sloping sides of the roof and the top of the ceilings below. One had a bed[1] and a window. A lean-to at the back, a coal-hole, and a dreary little lavatory tacked on behind completed the house. It appeared to me incredible that so much could have been packed into that toy box of a house.

Nothing daunted, my parents promptly set about moving into their new home. No sooner had the operation begun than their good humour and ingenuity were taxed by the 'apelike' antics of their Laurel and Hardy removal team: 'When we had viewed the premises and eaten some bully beef, we noticed the driver and his car to be in the ditch. The poor man had been feebly trying to jack himself out for a long time. A red-headed farmer (! Roberts) came to help, and in time we extricated the vehicle with sacks – Mary's idea.'

As the exclamation mark intimated, Harri Roberts (who, as Williams-Ellis had explained to Patrick during his exploratory visit, owned the farm at Croesor Fawr in the valley immediately below), was to become a close acquaintance – indeed, a warm and generous friend. It was appropriate, as Patrick and my mother were to discover on innumerable occasions, that their first meeting was occasioned by Roberts's putting himself out to help a couple whose attempts to surmount the rigours of wild Wales he observed throughout their stay with wry amusement.

> *Then the first lorry of stuff came – feverish activity – apparent impossibility of getting half of it in. The second load brought the bed. We were very worried about it,*

[1]The bed is the only fictional addition, being required by the circumstances of the letting in the novel.

but at first sight it had seemed likely that it would go up the stairs; however, Charles, after one abortive attempt stated that it was impossible and left it.

They went away at last, having delivered everything and having, miraculously, broken nothing. The only casualties were the satinwood desk, which was scraped, or rather rubbed, by its confining rope, and Granny's chest, which lost part of a leg.

The afternoon was spent wrestling with the intractable task of compressing their furniture, most of which had previously adorned the spacious three-storeyed Cottage in Chelsea, into the tiny compass of Fron Wen. Though my mother and Patrick were by nature markedly unmaterialistic, throughout their lives they entertained deep sentimental attachment to their possessions. While this had little or nothing do with their financial value (only *in extremis* did they ever sell objects of material worth), the tiny cabin in Cwm Croesor housed many precious items. In particular my mother's beautiful furniture evoked memories of prelapsarian childhood days at Appledore, while Patrick's skilfully garnered collection of seventeenth- and eighteenth-century books afforded him a gateway into remote regions of imaginative exploration.

After this upheaval Patrick returned in the lorry to the gateway of Cwm Croesor, from which the disgruntled removal men had finally managed to extricate their van. He travelled with them to Penrhyndeudraeth, where he recovered his motorcycle. The return journey provided him with his first experience of the problems of communication in the valley. The road was so rough that it proved almost impossible for the motorcycle to travel in top gear, while the final ascent to Fron Wen required the ailing creature to operate in bottom gear, causing an indecently rowdy clatter which dismayed Patrick as it shattered the silence of the empty valley.

But it was when circumstances appeared at their most dire that Patrick's good humour and resourcefulness tended to become most manifest. The scene is best described in his own words: 'One of the first things we did was to survey the bed and the staircase. It seemed an obvious possibility, and at the second attempt we got the divan three quarters of the way up. We were congratulating ourselves like anything when it stuck hard. However, by cunning tilts and thrusts it came all the way up. It was the most distinct triumph, and it looked surprisingly well (being so low) in our bedroom.'

A still greater struggle was involved in attempting to get The Cottage's metal air-raid shelter through the front door. It might be thought strange that they should have troubled to bring so cumbersome and weighty an object with them, but the ever-resourceful couple converted it into an invaluable prop which served a multitude of functions, ranging from dining table to ping-pong. As Patrick proudly observed: 'It is an immense boon, the shelter:

life would have been much more makeshift without it. 30/- for a great solid, unshakeable thing like that is cheap enough.' Visiting Fron Wen not long ago, I was touched to learn that its rusting remains yet survive, deteriorating in the farmyard below.

Having squeezed their belongings into the house, that evening my parents descended to visit the farm at Croesor Fawr. Barking sheep-dogs greeted their arrival, but within they received a gratifyingly warm welcome. Harri Roberts and his wife Bessie were away, she having been taken to the hospital in Portmadoc to be delivered of a baby. The scene which greeted them held nothing of that cold and cruel twentieth century which they had left behind, and deeply appealed to Patrick's sense of historical atmosphere.

> *We were taken into the lovely kitchen – fine dressers covered with willow pattern – long table that would fetch £100 in London – ugly, gleaming grandfather* [clock] *(very wide face – 19thC.) – leaping fire – vast stone floor. We sat down in state chairs by the fire. Elderly rustic (26 years in valley) apparently quite happy on bench by the wall. Conversation hampered by mutual incomprehension – old lady's English sketchy – she apologized for it. M. thought of apology for not speaking their language in their country, but did not bring it out. Milk produced and promised for the future. We were exceedingly pleased with the farm.*

In *Three Bear Witness* Patrick describes this scene almost exactly as it occurred in reality.

Fortunately the first ten days after their arrival were blessed with gloriously warm weather. Then on Sunday, 21 October (Trafalgar Day) the fine weather broke, bringing a foretaste of just how grimly harsh climatic conditions could be in North Wales. All that night it rained heavily, and the next morning the Croesor river could be heard roaring like a gale gusting through a forest, while waterfalls appeared overnight traced in silver down the steep sides of the valley. The third member of the household, Mrs Guinea, was brought in from her hutch outside and placed upon a windowsill, where she crouched contentedly watching her master and mistress at work. From time to time she was fed with pudding, which she devoured with evident pleasure.

By Tuesday torrents of rain came tearing up the valley from the sea with a ferocity which sent water coursing beneath the front door and spreading across the stone-flagged floor. Patrick hastily set to work sawing slates in an attempt to create a miniature flood barrier, but his handiwork proved only partially successful. Later he did succeed in creating a miniature brick dam which at least kept external water at bay. Winter lay ahead, and a remorseless battle against the Welsh weather had begun. A wild wind howled angrily up the length of Cwm Croesor, and the rain drenched down in driving torrents and spitting gusts which Patrick felt made even the hardy mountain sheep look depressed.

Despite this there was no checking the young couple's resilience and enthusiasm. A break in the weather permitted a quick climb up the mountainside behind the house. They inspected a little waterfall, where Patrick decided that a pool could be converted into a fine place for swimming. His imaginative ingenuity promptly set to work, picturing an improvised dam created from boulders, and he even contemplated using dynamite to enlarge the pool. His keen eye for nature, always restlessly observant, noted a magpie (rare, as he commented, on such exposed terrain), a kestrel, and small flocks of yellowhammers. The grimmer aspect of the wild was evidenced by a dead sheep, and two rams locked together by their horns, who had pathetically starved to death in consequence of their ritual combat.

Despite a violent south-west wind tearing along the mountainside, my mother and Patrick scrambled higher up the steep slopes of Moelwyn Mawr, until they gained a point where they could gaze out over a vast prospect extending beyond the other side of the mountain, with the sheen of the sea glimmering in the distance. A few days later they climbed the precipitous peak on the opposite side of the valley. Patrick took his journal with him, in which he recorded triumphantly: 'Monday 15th Oct. 45 We are on top of the Cnicht. 4.15.'

Although within days Chelsea was fast becoming a fading memory, such scattered items of private and public news as reached the couple were eagerly read and discussed. A packet of sugared almonds and Turkish Delight (unbelievable luxuries in those days of extreme austerity) arrived from their thoughtful friend Walter Greenway, who was then serving in Cairo. Jack Christopher, their OSS colleague while they were working for PWE who had returned to the States where he became an assistant professor of history at Rochester University, sent a parcel of dried figs and not long after another containing a large pot of jam and other delicacies.

The jam had been provided by a Mrs Koren, to whom Patrick composed appropriate thanks.

Couplets in favour of Mrs W. Koren, who sent (per JBC) jam to us in time of dearth:

All Attic virtues, beauty, wisdom, wit,
Take what you will, she doth excel in it.
All these and yet one more th'Atlantic dame
Hath to illume her noble spouse's name.
Mark there the Greek with Chian wine and oil
Comes bearing gifts, and see how vain his toil.
Yet here Transpontine Ceres freely sends
Imprison'd comfits, Polemarchus' blends,
And reaps not fear nor anger (see above)
But grateful intercessions and our love.
The pallid bread grows purple, and the dew
Of anxious gleed bespreads each wizen'd brow
Encrimson'd mouths gape sated at the last.
Such admirable tins of jams as these
Are apt to promote international pese.

Still more remote than The Cottage appeared Patrick's and my mother's wartime work with Political Warfare Executive. A two-day-old copy of *The Times* arrived, bearing news of the French general election of 21 October. French politics, in which they had been so deeply immersed during the previous three years, already belonged to a swiftly evaporating past. My mother mistook the deputy Louis Marin for an elderly Communist leader, and had to be reminded that he was in fact a staunch Gaullist. He had been viciously attacked by the Communist Party in 1940 for advocating resistance to Hitler, then Stalin's staunch ally. Consistently a moderate conservative in politics,[1] Patrick was delighted with the electoral success of the Mouvement Républicain Populaire, whom he regarded as 'a thoroughly decent lot'. He chafed a little at finding himself so far removed from events and resolved to write to his former Free French colleague Armand Goëau-Brissonnière, who had returned to Paris, for more exact information. However Patrick was never one to dwell inordinately on the past, nor was he greatly concerned with contemporary politics. Close interest in public events was already waning, and became thenceforward at best intermittent.

[1]As Stephen Maturin observes: 'I have had such a sickening of men in masses, and of causes, that I would not cross the room to reform parliament or prevent the union or to bring about the millennium. I speak only of myself, mind – it is my own truth alone – but man as part of a movement or a crowd is indifferent to me. He is inhuman. And I have nothing to do with nations or nationalism. The only feelings I have – for what they are – are for men as individuals; my loyalties, such as they may be, are to private persons alone' (*Master and Commander*, p. 147).

A much more interesting event in Cwm Croesor was the return from hospital of Mrs Roberts, with her new baby boy Alun. My mother at once went down to the farm to admire the new arrival, and again received a warm reception.

Within a fortnight or so of their arrival the little household at Fron Wen had settled down to a pleasing if laborious daily round. As Patrick remarked: 'We did nothing much today except live, which takes a lot of time here, though we are getting into a routine, and a very pleasant one, too.'

For Patrick, with his intense love and understanding of the natural world, Cwm Croesor appeared as enchanted a refuge as the happy valley of Johnson's *Rasselas*.

'This morning no less than four ravens flew over Fron, clamouring. Later two came back, plainly talking: the front bird (a hen, if the word is applicable to a raven, from her higher voice) went Kraak kraak kraak, and the other replied Krawk-krawk. I heard them even when they had gone out of sight beyond the Cnicht ridge. When there is no wind our valley is full of sound: the moo of a cow down by the water rings like a trumpet.'

He conducted one of his repairs on the stove and my mother baked some delicious cinnamon rolls. (She was a marvellous cook, with a brilliant gift for improvisation.) After supper in what Patrick termed grandly or humorously 'the drawing room' they listened to Mozart on the gramophone, which helped him to overcome his intense irritation at the contents of an 'impertinent' letter just received from his former wife. Never idle, he turned to adjusting their grandfather clock, whose regular tick and sonorous chime acted as melodic heartbeat to the isolated dwelling.

While establishing themselves in their snug refuge made incessant demands on time and energy, they had continually before them in their minds the long dreamed of plan to re-establish Patrick's literary career, which had fallen entirely into abeyance since his arrival in London five years earlier. Before leaving London he and my mother had worked against time to complete his book on voyages, and before their departure it was delivered with high expectations to Curtis Brown, his literary agent.

At last all appeared to be moving promisingly and on 23 November, just over a month after their arrival, Patrick recorded in high excitement: 'A day to be marked with a white stone . . . the post came. I opened a letter from Curtis Brown with some trepidation. Saw with resignation that Chatto had turned down the book of voyages, then with unseemly joy that a new firm, Home and van Thal had accepted it – £100 advance, 10% 3000, 15% 5000, 20% thereafter. How very pleasant and encouraging.' The contract itself arrived on 3 December, making that Christmas a very special one.

Pencil self-portrait of Patrick, sketched *c.*1937

elow left) Official passport photo of ıtrick O'Brian taken 23 June 1937

elow right) Patrick at Locarno 1937, when he was working as guide for the Workers' Travel ssociation. The photograph was ter used by his first wife Elizabeth divorce proceedings in 1945

Frieda and Howard Wicksteed,
Mary's mother and father

Appledore, the North Devon fishing village (*c.* 1798 by Thomas Girtin, Courtauld Gallery), where Mary's parents bought their house Staddon following Howard's recovery from his wounds during World War I

Lundy, visible from the grounds of Staddon, was Mary's favourite place outside Appledore, and the scene of her first meeting with Dimitry, her future husband

(*Left*) Count Dimitry Tolstoy-Miloslavsky, refugee from the Russian Revolution, who married Mary in 1934

(*Above right*) Mary and Nikolai (aged one) in May 1936 at Staddon
(*Left*) Mary in the Tyrol, 1938. Having spent their honeymoon there in 1934, Mary and Dimitry returned in 1938 to help Dimitry recover from a bout of pleurisy
(*Below*) Nikolai at Staddon in 1938, listening to his mother first telling him about Patrick: 'I have a friend who is a writer'

Sketch of Miss Potts by Patrick. Miss Potts had been a wedding gift from Mary's elder brother Binkie at the time of her first marriage to Dimitry

The Cottage, Chelsea: Miss Potts at work (pencil sketch by Patrick drawn during World War II)

Sketch by Patrick, *c.* 1940-41: Miss Potts, owl (Patrick) and the landlord of the Black Lion, Chelsea, where the ambulance unit in which Patrick and my mother served during the Blitz forgathered

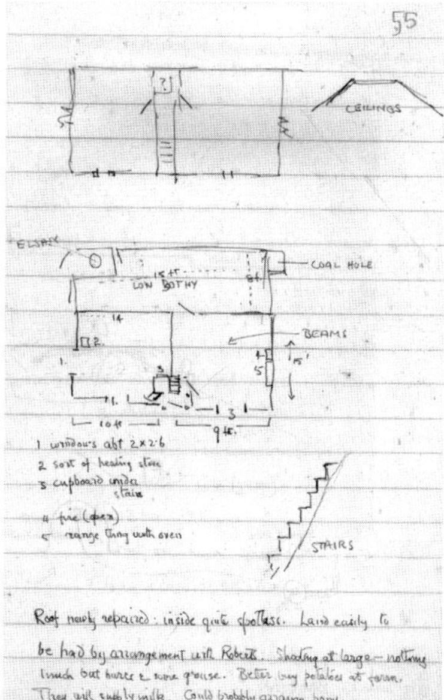

(*Top*) Patrick's fondness for doodling: a whimsical fancy from one of his rough notebooks from the early 1950s

(*Middle*) Page of Patrick's notes from his 1950s notebooks

(*Right*) Sketch drawn in September 1945 by Patrick of the interior of Fron Wen

The pseudo-medieval gatehouse at the entrance to the valley of Cwm Croesor, in which the O'Brians' removal van stuck at their arrival on 6 October 1945

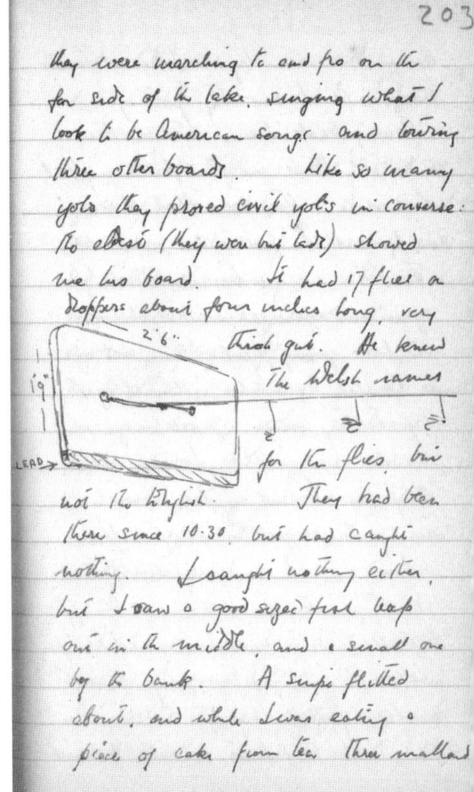

203

they were marching to and fro on the far side of the lake, singing what I took to be American songs and towing three otter boards. Like so many yobs they proved civil yobs in converse: the eldest (they were but lads) showed me his board. It had 17 flies on droppers about four inches long, very thick gut. He knew the Welsh names for the flies, but not the English. They had been there since 10.30, but had caught nothing. I caught nothing either, but I saw a good sized fish leap out in the middle, and a small one by the bank. A snipe flitted about, and while I was eating a piece of cake from tea three mallard

(*Above*) Fron Wen, where Patrick and Mary lived after World War II, in Cwm Croesor, Snowdonia

(*Right*) Patrick's description of the manner of fishing with an otter board (*estyllen*)

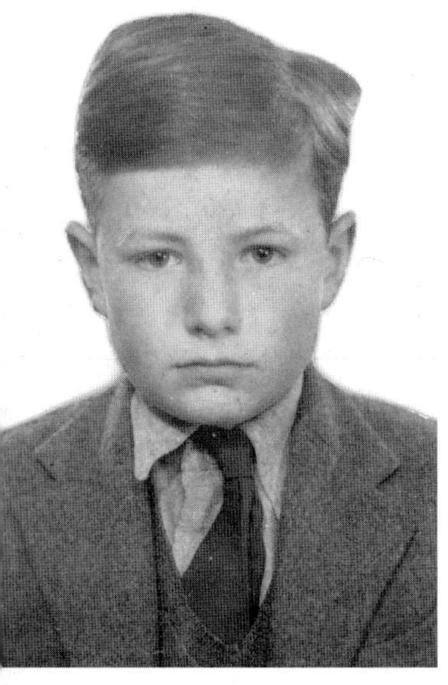

(*Above*) Patrick's son Richard Russ, *c.* 1947 (this photograph kept by Mary, who was devoted to him)
(*Right*) Captain Jack Jones, Master of the Ynysfor Hunt. Greatly admired by Patrick for his skill and leadership, he was probably a model for Jack Aubrey

Moelwyn Bank, the house in which Patrick and my mother lived from 1948 to 1949, showing the peak of the Cnicht above the left-hand gable

Collioure, postcard sent by Patrick to Mary on 12th July 1949

Cats of Collioure, whose outré appearance struck Patrick on his arrival at Collioure (crayon sketch by Willy Mucha)

The festival proved an unqualified success in every way. 'The goose: this noble fowl was M's handiwork from beginning to end . . . Christmas Day went very pleasantly indeed. The goose cooked to a turn – ambrosial. I had cut a wooden spoon out of the mahogany table leg for M. Compliant wood to carve.'

Despite their severe financial constraints, there were some luxuries which in those fortunate days remained affordable. 'M's Christmas present to me arrived the other day – Swift (ed. Hawkesworth 1756 4° 12v. calf). It is about four years since we first started trying to buy a good run, but I have not seen so handsome a set anywhere.' The first collected edition of Swift's works, it is indeed a splendid set of eleven volumes bound in contemporary calf, for which a delighted Patrick made room alongside the other resplendent leather-bound sets on his bookshelves.

After Christmas Patrick received encouraging news of his new publisher's apparent enthusiasm for his book: 'B. van Thal desires to get on with the book, say C. Brown. I shall go and see him. But why could he not write?'

On 15 January 1946 Patrick and my mother travelled to London to call on his new publisher, always a magical moment for an author at the outset of his career.

> *Van Thal was a surprise: dark, middle aged businessman with an indefinably scruffy and even bogus air – clothes coupons may have something to do with this. What puzzles me is his oddly uninformed air – can he know his business? A comforting thing is that he has O. Sitwell, C. Bax and Priestly* [sic] *on his list. He wanted the book shorter from the point of view of cost – wants it to be about 15/- rather than 1 gn. Or 30/-. Jettisoned poor Phillips (30,000 words)*[1] *I am sorry for it, but as van T. says we might be able to make a separate book of him. Van T. by the way, thought Phillips dull. M and I looked rather unsuccessfully in the BM for illustrations: I am not sure how they would turn out. Van T. does not think that they have to be strictly relevant – can afford 8. His office smells of paint.*

His exultation at once again finding himself a professional author seems to have led Patrick to accept with remarkable equanimity van Thal's insistence on discarding much of his labours. Disappointment lay ahead, however. In the event van Thal adhered all too literally to the terms of the contract: 'The

[1]Thomas Phillips's account of his voyage in 1693 and 1694 along the coast of Guinea and to Barbados (Awnsham Churchill and John Churchill, eds, *A Collection of Voyages and Travels, Some Now first Printed from Original Manuscripts, Others Now first Published in English* (London, 1732), vi, pp. 171–239). Patrick carefully annotated it in pencil, marking passages of especial interest and others to be omitted.

Publishers shall publish the said work at their own expense before Christmas 1947 . . . A sum of £100 . . . payable as to £50 . . . on May 1st 1946 and £50 . . . on day of first publication.' For various reasons (Patrick's journal conveys the impression that van Thal did not attach such importance to the book as he at first believed), publication was postponed until the last moment in the autumn of 1947, so that instead of the immediate £100 he had counted on, he had to wait until May, when after deduction of his agent's fee he received a cheque for £45. When weeks passed with no news of the publication date, Patrick wrote one of those insinuating enquiries with which publishers are all too familiar. The response was daunting: 'Van Thal, to whom I wrote asking news, replied with a degree of rudeness that left me speechless, at least metaphorically; he does not care for my prefaces and is causing his reader to prepare a new draft. S. C-B advises me to let him and them cope.'

My parents' natures dovetailed to an extent which I still find it difficult fully to evaluate. Each was lost without the other, even during brief periods of separation, and though they were deeply fond of their children and restricted circle of friends, they were most happy when alone together. With all its hardships, their four years' sojourn in Cwm Croesor offered them many pleasures. Given the physical travails of their existence, it could not be described as an idyll, but few people are so fortunate as to be content with idleness, and Fron Wen provided a haven in which they could remove themselves from the stigma of social condemnation and guilt. Though, as will be seen, Patrick's efforts to resume his *métier* as a writer were to encounter distressing difficulties, he became unconsciously immersed in an intellectual retrenchment and spiritual exploration which perhaps ultimately benefited him more than would have done the immediate success he craved.

They were each in their own way well adapted to cope with their new life. Though brought up in an atmosphere of wealth and privilege, my mother had always revelled in life in the open air, shooting rabbits with her brother in the fields above Appledore, galloping along the sands at Instow, or scrambling among the precipitous rocks of Lundy. Patrick, who had in contrast long been accustomed to poverty and isolation, had already experienced a comparable existence during his year in Suffolk at the beginning of the war. He was naturally resourceful and energetic, and the concept of practical self-sufficiency appealed strongly to his instinctive dislike of dependence on others who might at any moment malign or betray him.

Immediately after their installation at Fron Wen, Patrick insured the family treasures for the then considerable sum of £1,500, which included £500 for his books and £225 for my mother's furs and jewellery. This represented an amount considerably in excess of their total expenditure throughout their four years' stay in Wales, yet despite the unending struggle to maintain a near subsistence level of existence it was not until they finally came to move that they could be persuaded to sell anything. What my parents possessed they loved for their intrinsic worth, and as extensions of their own lives.

Though poverty was an inevitable concomitant of the life they had chosen, even while they fretted over their precariously balanced finances, the harsh struggle for survival provided compensatory stimulation in the form of challenges cheerfully encountered and overcome.

However, there had been a Fall, whose aftermath left a lingering canker which intermittently introduced distress into what might otherwise have been an untroubled Eden. My mother was denied access to her children, extending even to a prohibition on correspondence. Her marriage to Patrick had effected a reconciliation with her parents, who were concerned to help them in their new home. 'M's mama has suddenly taken to offering all sorts of things. I wish they may come,' Patrick noted. But beneath the surface their relationship remained irremediably tense and strained. Patrick felt ill at ease in their company, and resented what he felt to be their underlying coldness towards him.

Although they moved as far as they were capable towards treating them like any daughter and son-in-law the rift remained too great to be more than uneasily patched over. Patrick and my mother felt that they had been condemned out of hand and uncharitably treated as virtual pariahs. My grandfather's refusal to receive Patrick at Staddon earlier in the year was still a deeply wounding memory, and his denial of access to the capital he had placed in trust for my mother a continuing source of resentment. Patrick even went so far as to persuade himself that the decision arose from a deliberate desire to see them driven into exile. A passage in *Richard Temple* bears an application too obvious to require comment:

> The cottage . . . was dark, poky and damp, and it did not have a single one of the amenities of civilised life – but Canon Harler had not been concerned with her convenience: only with getting her firmly anchored at such a distance from his own home that she could not be a burden nor her poverty a reproach to him . . . he had never approved of her marriage and would lend its results no countenance. It is ludicrous to cite earth-closets, well-water and paraffin-lamps, particularly as Mrs. Temple was a pretty woman.[1]

Nor were relations improved by a demand Patrick made of my grandfather, which unfortunately went far to confirm the low esteem in which he held his

[1]*Richard Temple*, p. 48.

unwelcome son-in-law. Patrick was concerned to retain the lease of The Cottage in his own name. For three years he had enjoyed there a life of cultured refinement, fulfilling the highest expectations of his youthful yearnings beyond his wildest anticipation. It seems that even nominal retention of the house gave him a gratifying sense of well-being. Although the estate agents acting for the Church Commissioners swiftly discovered that their tenants had been replaced, they agreed to accept the change without formal ratification. But as the winter months passed by my grandfather found this anomalous arrangement unacceptable, and asked Patrick to accede to his taking over the tenancy. In the middle of March Patrick recorded: 'The post has been dreary recently: another demand from Mr W. about the lease – perfectly reasonable from his point of view, but galling from ours and shall have to acquiesce.' This he did, although my grandfather later told his son only after requesting £200 'key money'.

It is hard to conceive of a more misguided move. My grandfather would very likely have responded without demur had my mother requested the sum as a gift. Patrick's demand appeared a sordid combination of extortion and vanity. My grandfather acted with considerable generosity towards him and my mother, sending them substantial cheques and returning their payment of rates for The Cottage. It is a measure of the blindness of my mother's love for Patrick that she acquiesced in this demand.

All this served to exacerbate the already strained relationship between my mother and her parents, which the passage of time ameliorated but never fully cured. Relations were maintained on a formally cordial basis, which barely concealed an atmosphere of mutual suspicion. I do not recall my grandparents ever inviting Patrick to address them by their Christian names, and certainly at this time Patrick referred to them even in his diary as Mr and Mrs Wicksteed. 'Mrs W. is sending quantities of fine things,' he acknowledged, but went on to complain '(though she is unconsciously offensive about poor Cottage's alleged dirt in every letter – firmness from M.)'. Above all, the social gulf which he was convinced lay between them filled him with apprehensive awe.

Before going to London in January to see van Thal, he pondered: 'I hope it will not offend M's P[arent]s if I stay with Walter [Greenway], but I want to see W. and I rather dread putting foot in it some way at Cottage – need M's support' (my mother was suffering from a bad cold and sore throat). In the event Walter was unable to receive him, but fortunately my mother recovered and she and Patrick stayed with her parents after all. Patrick expressed considerable relief on their return to Fron Wen: 'It is wonderfully pleasant to be in one's own home again. The less said about staying at The Cottage the better: I wonder if I am as disappointing as a son-in-law as Mrs W. is as a mother-in-law? Though indeed I do not consider the relationship as real for a moment.'

My mother's capacity for self-delusion was such that she succeeded in persuading herself that she had been ill treated during her childhood, unconsciously ascribing her deep-rooted feelings of guilt to parental unkindness rather than her own desertion of her husband and abandonment of her children. Patrick understandably encouraged this view, and about 1960 addressed this note to her:

> Dearest M. you brood dark unhappy thoughts: they are essentially baseless & they arise from the old, unfounded impressions of disseminated guilt that your childhood was bathed in – unscrupulous, insecure people can easily make the sweet-natured young feel bad & inadequate, & those feelings can come to the top in moments of stress. I am not much of a creature, whatever in your kindness you may say, but such as I am, with all my faults, I am yours P. x.

During the first winter Patrick suffered recurring worry and distress over relations with Elizabeth and his young son Richard. He harboured increasingly bitter feelings against Elizabeth, who contrary to their agreement at the end of 1944 continued pressing him for money. Three weeks after their arrival, Patrick complained: 'The opposition is continuing her maintenance suit with remarkable effrontery: a beastly affidavit came today, and I must swear it tomorrow somewhere.' Correspondence between Patrick and 'Mrs R' was exchanged through the medium of their solicitors, provoking deep resentment, trouble, and (on Patrick's side) expense. In November he suffered momentary apprehension when he learned from his solicitor Baddeley 'that Mrs R.'s suit is left "adjourned generally", whatever that may mean: he is very wisely keeping Fron from her – what a miserable restless inquisitiveness she has. I dare say she will get it out of Richard sooner or later.' At his insistence, Baddeley withheld his address from Elizabeth. Since the house was not his and the furniture my mother's, he presumably feared that his sole possession of value – his precious library – could be adjudged an exigible asset.

As the winter wore on the dispute gradually petered out, presumably once Elizabeth was reluctantly obliged to concede that he had insufficient means to provide her with regular maintenance in addition to the substantial expense required to meet Richard's school fees.

Although these family problems remained a source of recurrent concern for both Patrick and Elizabeth they impinged only indirectly upon the lives of the young couple in Wales. Necessity and inclination led them to focus their thoughts and energies upon establishing themselves in their new home. Throughout his life Patrick gained almost as much satisfaction from intricate or arduous physical tasks as he did from writing. Indeed, there were marked similarities in his approach to both pursuits. Because of his pronounced antipathy to accepting instruction from others he derived much gratification from achieving success through his own unaided efforts. Both Jack Aubrey and Stephen Maturin display an engaging combination of exceptional competence in their respective professions, compounded at intervals by wild impracticality whenever they venture beyond the bounds of their particular skills. Such was the case with Patrick. The subtlety and finesse of his writing require no emphasis, but when he turned to manual labour the results lurched between masterful ingenuity and ludicrous failure.

Still, there can be no denying the energy which he and my mother devoted to setting the cottage in order. There was the arduous task of scraping what Patrick termed 'the vile ginger paint' off the massive slate sides of the kitchen fireplace and removing 'the wearisome whitewash' from the upstairs room and staircase, which was in so sorry a state as to require complete restoration. This task was largely entrusted to my mother who, contrary to her usual practicality, discovered her mistake in undertaking the task after laying the carpets, which had just been cleaned at the ill-affordable expense of £4 11. Next she set about whitewashing the entirety of the interior walls: a troublesome operation, in view of the quantity of furniture (to say nothing of the precious air-raid shelter) which had had to be crammed into the tiny dwelling. By the middle of December it contained not only much of the contents of the seven spacious rooms and extensive cellar of The Cottage in Chelsea, but in addition furniture and ornaments belonging to my mother which my grandparents had dispatched from Staddon before their move to London. These were discovered after lying unrecognised for a week at Penrhyndeudraeth station, the packages having been addressed in the name of 'Wicksteed'. As Patrick commented: 'It is remarkable how they have all melted into Fron, even M's wonderfully repellent Staffordshire dog.'

While my mother toiled at scraping and whitewashing the walls, Patrick when not assisting her applied himself to improving the internal facilities in his own inimitable way: 'I suspended the ironing table on hinges on the wall, M. having unfortunately seen something of the kind in an Ideal Homes Exhibition: it is not a bad job, really, but I proceeded on several unsound theories for good many hours.'

By far the most satisfying piece of work was that of arranging the book-shelves for Patrick's library. This generally proves a troublesome task, but in Patrick's case it involved additional problems of his own devising. By 6

November these had been all but overcome, and Patrick was able to admire his achievement with a glow of pleasure.

> *For a good deal of the time we have been very active with bookshelves, the brackets having at last materialised. But what a task it is plugging the walls. The only way is to put the brackets up first and the plank after: I wish I had done that at first. By now we have nearly all the books up, and we have used all our wood. They look exceedingly well, and sometimes I feel uneasily that I should not admire their mere aspect so.*

A fortnight later this most essential of installations was completed with characteristic ingenuity. After constructing a couple of shelves from an old potato shelf for the smaller books, Patrick was able to report a few days later that 'we have got the rest of the books up, and very well they look. M's pastry board made three for 12mo's and Penguins – it came apart by itself – the mahogany vile table made one, and one flat of the kitchen table slit in three finished the top long shelf. It will be sufficiently ludicrous if Mrs W. does get us the wood after all.' When not long afterwards my mother's fine dining table arrived from Staddon, the remainder of the 'mahogany vile table' served a wonderful variety of uses. Apart from providing bookshelves, Patrick contrived an apparatus more readily described than imagined:

> *The top is now a sort of sideboard – literally – sitting on hinged flaps. I wish it may be secure, but I have doubts. The hinges gave us hours of pain – by being the wrong sort; eventually I robbed the ironing board for a reasonable pair. The theory is that the top lifts off for use across the arms of the chair when I am writing.*

The heart of any less devoted wife might have sunk when her husband, eager to tax his wits with fresh undertakings, began 'soldering things'. When the top ring of his fishing rod broke, rather than spend sixpence replacing it at the shop in Portmadoc, he 'purchased the Smee (a patent solder and flux preparation) and, after many hours of practice, much loss of temper and the ring – once I had to prise up the bothy floor in search of it, not that it was there – I began the attempt. With quite exceptional luck it worked at once, gripping firmly in exactly the right place. If I never solder anything again I shall still feel a master plumber.' Thereafter he seized every opportunity for exercising his skill, toiling for hours at anything metallic, from the bath to his cigarette lighter.

It was not until early in the following spring that the interior of the house finally achieved a satisfactory state of order. On Lady Day, as the first lambs appeared on the hillsides, Patrick gazed contentedly upon the fruits of their labours. 'After many changes the drawing room has reached what must be its final arrangement. The moving of the shelves to accommodate the satinwood desk was a sad business, but it made us range the books anew and far more handsomely. The whole of Fron is wonderfully snug and inhabited now.' Patrick particularly delighted in the steady ticking and quarterly chimes of the great chamber clock, which for him gave life to the household.

The humble exterior of the tiny slate-roofed cottage provided no hint of the assembly of esoteric and valuable possessions with which it was crammed. It was perhaps appropriate (Patrick certainly seems to have found it so) that a household so redolent of the eighteenth century should have lacked every facility of the twentieth. The absence of a telephone meant that the nearest communication with the outside world was provided by a public callbox half an hour's walk away in Croesor village. However, *The Times* was delivered daily by a newspaper boy from Croesor, as were telegrams.

For much of the year every drop of water for cooking and washing had to be carried in buckets from a pool which the young couple had created by piling rocks to dam the flow of a small cataract descending the slope of the hillside above. During the winter this labour was eased following provision of a water butt by Mr Roberts, the farmer. Making it operative required Patrick's customary ingenuity. 'Today I tackled the butt. Of course the tap was too small for the bung hole, which dashed me very much: I made a kind of collar of sheet lead (it has been invaluable), lapped it in sacking, and rammed it home. The tap seems quite firm. The theory is that the tap's soundness will mould the lead exactly. If it doesn't work I shall try an inner ring of sacking.'

After further toil it worked satisfactorily, and drenching rain lashing down on the roof filled it within half an hour. Patrick entertained an ambitious project of sinking a tank under the spring, from which a pump-operated hose would run into a 100-gallon tank sheltered from frost in the bothy at the back of the house, but in the event the project never materialised. The primitive lavatory was situated in a rickety little lean-to shed at the back, invariably saturated with damp, and containing nothing more than a bucket which required regular emptying at a distance from the house. Winter sessions in this icy shed proved an uncomfortable ordeal, however much its visitors huddled themselves in heavy overcoats and woollen scarves. When Patrick came to describe the rudimentary arrangement of the heads from which eighteenth-century sailors relieved themselves directly into the sea in all weathers, he knew from literally bitter experience whereof he wrote.

A scheme for overcoming the lack of an electricity supply was likewise contemplated. Informed that it was possible to buy a windmill capable of providing sufficient power to light the house for about £30, Patrick reflected:

'It seems an awful lot of money when you consider the efficiency of oil lamps and the small amount of trouble they give. Yet there is the difficulty of getting a light high enough, and it is very convenient to switch a light on rather than grope wildly with matches.' Nevertheless this project was also abandoned, presumably on grounds of cost. In any case the concept of self-sufficiency exercised strong appeal, and the low, warm glow of paraffin lamps and candles enhanced the cosy atmosphere of winter evenings by the fireside, with wind and rain howling impotently about the walls.

Though of relatively primitive construction, the design of cottages like Fron Wen had evolved over centuries of grim experience of Welsh winters. The lower part of the house on the upper slope entered into the rock of the hillside. The hearth and its chimney were located at this end, which served to counter damp and cold arising from the subterranean foundations. The prevailing wind, which came tearing down the valley from the mountains in the north-east, was countered by bringing the rear roof of the cottage to ground level. One hot summer a cow was discovered wandering serenely upon the slates. Further visitations were prevented by the erection of a strand of barbed wire at the bottom. As additional protection against the weather, Clough Williams-Ellis had planted a screen of trees just beyond the building.

A small but effective coal-fired stove in the room to the right of the front door served for heating and cooking. Water for the famous bath, which in Patrick's fancy provoked the derision of the vulgar on their journey from London, took three hours to bring to singing point. Given the arduous labour involved in bringing it from the stream, it is understandable that baths were not a very frequent occurrence, only two being taken during their first fortnight. However, my parents took all these problems in their stride, and Patrick noted that apart from their hands, which were deeply ingrained with dirt, their bodies remained tolerably clean.

In November, a month after their arrival, with the major task of unpacking and sorting their belongings accomplished, Patrick gazed about him with deep but short-lived satisfaction.

> *We shifted the drawing-room around with immense success yesterday evening, and sat in it right comfortable for the first time: but today, where we were all prepared to sit happily for the greater part of the day, a wind sprang up, blew straight down the mad drainpipe chimney, and covered the room deep in smuts. When we came back from the waterfalls, where we had built dams in the afternoon, the room was even deeper in blacker smuts, and until the beastly thing went out it went on making tentative belches. I must endeavour to fix the end of the drainpipe to the top as a temporary measure until we can either have an open fire or an efficient stove.*

A week later the problem was overcome, though not without accompanying mishaps.

> *Mary had the moral courage to ask for the loan of a ladder at the farm; they were all complaisance, but vague. Young Mrs Roberts had to be called up to interpret – the old lady is unsound on any subject but the weather. We took the wrong ladder at first (I hope it was the wrong ladder) and I put my foot through a rung at once. This is the kind of hideous thing that happens with borrowed tools. The next ladder, a sound one, we unlashed rather uneasily from Cae'r Fynnon . . . With the ladder and some of the new wire clothes-line we fixed the top joint of the chimney, and in the morning cemented it. It seems pretty firm, and it works. There was a N.W. wind, which would have blasted straight down the old pipe, but not a smut appeared. Unless the chimney has some other vile tricks this makes the drawing room habitable, and very comfortable it is.*

The smuts appeared to have vanished for good, but the oven remained liable to recurrent problems. Patrick's diary entry for a chilly December day reads gloomily: 'Today I have done nothing at all except light the oven – something of an undertaking. In my anxiety lest the coke (tricky stuff – the coal all gone) should not ignite, I raised such an immense blaze that the oven was practically unusable . . . Mary has just pointed out that the oven is too cold for her cake. The fire has gone quite out. It is very frustrating indeed.'

Despite painstakingly acquired expertise, cold and damp remained recurrent afflictions. After their visit to my grandparents in London in January 1946 they returned to a freezing cold house, due to the fact that an expected fuel delivery had not occurred. As ever, Mr and Mrs Roberts came to the rescue with buckets of coal, but Patrick's and my mother's endurance was severely tested on innumerable occasions. Even in early summer the stone-slabbed floor was liable to sweat with damp for days on end. It says much for the vigour of their constitutions that they only rarely succumbed to illness and as time moved on they became as tough and resourceful as any of the native inhabitants.

CHAPTER FIFTEEN

The Untamed Land

The beginning of summer, fairest season;
Noisy the birds, green the trees,
Ploughs in the furrow, in the yoke,
Green the sea, dappled the landscape.

(Welsh *englyn*)[1]

Cwm Croesor today is a wild, lonely, and beautiful place, barely changed in appearance since my parents went to live there in 1945. The one melancholy difference is that it was then relatively well populated. Farming, as yet untouched by mechanisation, required numerous hands at busy times of the year. Save for the little village of Croesor, with its stone bridge, shop, chapel, and scattering of houses, its dwellings lie dotted about the three-mile valley. In such a closed and remote community thc inhabitants knew each other and their affairs intimately. Almost everyone had attended the village school and met at chapel on Sundays, while the exigencies of hill farming demanded much mutual assistance among the farmers at busy times of the year.

Bessie Roberts and Edgar Williams recall how the arrival of the O'Brians at Fron Wen provoked considerable curiosity and discussion in the locality. Who might this mysterious young couple be, why had they come to settle at this remote spot, and how did they maintain themselves? Differing opinions were voiced at farmhouse kitchen tables and cottage hearths. As Edgar Williams explained to me, 'people were a bit puzzled how they were actually

[1]*Kintevin keinhaw amsser. Dyar adar glas callet. Ereidir in rich. ich iguet. Guirt mor brithottor tiret* (J. Gwenogvryn Evans, ed., *The Black Book of Carmarthen* (Pwellheli, 1906), p. 33). *Englynion* are poems containing three-line verses, frequently descriptive of the natural world. Early examples such as this date from about the ninth century (cf. Kenneth Jackson, *Studies in Early Celtic Nature Poetry* (Cambridge, 1935), pp. 181–86).

managing to survive'. The favoured hypothesis was that 'O'Brian was actually in contact with the weather-reporting system[1] – and that was possibly because he spent lots of time in the telephone in the village'. While some came near the mark in believing 'that he was a writer, writing books', others maintained with equal conviction 'that he had been a pilot during the war, and had been injured and that he had a good pension because of his injuries'. Yet more colourful was the conviction 'that he had been a spy, and that he was hiding away . . . an English spy, because he never left, he didn't go anywhere – he kept out of sight, and didn't mix with the village and kept himself to himself'.

Edgar, who saw much of Patrick, concluded that he had probably been a schoolmaster. The wide extent of his knowledge, coupled with the didactic manner in which he was wont to correct and instruct a boy like him, aroused comparison with the village schoolmaster Ifor Owen. The mystery was sustained by the extent to which Patrick kept himself apart. While invariably polite and friendly in conversation, he generally maintained a discreet distance from the people of the valley, in particular making it plain that he disliked being questioned on personal matters. For days on end he would remain closeted within the cottage, emerging only to walk or cycle with my mother to Garreg or Penrhyndeudraeth to collect provisions, or make a telephone call from the kiosk at Croesor. From time to time he could be seen setting off on foot alone or with my mother, disappearing for hours in the mountains.

Initially he experienced some awkwardness on finding himself an object of undisguised curiosity throughout Cwm Croesor. This perturbed him, and he reflected irritably: 'What poor natural manners these village Welsh have – no ease, and a good deal of probably unintentional rudeness. They are not, from what little I have seen, a deferential race, as Taine (I think, or is it Brogan?) termed the English.' During a walk to Croesor village in search of a motorcycle battery, he observed that 'the natives still gape and turn, as on pivots, to continue staring'.

A related difficulty at the outset was to decide how to deal with the awkwardness of being unable to commune satisfactorily, or in many cases at all, with the local people. His and my mother's English origin appeared to mark them out as a semi-alien species: a distinction which was accentuated by the locals' courteous insistence on attempting to address them in English. When a shepherd greeted my mother in Welsh, Patrick remarked that this was 'the first time. They seem to detect un-Welshness from a great distance.' Typically, he pondered how to establish a correct etiquette. Riding his

[1]The Meteorological Office.

motorcycle up the valley a month after their arrival, he found that 'Most of the men hailed me in Welsh, which was awkward: to reply in English gives, I think, a faintly superior sort of an air to a conversation, and I fear to venture on scraps of Welsh, which might appear (a) unintelligible and foolish or (b) condescending.'

However the problem ceased to exercise him for long. Overt displays of inquisitiveness subsided once the novelty of their arrival had worn off, and the communal spirit which prevailed throughout the valley enabled Patrick to gain confidence in his position. He enjoyed being the outside observer, moving silently among the community, noting their special characteristics, while retaining a detachment and independence they were content to respect.

Now Patrick began to appreciate that, so far from possessing 'poor natural manners', the Welsh are generally characterised by remarkable social delicacy. In *Three Bear Witness* he remarked: 'That natural, unconscious fine breeding struck me again and again . . . When I was young, I was brought up in an ordinary middle-class home in London . . . but it was not until I came into Wales that I discovered the beautiful natural breeding Aunt Theresa assured me was the mark of nobility.'[1]

Throughout their time in North Wales, family finances remained on a precarious basis. By far the greater part of their annual income was provided by my mother's trust, and since the total approximated to the minimum level at which tax was due they were fortunately able to obtain the full rebate on her invested income.

The move from London and establishment of the fresh household at Fron Wen incurred unusually large expenditure, and at the beginning of February 1946 Patrick noted with alarm: 'The money position is a little frightening: we have spent about £250 in rather over 3 months.' That they were enabled to recover from this setback was largely thanks to financial support from my grandfather. However, in succeeding years Patrick's earnings dropped to almost nothing, and the household economy became almost entirely dependent on my mother's income.

Though Patrick was not extravagant by nature, he was as often as not hopelessly at sea in financial matters. My mother in contrast proved an adept accountant, and until her final illness meticulously maintained records of their income and expenditure on a monthly and annual basis in parallel account books. It was through her unremitting care that the household economy reflected the theory rather than practice of Mr Micawber. Thus their income for the year 1946 to 1947 amounted to £306/13/9d, while their expenditure totalled £306/1/11¼d.

[1] *Three Bear Witness*, p. 121.

Every item of expenditure was recorded on a monthly and yearly basis, ranging from regular accounts at the farm and grocery, to 1½d spent on some unspecified household necessity. Each month modest purchases were made at the grocery in Llanfrothen ('Roberts Siop Zinc'),[1] butcher ('Jones the Flesh') and baker. An account was also arranged with the farm, from which they obtained a range of necessities extending from daily milk to paraffin for lighting. Kindly Mr and Mrs Roberts at Croesor Fawr provided the impoverished couple with a regular supply of extras, for which they discreetly declined or avoided payment. With rationing still in full force farmers were officially restricted in what they might sell privately, or even retain for their own use. But in a region as remote as Cwm Croesor the law did not represent an unduly pressing consideration.

Throughout their four-year stay in the valley the O'Brians remained on terms of close friendship with their immediate neighbours, and after their departure the families retained affectionate memories of each other. Given Patrick's difficulty in sustaining social relationships, it was perhaps as well that linguistic difficulties ensured that intercourse remained at a rudimentary level. As he observed soon after their arrival, 'Roberts the farm . . . seems to be an admirable type – shy and reserved, but very kind and willing to help: speaks careful but imperfect English with a fine accent. His mother's English will not sustain anything of conversation.'

Harri Roberts's restricted command of the English language was liable to desert him altogether in moments of embarrassment or agitation, while the responses of old Mr Roberts were almost as perplexing as those of the virtually monoglot mother. 'Conversations with young R. quite successful, but subsequent interview with old R. difficult – he began by saying that he was sorry he knew so little English, and went on to exemplify this – dreadful difficulty with prepositions. I am left with only the most general notions of building a stone wall – he would say "Yes" to anything he did not understand.' Harri and Bessie's manner and conduct betokened only kindness and generosity. Early in their acquaintance Patrick remarked that 'nothing could be more pleasant than the farm people, thank Heaven', and this favourable estimate remained constant.

The fortuitous advantage afforded by the linguistic barrier is illustrated by a trifling exchange, which in other circumstances would probably have provoked lasting offence. In the early summer of 1946 Patrick began teaching

[1]Roberts's corrugated iron (*zinc*) shop (*siop*) was a better-stocked store than Siop Gôch ('red shop'), the post office in Croesor. In Welsh they were known as 'Bob Siop Sinc' and 'Evan Jones Cig' (from Welsh *cigydd*, 'butcher').

his son Richard to shoot with a home-made bow: 'We were seen, to our shame, by Roberts yesterday evening. He said . . . that as he had not the time we were welcome to pick up the wool lying around among the thorns; the merchant he said, comes around and buys it in sacks. We did not appreciate this suggestion, but no doubt he meant well and would have phrased it better had he a greater command of English.' An element of relief is detectable in Patrick's ascription of a well-meant suggestion to linguistic difficulty which, if proffered by an English farmer, he would have found intolerably demeaning. Although his propensity to take offence where none was intended reflected a deep-rooted sensation of vulnerability, if afforded adequate pretext he was inwardly relieved to be able to free himself.

Harri Roberts was an intelligent and observant man, with whom Patrick enjoyed conversing about life in Cwm Croesor as he took ever-increasing interest in the flora and fauna of the valley and surrounding mountains. Roberts had astonishing eyesight. On one occasion he pointed out a fox sunning itself on a rock shelf high up on the Cnicht. Patrick who could see nothing, was disinclined to believe him until he brought down his heavy brass telescope from Fron Wen and observed it for himself. That evening Patrick climbed the mountain with Roberts and his shepherd boy Edgar Williams, and Roberts expertly shot the fox. Its body was carried back to the farm for a young terrier to practise worrying. Roberts frequently provided Patrick with interesting information about birds, explaining their Welsh names and recounting local folklore and archaic customs. He believed, for example, that the coming of buzzards was a portent of bad weather, although Patrick did not find this borne out by experience. Another time 'Roberts . . . said . . . that formerly women working at the farms . . . were paid a fleece for a day's work and that they would take these fleeces to the factory to be made into flannel'.

Patrick also derived much information from the company of Edgar Williams, the *gwas* (farm boy) at Croesor Fawr. While Patrick encountered difficulty in establishing close relationships with people of his own age, he found Edgar in many ways an ideal companion with whom he could converse freely about the Welsh language, the customs and personalities of the valley, and natural life on the hillsides.

Like most boys in the valley Edgar attended the village school until he was fourteen, after which he went in 1946 to work on the farm for a few years: others found employment at the quarry. As was customary he lived in the farmhouse, where he received just over £1 a week and his keep. 'We were being fed in the farm – I suppose it wasn't too bad,' he told Patrick, although 'you were more or less on duty all the time'. Boys were engaged from the ancient Celtic festival dates of *Calan Mai* (May Day) to *Calan Gaeaf* (1

November), and paid at the end of each six months: 'if you left in between, you would probably forfeit your wages'.

Patrick was fascinated by the Welsh language, and 'very interested in the meaning of words, especially descriptive words'. Discussing the Cnicht, the great peak which towered above the northern flank of the valley, Edgar expressed doubt that a Welsh mountain could be named from the English word for 'knight'. Patrick in turn mused on its apparent similarity to the Irish word *cnoc*, 'a hill'.[1] Edgar suggested that a more appropriate name for the soaring peak would be *saeth*, 'arrow', which was that adopted by Patrick in his novel.

Any Welsh words or local lore which struck Patrick as of particular interest he jotted down in a notebook. He was intrigued to learn, for example, that every fox-earth bore its own name, which he carefully recorded. Thus Edgar explained that Llyn Cerrig y Myllt, a place notorious as a haunt of foxes, means 'The Lake of the Stones of the Wethers'. Like most people in Cwm Croesor, who spent their waking hours out and about in the valley, Edgar possessed an observant eye for wildlife. When Patrick remarked on a dipper he had spotted while fishing below the village, Edgar promptly informed him that they nested under the bridge at Croesor.

He also remembers Patrick's strong but unsentimental affection for animals. When one of Harri Robert's sheep-dogs developed epilepsy, which ordinarily required the animal to be put down, Patrick expressed his belief that their wartime diet of maize was the prime cause of the sickness, and procured some tablets which provided an effective cure. Discovering a fox suffering a painful death behind his cottage, he voiced strong objection to the use of poison. However, he changed his view when Harri Roberts quietly responded that the choice lay between the fox and his lambs.[2] Similarly for a time after his arrival Patrick expressed opposition to hunting, but on becoming acquainted with the reality swiftly converted into an enthusiastic follower of the local hunt.

At times Patrick and my mother found it easier to become fond and protective towards children other than their own. 'Mary could sometimes call at our house in the village and I know that my mother thought the world of her. We lived in the Chapel House then and the old track leading over the hills to Nantmor and Beddgelert went past the door,' Edgar remembers. He

[1] While I hesitate to differ from Edgar, a native Welsh speaker, the name *cnicht* surely derives from Old English *cniht*, 'knight'. The mountain is shaped rather like a Saxon or Norman helmet, and the term was borrowed into both Welsh and Irish in the medieval period. Patrick's etymology was certainly wrong: the Middle Irish cognate is *cníocht*.

[2] This exchange is reproduced in *Three Bear Witness*, p. 64.

worked at Croesor Fawr for about two years, and when he found that Mr Roberts could not afford to pay him the adult wage he left in 1948 for a bigger farm. My parents were sad to see him go, and in *Three Bear Witness* Patrick describes how 'he told me the tale of the great sow of Môn [Anglesey] and about an Irish princess in the Lleyn, stories that must have come to him straight from the Mabinogion, or from the verbal tradition before that . . . That poetic insight, continuity, feeling, is as real as the mist in the hills.'[1] At the end of the following year, when they had moved to France, my mother and Patrick sent Edgar a Christmas card, which his mother preserved for the rest of her life.

Farmers inevitably enjoyed luxuries which the continuance of strict wartime regulations denied the rest of the population. Not long after their arrival Patrick observed with relish: 'Another thing of interest was an immense dish of butter that Mary saw in the farm kitchen. 'We must do something about this. I saw a whole sheep, skinned, hanging casually in an ash tree. If the butter and the mutton are illegal, as I suppose they are, the Robertses will probably want to know us better before they sell any.'

A few days later 'M. took me to see the farm's newly killed pig – a fine sight – Roberts is an able fellow. Our idea was really to discuss fencing and the wall, so that we can get on with a kitchen garden – not that we were uninterested in the pig.' Harri and Bessie Roberts were not the people to let hungry neighbours go wanting, and promptly presented my mother and Patrick with 'some extraordinarily good ribs crammed with flavour, and some eminent brawn'. Even today Edgar Williams recalls from his boyhood that 'Mrs Roberts was famous for her brawn: she used to make brawn after the pigs. Anyone who tasted that would remember! I think I grew inches when I ate that!' The generosity of the Roberts family towards the little household at Fron Wen continued unabated during the years which followed, and the O'Brians maintained an account at the farm which rarely exceeded £2 a month. All this was much appreciated, and it is not hard to picture the contented gleam in Patrick's eye when he wrote: 'Mem. The shoulder of lamb from the Roberts – trout paste – Mrs Roberts' butter.'

Memories of the relative grandeur of The Cottage in Chelsea were eclipsed by the excitement of creating their cosy new refuge. Wherever possible Patrick and my mother sought to rely on the labour of their own hands. She trained herself to become an adept barber, regularly cutting Patrick's hair with a deftness from which I was to profit in subsequent years. 'If I could find

[1] *Three Bear Witness*, pp. 133–34. Today Edgar can still recite passages of the *Mabinogi* and lengthy Welsh poems, old and new.

a spinning wheel that really worked,' he mused, 'it would be a good present for M. Does not a distaff enter into it somewhere?'

Fortunately for my mother this fantasy was not pursued, and Patrick's pursuit of exotic artefacts was confined to less demanding curios. During a visit to Portmadoc in search of fishing gear, he could not resist buying my mother an elegant silver-topped cane, whose inscription 'Charles Metcalfe 1708' evoked the image of a forgotten dandy of Queen Anne's reign strolling into the coffee-houses of St James's Street. Such tangible everyday reminders of the distant past imparted a keen sense of immediacy to Patrick's imagination, and the acquisition of so personal an object established a physical rapport with its original owner.

There was little romance in the day-to-day management of their cottage economy. Though she never complained, it cannot have been very pleasant for my mother to be obliged to wash all their laundry in an 'unsatisfactory and muddy pond in the stream', nor can it have been easy to dry afterwards during the long wet winter months when the only resource was a clothes-line in the garden.

The readiest means of eking out their financial resources was to grow as much of their own food as possible. Minute though their garden was, rendering it productive proved no easy task. Over the winter its walls were repaired to prevent the incursion of sheep, and when spring finally arrived in the latter part of April it was time for Patrick to prepare the ground for sowing vegetables.

> *While I was waiting for old Roberts to advise me about the infernal well (he has not come yet, and I don't care to proceed) I incautiously started to destroy the box hedge – this was on Friday. This committed us to the arduous clearing of the end beds and, morally, to the beginning of proper gardening. I am trying to bastard-trench the right-hand plot, but it is a formidable undertaking, what with innumerable stones and lack of skill. The piece measures 66 ft × 12 or 13, which makes about three rods poles or perches. How mad the land measures are. At the present rate it should take about a month, provided my back lasts.*[1]

[1] The archaic measurement of the perch was legally established as a piece of land 16½ feet square. However there were local variations, and had he known of it I doubt Patrick would have resisted that employed in the early seventeenth century at Buckfastleigh in Devonshire, which was 'sixteen foot and one half inch and one barley corn square' (Andrew McRae, *God Speed the Plough: The Representation of Agrarian England, 1500–1600* (Cambridge, 1996), p. 184).

When Harri Roberts's father called unexpectedly he could barely conceal his amusement on observing the herculean task to which he found Patrick applying himself. When he gently attempted to explain that the correct way to prepare the heavy valley earth was to break up the topsoil, Patrick smilingly reassured him that he had 'read in a book' that deep-trenching was essential for the production of good crops.[1] Too polite to remonstrate, Roberts left him to the backbreaking labour of tilling his three rods, poles, or perches. Before long Patrick's regular use of the expression 'I read in a book' became proverbial among the amused population of Cwm Croesor.

Patrick's engagement in practical tasks was strongly coloured by nostalgia for a past era. Indoors, pursuing his favourite hobby of clock-mending, his mentor was *The Artificial Clock-maker*, published in 1732. For work in the kitchen garden he would consult Markham, John Worlidge's *Systema Agriculturæ: Being The Mystery of Husbandry Discovered and laid Open* (1687), and Cobbett's *Cottage Economy* of 1850. For shooting he relied upon Colonel Hawker's *Instructions to Young Sportsmen* (1838),[2] while *A General History of Quadrupeds* (1792), with its fine woodcuts by Bewick, informed his perception of wildlife. Meanwhile my mother at her stove produced delicious meals from Elizabeth Raffald's *The Experienced English Housekeeper, For the Use and Ease of Ladies, Housekeepers, Cooks &c.* (London, 1776).[3] This unaffectedly romantic approach to his daily round goes far to explain the striking manner in which contemporary knowledge and techniques are so

[1] '. . . if he dig it deep, and trench it, and meanure it, as is meet, either for Garden, Orchard, or Corn setting, then to delve half a rood in a day, is a very great proportion, because ordinarily to delve, as to receive ordinary Seeds, requires but one spade graft in depth, but extraordinarily to delve, as for inriching and bettering of the ground, and to cleanse it from stones, weeds, and other annoyances, will require two spade graft at the least' (Patrick's copy of *Markhams Farewell to Hvsbandry: Or, The Enriching of All Sorts of Barren and Sterile Grounds in our Kingdome* (London, 1649), p. 143).

[2] It was perhaps fortunate that Patrick lacked resources to attempt reconstruction of the extensive range of carriage-mounted artillery designed by the Peninsular veteran for bombarding wildfowl formations at long range.

[3] The copy is inscribed 'Mary her Book' in my mother's handwriting, and remained in regular use in her kitchen until in her later years she sadly became too ill to cook. It is noteworthy that Patrick made no reference to this work, upon which he drew extensively for descriptions of favourite dishes in his novels, in his foreword to the gastronomic companion to the Aubrey–Maturin novels by Anne Chotzinoff Grossman and Lisa Grossman Thomas *Lobscouse & Spotted Dog: Which It's a Gastronomic Companion to the Aubrey–Maturin Books* (New York, 1997). He approved their work, and I suspect the omission reflected his general aversion to revealing over-much of the sources of his knowledge, which might rob the illusion of its enchantment. His enthusiasm led him to make 'Mrs. Raffald, the housekeeping generalissimo' of the great house of Churleigh in *Richard Temple* (p. 228), while Sir Joseph Blaine's cook Mrs Barlow was 'Mrs Raffald' in the original version of *The Reverse of the Medal.*

effortlessly deployed throughout Patrick's later novels. When he came to apply himself to recreating a vanished world on paper, many aspects of eighteenth-century life represented familiar experience, physical as well as mental.

Patrick regarded his well-worn copy of *Markhams Farewell to Hvsbandry* with particular affection, both as a vade-mecum of which he made regular practical use, and as a source of that esoteric lore which he particularly relished. Markham's happy approach is manifested by this notice inserted at the beginning of his work:

> ADDITION.
> *An excellent way to take Moles, and*
> *to preserve good Ground from*
> *such annoyance.*
> Put Garlike, Onions, or Leekes, into
> the mouths of the holes, and they will
> come out quickly as amazed.

I would be surprised if Patrick did not essay whether this ingenious recipe worked as described. Certainly nothing would have delighted him more than to come face to face with an amazed mole. On the other hand it seems remarkable that Stephen Maturin never cited this remedy urged by the ingenious author: 'If your *Hound* as it is very natural to dogges be so costive that he can by no meanes skummer, you shall first take a peece of a tallow candle, about three fingers in length, and thrust it a good way into the ruell of the *Hound*, and then hold down his tayle hard a quarter of an hour or more, and then give it liberty, and when he hath emptied his belly, you shall give him to drinke five or six spoonefull of Sallet oyle, and will clense him sufficiently.'

A fault which cannot be ascribed to Patrick is lack of resilience. Having somehow succeeded in burying the thin layer of fertile topsoil in his garden beneath a foot of underlying clay, he found the ground virtually impermeable for planting. Temporarily baffled, he turned to walking and bird-watching with my mother, reading, and listening with her to their gramophone. During the first week of May a fierce wind raged unceasingly down the valley, and not until it had abated did Patrick return to the struggle with their garden plot. In order to remedy the condition of the soil which his labours had rendered intractable, he decided that the solution was to filter it to a sufficient depth by means of a sieve. This happened to be an article they lacked, but so trifling a difficulty did not deter Patrick. Under his instruction, my mother set about creating one from clothes-line wire. Unsurprisingly this proved a complex task, and it was not until a week later that 'We finished the famous sieve and went on with the garden a little'.

Shortly after this ingenious feat of craftsmanship was accomplished, heavy rain set in unceasingly for days on end, and planting did not begin until the start of June. Patrick laid down radishes (planting them at the new moon),[1] gladioli, lettuces, and parsley. During the next two to three weeks he was gratified to observe sprouts beginning to appear, but a month later he noted ruefully: 'They, the gladioli, look well, but the transplanted lettuces are static: the beans look but feeble. That garden is going to be a great labour. There is nothing for it but seiving [*sic*], though, and that requires drought.'

However, as the seasons passed, Patrick increasingly found himself mingling the trusty advice of Markham and Cobbett with practical experience. He even occasionally permitted himself to consult *The Vegetable Garden Displayed*, a wartime handbook published by the Royal Horticultural Society. Eventually he and my mother reached a satisfying point when almost all their vegetables came from their own garden. They further enriched the household economy by acquiring hens. The enthusiasm with which they tackled these tasks is suggested by the fact that expenses incurred in connection with the hens were classified in her accounts under the heading 'FUN', rather than as 'FOOD' or 'NECESSITIES'.

Patrick supplemented their diet from game in the valley. As Clough Williams-Ellis indicated when they took the lease of Fron Wen, there were few restrictions on shooting and fishing in Cwm Croesor. Patrick had brought with him the folding single-barrelled .410 shotgun my mother purloined from her brother, and relished the prospect of roving the hillsides in search of game for the evening pot:

> *Apparently .410 ammunition is to be had. I should dearly like to go up to the lakes with a dozen cartridges in my pocket: it adds a wonderful zest to a walk, even if one sees nothing, and the bringing home of a bird or two (for so indifferent a shot as I am) has something of a triumph about it.*

After purchasing cartridges in Portmadoc, Patrick and my mother set off up the mountain to the twin lakes of Llynnau Diffwys. His acknowledgement of being an indifferent shot had little to do with false modesty. Arrived at the lakes, a jack-snipe flew up before them out of a stretch of reeds.

[1] '. . . sow Lettice and Rhadish three or four days after the Full [Moon] and they will not run to Seed' (*Riders (1704) British Merlin*: 'Observations on June').

> *I had many a shot at him. Once I remember putting him up, missing him, seeing him pitch at the far, shingly end and going along after him. Arrived at the end we failed to flush him, and I was saying to Mary that snipe did lie very close when he got up within three yards of me, from the bare stony shore, and I missed him again.*

A second visit to the lakes found them enshrouded by dense wet fog, in which they became all but lost.

Although Patrick enjoyed intermittent success with his gun, it soon became apparent that shooting primarily provided sport rather than provender. 'It is sad to see how sterile these lakes are, and how destitute of game our valley is. I think that by now we should have seen signs of hares, grouse & even rabbits, but there seems to be nothing. But what do the foxes and ravens eat – apart from Roberts' poultry? Of course they travel far.'

From time to time he bagged a hare or rabbit for the pot, but that these were rare occasions is evidenced by the fact that his expenses for shooting for their first year at Fron Wen amounted to no more than £1/14/3d. From his preparatory school Richard wrote early in 1947, eagerly enquiring 'Has Daddy shot anything?' Occasionally Daddy did, and Edgar Williams, Harri Roberts's shepherd boy, remembers Roberts and Patrick returning from an expedition with a brace of hares. Each in turn invited him to sup. While the meat in the farmer's stew proved unpleasantly tough, that provided by Patrick and my mother was memorably delicious. Patrick explained to him that this was because he had hung the hare: a practice Edgar believed unknown to the valley.

Fish proved a far more rewarding source of sustenance. Not long after Patrick's arrival at Fron Wen, Roberts told him that the Croesor was full of trout. In the spring he began preparations to take advantage of this lavish source of free food.

> *Three or four days ago we went into Portmadoc by the bus . . . at the fishing tackle shop the man spoke of salmon and trout in the Glaslyn. Tickets for the season seem (conversation indefinite on account of his deafness) to be £2 for salmon and £10 for trout for the whole season. I bought a few flies and a damned expensive (5/-) cast. Then, inflamed by the thought of salmon, a beastly illiterate little book The Fishermen's Vade Mecum*[1] *for 12/6 – I have been regretting this ever since. The idea of catching a salmon is wonderfully attractive.*

[1] G.W. Maunsell, *The Fisherman's Vade Mecum* (London, 1944). Subsequently Patrick found the book more useful: 'I have learned from Maunsell how to whip – eminently gratifying – and I have whipped bits in the middle joint in the hope that this will stiffen the rod, perhaps it is imagination that I seem to be casting better last night. I am learning the blood-knot, too, but it is a brute.'

For the moment, however, he confined his attentions to the trout which lay near to hand. Although he had hunted game with his gun during his year in Norfolk, it does not appear that he had much opportunity for serious fishing. Initially he encountered problems: 'The Maesgwn [a tributary of the Croesor] produced nothing: I suspect that the trout despise my fishing.' Despite this he soon began to regard their river with proprietorial concern. Fishing one bright spring day near their home, he noted testily: 'Two men infuriated me by fishing the Croesor, which I regard as my own property, as calmly as if they owned it. One was quite amiable – said that a man had taken an 18lb salmon the other day in the Glaslyn.'

Lack of success never deterred Patrick, and soon, regardless of results, he derived exquisite pleasure from fishing. Before long a chance encounter one fine May day set him on the way towards becoming a proficient angler:

> *As for fishing the position is a good deal clearer. I did not catch any trout because my fly lacked point and barb: I had caught one tiddler with an old cockabondy*[1] *the other evening when* [Harri] *Roberts came and talked. Showed him my rod, he admired it – said 'Pray try a cast'. He formally demurred but eagerly began, making short, splashing, but accurate casts downstream (the wind was downstream). Very soon he threw out something – it looked to me as though he had been caught in a light tuft of grass and had brought it back on his backward cast, but in fact it was a trout. In some five minutes he had jerked out three, flicking them off the hook behind and going straight on with his fishing. The strike and the outward jerk were simultaneous. This is the usual way of fishing here: they generally use a 9ft. cast with three flies and fish them dry. It knocks all my ideas sideways.*

With the natural tact of his race, Roberts proved a helpful mentor for Patrick. He casually mentioned that at one time 'he used to catch salmon by putting a handkerchief round his hand and pulling them out', and explained that people in Cwm Croesor 'did not eat them, but would take perhaps twenty – they would sell some in Ffestiniog. Also the salmon would assemble "in hundreds" in a pool called the well in Garreg between the village and Rhyd.'

At first Patrick found it hard to adhere consistently to Roberts's example, from time to time reverting in frustration to his own idiosyncratic approach:

> *On Saturday, which was a lovely day, I went over into the Maesgwn proper and fished somewhat after Roberts' style. I killed two little trout, very handsome fellows, but only 6 inches long. There were two larger fish (perhaps caught up) in the*

[1] *Coch y bonddu*, an artificial fly used for trout fishing.

hawthorn pool, but nothing would tempt them. I got angry with them in the end, and chased them round the pool with the top of my rod.

Nevertheless his enthusiasm continued undaunted, and before long he was joined by my mother and (in school holidays) by Richard. Seeing an advertisement in *The Times*, Patrick sent off six guineas for a rod from Hardy of Alnwick for my mother. It was greeted with great excitement when it fortuitously arrived on their wedding anniversary, and not long afterwards Patrick noted with delight: 'The rod surpasses expectation: she [my mother] has improved beyond measure.'

Although their shared skills continued to improve, Patrick found it impossible to emulate the instinctive adroitness of the local inhabitants. 'While I was unprofitably fishing I watched the locals pulling beautiful great fish out, one at least 5lb., and I decided to go in for worming myself at all costs.' Patrick purchased a licence to fish for salmon in the nearby Glaslyn, where he 'dabbled in the left-hand, or gully, pool, and a friendly ancient fished over the rock. He caught and hauled out a lovely fish, almost pink on top, black spots, all above the strongly marked median or lateral line, nothing like the silver of the other sea trout I saw caught. He said that this fish alone was the true sewin, that sewin was not synonymous with sea-trout. Whatever it was, I would have given an eye tooth to have caught it.'

He persevered, and was rewarded two months later with a joyful triumph.

> *Today I caught my first sewin* [in the Glaslyn]. *He was about 10 oz (11¼") but he was vast compared with our little fellows . . . it was immensely gratifying, and I found it difficult not to hurry home at once to show him to M. We have just had him for supper: he was a lovely pink and tasted like the most delicate salmon. M. had caught a brown trout, so we can compare the taste. I think one could get tired of sea trout much quicker than brown T. Of Croesor fish I have caught but one – foul hooked – but M. has had 3, one a whale.*

Over the next four years Patrick devoted much time to and gained unfailing pleasure from fishing for trout along the grassy banks of the Croesor, and scrambling among the precipitous rocks of the Aberglaslyn in pursuit of sea-trout and salmon. He became as proud of his proficiency with the rod as ever he was with the pen, and was not averse to proffering instruction to his neighbours – occasionally with embarrassing consequences. On the lower Croesor one day he patiently explained the technique to a solicitor from Criccieth, who turned out to have been fishing the river for thirty years. Accompanying the solicitor was the secretary of the Glaslyn Angling Club, who invited him to give a talk at the Rotary Club at Portmadoc. Patrick disdained the offer: almost certainly because his acute shyness inhibited him from public speaking. Generally speaking the local people accepted his eccentric mannerisms with the same equanimity they accorded the vagaries of their weather.

While the patient skills required for fishing engaged Patrick's close attention, he derived equal pleasure from careful observation of everything around him. In high summer,

> *We went to the lower Croesor some days ago. It is strikingly beautiful, and there are some places where one might cast. The rowan, furze and heather by the wisby. Two adders, brown, one very large went away, t'other large average, remained and was slain – blue underneath – remained coiled and indifferent until prodded – mating? Red squirrels, one with yellow tail.*

At home in the evenings, when not occupied with the incessant work required about the house, he entertained himself by repairing his clocks, listening to music on the gramophone, and reading. Shortly before their first Christmas a friend named Jean sent a packet of records, which as Patrick noted with pleasure included 'Brandenburg no 6, a Mozart Concertante informie (whatever that may mean) Sheep may safely G'. However 'She had not been able to get the things I had asked for, which included Mozart's 39th (Beecham) Haydn's London and Clock, but her choice was very sure.'

Throughout his life Patrick's musical taste remained rooted firmly in the eighteenth century, only in exceptional cases extending beyond Beethoven in the nineteenth. In those early days he had a fine collection of 78 r.p.m. records for use on my mother's wind-up gramophone. Though the majority were classical music, he also enjoyed Fred Astaire, Paul Robeson, and other fine popular singers. Alas, the collection was discarded long ago when they were superseded by long-playing records, but I remember a haunting version of 'It was a Lover and his Lass' from Shakespeare's *As You Like It* delivered by a black American female singer. Patrick adored good music, but never succeeded in mastering an instrument. Once he bought a recorder, but good-humouredly demonstrated to me that playing more than a few notes lay beyond his powers.

After supper the couple would ensconce themselves comfortably in their armchairs by the open fire in the tiny shadowed room, a bare fifteen feet by nine. Recessed firmly into the rocky mountain slope, the cottage stood four-square and impervious to rain drumming heavily on the roof and gales gusting fiercely about its solid walls. The turbulence without made the little scene within appear the more secure, the only sound the regular ticking of the great chamber clock, with its reassuring quarterly strike. Here at least no unwelcome visitor might penetrate: Patrick had established a private lair, warmly remote from his childhood and youth. An oil lamp cast a mellow glow along the gilded spines of his beloved books, each one a cherished friend, glinting too upon the polished surfaces of my mother's graceful satinwood furniture.

Immersed one evening in *Treasure Island* ('a masterpiece') Patrick 'was interrupted at that point by a moth, which blundered so at the lamp that I had to put it out'. As a rare treat he would allow himself a cigarette, despite repeated periods of abandoning a habit he could ill afford. Two months after Christmas 1945 he noted ruefully: 'I have gone a month without smoking (apart from the three of Mr W[icksteed].'s cheroots) and I don't really miss it so very much – an occasional distinct hunger, and last night I dreamt of a cigarette – the essence seems to me a general rather than a specific resolution, and a determination not to let the mind dwell.'[1]

Patrick's reading was eclectic, ranging from Dickens, Henry James, Norman Douglas, and Swift to Cassell's Household Economy, a Victorian manual which he oddly found 'fascinatingly horrible'. *The Times* and *New Yorker* enabled him to keep in touch with the outside world. The latter was eagerly awaited and afforded much pleasure, not least because of the acerbic judgements he permitted himself:

> *two New Yorkers (good, but for a wart called E. Wilson – pretentious, earnest ape); I have read four New Yorkers in rapid succession instead of working. How good they are, for the most part, and how inexplicably horrible their advertisements are. They would be well advised to drown E. Wilson, though, and a dreary comic fellow called Perelman, who is laboriously facetious rather in Punch's less happy manner.*

In the spring he turned to the magnificent set of Swift's works my mother had cleverly found for his Christmas present: 'I read Gulliver again, or for the first time in the original. Is it such a good satire? Is the satirical part trite, sententious, drearily obvious – the king of Brobdignag an intolerable prig – the Hounhyms [*sic*] sad bores? One thing I am sure of, and that is that I dislike Swift's essays in lavatory humour.'

It must be acknowledged that Patrick could be a bit of a prig himself on occasion.

[1] 'I did get out once, to go to Pentref [Croesor], the village, for tobacco: I had not intended to do this, because I meant to give up smoking, but somehow the arguments in favour of tobacco presented themselves so strongly that I said I would just go down and see whether there was any good brand in the shop' (*Three Bear Witness*, p. 17).

Throughout their lives he and my mother devoted many hours to playing chess and backgammon, and at Fron Wen he applied himself to reviving the game which had enlivened otherwise tedious hours spent alone with his sister Joan during their three years' confinement at Albany Street. 'I don't know why it is,' he reminded himself in July 1946, 'but I left out the striking event of the halma men. Some time ago we cast them in lead, initially for R[ichard]'s benefit, and made a board; M and I have played furiously since then. M. usually wins. We followed the halma men by draughts, even more beautiful. M. wins at this, too.'

The combination of hard work and enjoyment of the adventure occupied the greater part of their energies over the first winter. Every day involved great expenditure of physical energy. This included the arduous labour required to maintain the rudimentary facilities of their household, extensive walking and climbing among the mountains, long fishing expeditions, and (as will be seen) hunting under conditions demanding extraordinary vigour and endurance. Regular journeys were made to the post office at Croesor, the stores at Llanfrothen, or still further to Penrhyndeudraeth to obtain provisions. During the long winter months it was necessary to walk down the valley twice a week, when snowdrifts and ice prevented the arrival of the baker's van, in order to collect bread in bundles. Edgar Williams remembers that my mother would quite often carry someone else's bundle as well; 'she really was energetic in that sense!' For any product out of the ordinary they had to travel to the nearest town, Portmadoc.

At first they relied on Patrick's trusty motorcycle, the Panther. Unfortunately Patrick and machinery, vehicles especially, all too frequently proved incompatible. 'Panther's battery is flat, and the elusive "Griffi" Williams would not come and cope,' he lamented. On another day 'Panther behaved abominably, quite refusing to start. Kindly men pushed her up two hills, but still she would do nothing. Lord, how I sweated, all covered up against the cold – there was a small white frost this morning. At last I went and bought a new plug and she started. She is an appallingly repulsive machine at times.' Recharging the battery or buying a new plug meant a five-mile walk to Penrhyndeudraeth and back (when the garage there was out of batteries, they had to walk the further three miles to Portmadoc), and after some months Patrick was compelled to resign himself to the fact that the wilful creature was proving more trouble and expense than she was worth.

Furthermore she was not the safest machine to operate on the rough and winding roads of the neighbourhood – above all with Patrick at the controls. On one alarming occasion, 'Panther behaved well, but I still find the hills difficult to manage, especially the bend by Bryn, where I nearly crushed Mary altogether by failing to change and going firmly backward.'

Eventually Panther was sold for £22/10s to the Penrhyndeudraeth garage man, and Patrick and my mother bought themselves bicycles upon which they relied as their sole means of transport (apart from the occasional bus) throughout the remainder of their time in Wales.[1]

Despite the satisfaction and pleasure derived from coping with their daily round of tasks, it was not long before Patrick became increasingly concerned by his lack of stimulus in his true *raison d'être*. In December 1945, a week after receiving news of the acceptance of *A Book of Voyages*, he noted in his journal: 'M. has started to tackle the dreary What comes after novel: I wish it may not cause her too much pain.' The allusion was to a work now apparently lost, which was probably among the writings he completed in the spring or summer of 1940 before joining my mother in London. He evidently did not regard it highly, and left it to my mother to polish as she typed it.

By the middle of February she had completed the work, which aroused a momentary surge of optimism.

> *The really important thing, though, is M's finishing and instant posting of the novel, now provisionally called Perfect Gold. I do not think, from the few pages that I have seen, that she has altered it enough, and I do hope it may not disappoint her in the event: it was poor material, or at least very uneven. Parts made me blush vily* [*sic*] *for shame – indeed, I could not bring myself to read it over for writhing. Then to the name: is it all right? I used to feel quite sure about it, but now I do not.*

A month later his agent's response arrived, which was unencouraging: 'Another letter was from Curtis Brown, whose reader thinks little of Perfect Gold on the rather curious ground of incoherence. C-B is trying Hutchinson, however.' Eventually 'Perfect Gold' sank without trace.

Meanwhile Patrick continued ransacking his old notebooks for further material which in polished form might prove suitable for publication. On 15 December he noted: 'I have just re-read that Samarcand tale. It is better than I had supposed, and it is well worth finishing. Suffers from want of central plot. It is hardly more than a series of incidents, more or less probable, fortuitously connected.' The allusion was to the children's adventure story which he had abandoned together with his family at the time of his abrupt departure in 1940. The hard winter had kept him busy with more practical tasks, and it was not until towards the end of April that he returned to the

[1]The bicycles were kept in an empty house below Bryn, as there was no room for them in Fron Wen.

work: 'I have been feeling guiltily idle recently, so I have made a new start on "Samarkand".'

However his resolution came to nothing, and the project was soon set aside. Four months later even the lively journal he had enthusiastically maintained since their arrival at Fron Wen ground to a halt. Its hastily written conclusion dwells on frustration at finding himself unable to improve the character of his son Richard (an account of whose stay is reserved for the next chapter), and anger at his publisher's dislike of the preface to *A Book of Voyages* – the only part of the work written by Patrick himself. One has the strong impression that he was assailed by bouts of lassitude, and although he read extensively he was growing conscious of the fact that he was no nearer undertaking creative work.

His interests ranged widely, and in order to be able to pursue the paths his fancy took he applied to join the London Library, that uniquely valuable private institution established in 1842 by Carlyle, Thackeray, and others seeking a refuge from what they felt to be the inadequacies of the British Museum. At the time of Patrick's application membership involved a somewhat pompous formal procedure, but he obtained a recommendation from his publisher Herbert van Thal. Despite this, Patrick acknowledged six months after their arrival that his reading had declined from Chelsea days: 'I don't know why it is, but I have never mentioned reading a single book in this diary, although my last had nothing else, except bank balance. We do not read very much, it is true, but it is not as bad as that.'

Meanwhile my mother suffered deep distress from her deprivation of contact with her children, together with the attendant coldness between her and her parents. Early in the new year Patrick recorded in his journal:

> *5.11.46 We go up tomorrow for M's trial; I cannot form an opinion of the outcome now, because we have moiled it over so that it is impossible to see it objectively. Sunday, February 17th. There is no point in recording the details of our horrible visit to London – we are neither of us likely to forget one moment of it. We have been home long enough now for it to have receded into the background; it is remarkable how Fron makes everything else seem very far away – but it has sunk deep.*

At the hearing my mother made formal application for the judgment denying her access to her children to be varied, presumably on the grounds that she was now married and able to receive us in a reputable household. After hearing evidence submitted by both parties, Mr Justice Wilmer ruled that it was still not in her children's interest that she should have access to them, but gave her leave to make a further application in three years' time.

Particularly galling to my mother and Patrick was the discovery that

Elizabeth Russ was secretly assisting my father to ensure the rejection of my mother's application. In the course of later proceedings Patrick's solicitors pointed out to Elizabeth's legal representative: 'You are no doubt aware that your client made a gross misuse of a letter the boy wrote to her in other proceedings in which she was not a party and did her utmost to hurt our client and his present wife, therefore it ill becomes her to speak of relations worsening.' Elizabeth claimed that all she had done was provide my father with the O'Brians' address at Fron Wen from one of Richard's letters. It is hard to accept this explanation at face value, since there is no conceivable way in which mere acquisition of my mother's address could have been of use to my father in presenting his case. It must surely have been something in one of Richard's letters (most likely a passing complaint) which was submitted as evidence that my mother would not make a good parent.

Making every allowance for my mother's moral culpability and her awareness that her elopement with Patrick could result in her being barred from seeing her children, it is impossible not to feel profound sympathy for the misery the separation caused her during the years of my childhood, the lasting consequences of which were to affect her deeply for the remainder of her life. In 1948 I was in my last year at preparatory school, a very happy and well-run little establishment called Hillside, overlooking Godalming in Surrey. One evening when my friends and I were awaiting the arrival of our Headmaster in his study, I regret to say that we seized opportunity to inspect the contents of his desk. There to my surprise I discovered a bundle of letters addressed to me by my mother. The Headmaster, Mr Whicker, was an upright and generous-minded man, but under the terms of the award he was obliged to intercept my mother's correspondence.

Recounting her memories of my mother to me, Harri Roberts's wife Bessie recollected 'she was a handsome lady . . . I was very fond of her.' She also recalled that at times she appeared 'down', and 'sometimes I could see she was wiping her eyes'. Once a man arrived at the farm asking for the O'Brians, and when Bessie afterwards remarked on it to my mother, 'she was very sad about it, I remember': 'there was something: she was very sad about it, because she cried when she told me that'. Although one cannot be sure, it seems not unlikely that my mother had been served with formal notification of the judgment.

The precarious state of the couple's financial situation is illustrated by the fact that the overall expenses of their unhappy visit to London for the court hearing cost them £54/3/6½d – more than a sixth of their annual income.

As Patrick's words on their return indicate, they could not continue brooding to no purpose over what they saw as the wrong which had been done, and there was besides much to distract them in Cwm Croesor. Although snow covered the mountain tops throughout the winter, in the spring an exceptionally heavy fall provided them with a novel pleasure. On 4 March Patrick wrote:

> *For the last week or ten days it has been really wintry ? wintery – beginning with a cruel frost and then on Friday morning we woke up to find the valley white. We hurried out with skis – the snow was just deep enough – and slid gently down the slope by Bryn. It was an extraordinarily clear day, brilliant sky, warm sun, dazzling snow. In the afternoon we went up beyond Moelwyn Bank to the best slope in the valley – much longer and steeper, but it had to be taken diagonally, which will be in the fault of all our slopes, I am afraid. The next day we were bolder, and with improvised sticks (broom and mop handles) we took to leaping, or at least surmounting, the path. I find it difficult to steer, M to balance. We would not offer a brilliant spectacle. It was great fun, though.*

Patrick dispatched a graphic account of their exploits to Richard at his preparatory school in Devonshire, who responded that 'I am glad that you went out skiing and I am sorry that Daddy went into a bush'.

Their social life in Cwm Croesor was severely restricted, largely by their own choice. Almost everyone living in Cwm Croesor was a tenant of Clough Williams-Ellis, and as Patrick had learned from the confiding naval officer he met on the train during his first exploratory visit, differing views were held about him. Not long after his arrival at Fron, he recorded without comment: 'Roberts says that W-E. is a bad landlord, and that agent Hardcastle fobs off all demands for repairs or does not reply.' This criticism appears unjust, since Williams-Ellis's low rents restricted the amount he could disburse on repairs. Patrick and my mother, for example, paid £8 a year for Fron Wen, while their annual rent for The Cottage had been £75.

As local magnate the personality and conduct of Williams-Ellis inevitably attracted gossip. Probably Roberts's complaint reflected no more than momentary irritation over some postponed repair, since in early January 1946 Patrick learned that 'It appears that Croesor is divided into at least two camps, the one containing Siop Goch [the Croesor shop] and the Smiths (anti W-Ellis) and the other the Roberts's, Siop zinc [Siop Goch's rival in Llanfrothen] and Griffi-Williams [a jack-of-all trades living at Croesor]. We seem naturally to be within the ambit of the second.'

Williams-Ellis had impressed Patrick with his learning and bearing when he visited Plas Brondanw in September 1945 to negotiate the lease of Fron Wen. Six months after their arrival the squire called to see how his tenants were faring. 'Unfortunately M was out, going to Garreg. He was very civil – we may build bothy and cut tree, furthermore his mason (not the most polished of men) will cope with the wall. He is going to Sweden, lucky devil – desires us to call when he returns in June.' Tellingly, Patrick confessed to having wished that my mother had been at his side during this visit by the local grandee. However, his politeness boded well for future acquaintance. By August Williams-Ellis was back in Wales, and returning one day with my mother to their cottage Patrick heard from his son Richard that he had paid them a visit. Gratified by this promising courtesy, Patrick lost no time in calling next day with my mother at Plas Brondanw. Sadly, the encounter proved disappointing. 'It was not very pleasant. I think we were exceptionally inopportune, but we did not deserve the unfriendly rudeness with which we were received. Mrs. W.E. was more civilised, but we were glad when it was over.'

It seems doubtful that any discourtesy was intended. Williams-Ellis may have been busy, and as Patrick had already discovered his manner was markedly eccentric. It was in just such circumstances as this, visiting 'the great house' where he was all too aware that his poverty was known, that Patrick felt most vulnerable. That Williams-Ellis did not intend to rebuff the young couple is indicated by their subsequent receipt of an invitation to dinner. Unfortunately this too proved something of a disaster. Walter Greenway informed me that Patrick was mortified on arrival to discover that everyone except himself was wearing a dinner-jacket. Doubtless his host did everything to put him at his ease. Still, matters were unlikely to have been improved by the presence among the guests of Williams-Ellis's brother-in-law John Strachey, then Under-Secretary of State for Air in the new Labour Government. A highly opinionated 'champagne socialist', who in pre-war days had flirted with Mosley's incipient Fascist movement before becoming an ardent apologist for Stalin, he was just the type to provoke Patrick's anger.[1] It is not difficult to picture him sitting awkwardly silent and inwardly seething, awaiting the moment of departure when he might deliver a tirade to my mother against the pretentiousness and pomposity of the company.

Patrick's animosity towards Williams-Ellis does not appear to have endured. In *Three Bear Witness*, where he might readily have introduced a grasping or arrogant landlord, he confined himself to remarking briefly that 'the local landowner lived in a house out of reach when he visited Wales

[1]His wife Amabel also exhibited the not uncommon combination of admiration for Stalin with inveterate snobbery. She published a memoir *All Stracheys are Cousins*, a title suggesting grandees on a par with de Vere, Stanley, or Mowbray.

(which was seldom), and his agent lived at the far end of the estate, ten miles beyond the big house'. A pair of drunken sailors named Williams and Ellis feature briefly in *The Commodore*, but had Patrick harboured adverse memories of his erstwhile landlord there can be little doubt that he would have afflicted them with haemorrhoids or had them hanged for buggery.[1]

Relations proved much more unsatisfactory with their immediate neighbour. Close by their cottage stood a substantial residential property called Bryn. It had a fair-sized garden and tennis court, and was even rumoured to boast mains electricity. Such a house provided a provoking contrast to the humble dwelling at Fron, especially since it was necessary for Patrick to pass beneath it every time he came and went from home. To compound his irritation, the owner of Bryn was an authentically pompous Englishman named Sydney Smith, grandly hyphenated to Whitehead-Smith, who sought to assert his social status by disparaging Clough Williams-Ellis. While he emerged from his drive in a car unique in the valley for its smartness, Patrick was obliged to rattle past his gate at first on his noisy and unreliable motorcycle, and subsequently on a humble bicycle.

At the New Year of 1946 Patrick recorded with disgust the 'ceremonial visit of Mrs Whitehead-Smith from Bryn – our taking tea with them – at the awful price of being obliged to ask them back. He is a repulsively confident fellow but extraordinary able with his hands – they are not people of any breeding, nor do they play bridge.' Accordingly he became 'the intolerable Smith' or 'that insufferable fellow Smith'. Later in the year Patrick learned with satisfaction that 'Smith is apparently a bad thing – owes money – is sued – Roberts loathes him'. When a pair of magpies began nesting in trees in his garden but prematurely departed, Patrick decided that this was because they were 'unable to abide Smith'.

This was one of those rare occasions when Patrick's condemnation appears to have been justified. Returning home past Bryn one winter evening, he came upon a dead branch lying in the road. Ever on the lookout for suitable firewood, he bent to pick it up and was about to proceed on his way when Smith shouted from his garden that it belonged to him, since it had fallen from one of his trees. Patrick flung it down in disgust and returned home in high dudgeon.

An unpleasant incident of this sort would irritate most people, but for Patrick it was an intolerable humiliation. He achieved his revenge by writing a short story entitled 'It must have been a Branch, They Said', which was eventually published with other tales reflecting his experiences in Wales by

[1]The amusing extent to which figures from Patrick's past are accorded punishment or praise in his later novels will be shown in due course.

Secker & Warburg in 1950 in the collection *The Last Pool*. The story recounts the experiences of a writer named McAdam during a day's hunting. The hunt is represented as a very grand one in the central shires of England, implicitly the Quorn.

Though McAdam is mounted, he feels ill at ease at the meet among the regular huntsmen in their red coats, and suffers embarrassment when he accidentally drops his hunting-crop. It was 'just as he was dismounted and grovelling' for the whip that a large arrogant man named Wilkes, mounted on a big chestnut, drove his horse against McAdam's, bawling: '*Will* you get out of my bloody way?' McAdam could think of no response, but felt deeply mortified and resentful: 'The big fellow was of a type McAdam had always disliked.'[1] However, when the hunt set off he put it out of his mind and joined with enthusiasm in the chase. Later in the day, following a good run, he found himself once again subjected to gratuitous abuse: this time by an opponent of blood sports. The self-satisfied moralist swiftly sped off in his car, leaving McAdam once again unable to deliver an effective riposte.

Patrick's description of his hero's reaction undoubtedly sprang from the heart. 'McAdam was saddened by this, for he always felt that he ought to have some ready answer, and none ever occurred to him until long after. Strong, unexpected disapproval put him at a loss . . .' When the arrogant Smith yelled at him over the garden wall of Bryn, Patrick had meekly dropped the branch, despite the fact that his neighbour was wrong both in law and manners. Not long after his brush with the pharisaical critic of hunting, McAdam came again upon the insufferable Wilkes, who 'treated McAdam to an offensive stare, a stare so offensive that McAdam felt inclined to resent it with some equally offensive remarks. He could think of nothing to say, however.' They separated, and the hunt continued until McAdam encountered Wilkes for a third time, this time riding directly towards him in a hazel coppice.

The two men were alone, and Wilkes's arrogance had become yet more insufferable. ' "Will you get out of my bloody way, you goddam sod?" he shouted, and the tone was so grossly insulting that McAdam's face flushed sudden red with anger.' Wilkes rode straight at McAdam, who, gripped by a sudden impulse of uncontrollable rage, lashed out with his crop with such force that its beak smashed into the man's skull, killing him instantly. As the body lay motionless upon the ground, 'McAdam looked at him without particular emotion . . . he felt no regret then or at any time after'. The title of the story indicates (a little implausibly) that the crime passed undetected.

The incident which inspired the story was recounted to me by Edgar

[1] *The Last Pool*, pp. 101–16.

Williams, who had it from Patrick himself. A chance mention by Patrick in his card index of birds shows that he and Smith were still on speaking terms in the summer of 1947, which would have been improbable following the unforgivable exchange. Since the fall of a sizeable dead branch is likely to have occurred in winter, it may be inferred that the affront occurred during the harsh winter of 1947–48. The date is significant, in view of the fact that this short story appears to be the only literary work completed by Patrick during nearly three years that he lived at Fron Wen.

With 'It must have been a Branch, They Said' we find ourselves again in the world of *Cæsar* and *Beasts Royal*, where an injured protagonist avenges himself on the unprovoked aggressor, reacting with such ferocity as to eliminate him entirely. Again, it is not hard to detect in the hulking bully Wilkes a further embodiment of 'Cousin Carew' (Patrick's father) in 'The Thermometer'.

Throughout those detested years when Patrick had lived in dread of his gigantic, authoritarian, and occasionally violent father, he was obliged to repress any overt expression of resentment. With his bitterness locked fast within his breast, he had learned from an early age that ingratiating evasion coupled with inward scorn and occasional carefully masked sarcasm provided his only means of coping with oppressive authority. As he grew older, he found himself enabled to give open expression to otherwise impotent anger through the medium of his fiction.

On Patrick's first visit to Cwm Croesor, Clough Williams-Ellis had pointed out various houses occupied by well-known writers. Although it would have not been difficult for him to obtain introductions, he was at pains to avoid meeting such people. To his awkwardness and apprehension in the presence of social or intellectual equals must be added the combination of poverty and his mounting inability to reactivate his literary career, which made social intercourse with a successful writer especially painful. On purchasing a second-hand bicycle for my mother, he learned that 'The owner has written a thriller, published by Hutchinson. He knew of me, and rapidly outlined his career, transactions and expectations – pathetic too.' Most likely the man sought no more than to be chatty and polite. Small wonder that Patrick acquired the reputation of a recluse, and once when fishing 'an odiously pushing fellow told me that I seemed an unsociable type'.

Patrick and my mother confined intimacy to a few select friends from Chelsea days. After the long isolation of their first winter they were glad to receive a visit in April 1946 from their friend Jean who had sent them the valued package of gramophone records. Barbara Puckridge, who had driven ambulances with them during the Blitz, also paid occasional welcome visits.

These relatively rare events were regarded as special treats, but on the whole their isolated existence suited Patrick well. Having gained an ideal soulmate in my mother, he found sufficient contentment in the enjoyment of her company, inhabiting a more satisfying imaginative world through his reading and communing with nature.

Unusual or picturesque aspects of local life never failed to intrigue him, and were carefully recorded in his journal, notebooks, and extraordinarily retentive memory. In Croesor, 'It was pleasant to hear them in the Post Office mingling an odd word of English in with their Welsh. "Buzz buzz buzz – unsweetened, four [ration] points . . . buzz buzz." Strangely enough they used English numbers sometimes.' Anything of a humorous nature pleased his fancy. Trudging home one day with my mother from Garreg, 'one of the blethering quarry cars gave us a lift. The driver (? Griffi Williams) was amiable but incoherent – expressed civility by a series of maniacal chuckles.' In Penrhyndeudraeth he was delighted by a noticeboard outside the Salvationists' meeting hall, which informed the faithful: '"Knee drill 7.30: Holiness 11.0" In English, oddly enough.'

Local places and place names excited his fancy in various ways. 'Over towards Arenig there is a place on the map called Rhobelly Big and another at hand called Bryn Pig,' he noted. Blaenau Ffestiniog he regarded for some reason as 'an abode of the damned', while the little fishing port of 'Portmadoc is a repulsive little town at first sight'. It was there that he 'met a dubious type in the shop who said that dinghies could be had for £10 – bade him let me know if he could find one at that price – he appears to be a semi-criminal semi idiot sort of longshoreman cum salmon netter'.

Patrick was delighted by the archaic customs. Each New Year Day morning the children of the valley would assemble and march from house to house, crying out for gifts of 'anything from treacle toffee to fruits or whatever they would be able to give for the children'.[1] It was on this occasion at the New Year of 1947 that Edgar Williams first met my parents. After a cool reception from Mr Smith at Bryn, who resented children shouting at his door early in the morning, 'in Fron that morning we had lovely hot mince pies'. Patrick was especially intrigued by the traditional song chanted by the children, 'and asked me to write it down in a book he had – write it down in Welsh'.

One day beside Llyn Llagi, a lake at the foot of a precipice to the north of Cwm Croesor, he came upon three young men engaged in a method of fishing he had never encountered before.

[1]For the custom of handing out the 'Kalend gift' (*calennig*) at the New Year (*Y Calan* or *Calan Ionawr*), cf. T. Gwynn Jones, *Welsh Folklore and Folk-Custom* (London, 1930), pp. 157–58.

> *There were three yobs who shouted to me . . . they were marching to and fro on the far side of the lake, singing what I took to be American songs and towing three otter boards. Like so many yobs they proved civil yobs in converse: the eldest (they were but lads) showed me his board. It had 17 flies on droppers about four inches long, very thick gut. He knew the Welsh names for the flies, but not the English.*

Intrigued by this ingenious device, Patrick made a careful note and later introduced it into his Welsh novel as an occupation for Dr Pugh.[1]

During one of their early walks to Garreg at the mouth of the valley, Patrick and my mother happened upon a rustic scene, which made a strong impression on him. The Garreg smithy was an ancient establishment, patronised in the eighteenth century by drovers from the Lleyn peninsula driving their herds across the rugged Aberglaslyn pass, who halted there to have their cattle shod while awaiting the fall of the tide to cross the estuary below Penrhyndeudraeth.

Venturing into the obscurity of an almost wholly darkened hut, they found the blacksmith labouring at his forge. Laughing nervously, the man explained in what little English he possessed 'that he could, given a plan, do anything in iron'. Patrick at once decided that he would have something constructed by this picturesque figure. A few days later they returned to the smithy, when Patrick presented him with a simple design for a fire stool wrought with their initials. It was by no means clear whether the village Vulcan understood a word of what he was told, and when they returned a month later they were greeted with an incomprehensible explanation as to why as yet nothing had been accomplished. By now it was December, and in April of the following year Patrick discovered that 'The smith has not yet made our firestool, but promises it, between wild chuckles, for next week.' 'Next week' proving to be more than two months, it was not until nearly eight months after he had placed his order that Patrick was enabled to record with pleasure: 'I forgot to mention the fire stool, which arrived on Friday night: it is a good piece of work – if I had been a little cleverer with my measurements it would have been even better. The smith would not be paid, but said with cackles that we should try it first.'

Though my mother was sociable and friendly with everyone with whom she came in contact, she too made no allusion to their antecedents or the reason for their coming to dwell in humble circumstances in so remote a spot. That the O'Brians were poor was well known, but not a matter for adverse reflection among a population few of whom enjoyed the luxuries of twentieth-century life.

[1] *Three Bear Witness*, pp. 71–73.

Living as they did in close proximity to the little community at Croesor Fawr, Patrick and my mother followed closely the events of the farming year, regularly lending what assistance they could as recompense for the unfailing generosity of the Roberts family. The season began in the spring with the departure of the cattle from their winter stalls to summer pastures. It was at this time also that the sheep, which were left to graze the hillsides throughout the winter months, being taken hay only when snow covered the ground, arrived at the lambing season. In April Patrick remarked that 'the weathers – or rather wethers – have come back from their winter quarters by the sea – Pwllheli. They are odd looking creatures, inefficiently horned and sometimes very small. The valley is full of antic lambs; they conduct themselves more as if they were going to grow into gazelles than sober sheep. One ran right up to us, and I picked it up – horrified ewe uttered something like a growl.'

Initially Patrick was struck by what he took to be the careless attitude of the farmers, but he soon came to appreciate that they knew what they were about.

> *A thing that surprises us here is the apparent casualness of their shepherding. The ewes lamb all over the place, seemingly unregarded: no doubt they know their own business best, but it disturbed one's idea of the shepherd with a crook, a dog and a flock. The other day a lost lamb cried hideously all the morning until it was taken up to be fed by bottle at the farm: Robert supposed it might have been separated from its mother by a lorry chasing one or the other down the road, or else that the ewe just did not care for the lamb – this happens, he said. Yesterday, however, I was going for water when I happened to notice a dog tearing a dead sheep above Fron – I thought the dog had killed it, for they do pursue them sadistically, obviously for fun, but it seems that this was the mother of the lost lamb, dead for a day or so. Then this morning, as we were going along the path to Rhosydd we saw a pair of ravens and a band of crows a little way ahead; there was a dead ewe, with its newly born lamb trying vainly to suck. The crows had already taken the ewe's eyes, though it was still warm – or had they or the ravens attacked it alive? We took the lamb, who came trustingly to hand, down to the farm. M. would not relinquish it except to Mrs Roberts – would carry it all the way. I can hardly suppose it would have survived the ravens' attentions long if we had not chanced by.*

In the late spring my mother and Patrick often had to rescue lost lambs and ewes trapped in ditches or caught up in barbed wire, although not always in time to anticipate deadly visitations by crows, black-backed gulls, foxes, and other predators ever on the watch for vulnerable prey. After the long winter the foxes were hungry and prowling in search of vulnerable lambs to feed their offspring. From the beginning of spring until June, when the last lambs were being born, the farmers roamed the valley with guns searching for foxes and their cubs. At Harri Roberts's invitation Patrick regularly accompanied these hunting expeditions with his little shotgun.

The first of the two major events of the farming year took place about the beginning of July, depending on the state of the weather. This was the sheep-shearing, which required collaboration among the farmers of Cwm Croesor. On the first occasion that this occurred after my parents' arrival Patrick was obliged to visit Portmadoc. My mother volunteered to join in the work traditionally assigned to women at shearing: 'M. went down to help feed the eighteen men, and appears a little worn by the experience. She carved up a whole lamb and an entire ham.'

In subsequent years Patrick also turned out to lend assistance. Although he could not help with the shearing itself, which required years of experience, he joined the men who ascended the valley slopes to round up the sheep and drive them down to the farm. In *Three Bear Witness*, Patrick includes a beautifully recounted description of the day's activities, almost every detail of which is taken from the life. The farmer's dog (Edgar Williams) calls at the cottage the day before to ask Pugh (Patrick) to meet Emyr (Harri Roberts) on the quarry road early next morning. In the grey light of dawn Pugh descends to find Emyr waiting with his sheep-dogs. Together they trudge up the mountainside, the farmer expressing his profound concern that clouds hanging on the mountains presage rain. Wet sheep cannot be shorn, and cancellation of the day's work would mean postponing the shearing until all the other farms in the valley had completed theirs. In addition the elaborate feast traditionally provided for the workers would be spoiled. 'A good wether is killed, a whole ham cut up, innumerable puddings made – a hundred preparations that go to waste if there is no one there to eat them.'

Pugh is allocated the apparently simple task of ensuring that the sheep follow the right route down the mountain, as the men and dogs drive them down from above. 'I was posted at a place where the sheep had a habit of plunging down the scree and breaking back into the mountain when they were driven: I was to head them to the pens at the top of the road.'

Unfortunately he succeeds in mishandling even this most simple of duties.

> A long wait alone in the cold wind: I allowed fantasies to take shape in my mind and when the first sheep appeared I was not ready for them. They were trotting uneasily towards my gap. Already they were quite close: when I came from the shelter of my rock, shouting and waving my stick to send them back, I was on

> their flank; the foremost bolted for the gap and the others followed him, rushing along with quick, springing bounces so near past me that I could have struck the last.
>
> This was very bad. I hoped that no one had seen me.[1]

Fortunately the expert drivers and their dogs succeeded in controlling the flow of hundreds of sheep and herded them into stone pens by the road. Shearing began immediately, and Patrick describes in realistic detail the great skill, speed, and endurance with which the men conducted their work. His own duty, which he found hard enough, was to mark the shorn sheep with black oil, using an iron stamp bearing the farmer's initials. The speed with which the sheep were delivered into his hands and the unrelenting physical strain of lifting and carrying them to the spot in the middle of the pen where he kept the pail and stamp left him utterly exhausted at the end of the day. 'On and on: sheep and more sheep. I had been doing this for ever. My stomach and my back were giving me a great deal of pain, the first from the pounds of food I had stuffed into it, the second from the bend and lift, bend and lift that had been going on the length of this unending day.'[2]

The second major collective task facing the farmers of Cwm Croesor was that of harvesting hay. This followed on the shearing as soon as a spell of fine weather permitted. At the beginning of August 1946 Patrick noted with concern: 'What a filthy summer this is being, and how wretched for Roberts, with hay being so vitally necessary now.' In the level meadows at the bottom of the valley on either side of the Croesor river harvesting was conducted by mowing machines drawn by pairs of horses, but on the steep rocky slopes of the mountainside the precious crop could only be gathered through long days of painstaking labour with scythes. An essential factor in its preservation was to ensure that it was properly dried, which was achieved by constantly turning it so that the underside was regularly exposed to the sun and breeze. Speed was vital, since were the crop to be spoiled there would be insufficient fodder to sustain cattle and sheep through cruelly cold winters, which in bad years were liable to continue late into the spring.

Even the most inexpert hands were welcomed, and Patrick and my mother dutifully joined the little group on the hillside for each day's work. While Harri Roberts and his father plied their scythes with skill between rocky outcrops and hollows, Bessie Roberts and the other women raked the grass into lateral rows. As each row was completed, they had to return to the beginning and work back turning the underside to the sun. This would

[1] *Three Bear Witness*, pp. 54.
[2] *Three Bear Witness*, pp. 52–60.

continue for two or three days until the hay was completely dry. In wet weather, the entire process had to be conducted again. This completed, the hay was raked into large heaps for collection, heaved with pitchforks into carts, and taken to the farm where it was unloaded and spread carefully in the barn.

Edgar Williams remembers that, while my mother handled the raking procedure with ease, Patrick worked well when employing the rake on his right, but unlike the others, who simply turned and worked back along the row shifting their grasp to the left, he returned to the beginning of the row and began again as before. For this he was subjected to good-natured teasing which he generally took well, although he once expressed annoyance when Edgar proffered advice. Patrick was not regarded by Mr Roberts as a particularly efficient worker, and it was probably his awkward manner of handling the rake which obliged him to wear gloves to avoid blisters.

Edgar also remarked a characteristic peculiar to Patrick, which he retained throughout his life. When a photograph was being taken of the group of harvesters, he hastily withdrew himself and my mother to one side in order to avoid appearing in the picture.[1] Another habit which provoked quiet amusement was his insistence on walking off a great distance when he needed to relieve himself.

With her country upbringing, my mother took naturally to farm work. Old Mr Roberts preferred her as a worker, finding her good with animals and able to turn her hand to anything. Patrick in contrast manifested awkward difficulties and not infrequently disappeared without explanation. Nevertheless he was generally concerned to help, particularly where the task required some ingenuity. Since the Milk Board insisted on immaculately clean barns, it was necessary to whitewash the walls by squirting them with lime from stirrup-pumps. Patrick designed goggles to protect himself from the splattering liquid by cutting a section out of a gas mask, and reproved Edgar for not similarly masking his eyes. He also proved of real use to Harri Roberts by acting as his unofficial amanuensis, writing out applications for renewals of leases and correspondence which had to be conducted in English.

The population of Fron Wen was increased by the arrival of a terrier from the farm, whom Patrick named Barkis after the carrier in *David Copperfield*. At first his presence was resented by the incumbent Mrs Guinea, who 'bit Barkis on the nose – it bled profusely – and I saw her make a direct and

[1]On 31 January 1993 Patrick wrote to Arthur Cunningham of the British Library: 'I have always disliked looking at a camera & most of my few photographs show a dogged, sullen fellow – a face that should not go down to posterity.' His instinctive dislike of being photographed is clearly expressed in *Richard Temple*, pp. 199–200.

determined run at him. Peerless pig.' Initial problems in training were swiftly overcome, and Barkis promised to prove a sporting companion. But sad to relate he was destined for a premature end before the year was out. In October Richard wrote home: 'I am sorry to hear that Barkies is ill it may be that bang on the head with daddy's cricket ball.' Unfortunately Patrick's erratic prowess on the improvised Fron Wen cricket pitch proved fatal, and a month later Richard wrote: 'I am so sorry that Dog Barkies is dead.'

Barkis was replaced by his sister Nellie, who happily lived on to become the proud mother of redoubtable offspring. Patrick further decided that Mrs Guinea required a companion, and ordered another guinea pig whom he fetched from the station at Penrhyndeudraeth on the pillion of his motorcycle. Although he was christened 'the Selected Specimen', he proved a grievous disappointment to one and all: 'The Selected S. is a tiny little white pig, rather weedy and rattish; not very lovable at first sight. Mrs G. will not let him in her house, and protects herself from his surely rather precocious advances by peeing in his face. They have been making an extraordinary din all the afternoon.'

The incompatibility proved insurmountable, and before long Patrick had to dispose of the new arrival.

> *I forgot to mention the demise of the Selected Specimen, whom I put down some days ago. He really was a disgusting little creature, runtish, abnormally highly-sexed, rat-like. Bewick, or the author of B's quadrupeds, must have seen guinea-pigs of that kind when he wrote "They have neither beauty nor utility to recommend them . . . Their habits and disposition are equally unpleasant and disgusting".*

Not long afterwards Patrick was disturbed to find that Mrs Guinea was growing unusually stout. 'Recently I have been trying to tame the pig by starvation (v. Crusoe and goat) It has had very little effect so far, except to make the pig excessively vocal and worried . . . she is very much too fat, rather alarmingly so even now, after three days of short commons.' The mystery was resolved at the end of January: 'To our intense surprise Pig produced young this morning – three, we think. I had supposed a guinea-pig to go 28 days, but this is at least 64. What a good thing we did not carry out the thinning treatment more thoroughly.' Evidently Mrs Guinea's emphatic intimations of maidenly displeasure had not proved effective.

She had produced two offspring, on whom were bestowed the curious names of Vrille and Protsch. They were later given to a pair of small boys in the village at Croesor, Arfon and Frank Jones, who were delighted with their new pets. Frank 'who speaks English . . . repeated that Griffi Williams' grandmother, on being told of guinea pigs, asked whether they laid eggs . . .

The farm apropos of Vrill, reported the Portmadoc opinion that g. pigs are "good for chasing rats".'

So it was that the O'Brians adapted themselves to the tenor of life in Cwm Croesor, where the only major changes were provided by the passing of the seasons and their effect on the farmers' yearly round, and the annual cycle of wildlife. The winter of 1946–47 was the harshest in living memory. Much of Britain suffered extensive flooding, and mountainous North Wales was held fast in the grip of heavy snow and bitter ice until late spring. For Patrick and my mother, so long as they possessed adequate fuel to heat their tiny snowbound refuge, the magnificent appearance of the landscape and unusual activities of the local wildlife provided ample compensation.

'In the very hard winter we were on the shore by Criccieth when a pack (14 of them) of swans came down in the sea quite near us. Their noise was more like the cry of a musical pack of hounds than any birds. They swam, holding their necks very straight.' Not every species was so well equipped to survive, and Patrick noted regretfully that 'I am afraid that the terribly severe winter of 46–'47 more than decimated the wrens here'. The deep drifts offered greatly improved facilities for skiing in comparison with the previous winter, and in March Richard wrote thoughtfully offering to make a sledge in his carpentry class as a present for his father's name-day.

At the end of 1946 a tragedy occurred in the valley. The father of Arfon and Frank, a man named Isaac Jones who worked as a night-watchman guarding the explosive stores in the quarry above the valley, died suddenly of pneumonia. Since there was insufficient space in the small house for all the family while the body was laid out in preparation for the funeral, my mother and Patrick offered to take in the widow's two younger boys at Fron Wen. Arfon vividly remembers the occasion. My mother and Patrick moved downstairs to allow the brothers to sleep in their bed in the loft. During the night they awoke, and were startled to find themselves lying in pitch darkness. The mystery was resolved when they found that a heavy snow, the first that winter, had covered the roof during the night and obscured the skylight. The gusting wind had driven a considerable amount under the slates into the room. Evidently this was a hazard to which my parents were accustomed, for the boys discovered that while they were sleeping oilskins had been quietly placed over their blankets to protect them from the layer of snow which covered their bed. Arfon also recalls the chilling experience of making his way through the snow to the ramshackle little lavatory at the back of the cottage.

Although neither spoke much English, my mother continued to take a close interest in the boys' welfare. Arfon called on them daily on his newspaper delivery round, and after my mother and Patrick moved to France two years later Patrick jotted down what they had left behind: 'Arfon & Frank / our lambs / our dogs'.[1] It is not hard to guess that the parentless boys may have filled in part the aching void caused by my mother's separation from her own children, who were of an age with the two Welsh boys.

The cruel weather continued until the April of 1947, when it was replaced by a fine spring heralding an exceptionally good summer. By the end of May the weather became so 'outrageously hot' that they walked up to the lakes at Llynnau Diffwys to swim; here Patrick was delighted to spot a ring ouzel and summer snipe. As in the previous summer, he devoted little or no time to literary work, and spent much of each day absorbed in his favourite occupations of fishing and bird-watching, varied by occasional treats such as a visit to Criccieth fair in June.

In October 1947 they received welcome visitors, when Walter Greenway arrived with his wife Susan. Walter was struck by the minuscule size of Fron Wen, and marvels now how space was found for him and his wife. Since Richard was also living there at the time, it must have been crowded indeed. Long deprived of congenial company, the O'Brians were delighted with the companionship, and long happy days were passed discussing clocks, books, naval history, and other shared enthusiasms. The two couples went on long walks in the mountains, and though Patrick vainly attempted to interest Walter in fishing, the latter shared his intense interest in bird-watching. Patrick was delighted to show him a barn owl he had earlier encountered 'on a beam staring at me haughtily', which they found occupying the same deserted building by the old quarry at Rhosydd. Walter greatly enjoyed his visit, having long accustomed himself to overlooking Patrick's contrary ways, but frankly acknowledges that little love was lost between his wife Susan and Patrick.

Patrick lent Walter a copy of C.S. Forester's *Hornblower* novels *The Happy Return*, *A Ship of the Line*, and *Flying Colours* bound together in a cheap wartime edition. Although he recommended them, Patrick privately disparaged Forester's work: 'Hornblower, I'm afraid, does not really wear very well. Forester is no longer content to tell a tale of adventure well: he must be clever, which is a pity.' He had criticised Forester before, though then on the grounds that he preferred 'the real thing': i.e. histories and biographies, many of which were fully as exiting as any novel. It does not appear that the idea had yet occurred to him that he might make comparable dramatic use of his own extensive knowledge of the eighteenth-century Royal Navy. Such inspiration as he could muster was confined to briefly

[1]They kept pet lambs (the favourite was named Bee) in a stone pen above Fron Wen.

contemplated projects of editing interesting texts from old authors, such as those he had selected for his *Book of Voyages*.

Overall, it was hunting which provided the principal recourse which enabled Patrick to survive with any equanimity the short days and long dark evenings of the bitterly cold and dank Welsh winters. Even so, all was not well with him. Strive as he would to divert himself with the 'Country Contentments' recommended by his mentor Gervase Markham, Patrick experienced worsening bouts of depression and frustrated anger, whose cause he was not altogether able to understand. On one occasion he recorded moodily: 'yesterday M. and R[ichard]. went over to Ceunant Côch – I sat by the fire in an ill humour'. On another, after a fierce wind had continued blowing for four or five days, he noted how 'it frets one's temper'. Not long after that, 'being in a nasty temper (I spend a lot of my days in simmering irritation now) I fished the Croesor'.

This malaise increased gradually but inexorably, until towards the end of his second year at Fron Wen there arose a crisis so acute that it became apparent that some radical remedy was essential for the recovery of Patrick's well-being.

CHAPTER SIXTEEN

Father and Son: A Tormented Relationship

> I was docile, I was plausible, I was anything but combative; if my Father could have persuaded himself to let me alone, if he could merely have been willing to leave my subterfuges and my explanations unanalysed, all would have been well . . . He had no vital sympathy for youth, which in itself had no charm for him. He had no compassion for the weaknesses of immaturity . . .
>
> (Edmund Gosse, *Father and Son: A Study of Two Temperaments*)

The nature of Patrick's relationship with his first wife Elizabeth must forever remain elusive. Although relations between them appear to have continued on at least an outwardly amicable level for some years after his leaving her in 1940, by the early spring of 1946 disputes over custody and maintenance provoked irreconcilable hostility. In the end all mention of Patrick's first marriage became subject to suppression as absolute as the *damnatio memoriæ* which officially removed tyrannical Roman emperors or disgraced senators from the historical record. This was almost certainly a major factor in his decision to suppress his past life and assume a new persona from the time of his arrival in Wales.

One problem which could not be banished was Patrick's relationship with Richard, who at the vulnerable age of eight found his loyalties torn between warring parents. His mother frequently reviled his father in his presence, and though Patrick's instinctive reticence and rigorous adherence to what he regarded as the proprieties led him to refrain from overt criticism, his cold aloofness spoke for itself. Since he was not in a position to understand what had turned his parents into embittered foes, Richard increasingly found himself a bewildered and largely unprotected victim in the gulf which had opened up between them.

It must be acknowledged from the outset that Patrick was constitutionally incapable of being a good father to a child. Many people who have suffered an unhappy childhood are determined to ensure that their own children should be spared such misery. Others, in tragic contrast, have their natures so gravely warped that they visit harshness upon their offspring comparable to that which they themselves experienced. In Patrick's case the exceptional quirks of his character were so profoundly rooted as to suggest that their origins lie in innate (genetic) psychological predisposition (there was much dysfunctionality in his family), exacerbated by the loss of his mother in infancy and his ensuing disturbed and unhappy childhood.[1] Of his sister Joan, her son Harry informed me recently that 'Her attitude to children was perverse believing that as she had had a miserable time she saw no reason why other children including her own should fare any better.' While Joan's other children would not accept this harsh judgement *in toto*, in varying degree they accept that her unhappy childhood marred her relationship with her own children. Michael had abandoned an illegitimate son in Australia, while Bernard shed his first wife and did not prove the kindest of fathers to his son Charles.

For a man whose writings exhibit such profound and varied insights into human nature, it is noticeable that children represented in Patrick's vision an alien and largely threatening race, whom he generally regarded with a confused mixture of fear and intolerance. They tend to be inadequately portrayed in his novels, where they feature either as snivelling little pests or coy miniature adults. In life those rare exceptions whom he liked, or at any rate tolerated, tended to be either timidly obedient or socially 'lame dogs' who could be safely patronised. What grated on his sensitivity were the untutored frankness and unpredictability characteristic of children. From long observation I gained the impression that the extreme apprehension which they almost invariably aroused in him was grounded in a similar reflex to that which provoked his dread and loathing of crowds, or finding himself in social situations he feared lay beyond his control. In any case, given his inadequate and fragmented experience of real childhood, it is unsurprising that Patrick encountered difficulty in comprehending or empathising with children.

So far as his son Richard was concerned, it was most unfortunate that

[1] 'The genes, then, are not for psychosis itself, but for a predisposition or temperament, which, among other things, increase the chance of developing a psychosis. There are slips and gaps, as it were, between the predisposition and the disorder. This view is known as the *temperamental threshold* position . . . (Daniel Nettle, *Strong Imagination: Madness, Creativity and Human Nature* (Oxford, 2001), p. 64). Dr Nettle further notes that 'There is an increased risk of psychosis and related disorders in those who became eminent in the creative arts . . . This conclusion would seem to confirm the hypothesis that the compensatory benefit that keeps the extremes of psychotic personality in the human gene pool is enhanced creativity' (p. 147).

there existed an additional factor. Throughout his life Patrick suffered intensely from an irrational fear of social inadequacy. He believed – possibly at the time, certainly afterwards – that his marriage to the working-class Elizabeth was a shameful descent into the social abyss. So far as the unwitting Richard was concerned, his life was all too often made wretched by his father's overriding concern that he should on no account manifest any trait that might be regarded as 'common'. Any lapse in that respect was immediately perceived by Patrick as undermining his own social status, confidence in which rested on desperately fragile foundations. A further factor to be borne in mind when considering this aspect of Patrick's mental constitution is its lack of any basis in reality. Nothing suggests any other member of the Russ family suffered from a sense of social inadequacy, nor indeed was there any reason why they should. They were of perfectly respectable origin, and several of them distinguished themselves in professional life.

It must be recalled just how complex and overridingly important a part questions of class played in English life at the time. There is probably no other country in the world in which its multifarious considerations pervade to such an extent almost every level of society. To find a parallel it is scarcely an exaggeration to suggest the taboo-ridden primitive communities described in Sir James Frazer's *Golden Bough*. Today's more fluid community is changed beyond recognition from that which lingered on from the early Victorian era into the 1950s.

Prevailing standards were set by the major public schools and ancient universities, and this code it was simply 'not done' to question. Naturally there were those who did so, sometimes vociferously, but their protests had little effect on public attitudes generally. The middle classes tended to regard poverty in one of their own order as bearing the taint of sinfulness. As C.S. Forester wrote in his autobiography: 'In the early nineteen-twenties one could only descend from the opulent middle-class to the ranks of casual labour via a prison.'[1]

The departure from Chelsea must have exacerbated Patrick's entrenched concern with social status. There, after all, he and my mother had lived in a sizeable house of exceptional age and beauty, which provided an ideal setting for my mother's lovely furniture and Patrick's impressive library. Their small circle of friends was without exception well educated and well bred, while their work for the Foreign Office provided him with a comfortable salary, professional prestige, and absorbing interest. Now all that was gone, and their poverty and isolation could not be ignored. This my mother

[1] C.S. Forester, *Long Before Forty* (London, 1967), p. 137.

could endure without repining, for so long as she was with her beloved Patrick she was happy. Possessed of a strongly independent character, and fortunate in coming from a background so secure as to enable her to dispense with outward marks of gentility, she felt no humiliation for herself and concerned herself with issues of status only to the extent that they affected Patrick.

Patrick's obsessive desire to establish his gentility may not appear much to his credit, but at least the rigorous extent to which he was concerned to banish his detested and despised past makes his determination to act as a good father to Richard the more laudable. His son was after all a constant reminder and embodiment of that past, and his presence in his home necessitated constant communication between Patrick and his former wife, which he found unspeakably distasteful. He fought hard in the courts to retain responsibility for his son, and save for a temporary breakdown in 1949 was scrupulous in facilitating his stays with his mother. Unless he felt real affection for Richard, there was no reason why he should not have accepted the court judgment in 1944 awarding the child to his mother's custody. Unfortunately his almost total inability to 'suffer little children' undermined the effects of his good intentions, and overall their relationship during Richard's childhood was to prove an unhappy one.

Following his abrupt departure from the family home in 1940, Patrick did not see his son until Richard and his mother returned to London in 1942. My mother, deprived of her own children, swiftly became devoted to the little boy, who returned her affection. However she regrettably failed to influence Patrick into adopting a more understanding attitude towards his son. Indeed, it does not appear that she ever attempted to do so. Possibly she hoped her conduct might set him an example, but this seems doubtful. Her reticence in this respect was just one facet of the undeviating respect, bordering on awe, with which she regarded her husband, with whom she rarely if ever disagreed. Possibly she simply viewed a mother's role as distinct from that of a father, and acted accordingly. This is borne out by Patrick's dispassionate reflections on his and my mother's differing treatment of Richard, and recalls the marked disparity in treatment he had himself experienced at the hands of his father and stepmother.

Nevertheless, according to his own lights Patrick was deeply concerned to do his best for his son. He was scrupulous in remembering his birthday, and three days before Richard reached the age of eight in February 1945 his father noted in his diary: '<u>Present for Richard</u>'. His earlier tactless gift of cod-liver oil provoked Richard's indignation over half a century later, but he appears to have forgotten or suppressed the fact that the gifts his father subsequently gave him on birthdays, Christmas, and other occasions were carefully selected as likely to appeal to a small boy. Richard retained affectionate memories of The Cottage in Chelsea, and when he learned in 1957 that my grandparents were leaving it for the country, he wrote to his father: 'Do you know who is buying The Cottage. Had I the money and opportunity I would like to buy it. Its one of the few houses in London that is attractive.'

At the beginning of 1945 Richard was sent to board at Southey Hall, a preparatory school near Exeter. In press interviews after Patrick's death he expressed resentment that 'My father never offered to help'. As the journalist conducting the interview explained: 'Richard had been sent to a boarding school in Devon by his mother . . . His mother found the fees increasingly difficult to pay . . .'

While he may not have been informed who paid his school fees, his regular requests for payment of school and other expenses were addressed exclusively to Patrick and my mother. During his first two terms at Southey Hall Patrick continued to receive his Foreign Office salary, but when he and my mother were reduced to poverty they reduced their personal expenditure to the barest necessities in order to maintain him at the school for a further two years. They sent him clothing, tuck, and small presents whenever they could afford them.

At the end of March 1946 Patrick noted in his diary: 'We had a disagreeable shock yesterday: the Bank sent £10 for which I had written, but observed that we were now overdrawn. We had supposed that we had £18 left.' It was pointed out earlier that their income and expenditure for the year 1946 to 1947 were precariously balanced at £306. What was not mentioned was that well over a third of the income (£123) was allocated to school fees and other expenses required for Richard, and what remained placed them in the poorest income bracket in Britain.

Richard now declares that his mother 'wouldn't ask my father for help – she loyally said he needed his money for "his art"'. However at the time Elizabeth stated on oath that Patrick 'paid the School fees but ceased to pay me maintenance by mutual agreement', because he could no longer afford to do so. Despite this her solicitors continued pressing Patrick hard on her behalf to provide her with financial support, which he did as far as he could. In March 1950, when Richard wrote describing his mother's difficulty in keeping their flat clean, Patrick arranged for her to be given a Hoover he had left at The Cottage on their departure for Wales. Ironically, Patrick's capacity to provide for Richard was reduced by solicitors' bills incurred in resisting his mother's financial demands.

Whether Elizabeth's accusations represented a consistent pattern of distortion, or the random angry misrepresentations of an injured woman, there is now no means of telling. Nor is it possible to assess how far her bitterness was exacerbated by her relationship with her lover Le Mee Power, whom Richard himself described as 'often drunk and violent'.[1] Elizabeth was unlucky in her choice of husbands, and her active resentment towards Patrick appears to have begun about the time she took up with Power, and increased thereafter. In the end his behaviour proved so intolerable that she was obliged to divorce him also.

Without seeking to justify Patrick's misconduct, there are further factors which, even if only moderately extenuating, it would be unfair to ignore. Far from attempting to influence Richard against his mother, Patrick scrupulously refrained from any allusion to dissension between his separated parents. Indeed, it was some time before he even told Richard that they were divorced. Towards the end of the Christmas term of 1945 Richard wrote guilelessly to Wales: 'Dear Daddy and Mary . . . I hope Mother will come down for Christmas day.' Over the coming years his letters to his father regularly included unselfconscious references to his mother, which he would scarcely have volunteered had he sensed they might provoke annoyance. Soon after arriving in Wales Patrick discovered that Richard was not writing from school to his mother. Concerned as ever in his emotionally clumsy way to do the right thing, he at once wrote insisting that the boy maintain regular correspondence with her.

Elizabeth rarely had difficulty in obtaining from Patrick means of providing those necessities which she regularly required for their son. In his first letter addressed to his father and stepmother after they had moved to their new home in France in 1949, Richard wrote: 'Here is a bit of news for Mary, I have growen out of my good old boots, I can't get them on though last two months I could, my Mother says please can I have several pairs of socks and some pyjamers.' Shortly afterwards he was gratified to report that 'the Pygams have come and are the right size'.

Other examples illustrate the extent to which Patrick and my mother met these continuing demands. In April 1950 Richard wrote to thank my mother 'for the letter and cheque, we will get the clothes at Hope Brothers about Wednesday', the clothes in question being presumably the uniform required for the new school he was on the point of attending. Less than a week later he reported further to his father: 'Yesterday I bought my cricket stuff it was very expensive . . .' His letters regularly included such requests, as often as not urged on his mother's behalf, and in every case of which record survives either funds or the articles themselves were supplied without questioning or delay.

[1]*Mail on Sunday*, 16 January 2000.

Nor was Patrick's concern for Richard's welfare confined to paying his school fees and attendant expenses. He and my mother wrote to him regularly (generally weekly), had him to stay at Fron Wen for lengthy periods during the holidays, bought him a bicycle, and in respect of material considerations were generous to a fault. In his first letter home he reported stoically: 'I went to Exeter on Thursday to the dentist. I did not like the drill, I only made one or two squeals.' The poor boy was having considerable trouble with his teeth at this time and over the next five years Patrick paid for regular visits to the dentist, Mr Murch.

Southey Hall appears to have been a well-run and happy school. Richard was a robust child of the type that thrives at preparatory school. Like all small schoolboys, he was confident that his parents followed every football match with obsessive interest, and regularly kept them informed of scores. The assurance that 'I have my revolver' will strike a responsive chord in the heart of every former schoolboy. The Headmaster, Mr Fussell, laid on occasional customary treats which Richard appreciated. In November 'We had a Filme of Rin-tin-tin [a celebrated canine star of the day] and then Rinty gave a beautiful jump, he knocked the wicked man clean off his horse.' As the end of the Michaelmas term of 1945 approached, Richard reported excitedly: 'The conjuror is coming tomorrow. We have been making all things like decorations for Christmas. How long am I coming to stay with you?' His letters continually expressed keen interest in all that passed at Fron Wen, and he was particularly solicitous concerning the pets. 'I hope Mrs Guinea will answer to me. It is a good thing that she is nearly tame,' he wrote soon after Patrick and my mother arrived in Wales, and shortly afterwards expressed relief on learning that 'Guinea is well and liked her journey in the basket'. The prospect of life in the wild Welsh countryside appeared enticing. Thanking his father for sending him drawings of the cottage at Fron Wen, he remarked appreciatively: 'I like the look of it.' 'It must be wonderful to see the sheep being rounded up,' he responded to a description of the flocks in Cwm Croesor being brought in for the winter.

The term ended early owing to an outbreak of chickenpox, and Richard returned to spend Christmas with his mother in Chelsea. In the New Year my mother travelled by train to London to accompany him on his first visit to Fron Wen. Unhappily his ten-day stay was to prove a melancholy precursor to future unhappy occasions.

Following Richard's return to Chelsea with his mother in 1942, he had come in contact with his father only on scattered occasions involving no more than outings to the park or tea at The Cottage. The decree nisi issued in December 1944 restricted their meetings to a maximum of six or seven days in the year, which meant that when Patrick was granted custody in August 1945 he had seen Richard for three afternoons that year. Thus when Richard arrived at Fron Wen for his Christmas holiday, he and his father had not been on terms of real intimacy since a time the boy was too young to remember.

Now matters were entirely different. Cwm Croesor was remote from the outside world, Patrick and my mother possessed not a single acquaintance of similar background, and the cramped conditions imposed by the tiny cottage meant that its three occupants were confined together without intermission or distraction. Such circumstances brought out all that was most damaging in Patrick. His vulnerable psyche required that he be in total control of his environment, a necessity to which my mother had long instinctively adapted herself. Inevitably the intrusion of a third party brought about constant stress, which could be allayed only by the exercise of extreme tact and self-restraint: qualities rarely found in small children.

The excited Richard was barely installed in Fron Wen when Patrick arrived at a gloomy estimate of his son's character. 'At the moment I am inclined to feel gravely disappointed in him; he is certainly rather vulgar and very ignorant: worse, I fear he is unpleasantly affected and wanting in character. Still, this may be temporary, and at any rate it is far too soon to form an opinion.'

Once formed, Patrick's opinion rarely changed. By the time Richard was due to be returned to London, his assessment could scarcely have been more damning. 'Alas I shall not be sorry this time that the holidays are over. He has some horrid ways and I fear a truly apelike and wholely [*sic*] superficial mind. Charming for perhaps five minutes in the day: not too bad with me, but downright repulsive with Mary or by himself. Is the school all right? Mary doubts it. It does seem that he needs more companionship.'

From my own observation of my parents' attitude to children, I cannot help thinking that Richard's principal 'crime' was to arrive from his first term at boarding-school bubbling over with juvenile enthusiasm and self-confidence. That it was my mother on this occasion who chiefly objected to his behaviour, despite her generally affectionate regard for her stepson, does not surprise me. She too could be intolerant of small children when the mood took her. Whether in this case her condemnation arose spontaneously, or through overprotective concern for Patrick's peace of mind, is impossible to tell.

What is unmistakable is the ludicrous irrationality of Patrick's criticism. How could he conceivably know that Richard was 'downright repulsive . . . by himself'? Indeed in his own odd way he was dimly aware of the injustice of his attitude: 'Yet my heart misgives me in the evenings, when he has gone to bed. I nag almost without cease, often unjustly or disproportionately. He has made one or two "quaint child" remarks, one where he honestly confused M's age and [her] temperature, then 99°. . . I asked "When do you start in history at school?" "We begin with Neptune and try to go on to the end of the book, but we never do." '[1]

The inverted commas placed around 'quaint child' are suggestive. They can only have been intended to imply that Richard was showing off. Yet Patrick plainly recognised that his mistake about my mother's age was genuine. In most parents the boy's remarks would have provoked affectionate amusement. Indeed, many years later Patrick humorously recounted the 'Neptune' story to me, without any reflection on the (unidentified) small boy who had proffered this naïve account.

What lay behind Richard's conduct was irrelevant to Patrick. He detested any exhibition of childishness in children, who were considered tolerable only if they conducted themselves as intelligent and respectful diminutive adults, which is what he believed himself to have been as a boy. Recently Richard himself has perceptively declared: 'He wasn't equipped to be a father. He didn't actively dislike me. I think there were occasions when he actually liked me.'[2]

Patrick also found fault with Richard's failure to appreciate the beauties of the mountain landscape. It would surely have been more surprising had the boy fulfilled this expectation at an age when football, secret codes, and enemy spies generally provide prime considerations of concern. Again, however, this contemptuous dismissal was followed by a concession that he might be expecting too much of the child.

> I am afraid it must have been a wretched holiday for Richard, really. A couple of moribund naggers, lessons, incessant correction. He is wonderfully resilient, though, which I imagine to be the compensating advantage of insensitivity. This is all very unkind about the lad. No tobacco and a cold must give one a jaundiced outlook. I am very fond of him really, I suppose – certainly of the ideal of R. – but obviously I expect too much.

To do Patrick and my mother justice, they had indeed been unpleasantly ill. One freezing cold day, with the Croesor river racing in high flood and vast icicles hanging beside the cataract, the three of them went for a walk along the valley. The spectacle was magnificent (though Patrick was predictably

[1] English readers of a certain age will recall the book in question. *Our Island Story*, by H.E. Marshall, begins: 'Once upon a time there was a giant called Neptune. When he was quite a tiny boy, Neptune loved the sea. All day long he played in it, swimming, diving, and laughing gleefully as the waves dashed over him.'

[1] *Mail on Sunday*, 16 January 2000.

irritated that Richard refrained from expressing admiration), but unfortunately my mother had a cold coming on. In consequence the expedition proved something of a disaster. As Patrick recorded, 'M. insisted on coming despite threatened cold – fell into bog, fell over forwards, slipped flat backwards, wet through. Temperatures running around 102° and a vile throat for the next few days. I got the cold part of it – have it at this minute damn it – very low.'

For Patrick a yet more harrowing experience lay before him. It will be recalled that in the middle of January 1946 he, my mother, and Richard travelled to London, where they stayed with my grandparents at The Cottage. Patrick regarded my grandfather with an awed apprehension which never abated in coming years: a state of mind so strong that he found himself unable even to criticise him in his diary. Instead he concentrated his fire on my warm-hearted and diffident grandmother.

The agonies Patrick experienced when staying with his parents-in-law serve in part to illuminate his troubled relationship with his son. While he believed himself (while never wholly confident) to have mastered the baffling intricacies of gentility, he lived in dread lest his son betray some strain of plebeian origins. 'Richard behaved quite well at The Cottage; I was on tenterhooks (whatever they may be – calthrops?) quite unnecessarily. He loved the vile little pantomime at the Chelsea Palace, with a truly dreadful principle [*sic*] boy. Why are the comedians always so unsuitably suggestive? Punch complained about it in about 1880.'

Poor Patrick! He and my mother had taken Richard to the pantomime at the Palace a year earlier without apparent concern: it was clearly the accompaniment of his in-laws which caused him such apprehension. Within a few days of this visit our grandparents took my sister and me to see the same pantomime. Doubtless, as tradition dictated, it included many cheerfully suggestive innuendoes. But in those more civilised days they were rarely excessively salacious, and much ribaldry in any case passed over the heads of small children. Above all, had Patrick really understood the upper class of my grandfather's generation, he would have realised that such innocuous vulgarity was unlikely to shock a regular attender at Edwardian music halls, who had revelled in performances by the likes of Marie Lloyd and George Robey.

Patrick's concern lest Richard subside into the dreaded slough of vulgarity, a descent which must inevitability contaminate him likewise, arose again when he and my mother saw him off to school at Waterloo station. 'Richard was rather subdued on the platform, but cheered up in the train. The other parents looked a motley crew, some downright common many dubious. Is Southey Hall all right? Cannot decide.'

Fortunately Richard appears to have been possessed of a robust (or, as his father interpreted it, 'insensitive') character, and was blessed at this time by being enabled to escape for the greater part of the year to the uncomplicated extrovert world of Southey Hall. Though a child's letters home provide no sure guide to his underlying feelings, the indications are that he was a happy schoolboy.

Patrick carefully conducted his duty as a parent – as he understood it. Care was taken to ensure that Richard was properly supplied with tuck, that essential commodity. For his birthday Patrick sent him a kite of his own construction. 'The kite is broken by the wind but it flew all the same,' Richard reported contentedly. His father, determinedly setting to work to provide a replacement, encountered characteristic problems: 'I was rash to tell R. that he should have a kite. Our combined efforts produced a most inefficient abortion, and now even that is kaput, having got trodden upon during the climax of whitewash scraping.' A week later matters were not much further advanced: 'Three or four days ago we went into Portmadoc by the bus: we failed in our main aim, which was to buy a cane for another kite.'

As the Lent term of 1946 drew to its close Richard wrote: 'There are 13 more days to the end of term and I will be glad when I come to meet you and go to Fron-Wen, the little cottage in Wales and be able to sail my kite and see the new guinea-pigs. They seem nice in the drawings of them.' Richard grew more excited as the holidays drew closer, calculating that 'there are only 5 more days to the end of term, I think . . .The holidays will be nice I hope for picnics. I am glad that the [guinea pig] children are well.'

At last the longed-for day arrived. Owing to confusion over the arrangements, my mother and Patrick were obliged to take a lift in a van over the mountains by Ffestiniog all the way to Shrewsbury. They arrived at the station just in time to meet Richard, 'who had travelled with a kindly, if common, Parent'. After a brief exploration of the town, whose then unspoiled medieval architecture delighted Patrick, they set off on the long journey home. 'The way back seemed very long but R. who had started in pain [toothache?] was in high spirits. We had taken poor wretched Protche [the guinea pig], which – especially considering the remarkable heat–was an error.'

Richard spent just over a fortnight at Fron Wen. He was a thoroughly normal, physically robust, and high-spirited boy – at least, when permitted to be. Considering the exceptionally disturbed circumstances of his upbringing, his temperament was remarkably equable, affectionate, and (save on one occasion when pressed beyond endurance) biddable. Academically he was not in the first flight, but neither was he backward for his age. He shared his father's enthusiasm for natural history, and eagerly participated in his and his stepmother's explorations of the surrounding countryside. In short, he was the sort of son of whom most fathers would have been fond and proud. Unfortunately Patrick was far from being a normal father. In old age he acknowledged himself to have been 'a sort of elderly child' in his early years, and in truth it might be said that from about the age of six he had scarcely known what it was to be a child at all.

A related factor in Patrick's treatment of his son may reflect the irrational shame with which he regarded his own childhood. He was ashamed of being alienated from his brothers and sisters and of what he considered to be his prevailing vices of weakness and compensatory slyness. The introduction of a third party into his cosy domestic ménage was clearly fraught with potential for friction. The needs and nature of a small boy – above all a son, on to whom most fathers tend to project deeply felt hopes and ambitions – might provoke difficulties of a peculiarly delicate and intractable nature. In Patrick's imagination there existed an ideal standard of boyhood, which he had never known but now sought to create in surrogate form. Richard's individuality, together with the need for a child to share his exploration of life with friends of his own age, made it impossible that he should meet his father's rigid expectations. The irreconcilability of their respective positions was all too often misinterpreted by Patrick as evidence of Richard's mulish stupidity, vulgar habits picked up from his humble home in Chelsea, or obdurate refusal to act the part nature intended for him.

All in all, the prospects for a happy relationship between father and son were not propitious, and it was with grim predictability that they deteriorated swiftly from the outset. Within twenty-four hours of Richard's second arrival at Fron Wen for the Easter holiday in 1946, Patrick gloomily confided to his journal:

> R, apart from being a little tedious over a lost ball, was thoroughly likeable all day. The thing is not to listen to the flow of mindless egotistic chatter (or artless prattle) rather than to try to quell it. Listening only drives me melancholy mad. It is plain that it is not Southey Hall that has a bad effect on his diction. Apart from one or two haiches his accent is perfect. Even more gratifying is the fact that so far, at any rate, he has shewn none of those dreadfully depressing little nastinesses of the 'aren't I a sweet little thing?' type – I am sure that they, the grosser vulgarisms and the cinema outlook on entertainment are solely Chelsea products.[1]

As ever, Patrick's analysis of Richard's behaviour betrays vastly more of his

[1] 'He had reached a silly age and he went to the cinema too often, but he was a good, loving boy really' (*Three Bear Witness*, p. 159).

own hopes, fears, and childhood privations than it reveals of his son's supposed inadequacies. It is hard to believe that he could have written as he did had he himself been accustomed to the 'artless prattle' of childhood. He could conceive of no expectation other than that children should be constantly attentive to the interests of their elders, and unstintingly eager to acquire their superior knowledge and manners: in short, they should strive not to act like children at all.

Patrick found Richard's recalcitrance incomprehensible. Was he not provided with every opportunity of enjoying those pleasures which he had himself been denied? The weather was glorious during the week that followed Richard's arrival in Cwm Croesor. Each day the trio roamed the valley and surrounding countryside, carrying food for the picnics to which Richard had looked forward with excitement as his term drew to an end. But once again the pleasure was soured somewhat for Patrick, when he found that Richard did not always react as he was convinced that he would himself have done at the age of nine, had he been afforded such opportunities.

> One thing against going out and about so much is that it multiplies the occasions on which R. can display his complete lack of interest in country matters. This is a pity, for (apart from the pleasure he loses) it seems to me that there is a close connexion between such knowledge and virtue. The lack of interest is surely abnormal – he whittled a stick while we (in a high state of excitement) tried to put an adder out of a patch of grass. I could go on at great length about the boy's imperfections, but what is the use? It would need some effort and it would only depress – I will break off now to try to drill a little knowledge of letters into his head. Not very successful lessons. Is Southey Hall any good at all?

The allusion to 'lessons' raises the most damaging aspect of the relationship between father and son during their time in Cwm Croesor. Even during Richard's relatively brief stay during the Christmas holidays, Patrick had felt impelled to instruct and improve his son through a formal curriculum of his own devising. It is hard to imagine a project more prone to disaster. Children nurture a natural sense of justice, which includes a provision that holidays be set apart from the rigorous round of school life. In class the child is protected by the company of his fellows, which provides the dual benefit of companionship in adversity and deflection of the schoolmaster's attention. Furthermore the relationship between parent and child is of a delicacy which makes its successful translation into that of teacher and pupil wholly exceptional. As if this were not enough, there could scarcely exist a person less suited to impart instruction than Patrick, who entertained only fleeting doubts of the efficacy and value of his methods.

There is no reason to believe that there was anything consciously cruel in Patrick's attitude. That he found Richard's boyish ways so tiresome and difficult of correction if anything confirms the sincerity of his commitment to a long-term programme of improvement.

Richard had been baptised as a Roman Catholic while attending the Servite School in Chelsea, and although Patrick was not himself a Catholic he was concerned to ensure that Richard attended church while staying with him. Finding a Catholic church was not an easy matter in Nonconformist Wales, but by June Patrick had managed to discover one in Portmadoc. Like so many other buildings in the neighbourhood it had been erected by Clough Williams-Ellis, and Patrick admired its architecture. He found the priest Father Crowley 'gentle, un-inquisitive and unassuming. It is a pity that the average priest in England (or Wales apparently) is not like the oldfashioned parson': i.e. not quite a gentleman! Fortunately Richard liked him, though this in turn aroused his father's recurrent misgivings: 'Richard and Fr. Crowley got along well: I hope this will not start any religiosity nor any of that repulsive sweet little thing business to which he is so regrettably prone.'

A telling indication of the bizarre dichotomy of Patrick's character is provided by his lack of shame in recording so unpleasant a reflection, while conceding that 'I spend a lot of my days in simmering irritation now'. However all appears to have gone well, and the extent of Patrick's conscientious concern to act in his son's best interests is illustrated by the fact that each Sunday he and my mother accompanied Richard on bicycles for the fifteen-mile journey to Portmadoc and back. Edgar Williams recalls seeing them return when emerging from the chapel in Croesor at 10 a.m.

Patrick noted a few days after Richard's arrival: 'April 1st. was good fun. Somehow R had not heard of All Fools' day, but he thought very highly of the idea – empty egg for my breakfast.' During a long walk across the mountain to the east to view the deserted slate quarries at Llyn Cwmorthin, he spotted some ponies and pondered: 'Would one be possible for Richard?' Back at home, he and my mother busied themselves in making him a bow and arrows. Tellingly, Patrick reflected how 'he would have loved a proper arrow that would have flown true when I was a youngling'.

Patrick's highest priority was to ensure that Richard be provided with that thorough education whose advantages in his eyes were inestimable, and he was persuaded that special measures were required to ensure his son's success. 'His virtual illiteracy appals me,' he complained at the outset of the school holiday. 'What is the use of his going back to school? He will only sit vacantly in form (as I did in maths) learning nothing and being the buffoon. I know that I could get him along quite soon, and I have written to Fussell [the Headmaster of Southey Hall] again.' The allusion was to a project which Patrick harboured of retaining Richard at home for a term, in order to bring him up to standard by individual coaching.

Patrick found the condition of childhood baffling to an extent that would be laughable were it not so tragic. 'I left Richard to do lessons by himself. One task was an essay on climbing, which on completion proved to be confined to the reflexion: "If it is fine no doubt you will take a piknik."' A day or so later the three climbed to the top of the Cnicht, where Patrick was mortified during their ascent 'to see other, repulsive, people on the peak'. To make matters worse, Richard brought home as a trophy the horned skull of a ram. 'Is R's pronounced taste for blood and bones quite healthy?' fretted his father. 'I did not like the way in which he asked whether he might go up and look at the remains of the ewe the other day – there was more than a hint of something unpleasant.' Not only would most fathers recognise a 'taste for blood and bones' as a normal symptom of boyhood, but the irrationality of Patrick's concern was displayed not long afterwards when, coming unexpectedly upon a particularly fine adder, he 'killed him as a specimen for M. & R. – one neat blow. I left him to bleed and finish writhing on a rock and went on reading.' Three weeks later, when Richard returned for the holidays, his father observed that he was 'immensely pleased with the adder, which is past its prime'.

However a few days later Patrick reported: 'R. very pleasant today. I must try to be more reasonable in my nagging. I hope it really has as little effect as it seems to have.' What he meant by 'pleasant' is not specified, but it is to be feared it involved little more than the boy's refraining from chattering in the next-door room while his father was trying to concentrate on Henry James.

On 15 April Richard returned to his mother in London, presumably with few or no regrets. His departure occasioned yet another of Patrick's revealing acknowledgements of the fog of incomprehension which clouded his relationship with his son.

> Richard went off yesterday, taken by M. to Ruabon as I funked the journey. There was, I'm afraid, a mutual relief perceptable: R. was curiously unpleasant for the last two days – indeed, even after he was told that he would be going to his mother on Monday. However, Fussell wrote most acceptably, saying that he would be grateful if I would keep R. for this term in order to get him to read fluently. I do hope that an uninterrupted four months will make him rather more of a human boy and less of a mindless, perpetually showing-off overgrown child.

It seems that by 'human' Patrick intended his ideal of the child as small adult:

an idiosyncratic view complemented by his indignation on discovering a nine-year-old boy behaving as an 'overgrown child'. This was not the most promising attitude to be adopted by a prospective tutor, above all when that tutor was the pupil's parent. However, Patrick prepared himself for the task in the sincere belief that he could improve Richard, while the latter on his return to Southey Hall guilelessly regarded the prospect of no school for a whole term with pleasurable anticipation.

My mother and Patrick set out on a beautiful morning in early May to meet Richard's train at Ruabon on his return from London. Once again he was in a state of high excitement at the prospect of seeing his beloved guinea pigs, and spending long sunny days fishing, picnicking, and watching birds. Patrick noted that 'He was charming all the way home, and delighted not to be going back to school – had thought it too good to be true.' Though Richard loved and missed his mother, the material conditions of life were far from easy in their cramped flat in Chelsea. Artlessly, he explained to his father that 'he went by himself to church in London as I had told him but his collection money had been taken from him [presumably by his mother] "because it was needed for food" '.

Four days' grace being allowed before the commencement of lessons, the boy enjoyed himself by the banks of the Ceunant. He ventured boldly into the river, despite the fact that he was 'rather frightened of the water: very naturally seeing that he cannot swim'. The deficiency very nearly proved disastrous on the following day, when Richard plunged into a deep pool. 'Fortunately we were at hand and fished him out at once. He had a lot of water in him and seemed aggrieved, he was incoherent for the first few moments, but soon cheered up. He is responsive to un-fussiness.' Unfortunately Patrick's recognition of his son's courage did not lead him to make any allowance for his real or supposed academic failings.

After two days of teaching, Patrick reported gloomily that 'R's education is proceeding . . . What a very slow process it is, and how very much there is to do. He does not know how to use his brain at all yet – no sense of analogy, either. We are reading Horatius and drumming home the multiplication table at present: I imagine this will go on for a long while. Yesterday was not too good – R. reduced to tears for the first time – but today's effort was much better. M. is coping with French; her method is in many ways better than mine, and seems to entail no bullying.' Once again it is telling to note the frank admission – and inability to learn from it. A problem may have lain in the fact that Patrick retained a deep love for Macaulay's *Horatius.*[1] If Richard

[1] On 3 March 1975 Patrick noted in his diary: 'I can still say long pieces of Horatius.'

did not display precisely the right degree of enthusiasm, that could only reflect lack of appreciation.

Patrick's complaints continued throughout the four months allotted to his relentless course. 'Richard's dreary education goes on. It is a sorrowful business all round.' The boy could not 'count beyond a hundred and he has incorrect notions on figures, 100,99 [*sic*] being 199. I spent this morning trying to remedy this. How agonizingly slow he is.'

My mother's gentle approach seemingly produced no better results, and little perceptible improvement was detectable in Richard's French. Patrick found it incomprehensible that his son could be unable to grasp a concept once it had been clearly explained, and feared lest he might not be merely deficient in education, but congenitally backward.

> Richard's education worries us. We have been going on long enough to be fairly sure that the excruciating slowness of apprehension is a settled feature of his mind. It is really dreadful. He seems almost incapable of learning. When I am hard with him he goes silly from fright; when I am mild he grows obnoxious and shows off. I don't suppose that my methods are faultless, but they can't be as bad as all that. I am afraid he is sub-normal. It may only be arrested – temporarily arrested development. God knows I hope so. The other day he quite stunned me with his wonderful casualness. I had found that he did not really understand figures, particularly above 100. I had explained all one morning long, and I left him in the afternoon with strict instructions to write the figures seriatim up to 1,000. This was supposed to drum the system right into him and to improve his writing of figures – I gave him a copy. When I came back (we had been to the hanger [a wood above the house], which is probably resented) he had reached 250 odd. Questioned, he observed that he had not gone on 'because it was too boring for me'. This earned him ten of the best. I detected his uncertainty, by the way, by getting him to use an index – he did not know that 246 came before 370 – no idea of relation. Reading is terribly slow, but we have now mangled 70 verses of Horatius. Poor Macaulay: I would not have done it had I known. Difficulty with schools of pronunciation. M's French [lesson] – the time now – is agony to hear. We feel old and wan.

Patrick's reference to giving his son 'ten of the best' may jar on contemporary sensibilities. However, he administered physical punishment relatively sparingly: certainly no more often than a boy might have expected at preparatory school in those days. In an affidavit submitted to custody proceedings in June 1949 Patrick declared: 'When it is necessary and this was twice in the last term I certainly chastize my son as he would be chastized at school.' Richard himself does not appear to have resented the punishment *per se*, as he has candidly explained in newspaper interviews:

'From my point of view he was teaching me mainly useless things. Arithmetic was OK. English was fine. But I couldn't see the point of Latin. He was a pretty rigorous teacher. He didn't like mistakes. If I made one, I would be told to put it right, and if I went on getting it wrong, he would cane me, but not heavily – don't run away with the idea that it was sadistic . . . He didn't give me a fully-fledged whacking as such but a stick was certainly wielded and it was a Malacca cane, I can see it right now. He was very strict and beat me if things got very bad. But I wasn't the easiest child in the world to teach.'[1]

Commenting on a letter from his solicitor Baddeley, Patrick angrily noted that Elizabeth ('the opposition') 'has the silly effrontery to say that R. has only been to two films, and those Disney films, in the past year. The boy's mind is a veritable palimpsest of vulgar cinema impressions – Bob Hope, Formby and others. And with extraordinary naïveté her solicitors sent poor R's membership card of the repulsive "cinema" club. I wish I had kept the *Times* special articles on the subject.'

The ascription of Richard's failure to achieve adequate progress in French and mathematics to his having enjoyed the exploits of Bob Hope and George Formby in the King's Road cinema appears ironic when I recall Patrick's laughter many years later when watching *Son of Paleface* on television. But that was in the exemplary company of my grandparents, whom he respectfully observed greeting Hope's antics with uninhibited hilarity.

Richard has subsequently acknowledged that there were compensations. Despite his father's success in converting even Macaulay's *Horatius* into something of a grind, its resounding rhythm and stirring story aroused his boyish enthusiasm. Away from the dreary schoolroom, Patrick imaginatively identified a mountain tarn below the grim crag of Yr Arddu with a name familiar from the *Lays of Ancient Rome*:

[1]*Guardian*, 27 November 2003; *Daily Telegraph*, 26 November 2003. Richard recalled an occasion when he received (surely justifiably) 'a judicious wallop with a walking stick' for throwing stones at a neighbour's cowshed (King, *Patrick O'Brian*, p. 132). Patrick's condemnation of his son's supposed failings, bitter frustration at the failure of his attempt to teach him, and consequent resort to violence, are accorded extraordinarily transparent treatment on pp. 112–20 of his novel *The Catalans*, which was published in 1953 at a time when he was on amicable terms with Richard. I am at a loss to understand Patrick's purpose in penning such an unpleasant diatribe, whose application my mother must certainly have understood and which his son might be expected to read. Possibly the indefensible harshness and sadistic brutality unsympathetically ascribed the fictional father indicate a bizarre attempt at exculpatory purgation: particularly as the depiction is far in excess of anything that occurred in reality. I doubt that his conscience was entirely easy. In 1983 he experienced a disturbing dream, 'in which I bullied small child quite disgracefully'.

Best of all pools the fowler loves
The Great Volsinian mere.[1]

Patrick loved the stirring rhythms of *Horatius*, and a desperate fight-scene in his *The Road to Samarcand* gleefully describes how 'through helmet skull, and bone the sword bit to the ground' – a passage whose provenance readers of the poem will at once recognise.

Richard's stay at Fron Wen in 1946 lasted from the beginning of May to the middle of September, which meant that the family was able to spend much time out of doors. There Patrick was at his best, eagerly sharing his interests with his son, and displaying genuine concern to provide him with congenial entertainment.

Before long the archery begun in the Easter holidays had become quite a success: 'Recently we have both grown childishly fond of shooting in the long bow. I began partly to play with R., then to show him how unwise he was to lose and break his bows and arrows and to spur him on to making his own. The didactic purpose has quite failed, but we have fun. We have made five beautiful arrows, two with raven's feathers, and we shoot easily fifty yards at a mark, sometimes nearly hitting it. Markham is our teacher.'[1]

Patrick's great success with Richard was the extent to which he enthused him with his own love of the countryside, above all its natural life. Observing, as he thought, kestrels nesting in a cleft above the Ceunant, he contemplated dangling Richard over the edge on a rope to inspect the spot. Happily the project was not put into effect, but Richard was more than content to participate in explorations such as most boys would enjoy, and under his father's instruction swiftly acquired real pleasure and considerable skill in observing and identifying birds and wild animals. Peering eagerly into a wheatear's nest, Patrick pleasantly recorded that 'there were about six gaping little visages (R. says zivages) plainly visible'. Richard encountered no difficulty in keeping up with his father and stepmother during their regular walks for miles across extremely wild country, and generally accepted the mishaps he not infrequently encountered with admirable stoicism.

Walter Greenway, whom Richard knew as 'Uncle Walter', thoughtfully sent him a present of a cricket bat. Patrick, who had played as a boy at Lewes,

[1] Almost certainly Patrick or my mother borrowed the idea of identifying local landmarks with names in *Horatius* from Kipling's *Puck of Pook Hill* (cf. the opening of 'A Centurion of the Thirtieth').

[2] Patrick's copy of Markham's *Country Contentments: Or, The Hvsbandmans Recreations. Contayning the Wholsome Experiences in which any man ought to Recreate himselfe, after the toyle of more serious business* (London, 1649) contains sound practical advice 'for shooting in the Long-bow'.

set about providing instruction. Richard proved a keen pupil, though not unnaturally his skill initially proved of limited success. Outside the classroom Patrick's strictures tended to be mild, and of Richard's cricket he commented that 'he has slightly more idea of using it [Walter's bat] than of fielding (in which his practice is to get out of the way of the ball as briskly as possible) or bowling, not that that is saying much'. Their play continued on a regular basis each summer, and two years later Patrick mentioned: 'This evening, when Richard and I were playing cricket, one raven sat on the skyline on the top of the Drws croaking at half-minute intervals for an hour or so, occasionally taking a short flight.'

In May the tranquillity of the valley was dramatically interrupted by the first VE Day anniversary, which was for some reason celebrated on 8 June, a month after the actual date. 'Today – R being excused lessons, though God knows there's little enough to celebrate about – we went to Arddu and Cerrig y Wyllt.' After their return from the mountains they watched from the garden of Fron Wen a curious display of mass jubilation on the part of the local people. 'As their celebration of Victory Day the inhabitants of Llanfrothen rushed up the Cnicht, like inverted Gadarene swine. We saw and heard them from a great way off. Afterwards they had tea at Blaencwm. We had a bonfire, which pleased R.'

The dreary curriculum imposed at Fron Wen was occasionally enlivened by other indulgences. At the beginning of July Patrick travelled to Portmadoc and bought Richard a bicycle. As with his swimming, the boy proved fearless in pursuing the exhilarating new hobby – to an extent which all but resulted in disaster: 'The first day Richard plunged over the wall by Bryn, a six foot drop, with the bicycle on top of him. Both escaped harm by some miracle. I soon got him good enough to go down to Port[madoc], but the first time he shot past me on the right angled hill and hurled off at the corner, again quite unharmed.'

By the middle of August, however, Patrick had characteristically come to revise his estimate of Richard's robustness. Barkis, the terrier who subsequently came to a sad end in consequence of Patrick's cricket practice, 'went fishing with M. and behaved admirably . . . The same cannot be said of R., alas. He seems to be getting progressively wetter and less manly. What to do? I am already too savage by far at lessons, but any relaxation produces tasteless drip and dreary showing-off. Ichabod.'

This was plainly unjust. Richard had taken to country life with fortitude and enthusiasm, but there are limits to the pleasure which a small boy can sustain confined to the company of two adults for months on end. That Richard might have been lonely seems never to have seriously occurred to his father: solitude had after all largely represented the normal order of things during his own childhood. At the end of May Patrick noted: 'I made a hazel rod for R., but he doesn't really care for fishing yet – too solitary.' Patrick persuaded himself that once Richard made a successful catch his interest would develop.

A few days later he confided to his diary a predictable development which aroused his deep concern.

> R. sets me a bit of a problem by striking up a violent friendship with Arvon.[1] I don't like to forbid it, although it isn't really suitable, he being so prone to bad influence and the Arvons being so very slummy (though decent lads, I think, in themselves). He is so very gregarious too, and is obviously filled with joy at the prospect of companionship. But he doesn't seem to have understood my general, rather vague discourse on unsuitability (nobody could be more truly democratic than R.) and I fear he is incapable of moderation.

It is impossible to read this transparently irrational complaint without feeling profound sympathy for Richard's plight. The contorted emphasis which Patrick's strange upbringing induced him to place on social distinctions provided one of the prime causes of his increasing estrangement from his son. Had Richard been permitted to enjoy a wholesomely boyish existence outside the stifling confines of the introspective little family group at Fron Wen, it would surely have gone far to ameliorate the deeply troubled relationship between father and son.

Eventually September arrived, when Richard returned to Southey Hall. While Patrick and (to a lesser extent) my mother tended to be harshly intolerant of behaviour which they regarded as characteristic of an unregenerate young barbarian, it frequently occurred (as I had occasion to observe) that in his absence the same child could become transformed into an object of uncritical affection.

On 5 October Richard wrote to 'Daddy and Mary' to thank them for 'the nice little bus, it is a great toy for me. I had two races with other boys and it won.' His letters were full of news which boys conceive as being of equal concern to their elders. 'I have scored 4 goals in the 2nd game it is not very easy to do it . . . do you think I can box as I want to learn to box there is another sport and that is fives.' Away from home he swiftly forgot the travails he had experienced, and was eager for news of life in Cwm Croesor. 'Is there any snow on the mountains yet, I don't think there is. How are M[r] and M[rs] Robts how are the dogs. Have you been to the Black rock sands yet.'

Either because Richard was performing better at school, or because he

[1] The boy who was subsequently looked after by my mother and Patrick after his father's death.

found the grind of tutoring tedious, Patrick appears largely to have abandoned the programme of holiday teaching which father and son found so insupportable.

For a while Richard's life moved on to a more regular and happier plane. While enjoying the normal pleasures of school life, he was eager to learn everything that passed in Cwm Croesor. He had departed at a time when conditions in the snowbound valley were at their worst, and wrote soon after his return to report that 'I came to school safely. I hope you are alright? Are the dogs and farm alright? It has snowed a little bit but not very deep.' In the holiday Richard enjoyed joining his parents in assisting the Roberts family in saving as many of their lambs as possible from the effects of the ferociously cold winter of 1946–47. Patrick found it all but impossible to enter into a warm relationship with his son in person, but in correspondence he was both affectionate and solicitously understanding of boyish requirements. Richard, having succumbed to one of those flu epidemics which provide a welcome break from lessons, wrote home to 'thank you for the torch, cake and letters. I am now up out of the sickroom. The cake and the torch were not broken. I will not forget "Treasure Island".' Patrick, who had read it in the previous year, was concerned that Richard should share his pleasure.

Despite his father's strictures on his cricketing ability (which were a bit rich, considering the fate of the unfortunate dog Barkis at his hands), Richard was eager to resume their games on the grass outside the gate of Fron Wen, and reminded my mother: 'I am looking forward for the holidays . . . Please could you ask Daddy if he could linseed-oil my bat . . . I am getting on in French. yesterday I was playing and I chepped one of my teeth Love Richard. P.S. I am breaking up on April 1st.'

His enthusiasm was sustained by practice during the Easter holidays, and on returning to school he reported to my mother: 'I have arrived safely. We have started Cricket. Please could I have some lettuce seeds? I have dug my garden and have put some radishes in. Please could you ask Daddy to oil my bat.' It is to be hoped that Patrick recanted his misgivings concerning his son's courage and enterprise, when he learned from Richard that 'I am in the boxing club. I hope you do not mind? The garden is going very well and my radishes are very big.' With the arrival of the summer term he also had opportunity to acquire a skill, the lack of which had all but cost him his life in the previous year. As he explained in the middle of June, 'I have started to use the swimming-bath and I ought to swim and float at the end of the term. I have taken three wickets in one over and I am going to use my bat. The weather is hot and it makes the swimming easier. I am glad to hear that you caught some whales.' The last reference was to an amusing account by Patrick of his catching some exceptionally small trout in the Croesor river.

Richard looked forward to displaying his newly acquired prowess at cricket in the holidays. 'The cricket is allright and I am going to learn to do over arm balls and I hope I will be good at it . . . We have not had much swimming because of some geese and one drowed itself . . . I have made a tray for you and I think it is big enough and I hope you will like it. The garden is not bad and the seeds are high. I am looking forward to the holidays.' Richard was a tough boy, well able to cope with life despite his traumatic childhood. 'Thank you for the jam and I eaten it. The boxing is not to bad with other poeple and Rolph has won another fight and it was with Gahagan . . . the exams are on 21st.'

While Richard forgot previous unhappinesses and eagerly anticipated his summer holiday, he was unaware of a dramatic decision which was about to effect a radical change in his life. In July Elizabeth received a letter from Patrick's solicitors informing her that he had decided to withdraw their son from Southey Hall at the end of term, and thenceforth intended to coach him at home with a view to his eventual entry into public school.

Patrick's explanation for his decision was that Richard's educational standard was so poor that he saw no alternative to undertaking the task himself, with my mother's assistance. Before beginning at Southey Hall in January 1945, he claimed, the boy's education had been erratic and sub-standard. In the course of subsequent legal proceedings Patrick explained that while working for the Foreign Office,

> I had no opportunity . . . of finding out how really backward the boy was. His school reports had been generally bad but until I had him at home and tried to coach him during the holidays I did not realise how backward he really was. I have tried various experiments, keeping him at home for a term and going through the books he had had at school. I discovered that Richard had never learnt the basis of any subject, he could not read properly and did not know what came after 100; he was then 9 years of age.

Although much may be urged against Patrick's approach to teaching, there can be no doubt that he was sincere in his belief that he was acting in his son's best interest by removing him from school. It has been alleged that concern for Richard's welfare was not the true reason for his withdrawal from school. Dean King states that 'Patrick and Mary could no longer afford to pay for tuition, room and board at Southey Hall'.[1] This appears fair comment, though only up to a point. The school fees were £45 a term,

[1] King, *Patrick O'Brian*, p. 127.

payable in advance. My parents' income and expenditure from November 1946 to October 1947 amounted to just over three hundred pounds. This included £123/3/4d for 'Richard'. Plainly the remaining £33/3/4d (which was in any case spent on his additional expenses at school and home) could not cover the Michaelmas term.

Though the decision to remove Richard from school may to some extent have reflected financial considerations, the prime cause appears to have been a genuine conviction on Patrick's part (earlier confirmed by the Headmaster of Southey Hall) that his son was academically backward and would benefit from intensive coaching at home. At the time of Richard's removal from Southey Hall Patrick entertained high expectations for the success of *A Book of Voyages*, which was to be published that autumn. He was due £45 as the second instalment of his advance, which would have exactly covered Richard's school fee for the Michaelmas term. Apart from this, it is not unlikely that an appeal by my mother to her father would have proved successful. The sum involved was after all relatively modest, and my grandfather was concerned for Richard's welfare. How school fees might be met in ensuing years was another matter, but my parents were perpetually placed in a situation where they could only consider the immediate future.

Richard himself, in so far as he had any say in the matter, was like most small boys prone swiftly to forget hardship and unpleasantness, and as each term at Southey Hall drew to its close found himself looking forward to returning to Cwm Croesor. His mother raised no objection at the time to his being once again taught by his father and stepmother.

Half the summer holiday was spent with his mother in Chelsea, and since Patrick adhered to the school timetable Richard may have found the days spent at Fron Wen enjoyable enough. But his father's resumption of tutoring for the Michaelmas term proved a harrowing experience for the unhappy boy. Enough has been seen of Patrick's own account of his approach to instruction to make it clear that his son's bitter recollections in later life were largely justified.

> 'The lessons were not easy,' he says. 'My father was a grim teacher. He had no spark, no motivation. It was learning by rote . . . I tried to stay out of his way. I wasn't enjoying myself with my father – I wanted to go back to London. I missed my mother and our dog, Sian.' His father was a hard taskmaster. When Richard burst into tears after stepping on a drawing pin, O'Brian sternly told him the fable of the Spartan boy who died rather than show pain.[1]

[1] *Mail on Sunday*, 16 January 2000. In *The Golden Ocean* (pp. 116–17) Patrick was to make use of the exemplary tale in a ludicrous context.

That this probably represented no more than a clumsy attempt at pedantic humour provided scant consolation to its recipient.

As in the previous summer, if Richard appeared particularly obtuse or idle, Patrick took a stick to him. His concept of teaching bore marked resemblance to that imposed by the father of Anthony Trollope, as recalled by the author in his autobiography.

> From my very babyhood . . . I had to take my place alongside of him as he shaved at six o'clock in the morning, and say my early rules from the Latin Grammar, or repeat the Greek alphabet; and was obliged at these early lessons to hold my head inclined towards him, so that in the event of guilty fault, he might be able to pull my hair without stopping his razor or dropping his shaving-brush. No father was ever more anxious for the education of his children, though I think none ever knew less how to go about the work. Of amusement, as far as I can remember, he never recognised the need. He allowed himself no distraction, and did not seem to think it was necessary to a child.[1]

Despite all this Richard later acknowledged that amid the prevailing gloom there were compensations. 'From my point of view he was teaching me mainly useless things. Arithmetic was OK. English was fine. But I couldn't see the point of Latin. He was a pretty rigorous teacher. He didn't like mistakes. If I made one, I would be told to put it right, and if I went on getting it wrong, he would cane me, but not heavily – don't run away with the idea that it was sadistic. I got on much better with Mary, my father's second wife. She was a fine person – good fun, pleasant, an excellent cook and, on top of that, extremely good-looking. In the holidays I would go back to my mother, who was now living in Chelsea, and my boxer dog, Sian. I missed my mother terribly when I was away from her. The dog used to sleep on my bed, and I missed the dog hugely, too.

'This went on for two years. I was living in a very remote area, and I didn't mix with other children, but a little boy out in the countryside can find his own entertainment. I didn't feel that I was missing out on a more conventional upbringing because I had no yardstick. Children are very resilient.'

In previous years Richard had celebrated Christmas with his mother at her flat in Chelsea, but in 1947 he spent it at Fron Wen. Patrick had for some time been following the local hunt, and his son accompanied him to the Boxing Day meet beside the wood of Craflwyn at the entrance to the beautiful valley of the Glaslyn near Beddgelert. It proved a good day for Richard's

[1] Patrick probably noted the parallel. In his diary for 20 October 1978 he noted: 'read in Trollopes charming autobiography'.

introduction to hunting. Failing to find a fox on the lower ground, the Master led the pack up the lower craggy slopes of Yr Aran, a lofty outwork of Snowdon to the north. By the time the hounds had conducted a vain search among marshy stretches from which streams emerged and flowed down into the Glaslyn, the field had been reduced to a dozen determined followers, who included Patrick and Richard.

There now followed a long, hard, and grinding ascent of the mountain, when about two-thirds of the way up to the peak the hounds struck a good scent leading directly to a large earth. The Master sought for some time to bolt the fox, but the terriers worked away in vain. It was decided to dig the animal out, which proved a lengthy and troublesome business. After the coldest period of waiting that Patrick had ever experienced on a hunt, with an icy wind gusting remorselessly across the mountainside, Captain Jones and his huntsman set to with a will, shifting great lumps of rock with their crowbars until they succeeded in releasing a trapped terrier. Finally they hooked out the fox – actually a vixen – which appeared to be dead and was accordingly flung over a crag down the slope. Thereupon she promptly revived, but the hounds were upon her and killed before she could run a hundred yards.

By now it was about three o'clock and growing dark, and father and son set off for home. To find their way across the wild trackless mountainside was no easy matter. Eventually they met two kindly women, one of whom advised them to cross over the Cnicht by Cwm Gelli Iago, while the other with equal conviction recommended going by road via Beddgelert. Patrick politely agreed with both, and chose the latter route. It was fortunate that he did so, since the ladies had omitted to inform them that they were themselves on the point of driving past Cwm Croesor. By the time Patrick and Richard had trudged in the darkness as far as Beddgelert, they overtook them in their car and gave them the lift it had not occurred to them to offer in the first place.

All in all it had been a rewarding day, not the least of whose pleasures was that of sitting down on their return to cold goose by the fireside in Fron Wen. Patrick recorded his ten-year-old son's stalwart performance with approval: 'Richard really followed quite well; was only rather sorry for himself from the cold twice, and did not appear in any way exhausted. Our foot distance was something between 16 and 20 miles.'

Exhilarating shared experiences such as this make it the more tragic that Patrick was incapable of establishing a wholly cordial relationship with his son during the latter's impressionable days of childhood.

CHAPTER SEVENTEEN

The Long Day Running

Some day we shall get up before the dawn
And find our ancient hounds before the door,
And wide awake know that the hunt is on;
Stumbling upon the blood-dark track once more,
That stumbling to the kill beside the shore;
Then cleaning out and bandaging of wounds,
And chants of victory amid the encircling hounds.
(William Butler Yeats, 'Hound Voice')

In the high summer of 1946 there occurred a chance event which was to have a profound effect on Patrick's life during the ensuing years that he and my mother lived in Cwm Croesor. There is also reason to believe that it made a significant contribution long afterwards to his greatest literary achievement. On Tuesday, 13 August

> hounds were seen passing Fron. I pursued them on bicycle and caught them – spoke [to] a tall young man, rather high[1] – referred me to his uncle, the master. He was an oldish gentleman, indistinguishable at first glance from a labourer, unshaven to a notable degree, but more amiable – Capt. Jones. Asked if I might come out; he said yes and will send me details of meets on postcards to be sent. Wynisfor? pack. On foot, of course. Hounds cream coloured, short-legged, various in size. Quantities of terriers, mostly tiny.

The correct name of the hunt, as Patrick shortly discovered, was the Ynysfor. It had a long history, the pack having been started in 1765 by John Jones, son of Thomas Jones, Rector of Trawsfynydd, and Jane, daughter of William Williams of Brondanw (ancestor of Clough Williams-Ellis). The hounds and terriers were of ancient Welsh stock, to which in the early twentieth century

[1] Major Edmund Roche.

was added a strain of Fell hounds from the Lake District. The area covered by the Ynysfor Hunt was extensive. While its heart lay around Cwm Croesor and the Glaslyn estuary, it stretched far inland into the mountains of Snowdonia, its meets on occasion being held as far apart as the Lleyn peninsula and Barmouth estuary.

Many tales were preserved in old hunting diaries at Ynysfor and local tradition of famous runs, noble hounds, and fearless terriers of former days. The strangest chase occurred in the 1890s, when the pack was pursuing a fox on the slopes of Moel Gest. The scent led them to a curious moss-covered hollow. The Master, Captain Jones's grandfather, came up and began poking about with his stick. To his surprise he discovered concealed among the bracken and brushwood an emaciated man clutching a bible and milk bottle, who proved to be a ship's captain from Portmadoc. Gripped by religious mania, he had withdrawn to this rude retreat, from which he emerged at night to buy milk from a neighbouring farm. It seems that running him to ground exerted a salutary effect on his mental stability, for he promptly recovered from his pious fervour and returned to his former occupation at sea.[1]

Captain Jack Jones, whom Patrick first met that summer morning below Fron Wen, had succeeded his brother Colonel Edward Bowen Jones, a legendary Master whose long reign stretched from 1901 to 1940. The present Master, as Patrick's description suggests, was a Welsh squire or 'gentleman farmer' of the old school. Descended from an ancient North Walian family, Welsh was his native tongue, and he entertained a particular interest in local folklore and customs. In the Great War he had served in the 6th Battalion of the Royal Welch Fusiliers, commanding 'D' Company of local Portmadoc men during the disastrous landings at Gallipoli. After the war he retired from the Army, but maintained close links with former comrades of all ranks. He was a respected magistrate, playing a prominent part in the affairs of the locality, where his genial and unpretentious manner gained him widespread popularity.

Jack Jones could scarcely have been more different from the cosmopolitan and sophisticated Clough Williams-Ellis,[2] much less Patrick's obnoxious English neighbour, Whitehead-Smith. On one occasion when the Ynysfor pack had killed a fox on land belonging to Williams-Ellis, a man working for the latter appeared and demanded the brush for his master, a guinea's bounty money being paid for foxes' brushes. Captain Jones promptly strode into the

[1] Cf B. Dew Roberts, 'The Ynysfor Hunt', *The Transactions of the Honourable Society of Cymmrodorion* (London, 1941), pp. 200–220.

[2] Williams-Ellis could not speak his native tongue (Jonah Jones, *Clough Williams-Ellis: The Architect of Portmeirion* (Bridgend, 1996), p. 13).

midst of the snarling pack, thrust his hand among the mass of snapping jaws, cut off the tail, and presented it to the man with the sardonic comment: 'You are enough of a tail [hireling] for Williams-Ellis!'

Captain Jones, a bachelor, lived with his sisters at their ancestral home of Ynysfor, situated on the levels by the River Glaslyn. The house, which was built in 1865, stood next to its predecessor which had been left empty but intact, evoking the atmosphere of a former age. The walls were liberally decorated with foxes' masks and brushes, oil portraits of former Masters, and paintings and photographs of their horses, hounds, and terriers. Prominent among the last was the immortal Juno, who in the 1860s had brought many a fox to an untimely end. Her fighting blood had been transmitted through generations of terriers to the current Bunt, Sandy, Crab, Nanny, Tiny, and their hardy fellows.

Dean King describes the Ynysfor Hunt as 'a social event for the upper crust'.[1] Nothing could be further from the truth, and the error is the more unfortunate in that it serves to confirm a misconception widely prevalent in today's urbanised Britain. A fair impression of the reality is provided by Patrick's account of what was regarded as an exceptionally well attended meet: 'The field was swollen to unusual proportions by the presence of a couple of very knowing old farmers and some local youths.' While tenant farmers like Harri Roberts preferred to track down foxes with guns on their own land during the cubbing season, they had good reason to support the hunt. As Patrick noted on another occasion: 'There were some farming people above the earth – they had lost five lambs to foxes in the last night or so.'

The chase was conducted on foot over vast tracts of mountain wilderness, sometimes being joined by individuals encountered upon the way. The wild terrain, savage climate, and long distances normally covered in a day's hunting meant that remarkable hardihood was required of the followers. After an hour or more of scrambling about mountain screes and negotiating marshy hollows, the field was generally reduced to a bare dozen capable of keeping up with the Master and his huntsman, and on at least one occasion Patrick and my mother found themselves the sole followers. This suited the temperament of Captain Jones. When rather more than the regular following arrived at a meet, Patrick observed him 'shaking off most of the field: I believe he loathes a field of any size'.

Nothing could be more different from the glamour which characterises many English hunts, whose elegantly dressed and well-mounted followers gather at meets held before the stately façades of country houses or in the

[1] King, *Patrick O'Brian*, p. 130.

marketplaces of ancient county towns, and whose hunt balls are major highlights of the local season. There was little in appearance or attire to distinguish the Master of the Ynysfor from his heterogeneous little band of followers. Following the pack one day, Patrick remarked with implicit emphasis on 'an elderly labouring man . . . [who] bore a marked resemblance to the Captain'. Jack Jones cared little for social or professional status, accepting a man for what he was. On learning that a youth in Cwm Croesor had volunteered to join his old regiment, but was not yet of legal age to enter the Brondanw Arms (known locally as 'The Ring'), the magistrate firmly marched him into the bar and ordered him a glass of beer.

Following the Captain's invitation, Patrick took up hunting with enthusiasm. The season generally extended from August or September until April. As often as not a long and taxing journey was required even before the hunt began, since meets were frequently held several miles away in the mountains. A regular assembly point lay beside Llyndy Bridge in the beautiful valley of Nant Gwynant. A typical example of what this involved for a follower like Patrick occurred one freezing morning towards the end of January 1948. At 8.30 he left the snug warmth of Fron Wen on his bicycle, pedalling down the valley into a blinding flurry of snow. On gaining the main road, he struggled to make his way up the steep ascent to Beddgelert against a driving north wind battering him relentlessly. Before long the snow turned into pelting rain, and by the time Patrick succeeded in forcing his machine through a furious north-westerly gale raging the length of Nant Gwynant and reached the appointed rendezvous, he had been riding for two hours through atrocious weather in what was, like its predecessor of 1946–47, one of the worst winters on record. And this was before the day's hunting began.

At least he was cycling along macadamised roads. Another time, having set off at his customary hour of 8.30 in the morning, he spent a long and somewhat frustrating day climbing about the mountain slopes on the southern side of Llyn Gwynant, where the hunt eventually made a satisfactory kill, followed by a fruitless exploration northwards into the wild precipitous valley of Ceunant Mawr. At last the party returned to Llyndy Bridge, where Patrick recovered his bicycle and set off home. However, at Nantmor he decided to leave the main road and take a short cut home by pursuing the course of the Roman road running from Caernarvon (Segontium) to the Roman fort at Tomen y Mur, which traverses Cwm Croesor on its way.

Patrick's 'short cuts' were symptomatic of his attitude to life, being based not on experience, still less advice, but on idiosyncratic notions of his own devising. He presumed that the Roman engineers knew what they were about, and following where units of their garrison had once marched represented a pleasing step into the past. He overlooked the fact that the Romans had not anticipated the bicycle, and found himself obliged to push his (actually my mother's) machine almost the entire way, hauling it up steep rocky inclines and crossing extensive tracts of mountain. He arrived home at dusk 'quite done up' and made a firm resolution that 'I will never, in any circumstances whatever, push a bicycle over the Roman road again'.

Depending on the season and the endless vagaries of Welsh weather, the air could be bright, clear, and invigorating – or bitterly chill and wet. It was not unusual before the pursuit had begun for Patrick's clothing to be sodden with pelting rain, which permeated downwards and before long filled his boots. Even without rain it was possible to spend an entire day soaked to the skin. Hastening on one occasion to catch up with hounds doubling back, Patrick and my mother had 'a sad to-do crossing the Croesor', which they found coursing in full spate.

None of this deterred Patrick for a moment. He revelled in the sensation of being at the peak of fitness and in the opportunities the hunt afforded him for viewing the remotest regions of the countryside and its wildlife. Scarcely a day passed in which he did not encounter some vignette and mentally store it away for future use, whether it was the refusal of grouse put up by hounds on the Moel Ddu to take to the air for fear of a pair of ravens circling overhead, or an evocative glimpse of their wily prey: 'A little while later I saw a dog-fox come delicately over the flat piece from left to right (like people on a stage) and he was in no sort of a hurry.'

Though Patrick's attention was never seriously diverted from the prime object of the day's exercise, his vigilant eye and retentive memory were always on the alert for objects of interest. Cycling to a meet with my mother on a fresh January morning, they heard an unfamiliar cry which proved to be uttered by the first choughs they had seen.

> They crossed the road again behind us, and one perched on a fence: his Post-Office red legs (slim and elegant) and beak were as clear as they might be. They were rather larger than I had expected them to be – decidedly bigger than jackdaws – and less elegant than the illustrations, though perhaps their feathers were puffed out from the cold. Their cry is most distinctive, a ringing sound, akin to a buzzard's as well as a kestrel's.

Patrick was fascinated by the creatures of the wild, but nurtured no urban sentimentality. No one could observe their conduct in their natural habitat with anything approaching the extent of his patience and perception without becoming aware that virtually every animal, bird, and reptile was engaged in an eternal search for prey to ensure survival. As for the fox, it was impossible to live in Cwm Croesor without appreciating the constant threat they posed to the livelihood of the hard-working hill farmers.

Another consideration which undoubtedly loomed large as a factor in Patrick's enthusiasm for the chase was the enthralling sensation of physically and mentally transporting himself into his beloved eighteenth century. Nothing had altered in the character of the Ynysfor Hunt since its establishment at the beginning of the reign of King George III, and the landscape and people too remained unchanged. The failure of the ugliness, cruelty, and vulgarity of the twentieth century to penetrate this wild paradise was immeasurably appealing to Patrick's imagination. So strong was his hostility to any intrusion by the outside world that a bystander whom he suspected of not being a native of the district was mentally accounted 'a sinister English person'.

Ever curious about local customs and beliefs, hunting provided him with extensive opportunity for conversing freely with shepherds, farmers, and a travelling blacksmith. He would question them closely about local lore, mentally registering and subsequently noting intriguing details. He was equally fascinated by the country characters with whom he came in contact. As one of the few regular followers to keep up with the hunt throughout the day, he came to know intimately the Master and his huntsman, Idwal Jones. For them he entertained unalloyed affection and respect, to an extent which he does not appear to have found possible at any other period of his life. Their all-consuming shared interest, combined with taxing physical exertion, assured a comradeship of equals among whom artificial social or intellectual constraints were altogether irrelevant. In the hunt each person fulfilled whatever role he might be allotted, and unless he were to prove idle or a consummate bungler he was accepted as integral a member of the team as any other.

At the opening of the 1948 season Patrick enjoyed a good day out among the hills to the south above Maentwrog, although the tall sodden heather and an oncoming drizzle left him soaked to the skin from the outset. He kept up with Idwal throughout the day – no easy feat, in view of the huntsman's long legs and inexhaustible endurance.[1] Towards the end of the day Patrick was afforded a characteristic glimpse of Idwal's doglike devotion to the Master, Captain Jones: '. . . we went on to Llyn Tecwryn. We saw nobody there but as we were going to a high place we saw the Captain disappear over the ridge

[1] In his story 'The Long Day Running' Patrick wrote: 'In front was the long-legged huntsman with his pole; four terriers with him. He walked fast, so fast with his long legs and unceasing springing stride that William Kirk, who came behind him, could keep up only by putting all his close attention to it, taking advantage of every easy step, watching the feet before and above him, concentrating all the time' (*The Last Pool*, p. 140).

above the Harlech Road. Idwal raced along and I kept with him but by the time we got there the Captain had vanished. Poor Idwal was getting worried, but it all came right in the end . . . Later I heard that they had killed the second fox – a vixen – in the earth at Gelli Grîn.'

Patrick had enormous admiration and respect for the Master. Jack Jones was a plain-spoken, roughly dressed, soldierly man with no concern for social pretensions. Although approaching his sixtieth birthday and thus nearly twice Patrick's age, he possessed a constitution so tough and resilient as to place him almost invariably foremost in pursuit of the fox. On his arrival at an earth, he was usually the first to set about opening it up with pickaxe or crowbar with a single-minded vigour exceptional in a man of any age.

Like most Masters, Captain Jones was given to blunt speech in the field. Patrick recorded instances from time to time, which clearly afforded him considerable amusement. After losing a fox among marshy hollows above Beddgelert in January, 'Capt. J. observes that the fox had probably been disturbed by "that fellow walking about like a goddam Fool this morning". Do not know to whom this referred, but perhaps Major Rhodes.' So far as Captain Jones was concerned, the value of a man was measured purely by the extent of his contribution to the concerns of the Hunt. Ideally he preferred to be accompanied by a select few followers possessed of sufficient endurance to keep up with the pursuit, who were prepared to obey his instructions to the letter.

He generally wore his service revolver in its holster, in case it should prove necessary to put down an injured hound. On one occasion a shepherd named Ben saw an exhausted fox loping by after a long chase, whose bedraggled condition excited his sympathy. When Captain Jones came up shortly afterwards, Ben declared that he would have shot the fox had he had a gun. 'If you'd have done that, I'd have shot you!' was the Master's sharp response.

Just as he never spared himself, so Captain Jones expected an unremittingly high standard of his hounds and terriers. 'Lucifer, a babbling, ill-conditioned hound, was addressed very severely indeed for giving tongue over some nonsense. The echo of "You bloody Sod" came prettily back from the rock-face.' Angered when some hounds set off on a trail of their own, 'the Captain inter alia, said "God damn and blast the whole pack"'. Such language was as much a property of his office as his bugle or crop, arising so naturally that it did not occur to him that it might provoke offence, even in a lady. One one occasion my mother, who was following without Patrick, found herself standing next to the Master beside an earth where a large vixen had gone to ground. 'Then the Captain said that if all the hounds were kept away he would bring out the bloody fox. He did, & it was torn to bits at once. The Captain was very pleased.'

The Deity Himself was not spared criticism when proceedings proved unsatisfactory. On the pack's failure to discover a scent, 'After quite a long time he called them off again . . . and observed that as soon as the Almighty would let him he was going home'. Often Patrick found himself at the receiving end of the Master's wrath. 'I kept fairly close to the Master, who was in a vile temper,' he wrote at the end of a hard day's run near Beddgelert. 'The Wainwrights and I stuck to the Captain's heels as he went round the top and on to an advantageous crag. Here he observed coldly that it was not much good all standing together like a flock of bloody sheep, directed W. and his son to a higher, more remote crag, and stalked off to a privy eminence. This left W.'s daughter and me rather at a loss on the original rock.' After a momentous occasion when Patrick became separated from the hunt and eventually returned home alone, 'the Master . . . reproved me in unmistakable tones for not having left a message the other day'.

Throughout his life Patrick burned with anger when he fancied himself recipient of the most insignificant of slights, and his happy acceptance of the Master's ferocious rebukes appears astonishing. Though Captain Jones's expletives could not reasonably be regarded as personally insulting, liberally distributed as they were on any occasion which aroused his wrath, Patrick would not have tolerated this in any other circumstances. Yet it is a remarkable fact that he accepted the most peremptory of commands and roughest of abuse from the Master of the Ynysfor Hunt without a tinge of resentment. Indeed, the manner in which he recorded instances in his hunting journal indicates that they gave him positive pleasure, being regarded almost as compliments.

The exception frequently proves the rule, and Patrick's sensitivity remained so rigid from childhood to old age that this unique instance deserves consideration for the light it throws upon his character. Much must be ascribable to Captain Jones's superlative mastery of his art, which never ceased to provoke his admiration. The Master was rarely at fault in sensing the most promising spot to find a fox, the likely direction of its running, the juncture at which it might be expected to double back, the likely choice of the earth for which it was making, or the strategic positioning of his followers to check its course – particularly when it was heading for one of a number of notoriously impregnable earths. After the conclusion of a day's hunting at an earth above Dinas Ddu near Aberglaslyn, Patrick remarked: 'It was a place (surely one of the very few) where the Captain had not killed a fox before.'

Patrick committed himself to the select group upon whom the Captain relied. He was treated no differently from Idwal and the belman, and regarded acceptance by such a man as an unconscious compliment. Nothing could differ more from the Master's consummate qualities of leadership and skill than the formal hierarchy of rank which Patrick found so intolerable during his brief service in the Royal Air Force.

More than half a lifetime's experience enabled me to observe the extremity of Patrick's insecurity when visiting even the closest of friends or relations. His sensation of exposure on alien territory, where he found himself lost for emotional landmarks and vulnerable to unanticipated threats, was unmistakable. He displayed relative confidence of his ground only when receiving people in his own home or entertaining at a restaurant or club, where his position as host enabled him to retain control of the situation. But even then his guard could never be entirely lowered, for who could tell when some insufferable guest might not overstep the mark and challenge his precariously established authority? In marked contrast I could not help but note, accompanying him as I did over many years on long walks in the Pyrenees, the extent to which his jealously maintained guard fell away under open skies. How far this arose from the circumstance that walkers rarely address each other face to face, absence of constraints imposed by enclosure within four walls, or removal of apprehension of interruption by a third party, is difficult to assess with precision. All I can vouch for is the fact.

With regard to Captain Jones, the colourful excoriations to which Patrick submitted with such good humour occurred exclusively during the excitement of the chase. Off the field the Master was courtesy itself, wholly transformed from the dynamic single-minded leader furiously urging on his huntsman and pack in pursuit of an elusive prey, whose speed and cunning often proved a match for those of his pursuers.

As a Welsh squire of ancient lineage, whose ancestors had lived at Ynysfor and hunted the mountains of Snowdonia for centuries, Captain Jones possessed an instinctive air of authority. From Patrick's point of view it was advantageous that he was himself effectively a foreigner, dwelling among an indigenous population who neither knew nor cared anything about his English background. It is inconceivable that he could have enjoyed a comparable relationship with an English Master of Foxhounds, when he would have felt himself inescapably allotted his grade in the social hierarchy.

During visits to the house at Ynysfor, Patrick and my mother always received an unaffectedly warm welcome from Captain Jones and his sisters. A lifetime's familiarity with the region made their host a fund of information about its wildlife, providing Patrick with congenial material for conversation. 'Capt. J. told me that buzzards are very found of grass-snakes and that they are often to be seen carrying them to their young,' reads a characteristic entry in the card index where he recorded his observations of bird life.

On one memorable occasion in the field 'Mary was given the brush –

contretemps with Ranter – by the master, very handsomely. This made her very attractive to hounds and terriers.' Patrick stood contentedly by, as my mother in the full bloom of her health and beauty gracefully acknowledged the honour. The setting of the improvised ceremony was one of dramatic grandeur, with fierce gusts of snow and rain buffeting the lonely little group gathered on a gaunt slope below the summit of the Moel Ddu. Proud as he felt, Patrick's attention was diverted by harsh cries from a pair of ravens circling overhead. 'Perhaps I imagine it,' he reflected, 'but it seems to me that ravens are particularly excited by the presence of a pack of hounds. Several times I have noticed how clamorous they are when hounds are in the high rocky places.'

For Patrick his runs with the Ynysfor hounds provided bright moments of unalloyed pleasure during the gloomy season of the year, when as time went by his spirits were sinking ever lower. In the field his physical and mental energies were challenged to their extremity. He possessed every justification for priding himself on the skills he had acquired, while the noble sport provided him with unrivalled opportunity for his constant observation of the natural world in some of the wildest terrain in Britain. It was the sole time in his life that he found himself working for a common purpose with a set of men united by mutual respect, from which the awkwardness which normally bedevilled his social relationships was entirely absent.

Patrick devoted two stories in *The Last Pool* to his experiences with the Ynysfor Hunt. In 'The Steep Slope of Gallt y Wenallt' he describes how, at the opening of the meet: 'The Master came out of the farmhouse. He was of an ancient family and his ancestors had hunted this country above two hundred years. He had an eagle's nose and eye, and his moustache curled with a magnificent arrogance. He wore a very old cloth cap and his torn Burberry hid his horn and the whip that he carried over his shoulder. Sometimes he would fly up in a towering choler – shattering was his invective then – but he would speak with a kind gentleness at other times, and that would strike a man equally with his anger. He spoke to the huntsman in Welsh . . .'[1]

Edgar Williams, then the farm boy at Croesor Fawr, recognises the description as that of Captain Jones to the life. Patrick's affectionate admiration for the man is also patent in 'The Long Day Running'. Like 'The Steep Slope of Gallt y Wenallt', the story adheres closely to the events of a day's hunting in which he participated. The meet was held at Hafod Llan on 2 March 1949. It comprises the final entry in Patrick's hunting journal, and was the last he attended.

[1] *The Last Pool*, pp. 122–23.

This time Patrick introduced himself under the name of Kirk, and once again Captain Jones is depicted in palpably recognisable guise: 'The Master, lower down the slope, did not like to be followed, and it would have taken a bolder man than Kirk to have spoken to him uninvited. He was more than usually taciturn that morning, and his terriers, who knew his mood, came soberly at his heel. He was hunched in his old leather patched coat, and his long moustache bristled as he went.'[1]

When the Master and huntsman stop to examine an earth within which they believe a fox to have taken refuge, Kirk is struck by the manner in which they communicate with each other. 'The Master . . . spoke to Gerallt [the huntsman]. His head was turned and he did not raise his voice but Gerallt knew very well what he said, and replied in the same tone. Kirk was more accustomed to shouting, and this almost telepathic communication, so usual in mountainy people, never failed to surprise him.'[2]

A similarly instinctive reaction characterised the manner in which the Master conducted his pursuit of the fox: 'it was well known that he was second cousin to the fox: at all events, he seemed to know where any fox was going, and he was almost invariably up as soon as any man, and with far less effort'. Captain Jones's propensity for colourful language is readily recognisable: 'Some of the hounds that had broken back began hunting on a frivolous line, and the Master lifted them with the harshest rating. "Aah, you bloody rebels," he cried. "Lucifer, Lucifer, God damn and blast that bloody Lucifer." '[3]

Patrick's concern to portray Captain Jones as realistically as possible is illustrated by his scrupulous concern for accuracy of detail. Thus when he wrote the story he described the Master as carrying his whip 'over his shoulder'. However in the proof copy he corrected this to 'slung under it' – an alteration of no dramatic concern presumably inserted in order to approximate more closely to reality. Furthermore he appears to have been concerned to include nothing which might appear remotely detrimental to the Master. Thus he deleted the sentence referring to the Captain's occasional 'towering choler' and 'shattering invective', despite its relatively innocuous application.[4]

There could exist no greater contrast between Patrick's sensitive concern to portray Jones in as kindly and admirable a light as possible, and the neutral or hostile descriptions of virtually everyone else who features in his stories of *The Last Pool*. Patrick made extensive use of his hunting experiences in his

[1] *The Last Pool*, pp. 140–41.

[2] *Ibid.*, pp. 148–49.

[3] *Ibid.*, pp. 150, 153.

[4] For some reason Patrick's proof corrections were largely ignored by the publishers.

fiction, but there are indications that the hold which Captain Jones secured in his affections led to his reappearance long after the scope of his writing had moved to other fields. It is surely his voice that is heard addressing Dr Maturin in the hunting scene at the beginning of *Post Captain*, when Stephen accepts with equanimity a rough rebuke from the Master: '"You sir – on the mule," cried old Mr Saville's furious voice. "Will you let the God-damned dogs get on with their work? Hey? Hey? Is this a God-damned coffee house? I appeal to you, is this an infernal debating society?"'[1]

I believe the Master of the Ynysfor Hunt played a more fundamental part in Patrick's fiction than that of affording realism to his descriptions of fox-hunting. One of Captain Jones's most remarkable characteristics, as Patrick frequently remarked, was his instinctive authority and skill as a leader. Not only was he master to perfection of the skills of his profession, but, as Patrick observed, he seemed to possess the power to enter the mind of the most wily of foxes, unfailingly anticipating its every move. To these qualities were added inexhaustible vigour and total absence of fear, which made him ever the first to enter into any situation of danger.

Patrick gained security in an accepted and justly administered order, antithesis alike of arbitrary subjection and anarchic turbulence. Finding no secure refuge in the world, he sought it first in animal realms far removed from the oppressive society of human beings. Later in early manhood he rediscovered it in that century-long Age of Reason, whose placid surface lay spacious and serene between the violent social, political, and intellectual storms of the seventeenth and mid-nineteenth centuries. And, upon that still ocean, what more ideally ordered refuge was there to be found than that which obtained aboard the highly structured microcosmic world of a British man-of-war?

A number of factors made life on board ship a stimulating setting for a novel, some of which Patrick outlined in the text of a lecture which he delivered on several public occasions:

> And when you come to think of it, there are few better places for observing the development of relations between men than a ship, above all a sailing-ship, a man-of-war in Nelson's time, when the people aboard lived so very much on top of one another, when they might travel for weeks, and months, and almost years seeing no one else, and when no one could get away. It provided a hothouse atmosphere in which the plants of good and evil, love or liking and hatred, close comradeship and its reverse could grow fast and without

[1] *Post Captain*, p.16.

> distraction from outside sources, there being no outside sources apart from the weather and the enemy (neither of them, admittedly, negligible).

All this is of course true, though like most authorial exegesis probably reflects retrospective rationalisation more than the reality of inspiration. However, this brief catalogue omits one of the most significant factors of naval life: one permeating Patrick's naval novels, which he renders with particular skill. This was the high degree of discipline, generally very effective, which enabled a ship's captain and a handful of officers and marines to exercise authority and impose a common purpose on several hundred powerful and untutored men trained and accustomed to violence, a high proportion of whom had been pressed into the service against their will.

The constant maintenance of this rigid hierarchy, regularly tested in the most dangerous and difficult circumstances imaginable, is implicit in almost every exchange that occurs on board ship, to which the equality permitted by the friendship between Jack Aubrey and Stephen Maturin provides a striking exception. It was clearly an aspect that fascinated Patrick, to which he often drew explicit attention. In particular he often contrasted the rigorous but intelligently applied discipline maintained by Captain Aubrey with the brutal and often counter-productive regimes imposed by 'flogging' captains, such as the real-life Captain Pigot of the *Hermione* (whose crew mutinied and butchered him in 1797), or the fictional Captain Corbett who comes to an untimely and well-deserved end in *The Mauritius Command*.

Aubrey's ability to run a 'taut ship', i.e. one administered as harmoniously as is commensurate with strict discipline, is paralleled by his combination of scientific understanding of the correct handling of a vessel with intuitive ability to assess in an instant whatever action is appropriate: '. . . although his behaviour was composed, reserved and indeed somewhat severe – his orders cracked out sharp and quick as he sailed her hard, completely identified with the ship. He was on the quarterdeck, yet at the same time he was in the straining studdingsail-boom, gauging the breaking point exactly.'[1]

Although there could be no question as to who was in command, the special circumstances of this finely tuned microcosm of society led to a curiously deep camaraderie, whose most prominent feature was the widespread mutual respect extending among all ranks, from captain to loblolly boy. 'All through his naval life he had observed the attachment, even the affection, that spring up between men who had been through a serious sea-fight together, and the very valuable change in the relationship between the hands and the officers, a change that worked both ways . . . naval custom

[1] *HMS Surprise*, p. 141.

ruled out much in the way of conversation between them, but the special relationship, the esteem, was most certainly there.'[1]

One of the great strengths of Patrick's portrayal of Jack Aubrey lies in its absence of sentimentality. While Jack finds the concept of flogging distasteful in the abstract, he nevertheless unhesitatingly orders the lash to be applied when he believes it necessary. Though judiciously tactful in his treatment of his subordinate officers, he is frighteningly authoritative in correcting any failure of seamanship or infringement of discipline. His outbursts rarely provoke offence, since his officers and men entertain so high a regard for his judgement and skill that they happily accept reprimands rarely delivered without justification: '"Avast that God-damned ——— foolery, God rot your ——— eyes," he called out in an enormous line-of-battle voice. He rarely swore, apart from an habitual damn or an unmeaning blasphemy, and the men . . . fell perfectly mute, with nothing more than the rolling of an eye or a wink to convey secret understanding and delight.'[2]

Patrick's skill and delight in bringing to life a world administered on the basis of firmly imposed authority presents a striking contrast to all the obvious manifestations of his character. As a child his experience of authority had been far from happy, and deeply resented. Those who had exercised power over him had in his view employed it unsympathetically, irrationally, and not infrequently brutally. One recalls in particular his harsh treatment at the hands of his father and the flogging Headmaster of Lewes Grammar School.

All in all, it might appear surprising that one of Patrick's finest literary creations should have been a man allotted virtually unrestricted power over everyone about him, and that he was so clearly attracted to the re-creation of a miniature society structured in rigorous hierarchical order. However, the paradox vanishes when one takes into account the unalloyed happiness which Patrick derived from following the Ynysfor Hunt, and his unqualified admiration for Captain Jones. Like Jack Aubrey, Jack Jones exercised no-nonsense, efficient control over the members of the Hunt. When they acted with less than the exemplary diligence or intelligence he expected, they were content to accept the rough side of his tongue. Above all Captain Jones shared with Captain Aubrey a masterly ability to imbue his followers with a portion of his own superlative professional and instinctive skills.

Added to these factors was the overwhelming excitement of the chase, calling as it did for a man's physical and mental faculties to be engaged to their uttermost extent. In the Aubrey–Maturin novels attention is repeatedly

[2] *The Surgeon's Mate*, pp. 159–60.

[2] *Master and Commander*, pp. 267–68. Cf. *The Far Side of the World*, p. 142.

drawn to Jack's transformation in battle. One passage may stand for innumerable others:

> . . . Jack Aubrey's mind was too taken up with the delicate calculations of the coming battle for conversation: he stood there, wholly engrossed, working out the converging courses, the possible variants, the innumerable fine points that must precede the plain hard hammering, when everyone would be much happier. On these occasions, and Stephen had known many of them, Jack was as it were removed, a stranger, quite unlike the cheerful, not over-wise companion he knew so well: a hard, strong face, calm but intensely alive, efficient, decided, a stern face, but one that in some way expressed a fierce and vivid happiness.

It is surely not for nothing that in the same novel from which this passage is taken Jack himself likens the exhilaration of combat to 'fox-hunting at its best . . . fox-hunting raised to the hundredth power'.[1]

All this is not to suggest that Jack Aubrey is simply a fictional portrayal of Jack Jones. There are significant aspects of Aubrey not found in Captain Jones. What Patrick took from the Master of the Ynysfor were his natural authority, his expert handling of men, and his proficiency in conducting an activity which required a harmonious balance between professional experience and inspired skill.[2]

The genesis of Jack Aubrey is to be found in Jack Jones, a possibly unique figure of unqualified admiration in Patrick's life. Subsidiary factors in Jack's character may have derived from Captain Jones's successor, his nephew Major Roche. Though Roche lacked his uncle's supreme skill in the chase, he possessed other qualities characteristic of Jack Aubrey. A former officer in the South Wales Borderers, he was, according to those who knew him, good-looking, imposing, authoritative, cool, calm, and witty. That Patrick admired him as well as his uncle is clear from frequent allusions to him in his hunting journal, and the fact that the dedication to his short story 'The Steep Slope

[1] *The Ionian Mission*, pp. 62–63, 185. 'A gunboat fired: deep, booming note – the voice of an old solitary hound' (*Master and Commander*, p. 272).

[2] Earlier in his literary career Patrick unmistakably drew upon Captain Jones's qualities of leadership in his portrayal of the historical Commodore Anson. 'He appeared to be made of iron and oak, quite unchanging, except that he grew a little more affable as things grew even worse. Peter [the young hero of the tale] had an immense respect for him, and although they did not often speak, a real affection: the Commodore held the ship together, and the officers drew strength from him. In the very worst of times there was no hint of anarchy: the routine of the ship went on in the most orderly manner that circumstances would allow. Everything that could be done was done, in a seamanlike fashion, quickly, with no thought of argument' (*The Golden Ocean*, 1956, p. 130).

of Gallt y Wenallt' reads: 'For Major Edmund Roche, M.F.H., and the Ladies of Ynysfor'.

All in all, it is hard to overestimate the effect which his three seasons of following the Ynysfor Hunt exercised on Patrick's imagination.

> They stood watching and the whole pack crossed in front of them on the flat ground below, not five hundred yards away: there was not a hound but spoke and the music echoed from Moel y Gigfran behind and from a ragged cliff in front, echoed and reverberated, though torn by the wind. It was a rare, fine sight and a sound to dwell in a man's ears for ever.[1]

[1] *The Last Pool*, p. 148.

CHAPTER EIGHTEEN

Moelwyn Bank

> The youth of genius is that 'age of admiration' . . . when the spell breathed into our ear by our genius, fortunate or unfortunate, is – 'Aspire' . . . but this sunshine of rapture is not always spread over the spring of the youthful year. There is a season of self-contest, and doubts, and darkness. These frequent returns of melancholy, sometimes of despondence, which is the lot of inexperienced genius, is a secret history of the heart . . .
>
> (Isaac D'Israeli, *Miscellanies of Literature*)

At the beginning of 1948 Patrick and my mother had been living for two and a half years in the cramped confines of the tiny cottage Fron Wen, where they had been joined by Richard in July of the previous year when his father decided to undertake his teaching at home. While they derived considerable satisfaction from their modest and frequently arduous pastoral existence, Patrick's entry into the third year of his life of exile without any manifestation of literary productivity brought increasing emotional tension. My mother's faith in his talent remained undimmed: but for her unwavering support it is improbable that he could have continued. Nevertheless with each winter that passed it became harder to justify the failure to produce his long-awaited *chef d'œuvre*. Indeed, it was largely the expectation of staging a dramatic revival of his pre-war literary success which enabled him to endure his humiliating poverty with relative equanimity for so long.

His *Book of Voyages* had finally appeared in the previous autumn, but apart from the welcome arrival of the remaining £45 of his advance appears to have brought him little satisfaction. Patrick and my mother had attached great hopes to it when they were working against time to complete their researches in the British Museum before departing for Fron Wen in the autumn of 1945. However, the initial excitement of finding a publisher soon after their arrival was soon dissipated by van Thal's subsequent lack of enthusiasm and prolonged postponement of publication. The book was savagely cut and much of their extensive labour consequently wasted. It received scant attention from reviewers, and shortly after its appearance Home and van Thal sold their business. No prospect of a fresh commission offered itself, and Patrick was unable to settle on a constructive new venture.

Probably the most striking aspect of his adventurous time in North Wales is how little of it was devoted to literary endeavour. This at first sight appears surprising. Given his precocious achievement in publishing well-received books at an age well before the most committed of authors has even attempted serious work, it might be imagined that a life remote from distraction in North Wales would provide him with ideal opportunity to practise his craft and resume his literary career. It is clear that at the outset he did entertain high hopes of a productive recovery.

Describing Patrick's life in Wales, Dean King writes that he 'worked on an anthology, which would be published in 1947 as *A Book of Voyages*', following which he 'moved on to writing fiction . . . The major literary achievement of O'Brian's three years on the far side of Offa's Dyke would be his celebrated novel *Testimonies*, published originally in Britain as *Three Bear Witness* in April 1952. The more immediate product was a collection of short stories written in Cwm Croesor, which would eventually be entitled *The Last Pool*.'[1]

The impression conveyed is one of continued application to writing, from which gardening and field sports provided invigorating relaxation. In the absence of evidence to the contrary, it would be natural to assume that Patrick's literary career in Wales followed a consistently evolving pattern. Such was the picture he himself drew in retrospect long years afterwards: 'In Wales I had put together a volume of short stories (a delightful burst of real writing after so many years of official reports) and an anthology of voyages.'[2]

In reality this impression is delusive, and it seems that his customary over-sensitivity led him to suppress the grave crisis he experienced at the time. In later years he was wont to assert publicly that his writing flowed with ease, which was broadly true. That there should ever have been a time when he encountered great difficulty even in putting pen to paper was something to be regarded with shame, an acknowledgement of fallibility. Despite the fact that many aspects of their life in Wales gave Patrick and my mother intense pleasure, and that there was much in their struggle for survival that they could look back upon with justified pride, they rarely talked about their experiences of those four years. I find this especially remarkable in my case,

[1] King, *Patrick O'Brian*, pp.113, 123, 133.

[2] Cunningham (ed.), *Patrick O'Brian*, p. 17.

given my absorption in Welsh history and legendary lore, and how soon it was after their time in Wales when first I came to stay with them.

During the years that he lived at Fron Wen Patrick's efforts to revive his writing career had proved almost entirely abortive. It seems that all, or almost all, that he wrote in Wales for publication was composed during the last year of his stay. What he did eventually accomplish did not amount to much in terms of quantity, and there is every indication that throughout most of the four years he spent in Wales he suffered grievously from a protracted attack of writer's block.

The high hopes of building on the success of *The Book of Voyages* within a few weeks of their arrival in Wales in 1945 were dashed by the frustrating two years' delay before its publication. This disappointment was compounded by Patrick's agent's inability to secure a contract for a revised version of the novel provisionally entitled 'Perfect Gold', which he had written several years earlier. He also found himself incapable of completing *The Road to Samarcand*, although he was to do so later with considerable success.

The sole literary achievements of Patrick's four years in Wales were the eventual publication of *The Book of Voyages* in 1947, and the collection of thirteen short stories published the year after they left Wales, *The Last Pool*. This last amounts to some 56,000 words, and considering that once Patrick applied himself to a tale he generally wrote 1,000 words a day, his production rate was by any standard exceedingly modest.

Nor is this the whole of the matter. Two of the stories were written long before his move to Wales, 'The Return' having been completed at the end of 1939 and 'The Dawn Flighting' in the spring of 1940. Reasons have been given for inferring that it was also then that Patrick composed another tale in the collection, 'The Trap'. With less certainty it was suggested that the two delightful Irish tales, 'The Green Creature' and 'The Virtuous Peleg', were written during or shortly after his visit to Ireland in 1937. Finally, three of the remaining stories represent almost verbatim renderings of events he had himself experienced, to greater or lesser extent expanded from his journals.

The story 'It must have been a Branch, They Said', which originated in the unpleasant difference between Patrick and his neighbour Whitehead-Smith, is the only work (some 4,200 words) possibly written at Fron Wen. However, it too may have been composed after my parents' departure from the cottage in the early spring of 1948, given Patrick's devoted commitment to hunting over the winter, and the time he spent from the New Year onwards preparing the garden of the house into which they moved that spring.

Thus two and a half years passed by, during which Patrick was unable to apply himself seriously to any literary endeavour. On the other hand, in marked contrast to these indications of mental desperation his enthusiasm for fishing and observation of wildlife continued unabated. The indications are that he effectively abandoned his flagging attempts to revive his writing, and diverted his physical and imaginative energies into field sports, walking, natural history, maintenance of the house and garden, and reading solely for pleasure.

Although he abandoned his journal after a few months, he maintained a card index ('borrowed' from his office in Bush House) in which he inserted careful observations on birds, and after a time began compiling his detailed hunting journal. Although he drew extensively on these when he came to write his sporting tales, that does not appear to have been his intention at the time. The journal bears every indication of having been written without extraneous purpose. In 1948 and 1949, on the other hand, he carried a notebook in which he jotted down ideas and notes about country life to develop into stories.

In the novel he subsequently wrote based upon his experiences in Wales, its protagonist explains: 'So what consolations I had, I took. I read and I fished – writing was out of the question, and I packed away the dreary, unprofitable sheets [of a projected book on bestiaries]. These two things made life tolerable on good days. No, it is excessive to speak like that – I passed delightful hours up there [fishing] . . .'[1]

This is unmistakably Patrick himself speaking, and it is plain that for all his efforts he was unable to rid himself of a frustrating consciousness of failure. By the river and in the mountains he found consolation for mind and body, but back in the tiny cottage he became prey to deep-seated gloom. As two winters passed by with no return of creative inspiration, he succumbed increasingly to bouts of bitter depression and sudden outbursts of rage. He and my mother became convinced that a change of setting was urgently required, all else having failed to restore his imaginative faculties. Now an unexpected opportunity presented itself. Not long after their installation at Fron Wen, Patrick learned from Mrs Roberts that 'some pleasant people are going to take Moelwyn Bank'. He expressed a hope that 'this may be so, and that we may have some bridge, but it is not to be depended on'. In fact the event did not transpire, and Patrick thought no more about the matter. Moelwyn Bank, a solidly built nineteenth-century house of modest but comfortable proportions, is situated beside the Croesor river above the Robertses' farm. In the days when the quarry was being worked, it had been home to the quarry-master's deputy. Then came the war, when the quarry was converted into an explosives dump, and Moelwyn Bank became a refuge

[1] *Three Bear Witness*, p. 68.

for evacuees. When they in turn departed it remained empty and neglected. For all this, compared with Fron Wen it represented a substantial house with considerable potential.

At the end of 1947 the O'Brians were able to take over the lease of Moelwyn Bank in the following spring. The prospect breathed new life into their troubled existence. First and foremost, there was the excitement of moving into a proper house, in which they could expand, laying out to full effect their furniture and other effects. Above all it would provide Patrick with his own study in which he could devote himself exclusively to his work. As an additional benefit, he would no longer have to suffer the humiliation of living under the lee of the substantial property at Bryn, where the Smiths lorded it in vulgar pride.

Finally there was the exhilarating prospect of possessing a real garden at front and back of the house boasting a fine greengage tree, with the possibility this presented of increasing the extent to which the household might be fed from its own produce. No sooner had they arranged to take the lease at the next quarter than they set about preparations for making the garden as productive as possible. Almost every day Patrick descended the hill, frequently before breakfast, in order to prepare the ground for the spring.

On 22 January he began digging and manuring a section with dung provided by Harri Roberts from Croesor Fawr, and on 3 February he recorded with pride: 'Finished plot A'. Meanwhile inside the house he and my mother planted boxes of Ailsa Craig onions, and set out some 300 potatoes in trays together with twenty-four broad beans from their crop at Fron Wen. Their work continued, despite the fact that the valley remained snowbound until March, and on 9 February Patrick noted that it had become sufficiently light to continue gardening after tea. By early March the time had arrived for planting and sowing, and an impressive array of artichokes, beans, lettuce, radishes, parsnips, parsley, onions, and shallots was set out in rows in 'ground in perfect condition', as Patrick noted with satisfaction. Nor were there only plants to be considered. The chicken coop which had been installed at Fron Wen some time before was transported to its new site. At the beginning of the month three goose eggs were placed under one of the hens, and from these a few weeks later three tiny goslings emerged.

This energetic activity was only interrupted by Patrick's continued support for the Ynysfor Hunt. Once or twice a week he spent the day tirelessly following the hounds among the mountains, often accompanied by my mother. Weather conditions were generally appalling during those early months, ranging from icy cold to drenching rain. After a day spent scrambling across precipitous slopes and marshy hollows, he would bicycle home to enjoy a hearty supper with my mother and tumble straight into bed

– normally with no bath, unless my mother had remained at home and brought back sufficient buckets of water from the stream to fill the copper on the stove. Next morning he would rise at first light and hasten down the hill to the garden of Moelwyn Bank. So far from being daunted by the task, he was filled with renewed energy. Nothing delighted him so much as a fresh challenge stretching his mind and body to the utmost. While turning frozen or sodden earth beside the house, his watchful eye was ever alert to the sounds and sights of nature's renewal. At the beginning of March there was a spell of unusually fine weather, with perfectly clear mornings and no wind. Looking up, he saw two choughs flying overhead, 'with something of that undulating flight of a wood pigeon or (to a lesser degree) a jay'.

In general Patrick's health and vigour were remarkable. However, just as he and my mother were on the point of moving down the hill into Moelwyn Bank he was struck by an unexpected blow. He was seized with excruciating pains in his stomach, and the doctor who eventually arrived from Penrhyndeudraeth diagnosed an acute attack of appendicitis. An ambulance was ordered, and on its arrival at the farm Harri Roberts and Edgar Williams went up to Fron Wen. There they carefully bore Patrick down the precipitous ladder from the loft where he and my mother slept, and down the road to the farmyard. By now he had suffered two or three hours of agony, and was raving and uncharacteristically swearing. He was taken to Portmadoc hospital, where the operation had to be performed at once.

By the time of his return my mother was ensconced in Moelwyn Bank, which Edgar Williams recalls her decorating during his absence. She and Patrick were delighted by the prospect of restoring the long-abandoned house to good order, in addition to making their new garden fully productive. Assisted by Edgar and Richard, they set to work scraping and painting walls.[1] Patrick relished the prospect of having a private study for his writing, undisturbed by the need for it to double up as dining- and sitting-room, as in the cramped confines of Fron Wen. One of his first tasks was to erect bookshelves the height of one of the walls, so that at last his precious library could be set out in proper order. With all material obstacles removed, it seemed at long last as though the ever-increasing difficulty he had experienced in applying himself to his literary *métier* would shortly be set firmly behind him.

The move significantly stretched Patrick's and my mother's financial resources. The rent for Fron Wen had amounted to no more than £8 per year, and the rates less than £1. At Moelwyn Bank they now paid £31 rent

[1] Characteristically, Patrick did not adopt so commonplace a course as buying a scraper, but painstakingly created his own by breaking the blade of a breadknife and sharpening the end.

and £5/18/6d rates, while the move itself cost £7/13/od. In addition they were faced with a heavy medical bill of £19/19/od in consequence of Patrick's appendicitis operation, which could not have been anticipated. Despite this my mother's skilful budgeting confined their expenditure for 1947–48 (her annual accounts ran from November to October) to £276/18/7½d, while their income was a relatively healthy £311/8/2d.

Initially the move appeared to justify expectations. It was quite likely soon after he was settled in his new library that Patrick composed the story 'It must have been a Branch, They Said'. Now that he too occupied a house of comparable proportions, he could indulge in cocking a gratifying literary snook at his former neighbour.

Probably next in order of composition was 'The Drawing of the Curranwood Badgers', which bears internal indications of having been written at Moelwyn Bank. The greater part of the story consists of a straightforward account of a badger hunt in Ireland, depicted with Patrick's customary verve and graphic evocation of landscape and atmosphere. Its conclusion is however grimly sinister, reflecting his predilection for ending a short story with a Gothic twist. Three terriers introduced into a badger's holt are hideously mauled. Peering into the entrance, the huntsman and his companion realise with mounting horror that the unseen creature within is no badger, but something indescribably monstrous and evil.

Edgar Williams plausibly suggests that the story was inspired by an incident when he, Patrick, and Harri Roberts were out shooting foxes. Tramping northwards beneath the precipitous cliffs of the Cnicht, they entered a strikingly wild and desolate valley named Cwm Foel. There they found what appeared to be a fox's earth, into which Roberts tried to introduce the older of two terriers he had brought with them. The veteran dog proved uncharacteristically reluctant to descend into the chasm, and the youngster was dispatched in his place. After a time a terrified yelping echoed back up the tunnel, and the men set to work frantically digging and prising up heavy stones. Eventually they managed to reach the dog, who was discovered severely mauled and bloodied. Though they did not succeed in exposing his adversary, the sound of a badger scraping fiercely underground with his great claws had been clearly heard. Dusk was descending and as the party set off home for Croesor Fawr Patrick remarked on the eerie setting of Cwm Foel, a silent gloomy hollow sunk beneath the shadow of the grey crag. The sinister atmosphere was increased by the uncanny sensation afforded by the unseen subterranean predator which had mutilated the unfortunate terrier. It was a weird scene reminiscent of unworldly menace as old as *Beowulf*: one very likely to impress itself on Patrick's imagination, with his marked proclivity for the wild and exotic. The dramatic incident witnessed by Edgar Williams possibly occurred on 4 June 1947, when Patrick mentions an expedition 'looking for cubs' with Roberts and 'Edgar the gwas', though doubtless there were other such occasions.

When Patrick came to dramatise the event, he made two primary alterations to the original episode. In his story the chase takes place, not in the barren mountain hollow of Cwm Foel, but in the eponymous Irish wood of the story's title. It is a primeval grove: wild, unchanged, and remote from human habitation. Yet it contains 'self-sown strangers, rhododendrons and barberries and many others that thrived there and looked both elegant and surprising in the season of the year'. Rhododendrons are notorious in North Wales for the extent to which they colonise the immediate vicinity of large houses, into whose gardens they had been introduced in the nineteenth century.[1] Twice when following the Ynysfor Hunt Patrick remarked on the presence of rhododendrons in contexts reminiscent of his story.

On 14 January 1948 at Dolfriog Bridge, in the Nantmor valley over the ridge to the north of Cwm Croesor, after much initial working about the woods the hunt encountered 'trouble with the terriers in the rhododendrons'. This was followed by an event reminiscent of Patrick's tale:

> Hounds took a dubious line to an earth thereby – said to be badgers . . . M and I kept with the master, who presently found the fox (perhaps two) at home in a big earth under a crag . . . Bunt and the little white bitch went down – devilish scufflings far below. It was a very long time before they came out again (Capt. J blew his horn down the hole) and it was not until we were going away that they emerged from unexpected places. The white bitch was so earthy as to be unrecognisable.

The last sentence recalls Patrick's description in his story of a terrier emerging from the earth so 'sandy red with the earth' as at first to be unrecognisable.

The sinister primeval wood of the story looks much as though it was inspired by a meet which Patrick attended two months later: 'We went up the path by Plâs Gwynant and hounds worked through a great deal of rhododendron undergrowth and scrub without finding anything – all this in what had been well-timbered country, but is now a hideous wreckage of rotting felled trees, larches and Scotch pine for the most part.' Here we find the combination of the uncanny atmosphere of the wood with the rhododendrons which features in the fictive Irish setting of Patrick's

[1] F.J. North, Bruce Campbell, and Richenda Scott, *Snowdonia: The National Park of North Wales* (London, 1949), p. 226; Richard Mabey, *Flora Britannica* (London, 1996), p. 158.

tale. He also remarked upon a badger's holt which they passed shortly afterwards.

It looks as though the episode in Cwm Foel from which the story germinated passed through two stages in its evolution. Patrick's decision to shift it from its original mountain setting to a wild wood in a valley may have reflected his use of Cwm Foel as the setting of another story ('Naming Calls') in the same collection. For dramatic purposes he decided to replace the desolate upland hollow with the gloomy ravaged wood in Nant Gwynant.

A more radical change was the transposition of the story from Wales to Ireland. Throughout the story events are seen through the eyes of Gethin, a North Walian who has recently found employment as a gardener with Mr Burke, a Master of Foxhounds in the West of Ireland. While allusions to Irish life are cursory and superficial, Gethin's upbringing and outlook are recounted in vivid and well-informed detail, to an extent which appears superfluous and even incongruous in an Irish sporting tale. One of the fictional terriers, Crab, bears the name of a real-life counterpart in the Ynysfor Hunt, and it is tempting to identify another named Biddy, whose experience and courage receive particular emphasis, with Patrick's own beloved Buddug, who was born at Moelwyn Bank on 1 April 1948.

All this intimates that Patrick wrote the story after he had moved to Moelwyn Bank in the early summer of 1948, and that in its first form it was set in North Wales. Only when he came to revise the stories for publication in the following year did he decide to relocate it in Ireland, and effected minor alterations towards that end. Since the collection contains two other stories about hunting in the mountains of Snowdonia, but none in Ireland, his motive for the transfer very likely reflected a perceived need to ring the changes.[1] If so, it suggests the intriguing possibility that this trifling consideration may have exerted disproportionate influence on the attribution to Patrick of Irish identity. It was seen earlier that his publishers (particularly in the United States) and his readers were strongly influenced to accept this assumption by a favourable review of *The Last Pool* written by the well-known Irish writer Lord Dunsany, who described it as a 'charming book by an Irish sportsman . . . a genuine collection of tales of the Irish countryside'.

One wonders whether Dunsany would have made this assumption had 'The drawing of the Curranwood Badgers' retained its originally Welsh setting, alongside 'The Steep Slope of Gallt y Wenallt' and 'The Long Day Running'.

[1] In November 1952 Patrick jotted down a memorandum about a story originally set in London: 'I will change that inferior story about George to a setting in Dublin and send it to Irish Writing . . .'

During the weeks that followed the establishment of their new household, life was full of bustle. Keen to show off their fine new house, they invited Walter Greenway to stay immediately after their installation at the end of March. As on the previous occasion, he and Patrick eagerly discussed topics of common interest – clocks, books, naval history. Patrick told him that he contemplated writing a collection of short stories about hunting, shooting, and fishing. This confirms that they remained as yet unwritten, and that the project was linked to the fresh start in the new house. It is clear too that he was casting about for suitable topics on which to write. Thus he discussed a project of republishing all or part of Anson's chaplain's account of his great voyage around the world, but this unimaginative scheme was dashed when Walter discovered in the bookstall at Barmouth station on his return journey that it had recently appeared as a Penguin paperback.[1]

They set off on long walks together. The previous time he had come to stay Patrick had only just discovered the existence of the Ynysfor Hunt, but having now enjoyed his second winter as a follower he invited Walter to join him for a day's hunting.

On 3 April the two friends left the cottage at eight o'clock in the morning. After tramping for two hours along a largely trackless route leading northwards over the mountains from Cwm Croesor to Nant Gwynant, they arrived at the meet beside Llyn Gwynant. Captain Jones threw off the pack at the bottom of the wood skirting the north side of the lake, and the hounds worked quickly up the steep slope towards the mountain Gallt y Wenallt towering above. Idwal the huntsman, accompanied by Patrick, Walter, and Major Roche, made their way up to a lofty crag which provided a good vantage point overlooking the wood and the lake. Beneath them they could hear the hounds giving tongue, and a moment later a dark brown dog fox emerged from the trees. Patrick noticed that 'he was quite unhurried and he looked up at us in a considering manner before he went away towards Cwm Dyli' on the far side of the mountain behind them. It was a magnificent scene. Above them the summit of Gallt y Wenallt lay covered in snow, which also mantled the great rampart of Y Lliwedd stretching away to the north-west up to the impassive height of Snowdon.

Idwal at once ran down to the wood to lay the hounds on the trail, which they had evidently lost in the wood. Meanwhile Patrick and his companions made their way around the edge of the mountain in the direction taken by the fox. They were well above the snow line, but so long as they moved among the rocks beneath the summit they were able to obtain precarious footholds.

[1] *Anson's Voyage round the World*, edited by S.W.C. Pack.

However it was not long before they came 'to a grassy slope, tilted at an angle of about 55° and covered with some two inches of snow. We were soon in difficulties: nearly all the few rocks on the surface were loose, and the uninterrupted slope down to the wood looked exceptionally menacing. Sometime after it had become a matter of proceeding crabwise Major R. turned up for the ridge. I did not appreciate the fact that he was making for the peak,' wrote Patrick next day, 'and thought I would be well advised to try to go down below the snow to join the kennel huntsman. After about ten paces, or rather shuffles, for I was in a squatting position all the time, I began to slip, at first slowly, then with a sickening impetus: I had gone perhaps a hundred feet before one foot came up against a firm rock and I stopped in front of a little precipice.'

By this time Patrick was on his own. While Major Roche had ascended the crag in order to discover the direction taken by the pack, Walter had seized the opportunity afforded by a dry stone wall to assist his descent, and was fortunate enough to come across the hounds passing in full cry on an apparently good scent which took them back through the wood of Penmaen Brith beside the lake, and then on up through the precipitous valley of Cwm Llan until they were brought to a stand before its waterfall. The fox had ensconced himself on a rock among the trees, from which as Patrick had noticed he observed (presumably with satisfaction) his pursuers racing back along the scent he had laid when passing through the wood an hour earlier.[1]

The rest of the field came up shortly afterwards, and Walter joined them for tea provided by the hospitable mistress of the farm at Hafod Llan. As time passed by without Patrick's reappearing, they grew alarmed and set out to search the upper reaches of Cwm Llan. Walter was especially concerned, fearing that he might inadvertently have left Patrick stuck somewhere near the point where they had separated, and made numerous laborious casts about the steep and trackless slopes. But he was nowhere to be found, and with darkness coming on Walter was compelled to abandon his search. Filled with apprehension and compunction at not having remained with his friend, he trudged back through the dusk to Cwm Croesor. It was not until seven o'clock that he arrived at Moelwyn Bank in a state of utter exhaustion and, much worse, acute fear that Patrick might all this time be lying severely injured or even dead on the mountainside. When he reached the gate of the house, to his intense surprise and relief he discovered him standing in the garden anxiously awaiting his arrival. Though Walter was understandably

[1] It may well have been this glimpse which inspired the conclusion of 'The Long Day Running', in which the protagonist of the story cannot bring himself to betray an exhausted fox crouching unobserved on a ledge.

not best pleased when he learned that Patrick had for the past two hours been comfortably sitting in his armchair by the fireside, he swiftly forgave him when he discovered what had happened.

Patrick explained that at the time of their separation on the mountainside he had assumed that Walter and Roche were still following him, and when he came to realise that he had left them behind it was too late to turn back. Feeling very shaken after his alarming slide down the snow-covered grassy slope, he decided that his best course would be to reascend the mountain diagonally and cross over by way of the bare rocky crags on its summit. This plan, which with hindsight he acknowledged to have been thoroughly misguided, very nearly led to disaster. His climb involved a perilous scramble, during which he might easily have tumbled to his death.

> What I had supposed to be the top was a false crest, and the crags that had seemed so close together and scaleable were separated by wide shockingly steep grassy patches, and even without any snow they would have been sufficiently difficult to climb. I was soon in a bad way – hands with neither feeling nor strength, clothes soaked and spirit rather oppressed by the drop below. If the weather, which had been rather misty up till then, had not cleared up wonderfully, I should probably have been done for. As it was, the snow below me melted to such an extent that after I had decided to try to go down rather than up, there was only about 100ft. of it to traverse.
>
> For most of this time I had not, I fear, been paying much attention to hounds: once I had come face to face with them very near the top, and once I had seen them running very fast back along the top of the wood – this was the last I saw of them.

With the melting of the snow he was able to descend to the foot of the mountain with relative ease, and as he gained level ground he felt the hideous burden of fear and exhaustion lift as though it had never been. In a nearby gully he was excited to observe a group of ring ouzels. 'Their white gorgets in both cocks and hens, were unexpectedly plain, clearly visible from a hundred yards and more. The hen is perhaps a little browner – lighter – than a hen blackbird. They were fairly unconcerned at my approach: four flew away when I was within about 50y[ards]. but one pair stayed in a bush. I could not tell how many of each sort there were, as they were continually appearing from behind rocks, but I think there were more cocks than hens.'

While it is doubtful whether my mother or Walter considered the obsessive ornithologist's account of the ouzels adequate compensation for the fright Patrick's disappearance had caused them, Stephen Maturin would undoubtedly have understood. He would also have sympathised with another factor in Patrick's predicament. Like Maturin, Patrick was prone to attacks of vertigo, and that he was able to overcome his condition in such testing circumstances is a measure of his fortitude as well as his endurance.

At the next meet a few days later, the Master reproved him in no uncertain terms for not having had the consideration to call at the farm where the meet was held to leave word of his safe descent from the mountain. Patrick accepted the reproof, privately acknowledging that 'It was dull of me not to have gone back by way of Hafod Llan, where I could have left a message.'

At the time, he was so shaken that he confessed that 'I hardly cared whether I saw a hound ever again', and referred to it nearly a year later as 'that horrible day of snow'. Nevertheless it was too dramatic an event not to be put to creative use, and not long afterwards he turned it into the short story entitled 'The Steep Slope of Gallt y Wenallt'. He added almost no fictional elements, and the tale vividly recounts the events of that unforgettably terrifying day with scrupulous accuracy. Patrick cast himself as 'Brown' and Walter Greenway as 'Gonville' – he had attended Gonville and Caius College at Cambridge.

At the outset of the story Patrick describes how Brown and Gonville, beginning their walk from Cwm Croesor to join the meet, engage in a desultory dispute about the extent to which birds are aware of the speed at which they fly if their surroundings are obscured by cloud or darkness. This too was based on reality. Three weeks earlier Patrick had watched a raven pass over their cottage and enter a cloud hanging low along the wall of the valley. The bird plunged straight into the obscurity with such evident confidence that Patrick presumed it would gain the crag towards which its flight was directed. 'He croaked just as he went into the cloud: may this be connected? Conceivably the re-echoing swish of their wings (uncommonly sonorous on a calm day) may do for ravens what the squeak of a bat is said to do for them.'

Walter disputed his theory on scientific grounds: a contradiction which predictably displeased Patrick. In the story he represents Gonville as advocating his view 'in a dogmatic voice', while Brown 'did not believe what he was told, but . . . unable to refute it' abandoned the acrimonious discussion. This exchange, together with the manner in which Patrick represented it in his story, provides a perfect illustration of his character. His knowledge was largely acquired through observation and intuitive speculation, which could (as in this instance) be wrong. Any attempt to correct him or present an alternative view based on scholarly knowledge was almost inevitably deeply resented. In his story Patrick simply says that Brown fell silent and 'did not quarrel with him'. In the case of the real Patrick such a silence was more often than not accompanied by something like Maturin's 'reptilian glare', indicating that his interlocutor had displayed ignorance and overstepped the bounds of good manners.

Walter Greenway, justifiably confident of his intellectual capacity, took such rebuffs in good part. When he came to stay with my parents a few years later in their little flat at Collioure, he protested to Patrick at the unsympathetic depiction of their passing conversation. Patrick promptly apologised, and since he was genuinely fond of Walter it may be wondered why he gratuitously chose to include this unflattering portrayal in a tale manifestly describing a real incident, which Walter was bound to read on publication. The answer seems to be that for many years Patrick employed his writing as an *apologia pro vita sua*, an obsession which extended even to taking the opportunity of correcting so trivial a slight as that to which he fancied his friend had subjected him. Certainly he did not anticipate that the story might cause offence, as can be seen from its dedication: '*for Major W.M. Greenway, R.A.*'.

If the motive for making the perilously expensive move to Moelwyn Bank was that of reviving Patrick's flagging literary career, initially the experiment appeared successful. The transformation of the lengthy entry in Patrick's diary describing his adventure on the slope of Gallt y Wenallt into the short story might not appear to have required much creative effort. However, only authors who have suffered the nightmare experience of writer's block are likely to appreciate the great gain which this seemingly small step represented.

Meanwhile, despite the resolution expressed following his terrifying experience on the edge of Gallt y Wenallt, Patrick continued to follow the Ynysfor Hunt with undiminished enthusiasm. Four days later, as he was returning after a vain chase down the steep descent along the ridge which bounds the north side of Cwm Croesor, another follower inadvertently 'bowled a rock on to my right leg, which damped my ardour'. Yet two days later he and my mother spent an hour bicycling hard against the wind not to miss a meet at Cwm Meillionen in the Glaslyn valley. By the time they came to make the return journey they had spent four and a half hours chasing about the wilderness skirting Moel Hebog. In the following week Patrick spent a still more arduous day with Captain Jones, following scents which took them about the mountains on either side of the Glaslyn north of Beddgelert. (On this occasion my mother remained at home, having injured her back.) No sooner had Patrick returned home than he cycled to Penrhyndeudraeth station to meet Richard, who had returned from the Easter holiday with his mother in London.

Initially Richard found much about his new home at Moelwyn Bank which made a pleasurable change from Fron Wen. Its much larger premises allowed him a degree of privacy within the house which had been impossible in the tiny cottage. Although he still found his father grim and distant, particularly indoors, he derived considerable consolation from my mother's affection and the freedom he enjoyed in the valley.

Overall it would be wrong to suppose that Richard's life was entirely unhappy. Despite Patrick's manner of teaching, his varied and rich store of knowledge could not fail to stimulate the interest of a lively and intelligent boy. His father encouraged him to explore his extensive library, where the boy discovered books which enabled him to escape into realms of imaginative exploration. Richard found French lessons with my mother a pleasurable experience, her fluency in the language and fondness for her stepson making her an ideal teacher. As Patrick had frankly acknowledged at the outset of their first attempt to tutor Richard, her approach proved as successful as his was counter-productive.

In the evenings the little family created its own entertainment, playing the swift-moving card game Racing Demon, or ping-pong (at which Patrick was an adept and keen player)[1] on the treasured air-raid shelter. Alternatively they would read or listen to the radio or gramophone, or my mother would play the accordion, singing traditional favourites from Ernest Newton's *Community Sing-Song Book*. On such occasions Patrick could be a delightful companion. Curiously, he rarely evinced in games that ferocious competitiveness which lay never far from the surface in ordinary social intercourse.

Richard was very fond of animals, as were his father and my mother. Three weeks before their arrival at Moelwyn Bank their much-loved terrier Nellie, sister to the lamented Barkis, had given birth to a litter of five puppies. Of these one was retained, a bitch christened Buddug, who for years to come succeeded Miss Potts as my mother's and Patrick's most cherished companion. She was indeed a lovable and affectionate creature.[2]

Later in the year my mother bought another two puppies, this time corgis. They were of good stock, costing six guineas each and subsequently registered with the Kennel Club. The first, who was born in Aberystwyth

[1] At the age of eighty, not having played for half a century, he put up a very good showing against our well-practised teenage son Dmitri.

[2] *Buddug* is Welsh for 'victory', a later form of the name of the formidable Boudicca (long incorrectly known as Boadicea), who so valiantly resisted the Roman occupation. With such an illustrious precursor, our own Buddug would not have been best pleased at finding herself described as 'a Welsh farmyard terrier . . . not pedigreed' (King, *Patrick O'Brian*, p. 127). In fact, as Patrick proudly recorded in his 'Kennel Book', she was a hunt terrier of impeccably distinguished ancestry.

and arrived in October, bore the fine name Nanw Esgidiau Gwynion. Two months later another bitch arrived, this time bought from a friend of my mother's family in North Devon. Born 'Zenda of Eversleigh', she was rechristened with the good Welsh name of Bronwen y Moelwyn. Despite undergoing initial bouts of hysteria, Bronwen went on to parade her elegant proportions at the Blaenau Ffestiniog show in April 1949.

Not content with these three additions to the household, the family also acquired a cat, whom Patrick named Hodge after his admired Dr Johnson's pet. Finally, my mother and he gave Richard a fine white angora rabbit. With the hens and geese, it was a crowded and at times noisy household. The most regrettable factor in Richard's life was the unnatural deprivation of companions of his own age. As has already been seen, Patrick's obsessive delusions regarding social propriety led him to prohibit his son from forming friendships with the boys of the valley.

One of the annual treats which Patrick and my mother permitted themselves was a visit to Criccieth fair, which took place every Midsummer Day. The trip required a pleasant twelve-mile bicycle ride through Portmadoc to the pretty seaside town, with its thirteenth-century castle overlooking Tremadoc Bay. This was the first time that Richard accompanied them, as in previous years he had been away at school. Patrick, who was not entirely consistent in his self-imposed rulings, invited the Robertses' young son Gwynfor to join them. The two boys spent a happy day enjoying the customary fairground delights of roundabouts, coconut shies, and ghost trains. However, when the time came to depart, they were nowhere to be found. After a vain search among the milling crowd, Patrick and my mother reluctantly returned home. Gwynfor, who had become separated from Richard, eventually arrived at the farm, having taken the bus to Penrhyndeudraeth and walked home. Harri Roberts promptly offered to drive the anxious Patrick back to Criccieth, where they found Richard awaiting them. Though he received a stern rebuke, it had been a thoroughly enjoyable day.

Whether it was this incident, or a general dawning awareness which led Patrick to acknowledge his son's needs in this respect, it was decided that he required companionship. My mother approached her good friend Barbara Puckridge, then living at Haslemere in Surrey, to enquire whether her young son James would like to spend part of his summer holiday with them. Barbara readily agreed, and as James recently explained to me, 'I was invited, or *caused* to go and spend my summer holidays in Cwm Croesor in that lovely cottage.'

James travelled alone on the nine-hour train journey from Paddington. He was met at Penrhyndeudraeth station and brought to Moelwyn Bank, where he met Richard for the first time. His impression was that the boy, who was nearly two years younger than him, 'didn't seem to have the sort of friendships in school that I had. He seemed to be a rather withdrawn boy, and he welcomed my being there.' This was understandable since, as Richard explained once they were alone together, he was permitted little or no social contact with other children in the valley. He confided: 'thank God I've got someone to play with, because I'm not allowed to play with them!'

The two boys soon became good friends. Despite the fact that the weather was wet, cold, and miserable for much of the time, James recalled that 'we had a lot of fun together. We fished a lot, we walked a lot, we shot a lot: we had endless outdoor fun.' Indoors matters were very different. There Richard became subdued and almost mute, above all when his father was in the room. Generally Patrick appeared cold and withdrawn, but if his son did anything that irritated him he would shout at him fiercely. My mother impressed upon the boys that on no account was he to be disturbed in any way. 'I think that the old adage that children should be seen and not heard was very much in play. In Patrick's household he did not wish to see the children: he didn't even want to tolerate them, if he could help it. Meals were very tense, always very tense.' Even in the garden the boys had to act with extreme caution. If a football were accidentally kicked against the wall of the house, Patrick 'would come rushing out shouting'.

Such was the grim atmosphere which prevailed in the house at Moelwyn Bank. However, no greater contrast could be presented between Patrick at home and Patrick out and about in the countryside. 'We often used to walk prolific distances, because Patrick loved to walk.' He and my mother took the boys up into the mountains, picnicking, fishing, and observing wildlife. During these expeditions James invariably found Patrick a delightful and inspiring companion. 'He was full of charm and enthusiasm and encouragement, and everything you can imagine. Absolutely the opposite to his personality in the house. I would have said that he was even content to have children around him. He was more than content, because he would cause us to come for long walks with him. Then he would talk, and be much more open. Very different.' Far from expecting the boys to remain attentive, he invited and welcomed their comments, at times displaying genuine interest in their opinions. Despite the chilling atmosphere imposed by Patrick within the house, James's overall recollection of his summer holiday at Moelwyn Bank was that 'it was fun, I enjoyed it: it was a very different life'.

Patrick's description of one of several walks in May 1949 to Llyn Croesor, a lake beyond the quarry at the end of Cwm Croesor, provides a characteristic example of the varied delights such excursions provided.

> Such a pleasant warm day. We went up and M. waded first to the island and found a nest with three eggs. They were extraordinarily large, very nearly as big as a Greater Black-Back's, and the one we brought home (Bron [the corgi Bronwen] had picked it up and cracked it) weighed 3½oz. – it was addled. Then Richard found another, also with three in, but smaller by far: his weighed 2½oz. – it was fresh, but it could not be blown and in the end I crushed it. However, he ate it fried, and very good it was. There were four other nests, three well-made, above a foot across and raised as much as 3″, and one but rough. There were pellets, too, and a good deal of grain, fish-bones and a strange candle-wax-like substance as well as droppings. The birds were not unduly agitated, and moaned rather than screamed. After we had waded back Richard found another nest on the peninsula at the far end of the lake, with one medium-sized egg in it. The nests were not cleverly made or woven and lined – just dry grass heaped and hollowed, but substantial, solid affairs, rather than the wisps I had expected.

To which my mother added: 'I noticed two or three of the nests were built largely of lichen-like moss, in big lumps.'

Although the departure of James left Richard companionless and unsupported, there remained compensations. He assisted in the garden (an activity he had enjoyed at Southey Hall), looked after and played with the dogs, cat, and his rabbit, was free to fish in the river, roam the valley slopes shooting rabbits, and bicycle about the valley.

The encouraging resurgence Patrick experienced after Walter Greenway's visit proved temporary, and before long the dread spectre of writer's block returned to haunt him throughout the summer. The extent of his affliction is indicated by the fact that he and my mother occupied separate bedrooms at Moelwyn Bank. Throughout his life Patrick suffered from bouts of insomnia, but in no other home did he sleep separately from her, which suggests that at this time it became acute. That Patrick was deeply troubled was evident even to young James Puckridge during his stay in late August and early September. He could not help observing the obsessive extent of her concern for his peace of mind. 'I believe that she really thought that we were interfering with his life if we upset him. And she didn't want anything to upset him. Either that, or she was desperate for him to come up with something or other – but I've no idea! I never saw any evidence that she didn't have huge respect for him. Because . . . she was an extraordinarily peaceful person, and lovely and serene sort of person. But when he was around, she was almost cowed by it.'

Patrick gave every indication of living on his nerves while in the house, when he usually withdrew to his study to pursue his 'writing'. However, as James sensed and the evidence indicates, ideas simply refused to flow, and he faced that nightmare experienced by almost every writer at some stage in his life: the poised pen, the blank sheet of paper – and the creative flow stifled at source. In *Three Bear Witness* the protagonist is a university don who has taken a small cottage (modelled on Fron Wen) in a Welsh valley in order to recover his physical health and mental equilibrium. As he explains:

> It was not that my duties in the university took up so many days in the term, nor that my research carried me along at an exhausting pace; it was my tutoring that wore me down. The young men who came to me did not seem to do very well, and my responsibility for their lack of improvement worried me more and more. It had come to the pitch where I was spending more time over their essays than ever they had spent; and with indifferent health I found that this frustrating, ungrateful task had become an almost intolerable burden . . . I hoped to make so complete a break with my established habits and discontents that I should return . . . to the writing of my book . . . with enough zeal to carry me through . . . the next few chapters.[1]

Here there is plainly an allusion to the embittered frustration experienced by Patrick as a consequence of his unfortunate attempt to instruct Richard, which he seems to have fastened upon as the cause of his inability to write. Although this was more likely symptom than cause, Patrick's harsh and unimaginative approach must have been deeply affected by the psychological crisis which afflicted him so sorely throughout his time in Wales.

Even young Richard noticed the effect of his father's state of introverted detachment: 'My father was a grim teacher . . . He wanted me to be quiet especially when he said he was "thinking". When he was thinking he would switch off completely. His eyes changed, his stance altered. It was as if he was on a different planet.'

Yet that his father was capable in happier circumstances of proving an effective teacher was acknowledged by the boy himself only four years after the conclusion of his detested course in Wales. With an important examination pending, he wrote on 23 September 1953 to their new home in France: 'if Dad is willing, I would like him to teach me Latin and Greek so that I could pass in them. I have got to pass.'

The frustration and depression which constantly dogged Patrick throughout the four years he spent in Wales caused him at times to become excessively provoked to an extent beyond what might have been the case had

[1] *Three Bear Witness*, p. 10.

he been able to achieve an intellectually satisfying existence. His nagging sense of failure can only have been exacerbated by the bitter disappointment which followed not long after the move to Moelwyn Bank, upon which such high hopes had been built.

It was not until after James Puckridge's departure at the beginning of September that Patrick achieved a second breakthrough in his writing. He completed two further stories, both of which revolve around graphically described fishing expeditions. That he switched to this theme is unlikely to have resulted from chance. His two earlier stories describing days spent following the Ynysfor Hunt were written shortly after the close of the hunting season, while he devoted much time in the summer to fishing the Croesor and the Glaslyn.

'The Last Pool' recounts the mounting excitement of a day's salmon fishing, with a tragic conclusion. The name given to the eponymous pool and another mentioned in connection with it imply an Irish setting, but this factor barely impinges on the tale. The description is clearly based on Patrick's own experience in Wales, and is almost certainly based on a pool in the pass of Aberglaslyn where he occasionally fished for salmon.

'The Happy Despatch' is distinguished from the other stories Patrick wrote in 1948. Though a fishing expedition plays a significant part in the story, it is incidental to the main plot. Its principal theme is the fundamentally honourable nature of its protagonist, a man doomed by his lack of guile and inadequate judgement to a life of wretchedness which eventually culminates in disaster. The story is replete with themes which recur in Patrick's subsequent fiction, and like them contains much that is transparently autobiographical.

Woollen, the character about whom the story revolves, 'had been gently bred, of no particular family, but a gentleman'. Socially and financially inept, and after retiring from an ineffectual career as an army officer he makes a brief and unsuccessful attempt to establish himself in business. Before long a dishonest employer cozens him of most of his savings, and with a small annuity as his sole remaining resource he is compelled to retire to a remote valley in the west of Ireland. Yet again his naïvety leads him into being deceived, this time by the local landowner, the cabin he rented proving barely inhabitable and its ground incapable of maintaining the smallholding from which he had intended to make his living. His pathetic attempt at farming is an utter failure: 'his neighbours . . . would not teach him anything, and, being town-bred, he knew almost nothing of any value'.

He finds himself shunned as an Englishman and his property damaged by the local people. His mild consciousness of his status as a gentleman has inadvertently led him into total isolation. 'Woollen, of his own act, had effectually closed the door of silence upon himself. He had thought it best to maintain his status by a certain stiffness – after he had asserted his gentility, he could unbend to the two or three half-gentlemen of the neighbourhood. He never had the opportunity. His poverty was quickly discovered and they felt themselves outraged. Even the poorest of his neighbours considered himself affronted. Woollen had picked up . . . a kind of superficial arrogance – a protective colouring of which he was wholly unconscious – and this unconciliating manner, and his other overwhelming disadvantages, rendered him perhaps the loneliest man in the county.' Fate had treated him with brutal injustice, for behind his awkward exterior lay 'a simple honesty that would put nine men out of ten to shame at the judgment seat'. His misery increased until 'there were times when it seemed to him that he hardly belonged to the human race at all, the more the pity, for he was a sociable creature by nature'.

Although Woollen acknowledges that his predicament has arisen in large part from his needless prickliness, he assigns much of the responsibility for his isolation to 'his horrible wife'. Words can scarcely be found to describe the squalid depravity of her nature. She was 'a deathless shrew . . . she did not wash: she had many disgusting personal habits. Woollen had married her in haste a great many years since; she had been employed in an inferior boarding-house at the time.' Totally lacking in any redeeming quality, 'She was unbelievably ignorant, and her tiny mind had narrowed with the passing years to the point of insanity.'

Though written in the third person, the story reads as a sort of confessional. Woollen's hatred and contempt for his wife lead to an horrific incident, which is recounted without a hint of regret. Fishing affords him his sole opportunity for relief in a situation which grows more desperate with every year. 'Once she had broken his rod, and he, moved out of himself, had beaten her almost to insensibility with the butt-end. This had earned him one undisputed day's fishing a week, for a deep voice had warned him, against his convictions, never to apologize for this outburst, nor, indeed, to refer to it.'

Ground down by poverty and failure, Woollen longs desperately to depart 'to some happier place where children would not shriek after him with stones'. But all appears to no avail. 'Poverty had brought him there, and poverty chained him there.' Then a day comes when he sets out for one of his days' fishing, as ever 'as excited as a boy'. His destination is a wild ravine among the mountains with which he is familiar, where he begins casting for trout in a stream below a prehistoric stone circle. After a graphically realistic account of the fishing, the story takes a dramatically unexpected turn. A shift in the course of the stream uncovers a stone chest containing a massive hoard of gold coins. Recognising that this offers him unique opportunity for escape from his detested incarceration in the valley, he adopts frantic measures to conceal the treasure, and starts off with as much gold as he can carry.

The pass leading to the neighbouring town narrows at its final point to a dark chasm. Here, as in 'The drawing of the Curranwood Badgers', the story abruptly concludes on a note of horror: 'But in the pass he met the keeper of the hoard.'

The description of Woollen bears marked resemblance to Patrick's self-portrait in *Richard Temple*. Well-bred but poverty-stricken, his innate generosity and kindness make him a type of holy fool, readily deceived and abused by his fellow-soldiers, his employer, his landlord and neighbours, and worst of all by the gross and vicious woman to whom he is shackled by an undeserved stroke of abominable ill luck. His effort to maintain his social position in face of ever-increasing poverty serves only to increase an isolation unnatural to his mildly sociable character. The valley which he inhabits in County Mayo is an almost exact replica of Cwm Croesor, and his untutored and unsuccessful efforts to establish the smallholding which provoke the derision of his neighbours echo Patrick's own inexperienced attempts at gardening. As an additional revealing touch, his unscrupulous landowner bears the name Harler, which is also that of the hero's snobbish and unsympathetic uncle in *Richard Temple*.

Fishing leads Woollen to discovery of a glittering treasure promising release from all his suffering. It is precisely at this moment that grim fate appears to destroy him. The melodramatic ending represents a familiar feature of Patrick's writing, but here a deeper symbolic significance is unmistakable. Fishing and hunting in the open countryside provide absorbing sensations of liberation and achievement, but disillusionment and failure lurk hard by and ultimately prove inescapable.

Though the story is not one of Patrick's most successful, it repays attention for the light it sheds on his character generally, and in particular his state of mind at this critical juncture of his life. On 23 September 1948 Patrick sent 'The Last Pool' and 'The Happy Despatch' to the magazines *Britannia and Eve* and *John O'London's Weekly*. The likelihood that they were written not more than a few weeks before that date is confirmed by a chance allusion in the account of Woollen's sorry struggle to make a profit from his garden. The catalogue of his failures includes an attempt to keep bees. Spiteful neighbours repeatedly overturn the hives, so 'that he was hardly sorry when the survivors died of Isle of Wight disease'. This specialised knowledge of apiculture is incongruous. How might a man as ignorant of husbandry as Woollen have known the beekeepers' term for acarine disease? The anomaly is readily explained by the fact that in the previous month Patrick had himself installed bees in the garden at

Moelwyn Bank. With his usual thoroughness he had conducted research into their care, purchasing carbolic acid, glycerine, and oil of wintergreen from a firm in Scotland to preserve his hive from mites carrying infestation.

Woollen's ugly, spiteful, stupid, and lazy wife is little more than a vindictive and implausible caricature. Her counterpart is found in Richard Temple's mother, a sluttish, alcoholic nymphomaniac, whose condition degenerates so far that she has to be confined in an asylum. There can be little doubt that these tawdry and malicious women who destroy, or all but destroy, a high-minded and deeply misunderstood hero represent caricatures of Patrick's first wife Elizabeth. The revolting account of Woollen's beating his wife with the butt of his fishing rod derived from a literary source, whose application to his own predicament struck him as apt.

There is reason to believe that Patrick wrote 'The Happy Despatch' under the influence of the Irish writer Liam O'Flaherty's novel *Skerrett*. Published in 1932, it tells the story of a schoolmaster, David Skerrett, who takes up a post teaching on a remote island off the coast of Galway. A man of formidable energy and intellect, he initially proves successful in improving educational facilities and generating co-operation and purpose among the insular community. At the outset he collaborates happily with the village priest, Father Moclair, a man outwardly of imposing personal authority, but within proud, cunning, and avaricious.

Gradually Father Moclair comes to view him as a rival: they fall out, and a battle of wills develops for domination of the island community. Skerrett's physical and intellectual vigour sustain him for a time in his unequal struggle against the all-powerful priest and the superstition and ignorance of the islanders which provide the basis for his tyrannical rule. However Skerrett is gradually dragged down and ultimately destroyed, his downfall being caused as much by the uncompromising nobility of his character as by the venerated office and machiavellian scheming of his principal adversary.

Patrick possessed a copy of *Skerrett*, which appears to have exercised considerable influence on his literary development. Related themes of the novel found in his own work include the arrival of an intelligent and upright stranger in a remote and primitive community, from which his very virtues assist in alienating him, his resolute refusal to compromise his principles, and his marginalisation and eventual isolation within a society for whom he wishes nothing but good.

Skerrett's physique and morale are weakened by the relentless struggle, until he reaches the point where he finds his energies entirely sapped. His health begins to fail, and at the instigation of the priest he and his school are boycotted by the primitive islanders, until he withdraws cooped up sick and alone in an isolated cottage. 'Now he realised that his whole life had been an utter failure. All that he had touched had been accursed. One after the other, everything he held dear had been taken from him. He had been gradually stripped until he now stood alone in this tiny cabin on a lonely crag, by the edge of the ocean.'

Driven to despair and near-insanity, he resolves to kill Father Moclair. Painfully, he drags his weakened body down the hill and along the road in an implicit Calvary: 'The children pelted him with stones and shouted insults.' When he bawls out his impotent threat to kill the priest, he is promptly bound by the bystanders and hauled off to a police cell. There the doctor certifies him as insane, and a few days later he is removed across the sea and confined in the county asylum. 'There his proud heart broke after six months and he died in the asylum hospital. But he died undaunted as he had lived. The very last words he was heard to utter were: "I defy them all. They can't make me bend the knee." '

In a brief epilogue, O'Flaherty contrasts Skerrett's achievement with the hollow victory gained by Father Moclair: '. . . the nobility of Skerrett's nature lay in his pursuit of godliness. He aimed at being a man who owns no master. And such men, though doomed to destruction by the timid herd, grow after death to the full proportion of their greatness.'

Whatever chance it was that drew Patrick to read *Skerrett*, it is not hard to picture the immediacy of its appeal to his tormented spirit: elements of the story appear to varying extent in Patrick's most intensely autobiographical novels, in particular *Three Bear Witness*, *The Catalans*, and *Richard Temple*. The parallels were obvious: was he not himself a solitary, high-minded intellectual stranger, driven by poverty to dwell in isolated squalor, shunned and scorned by high and low alike? Furthermore in Father Moclair the author provided a remarkable counterpart of Patrick's father. 'The priest was a tall man, over six feet in height . . . strongly built, handsome in appearance, of striking personality.' His office and keen intelligence combine to confer upon him an authority hard to resist. At the same time, 'he walked with a riding crop, which he carried between his clasped hands behind his back', and does not hesitate to resort to physical violence where his moral authority appears inadequate. When Skerrett remonstrates truculently with him in church, the powerfully built priest strikes him a terrible blow.

Skerrett's wife in the end turns to whiskey, and becomes a hopeless drunkard. Their relationship deteriorates drastically, leading to a hideously violent scene. 'Skerrett lost all patience and beat his wife severely when she came home drunk one evening; but this only drove her to further excesses . . . He now conceived a deadly hatred for his wife, whom he regarded as the cause of all his misfortunes.' Her condition continues to worsen, until the relationship reaches a point of no return.

> All decent human intercourse between them had entirely ceased. Each hated the other bitterly . . . Kate had grown into a most disgusting slut. She made no effort to keep herself clean. In fact she made herself look as unseemly as possible in order to madden her husband . . . The house got into a state of gross disorder, as Kate took pleasure in spoiling whatever the servant made clean. She took especial delight in ruining Skerrett's books, burning some, mutilating others.

In Patrick's 'The Happy Despatch', Woollen's wife, who for no discernible reason 'hated fishing', maliciously breaks one of his rods, which provokes him into giving her a vicious beating.

Patrick asserted to his brother Victor that Elizabeth, his senior by four years, had trapped him when very young into a loveless marriage by claiming she was pregnant. It is not difficult to picture the impact upon Patrick of O'Flaherty's account of Skerrett's marriage. 'She [Skerrett's wife Kate] was a year older than himself and their marriage had been forced by her becoming pregnant through a previous intimacy.[1] He had taken her without love, finding her handy to his passion . . . and he was not particular about the object of his lust. When she miscarried and he found himself tied needlessly to a dull and unattractive woman, indifference became hatred in him.'

Overall 'The Happy Despatch' reads like a rendering of the central theme of *Skerrett*, modified to accord with Patrick's circumstances. While Skerrett is a passionate, energetic, and not infrequently violent reformer, who provokes equally strong reactions in the oppressive authority against which he pits himself, Patrick's essential passivity led him to create the image of a quiet and honourable man of letters, a Man of Sufferings whose calm virtue attracts the irrational resentment of all about him. What he shared with Skerrett was an indomitable determination to conduct himself honourably in face of all that an unjust and omnipotent fate might fling at him.

That an acclaimed contemporary novelist could effectively exalt failings into virtues in a character with whom Patrick could so closely identify, offered an unexpected road to public vindication. Whether it was an altogether beneficial influence is for critics and readers to judge. Three of his subsequent novels, *Three Bear Witness*, *The Catalans*, and *Richard Temple*, together with several short stories, betray in varying degree his driving need

[1] It will be recalled that Elizabeth may have been pregnant with another man's child when she first met Patrick.

to subject his own character and past life to intensive examination and exculpation. It is fortunate indeed that he did not abandon that other avenue of escape which he had discovered in early childhood, when he boldly turned his back upon sombre regions of reality to write *The Road to Samarcand*, *The Golden Ocean* and *The Unknown Shore*.

Six days after posting 'The Last Pool' and 'The Happy Return' to prospective publishers, Patrick travelled with my mother to Ynys Gifftan, a small island situated in the estuary of the Traeth Bach across the water from Clough Williams-Ellis's baroque village of Portmeirion. As Edgar Williams remembers, 'he had great hopes of becoming a farmer, and he was going to rent an island . . . called Ynys Gifftan . . . And he actually went there to the dispersal sale with Harri, the farmer, to assess the possibility of earning a livelihood, by farming there. But I think he was eventually put off the idea because it's a tidal little island, and you can go there only on certain tides.'

While they were inspecting it Patrick's attention was drawn to a horse grazing nearby, and on being told that it was used for transporting goods to the mainland observed that it was presumably accustomed to crossing the sands at low tide. Pondering the matter further, he remarked that 'its tail was sadly put'. This subsequently afforded a topic of amusement in Cwm Croesor, when Harri Roberts came to recount Mr O'Brian's fanciful notion that the length of a horse's tail could affect its working capacity. In fact his attention was attracted by all manner of things which had nothing to do with the practical concerns of farming. What chiefly drew him were flocks of water wagtails, and he pointed out a dead heron to my mother as they crossed the marshy tract of the Glas Troeth to reach the strand. On arrival much of his time on the island was taken up with an earnest debate with my mother as to whether some birds in the distance might not be tufted ducks.

Despite this, the project was seriously contemplated. Its abandonment is unlikely to have resulted from Patrick's concern with the length of the horse's tail, and the most probable explanation is that they were reluctantly compelled to accept that so unpredictable a venture would be too costly.

Since the date for renewal of the lease of Ynys Gifftan was imminent, there was no time to learn how Patrick's two stories would be received by the editors to whom they had been sent. The fact that he seriously considered engaging in full-time farming suggests that he had reached a point where he was compelled to acknowledge that he could no longer regard his literary prospects with confidence. In the event both stories were rejected, and as Arthur Cunningham of the British Library points out: 'Britannia and Eve: a monthly journal for men and women . . . ran from 1929 until, I think, the early 1950s. I have looked at some issues from the early 1930s and it seems to have been a mix of features and fiction. Fairly middle brow with the emphasis in the fiction on action and adventure, though with some respected names from the period. I wouldn't have thought "The last pool" was at all their sort of thing, so perhaps submission was a mite desperate?'

In view of the fact that none of the short stories which Patrick had composed in Wales up to this time appears to have found a publisher, Cunningham's conjecture appears plausible. Though Patrick and my mother were invariably imbued with high hopes for the success of each successive literary venture, by the autumn of 1948 all he had achieved after three years were three unpublished stories written that spring and a further two in recent weeks. Nor does it appear that he could discover any means of extending his inspiration beyond the restricted themes of hunting and fishing.

This low point in their fortunes appears reflected in the two stories which Patrick completed just before he reluctantly decided not to take up the lease of Ynys Gifftan. He and my mother must have been seriously considering their plan to farm the island for some time. On 14 September they had conducted a preliminary inspection, and the fact that they returned on Michaelmas Day (the quarter day when farm leases were renewed) suggests that they continued indecisive up to the last moment.

The themes of the two stories are strongly indicative of his state of mind at the time. In 'The Last Pool' a fisherman engages in a prolonged struggle to land a salmon, which eventually takes the hook – only to drag him down to his death with 'a vast galvanic lunge'. In 'The Happy Despatch' a man dogged by poverty and misfortune discovers a pot of gold during a fishing expedition, and meets annihilation at the very moment of his escape.

Add to this James Puckridge's memory of Patrick's nervous tension while attempting to write, and it is hard not to conclude that in writing these two stories Patrick had strained his creative energies to their limit, and was forced to acknowledge that his work as an author appeared once more to have reached a dead end. The disillusionment was enhanced by the high expectations which he and my mother had entertained on moving into Moelwyn Bank.

The new hunting season opened in the same month that Patrick and my mother returned disappointed but resigned from Ynys Gifftan. In this third season of Patrick's following the Ynysfor, a sudden and terrible tragedy occurred. The entries in his hunting diary provide a vividly detailed picture of each occasion he or my mother spent following hounds. Then, towards the end of 1948, there appears this stark record: 'November 3$^{rd.}$ was the black day.'

Neither Patrick nor my mother was present when the disaster occurred.

On the previous day Captain Jones had been hunting south near Dolgelley, on the wooded slopes of Penmaen overlooking the Mawddach estuary. During the pursuit he lost a hound, and next day returned with his nephew Major Roche and huntsman Idwal to resume the search. They took a dozen hounds with them, who before long discovered the scent of a fox which they pursued up the mountainside. The trail led to a crevice beneath some huge boulders. By this stage Major Roche had become separated from the Master and Idwal, who began levering aside the stones with iron bars.

They were joined by the local Deputy Chief Fire Officer of Dolgelley and one of his firemen, both keen followers to hounds. After toiling at the entrance for some time it became plain that it was impossible to penetrate the fox's refuge. The party waited for a while to see if the animal would emerge, but when nothing transpired Captain Jones decided to smoke it out. Collecting some bracken, he stuffed it into the hole and put his hand into his pocket to take out his matches.

The Fire Officer, Mr Roberts, warned him that he did not like the look of two huge boulders poised above the entrance. Just as Captain Jones assured him that they were quite firm, one of the rocks dislodged itself from the slope and rolled over him, crushing him to death on the spot. Idwal was also injured though fortunately not seriously.[1]

Patrick's distress on learning of this dreadful news was acute. To Harri Roberts he remarked: 'Captain Jones was not the sort of man to die in bed.' The comment indicates the high estimation in which he held the Master's resolution and intrepidity, but its inadequacy as an expression of the depth of his feeling reflects the extent to which the tragedy affected him. Indeed, I suspect he felt it even more than the death in action of his brother Mike, whom he had after all barely known.

Captain Jones was succeeded as Master of the Ynysfor by Major Roche, who was unable to hunt until a month after the tragedy. In the interval he pressed Patrick to assist the huntsman: an indication of how adept Patrick had become in his third year as a follower. On 24 November he met Idwal and the hounds at Bwlch Gwernog, across the ridge to the north-west of Cwm Croesor, and together they walked up the wooded valley of Nantmor. The faithful huntsman, unable to conceal his distress at the loss of his beloved Master, confided to Patrick that he 'had been exercising hounds on Moel Ddu last week and he had had a very good hunt by himself, killing a dog fox in Gorseddau Quarry: he said, "It gave me a rotten feeling – I could have sworn I heard him shouting 'Get the bloody bastard out of Foel Hebog.'" (I

[1] *Caernarvon and Denbigh Herald and North Wales Observer*, 5 November 1948. I am grateful to Edgar Williams for providing me with a copy of the article.

am not quite sure that I have that exactly right, but it was certainly very like.)'

Major Roche took the field ten days afterwards, but though Patrick liked him and continued to follow hounds for the remainder of the season, the spirit of the Ynysfor Hunt could never be the same without the inspiring leadership of Captain Jones. Towards the end of February 1949 Patrick was disturbed by 'Words between Roche & Idwal [which] made things very uncomfortable'. Whilst the experienced huntsman would have accepted without a murmur any reproof, however violently expressed, from his old master he could not entertain similar respect for his successor. Time did nothing to heal the wound, and considerable local scandal arose when some time later Roche discharged Idwal as huntsman.

Hunting now began to lose its appeal for Patrick, and his attendance became less regular than in previous years. At the end of the month he went to a meet in Nant Gwynant, but by now found himself 'so much out of training' that at the end of the day 'I was sadly wearied before I got up to the top of the Croesor ridge'. After the New Year he followed the hounds only three times, the last occasion being on 2 March. Towards the end of 1948 Patrick had resolved upon escape from the valley in which he had come to feel trapped.

CHAPTER NINETEEN

The End of the Road

> . . . however, my brother, let us be patient, and endure a while; the time may come that may give us a happy release; but let us not be our own murderers. With these words Hopeful at present did moderate the mind of his brother; so they continued together in the dark that day, in their sad and doleful condition.
>
> (John Bunyan, *the Pilgrim's Progress*)

As they approached the fourth year of their stay in Cwm Croesor, my mother and Patrick decided to tear up roots they had originally put down so firmly. Although their unfailing tenacity and resourcefulness had enabled them to overcome the material privations of their lives, the essential problem remained unresolved. By the late autumn of 1948 nearly three years had passed without any material improvement in Patrick's literary prospects. Their final attempt to obtain success through the move to Moelwyn Bank had failed to achieve its end, and there was no alternative to their leaving North Wales in order to begin their lives afresh a second time.

In his biography Dean King explains the grounds for this decision as follows:

> It was a fine, sunny early summer, and O'Brian, now thirty-five, polished up his short stories. But he and Mary, no longer so world-weary, also considered moving. Cwm Croesor had offered them the simple, clean life that they had coveted after the war and a degree of freedom within their means. But life in the Welsh valley, which was cold and damp much of the year, aggravating ailments, was remote, harsh and monotonous. They had also to consider Richard's welfare. So far, his boyish transgressions were minor . . . but Richard would soon need the company of children of his

> own age, proper schooling, and additional activities to occupy his teenage mind.[1]

No authority is given for this insight into my parents' thinking, and most of its conjectures appear to me misconceived. So far from having been world-weary at their arrival, they had thrown themselves into their Welsh adventure like two high-spirited adolescents. The move to Cwm Croesor in 1945 was not instigated by desire to find a simple, clean life, but by the lack of any alternative compatible with their financial position. If, as appears, the statement that Patrick 'polished up his short stories' is intended to imply that they had been completed by that time, this again is incorrect. The polishing took place in August 1949, nearly a year after he and my mother had decided to move to France.

The reference to 'cold and damp much of the year, aggravating ailments' as a contributory factor appears to reflect misapprehensions concerning Patrick's health throughout his lifetime. It has been seen how remarkable was the extent of his vigour and endurance, above all in the hunting field. Edgar Williams, who was out and about with him in the valley in all weathers, never noticed in him any sign of debility. There were periods of his life when he suffered from asthma, but nothing suggests that the Welsh climate exercised an adverse effect on his health. Occasional colds and the appendicitis attack in the spring of 1948 appear to constitute the sum of his maladies. In *Three Bear Witness*, written soon after their arrival in France, Patrick dwelt on the 'keen, fine air, a pleasure to breathe' of Cwm Croesor. During their first year in the valley their doctors' bill amounted to £1/14/7d, in the second £1/11/7½d, and in the third £23/17/8d. Since the last included £19/19/0d for Patrick's appendicitis operation, the couple can scarcely be regarded as chronic invalids.

Perhaps the strongest reason for dismissing their state of health and the relative cheapness of life in France as primary reasons for moving lies in the fact that in 1953 and 1954 they became dissatisfied with their life in the south of France and planned to move again. Then they engaged in much time and effort to buy or rent houses in rainy and windswept Cornwall, Ireland – and Wales!

The decision to leave Wales arose from a second recognition of Patrick's agonising failure to recover his literary talent. This may appear surprising. As

[1] King, *Patrick O'Brian*, p. 132. It has been suggested that the move to Collioure was 'perhaps, in order to be a long way from the family he had abandoned' (*Daily Mail*, 3 November 2003). In fact, much of Patrick's time in the summer of 1949 was occupied by a struggle to gain custody of his son Richard in order to take him to live with him in France.

a boy and adolescent his imagination had soared like the peregrine falcon in *Beasts Royal* over cliffs and sea, entering the minds of birds and beasts and conjuring up convincing images of an exotic India which he had never visited. When he first resumed his writing after settling in at Fron Wen, he attempted to take up where he had left off when the war interrupted his work, but the effort had proved largely unavailing.

Over the last winter in Cwm Croesor Patrick became increasingly disenchanted with his existence, and with the death of Captain Jones on 3 November 1948 his most effective solace – hunting with the Ynysfor – swiftly lost its spell. In the next month Patrick and my mother began discussing whether the time had not come to make an entirely clean break from their present unproductive existence. The valley lay gripped in the snow and ice of the fourth winter they had lived there, and sunny France suddenly presented an enthralling alternative. Richard was greatly excited by the prospect, and told his mother the news when he went to stay with her for the last part of December. According to her, he was despondent when the time came for him to return to Wales, and it is clear that the morale of the household at Moelwyn Bank had sunk very low.

In March 1949 my mother was away for some time in London, looking after her mother who was ill. Patrick carried a notebook with him on his walks, in which he jotted down random ideas for fresh literary ventures. The first of these looks as though it was inspired by her absence: an occurrence which invariably aroused feelings of anxiety: 'A very loving pair – one dies and the other grieves sorely – the swish of the silk skirt'.

However nothing further came of this, and instead he contemplated a gloomy horror story. 'A man is writing a very horrid tale, it comes hard and his concentration creates the Thing he is writing about. Gaiety at noon – fading with the light. He writes at night. Suspicion of madness – changes the tale – It changes. Utterly weary and terrified he tries to write a godly ending, but the words do not run that way: he re-reads the end and is aware that it is now inevitably in train – he is right.' This looks like a premature version of the story 'Naming Calls', which Patrick wrote a month or so later. The disturbed frame of mind of the author in this summary, and his sensation of entrapment by his work, reflected Patrick's own emotional turmoil at this time.

When my mother returned to Moelwyn Bank, she found Patrick in even lower spirits than before. A note in mirror writing on the cover of his notebook indicates that he was taking medication: 'I was taking rather much/But it worked out perfectly well'. His lack of literary progress was apt to bring on psychosomatic disorders, and it looks as though he experienced an unpleasant attack at this time.

In *Three Bear Witness* the Patrick-figure Pugh falls sick, and the description of his ailment suggests a painful memory of the mental and physical state which eventually drove Patrick to leave the valley: '. . . my old illness began again: it was not very bad, but enough to make me feel rather ill all day and to stop me sleeping at night. Something was wrong with my digestion, as I have said before, and whatever it was (doctors were vague and contradictory) it was linked in some way with my nervous system, and, whenever the one went wrong, the other betrayed me.'[1]

Unsurprisingly the local doctor was unable to diagnose any physical cause, and Pugh acknowledged that his sickness might be regarded by others as hypochondria. Still more suggestively, he accepts its close connection with his inability to continue his literary work. 'I would find myself as nervous as a cat, unequal to my food, useless for reading or settling to any sort of work. As for my book, it had dropped into the utter distance . . .'

Alone with his trouble, Pugh is himself at first uncertain whether he is really sick.

> . . . there was a whole week when I dragged myself about, either unaware that I was seriously ill or denying it to myself. By the end of the week I had let everything slide; the cottage was in a horrible mess, but I lacked the courage to start setting it in order: even the effort of getting the milk from the farm was too much at the end – besides, I no longer possessed a milk jug that was not crusted with sour milk. I just sat over the fire and drank pot after pot of weak tea, letting time pass over me, day and night . . .[2]

Incapable of maintaining even this feeble struggle, he takes to his bed, where he lies in the grip of a debilitating lethargy. 'In these long silent days my mind revolved with a curious motion, slow and dispassionate, following no logical pattern.' He began to accept the possibility of death: a prospect which he contemplated with resignation rather than fear.[3]

In the early months of 1949 Patrick's notes indicate that he was casting about with increasing desperation for a theme which he might develop into dramatic form. But no sooner did he happen on a promising idea than his inspiration failed him. Though my mother stayed in Chelsea for only two or three weeks and returned at the end of the month, so relatively brief a separation would have disturbed his peace of mind even had he not been experiencing a particularly low period in his life. On this occasion

[1] *Three Bear Witness*, p. 61.
[2] *Ibid.*, pp. 109, 114.
[3] *Ibid.*, p. 115.

his agitation was probably exacerbated by the fact that she was staying with her parents, whose influence he feared and resented.

Patrick was not alone in Moelwyn Bank, since Richard remained with him. Relations between father and son were not unremittingly difficult. On 23 March Richard sent my mother in Chelsea a cheerful report of recent happenings at Moelwyn Bank: 'I hope that Step-granny will be up soon and that you well. How awful of Buddug to bite the big, black poodle, I hope she did not hurt it. All the animals are well. I took Bun [his angora rabbit] out yesterday and I had a job to catch her. Daddy has made a cross-bow but for all his pains it does not go far. By the wall where Bron [the corgi] hurt her foot I have seen a snipe twice and I went with the cross-bow and it was not there. I gave the meat to Mrs Roberts and she brought it up with two puddings. Please come back soon as I miss Bud. I did not know where you had put Daddy's cake [for St Patrick's Day] and I had forgotten where I had put the grapefruit.'

Their explorations of the surrounding countryside continued, and Richard continued his intelligent interest in natural history. He was allowed to borrow the shotgun, with which he set out eagerly stalking rabbits in the fields. It was probably observing this that led Patrick to contemplate writing a story based on the shooting experience of 'A boy with a .410 . . . The boy is the vicar's son – Christmas holidays.'

He proposed to set the episode near the sea during a bitterly cold winter, with 'the waves curling over and the knife-edged dunes to the lee of everything'. He jotted down evocative features of the snowbound landscape, in wording which indicates a real-life situation: 'I could bring in those harriers, perhaps to keep the geese down. That starved pigeon.' He can only have had in mind the countryside around the cottage which he had shared with Elizabeth and their children in Norfolk during the icy winter of 1939–40, when he had himself regularly ventured out with the same .410 to shoot game for his poverty-stricken household. The idea of extrapolating his own hunting experience into an adventure involving a small boy suggests Patrick's constant desire to reinvent his own childhood, indulging the illusion of boyish experiences he had been denied in reality.

This story also never came to fruition, and Patrick turned to confront a psychological problem of which he had long been uneasily aware, and which his recent experience led him to contemplate more directly. In his notebook he remarked, 'The sense of déjà vu. Being at a remove from reality, so that the world is like a picture or a back-cloth.' In itself this provided insufficient grounds for a story, and Patrick added what might otherwise appear an inconsequential afterthought: 'The sawn off tree and platform used . . . for pigeon-shooting.'

There can be no mistaking the fact that the first reflection represented his primary concern, while the second (possibly deriving from an unrecorded event in his past) provided a theme to give the story structure. This time the idea took off, and appeared in due course as the final story in *The Last Pool*. Entitled 'The Little Death', it revolves around the experience of a war veteran named Grattan, who ascends just such a platform to shoot pigeons. His brief attack of vertigo and fascinated observation of birds reflect Patrick's own experience. Grattan spots a plump pigeon within easy range of his gun. But even as he prepares to shoot it, a horrifying memory flashes into his mind of a crashed Messerschmitt exploding on the ground with its pilot trapped inside. 'While I live I shall never kill another living thing,' he says aloud, and deliberately shoots wide, scaring away his prospective victim. Patrick dedicated the story to Maître Armand Goëau-Brissonnière, the French Resistance leader who had been his valued colleague and friend during his service with PWE.[1]

The principal interest of the story lies less in the theme of sudden compunction which unexpectedly grips the war-wearied protagonist, than in the reflections which pass through his mind while he waits. His main concern, symbolised by his distancing upon his elevated perch from the world below, is best conveyed in Patrick's own words:

> . . . that feeling of being at one remove from life, or rather from one's surroundings, so that they look as little real as the back-cloth of a pantomime . . . It was something remotely like one of the stages of drunkenness when a man seems to stand a little to one side of himself, listening to what he says and watching himself, but without a great deal of interest . . . it had waited upon him now and then from boyhood, and since he had come home from the war it had been at his elbow most of the time . . . if he had wanted to he would have found it very difficult to describe what it was, the thing that interposed itself between him and ordinary life, so that with an indifferent eye he saw everything strange, so that sounds and impressions came through to him as if they travelled more slowly: the something that gave him an inner life of far greater reality than that which went on around him at the same time and in which he took part with the rest of him.

This story was a harrowing exercise in catharsis, with Patrick mercilessly

[1] In 1950 Patrick sent Goëau-Brissonnière (by then a successful lawyer in Paris) a copy of *The Last Pool*. This was acknowledged by his secretary on 24 October with promise of a long letter, which in the event never materialised.

applying the surgeon's knife to his own *condition humaine*. Of late he had become conscious of his unnatural isolation, and sought to analyse its genesis and evolution. In the story Grattan had first become conscious of this peculiar trait as a growing boy, and it affected him intermittently until the end of the war. Thereafter it gradually closed in upon him until he experienced a claustrophobic divergence between himself and the world outside. Over the past year his solipsism had become so acute as to inspire mounting dread of some impending but indefinable catastrophe. This apprehension appeared at once terrifying and enticing – enticing, because the tension of approaching the unknown bourne was becoming intolerable.

These successive stages in Grattan's psychological evolution tally with Patrick's own experience. His romantic adventures with my mother and their happy domesticity in The Cottage at Chelsea combined with their shared absorbing work for the Ambulance Service and PWE to make his life from 1940 to 1945 the period when he had been most sociable and contented. His professional work, though not very exacting, engaged sufficient of his time and thought to justify postponement of any attempt at fresh literary ventures, while he obtained intellectual satisfaction from increasing his library and reading widely without being obliged to hold a specific end in view. All this abruptly changed after the war, when he found himself immured in unprecedented isolation in North Wales. Of course he had my mother as a close and beloved companion, but their union was so intense that she all but constituted an extension of his own personality. Significantly, she makes not even a fleeting appearance in Patrick's two books which draw on his life in Wales, *The Last Pool* and *Three Bear Witness*.

Patrick's spirits appear to have fallen to their lowest ebb during my mother's absence, and only partially revived with her return. As ever, bird-watching provided a welcome distraction (on 27 March he remarked how the mountains were full of skylarks singing sweetly), and soon after she came back they were cheered by the arrival of old friends from Chelsea days, Francis Cox and his wife. Cox was a painter, and Patrick was eager to point out the beauties of Cwm Croesor and its fascinating bird-life, such as the merlin which unexpectedly approached within ten yards of them while they were walking past Clough Williams-Ellis's house at Plas Brondanw.

At this time the simmering discord between Patrick and Elizabeth now flared up again. Under the terms of the judgment of 20 August 1945 Patrick had been granted custody of Richard, on the grounds that Elizabeth was living in adultery with Le Mee Power. Richard was to live with her for half the school holidays, provided she honour her undertaking that he should not be permitted to come in contact with her lover.

Now, on 26 April, Elizabeth filed a petition requesting the court to review the case in light of 'radical changes' which had occurred since, both in her circumstances and those of her son. At the time of the 1945 judgment Richard was attending Southey Hall. His withdrawal in July 1947 to be tutored by his father 'in a remote Welsh district' was, she stated, 'detrimental to the welfare of the boy, and has increased difficulties over the arrangements for access . . .' Furthermore she alleged that Patrick 'had, almost from the beginning, adopted a vexatious attitude over the matter of access that caused me constant anxiety, distress and even actual ill-health'.

Elizabeth asserted that Patrick raised so many objections and obstructions to Richard's visits as to make her life intolerable. Eventually in March 1948 their solicitors concerted an agreement laying down precise dates and train timetables for the visits, so precluding room for misunderstanding and further recriminatory exchanges. She accepted that this arrangement had worked perfectly for a year until the current Easter holiday.

On 5 April 1949 she arrived as arranged at Paddington station, only to find that Richard was not on the train. Surprised and alarmed, she immediately contacted the police, who on investigating the matter informed her that he was still at his father's home. (Patrick told Richard that the constable had called to enquire about one of their dogs.)[1]

The first news from Moelwyn Bank came in the form of a letter written by my mother ten days after Richard's failure to arrive.

> Dear Mrs. Russ,
> I thought you might like to hear that Richard is very well indeed; he is quite fat, and is always in excellent spirits. He sees plenty of other children, and leads the healthiest of lives, being out-of-doors for a long time every day and eating a great deal of country food. He sleeps all night every night. He always receives your letters. He has done so well in his lessons this last year that we shall soon be able to send him back to school. Richard is devoted to you and often speaks of you with evident pleasure.
> Yours sincerely, Mary O'Brian

Elizabeth instructed her solicitor to find out why the agreed arrangement had been broken. He was informed that Patrick had recently discovered that she was violating her undertaking 'that the child be not brought into contact with the man with whom she is living'. Accordingly Messrs Baddeley Wardlaw proposed that, unless she agree to Richard's 'ceasing to come to her for half the school holidays', application would be made to rescind the original order,

[1] This was presumably the occasion related by Richard to Dean King (*Patrick O'Brian*, p. 136).

when 'we will advise our clients to take such opportunities as offer themselves in the future to let your client and Richard meet on suitable occasions'.

This led an indignant Elizabeth to respond with an application for custody of her son to be restored. John Le Mee Power had finally obtained a legal separation from his wife, and they planned to marry on 7 May. So far as his contacts with Richard were concerned,

> the true facts are that Mr. Power has always left the flat for the whole period of access and lived elsewhere, often right out of London, and never came into direct or indirect contact with the boy. At Christmas last however, when I knew that within a very short time I would be marrying Mr. Power, I thought it proper to invite Mr. Power to visit the flat on three occasions during the fortnight for tea. He also called once to collect some papers and on another occasion by pure accident they met in a Butcher's Shop. It did not occur to me that this would be regarded as a breach of the undertaking I had given and which I had with utmost conscientiousness observed, for I felt that the time had come to begin to prepare the boy for the changed situation he would soon meet by letting him have this slight and informal contact under conditions that seemed to me entirely appropriate and natural.

Elizabeth recapitulated a series of complaints about Richard's treatment by his father and stepmother, including assertions that Richard invariably arrived in London without any change of clothing or ration card, and that correspondence between them was prevented or intercepted. As evidence of this she submitted a letter which she claimed arrived in an unstamped envelope received from Richard at Moelwyn Bank, in which he mentioned 'I write this letter on the sly'.

Elizabeth also asserted that Richard was subjected to a regime at once so harsh and negligent that he suffered nightmares and had become so 'desperately unhappy with his father and his wife' as to contemplate committing suicide. 'He complains that his father beats him with a Malacca cane and shouts and bullies him, and that his wife screams at him. He has spoken more than once of being "pumped about Mr Power" and says that they never play with him.' He no longer loved his father, and his overwhelming desire was to return home to live permanently with his mother. Such behaviour on Patrick's part, she concluded, was

> what I was bound to expect from knowledge of the Respondent who, during the period of our marriage, treated me very repressively, not allowing me to have a newspaper, to visit a Cinema, or to listen to a wireless. He is a man with a

> passion for culture that overrides all human considerations and although this passion for culture is quite evidently sincere and well meant it is bound to impose intolerable emotional pressure on a young and sensitive boy. I am perfect satisfied that the Respondent has no intention whatever of being unkind to his son and that he believes his attitude and his methods with the boy are for his ultimate benefit; but in fact the effects are obviously bad.

From what is known of the matter, at least the last two sentences appear fair comment.

With regard to my mother, Elizabeth continued:

> I am informed and verily believe that the Respondent's present wife, who is a Divorced woman and has two children, is deprived by Order of this Honourable Court from even having access to her own children, and this leads me to believe that there must be valid and cogent objections to her having the care of any child.

This confirms that Elizabeth continued being advised and assisted in the background by my father, from whom alone this information could have derived. My mother had been granted leave at the hearing in February 1946 to reapply for access in three years' time, and Elizabeth had evidently been privately notified that she had not succeeded.

Elizabeth requested the court to grant her custody of her son. She was now self-employed, and in a position to provide Richard with a home where he could have his own bedroom. She accepted that the holidays should be shared as before, and unless his father was able to find him a suitable school she would arrange for her son to be educated locally.

Patrick responded on 2 June with an affidavit in which he recapitulated the lamentable state of Richard's education on his arrival in London, the care and expense he had provided in sending him to boarding-school, and his decision to coach him for entry to public school: 'I do state that had he not been taught very patiently at home and unlimited pains taken by my wife and myself he would have remained one of those unhappy boys who are always at the bottom of their form throughout their preparatory schooldays and would never pass into a public school at all . . .'[1]

This last sentence is revealing. For had Patrick himself not been 'one of

[1] Walter Greenway attested in an affidavit that 'I know nothing of Richard's mother, but it struck me when I first met the boy [in 1945] that he was very backward and that this could only be attributed to his upbringing up to that time and I was forced to the conclusion that . . . [his mother] had neglected him'.

those unhappy boys who are always at the bottom of their form . . . and . . . never pass into a public school at all'? In fact his claims for Richard's educational progress do not appear exaggerated, and Elizabeth herself accepted that the 'tuition has been successful from an academic point of view'.

Elizabeth firmly rebutted a further charge 'that Richard has been allowed by me to play in the streets and pick up undesirable play-mates . . . I live in King's Road Chelsea where it would be suicidal to allow a young boy to play and I, in fact, never allowed Richard to cross a road alone without my being with him as he has become unused to London traffic.' This denial is difficult to reconcile with Richard's own memories of roaming 'the streets of London with other boys, gathering and swapping shrapnel after bombing raids and dazzling drivers by reflecting the sun with shards of broken mirrors. While the homeless foraged outside the charred shells of buildings, he chased after Mitsy, his pet Yorkshire terrier, who was prone to getting picked up by the dog-catcher.'[1]

It is true that this was at an earlier period during the war, but if he was permitted such licence during the air raids it seems a little implausible that it should have been withdrawn in peacetime when he was several years older. Possibly Elizabeth was being needlessly defensive. I stayed frequently around the corner with my grandparents at the time Richard supposedly had to be shepherded across King's Road, and was allowed complete freedom to walk or bicycle where I wished. I do not recall negotiating the King's Road as being remotely dangerous, let alone 'suicidal'.

Patrick acknowledged (significantly without specifying why) that 'the question of letter writing has always been a difficult one', but denied that Richard was restricted in corresponding with his mother. As for the letter submitted in evidence by Elizabeth, 'The words "on the sly" can only mean that he was supposed to be doing his lessons when he wrote the letter.' Patrick and his solicitors strangely overlooked the relevance of another sentence in Richard's letter: 'I am very sorry not to have writen [*sic*] before but I had no time.' As my mother commented in her affidavit, 'I am afraid he is like most normal boys, a bad correspondent.'[2]

As to whether Richard's life at Moelwyn Bank was beneficial or detrimental to his well-being, Patrick painted a glowing and (so far as it went) accurate description of life in Cwm Croesor:

[1] King, *Patrick O'Brian*, pp. 93–94.

[1] On 2 March 1946 Richard wrote from school to Patrick and my mother 'I am very sorry that I have not written for so long', his previous letter having been sent on 26 January.

> Whilst here he has a natural life, lessons and good healthy sport.
>
> I have never heard my wife scream at Richard and am quite certain this is untrue.
>
> The allegation that we do not play with him is not true. I have taught him fly-fishing, taken him hunting when hounds meet conveniently near and taught him to handle a gun. I have got him interested in nature study and have shown him every local bird, including some very rare ones, whilst indoors my wife and I have spent innumerable hours playing games with him such as table tennis, Racing Demon and other kinds of Patience, and games such as lexicon and Pope Joan as well as Draughts, Halma and rudimentary chess. My son has a good many books, music and we have sing songs and of course the wireless.
>
> He has two gardens, a white rabbit a ewe and a lamb and a cat of his own. There are three dogs in the house. Cricket is unfortunately generally limited to practice at the nets. I play it with him throughout the Summer and sometimes we can manage to assemble quite a team.
>
> He has also learnt to swim and together we have climbed every nearby mountain.

Originally Patrick had hoped that Richard could enter Dartmouth with a view to serving in the Royal Navy, 'but it soon became obvious that he would not reach the standard necessary, I therefore concentrated on bringing him up to the level of the Public Schools Common Entrance Examination in order that he could go to Wellington for which he was entered and that he would eventually make the Army his career if he showed no other bent. Recently however the Master wrote to me declining to accept Richard although he was entered in 1945, on the grounds that my wife's son by her former marriage was joining the school on the 21st January 1949 . . .

'This is most unfortunate as I do not think that another public school within my means would be suitable for Richard even if he could be got in at a later date. For a number of personal reasons I was prepared to make considerable sacrifices such as taking a salaried position, which would mean a great interruption of my writing, for a number of years to keep Richard at Wellington. Being baulked of Wellington, therefore, it is my intention to go to live in France in order that he may be educated at a Lycée . . .'

After explaining the advantages he believed this course of education would confer on his son, he alluded to what he regarded as the grave danger attendant on spending too much time with his mother. 'I have no wish to break the relationship between Richard and his mother, but I think it would be more to his advantage to see less of her as she drinks heavily, is often seen drunk and from time to time Mr Power is in an equal state of intoxication.'

According to my mother's affidavit, on his first arrival at Fron Wen

Richard 'settled down very quickly with us . . . and became very affectionate towards me. He at first evinced surprise when he discovered that my husband and I did not leave him alone in the house after he was put to bed and told me that "she always went out to the pubs". On one occasion I heard him singing "Nag, Nag, Nag" and on being asked to explain he replied that was what John Le Mee Power said to his mother.'

She concluded: 'We have talked to him of the likelihood of going to live in France and he seems very interested and pleased and is looking forward to it.'

Elizabeth responded on 18 June with a recapitulation of her early struggles to provide Richard with the best education she could afford, and reminded the court that any difficulties had arisen in consequence of her desertion by her husband. She reiterated her complaint that Patrick's recent decision to discontinue the agreed arrangement for access which had proceeded smoothly in the previous year was based on specious pretexts unconnected with the cause alleged, and countered the various allegations levelled against her.

Although it was inconsiderate of Patrick not to have warned Elizabeth in advance that Richard would not be arriving as expected on 5 April, the reason for his reluctance to allow the boy to see his mother appears to have been genuine. In his first affidavit he declared that 'It was very near to Easter 1949 when I first became aware that Richard was being brought into contact with the man with whom his mother lives.' Clearly somebody must have provided Patrick with this information, and fortunately it is clear who that was. As noted earlier, just before Easter their old Chelsea friends Francis Cox and his wife came to stay at Moelwyn Bank. They lived in a flat immediately below that occupied by Elizabeth Russ at 237 King's Road, so were familiar with much of what passed in her household. The fact that they were on good terms with her would explain why Patrick forbore to cite the source of his information.

Patrick had reason to be disturbed by Elizabeth's violation of her undertaking not to bring Richard into contact with her lover, who appears to have been a disreputable character. Patrick declared that 'from time to time Mr Power is in . . . [a] state of intoxication'. There appears no good reason not to accept that it was his discovery that Elizabeth had secretly brought Richard into contact with Power that accounted for his sudden decision to prevent him travelling to London on 5 April.

Elizabeth's account of the few formal meetings she claimed had taken place between Power and her son is open to question. In her first affidavit she accused Patrick of 'pumping' Richard for information about Power. Patrick's response was that 'on the only occasion that I ever spoke to Richard about Mr Power the boy told me that Power had complained about the noise made by the cats in the early morning'. Here Patrick appears to have overlooked an implication helpful to his case, since it might be enquired what Power was doing in the flat at such an hour.

Elizabeth vehemently denied the accusation that she herself was frequently drunk, explaining that the only occasions she visited public houses was to view exhibitions given by artist friends. At such events she confined herself to a glass of light ale, and never touched spirits. Today Richard emphatically denies that she drank to excess: 'I never, never saw her the worse for wear. She was quite definitely not a heavy drinker.' Nevertheless she may have accompanied Power during his drinking sessions.

CHAPTER TWENTY

A Place in the Sun

To kinder skies, where gentler manners reign,
I turn; and France displays her bright domain.
Gay sprightly land of mirth and social ease,
Pleas'd with thyself, whom all the world can please –
(Oliver Goldsmith, 'The Traveller')

All in all, the situation with regard to Patrick's relations with his first wife and son was far from being as one-sided as it has been represented. Richard's excitement at the prospect of living with his father and stepmother in France (provided he was able to continue seeing his mother regularly) suggests that, though his father was from from being an ideal instructor, it was as much the loneliness of his existence in North Wales as anything else that made his life miserable. Nor does it appear that he was so consistently unhappy as his subsequent memory suggested.

In addition to her original request to be reassigned custody of her son, Elizabeth earnestly urged 'the Court not to consider permitting Richard to receive his further education in France', on the grounds that experience led her to fear the consequences of his removal from the jurisdiction of the court, and her belief 'that he would be thoroughly unsettled by being transplanted in the way proposed'.

The case was set down to be heard in July. These depressing and time-consuming proceedings were little conducive to inspired creativity, but Patrick continued casting about for some fresh topic to inspire his muse. On 24 May an unexpected drama brought excitement to Cwm Croesor, when a helicopter carrying material for repair of the dam at the quarry crashed. Fortunately the pilot miraculously escaped. Patrick walked up to observe the wreckage, and briefly considered weaving a tale about the incident. 'That half-witted Londoner guarding the helicopter – could vanish. Rather commonplace, perhaps, unless I first described the place and the thing, then as something quite different, have the machine crashing up there and the man disappearing, and let the connection make itself. Or perhaps it would be better the other way around, ending "But when I came up again there it was not there." '

Like its predecessors, the project went no further. Strive as he would, Patrick's inspiration failed him almost every time he attempted to get it off the ground.

My mother's visit to London in May seems to have distressed Patrick as much as the occasion of her previous absence in March, leading him once more to compose a story reflecting his agitated state of mind. His final story reads like a defiant farewell to an episode in his life which he had come to regard as a miserable failure. Walking some time before through the desolate valley of Cwm Foel beneath the north face of the Cnicht, on his way to the remote upland lake of Llyn yr Adar, he had seen an uncanny image which he was to describe with telling effect in *Three Bear Witness*. He had remarked on the unusually sinister atmosphere of the place in 1947, when he heard a terrier being savagely mauled by an unknown subterranean adversary. Revisiting the spot on a subsequent occasion, he noted a ruined cottage set in a cliffside, named 'Llys Dafydd y Foel' after the hero of a wild local legend. Patrick recorded in his notebook the overall air of grim solitude: 'It is a sunless valley. The bare black floor of the lake at the top. The bubbles of marsh gas rising in the water. The bog at the top, and the huge rocks that lie on the one side.'

It was this experience which inspired his final short story written in Wales, 'Naming Calls'.[1] The protagonist is one Abel Widgery, who rents Llys Dafydd 'to spend the long vacation reading hard, essential, indeed, if he were to stand any chance of a good degree. Scarcely less important to him was the opportunity of bird-watching.' Widgery is immediately recognisable as Patrick himself, and while the situation of the cottage is that of Llys Dafydd, the building itself is unmistakably modelled on Fron Wen. Widgery's experience precisely echoes Patrick's first arrival in Cwm Croesor: 'the first week had passed in ceaseless activity; bookshelves, the windows, the defective chimney, the unfamiliar cares of housekeeping, these had kept him busier than he had been in his life'.

A week after his arrival Widgery rises with the dawn in a sunny frame of mind. While dressing he is struck by the appearance of two choughs on the grass just outside his window – just as was Patrick on 17 May 1949 when writing the story. For some reason they induce a feeling of unease, and the sky ominously clouds over.

[1] *The Last Pool*, pp. 161–74.

> This day was to be the beginning of his reading programme, but after he had washed up he had no inclination to read. The pages went slowly over, and in the end he found that when he had finished a paragraph he had no idea what had been said, although he had conscientiously formed each word with his lips. He closed the book and started on his lecture notes: they seemed either trivial and obvious or obscure to incomprehensibility. His eye roved vacantly and slid down to his watch; it was unthinkable that so few minutes should have passed, but when he held it to his ear the watch was ticking . . . Widgery passed the rest of the day, a very long day, going over and over the old ground of his lecture notes. His acquired knowledge had never seemed so unprofitable, and by the time he lit the lamp he knew that he had done little or nothing of use.

Retiring early to bed, Widgery is unable to sleep, despite the soporific effect of rain beating on the roof and the roaring of nearby watercourses. 'After a long spell of determined stillness, with vacant mind and relaxed body, he resigned himself to waking and let his mind run idly where it liked. It chose, as it so often did, to run over those shameful occasions which he would most like to blot out, those dreadful things that made him blush in the dark: the joke he had made which the unsmiling company thought to be in poor taste, the time when he found himself impotent, his arrival in a suit when everyone else had a dinner jacket on – these, and many like them, repeated their well-known lines, no word forgotten, no humiliating nuance overlooked, every possible consequence magnified.'

Readers could not be expected to know of Patrick's own agonising shyness in company, his terror of perpetrating social gaffes, or his occasional fear of impotence.[1]

Abel Widgery's thoughts pass from these tormenting reflections to memories of his childhood, which before long focus on his father, 'a formidable, roaring tyrant – it was only since he had gone to the university that Abel had begun to realise that there must have been something very strange about his father's life, and stranger still about his death, and the manner of it.'

He recalled a conversation between two servants, one of whom had begun to speak about his father's death. But before she could speak his name, the other urgently interrupted with the warning: 'Naming calls, you know. God between us and harm.'

The allusion was to the widely attested belief in early and primitive

[1] He never rid himself of such fears. In 1984, for example, he recorded in his diary: 'A long, long, v long night, waking at 3 persuaded it was 7; wretched hours too, with the usual going-over of slights, humiliations, misdeeds, crimes, failures . . .'

societies that the name is identified with the person, and that uttering that of a recently dead individual could conjure up his ghost. An ingenious precaution for frustrating this danger lay in changing the name of the dead person, so that the ghost might not realise that it was his that was being taken in vain.[1] The concept appears to have had a strong influence on Patrick's imagination. Of Jack Aubrey he wrote that 'the deepest of his private superstitions, or ancestral pieties, was *naming calls*'.[2] One wonders whether something of this consideration may not have affected Patrick's decision to abandon his paternal surname in 1945, and his insistent determination to conceal and rearrange his past. That the transformation was prompted in part by irrational motives is suggested by his apparent lack of consideration of the constant vulnerability to public exposure to which the pretence inevitably exposed him.

Returning to 'Naming Calls', recollection of the 'exquisite horror' which the fearful exchange between the two women had excited in his infant imagination inexorably draws the restless sleeper into a further obsessive reverie.

> He recaptured the feeling now; the words had an awful value of their own, and the course of years had enhanced this. He repeated them now, with a sense of growing insecurity. He felt a powerful temptation – temptation, because he resisted it as though it were an evil sin – to say his father's name aloud. He made a strong effort and changed the current of his thought. In the early morning he dropped into a series of uneasy dozes, and he dreamt of the far-off horror of his father, and he shouted, so that he awoke suddenly, with the sound of his cries still in the room. With a sudden burst of energy, he got up and lit the lamp, and in the light the terror of nightmare receded and his sense of proportion returned. He knew that he must have been talking in his sleep again, as he had done from his schooldays.

Widgery dozed again fitfully, and when he reawoke it was to find the morning still dark, while the heavy rain which had lashed the house throughout the night had greatly increased. A fierce wind drove it passionately across the valley, and a dozen new cataracts appeared frothing

[1] For accounts of the belief recorded around the world, cf. Sir James George Frazer, *Taboo and the Perils of the Soul* (London, 1911), pp. 349–63; *Aftermath: A Supplement to the Golden Bough* (London, 1936), p. 280; *Totemism and Exogamy: A Treatise on Certain Early Forms of Superstition and Society* (London, 1935), ii, p. 535; *Totemica: A Supplement to Totemism and Exogamy* (London, 1937), p. 19.

[2] *HMS Surprise*, p. 309; cf. *The Reverse of the Medal*, p. 66. Patrick was evidently aware of the superstition at an early age, since he mentions it at the beginning of *Hussein* (1938).

white down the mountainside. Water welled up between the flagstones of the floor and flowed away beneath the door.[1] After rearranging the room as best he could to protect himself from the damp, Widgery attempted to restore his equanimity by resuming his studies, for which he had prepared a careful plan. 'He made a conscientious attempt to follow it now, but it would not answer, and before long he was gazing out of the window, with his elbows on the sill and his legs astraddle to avoid a growing pool.'

For long he gazed out upon the wild turmoil of the tempest raging in the valley, until 'his mind quite abstracted itself from the scene outside and wandered off into the vaguest day-dreams. "Naming calls," he found himself repeating, and as he said it he was conscious of a strong disinclination to turn from the window to the gloom behind.' Making a strenuous effort to resume his work, 'he plodded on to the end of the afternoon's programme, although his eyes were pricking with tiredness and his mind heavy and unreceptive. Loss of sleep always made him feel like this, and now, when he closed the book he closed his eyes too, for they hurt, and his head ached: he was asleep in a few minutes.'

A moment later he was woken by an exceptionally ferocious blast of wind, which struck the house with such malevolent force that the strong stone-built structure shuddered. As the tempest grew ever more violent, Widgery's secret dread became subsumed into an overwhelming sense of physical fear. When night eventually returned, his watch unexpectedly stopped and the absence of its familiar tick accentuated his increasing sense of timeless isolation. Although there were indications that the storm was preparing to subside, three exceptionally savage gusts of wind buffeted the cottage more violently even than before. High overhead on the mountainside a vast mass of rock gradually shifted, as a newly created torrent began to undermine its foundations. Moving at first slowly, it detached itself at last, gathered impetus, and plunged with a terrible grinding roar down the scree.

Though Widgery heard the dreadful noise, it barely impinged on his consciousness. He 'sat listening, with a strained anxiety. An instant horror caught his breath. There was something outside the door, he said . . . The twilight faded, and still he sat rigid, listening and listening . . . He was listening for a little grating sound, no more, but horrible beyond words.

' "What did I say in my asleep?" he asked for the hundredth time, though by now he knew full well.

'There was an old cough outside, a little scratching sound and the door creaked with a pressure that was not that of the wind.'

[1] On 23 June 1946 Patrick noted in his journal: 'All the slate[s] in Fron have exuded water all day long, and will not dry.'

Unable to take his eyes from the door, he remained gripped in his chair by nameless fear. There was a long, seemingly endless pause while he awaited the inexorable arrival of the approaching intruder. Then, all of a sudden, it happened.

'The scratch, a little grating knock, a pause, then a battering, furious smashing on the wood, the frail wood, and there no more than a hasp to keep it. Abel shrieked high and the door burst open, swinging wide and shuddering on its hinges.'

As an exposition of Patrick's state of mind at this time, this narrative could scarcely be more revealing. However painstaking his preparations and strenuous his mental striving, Widgery finds his capacity for work stifled from the outset. Bird-watching provides a gratifying digression, but nothing can overcome his inability to concentrate on the work upon whose completion his success and peace of mind depend. He encounters constant difficulty in sleeping, and during long hours in the stillness of the night his thoughts are constantly drawn to recollections of incidents involving humiliating failure.

These random instances of inadequacy become gradually focused on childhood memories, dominated by the terrifying figure of his father, that 'formidable, roaring tyrant' who had reduced his early life to misery. Though absent in body he threatens ever more ominously to return in spirit. His son's pathetic attempt to achieve security and success by withdrawing to a remote refuge was doomed from the outset. The storm raging against his frail retreat with fury becomes with each savage assault ever more overtly an elemental evocation of his father.[1] Gripped by ineluctable tension, he can only sit frozen in his chair, until the door bursts open to admit the monstrous figure bent upon his annihilation.

The storm is described with wonderful realism, and Patrick must have witnessed countless such scenes while living at Fron Wen and Moelwyn Bank. However, the whole is a metaphorical account of his state of mind in May 1949. My mother had returned to stay with her parents in London and, save for Richard, Patrick was on his own. Despite every effort, he had become virtually incapable of creative writing. As every writer who has undergone this traumatising experience will recognise, prolonged bouts of writer's block are frequently accompanied by an acute sense of impending obliteration, creation appearing the fundamental expression of being. At the same time he constantly engages in fruitless self-analysis in a desperate search for a solution to his debility.

[1] Elsewhere Patrick describes a figure clearly recognisable as his father as 'a ferocious domestic bully . . . a force of nature' (*The Catalans*, p. 86).

The opening chapters of this book indicate why Patrick evoked the figure of his father, whose enormous size, unpredictable outbursts of rage and violence, and forbidding personality had imbued Patrick's childhood and adolescence with fear and resentment. His financial ineptitude and lack of concern for the interests of his children had resulted in Patrick's being denied a full education and place at university. But for the endemic lassitude induced by prolonged periods of isolated confinement in childhood, and deprivation of public school and university training, what might he not have achieved with those exceptional talents with which he felt himself endowed?

In comparably autobiographical stories, such as 'The Happy Despatch' and *Three Bear Witness*, the Patrick-figure features as a middle-aged man. In 'Naming Calls', however, Abel Widgery is an undergraduate. This is mentioned at the beginning, but nothing that follows conveys the least impression of youth. It is decidedly incongruous that a young man should catalogue among the most embarrassing moments of his life gauche perpetration of tasteless jokes, the lack of a dinner-jacket on a social occasion, and lapses in sexual adequacy! Nor would one expect a twenty-year-old undergraduate to abandon bird-watching because 'his knees, which were thin, began to hurt him'.

The significance of Patrick's making his hero an adolescent boy whose tyrannical father's spirit cruelly denies him opportunity of gaining a university degree is patent, as is his transformation of the father from malevolent individual into an irresistibly destructive elemental power. Before his departure, Patrick decided to fire a last defiant salvo at the figure whom he identified as the underlying source of his misery and failure.

What led my parents to fasten on the little fishing town of Collioure at the foot of the Pyrenees as their future home I do not recall. Patrick had picked up information about the town during the course of his extensive researches on France while working for PWE. In a report he compiled in May 1944 on 'Mediterranean France', he noted: 'Between the Spanish frontier and Collioure the Pyrenean range meets the sea abruptly and forms a stretch of coastline with alternating cliff and cove. North of Collioure the coastline is flat and an almost smooth arc stretches 195 miles to the Rhone delta.' He had always been deeply interested in art, and the picturesque medieval walled town with its striking seaside church and clocktower had long provided a favourite subject for painters of the calibre of Derain and Matisse.

After some discussion Patrick and my mother decided that Patrick should scout out the terrain, just as he had done in preparation for the move to Wales four years earlier. The court hearing over custody of Richard was due to be heard on 7 July, and he could attend that before crossing the Channel. At the end of June he travelled by train to London, eagerly observing birds from his carriage window, and as ever plagued by unsavoury fellow passengers: 'They were [a] nasty lot in the carriage – Brummagem and a discontented fellow who took off his boots.' At the capital, he lodged at the Volunteer, a Chelsea pub he and my mother had frequented during the war. His quarters settled, his first move was to make a pilgrimage to 50 George Street and Marylebone Grammar School, where his literary career and education had enjoyed their respective geneses. From this it appears that not all his childhood memories were unhappy, but it is significant that he went to look at the house where he had once lived with his father, while he did not trouble to visit his father and stepmother who were at the time living within each reach in Ealing.

Returning from the Grammar School down Baker Street, Patrick suffered one of those minor embarrassments to which he was peculiarly prone: 'I became aware that I was undone: turning into a doorway to cope I peered at the name by the bell "Association of Funeral Directors of Gt. B".'

By the time he returned from his walk he was sweating profusely. He retired to his bedroom, ate his remaining sandwiches and cake, and went to bed. Excitement at the prospect of the coming adventure kept him awake for much of the night.

Next morning, following an apprehensive visit to the bank, he strolled up King's Road to Peter Jones. There he bought trousers and shoes (reduced by £1), 'but was I wise with the pyjamas? Doubt it now.' From Sloane Square he walked to Victoria, only to discover that confusion over his ticket reservations meant he would have to return next morning to sort them out. Travel for Patrick invariably proved a hazardous business in one way or another. Finding no solace in a visit to the Tate Gallery, he cheered himself by calling on their old friend Barbara Puckridge, with whom he reminisced about 'times that were certainly very dull years ago, but which have brightened up a lot now'.

The court hearing was next day, and that morning a nervous Patrick shaved with care and made sure that his shoes were perfectly polished. Arrived too early at the Law Courts, he found his solicitor Baddeley was not there, and his only companions during the long wait were 'a dreadful little man who undertakes their criminal business, I imagine, and a young articled clerk'. Eventually the barrister briefed by Baddeley arrived. Mistaking the clerk for Richard, he clasped his hand and enquired genially: 'is this the young fellow?'

After further delay they were ushered into the courtroom, where Patrick encountered Elizabeth 'looking yellow and disagreeable'. There followed what Patrick described as 'long stupid meandering with pleasant but wrong-headed judge', in the course of which he feared that in delivering his testimony he 'spoke rather too loudly and confidently'. After hearing submissions from both sides, Mr Justice Pilcher ruled: 'It is ordered that the Petitioner's summons sworn the 27th day of April 1949 for Custody of Richard Russ be adjourned, that the Petitioner be released from her undertaking in the Order herein dated the 20th day of August 1945 and that the Respondent be at liberty to take the said child out of the jurisdiction of this Court to France for half of the Summer Holidays, the Respondent undertaking to return the said child within the jurisdiction at the end of the said period.'

Although relieved at the decision, Patrick was disappointed at not having been awarded custody: 'Inconclusive and unsatisfactory result, but I am sure he [the Judge] means to do right.'[1]

Seeking to efface this unnerving experience, Patrick called at the National Gallery, where he found the Rembrandts and 'dozens and dozens of great noble masterpieces' infinitely refreshing. Cheerful too was a visit to the bank, which he reached with one minute to spare, having forgotten about early closing. To his great relief their account proved to be in credit, and he clasped his travellers' cheques and cash with such glee that he suddenly felt 'ashamed to be seen dandling and rustling them'. He could not resist crossing over to Charing Cross Road and browsing among the bookshops, where he found nothing sufficiently inviting to deplete his modest resources. Ten minutes' walk away Patrick visited another place which had played a significant part in his life. At Bush House he made enquiries after his former colleagues in PWE, only to find that virtually all had departed for other employment, marriage, or (in one case) death.

Early next morning Patrick gobbled down his breakfast at The Volunteer, felt relief at the modest bill of £1/17/6d, sprinted to catch a number 2 bus, and arrived at Victoria just in time to queue for his ticket. Matters did not go according to plan.

> Things began to go badly at Victoria, however. There was one old deliberate man at the receipt of parcel baggage – ¼ hr. – then like a fool I got into the wrong queue – rumours – dartings to the ticket queue, out of it, back again – brisk determination on part of clock to do us all down – agitated Frenchwoman anxious to return to Lille as quickly as possible – English cold and secretive – repulsively reserved – their cooking – never make charming bêtises – repulsive Americans – kind interpreter called us out of the queue – clock still putting up

[1] Elizabeth was eventually allotted custody on 14 November, when the court granted her 'care and control' of her son 'until further order'. This meant that from the Michaelmas term onward Richard attended school in London.

> a gallant fight – efficient, brisk clerk – ticket . . . at 9.20 . . . Lost ticket between office and barrier – in other pocket. No seat of course – train packed . . . Young Dutch with remarkable bosom & roving eye.

Once the train reached Sussex, Patrick could relax and observe the countryside. As he had noted during his passage through Wales, much hay remained uncut. He glimpsed a family of partridges, 'the chicks no bigger than hens' chicks of a week', and also many magpies – 'too many to be ominous any more'. Rattling on through the countryside, he suddenly came on a sight that brought a catch to his heart: 'Lewes – first recognised our quarry. They are doing something to the Castle.'

Finally they arrived at Newhaven, where despite its being high summer the weather was cheerless. After an hour's tedious examination of passports, 'Fair stands the wind for France. Damned cold. Horrible shipmates, one and all – one very loudly "not used to travelling 3rd". Nor anything else.'

As recompense he gazed at the magnificent expanse of white cliffs stretching from the Seven Sisters to Beachy Head, which must surely again have drawn his memory back to those far-off happy years at Lewes. The voyage passed uneventfully. 'Sea – grey, grey. England vanished undramatically, France appeared furtively while I was at lunch – 6/-, indifferent. Some souls were sick – 3 I saw.'

Disembarking at Dieppe, Patrick was delighted to be back in France, for the first time since he travelled to Locarno in 1937. He found the town still sadly ruined from fierce fighting during the abortive Allied landing in 1942. He conducted his usual careful observation of the countryside as the train rolled on through Picardy; once arrived at the gare St Lazare he rushed forth to stroll delightedly about the beautiful streets: 'wander like an amazed ass in Boulevard Hausmann [*sic*]'. The house in Cwm Croesor seemed a world away, and Patrick was determined to make the most of his brief stay in the world's great capital. Taking the métro to Châtelet, he ascended and strolled across the Île de la Cité. In the Boulevard Saint Germain he treated himself to a good dinner of *bœuf bourguignon* and *pelure d'oignons* at 220 francs. His spirit warmed by the accompanying wine, he 'rashly (partly because of poor feet) take sordid room in rue des Carmes – emerge, indulge in Grand Marnier with my coffee – 150 fr. not to be repeated'. Passing a stall where Frenchmen were hurling darts wildly at various targets, 'throw darts with some success for nougat (retain piece for M)'. Late into the night he roamed ecstatically along the banks of the Seine, gazing upon Notre Dame from different vistas. Finally, wearied after his long day, he retired to bed, where however he found little peace. 'Notre Dame has just struck two, followed by other clocks, one of a different opinion. I cannot sleep, despite aspirins and a great deal of exercise: it would perhaps have been wiser to have chosen a quarter less densely packed with traffic and dogs.'

Waking from time to time, Patrick took up his notebook and jotted down reflections overlooked when compiling his diary. He was intrigued to note 'after London the almost complete absence of whores – in the streets, I mean. mem, also, the typically French lavatory here – unusable for serious purposes. MM. les locataires sont priés de ne pas jeter des journaux, tampons et. dans le Waters. Messieurs have however removed the seat, which in an inverse sort of way appears to be cutting off their noses to spite their ff. [*fesses*?]'

Next day Patrick continued pertinaciously pacing the streets and viewing the grand sights of the beautiful city, but by the end of the day was completely exhausted from lack of sleep on the previous night, as well as suffering from sweltering July heat and agonies inflicted by his new shoes. The next night he found himself quieter, if more expensive, quarters, and on the following evening took the night train for the Mediterranean.

Patrick congratulated himself on handling the journey 'in a masterly style', whatever that meant. Actually it followed the customary pattern. 'I had dinner on the train – passable (Nescafé) – with damned unpleasant neighbours, and the people in my carriage were a sad lot, too. Immense thirst – hurried descent at Limoges for mineral water – usual complete loss of carriage and consequent panic. Found it somewhere about 1 a.m. or 2. Neighbours all strongly inclined to snore, push, lean, and smack their lips.' There were compensations, however. 'It was wonderful weather. As the train (electric most of way) ran down through the middle of the country the sun was setting on the right hand, and at once the full moon rose on the left. The rush of warm air was delightful on one's face gazing out of the window.'

Dawn was breaking by the time the train reached Toulouse, and Patrick studied birds and rural life from his window. Viollet-le-Duc's magnificently restored ramparts and towers of Carcassonne were denounced as 'too improbable to be countenanced'. At Narbonne he was entranced by glimpses of the sea and the great saline lakes, before they sped southward along the Mediterranean coast towards Spain. At last the train emerged from the short tunnel after Argelès, and clattered to a halt at the little station of Collioure.

Patrick descended into blazing sunshine on the platform, and made his way down the Chemin de la Gare into the town. His wondering admiration for everything he saw suggests that he knew little about the place when he and my mother contemplated it as a prospective location for their new home. Certainly it does not appear that he had received a description from anyone who knew the place at first hand. But now he had arrived. It was 13 July 1949.

'It would have been easy to miss Collioure altogether, but I did not . . . The place is really amazing – one wanders gaping. A two lobed harbour, fortified in the grand late medieval manner, rose coloured roofs, blue and pink houses, streets with hardly room to pass, strong smell of the sea, nets, black ancient women, blue, inactive sailors with their espadrilles tied above their ankles.' The young fishermen appeared especially elegant in their blue cotton trousers, *espadrilles* (blue or black rope-soled slippers), and singlets.

Excitedly he sent my mother a postcard, written in slightly faulty French: 'Thursday morning. I have arrived after a pretty troublesome journey . . . The village is altogether absurd – alleys seething with silent disreputable people – strange cats, with thin bodies and something eccentric about their bearing. The town seems to be populated with hundreds of pirates retired or on strike.'

Patrick bought bathing trucks and immediately went for a swim. 'The water was perfectly clear, with aquarium fish in it – joined them – quite delightful,' he noted in his journal. Next he had lunch at La Frégate, but after discovering the price of the meal and observing the waiters' surly attitude towards the tourists, to say nothing of the unappealing appearance of the tourists themselves, he decided it was not the place to stay. Fortunately he found private lodgings 'carried on by three old women in a very haphazard manner'. Now comfortably settled and freed of his suitcase, Patrick began the thorough reconnaissance he was accustomed to perform when contemplating a new habitation.

Excitedly he pictured Richard joining him and my mother in this seaside paradise, and sent his son two postcards of aerial photographs of Collioure. On the first he explained: 'The scrubby looking things on the right hand bottom corner are vineyards', and on the second: 'At the end of the jetty is a light – it flashes green. The tall thing is the church tower.'

It was not only the architecture, but the people of Collioure who appeared to belong to a happier bygone age. He was delighted to discover in the square a group of men and girls unselfconsciously circling gracefully in the local dance, the *sardane*, its shrill entrancing music played on a gramophone at the entrance to the cinema set within the town wall. That evening, despite his exhaustion after a sleepless night on the train, he could not resist the attraction of a noisy disturbance which arose immediately below his window: 'It is 10.30, and the entire child population, as well as all the adults, are in a state of intensely vocal excitement about the fate of Cindrelle – the old Queen is being difficult . . . They are lovely puppets, with tremendous grand high-theatrical tones.'

Next day being the *quatorze juillet*, Patrick watched a band playing in the square, children on parade proudly brandishing tricolour flags, fiddlers marching, 'and that strange oboe-like shrill pipe' which provides the marked refrain of the *sardane*.

In the shops Patrick compiled a careful catalogue of food and its prices. The culinary utensils he found especially pleasing, and was much taken with charming local pottery cooking vessels, plates, and bowls. Food prices varied not too unfavourably in comparison with those at home, and a small iron omelette pan cost a mere 90 francs, while a broom ('witch's type') could be had for 145. Generally speaking, saucepans and other cookery items appeared much cheaper and better than in England.

There were more weighty practical considerations, however, which required careful thought. Patrick's wartime service with PWE had perfected his French. However, he found this of restricted utility in a region where he discovered that almost everyone spoke as their first tongue Catalan, a romance language distinct from French and Spanish. A much more serious problem lay in the difficulty of finding anywhere to live. On enquiring in a shop, he was informed that his chances were 'hopeless', since there were already too few houses for the population, many of whom gained additional income from letting rooms to visitors during the summer. He was advised to try 'further south', which was hardly encouraging in view of the fact that only three villages lay between Collioure and the Spanish frontier. Expeditions to two of them, Port-Vendres and Banyuls, proved disappointing. 'I did not care for Port-Vendres – empty, centre-less, commercial – nor very much for Banyuls, which has rather a sordid air to it after Collioure.'

At first the quest appeared hopeless, which was all the more disappointing now that Patrick was convinced that he had happened upon the ideal haven where he and my mother might settle. During the next couple of days, however, he was fortunate enough to meet an Englishman named Whitelaw, who introduced him to his friend Mel, an American, who was accompanied by his mistress Francesca. Mel was a graduate of New College, Oxford, while Whitelaw had attended Corpus Christi, Cambridge. They were familiar with the town, and in no time at all showed him quarters which appeared both suitable and available.

Patrick was delighted with his new friends, who could not have been more amiable, and sat up drinking with them on the beach until two o'clock in the morning, watching the moon come up over the castle of Saint-Elme on the summit of the hill overlooking the faubourg on the southern side of the bay. Suddenly all appeared to be going swimmingly. Whitelaw and Mel generously invited Patrick to join them for the next fortnight in rooms they had rented in the rue Quintana, which meant he could save a substantial part of his scanty funds and conduct a thorough exploration of the possibilities offered by the town.

The morning after moving in with his new friends, Patrick woke early and sat on his bedside pondering all that Collioure had to offer. There were the prickly pears with their gorgeous yellow flowers, swallowtails flitting across the rooftops, and gaunt suspicious cats who prowled the streets. With their beloved Buddug in mind, he noted that the townspeople 'must be reasonably good with dogs, for the good beasts are fat and trusting'. His musing was interrupted by another manifestation of the unchanging character of life in Collioure. 'An admirable person has just gone by, blowing on a horn and announcing in a fine clear voice what is for sale when – grand choix de poissons à la Place – had a gendarme-ish hat.'

Still Patrick could find no permanent dwelling. By the end of the month he was becoming increasingly desperate, crossing the frontier at Port-Bou and making an expedition down the Spanish coast. However there was nothing to be had there either, and he returned disconsolate. To my mother he sent a postcard of a bullfight, with the laconic comment: 'An uncomfortable way of earning a living, is it not?'

At that time few households in Collioure possessed running water, and the inhabitants of 14 rue Quintana shared the facilities of a tap and *bassein* in the garden of a neighbouring house in the rue de Soleil. One day Odette Bernadi, a beautiful dark-haired twenty-two-year-old *Colliourencque* was washing clothes in the *bassein*, when she noticed a good-looking young stranger standing next to her. From his accent she understood him to be English, and he told her that she lived in a truly beautiful town – *formidable*! Odette's husband François was a sculptor well known in the locality, and the couple immediately became friends with Patrick and his companions. Since they knew everyone in the little town, they were soon able to find a suitable place for my parents to stay on arrival.

Patrick's reconnoitring expedition had led him all unknowing to set foot for the first time in the town that he and my mother were to know and love for the next half-century. Furthermore, in Odette he had found a steadfast friend, who still remembers them with devoted affection. He could not wait to bring my mother the glad news. On returning to Moelwyn Bank at the beginning of August, he enraptured her with his account of the beauties of sun-drenched Collioure and the friendships he had already established during his brief stay. No difficult decision was required, and immediate preparations were made for their final departure from the valley where they had known much happiness but also frustrated disappointment.

Patrick had polished his collection of short stories, and now he sent them to his literary agent Spencer Curtis Brown in London. Curtis Brown submitted them to the respected publishing firm Secker & Warburg, who replied on 17

August with encouraging news: 'We have now read and admired the remarkable stories of Patrick O'Brien [*sic*], at present entitled COUNTRY CONTENTMENTS, and would certainly like to publish the book.' Their only reservations were that they did not like the title,[1] proposing instead that of one of the tales in the collection, *The Last Pool*, and suggested altering 'the ending of two or three of the stories, which do not appear quite to come off'.

Finally a request was passed on from Roger Senhouse, Patrick's appointed editor, for 'some information about the author'. In future years Patrick would go to considerable lengths to avoid providing such material, but on this occasion he provided what he described as 'some biographical scraps' by return of post which Warburg extolled as 'excellent'. On 5 April of the next year Patrick was urged to 'send us as soon as possible your biographical details, i.e. date and place of birth, education, appointments held and any other relevant information . . . speed is of the essence'. It appears that the 'scraps' he submitted earlier had been mislaid, and either Patrick failed to replace them or the matter was overlooked.

Curtis Brown responded to Secker's enthusiastic acceptance with appro priate delight, but rigorously insisted on more equitable terms in the contract. Warburg had cited as example their contract with Angus Wilson, whose collection of stories *The Wrong Set* they had recently published. The agent rejected the comparison, pointing out that Wilson's book had been his first, whereas 'O'Brian . . . has had two books published, one by the Oxford University Press [*Hussein*] and one [*A Book of Voyages*] by Home & van Thal'.

Since Curtis Brown had provided the formal attestation for Patrick's change of name by deed pool, he was naturally apprised of his earlier literary work accomplished under the name of Russ.[2] Warburg might well have wished to see the books in question, in which case they would at once have discovered Patrick's change of name. This suggests that he was not then so deeply concerned to keep it secret as he was to become in later years, indicating yet again his change of identity may have been much more lightly assumed than has been imagined.

What with their imminent move to the Mediterranean and his belated recovery as an established author, these were heady days for Patrick and my mother. The time had finally arrived for them to say goodbye to Moelwyn

[1] Patrick had appropriated it from his seventeenth-century mentor Gervase Markham.

[2] Given his concern to emphasise Patrick's literary credentials, it seems odd that Curtis Brown made no mention of Patrick's two earlier publications, *Cæsar* and *Beasts Royal.* Possibly Patrick had come to regard them as mere juvenilia, which could detract from his credibility as an author.

Bank and Cwm Croesor, where they had experienced so much adventure and hardship, pleasure and pain. They made a round of fond farewells to all their kind friends, above all the Roberts family at Croesor Fawr, with whom they promised to keep in touch. The corgis Bronwen and Nanw were given to neighbouring families, and Richard's white rabbit, who would not have been happy in London, was presented to Edgar Williams's young brother Gwilym. Edgar himself received the accordion with which my mother had whiled away many an evening. Although at the time he nurtured a secret hope that he might receive the .410 shotgun he had often been permitted to borrow, he still preserves the accordion in affectionate memory of his departed friends. He remembers too Patrick's jocular remark, when he called at his parents' house to say goodbye: 'If you are going to be poor, it is better to be poor in a warm country.'

Together they travelled to London, where they stayed with my mother's parents at The Cottage for three weeks. On 24 August Frederick Warburg 'had a very pleasant lunch' with Patrick, as he informed Curtis Brown the next day. Increasingly confident of his new author's talent, he accepted without demur the latter's proposals for improved contractual terms, and went on to discuss Patrick's future prospects.

> I am not quite clear what option clause you have in mind for the agreement, but O'Brien [*sic*] told me that he plans to write a full length novel with a Welsh background, and we should surely have an option on this? We should surely also have an option, no doubt, on another collection of short stories, should he write one; but I gathered that in this field he had, for the moment, written himself out . . .
>
> I am really very grateful to you for putting this most unusual book our way and very much hope it will have the success it deserves.

It is revealing to note Patrick's explicit reference to the protracted anguish which lay behind completion of his present collection.

Back at The Cottage Patrick worked hard on Warburg's suggested improvements, and returned him the corrected manuscript four days later, accompanied by a suggestion that the book be retitled 'Dark Speech upon the Harp'. Warburg rejected the proposed title, insisting on that under which it eventually appeared, *The Last Pool And Other Stories*. Although Patrick's brief autobiographical notice never appeared (another instance of his reticence in this regard?), correspondence between him and the publishers shows that the dust-jacket 'blurb' was Patrick's work. It includes this telling passage: 'Every solitary angler . . . may feel himself on the fringe of a world that does not wait everywhere for nightfall; and more especially, *when he has hoped to leave behind the discords of modern life and is trying to escape from himself*, will this feeling come upon him' (italics inserted).

Meanwhile my mother secretly arranged the sale of all the beautiful satinwood furniture, china, and other valuable household goods given her by her father. Their financial situation was now stretched to its limit by additional expenditure incurred by the move to France. My grandfather did not discover this until later, when it caused him considerable anger and hurt. This represented yet another tactless move which increased the damage to relations between parents and daughter. Had my mother explained her predicament frankly, I feel confident that her father would have bought them himself – very likely returning them to her subsequently as a gift.

At the beginning of the second week of September the couple set off for France. During a brief stay in Paris *en route*, Patrick wrote to his editor Roger Senhouse (whom he addressed as 'Spenhouse') with a brief query as to whether he could not suggest a substitute for what he had come to regard as the overly facetious 'Prawn' (i.e. the Quorn) as a name for the élite hunt in 'It must have been a Branch, They Said'.

Patrick wrote the letter sitting with my mother in the Paris sunshine. 'I wish I could convey some of the pleasure it is to sit here in the Luxembourg: there are bloated wood-pigeons in every tree almost, and children playing just at the right distance [!]' Secker replied: 'What about "the Rutland" to take the place of "the Prawn"? I happened to put this to Nancy Mitford, with whom I was lunching, and it won her approval. It seems to me to give a whiff of the Shires that is required, and was suggested by David Farrer [Senior Editor at Secker & Warburg].'

A week later the contract arrived for signature. It provided that 'The author undertakes to write a book on Southern France and to proceed to France within the next two months in order to collect material for such a book . . . the Publisher undertakes to pay to the Author forthwith £75 . . . towards the expenses of the Author's visit to France.' Secker had originally proposed paying an advance of £100 in two instalments, but Curtis Brown had persuaded them to make an arrangement more in accord with Patrick's current requirements.

Patrick could finally feel that he had turned the corner after his long dark days in Wales. He and my mother had exchanged the damp stone house at Moelwyn Bank for a cheerful bustling medieval town by the sparkling Mediterranean, while Patrick's career as an author appeared firmly re-established. At long last he could escape that oppressive presence which had stalked him throughout his childhood and beyond. Even his flight to remote North Wales had not enabled him to shake off a pursuer who dogged his every footstep, destroying his happiness and crushing his hopes at every turn.

A bare five months before their descent at Collioure station, in 'Naming Calls' Patrick had pictured Abel Widgery crouching immobilised by fear within his isolated mountain retreat, incapable of evading annihilation at the hands of the elemental demon remorselessly lurking in the shadows. Now he and his beloved Mary were far from the frowning precipices and angry storms of Cwm Croesor. Richard would join them during school holidays, having expressed excitement at the prospect. As they descended the Avenue de la Gare into the waking town, the benign southern sun rising beyond its ancient ramparts presented a bright new dawn.

BIBLIOGRAPHICAL NOTE

All page references to Patrick O'Brian's works are to the first editions of his cited works, which are as follows.

Cæsar: The Life Story of a Panda Leopard (London, 1930).
Hussein: An Entertainment (Oxford, 1938).
Beasts Royal (London, 1934).
A Book of Voyages (London, 1947).
The Last Pool And Other Stories (London, 1950).
Three Bear Witness (London, 1952).
The Catalans (New York, 1953).
The Road to Samarcand (London, 1955).
Lying in the Sun and Other Stories (London, 1956).
The Golden Ocean (London, 1956).
The Unknown Shore (London, 1959).
Richard Temple (London, 1962).
Master and Commander (London, 1970).[1]
Post Captain (London, 1972).
H.M.S. Surprise (London, 1973).
The Mauritius Command (London, 1977).
Desolation Island (London, 1978).

[1] It is unclear whether the British (Collins) or US (Lippincott) edition is the first. Arthur Cunningham's bibliography suggests the latter, noting that the Lippincott version terms itself 'First Edition' and their advance publicity announced 24 November (1969) as the planned date of issue (A.E. Cunningham, ed., *Patrick O'Brian: Critical Appreciations and a Bibliography* (Boston Spa, Wetherby, 1994), p. 121). However copies of the British edition were in print no later than 28 November 1969, when Patrick's editor Richard Ollard wrote to tell him he had 'just seen the first samples of MASTER AND COMMANDER and I hope that you will be as pleased with its appearance as I am . . . it looks to me well printed and well bound'. My mother kept the Collins edition for her personal collection, which normally indicates that it was the first published. The Collins text contains a number of corrections Patrick made to the Lippincott galleys used by Collins for their edition.

The Fortune of War (London, 1979).
The Surgeon's Mate (London, 1980).
The Ionian Mission (London, 1981).
Treason's Harbour (London, 1983).
The Far Side of the World (London, 1984).
The Reverse of the Medal (London, 1986).
The Letter of Marque (London, 1988).
The Thirteen-Gun Salute (London, 1989).
The Nutmeg of Consolation (London, 1991).
Clarissa Oakes (London, 1992).
The Wine-Dark Sea (London, 1993).
The Commodore (London, 1994).
The Yellow Admiral (London, 1997).
The Hundred Days (1998).
Blue at the Mizzen (London, 1999).

I have used the British edition of Dean King's *Patrick O'Brian: A Life Revealed* (Hodder & Stoughton, 2000). The only other published work which concerns Patrick's life is a privately printed memoir by his elder brother Bernard ('Bun'): *Lady Day Prodigal* (Victoria, BC, 1989). At Patrick's insistence it has little to say about him directly, but provides precious glimpses of his childhood by one who was close to him at the time.

Patrick's son by his first marriage, Richard Russ, provided Dean King with memories of his childhood and youth. He also gave two lengthy interviews to the press. Although he quarrelled irrevocably with his father in 1963, there is no reason to doubt the overall reliability of his account where it concerns matters he himself witnessed. That he too perpetrates minor errors over dates and other factors is natural, and cannot call in question his general value as a witness. Paradoxically, in some respects I know more about his early childhood than he himself remembers. Not only do I have Patrick's journal describing their time together in Wales when Richard was aged nine, but my mother (who was very fond of him) preserved every letter he wrote to them from 1945 onwards.

There are points on which Richard's memory conflicts with other evidence, which I would have liked to discuss with him. However he politely but firmly explained that his rift with his father led him to decide to have no contact with anyone connected with his father. I respect his decision, but this unfortunately means that I have been obliged on occasion to arrive at judgements without being able to consult him. I hope that nevertheless he will feel that I have treated their delicate relationship as fairly as possible in the circumstances.

The greater part of my information derives from private papers. Unless otherwise stated, these are in my possession. Unfortunately unusual circumstances prevent my providing details which would no doubt interest readers.

I have copies of the diaries which Patrick kept from 1969 to 1998. Before his death Patrick gave me his library, which is not only an invaluable mine of information in itself, but contains a wealth of scattered notes, sketches, etc. which he inserted as bookmarks. I also engaged in continual correspondence with Patrick and my mother from the time of my first visit in 1955 until the last year of Patrick's life in 1999.

A number of individuals provided me with helpful information, which is acknowledged in the text. In particular numerous members of the Russ family assisted me generously with memories, photographs, copies of correspondence, and other documents which were of the greatest help in reconstructing Patrick's early life.

Finally, I have made extensive use of some of Patrick's early published fiction, which without doubt contains a great deal of autobiographical material. In one case, that of his short story 'The Thermometer', his preparatory notes explicitly state this to be the case. The three most important sources in this respect are his novels *Three Bear Witness*, *The Catalans*, and *Richard Temple*. While it goes without saying that they cannot be arbitrarily or uncritically employed as sources for Patrick's own life, I have adopted two fundamental approaches. In the first place it is at times possible to confirm the autobiographical elements from independent sources. Secondly, contradictions and inconsistencies are usually explicable as inadvertent obtrusions from Patrick's own life into narratives whose principal function (conscious or unconscious) was to explore and analyse his confused early life and character. However no general rule is applicable, and I have endeavoured to justify each interpretation in its own context.

ACKNOWLEDGEMENTS

I would like to thank the following friends, relatives, helpers, and institutions, without whose help much of this book could not have been written.

Miss Libby Adams, Archivist at the University College London Hospitals NHS Trust; Mrs Christine Ashby (née Welch); Mr Martin Ashby; Mr Stuart Bennett; Dr Colin E. Blogg; Mme Odette Boutet; Mr Robert Bucknell; Mr Philip Bye, Senior Archivist of East Sussex County Council; Mr John A. Cole; Mrs R. Cox of the Records and Historical Department of the Foreign & Commonwealth Office; Mr Michael Cullis CVO; Mr Arthur Cunningham; Dr Christopher Dowling of the Imperial War Museum; Mr Ben Fenton; Mrs Carolyn Findell; Professor M. R. D. Foot; Mr R. B. Ford, Manager of Kenilworth Court; Mr Alan Gater; Mrs Jane Goddard; Mrs Philip Goodman; Mrs Linda Green; Brigadier Walter Greenway; Miss Julie Gregson, Local History Archivist at Wandsworth; Dr Jane Harrold of Dartmouth Naval College; Mr Michael Harte; Mr Arfon Jones; Mr Ian Jones; Mrs Diana Keast (née Harman); Miss Jennifer Macdonald, City of Westminster Archives Centre; the London Metropolitan Archives; Dr Martin Maw, Archivist to the Oxford University Press; Mr Angus McGeoch; Mr Edward McNeal: Mr Edwin Moore; Mr Andrew Murray; Mr and Mrs Richard Ollard; Miss Elaine Pankhurst, Personal Assistant to the Registrar, Birkbeck College; Mr William Podmore, Archivist of the John Lyon School; Mr James Puckridge; Mr Ken Ringle; Dr Philip Rizzo; Mrs Bessie Roberts; Mrs Primrose Roche; Mrs Jacqueline Rowe, Headmaster's Secretary at Shebbear College; Mr Charles Russ; Mr Harry Russ; Mr Mick Russ; Mrs Saidie Russ; Mr Stephen Russ; Mrs Gwen Russell-Jones; Mr John Saumarez Smith; Mr Richard Scott Simon; Mr S. B. Taylor of the Royal Air Force Personnel Management Agency; Mrs Myrtle Ternstrom; Count Ivan Tolstoy-Miloslavsky; Father Eric J. Tomlinson; Miss Sara Waterston; Mr Ron Welford; Mrs Elizabeth Y. Wickstead; Mr H. F. S. Wicksteed; Mr and Mrs Edgar Williams; Mr Hugh Winkler; Mr John Yeowell.

This book has taken so long to prepare that I may well have overlooked further kind helpers and advisers, to whom I extend my apologies and thanks. While it would be invidious and unhelpful to specify individual contributions, varying enormously as they did in their range and extent, I cannot avoid singling out Oliver Johnson, my sympathetic but firm editor at Century, who displayed exceptional patience as my book gradually extended itself from a simple personal memoir to a lengthy biography, and devoted great care and skill to editing a long and at times complex text, in which constant fresh discoveries acquired over a period of nearly four years required subtle changes in interpretation which I had not always been observant enough to sustain with requisite consistency.

Above all, it would be impossible to overestimate the contribution of my dear wife Georgina. Not only had she sustained me without ever faltering in my frequently desperate battle against the English judiciary and Establishment which has prevented my writing a book since 1988,[1] but continued my constant guide, wise adviser, and loyal helper throughout the difficult task of bringing this book to as satisfactory a conclusion as possible. Since she also knew Patrick and my mother intimately from the time of our wedding in 1971, her memories and psychological intuition made her as ideal a consultant and adviser as could be wished.

This said, any faults which have survived her and Oliver's penetrating examination must be laid at my door. This is not the customary polite disclaimer, but regrettable fact.

[1] From 1990 my book *The Minister and the Massacres* was censored in Britain – almost exactly two centuries after the covert prohibition of Thomas Paine's *The Rights of Man*. Cf. John Keane, *Tom Paine: A Political Life* (Boston, MA, 1995), pp. 346–48.

INDEX

Ainsworth, Beryl 183
Ainsworth, Joan 183, 265
Albany Street, no. 144 117–19
Alexander the Great 224–5
Annesley, James 297
Anson, George Anson, Baron 51–2, 449
Appledore 214–19
Ashbrook, Mrs 20, 23, 27, 35
Ashdown Forrest 136
Atterbury, Mrs 284
Aubrey, Jack 26, 56–7, 63, 90, 96–7, 165, 263, 278, 299, 319, 358, 436–8
Austen, Jane 99–100, 295
Austria 222, 263

Banyuls 495
Barrow, Tobias 132–3
Battersby, Chris 213
Bayley, John ix
Beaumont Street, Marylebone 28–9, 30, 58, 82
Beck, Dr Leslie 279, 281
Becker, Stephen 99
Belem (renamed *Fantome II*), yacht 159–61
Belfast 174
Bengal Lancer (Yeats-Brown) 125
Bernadi, Odette 496
Binyon, T.J. ix–x
Birkbeck College 119–20, 123
Birt, José 156
Blakeway, Reverend Bennett 62
Blitz, the 245–6, 249–51, 254
Brighton 93–4, 100
British Museum 186–7
Bryn 385
Burney, Fanny 295–6
Burns, Eric 327
Bush House 269, 274, 289, 491
Byatt, A.S. ix

Carcassonne 493
Carew, Cousin 31–3, 35–8
Center, William 176
Chester 120
Christopher, Jack 281, 350
Chums (magazine) 116
Clapp, Mrs 35–6, 37–8, 172
Clark, Kenneth xi
College Road, no. 10 10–11, 14
Collingwood, Thomas 68
Collioure 93, 227, 453, 489, 493–6
Commodore, The (Forester) 299
Conrad, Joseph 299
Cottage, The 274–7, 282, 284, 289–93, 334, 341, 342, 343, 356, 383, 407, 498
Cox, Francis 475, 482
Criccieth fair 455
Critical Appreciations (British Library, 1994) 65–6, 80–1, 157–8, 329
Croesor Fawr 349, 390
Croesor village 363, 379, 383, 388
Crowborough 135–7, 138–9
Crowley, Father 410
Cunningham, Arthur 80, 279, 329, 465–6
Curiosities of Literature (D'Israeli) 109–10
Curtis Brown, Spencer 315, 334, 352, 354, 380, 496–7, 498, 499
Cwm Croesor 337–8, 345, 352, 363–4, 371, 383, 391–3, 395, 470
Cwm Foel 446–8

Dawson, Lord 21
de Salis, Charles 255
de Zulueta, Father 260
Dean Close School 9
Dickens, Charles 14–15
Dieppe 492
Dublin 81, 173, 175, 177
Dunsany, Lord 323–4, 325, 448

Eastes, Dr Thomas 5
Edgehill College 28, 64

Evelina (Burney) 295–6
Fantome II (former *Belem*), yacht 159–61
Far Side of the World, The (film) x

Farnol, Jeffrey 100–2, 203, 206
Farrer, David 499
Father and Son (Gosse) 109
First World War 7–8, 12–13, 16–17, 213–15, 425
FitzGerald, Peregrine 165–8
FitzGibbon, Theodora 253, 275, 289–91
Fitzmaurice Place 255
Fool of Quality, The (Brooke) 297
Ford Field Cottage 136–7
Forester, C.S. 396, 400
France 470, 482, 492–6: *see also* Collioure
Fron Wen 346–9, 352, 354, 358–62, 365, 377–9, 383, 393–5, 395, 440, 445, 484
Richard's visits 404–5, 408–12, 413–19, 421–3, 480–1
Fussell, Mr 404

Gadds Cottage 198–200, 207–10, 239–40, 241–2
Gade, Felix W. 220
Gallt y Wenallt 449–53
Garreg 389
Gay, Charles 142
General Strike, 1926 71
Gentlemans Magazine 51–2, 99, 297
George Street, no. 50 82, 490
Gertrude Street, no.24 157, 196
Goddard, Leonard Morse 17–19
Goëau-Brissonière, Armand 280, 351, 474
Grace 'Aunt' 19, 20, 27, 66
Greenway, Susan 396
Greenway, Walter 222, 230–1, 282–4, 294, 320, 350, 384, 396, 416–17, 449–53
Guinness, Colonel Arthur 159–61

Hamlyn, Mrs 29
Hancock, Dr 301
Harman, Martin King 219
Herbert, Violet 195
Heston, Charlton x
Heywood Hill Literary Prize 64
Hicking, George 212
Hidden Power (Charles Russ) 115
Hill, Ethie 29
Hill, Trixie 29
History of Rome (Goldsmith) 206–7, 298
Horowitz, Mark 304, 326–8
Horton Rectory 46, 62–3
Hotel Quisisana 182–3

Ireland 140, 174–6, 177–8, 181, 331–2, 448
Italy 140

James, Henry 295
Jerome, Jerome K. 70
John Lyon School for Boys 11, 23
Jones, Arfon 394, 395–6
Jones, Frank 394, 395–6
Jones, Idwal 429–30, 449, 467, 468
Jones, Isaac 395
Jones, Captain Jack 423, 425–6, 426–7, 429–33, 433–5, 437–8, 449, 467, 471

Kaberry, Charles 174, 175, 182
Keast, Diana (*née* Harman) 262
Kenilworth Court, 146 58–60
King, Dean (*Patrick O'Brian: A Life Revealed*) xi, xi–xiv, 63, 113, 131–2, 140, 156, 158, 173, 190, 209–10, 211–12, 234, 285, 304, 316, 322, 328, 420, 426, 441, 469–70
King's Road
no. 301 196, 198
no. 237 260, 479
Kipling, Rudyard 116, 120–1, 124–5
Koren, Mrs W. 350–1

Lackstead, Geoffrey 113
Lady Day Prodigal (Bernard Russ) 6, 16, 16–17, 18, 19–20, 30–1, 35, 40, 63, 74, 76, 90, 107–8
Lahore 214
Lawrence, T.E. 186
Le Mee Power, John Cowper 311, 403, 475, 477, 480, 481, 481–2
Lewes 71–3, 95–105, 492
Lewes Grammar School 72–6, 90, 92, 105
Lichfield 343–4
Lloyd George, David 103
Llyn Croesor 456–7

Llyndy Bridge 427
Llys Dafydd y Foel 484
Locarno 182–3, 185, 196
London 245–6
London Auxiliary Ambulance Service (LAAS) 240–1, 244, 250–1
London Library, the 381
London Lodge 29
Love Lessons (Wyndham) 149, 155, 246
Luckett, Dr Richard 159
Lundy 219, 220–1

Male Lock Hospital 15
Mandeville, Sir John 296
Mann, Jessica 190
Maria Grey day school 19, 23
Marin, Louis 351
Marylebone Grammar School 67–71, 73, 490
Maturin, Stephen 52, 89, 90, 97, 101, 155, 165, 166, 168, 263–4, 299, 358, 451–2
Mel (American in Collioure) 495–6
Melbury Lodge, Kempsey 49, 50–1, 52, 55–6, 57
Milford, Sir Humphrey 191
Mitford, Nancy 499
Moelwyn Bank 443–6, 449, 453–9, 469, 473, 479–80, 497–8
Moelwyn Mawr 350
Myers, Kevin 329–30

Natural History (Wood) 67, 85, 116
Naval and Military Memoirs of Great Britain from 1727-1783 (Beatson) 283
Naval History of Great Britain, from the Declaration of War by France in 1793, th the Accession of George IV (James) 283
New York Times Book Review ix
Newhaven 492
Newton, Mrs 20, 24

Oakley Street, 2a 156
O'Brian, Mary (Countess Tolstoy *née* Wicksteed)
  literary role 41, 211–12
  family background 212–16
  character 212
  birth 214
  childhood 216–20
  marries Dimitri Tolstoy 220–3
  Russian Orthodox faith 223–4
  first meets Patrick 223
  begins relationship with Patrick 225–39
  LAAS service 240–1, 244, 250–1
  war-time relationship with Patrick 246, 248–9, 252–4, 256, 261–2, 282, 291–2, 300
  divorce 256, 260
  PWE service 269–70, 279, 280
  visits parents with Patrick 305–7
  marriage to Patrick xi–xii, 315
  visit to Ireland 331–2
  move to Wales 341–52
  life in Wales 352, 354–5, 358–9, 362, 363–97, 440, 445, 471, 475
  relationship with parents 356–7
  1946 access hearing 381–2
  relationship with Richard 401, 404, 413, 414, 422, 454, 456, 481–2
  and the Ynysfor Hunt 430, 432–3
  Elizabeth's opinion of 478
  move to Collioure 497–500
O'Brian, (Richard) Patrick (formerly Russ)
  short stories: *see* short stories
  works: *see* works
  critical acclaim ix–x
  privacy x–xi
  status x
  Picasso biography xi, 324
  press attacks xi, 332
  death of xii
  character xiv, 25, 70, 88, 148, 149, 399
  family background 1–4
  birth 4, 6–7
  siblings 4
  childhood 11–12, 17, 18–19, 21–2, 23–7, 29–60, 65–6, 81–4, 91–2, 148–9, 399, 409
  death of mother 13–15
  sailing experience 18–19, 157–63, 168–9
  relationship with siblings 24–5, 81
  siblings education 28, 58, 64, 138
  portrayal of father as Cousin Carew 36–7

death of father 41
attachment to mother 46
doubts about paternity 46
relationship with stepmother 54–5, 61–2
education 61–79, 82–4, 90–1, 92, 105, 119–20, 123–4, 478–9
Royal Naval College entrance examination 77–8
poetry 86, 96, 251–4, 351
juvenile love 88–9
and corporal punishment 90–1, 414–15, 422
'autobiographical' novels 91
childhood reading 97–8, 99–100, 112–13
literary influences 100–2, 124–5, 462–4
adolescence 108–13, 117–19
relationship with father 110–12, 119, 137–8
sadistic streak 122–3
and death 126–7
RAF service 129–35, 183, 319
on friendship 131, 165
possible nervous breakdown 134
leaves home 139–40
Chelsea life 140–51, 184
children 140
meets Elizabeth Jones 153–4
first experience of love 154
marriage to Elizabeth Jones 140, 156–7, 265–6, 464
attempt to go whaling 161
vertigo 167–8, 452
birth of first child 170–2
and communism 176–7
love of Irish literature 177–8
infidelity to Elizabeth 183–5
bestiary research 186–91
bicycle theft 192–3
birth of Jane 196–8
leaves Gadds Cottage 208–10
in the Ambulance Service 210, 242, 248, 250–2
first meets Mary 223
begins relationship with Mary 225–39
illness of 1939 233–7
returns to Gadds Cottage 239–40
gun 241–3
war-time relationship with Mary 246, 248–9, 252–4, 256, 261–2, 282, 291–2, 300
PWE service 254–6, 269–74, 279–81, 317, 351
divorce 260–1, 284–6, 293–4, 309–10
fear of losing Mary 262–4
conceals affair from Elizabeth 264–8
on marriage 267–8
as firewatcher 273, 276
intelligence reports 281
war-time reading 295–300
Thomas Cary outline 300–1
illness of 1945 301–2
financial crisis 303–5, 317, 334
relationship with Mary's parents 305–9
custody case 311–14
marriage to Mary xi–xii, 315
change of name xi, 26, 315–24, 497
reinvention of self 317, 328, 330–2
identification as Irish 322–30
biographical notices 324–6, 497
Horowitz interview 326–8
move to Wales 341–52
establishes self in Wales 352–62
life in Wales 363–97, 440–68, 469–73
attempt to plant vegetables 370–3
shooting 373–4, 416
fishing 374–7
musical taste 377
fire stool 389
malaise 397
attitude towards children 398–9
relationship with Richard 398–423, 456
fear of social inadequacy 400–1, 485
financial support for Richard 402–4
Richard's visits to Fron Wen 404–5, 408–12, 413–19, 421–3, 480–1
tutors Richard 409–10, 411–12, 413–19, 421–2, 454, 458, 476, 478–9
1949 custody hearing 414–15
withdraws Richard from Southey Hall 420–1
and the Ynysfor Hunt 424–39, 444, 447, 449–53, 467–8
on life aboard ship 435–6
writer's block 442–3, 457–9, 470–1, 483–4

appendicitis 445
Richard's visits to Moelwyn Bank 453–8, 473, 479–80
visit to Ynys Gifftan 465–6
decision to leave Wales 469–71
doctors bills 470
health 470
disenchantment 471
custody review 475–82, 483, 489–91
final days in Wales 483–9
journey to Collioure 491–3
reconnoitres Collioure 493–6
move to Collioure 496–500
Ollard, Richard 139, 211, 330–1
O'Mara, Miss 27
Oxford 139

Padua, University of 281
Paris 492–3, 499
Patrick O'Brian: A Life Revealed (King) xi, xii–xiv, 63, 113, 131–2, 140, 156, 158, 173, 190, 209–10, 211–12, 234, 285, 304, 316, 322, 328, 420, 426, 441, 469–70
Penrhyndeuraeth 335, 345, 388
Picasso, Pablo xi
Pierce (Welsh taxi owner) 345–6
Pilcher, Mr Justice 491
Political Warfare Executive (PWE) 254–6, 269–74, 279–81, 295, 317, 351
Polsky, Father Michael 224
Port-Vendres 495
Portmadoc 388, 410
Portmeirion 335–6, 340, 345
Prajadhipok, King of Siam 218
Priory Crescent, Lewes 71–2, 93
Proffitt, Stuart 211
Puckridge, Barbara 387, 455, 490
Puckridge, James 455–8, 459, 466

Redcliffe Road, Chelsea 145–6, 153, 155, 246
Roberts, Bessie 349, 352, 362, 363, 366, 369, 382, 498
Roberts, Gwynfor 455, 498
Roberts, Harri 347, 349, 360, 362, 366–7, 368, 369, 374–5, 392–3, 426, 445, 446–7, 498
Robinson, Lieutenant William Leefe 8
Roche, Major Edmund 438–9, 449–51, 467–8
Rountree, Harry 85
Royal Air Force 129–35, 183, 319
Royal Naval College, Dartmouth 77–8
Russ, Bernard 4–5, 9, 28, 46, 49–51, 58, 59, 64, 67–71, 72, 82, 92, 102–3, 162–3, 195, 318–19, 320, 399
Lady Day Prodigal memories 6, 16–17, 18, 19–20, 30–1, 35, 40, 63, 74, 76, 90, 107–8
Russ, Charles 2–4, 5–6, 7, 9–11, 15, 17, 20–3, 24, 28–9, 30–1, 36–7, 41, 44, 47–8, 55–6, 57–60, 66, 79, 82–4, 86, 103, 106–7, 110–12, 115, 119, 134, 137–8, 156, 288
Russ, Charles, Jr. 30–1
Russ, Connie 59
Russ, Elizabeth (*née* Jones) 140, 153–4, 156–7, 168–9, 170, 172, 174, 195, 196, 233, 257–61, 264–8, 278, 284–6, 293, 309–14, 357, 382, 398, 402–3, 464, 475–82, 483, 490–1
Russ, Emil 29, 113
Russ, Godfrey 6, 11, 22, 28, 48, 57–8, 71, 258, 260
Russ, Jane Elizabeth Campaspe Tudor 196–8, 208, 224–5
Russ, Jessie (*née* Goddard) 4–5, 6, 11, 13–15, 40, 46
Russ, Joan 15–16, 22, 49–50, 51, 54, 59–60, 92–3, 104, 107, 114, 117–19, 122–3, 135–6, 138–9, 195, 266, 287–8, 399
Russ, Karl (Charles) 1–2, 10
Russ, Michael 11, 58, 58–9, 71, 107, 108, 114, 277–9, 318–20, 399
Russ, Nora 30, 59, 60, 170
Russ, Olive 58, 59, 60, 106–7
Russ, Richard Francis Tudor 170–2, 195, 208, 210, 258, 259–60, 278, 285–7, 293–4, 300, 315–16, 376, 381, 383, 398–423, 475–82, 483, 500
relationship with Mary 401, 404, 413, 414, 422, 454, 456, 481–2
visits to Fron Wen 404–5, 408–12, 413–19, 421–3, 480–1
visits to Moelwyn Bank 453–8, 473, 479–80
Russ, Sadie 106, 266

Russ, Sidney 3, 9, 21, 107
Russ, Victor 4, 6, 9, 10–12, 12–13, 20, 22–3, 23–4, 53, 58, 106, 198
Russ, William 21
Russ, Zoe (formerly Center) 46, 48–9, 54–5, 57, 59, 61–2, 71, 73, 77, 79, 106, 108, 113, 135, 156, 288
Russell, Harold 287–8

Scaliger, Joseph 109–10, 112
'Scotch Annie' 35–6
Seaford 92–3, 97, 102
Sealand, No.5 Flying Training School 129–30, 133
Seattle 195
Secker, Martin 207, 499
Second World War 199–200, 210, 240–2, 244–68, 269–94, 295
Senhouse, Roger 497, 499
Shebbear College 2–3, 28, 58, 64
Shelmerston 217
short stories
 The Thermometer 31–41, 44, 45, 84, 111, 117, 172, 234
 The Walker 93
 A Tale about a Peregrine Falcon 94–5, 120
 Old Cronk 95
 The Little Death 96, 474–5
 The Trap 100–1, 205–7, 442
 Skogula - The Sperm Whale 116–17
 Wang Khan of the Elephants 120–1, 125
 The White Cobra 121–2
 The Happy Despatch 132, 459–62, 464, 466, 489
 Cheetah 137, 174
 The Snow Leopard 137, 194
 The Dawn Flighting 156, 204–5, 442
 Noughts and Crosses 163, 165
 Two's Company 165
 The Green Creature 179–82, 325, 442
 The Virtuous Peleg 179–82, 442
 No Pirates Nowadays 181, 200–1, 301
 The First Story Teller's Tale 194
 One Arctic Summer 195–6, 200, 223–4
 The Return 201, 205, 442
 untitled crusading tale 202–4
 untitled tale of Moshe Ahrens 202
 Samphire 229
 George 235–9
 The Sorrow and Woe 267
 Not Liking to Pass the Road Again 324
 It must have been a Branch, They Said 385–7, 442, 446, 499
 The Long Day Running 433–4
 The Steep Slope of Gallt y Wenallt 433, 439, 452–3
 The Drawing of the Curranwood Badgers 446–8
 The Last Pool 459, 461, 466
 Naming Calls 471, 484–9, 500
 untitled shooting tale 473
 Noughts and Crosses 163, 165
Simon, Richard Scott 211
Skerrett (O'Flaherty) 462–4
Smithers, Dr 301–2
Snow, Richard ix
Southey Hall 293–4, 402, 404, 408, 418, 420–1
St Clair, William 331
Staddon 216–18, 244, 308–9
Stevenson, Robert Louis 299
Strachey, John 384
Sutherland Avenue, no. 54, Maida Vale 61, 73, 106–9, 114–15, 117

Taaffe, Edward H. 156–7, 163, 164–5
Targ, William 325
Thomas, Dylan 140
Tolstoy, Ivan 291–3
Tolstoy, Leo 14–15
Tolstoy Miloslavski, Count Dimitri 220–3, 229, 238, 256, 260–1, 309, 382, 478
Tolstoy, Nikolai 221, 382
Trollope, Anthony 296, 422
Tunbridge Wells High School 138
Twilight of the Gods, The (Garnett) 181, 186

Upper Cheyne Row 261–2, 274–5
Uxbridge, RAF Inland Area Depot 129

van Thal, Herbert 352–4, 381, 440–1
Verne, Jules 98
Volunteer, the 490, 491

Walden 4–5, 9–10

Wales 168, 233, 334–40, 341–62, 363–97, 440–68, 469–73, 483–9
Warburg, Frederick 498
Wayne, Philip 68
Weir, Peter x
Welch, Bertha 16, 26–7, 49–50, 106
Welch, Christine 26–7, 50
Welch, Frank 16, 26–7, 49–50, 106
Welch, Margaret 107
Welford, Ron 70
Wellington College 294, 480
Wheatley, Keith 162
Whitehead-Smith, Sydney 385–7, 388
Whitelaw (Englishman in Collioure) 495–6
Wicksteed, Francis 213
Wicksteed, Frieda Mary (*née* Hicking) 29, 213, 218
Wicksteed, Howard 29, 212–16, 218, 305–9, 342, 355–6, 407, 499
Wicksteed, Howard 'Binkie' 213, 230, 238–9, 241–3
Willesden Lane, no. 276 17, 19–20, 23–4, 27, 28, 29–30
William Again (Compton) 53–4
Williams, Edgar 363–4, 367–9, 379, 388, 393, 410, 445, 446–7, 465, 470, 498
Williams, Gwilym 498
Williams-Ellis, Clough 168, 334–9, 345, 383–5
Wilson, Angus 497
Wimpole Street 82
Woburn 279
'Woolcombe House' 63
Workers' Travel Association 182–3
works: *see also* short stories
 Cæsar: The Life Story of a Panda Leopard (1930) 80–8, 113–14, 125, 126–7
 Beasts Royal (1934) 94–5, 124–6, 131, 135, 137
 Hussein: An Entertainment (1938) 12, 81, 173–6, 182, 185, 191, 194, 195
 Perfect Gold (lost novel of 1945) 380, 442
 A Book of Voyages (1947) 302–3, 324, 333–4, 352–4, 381, 440–1, 442
 The Last Pool And Other Stories (1950) 178–82, 205, 207, 323–4, 324, 386, 433–4, 441, 442, 448, 474, 475, 496–7, 498–9
 Three Bear Witness (1952) 181, 189–90, 318, 337–8, 346, 365, 369, 384–5, 391–2, 441, 443, 458, 463, 464–5, 470, 472, 475, 489
 The Catalans (1953) 14, 25, 44–5, 45–6, 55, 111–12, 171, 172, 190, 266–7, 309, 324, 463, 464–5
 The Road to Samarcand (1955) 18, 181, 201, 209–10, 229, 244, 247, 380–1, 416, 442
 Lying in the Sun and Other Stories (1956) 238, 324
 The Golden Ocean (1956) 51, 165–8
 The Unknown Shore (1959) 51, 132–3
 Richard Temple (1962) 26, 41–4, 46–7, 54, 55, 61–2, 64–5, 72, 73–5, 77, 79, 88–90, 99, 103–4, 111, 125, 126–7, 133, 140–9, 152–3, 154, 155–6, 171, 184, 191–4, 196–8, 225–9, 234–5, 238–40, 240–1, 247–9, 254–5, 259, 262–3, 266, 270, 276–7, 280, 308, 355, 461, 463, 464–5
 Master and Commander (1970) 90, 166, 438
 Post Captain (1972) 56, 96–7, 435
 The Mauritius Command (1977) 319, 436
 The Surgeon's Mate (1980) 265
 The Reverse of the Medal (1986) 155
 The Letter of Marque (1988) 27, 97, 101
 The Thirteen-Gun Salute (1989) 27, 90
 The Wine-Dark Sea (1993) 27
 The Commodore (1994) 156–7
 The Yellow Admiral (1997) 26, 52, 56–7, 103, 157
Wrong Set, The (Wilson) 497
Wyndham, Joan 149, 155, 184, 246

Yeats-Brown, Major F. 125
Ynys Gifftan 465–6
Ynysfor (house) 426, 432
Ynysfor Hunt 422–3, 424–39, 444, 447, 449–53, 466–8